Masterpie

THE PEACEFUL END OF ...
IN EUROPE, 1989

NATIONAL SECURITY ARCHIVE
COLD WAR READERS

Series Editor
MALCOLM BYRNE

Previously published:

THE PRAGUE SPRING '68
UPRISING IN EAST GERMANY, 1953
THE 1956 HUNGARIAN REVOLUTION
A CARDBOARD CASTLE?
FROM SOLIDARITY TO MARTIAL LAW

Masterpieces of History

THE PEACEFUL END OF THE COLD WAR IN EUROPE, 1989

Edited by
**SVETLANA SAVRANSKAYA, THOMAS BLANTON,
AND VLADISLAV ZUBOK**

Editorial Assistant
ANNA MELYAKOVA

C E U PRESS

Central European University Press
Budapest New York

Paperback edition published in 2011 by
Central European University Press

An imprint of the
Central European University Share Company
Nádor utca 11, H-1051 Budapest, Hungary
Tel: +36-1-327-3138 or 327-3000
Fax: +36-1-327-3183
E-mail: ceupress@ceu.hu
Website: www.ceupress.com

400 West 59th Street, New York NY 10019, USA
Tel: +1-212-547-6932
Fax: +1-212-548-4607
E-mail: mgreenwald@sorosny.org

ISBN 978-615-5053-40-5 paperback
ISSN 1587-2416

LIBRARY OF CONGRESS CATALOGING-IN-PUBLICATION DATA

Masterpieces of history : the peaceful end of the Cold War in Eastern Europe, 1989 / edited by
Svetlana Savranskaya, Thomas Blanton, and Vladislav Zubok.
    p. cm.—(National Security Archive Cold War readers)
    Includes bibliographical references and index.
    ISBN 978-9639776777 (hardbound)
1. Europe, Eastern—History—1945-1989—Sources. 2. Europe, Eastern—Politics and government—1945-1989—Sources. 3. Soviet Union—Foreign relations—1945-1991—Sources. 4. United States—Foreign relations—1945-1989—Sources. 5. Cold War—Sources. 6. World politics
—1985-1995—Sources. I. Savranskaya, Svetlana. II. Blanton, Thomas S. III. Zubok, V. M. (Vladislav Martinovich) IV. Title. V. Series.

DJK50.M383 2010
947.0009'048--dc22

2010008972

Printed in the USA

Table of Contents

DOCUMENTS

Preface and Acknowledgements

This book is the culmination of an ambitious 15-year project to open up the previously secret Cold War files of Eastern Europe and the former Soviet Union, as well as those of the United States and its allies, and to use those primary sources to produce a new multi-lingual, multi-archival, multi-national history covering the most important flashpoints in the Soviet bloc and the ultimate, remarkable end of the Cold War.

We chose for the title of this book a revealing quotation from the Canadian scholar Jacques Levesque, who so presciently—well before many crucial primary sources were available—defined the key historical and analytical questions about the denouement of the Cold War in his book, *The Enigma of 1989* (University of California Press, 1997). As Professor Levesque wrote on the second page:

> Very little in the Soviet legacy is remembered, in the current context, as having been positive. With some irony, the way the USSR separated itself from its empire and its own peaceful end may seem to be its most beneficial contributions to history. These episodes are, in any case, masterpieces of history.

By using this wonderful phrase as our title, we certainly do not claim that our own work belongs on the masterpiece spectrum, but rather that the documents, dialogue, and analysis presented in this book do answer some of the most important questions that Professor Levesque posed and that we used to frame our own research agenda. That agenda grew from our close collaboration with many partners who were already prying loose the historical record throughout Eastern and Central Europe, as well as the former Soviet Union. Our partners sought with us to understand the crises of communism—primarily during the years 1953, 1956, 1968, 1980–1981—that culminated in the miraculous year of 1989. And yet it was exactly the repressive experience of those earlier flashpoints that made the peaceful conclusion of the Cold War seem so unlikely and—when it happened—such a masterpiece.

The books that precede this one in the series of National Security Archive Cold War Readers[1] through CEU Press tell the stories of those earlier crises in documents, and provide indispensable contextual history for the phenomenon

---

[1] Ostermann, *Uprising in East Germany;* Békés, Byrne and Rainer, *The 1956 Hungarian Revolution*; Navrátil et al., *The Prague Spring 1968*; Paczkowski and Byrne, *From Solidarity to Martial Law*; Mastny and Byrne, *A Cardboard Castle?*

of 1989. In the introductions and acknowledgments of those books, the careful reader will find the names of those on whose shoulders we stood—scholars, researchers, archivists, translators, former dissidents, former officials—all of whom helped in some way to open the secret files, bear witness to the events, provide explanations, atmosphere and analysis for the primary sources, and produce extraordinary cross-fertilized collections as well as "supernova" conferences that made headlines around the world. These books and the research projects they grew from led us to the present volume. Our partners in each of those adventures in scholarly spelunking urged us to take on the 1989 revolutions, which resulted in our organizing, co-sponsoring or participating in international conferences in venues from Potsdam to Timisoara, and from Providence, Rhode Island, to Saratov, Russia. We owe our thanks to the visionary philanthropists who underwrote these conferences and our work over these many years, especially the Carnegie Corporation of New York, the John D. and Catherine T. MacArthur Foundation, the Open Society Institute, the Central European University, the German Marshall Fund of the United States, and the Ford Foundation.

The scholarly meeting that is at the center of this book was both the chronological mid-point and truly a programmatic high point for the overall project. It followed our joint efforts to dramatically expand the historical record on each of the crises of what our Polish colleagues call "The System"—meaning the Stalinist regime imposed on Eastern Europe. Our partners from the region in particular were most curious about what exactly the superpowers had been up to in 1989, when Poland held free elections, Hungary opened its borders, the Berlin Wall fell, and the Czechoslovaks sent a political prisoner to the presidency. Why did the Soviet Union not intervene with force to stop the revolutions of 1989? When exactly did the Soviet Union decide—and did it do so explicitly—to renounce the Brezhnev Doctrine of intervention in Eastern Europe? How could a system founded on repression give up its empire largely without violence? What was the Gorbachev strategy towards the socialist camp, and how did it change over time? What happened to the U.S. policy of differentiation, which made Stalinist Romania into America's closest friend in the region? What was the role of the United States in Moscow's decisions, and in the multitude of interactions with East Europeans, both dissidents and officials, in the late 1980s? Was the possibility of a superpower condominium ever considered, as in the Yalta discussions at the end of World War II?

To address these questions, we gathered together a handful of the most well-informed eyewitnesses to the superpowers' roles in the events of 1989—top Soviet officials Anatoly Chernyaev, Georgy Shakhnazarov, and Sergei Tarasenko, and senior U.S. officials Jack Matlock and Douglas MacEachin (their biographies are given in the "Main Actors" section of this book). We surrounded them with inquisitive scholars from Central and Eastern Europe, the former USSR, the United States and Canada, and a thick briefing book of the best documents available at the time from all sides, and engaged them in a mutual interrogation. The site of the encounter was the Musgrove conference center on St. Simons Island, Georgia.

This book centers around the three days of dialogue that took place at Musgrove in May 1998. At its heart is a slightly edited version of the transcript of the discussions. By "edited" we mean primarily that we have reduced the input of the scholars. Because these sessions have remarkable historical value as oral history, especially since one of the leading participants, Georgy Shakhnazarov, has since passed on, our bias was naturally to keep the words of the veterans intact. We also cut discussions that took us too far beyond 1989—for instance, to 1991 and the fracturing of the Soviet Union—or that inconclusively debated issues like the Politburo's foreknowledge of the April 1989 Tbilisi violence, which the primary sources have now put to rest.

Since the Musgrove meeting, we have acquired thousands of pages of additional primary sources that answer many of the questions posed in the dialogue, and flesh out dramatically the accounts given by the veterans. The very best of that documentation is published here, most of it for the first time in English, and much of it for the first time in any language. Simultaneously with this publication, we are launching a Web companion site at www.nsarchive.org, which includes a more substantial piece of the historical record.

We consider the documents published in this volume to be the "greatest hits" of the much larger universe of sources that help us understand the end of the Cold War. Scholars have already pointed out the irony that "historians now have available, at least on the Soviet side, more primary sources on the end than on the beginning or the middle of the Cold War."[2] Our selection for this book emphasizes Soviet documents from the highest levels, both because of their relative rarity and because of the unique role Mikhail Gorbachev played as general secretary of the Soviet Communist Party in a highly centralized system. We sought to include the interactive documents—the notes of Politburo meetings and diplomatic sessions, the memoranda of conversations, the advisory opinions—which argue for particular positions or roads not taken, rather than the one-dimensional formal protocols or decision directives which are usually short on substance and long on bureaucratic jargon. We also looked for evidence of what these leaders said to each other in private talks or closed-door sessions. And we focused on documents that were illustrative of issues that came up over and over, and therefore were representative of the larger body of available documents too lengthy to include here.

We selected these materials from the National Security Archive's collection of tens of thousands of pages of sources on the end of the Cold War, which in turn were amassed from archives all over Eastern Europe and the former Soviet Union, as well as from U.S. government and Western European sources. Appended to each document in the book is a specific source citation, but here we want to provide some context for those citations, and give credit where it is due.

---

[2] Painter, "The End of the Cold War," 491.

Probably the most important single source for this volume has been the Gorbachev Foundation in Moscow, which began publishing its primary materials as early as 1993, including transcripts of summit meetings such as Malta and Reykjavik. During the 1990s, the Gorbachev Foundation was a haven for scholars, providing unique access to documents as well as to eyewitnesses, many of whom were writing their own memoirs and commentaries on the Gorbachev period. In 2006, the Foundation published an extremely useful edited volume of transcripts from the Politburo meetings of the Gorbachev era.[3] Although current political and archival conditions in the Russian Federation have severely limited access to this kind of material, the Foundation deserves our thanks for making possible so much of the new scholarship on the end of the Cold War.

We also relied on the extraordinary generosity and intellectual openness of Anatoly Chernyaev, who donated to the National Security Archive his historic diary of his years in the Central Committee, including six years at Gorbachev's side. Anatoly Sergeyevich's notes of Politburo discussions, of brainstorming sessions with Gorbachev and his advisers, and of the general secretary's meetings with foreign leaders—on file at the Gorbachev Foundation—have proven invaluable for our efforts to document, analyze and understand the dramatic events of the late 1980s.

Georgy Khosroyevich Shakhnazarov not only contributed his insights to the Musgrove dialogue, but shared with us key memos he had written to Gorbachev. We also found highly relevant documentation in the collection amassed by the historian and former general, Dmitry Volkogonov, which his family donated to the Library of Congress in Washington D.C., and in the "Fond 89" collection (based originally on the records of the trial of the Soviet Communist Party in the early 1990s), which was published through the collaboration of the Hoover Institution (Stanford University) with the publishing firm Chadwyck-Healey and the Russian Archival Service (*Rosarkhiv*). Professor Jacques Levesque donated from his personal collection the planning memos produced in early 1989 by the Central Committee's International Department and by the Foreign Ministry.

In a pioneering example of highest-level openness, former West German Chancellor Helmut Kohl took the initiative in 1998 to publish a large volume of German documentation of his conversations with other leaders about the end of the Cold War and German unification.[4] Instead of the usual 30- or 40-year rules for release of documents, this 10-year standard would revolutionize the use of primary sources for contemporary history, not to mention accountability for leaders. Fortunately, in the formerly communist countries of Eastern Europe, such openness is now the rule for records of that era, and our partners at the Institute for Political Studies of the Polish Academy of Sciences; the Cold War Research Group and the 1956 Institute in Hungary; and the Czechoslovak Documentation

---

[3] Chernyaev, *V Politburo TsK KPSS.*
[4] Küsters, *Dokumente zur Deutschlandpolitik.*

Centre and Institute for Contemporary History in Prague all provided us with remarkable primary sources from those countries' Politburo and Central Committee records, opposition movements, and secret police files, a selection of which are included in this book and all of which informed our research.

As always, we warmly acknowledge our partnership in exploring documentation from "the other side" of the Cold War with Christian Ostermann and the Cold War International History Project at the Woodrow Wilson International Center for Scholars in Washington DC.

The National Security Archive's trademark approach to American documentation focuses on the U.S. Freedom of Information Act, and during the course of this investigation we filed hundreds if not thousands of FOIA and declassification requests with agencies of the U.S. government as well as the Ronald Reagan Presidential Library (Simi Valley, California) and the George Bush Presidential Library (College Station, Texas). Many of those requests are still pending today, but the ones already processed have produced such useful materials as the U.S. transcripts of Reagan–Gorbachev summits and a wide range of CIA intelligence analyses of the Soviet Union. We are particularly indebted to the archivists of the presidential libraries for making these documents available to us, and to Catherine Nielsen, formerly of the National Security Archive, who handled the organization's numerous related FOIA requests.

Special thanks to Lisa Thompson for preparing the index.

The essays that precede the Musgrove dialogue and the documents in this volume seek to answer as explicitly as we can the questions that we and our partners posed at the beginning of this project. How did the Cold War end so peacefully? What were the roles of the superpowers? Since this book does not attempt to document the actual course of the revolutions of 1989, but rather to explain the behavior of the superpowers, the two essays take their frames from Moscow and Washington, respectively.

For Moscow, this collection presents the most conclusive evidence to date that the Soviet leadership made the critical choices about Eastern Europe much earlier than historians previously understood, that Gorbachev's vision for Europe—"the common European home"—drove his decisions and tactics for Eastern Europe, and that the use of force to preserve the Soviet empire in Eastern Europe was never an option for Soviet reformers. Among other major findings, this volume shows how economic factors such as the falling price of oil influenced the Kremlin's reassessment of the strategic value of Eastern Europe, as Moscow came to see the "fraternal allies" more and more as burdens rather than assets. The evidence here reinforces arguments that the power of ideas was more important in guiding the Kremlin's new thinking than concerns over the balance of power or the realist conception of national interests.

For Washington, this book argues that U.S. engagement with its traditional Soviet adversary—especially that of President Reagan with Gorbachev in their discussions of nuclear weapons—was more significant than U.S. pressure (defense buildups, proxy wars, or anti-communist rhetoric) in contributing to the major changes in Kremlin policies in the late 1980s. By relieving the Soviet sense of threat, the Reagan–Gorbachev discourse on arms reductions and the abolition of nuclear weapons reinforced Gorbachev's "new thinking" mindset and enabled faster progress on reform both domestically and in foreign policy. In contrast to the interactivity between Washington and Moscow during the Reagan years, the transition to the George H.W. Bush administration was in fact the second coming of the "hawks," clustered around a cautious president, and the resulting "pause" in U.S.–Soviet relations during 1989 left a vacuum in Eastern Europe into which the dissidents and the reform communists rushed. In making possible that outcome, the pause—more a consequence of presidential tentativeness than White House grand strategy—helped change the world, and thus was greatly, if unwittingly, beneficial. But it had significant costs as well, weakening Gorbachev's political standing at home and leading the players to miss opportunities for dramatic arms reductions and the integration of the USSR (and later Russia) into Europe.

Our real purpose in preparing this book is to encourage and guide further scholarship on these issues, since we see this collection as a starting point for much more work. For us, the dialogue, the documents and the analyses show what 10 years of research have added to our knowledge—from the point at which the original Musgrove dialogue took place, all the way to 2009, this 20th anniversary of the year of miracles and "masterpieces of history."

SVETLANA SAVRANSKAYA
THOMAS BLANTON
November 9, 2009

FOREWORD

Anatoly S. Chernyaev

This book is based on the materials of a conference that took place in a picturesque spot on the shores of the Atlantic Ocean off the state of Georgia—the Musgrove Plantation—in May 1998. That conference was probably one of the most significant ever held by the National Security Archive. It was organized by Tom Blanton, director of the Archive, and his colleagues. They courageously entered a subject, which allowed them to discover the origins, the motives and the circumstances of a turning point in world history—the cessation of the Cold War and of an ideological confrontation that had been suicidal for mankind.

The Archive exhibited an enviable persistence and piercing energy, which deserves the highest praise for its dedication to work and truth, and for overcoming numerous obstacles created by bureaucrats and other excessively cowardly and greedy custodians of the truth about the past. The documents for this book were compiled in a painstaking process from the archives of several countries by the scholars participating in the project, through Freedom of Information Act requests by the National Security Archive, and through donations by the conference participants.

The proceedings of the conference and the documents—Soviet, American, and East European—together create a rare volume and significant pool of evidence about that time. They provide an opportunity for an unbiased reader and scholar to build an adequate understanding of Gorbachev's policy toward those countries, and about his "new thinking" in general. They show that the principle of freedom of choice announced by Gorbachev—which was used primarily by those countries—was his sincere conviction. In addition to the withdrawal from Afghanistan, and perhaps no less so, this opened the road to *understanding* in the West, and therefore, to *trust*, which became the decisive factor in the movement toward crucial change throughout the international arena, and toward the cessation of the political and ideological Cold War. This was because that principle essentially contradicted the central Soviet doctrine, which interpreted world politics as a function of the international class struggle, and repealed the principle that was in effect at the time—that what is good for you should be bad for the opposite side.

Gorbachev, during his first meeting with the leaders of the alliance after the funeral of his predecessor, Konstantin Chernenko, announced to them that from now on they should proceed from the assumption that there would be no control from Moscow, and that they would not be getting any directives from there either. Let them be responsible for their actions to their parties and to their peoples, and that was all. It was then that he put an end to the "Brezhnev Doctrine," then confirmed that position at the October 1985 conference of the Warsaw Treaty Organization's Political Consultative Committee in Sofia. And he never, throughout all the years of *perestroika*, retreated from that position, even though his colleagues from the socialist countries, having felt the dangerous nature of that freedom, repeatedly tried to pull Moscow into their own affairs.

Another extremely important point, even though it derived from the "freedom of choice" principle, was the rejection of the use of force in international relations and the ban on utilizing Soviet armed forces on foreign territories. Many people did not believe this at first, and those in the leadership of our allied countries simply did not want to believe it. However, when Moscow did not react to the mass exodus of East Germans across the borders of Hungary and Czechoslovakia, and when later it did not allow the troops stationed in the GDR "out of the barracks" against the powerful popular movement for German reunification, which brought down the Berlin Wall, everyone became convinced that Gorbachev's deeds did not diverge from his words. And then the so-called "velvet revolutions" unfolded, and independent states emerged very quickly.

Gorbachev was not very interested in the changes that began in Eastern Europe. He used to say, "They are sick and tired of us, and we are no less so of them; let them live on their own, then everything will come out right." However, it did not turn out the way he hoped. We received no appreciation from the "fraternal countries." They turned away from us and turned their faces to the West. This was where one of Gorbachev's mistakes caught up with him: he continued to believe in the appeal and the "gravitational force" of the idea of socialism, as such. However, our allies were no less sick and tired of socialism than they were of Soviet paternalism, especially because that socialism was in reality the Stalinist–Brezhnevist model that had been imposed on them, and that was alien to them both historically and ethnically.

Nonetheless, Gorbachev naturally imagined those new states as an integral part of the "common European home." He announced that idea for the first time in Prague—not just in any location—in the spring of 1987. And from then on he tried to convince each of his interlocutors—whether it was François Mitterrand, Hans-Dietrich Genscher, Johannes Rau, Gro Harlem Brundtland, Felipe Gonzalez, Giulio Andreotti or those of a lower rank—of its promise. He could not imagine how to overcome the division of Europe, or the European future, in any other way. President George Bush eventually came to share this idea, otherwise the European CSCE Paris summit of November 1990 would not have taken place, and the famous Declaration for Europe would not have been signed by 34 states, including the United States and Canada.

For Gorbachev, that was the pinnacle of his European policy, which he always saw as the most important and perhaps the decisive (always together with the United States) part of the transition to a peaceful period in world history.

One can only guess how his design for a common European home would have turned out had the Soviet Union survived as a great peace-loving democratic power. However, history has demonstrated that Europe, and even the world, were not yet ready to accept the "new thinking"—even individual elements of it, let alone in its entirety. The process of integration in the western part of Europe turned out to be more complex, difficult and contradictory than it appeared in the late 1980s. And yet, Gorbachev acted "ahead of his time," believing in his idea of the common European home, which perhaps did not go to waste.

The materials in this book show that Western leaders, especially the Americans, did not trust Gorbachev for a long time: at first they believed that his "new policy" was nothing more than another Kremlin trick and the ambitions of a young leader. Later, when they came to trust his sincerity, they did not believe that he would be able to do what he wanted, the way he wanted. That circumstance—in which the West only with great delay recognized the "usefulness" for its own purposes of Gorbachev's *perestroika* and then only very timidly demonstrated its willingness to support it or even to provide help—contributed to his inability to cope with the crisis and to solve the historic task of preserving the Soviet Union in its new, democratic form.

The book is valuable also because the documents collected in it can be viewed through the prism of the discussion and polemics at the conference, where many things were clarified, developed, and even refuted.

The organizers of the conference chose—precisely for this purpose—the most appropriate and persuasive method. They brought together at one table, face-to-face, scholars from different countries, as well as experts and people who participated directly in the events of that time that were marked with the name of Gorbachev and *perestroika* in the USSR, and those who were connected with the work of presidents Ronald Reagan and George Bush (the elder) in the United States. At Musgrove, among other similar conferences and meetings, this combination turned out to be especially expressive and fruitful.

On the one side were the Americans led by the conference mediator, Tom Blanton, who, in addition to his own brilliant interventions, posed very sharp and professionally irreproachable questions. (In any serious conversation that is a great feat in itself!) The former U.S. officials comprised the wise and knowledgeable professor Jack Matlock, former State Department official and U.S. ambassador to Moscow, and the respected intelligence officer and author, Doug MacEachin, in 1989 the CIA's leading Soviet expert. On the other side were two former assistants of the CC CPSU general secretary and president of the USSR—Anatoly Chernyaev and Georgy Shakhnazarov (now deceased)—the former assistant to Eduard Shevardnadze, Sergey Tarasenko, and two historians from the Russian Academy of Sciences. On the third side were prominent Western scholars, especially the well-known expert on the subject, Jacques Levesque, and scholars from the countries of Eastern Europe, especially Andrzej Paczkowski, Vílem Prečan, and Csaba Békés, whose contributions made it possible to see the problems from a somewhat different perspective than they appeared to the "main protagonists." The clash of opinions was made more pronounced and even somewhat bitter by the scholars of Soviet origin but who already possessed an American mentality.

The polemics were further enlivened by sharp confrontations among ... the Russians themselves, among whom were some who had hidden as well as explicit ill feelings towards Gorbachev's policy.

Thanks to the art of "managing" the discussion, the sensitivity and the good sense of humor exhibited by Tom Blanton as chairman, the comparison of facts, opinions and positions assumed an extremely sincere, lively, often sharp, but always correct character. The hosts succeeded in creating an atmosphere of tolerance for every opinion, an honest approach to any detail of a problem in any of its twists and turns, which provoked the kinds of spontaneous thoughts, reminiscences, and discourses that the participants themselves probably could never have "planned" beforehand. This circumstance enriched the main theme with often unexpected details, which gave the discussion the unique and colorful feel of "being there" and, I would also add, a certain "cheerfulness." It is not without reason that laughter was heard often at that table.

The conference uncovered a lot that was new not only in terms of factual material, but also in terms of arguments substantiating the policy of "new thinking" and the reactions to it in other countries. It also raised doubts—if not about its goals then about the methods of its implementation at particular stages and in certain cases.

In short, this book, based on the Musgrove conference together with the documents included in it as an integral part, represents rare historical evidence of how and why the ideas and decisions that led to the ending of the Cold War were born, and which concrete consequences of the accomplishments of that period were especially significant for different countries, and for the entire world.

Thinking about Musgrove today, I would like once again to express my deep gratitude to Mr. Smith Bagley, who made his beautiful, picturesque estate available for convening that conference.

And once again, my deepest bow to the main organizers, who also prepared this volume. All that is left for me to do is to express my regret that publication of such a unique book was delayed for ten years.

FOREWORD

Jack F. Matlock, Jr.

The conference held at the Musgrove plantation on Georgia's southeast coast in 1998 illuminated one of the most important periods in 20th century history: the liberation of the countries in Eastern Europe from Soviet control. The fact that this episode occurred peacefully near the close of a century filled with violence and following over four decades of East–West confrontation made the event worthy of the most careful study. The National Security Archive rendered a service to historians and the public as a whole when it gathered declassified source material from both Soviet and American archives and invited scholars and several former officials to examine the historical evidence, comment on it, and discuss its implications. One of the scholars who attended the conference, Jacques Levesque, had published a book on the events discussed at Musgrove which he entitled *The Enigma of 1989*. The task of the conference was to take some of the mystery out of that enigma.

Although the conference took place 10 years ago, publication of these documents and of the record of discussions is both necessary and timely. It is necessary because groundless myths have arisen regarding the way the Cold War and the division of Europe ended; it is timely because these myths have produced dangerous distortions in current American and Russian policy.

The unfounded conviction that the United States and its European allies "won" the Cold War and "defeated" communism by the application of military and economic power, and that, as a consequence, the United States has the means—if it has the will—to police the world and to create, wherever it wishes, governments that mirror its own, lies behind many of the mistakes American deciders have made since the turn of the century. The facts are that the Cold War ended not as the victory of one country over another, but as the result of successful negotiations benefiting both sides. It was not a defeat for the Soviet Union, for the Soviet leader made no agreements that were not in his country's interest.

It is to Gorbachev's credit that he was able to recognize that the policies he had inherited were not in his country's interest. It is to the credit of Ronald Reagan, George H.W. Bush and their Western colleagues that they aimed to change Soviet behavior, not to destroy the Soviet Union or replace its regime. They offered conditions for ending the Cold War that were consistent with the national interests of a Soviet Union at peace with its neighbors.

Communism ended in the Soviet Union not as the result of Western military pressure but in response to internal reforms in the Soviet Union that would have been possible only if the Cold War were ending. The subsequent break-up of the

Soviet unitary state was caused by internal factors and could not have taken place if the Cold War had not ended.

Myths about a quasi-military victory by the West in the Cold War have also had a damaging impact on current Russian thinking and the policies of the current government. If the Cold War ended in a "victory" of the West and Western pressure destroyed the Soviet state, then Gorbachev was duped and surrendered Soviet (and Russian) interests when he came to terms to end the Cold War. This has fed anti-Western and anti-American sentiments in Russia and made it more difficult to find a way to cooperate in the interests of both countries.

For these reasons, understanding how "1989" happened is essential if one is to benefit from the lessons the Cold War and its end should have taught us. In making available to scholars and interested members of the public the Musgrove documents and discussions, the National Security Archive has once again helped us reach a more reliable understanding of the past in order better to deal with the problems of the present, and of the future.

Acronyms

ABM Treaty	Anti-Ballistic Missile Treaty
CFE Treaty	Conventional Forces in Europe Treaty
CSCE	Conference on Security and Cooperation in Europe
ČSSR	Czechoslovak Socialist Republic
CDU/CSU	Christian Democratic Union/Christian Social Union of Bavaria
CMEA	Council for Mutual Economic Assistance
COCOM	Coordinating Committee for Multilateral Export Controls
Comintern	Communist International
CPCz	Communist Party of Czechoslovakia
EC	European Community
FRG	Federal Republic of Germany
GATT	General Agreement on Tariffs and Trade
GDR	German Democratic Republic
Gosplan	State Committee for Planning, USSR
GRU	Main Intelligence Directorate, *Glavnoe Razvedyvatel'noe Upravlenie*
HPR	Hungarian People's Republic
HSWP	Hungarian Socialist Workers Party
IMF	International Monetary Fund
INF Treaty	Intermediate-range Nuclear Forces Treaty
KGB	Committee for State Security, *Komitet Gosudarstvennoi Bezopasnosti*
KNDR	Democratic People's Republic of North Korea
Komsomol	Communist Union of Youth, *Kommunisticheskii Soyuz Molodezhi*
MFA	Ministry of Foreign Affairs
NATO	North Atlantic Treaty Organization
PB	Politburo
PCC	Political Consultative Committee
PCI	Communist Party of Italy, *Partito Comunista d'Italia*
PDPA	People's Democratic Party of Afghanistan
PUWP	Polish United Worker's Party
PRC	People's Republic of China
PPR	Polish People's Republic
RENAMO	Mozambican National Resistance, *Resistência Nacional Moçambicana*
SALT	Strategic Arms Limitation Talks

SDI	Strategic Defense Initiative
SED	Socialist Unity Party of Germany, *Sozialistische Einheitspartei Deutschlands*
SFRY	Socialist Federal Republic of Yugoslavia
SPD	Social Democratic Party of Germany, *Sozialdemokratische Partei Deutschlands*
SRR	Socialist Republic of Romania
START	Strategic Arms Reduction Talks
STR	Scientific-Technological Revolution
TASS	Telegraph Agency of the Soviet Union
UNESCO	United Nations Educational, Scientific, and Cultural Organization
WTO	Warsaw Treaty Organization

Chronology of Events[1]

1985

March 11: Mikhail Gorbachev is named general secretary of the Communist Party of the Soviet Union (CPSU) after the death of Konstantin Chernenko.

March 13–14: Gorbachev meets with foreign leaders, including leaders of socialist states. In his memoirs, Gorbachev writes that he announced to the fraternal leaders that the old policy of Soviet patronage was over and that the allies were responsible for the situation in their respective countries.

April 23: The Plenum of the CPSU Central Committee, which officially launches the policy of *perestroika*, convenes.

May 7: The CC CPSU promulgates a resolution "On Overcoming Drinking and Alcoholism," one of Gorbachev's early social reforms.

May 22: The 30th Anniversary summit of the Warsaw Treaty Organization (WTO) in Warsaw renews the treaty for 20 years.

June 29: Eduard Shevardnadze is appointed Soviet foreign minister.

August 28: *Time* magazine publishes an interview with Gorbachev—his first of this length—which includes an extensive discussion on international issues.

September 19: Gorbachev meets with President of Finland Mauno Koivisto in Moscow.

October 21–23: At a session of the WTO Political Consultative Committee (PCC) in Sofia, Gorbachev discusses the prospects for integration within the Council for Mutual Economic Assistance (CMEA) and the state of affairs in the international communist movement.

November 19–21: Gorbachev and President Ronald Reagan hold their first summit, in Geneva. The two agree in principle to a 50-percent reduction in strategic offensive weapons. The most important result of the summit, however, is that it allows both leaders to establish a personal connection and find a common interest in the abolition of nuclear weapons.

December 24: Boris Yeltsin is elected first secretary of the Moscow Party Committee at Gorbachev's recommendation.

[1] Compiled and edited by National Security Archive staff: Svetlana Savranskaya, Gregory F. Domber, Catherine Nielsen, Vladislav Zubok, Thomas Blanton, Malcolm Byrne, William Burr, Kevin Symons, Matthew Talbot, Anna Melyakova.

1986

January 15: Gorbachev announces the Program for Comprehensive Elimination of Nuclear Weapons by the Year 2000.

February 25–March 6: The XXVII Congress of the CPSU takes place.

March 12: Gorbachev meets with Fidel Castro.

April 26: The Chernobyl nuclear accident occurs, demonstrating to Kremlin leaders and their allies the potential effects of a nuclear war.

May 20: Gorbachev meets with Prime Minister of Spain Felipe Gonzalez.

June 9–10: At a PCC session in Budapest, Warsaw Pact leaders discuss problems in the alliance, such as the lack of genuine coordination and cooperation among allies, as well as the urgent need for integration within CMEA.

June 13: The Soviet Politburo discusses the issues raised at the PCC meeting in Budapest. This is the group's first full-fledged discussion of the socialist countries since Gorbachev's accession to power. Gorbachev focuses on the economic crisis and the need for Western credits.

July 1: Gorbachev attends the X Congress of the PUWP in Warsaw and meets with PUWP leader Wojciech Jaruzelski.

August 19: The Central Committee passes a resolution allowing 20 ministries and the 70 largest enterprises of the USSR to establish direct contact with foreign partners and to create joint ventures. The decision is a step in the direction of deeper integration of the socialist bloc.

September 18: Gorbachev travels to Stavropol *krai* where he meets with party activists and promotes economic reforms and accountability in the Soviet Union.

October 11–13: The U.S.–Soviet Summit in Reykjavik takes place. Reagan and Gorbachev come close to an agreement to abolish all strategic offensive weapons but fall short because of Reagan's insistence on keeping SDI (the Strategic Defense Initiative) and Gorbachev's inability to compromise on SDI research and testing.

November 10–11: At a meeting of heads of CMEA countries in Moscow, a frank discussion takes place about the general economic crisis, failed efforts at integration within CMEA, and the need for serious economic reform.

December 23: Academician Andrei Sakharov is allowed to return to Moscow from his internal exile in Gorky.

1987

January 29: The Soviet Politburo discusses the results of a recent conference in Warsaw of Central Committee secretaries from socialist countries on international and ideological issues. Members point to the growing pro-Western orientation of Eastern Europe.

February 10: The USSR announces that it has pardoned 140 individuals convicted of subversive activities. This marks the largest release of political prisoners since 1956.

February 19: Reagan lifts economic sanctions on Poland.

February 27: The Yugoslav government places emergency controls on wage levels; nationwide strikes break out.

March 15: Up to 2,000 demonstrators in Budapest mark the anniversary of the 1848 uprising against Austrian rule, and call for more democracy in Hungary.

March 28: Poland announces price increases of between 10 and 100 percent on basic foodstuffs, cigarettes, fuel, alcohol, transportation, and postal services.

March 28–April 1: British Prime Minister Margaret Thatcher visits Moscow. Her highly critical views of Soviet human rights violations and continued military involvement in Afghanistan are given full coverage in the Soviet media.

April 9: Gorbachev visits Prague to meet with CPCz leader Gustáv Husák.

April 13–16: U.S. Secretary of State George Shultz arrives in Moscow to negotiate on arms control. He meets with Gorbachev, Shevardnadze and Chairman of the Council of Ministers Nikolay Ryzhkov.

April 23: GDR leader Erich Honecker publicly rejects the idea that East Germany should emulate Soviet political and economic reforms.

May 6: The U.S. and USSR agree to establish Nuclear Risk Reduction Centers in their respective capitals.

May 9: The CPSU Politburo, with Marshal Sergey Akhromeyev in attendance, discusses a new WTO doctrine.

May 25: Gorbachev visits Romania and makes a speech explaining the reform process in the Soviet Union.

May 28: Eluding vaunted Soviet air defenses, West German peace activist Matthias Rust lands a small private plane near Red Square.

May 30: USSR Defense Minister Sergey Sokolov is fired and replaced by Dmitri Yazov. The chief of Soviet air defenses and other generals are also replaced, reportedly as a result of the Rust incident.

June 2: Reagan informs Congress that Romania and Hungary should be offered most-favored-nation (MFN) status.

June 5–6: East German youth and police clash when crowds approach the Berlin Wall to hear an outdoor rock concert on the western side.

June 8: Pope John Paul II visits Poland.

June 12: During a speech in West Berlin, Reagan intones, "Mr. Gorbachev, tear down this wall."

June 25: Hungary announces that President Pál Losonczi and Prime Minister György Lázár will retire. Miklós Németh becomes president and Károly Grósz prime minister.

June 25–26: Gorbachev strengthens his position by promoting three supporters to full membership in the Politburo—Party Secretaries Aleksandr Yakovlev, Viktor Nikonov, and Nikolay Slyunkov—and by reducing the role of his chief rival, Yegor Ligachev.

June 26: The Central Committee of the Yugoslav League of Communists meets in Belgrade to discuss problems in Kosovo.

July 20: Hungary raises prices 10–29 percent on certain consumer goods and services to help combat its hard currency trade deficit.

July 28: In a speech to the Central Committee Plenum in Sofia, Bulgarian leader Todor Zhivkov calls for a reduction of the Party's role in the government and the economy.

September 1: Honecker begins a much-awaited visit to West Germany.

September 17: Shevardnadze and Shultz agree in principle to the elimination of INF missiles.

September 17–19: The Hungarian Parliament approves cutbacks in subsidies to state-run enterprises and the introduction of personal income taxes and a value-added tax.

October 5: A state of energy emergency is declared in Romania.

October 23: Shultz meets with Gorbachev in Moscow to discuss INF issues.

November 2: At a celebration of the 70th anniversary of the Bolshevik Revolution, Gorbachev denounces Stalin's legacy, defends *perestroika*, and announces his intention to seek a strategic arms agreement with the U.S.

November 11: At Gorbachev's request, the Moscow Party Committee removes Yeltsin as first secretary.

November 15: A general wage freeze and price increases are implemented in Yugoslavia, setting off a buying panic that devalues the Yugoslav currency. On the same day, several thousand industrial workers riot in Brasov, Romania, over mandated pay cuts.

December 7–10: At the Washington summit, Reagan and Gorbachev sign the INF treaty, mandating the removal from Europe of 2,611 intermediate-range missiles. For the first time ever, the actual number of nuclear weapons delivery systems has been reduced.

December 17: Miloš Jakeš succeeds Husák as general secretary of the Czechoslovak Communist Party.

1988

January 11: Gorbachev agrees with Jakeš that there are no grounds to reassess the events of 1968, including the Soviet-led intervention. He adds that the attempt by supporters of the "Prague Spring" to present themselves as "legal heirs of Soviet *perestroika* is nothing more than a blow at our *perestroika*. We are carrying out *perestroika* within the framework of socialism and to reinforce socialism."

February 1: Prices on approximately half of Polish goods and services are raised 27 percent, including a 100-percent rise for gas and electricity, and a 200-percent jump for coal. Thousands in Warsaw and Gdańsk protest.

February 8: Gorbachev announces on national television a plan to withdraw troops from Afghanistan beginning May 15, 1988, and ending February 15, 1989.

February 22: Shultz meets with Gorbachev in Moscow to discuss the Soviet withdrawal from Afghanistan. Gorbachev rejects Shultz's presentation of Pakistan's desire for an interim government in Kabul.

February 29: Bulgaria holds regional and municipal elections allowing, for the first time, more than one candidate per position.

March 10: At a Politburo meeting Gorbachev announces that the USSR will provide 41 billion rubles of annual assistance to socialist countries and clients around the world, including 27 billion rubles to Cuba.

March 13: *Sovetskaia Rossiya* publishes the "Nina Andreyeva letter" attacking *perestroika* in language borrowed from the speeches of Andrei Zhdanov.

March 24–25: The Politburo holds an intense discussion on Nina Andreyeva's letter and *glasnost*. There is a split between radical and more cautious reformers.

April 14: The Geneva Accords on Afghanistan are signed, calling on the USSR to remove half of its forces by August 15, 1988, and the remainder by February 15, 1989.

April 25–27: Thousands of Polish workers strike demanding higher wages. Strikes spread across the country, including the shipyards in Gdańsk, and continue until mid-May.

May 22: János Kádár is removed as Hungarian Communist Party secretary and is replaced by Károly Grósz.

May 29–June 1: The Gorbachev–Reagan summit takes place in Moscow.

June 28: In his address to the XIX All-Union Conference of the Communist Party, Gorbachev calls for restructuring the government, putting in place a strong president picked by a more representative legislature that would replace the Supreme Soviet. He also advocates term limits for high officials, more authority for the local soviets, multi-candidate elections, and a ban on communist party interference on economic issues.

July 4: The XIX CPSU Conference passes resolutions on political reform. In discussions of the draft, Gorbachev insists on including his own language. The resolution represents a political victory for the reformers.

July 11: Gorbachev visits Poland. He makes a speech before the Sejm which alludes to the XIX CPSU Conference and the deepening Soviet reform. At a dinner with the Polish party leadership he gives an extensive description of his Common European Home idea.

July 25: In a speech to the Ministry of Foreign Affairs, Shevardnadze rejects the class struggle as the basis for Soviet foreign policy.

July 30: The Yugoslav government orders an end to recent demonstrations by minority ethnic Serbs in Kosovo who claim mistreatment by the region's ethnic majority.

August 14: Police in Gdańsk clash with protesters marking the eighth anniversary of the founding of Solidarity. Strikes begin anew, particularly in the mining industry.

August 31: Solidarity leader Lech Wałęsa meets with Interior Minister General Czesław Kiszczak and notes that progress is being made towards initiating negotiations between the government and the opposition. After the meeting, he urges an end to nationwide strikes.

September 26: Poland's Central Committee appoints Mieczysław Rakowski prime minister. He succeeds Zbigniew Messner who resigned after criticism over his conduct of the economy.

September 30: The CC CPSU Plenum implements radical structural and personnel changes in the Central Committee. Gorbachev replaces Gromyko as president (chairman of the presidium of the Supreme Soviet); Gromyko is then retired by the CC. Ligachev receives a new assignment as party secretary for agriculture. Vadim Medvedev (secretary for science and technology) takes over responsibility for ideology and propaganda. Anatoly Dobrynin is retired as CC secretary in charge of foreign affairs and replaced by Aleksandr Yakovlev. Viktor Chebrikov is replaced by Vladimir Kryuchkov as head of the KGB and given the post of secretary for legal affairs. Mikhail Solomentsev loses his position as chairman of the Party Control Committee and his membership in the Politburo. Anatoly Lukyanov is confirmed as Soviet vice president.

October 6: Following suggestions from his adviser, Georgy Shakhnazarov, Gorbachev proposes that the Politburo begin to devise a "thoughtful" strategic approach toward Eastern Europe in case of a general crisis there. "We should not bury our heads in the sand like an ostrich," the leader declares.

October 10: Czechoslovak Premier Lubomír Štrougal resigns. Ladislav Adamec takes over the post the following day.

October 14: Deputy Director of Central Intelligence Robert Gates delivers a pessimistic address about Gorbachev's ability to reform the USSR. Shultz later assails him for giving a speech on policy and tries to have him fired.

October 31: The Polish government announces it will begin shutting down the Gdańsk shipyard. Wałęsa calls the move a "political provocation." The government claims it is for economic reasons.

November 6: Wałęsa threatens to call nationwide strikes unless the closure of the Gdańsk shipyard is called off; however, the following day the strike is indefinitely postponed after a meeting between Solidarity officials and shipyard management.

November 8: George H.W. Bush is elected president of the United States.

November 23: The Central Committee of the Socialist Workers' Party in Hungary names Németh to replace General Secretary Grósz as premier.

December 7: In a landmark speech at the United Nations, Gorbachev announces plans to shrink the Soviet military by 500,000 troops and endorses the "common interests of mankind" as the basis of Soviet foreign policy. He enunciates a decision to allow Eastern Europe to evolve "without Soviet interference." Afterwards, Gorbachev lunches with Reagan and President-elect Bush at Governors Island in New York harbor.

December 7: A devastating earthquake in Armenia kills 25,000 and leaves half a million homeless. Gorbachev cuts short his New York visit and returns to the Soviet Union. At Christmas, Bush sends his son, Jeb, and grandson, George, to Armenia to inspect the damage and determine how the U.S. might help. For the first time in years, the Soviet Union accepts foreign assistance.

December 18: Henry Kissinger meets the U.S. president-elect and his advisers, James Baker and Brent Scowcroft. He suggests negotiating a deal with the Soviets on Eastern Europe and offers himself as an emissary.

1989

January 11: The Hungarian Parliament votes to allow freedom of association and assembly, an important step in permitting the formation of independent political organizations and parties.

January 15: A demonstration in Prague commemorates the twentieth anniversary of student protest-suicides following the 1968 invasion. Police break up the protest and make arrests. Václav Havel is arrested the next day and charged with inciting the demonstrations with comments that were quoted on foreign radio broadcasts.

January 16: Kissinger meets with Yakovlev in Moscow. He compares the situation in Eastern Europe to that preceding World War I in which the Great Powers set off a chain reaction which led to war. To avert catastrophe, he proposes high-level negotiations to reach a set of both formal and informal understandings. Yakovlev agrees that negotiations should take place.

January 18: Kissinger meets Gorbachev in the Kremlin and presents his proposal for an understanding on Eastern Europe. He also delivers a letter to Gorbachev from Bush. Gorbachev is ambivalent about the initiative and wants to make sure that it is actually supported by Bush.

January 18: The CC PUWP grants the banned Solidarity trade union a two-year probationary period with the possibility of legalization to follow.

January 21: Gorbachev reports to the Politburo on his meeting with the Trilateral Commission.

January 22: Speaking on ABC Television's news program "This Week with David Brinkley," Scowcroft says that Gorbachev seems "interested in making trouble with the Western Alliance" and may be trying to throw the West off its guard to give the USSR time to rebuild its economic and military strength and prepare for a "world Communist offensive." He adds, "I think the Cold War is not over."

January 23: Honecker announces a 10-percent reduction in GDR military spending by 1990.

January 23: Bush calls Gorbachev to promise no "foot-dragging" in the improvement of relations. Gorbachev is encouraged by the call and tells several aides that he believes he can deal with Bush "as one human to another."

January 24: At a Politburo meeting, Gorbachev instructs Yakovlev, as head of the Politburo's International Commission, to conduct "a situational analysis" of Eastern Europe with scholars from think-tanks.

January 26: A letter to Prime Minister Adamec signed by 692 Czechoslovak cultural figures demands Havel's release.

January 27: Representatives of the Polish government, Solidarity, and the Catholic Church meet to negotiate political and economic reforms.

January 28: Imre Pozsgay, a member of the Hungarian Politburo, calls for a reappraisal of the 1956 revolt.

January 28: Kissinger meets Bush, Baker, and Scowcroft at the White House to report on his talk with Gorbachev in Moscow and discuss Kissinger's plan for Eastern Europe.

February 6: "Roundtable" talks between the Polish government and representatives of Solidarity begin.

February 10–11: The Hungarian Party's Central Committee formally endorses the idea of a multiparty system.

February 15: The USSR completes its military withdrawal from Afghanistan on schedule.

February 20–21: The Hungarian CC approves a new constitution omitting mention of the leading role of the Communist Party.

February 21: Havel is sentenced to nine months in prison for his alleged role in inciting riots earlier in the year.

March 1: Six former prominent members of the Romanian Communist Party send an open letter to Nicolae Ceauşescu accusing him of discrediting socialism, ruining the economy, and failing to observe the 1975 Helsinki Accords.

March 5: Thousands demonstrate in Moscow in support of Yeltsin's candidacy for the Parliament.

March 7: Baker receives Shevardnadze at the U.S. ambassadorial residence in Vienna for their first private meeting. He tells the Soviet minister, "We really hope that you succeed."

March 16: The CC CPSU adopts an agricultural reform program that would break up the central agricultural ministry and allow individual farmers to lease farmland.

March 17: The Hungarian Central Committee approves a new program of action which supports the principle of free elections.

March 26: Elections to the new Soviet Congress of People's Deputies take place. Many Party and military officials lose to independent candidates. Yeltsin wins the Moscow at-large seat with 89 percent of the vote. Andrei Sakharov also overwhelmingly wins a seat.

April 5: The Polish government and Solidarity reach an agreement on political and economic reforms, including the holding of elections in the summer and a restructuring of Parliament. The agreement also calls for strengthening the presidency.

April 6: In a private meeting in London with Thatcher, Gorbachev denounces Bush's "pause" as "intolerable." Thatcher urges patience but immediately sends a message to Bush describing how upset Gorbachev was and commenting that the ongoing U.S. policy review is indeed taking a long time.

April 7: The Polish government and Solidarity sign the Roundtable accords.

April 9: Soviet troops kill 20 Georgian nationalist demonstrators in the capital city of Tbilisi.

April 12: Ceaușescu announces that his country's foreign debt has been paid ahead of schedule.

April 15: Hu Yaobang, a respected Chinese Communist Party leader, dies. Over the next several days, tens of thousands of students gather in Tiananmen Square to mourn his death. The gatherings turn into demonstrations for democracy and freedom of the press.

April 17: Poland's Solidarity trade union is legalized.

April 20: The CPSU Politburo in a heated discussion denounces the use of military force in Tbilisi. Gorbachev claims he did not know about the decision to employ troops and blames it on the Georgian party leadership.

April 21: During a Politburo meeting on Afghanistan, Gorbachev opposes a proposal by Shevardnadze and KGB chief Kryuchkov to come to the rescue of the Najibullah regime by means of an aerial strike on rebel bases.

April 25: One thousand Soviet tanks leave Hungary. This marks the first stage of the planned Soviet withdrawal of 50,000 troops and 10,000 tanks from Eastern Europe by 1991.

May 2: Hungary begins dismantling the barbed wire on its borders with Austria.

May 5: The USSR announces it has withdrawn 1,000 tanks from East Germany.

May 8–9: The Hungarian CC votes to remove Kádár from the post of party first secretary and from the Central Committee.

May 11: The CPSU Politburo discusses a proposal by the Politburo commission on the situation in the Baltic republics. Gorbachev emphasizes that "force does not help in this business. We have accepted that even in foreign policy force accomplishes nothing. But internally especially—we cannot and will not resort to force."

May 13: Several thousand students start fasting at Tiananmen Square to pressure the Chinese government to meet their demands.

May 15–18: Gorbachev visits China for the first Sino-Soviet summit in 30 years and announces the "normalization" of relations.

May 17: Václav Havel is released from prison.

May 17: The Polish Sejm votes to give the Roman Catholic Church legal status.

May 18: The Lithuanian Supreme Soviet declares sovereignty.

May 20–21: Bulgarian authorities put down protests against the government's policy of forced assimilation in the south. Over 100 ethnic Turks are killed.

May 25–June 9: The new Soviet Congress of People's Deputies meets for the first time and elects Gorbachev president. The congress is televised and has a powerful impact on Soviet viewers. One of the first cases taken on by the Congress is the use of force against demonstrators in Tbilisi and the question of Gorbachev's involvement in giving the order.

June 3–15: Violent ethnic riots occur in Uzbekistan.

June 4: Solidarity wins decisively in free parliamentary elections. The union wins 92 of 100 seats in the Senate and 160 of 161 available seats in the 460-seat Sejm.

June 4: Chinese government troops with armored vehicles crush protests in Tiananmen Square, killing hundreds.

June 13: The Hungarian "Roundtable" talks begin.

June 16: Imre Nagy, the reform prime minister during the Hungarian revolution who was executed in 1958 and interred in an anonymous grave, is ceremonially re-buried.

June 18: A runoff election is held in Poland. Solidarity captures seven of eight unfilled seats in the Senate and the single open seat in the Sejm.

June 19: START negotiations resume in Geneva.

June 22: The Hungarian CC reorganizes the leadership of the party, creating a four-member Presidium consisting of Grósz, Pozsgay, Németh and Rezső Nyers.

June 30: Jaruzelski announces that he will not run for the presidency of Poland.

July: Shevardnadze visits Budapest. He tells Hungarian leaders: "Do what you think is best to preserve the position of the party."

July 1: Speaking on Soviet television, Gorbachev warns of ethnic conflict breaking out in the USSR.

July 4: The Polish Parliament convenes. Premier Rakowski and his cabinet offer their resignations but agree to stay on as caretakers.

July 6: Former Hungarian leader Kádár dies. On the same date, the Hungarian Supreme Court rehabilitates Imre Nagy and his associates.

July 6: Addressing the Council of Europe in Strasbourg, Gorbachev says the USSR will not block reform in Eastern Europe and will promote comprehensive European political and economic integration in the framework of a "common European home."

July 7: In Bucharest, Gorbachev speaks to Warsaw Pact leaders and seems to accept the changes in Poland and Hungary. Ceauşescu openly complains about "disunity" within the alliance.

July 9–13: Bush is hailed by crowds in Poland and Hungary. However, his cautious speeches, designed not to offend the Soviets, are later the subject of criticism.

July 10: In the USSR a wave of mining strikes begins and continues for several weeks.

July 10: Bush meets with Jaruzelski in the morning and tells him he thinks the Polish leader might be able to "assist in a process, an evolution," in Poland. Jaruzelski subsequently reverses his earlier decision not to run for the presidency. Speaking before Parliament, Bush pledges $100 million in aid to underwrite private enterprise development. Bush also meets with Wałęsa in Gdańsk.

July 12: Meeting privately with Grósz, Nyers, and Németh in Budapest, Bush tells the party leaders that he does not want to force them to "choose between East and West." He also meets with opposition leaders.

July 14: Wałęsa offers his support to Jaruzelski in his bid to be Poland's president.

July 14: The CPSU Politburo debates a draft proposal to transform the USSR into a looser federation with a larger degree of republican autonomy.

July 19: Jaruzelski is elected president of Poland.

July 22: The Lithuanian Parliament declares the 1940 Soviet annexation of the Baltics illegal.

July 25: Jaruzelski invites Solidarity to join a coalition government.

July 30: The "Inter-regional Group of Deputies" is formed in the USSR Supreme Soviet by Yeltsin, Sakharov, and others.

August 16: Solidarity and the United Peasants' and Democratic Parties agree to form a coalition government. Jaruzelski demands only that the PUWP be guaranteed the defense and interior portfolios.

August 18: Yakovlev holds a press conference to denounce "unequivocally" the 1939 Nazi–Soviet Pact which led to the annexation of the Baltics. However, he states that the Soviet government still considers the Baltics a part of the USSR and will resist any attempts to dislodge them from the Union.

August 21: In Prague, 3,000 demonstrators mark the 20th anniversary of the Warsaw Pact invasion. Security police break up the demonstrations.

August 24: Tadeusz Mazowiecki becomes the first noncommunist Polish prime minister since the early postwar period.

September 8–10: Rukh—the nationalist movement in the Ukraine—holds its constituent congress in Kiev and displays the banned blue-and-yellow flag of independent Ukraine.

September 10: Hungarian authorities announce they will no longer prevent East German citizens from crossing Hungary's border into Austria, a move that eventually makes it possible for 180,000 East Germans to reach the West.

September 11: Mazowiecki nominates a cabinet in which representatives of the PUWP are a minority.

September 19: The Hungarian government and opposition representatives reach an accord to create a multiparty system in 1990. The agreement provides for a unicameral legislature to be filled by free elections, a strong presidency with the authority to choose the premier, and the legalization and granting of rights to political parties.

September 22–23: Shevardnadze and Baker meet at the latter's ranch in Wyoming. They discuss START, chemical weapons, regional conflicts, and independence movements in the USSR.

September 23: The Azerbaijan Supreme Soviet makes Azeri the official language of the Republic, reasserts sovereignty over Nagorno-Karabakh, and reaffirms Azerbaijan's right of secession from the USSR.

October 6: Gorbachev meets with Honecker in East Berlin and advises that he begin a reform program. He later tells aides that Honecker "can't stay in control" and must go.

October 7: The Hungarian Communist Party formally dissolves, renaming itself the Hungarian Socialist party and adopting democratic socialist politics instead of Marxism.

October 9: Over 70,000 East Germans demonstrate against their government in Leipzig. Local communist leaders refuse to attack the marchers.

October 12: The Polish government announces new anti-inflationary measures and promises the "full introduction of market mechanisms and institutions" in 1990–1991.

October 17: Honecker is forced to resign both as general secretary and head of state. He is replaced by Egon Krenz, the former security chief and youngest member of the Politburo.

October 23: Hungary adopts a new constitution permitting a multiparty system, scheduling elections for 1990 and changing the country's name to the Republic of Hungary. Acting president Mátyás Szűrös declares the 1956 Soviet invasion to have been illegal.

October 23: Between 200–300,000 East Germans demonstrate against the government in Leipzig.

October 26: Shevardnadze calls for the dissolution of NATO and the Warsaw Pact.

October 28: About 10,000 protesters gather in Wenceslas Square in Prague to mark the 71st anniversary of the formation of Czechoslovakia. Demonstrators ignore demands to leave the square. Riot police storm the crowd and arrest 355 demonstrators.

October 31: Facing growing economic problems, Krenz authorizes secret meetings with West Germany to obtain emergency loans in exchange for a certain liberalization of movement between the two Germanys.

November 1: Gorbachev meets with Krenz at the Kremlin and calls on him to speed up reforms and open borders to "avoid an explosion." The GDR does so with respect to Czechoslovakia the same day, and two days later Czechoslovakia allows the transit of East Germans to the West.

November 3: The Bulgarian environmental group Eco-Glasnost holds pro-democracy demonstrations in Sofia. An estimated 9,000 protesters attend the event.

November 4: A crowd of 500,000 East Germans demonstrates for democracy in East Berlin.

November 7: East German Premier Willi Stoph and his cabinet resign.

November 8: Hans Modrow is named the new premier of East Germany.

November 9: The CPSU Politburo debates a proposal to grant Lithuania, Latvia, Estonia and Byelorussia the right of "economic self-accountability."

November 9: Helmut Kohl visits Warsaw. Wałęsa expresses concern that the opening of the wall between East and West Germany will divert FRG resources to the GDR and away from Poland.

November 9: The GDR announces the opening of all borders, including the Berlin Wall. Berliners from both sides cross through the eight check points, and began to chip away at the concrete and steel barrier.

November 9: Zhivkov, general secretary of the Bulgarian party since 1954 and president since 1971, is deposed and replaced by Petar Mladenov.

November 13: The East German Parliament, the *Volkskammer*, confirms that Modrow will replace Stoph as premier.

November 17: Modrow disbands the East German Ministry for State Security.

November 17: Mladenov is elected president of Bulgaria.

November 19: Civic Forum is formed in Prague as an umbrella opposition organization.

November 20: Mass demonstrations take place in Prague's Wenceslas Square.

November 21: A closed-door meeting is held between Czechoslovak Premier Adamec and the leaders of Civic Forum. Havel later announces that Adamec promised not to impose martial law and to investigate charges of brutality by the security forces.

November 23: Deposed Czechoslovak leader Alexander Dubček makes his first public appearance in 21 years at a 70,000-person anti-government demonstration in Bratislava.

November 24: Ceauşescu is elected to another term as general secretary. He calls the party the "vital center" of Romanian life.

November 24: Jakeš and the rest of the Politburo and Secretariat resign their party posts. Karel Urbánek is named the new CPCz leader.

November 28: Kohl unveils his 10-point plan for German reunification.

November 28: In Czechoslovakia, Adamec, now serving in a caretaker role after resigning on the 24th, pledges that the communists will give up their monopoly on power.

November 29: The Czechoslovak Parliament removes the clause in the Constitution concerning the "leading role" of the Communist Party.

November 30: Speaking in Rome, Gorbachev calls for a "common European home."

December 1: Gorbachev meets with Pope John Paul II and promises to reestablish diplomatic relations with the Vatican and enact a law guaranteeing freedom of conscience and the legalization of the Ukrainian Catholic Church.

December 1: The East German Parliament abolishes the Communist Party's special status.

December 2–3: The Malta summit takes place. Gorbachev tries to get Bush to commit to his idea of the gradual transformation of Eastern Europe with the close cooperation of the superpowers in order to prevent instability. The U.S. president states that he will not "jump on the wall," but pressures the Soviet leader on regional conflicts, especially in Central America. Gorbachev suggests recognizing the primacy of common democratic values rather than Western ideals in the final communiqué.

December 3: The East German Politburo resigns, including Krenz and Modrow. Krenz is reinstated as general secretary, Modrow as premier; Honecker and Stoph are expelled from the party.

December 3: Civic Forum rejects Adamec's proposal for a cabinet headed by him and including non-communists.

December 4: Gorbachev meets in Moscow with leaders of the Warsaw Pact nations. Bulgaria is represented by Mladenov; Czechoslovakia by Urbánek; East Germany by Krenz and Modrow; Hungary by Nyers; Poland by Mazowiecki; Romania by Ceauşescu. They issue a condemnation of the 1968 invasion of Czechoslovakia, although Ceauşescu refuses to sign on.

December 5: A new Czechoslovak cabinet is formed with a non-communist majority.

December 6: Krenz resigns as East Germany's head of state and chairman of the council on national defense. Manfred Gerlach is named interim president.

December 7: The East German government announces multiparty elections scheduled for May 6, 1990.

December 7: Jakeš is expelled from the Czechoslovak Communist Party.

December 7–9: Independent opposition groups in Bulgaria merge to form the Union of Democratic Forces.

December 9: Gregor Gysi replaces Krenz as East Germany's communist leader.

December 10: Husák, leader of the Czechoslovak Communist Party from 1968 to December 1987 and president since May 1975, resigns the presidency.

December 11: Bulgarian leader Mladenov announces support for free elections and pledges to end the Party's leading role in society.

December 12: The second session of the USSR Congress of People's Deputies convenes. Gorbachev refuses to discuss the elimination of Article VI stipulating the leading role of the Communist Party, and hounds Sakharov from the podium.

December 13: Zhivkov is expelled from the Bulgarian Communist Party.

December 13: Twenty-four Western nations announce a $1 billion emergency fund for Poland's economy.

December 14: Andrei Sakharov dies.

December 14: About 20,000 protesters surround the Bulgarian Parliament building and demand an end to the Communist Party's political monopoly.

December 17: Romanian security forces fire on demonstrators in Timisoara.

December 18: The European Economic Community and the Soviet Union sign a 10-year commercial agreement.

December 19: Modrow and Kohl meet in Dresden.

December 22: After a speech in Bucharest's main square, the Romanian dictator flees in a helicopter. The "National Salvation Front" declares itself to be the new government. The Soviets hail the overthrow of Ceauşescu as reflecting "the will of the Romanian people."

December 23: The Brandenburg Gate is reopened in Berlin.

December 23: Provisional Romanian leader Ion Iliescu declares himself in favor of a renovated socialism. He calls for a program of action that commits itself to promoting the "common values of humanity."

December 24: On NBC Television's interview program "Meet the Press," Baker says the United States will not object if the Warsaw Pact intervenes in Romania. On the same day, in a conversation between Soviet Deputy Foreign Minister Aboimov and U.S. Ambassador Jack Matlock, the Soviet diplomat responds to the idea that Moscow should consider becoming militarily involved in Romania by suggesting that the USSR is offering the Brezhnev Doctrine to the United States "as a gift," adding that Soviet use of force in Eastern Europe is out of question.

December 25: Ceauşescu and his wife, Elena, are executed after a hasty trial before a military tribunal.

December 28: The Czechoslovak Parliament elects Dubček as chairman.

December 29: The National Salvation Front—Romania's provisional government—announces that Romania is no longer a communist state.

December 29: Havel is elected Czechoslovakia's new president. Dubček becomes speaker of the Federal Assembly.

Sources

Beschloss, Michael and Strobe Talbott. *At the Highest Levels: The Inside Story of the End of the Cold War* (Boston: Little, Brown and Company, 1993).

Blanton, Thomas, William Burr and Vladislav Zubok, eds. "Chronology," *Briefing Book for the CNN "Cold War" Television History* (unpublished, July 1997).

Dawisha, Karen. *Eastern Europe, Gorbachev, and Reform* (New York: Cambridge University Press, 1990).

The Foreign Affairs Chronology of World Events: 1978–1991, 2nd ed. (New York: Council on Foreign Relations Press, 1992).

Garthoff, Raymond L. *The Great Transition: American–Soviet Relations and the End of the Cold War* (Washington, D.C.: The Brookings Institution, 1994).

Gates, Robert M. *From the Shadows: The Ultimate Insider's Story of Five Presidents and How They Won the Cold War* (New York: Simon and Schuster, 1996).

Lévesque, Jacques. *The Enigma of 1989: The USSR and the Liberation of Eastern Europe* (Berkeley: University of California Press, 1997).

Matlock, Jack F. Jr. *Autopsy on an Empire: The American Ambassador's Account of the Collapse of the Soviet Union* (New York: Random House, 1995).

Oberdorfer, Don. *The Turn: From the Cold War to a New Era: the United States and the Soviet Union, 1983–1990* (New York: Simon and Schuster, 1992).

Shakhnazarov, Georgy Kh. *The Price of Freedom. Gorbachev's Reformation As Seen by His Assistant* (Moscow: Rossika-Zevs, 1993).

Shultz, George P. *Turmoil and Triumph: My Years as Secretary of State* (New York: Charles Scribner's Sons, 1993).

The Union Could Have Been Preserved. Documents and Facts on the Policy of M.S. Gorbachev to Reform and Preserve the Multinational State (Moscow: Act Publishers, 2007).

The Logic of 1989: The Soviet Peaceful Withdrawal from Eastern Europe

By Svetlana Savranskaya

The Cold War came to an end in the exact geographical region where it began. In 1989, Eastern Europe became the epicenter of breathtaking changes that went beyond all Western expectations, Soviet fears, and the hopes of the East Europeans themselves. The non-violent and even harmonious nature of the change was naturally welcome but it was also puzzling to contemporaries, just as it still is to students of international politics today, who see it as a kind of beautiful aberration from the *realpolitik* perspective. Indeed, the most unexpected and seemingly illogical aspect of the East European transformations was the peaceful Soviet reaction to them. Moscow's permissive and even encouraging stance toward these developments in the summer and fall of 1989, embodying Mikhail Gorbachev's ultimate rejection of the use of force, is difficult to explain in terms of traditional power politics.

This puzzling outcome, or in Jacques Levesque's words, "the enigma of 1989,"[1] raises further specific questions. When did the change in Soviet policy toward Eastern Europe actually take place? What were the main factors determining Moscow's response to the unfolding crisis in the region in 1989? Why did the Gorbachev leadership act seemingly contrary to the long-standing Soviet interest of keeping a security belt along its Western border? How did the assessment of the strategic value versus cost of the alliance change in the late 1980s? Was the use of force ever seriously considered? What other possible scenarios did Soviet decision-makers imagine?

In response to Levesque's intellectual challenge, I would argue that the peaceful Soviet withdrawal from Eastern Europe was not at all an enigma. In fact, looking at all the available evidence, it probably was the most rational and reasonable policy to pursue at the time, following logically from Gorbachev's own thinking, his domestic and foreign policy priorities, the advice he received, and the course of events unfolding in Eastern Europe in 1989, in which the main role was played not by the superpowers but by the politicians and citizens of those countries. Using force in Eastern Europe in 1989 would have been senseless, ineffective and probably political suicide for Gorbachev, because it would have meant sacrificing everything he had fought for and achieved with *perestroika*, both domestically and internationally. In fact, a careful reading of Levesque's *Enigma* reveals that the author himself, the title notwithstanding, draws the conclusion that by 1989 the resort to force by the USSR would have been both

---

[1] Levesque, *Enigma*.

1

highly unlikely and counterproductive. Most of the recent document-based studies of the end of the Cold War share that view to some extent.[2]

The Soviet reluctance to use force or even pressure can only be puzzling if seen from within two common analytical frameworks. The first, which often serves as an implicit point of reference when the Soviet peaceful withdrawal is described as surprising, is the traditional realist perspective—in which one derives expectations from an abstract notion of the balance of power and assumed security interests without analyzing the actual dynamics of events or the personalities of the actors. The second framework is a narrowly focused examination of the history of the Soviet policy toward Eastern Europe which incorporates heavily deterministic tragic historical precedents and metaphors, such as the Soviet interventions in Hungary in 1956 and Czechoslovakia in 1968, and the image of soil sanctified by the blood of Soviet soldiers who died in World War Two (often invoked by Soviet hardliners). This framework presumes that Eastern Europe must always have been of the highest priority for Soviet decision-makers.

Since the East European countries were the USSR's most important allies, and (in view of a possible military conflict on the European continent) a strategically vital sphere of influence, one would expect that the Kremlin leadership would have used all means at its disposal—beginning with diplomatic and political measures, but including military if all others failed—to preserve the unity of the socialist commonwealth. However, the documents and witness accounts suggest that the new Soviet rulers made decisions on the basis of norms and beliefs that often contradicted such narrowly defined security considerations. In fact, Gorbachev and his close advisers redefined traditional security concepts on the basis of a new liberal internationalist vision and normative concerns that were highly original in the Soviet context. Strictly speaking, if one does not take account of these changes, then Soviet behavior in Eastern Europe in the late 1980s indeed makes no sense from a *realpolitik* point of view.[3]

However, new evidence obtained by the National Security Archive in the last ten years allows one to take another look at the end of the Cold War in Europe and provide more detailed answers to the questions posed above. These materials have surfaced as the result of a fruitful collaboration with the Gorbachev Foundation, our partners in Eastern Europe, as well as from oral history conferences and U.S. Freedom of Information Act requests. Over the last twenty years, numerous

---

[2] See especially Brown, *The Gorbachev Factor*; Leffler, *For the Soul of Mankind*; Grachev, *Gorbachev's Gamble*, and Zubok, *A Failed Empire*. For an excellent analysis based on documents from East European as well as Russian archives see Kramer, "The Collapse of East European Communism." This view was also shared by the analysts of the CIA Soviet desk (SOVA) as early as 1989: see MacEachin, Musgrove transcript, 171–173.

[3] For a discussion of Gorbachev's foreign policy from a realist standpoint see Wohlforth, *The Elusive Balance*, 18–32, 252–292 and Wohlforth, *Cold War Endgame*.

eyewitnesses published their accounts of the events of 1989, which illuminate our view of those events.[4]

The new documents, including the extraordinary collection presented in this volume, along with numerous eyewitness accounts, show that real change in Soviet policy toward the region began much earlier than is usually perceived, practically within the first few months of *perestroika*; that economic factors played a very important role in the redefinition of the value to Moscow of its smaller partners; and that the use of force was never seriously considered as a way to keep the alliance together. Interaction with Western leaders, especially U.S. presidents played a major role in providing a context of trust and success in arms control in which later Soviet decisions on Eastern Europe were made.[5] When looking at the record, one can see the overriding importance to Gorbachev and his allies of the idea of the common European home, which for them meant the USSR's economic and political integration into Europe, and how that priority structured many of the other choices the new leadership made, including the peaceful withdrawal from Eastern Europe. The explanation of the Soviet withdrawal would be incomplete without mentioning the evolution of Gorbachev's own thinking over the first four years of *perestroika*. Gorbachev of 1985 was not Gorbachev of 1989.

FAREWELL TO THE BREZHNEV DOCTRINE

From his very first days in power, Mikhail Gorbachev generated hopes for reform and liberalization in the countries of Eastern Europe. At the same time, both domestic and international observers in the mid-1980s had every reason to be skeptical about his stated intentions, which were perceived in the context of post-WWII Soviet behavior in the region—behavior that included the imposition of Soviet-style regimes by force and armed interventions when those regimes were seriously challenged by domestic opposition. Under those conditions, repudiation of the Brezhnev Doctrine was a necessary first step before Gorbachev's new thinking could become credible internationally. Reform communists and dissidents in the East European countries waited for Gorbachev to make a public statement to that effect, and journalists dogged him repeatedly on the subject during foreign trips.[6] Primary sources show that the new leader expressed his intention to reverse Moscow's traditional behavior within the circle of his advisers and to allied leaders early in his tenure, even though visible changes in policy

---

[4] The most valuable memoirs of the end of the Cold War used in this essay are Gorbachev, *Zhizn' i reformy*, Chernyaev, *Shest' let*, Medvedev, *Raspad*, Shakhnazarov, *Tsena svobody*, and memoirs of the British and the U.S. ambassadors to the Soviet Union, Braithwaite, *Across the Moscow River*, and Matlock, *Autopsy on an Empire*.

[5] On the importance of interactions with U.S. presidents to Gorbachev and his reassessment of external threat, see Thomas Blanton's essay in this volume.

[6] Musgrove transcript, 131, 138.

appeared more tentative for the outside world. The early years, before 1989, in fact, showed signs of both continuity and change in Soviet policy toward the region although the style of the dialog within the Warsaw Pact changed noticeably already in 1985.

It is not clear whether these changes were immediately obvious to the socialist leaders, because Gorbachev often used terminology in meetings with them that was similar to his predecessors'. Even while he made bold new policy pronouncements about freedom of choice and independence of each state, he managed for a long time to preserve a degree of ambiguity, especially in his private conversations with East European leaders, as to the limits of Soviet tolerance of threats to the "preservation of socialism."[7] It was expected that the new general secretary would begin his term with broad initiatives to reinvigorate the socialist bloc, where disgruntled feelings had been building under the surface during the early 1980s. What made his initial policy declarations on Eastern Europe less conspicuous was the order of his priorities upon assuming the leadership. They were domestic economic reform, arms control and withdrawal from Afghanistan.[8]

Even though Eastern Europe as such was not quite as high on Gorbachev's list of concerns, he understood that change there was overdue and he believed that as a good communist he could not afford to appear to be neglecting his socialist allies. At the same time, as Gorbachev's adviser and spokesman Andrei Grachev pointed out, the "apparent tranquility" of Eastern Europe in 1985 did not call for an urgent action and allowed the Soviet leader to postpone decisive steps and confronting difficult issues that came to haunt them later in 1989–1990.[9]

In his most recent book, Gorbachev emphasized that the intention to transform relations within the socialist bloc was indeed one of the earliest and most important concerns of *perestroika*: "[F]rom the very beginning we made it our rule that each of the members of the CMEA and the Warsaw Treaty would be independent in their decisions and that what happened with the 'Prague Spring' in Czechoslovakia should never be repeated—when the people wanted to build socialism 'with a human face' independently and we responded to that with tanks."[10] New evidence corroborates this statement: Soviet policy toward Eastern Europe began to change soon after his election as general secretary.

Gorbachev took the first step in this direction during conversations with the leaders of the fraternal countries while they were in Moscow for Konstantin Chernenko's funeral from March 12–15, 1985. Gorbachev notes that it was at the first of these meetings that the idea of "rejecting the Brezhnev Doctrine" was broached.[11] Although we do not know all the details of this meeting—the transcript is still unavailable and only Gorbachev's report to the Central Committee

---

[7] Document No. 50, Mikhail Gorbachev and Miklós Németh Conversation, March 3, 1989.

[8] Grachev, *Gorbachev's Gamble*, 55.

[9] Ibid., 114.

[10] Gorbachev, *Ponyat' perestroiku*, 33.

[11] Gorbachev, *Zhizn' i reformy*, vol. 2, 312.

secretaries has been declassified[12]—all key Soviet observers point to its exceptional importance. Gorbachev spoke informally, listening to his counterparts' concerns and emphasizing the need for a new level of coordination among the leaders on economic and political issues. According to Chernyaev, Gorbachev told his colleagues that they were responsible for their policies only to their own people and to their parties. That conversation occurred immediately after Chernenko's funeral. "Literally, on the next day," Chernyaev recounted at the Musgrove conference, "he gathered all of them in his office in the Kremlin, and told them that from then on there was no more Brezhnev Doctrine, that kindergarten was over." "Where you go, how you get there—that is your business, I will not interfere. I will not interfere even when you ask me for it."[13] Already at that meeting, as Gorbachev reported to the secretaries, the splits within the community were obvious: the Soviet participants spoke very highly about Wojciech Jaruzelski and János Kádár's speeches, but negatively and even condescendingly about Nicolae Ceaușescu's objections to renewing the Warsaw Treaty for the next 20 years. Gorbachev took Jaruzelski's ideas about the need for more informal contacts among socialist leaders very seriously and suggested that the CPSU Central Committee follow up on this issue.

The April Plenum of the Central Committee was another important event for Gorbachev and his policy of new thinking. Although it was mainly used as the occasion to officially launch *perestroika*, the expressed need for change left no sphere of economic or social life—or policy area—untouched. The Plenum also made significant personnel shifts, elevating Gorbachev's supporters to higher levels of political power, and sent signals throughout the system that a real transformation was forthcoming. The discourse stayed well within the framework of the socialist idea, but the fresh style and decisiveness of the new leader were unmistakable. In the Soviet system, the power and authority of the general secretary remained such that no opposition to his innovations was anticipated, but at the same time no deviation from the socialist mainstream on his part was expected either. As was the practice, the proceedings of the Plenum were widely read and interpreted by Moscow's allies. Therefore, even though the Plenum did not deal with Eastern Europe specifically, the winds of change were felt throughout the region.

The next indication of change in the Soviet position toward Eastern Europe came at the end of June 1985, when Gorbachev took strong action in response to an article in *Pravda* signed by "Vladimirov" that attacked the new policies unfolding in the socialist commonwealth.[14] The author of the piece was the conservative first deputy head of the Central Committee's Department for Liaison with Ruling Communist Parties, better known as simply "the Department" [*Otdel*], Oleg Rakhmanin. The article argued against "national models" of socialism in

[12] Document No. 1, Gorbachev's Conference with CC CPSU Secretaries, March 15, 1985.
[13] Musgrove transcript, 121.
[14] *Pravda*, June 21, 1985; Document No. 2, Diary of Anatoly Chernyaev, July 5, 1985.

fraternal countries, blamed them for promoting harmful tendencies toward nationalism and even Russophobia, and called for strengthening discipline within the socialist camp. It was especially critical of the Hungarian reforms and Budapest's economic ties with Western Europe. According to Georgy Shakhnazarov, who was at the time a deputy head in the same CC section, the article was seen in Eastern Europe as a "reinstatement of the Brezhnev Doctrine."[15] The Department immediately started receiving calls from the allies asking if the piece truly represented Moscow's position.

Gorbachev, meanwhile, correctly saw the article as seriously undermining his new approach to the region, and even his image, making him look like a "monster who ha[d] come to power."[16] Deciding that he needed to "extricate" himself, he contacted certain allied leaders on a "pretext" to make sure they knew the article was not a reflection of Kremlin opinion.[17] At a Politburo session on June 29, he made his displeasure and embarrassment known, subjecting Konstantin Rusakov, the head of the Department and Rakhmanin's superior, to particularly scathing criticism. He later replaced Rusakov with a like-minded reformer, Vadim Medvedev, and Rakhmanin with one of the Kremlin's most radical thinkers, Shakhnazarov. This incident and subsequent personnel changes were widely discussed in the Central Committee apparatus and viewed as unambiguous evidence of a new approach to Eastern Europe on the part of the general secretary.

If the signals were not yet clear outside the Kremlin, on October 21, 1985, at a meeting of the PCC, Gorbachev provided a lengthy analysis of the state of the international communist movement, suggesting that it was going through difficult times, and that each communist country now had to interpret the situation independently. Gorbachev also announced a new approach to the allies: the development of relations based on equality and respect for national sovereignty and independence, as well as mutually advantageous cooperation in all spheres. He stressed that these new principles also meant that the ruling parties bore full responsibility for conditions in their respective countries.[18]

Thus, Gorbachev's first year already served notice that the new general secretary was serious about changing the state of relations among the partners in order to make them more equal and mutually beneficial. Of course, for a group accustomed to taking orders from Moscow and aware of the ever-present possibility of armed "fraternal assistance," those signals were not immediately seen as *carte blanche* to strive for genuine independence or reforms. But the difference in style was noticed both within the USSR and abroad, and the apparent new Soviet flexibility became a source of hope and—for hardliners—concern throughout Eastern Europe.

---

[15] Musgrove transcript, 123.
[16] Ibid., 124
[17] Document No. 2, Diary of Anatoly Chernyaev, July 5, 1985.
[18] The Diary of Anatoly Chernyaev, October 19, 1985, http://www.gwu.edu/~nsarchiv/NSAEBB/NSAEBB192/Chernyaev_Diary_translation_1985.pdf.

Gorbachev's new approach did not escape resistance at home, notably from a cohort of apparatchiks who were used to treating the East European countries essentially as vassals. In order to alter relations within the bloc, Gorbachev first had to break the inertia of old-style thinking within his own diplomatic corps and the Central Committee apparatus. He attempted to do just that at a meeting with Foreign Ministry officials and ambassadors in May 1986. In a forceful statement, he announced a new era of dealings with the socialist community: "[T]he time when we helped them to form their economy, their parties, and their political institutions is past [...] we cannot lead them by the hand to kindergarten as we would little children." He declared that he was willing to trust "their search for national approaches, even though some steps that our friends take might be detrimental to the common cause." He also called for greater policy coordination and mutual respect within the alliance, and specifically promoted the creation of an institution of multilateral working meetings at the leadership level.[19]

Ironically, these changes were mostly felt internally, while for outside observers it appeared that Eastern Europe was treated with a benign neglect, or what Levesque called "immobilism" almost until the end of 1988.[20] The reasons for this cautious behavior could be that on the one hand Gorbachev did not see an acute crisis in his own backyard, and that on the other he felt quite uncomfortable making any decisions that would amount to interference in the domestic affairs of the allies. The fact that Gorbachev's closest supporter in the top leadership, Alexander Yakovlev, and his foreign policy adviser, Anatoly Chernyaev, were more interested respectively in domestic liberalization and relations with capitalist countries must have contributed to his relative lack of attention to Eastern Europe, among other factors. Chernyaev remarks on Gorbachev's seeming unwillingness to deal with his socialist counterparts in his memoir: "As far as the 'socialist commonwealth' was concerned, I did not notice any special interest to it on Gorbachev's part. [...] I felt that he interacted with the leaders of socialist countries without enthusiasm, only with difficulty agreed to visits, and obviously was not inclined to demonstrate 'his leadership role'."[21] The most important issue for Gorbachev, as far as the socialist bloc was concerned, was the absence of real integration in CMEA, which at the time seemed to be repairable.

Returning from a PCC meeting in Budapest in June 1986, Gorbachev presented to the Politburo a summary of the speeches made by the socialist leaders and his own impressions about the problems confronting the member-states. He spoke with optimism and approval about the growing independence of the allies because "they are still drawn to us," and about the interest in a dialogue with the West, which did not seem problematic to him. He then talked at some length about the economic problems in CMEA. This topic had taken up one-third of the

[19] Document No. 4, Mikhail Gorbachev Speech to Ministry of Foreign Affairs, May 28, 1986.
[20] Levesque, *Enigma*, 52.
[21] Chernyaev, *Shest'let*, 81.

time at the PCC and produced a genuine discussion, which in itself was a change from the formal speech-making of previous PCC meetings.

The main problem facing CMEA, according to Gorbachev, was the lack of integration between socialist countries and their resulting reliance on bilateral agreements, a function of the general inclination to "avoid questions of integration." A major issue was the creation of mechanisms for coordinating decision-making on foreign policy, especially on economic matters. Gorbachev stressed the independence of the allies and the need to restructure economic relations "exclusively on mutually beneficial grounds." Another issue that came up repeatedly was the economic relationship between the socialist countries and the West, especially West Germany. ("Everyone wants to get closer to the FRG," he noted.) Gorbachev spoke warily about such ties without prohibiting them outright, suggesting that Kádár should "lean on our shoulder, it will make it easier with the West as well." The Soviet leader believed in improving integration in CMEA first, and then dealing with the EEC collectively, bloc-to-bloc, arguing that the long-term view of integration between those two organizations was the best way out of the existing economic predicament. Importantly, even though economic problems received detailed treatment, Gorbachev did not see the situation as a general crisis, nor did he perceive the East European allies as a liability or a burden. At the Politburo, he expressed his strong belief that with the Soviet Union providing the model and leading the way, the East Europeans would follow and remain valuable partners in a reformed socialist alliance.[22]

Probably the key document that gives one an insight into Gorbachev's own early thinking on Eastern Europe is the long memorandum that he sent to Politburo members on June 26, 1986, for discussion at the Politburo session on July 3.[23] As a personal memorandum of the general secretary (drafted by Shakhnazarov and Medvedev), it is quite a unique document. In it, Gorbachev reaffirmed that CMEA was lacking genuine integration, and observed that a significant change of leadership was taking place in most countries of the Eastern bloc. He underscored the USSR's special responsibility for the fate of world socialism and the need to lead by example, not by imposing its will. The memo described economic integration as the main task, including real coordination in foreign policy and the sharing of experience and information about internal policies, among other priorities. Gorbachev concluded with a suggestion that there should be a discussion of Eastern Europe at the Politburo followed by instructions to the Ministry of Foreign Affairs, the KGB and the relevant departments of the Central Committee to develop a strategy of relations with the socialist countries.

Ironically, this document ended with a call to make relations with the allies a top priority of the Soviet Union, which at the time they obviously were not. One may guess that Gorbachev felt that he was obligated to regard them as an

---

22 Document No. 5, Notes of CC CPSU Politburo Session, June 13, 1986.
23 Document No. 6, Memorandum from Mikhail Gorbachev to the Politburo, June 26, 1986.

uppermost concern for both ideological and strategic reasons, and yet his heart was elsewhere. The June 26 memorandum was the first of his numerous calls to the leadership for a new coordinated strategy toward Eastern Europe. Yet no concrete steps in that direction were made until early 1989, when by all measures it was already too late—events were overtaking even the most ambitious strategies. It was one thing to have a bold new vision but another thing to develop a government policy that would implement it.

In order to strengthen communist reformers in the East European countries, the Soviet leader had to address the issue of past Soviet interventions in the region, such as the suppression of the Hungarian revolution of 1956 and the Prague Spring of 1968. He was presented with an ideal opportunity to do so when he traveled to Prague in April 1987, where euphoric crowds cheered Gorbachev but acted as if his Czechoslovak counterpart, Gustáv Husák, was not even there.[24] There was widespread hope in the country that Gorbachev would change the official interpretation of the Prague Spring as a counterrevolution instigated by outside elements. And yet he chose not to do so, holding fast instead to the standard formulas. From the documents, we now know that there was strong pressure from the Czechoslovak leadership on Gorbachev not to amend the interpretation, because as Vasil Bil'ak stressed, "it could become a catastrophe for Czechoslovak society."[25] According to Vadim Medvedev, who accompanied Gorbachev to Prague, the Soviet delegation was acutely aware that they were stepping into the midst of an intense internal political debate about change in the leadership, which had been "dictated by the 1968 syndrome." In fact, while Gorbachev was meeting with Husák, Bil'ak and Miloš Jakeš were talking to Medvedev in a separate room about the importance of keeping the official version of 1968 unchanged.[26]

The decision was made not to offer a public statement on the issue so as not to interfere in the domestic political struggle. In his private meetings with Czechoslovak officials, Gorbachev only carefully stated that it was up to them to allow political rehabilitation of individuals expelled from the party for their participation in the events of the Dubček era. Zdeněk Mlynář, the émigré Czech intellectual who had been Gorbachev's classmate and close friend at Moscow State University, analyzed the matter and concluded that Gorbachev himself had become a hostage of the Brezhnev Doctrine—of "Brezhnev's strangling embrace," as Mlynář put it. "But he cannot do anything about it—inheritance always carries with it negative issues as well." Thus, the Soviet leader could not publicly abandon the Husák regime whose political identity was tied to the old reading of events—"the dead body of the Prague Spring lying in the mausoleum."[27]

[24] Document No. 11, Report on Mikhail Gorbachev's Visit to Czechoslovakia, April 16, 1987.
[25] Conversation between Alexander Yakovlev, Miloš Jakeš and Vasil Bil'ak, November 14, 1989, GARF, Fond 10063, Opis 1, delo 257.
[26] Medvedev, *Raspad*, 148–150.
[27] Zdeněk Mlynář, 1987, translation on file at Gorbachev Foundation Archive, Fond 5, opis 1.

That assessment rings true in retrospect. The duality of aspirations for change and feelings of responsibility for the Soviet-installed regimes comes through in both documents and memoirs. While Gorbachev was ready to renounce the policy of intervention early on, he was ambivalent about doing so publicly because, among other reasons, he was concerned about possible efforts by the West to capitalize on his flexibility and to try to encourage overly rapid change in the region. This was an issue that came up repeatedly in Soviet leadership discussions during the period.

At the same time, gradually, Gorbachev began to rely on West European and U.S. leaders as his peer group. In certain later conversations with Western heads of state, he openly pleaded for support, asking them to use their political weight to warn others (usually meaning the U.S. president) against interfering in Eastern Europe.[28] This pattern had the effect of strengthening Gorbachev's identification with Western Europe. Margaret Thatcher and François Mitterrand became especially trusted partners on the German issue and on the evolution of Eastern Europe. Gorbachev repeatedly indicated in his conversations with the French president that the USSR accepted evolutionary processes of change, and was not considering the use of forceful methods in dealing with its allies.[29]

During the period 1985–1988, the Soviet leadership tried to encourage reform in Eastern Europe while keeping it within limits so that it would develop within the framework of gradual change on the continent—as Gorbachev would say, "in the European process." For this, reaching a good understanding with West European leaders was essential. Meanwhile, however, the Warsaw Pact partners often felt confused and unsure of Gorbachev's true intentions. As was the usual practice, they studied every development and innovation in the USSR, especially the speeches and publications of the general secretary. The local populations also watched Gorbachev and associated their hopes for domestic liberalization with him, thus putting pressure on their own conservative leaderships. The ideas of the new Soviet party leader also captured the imagination of those who were still hoping to build socialism with a human face—the reform communists within the ruling parties. However, a very different reaction came from conservative bastions, such as the GDR, where Erich Honecker decided not to publish the proceedings of the January 1987 CPSU Plenum for fear that the Soviets were going "too far."[30]

While domestic pronouncements of the new policy were quite daring, and there are no grounds to doubt the sincerity of Gorbachev's desire to reform the socialist bloc, his approach lacked a unified strategy and proceeded mostly on an *ad hoc* basis. The Gorbachev leadership rejected the Brezhnev Doctrine in dealing with its allies, but as Mlynář pointed out, to a certain extent they remained captive to their own past, unable to withdraw support decisively even from the most

---

[28] Some of the most pronounced examples are in the following conversations: with Margaret Thatcher on September 23, 1989 (Document No. 85); Helmut Kohl on November 11, 1989 (Document No. 103); and François Mitterrand on November 14, 1989 (Document No. 104).

[29] See Gorbachev–Mitterrand conversations in Document Nos. 71, 72, 74.

[30] Gorbachev, *Zhizn' i reformy*, vol. 2, 408.

notoriously repressive leaders, Ceauşescu and Honecker. This ambivalence and lack of consistent focus contributed to an uneven pattern of progress in the region.

GORBACHEV'S VISION AND HIS TEAM OF VISIONARIES

Although Gorbachev's East European policy lacked a detailed strategy, it was guided by a coherent vision that was articulated at an early stage and was consistent with his overall philosophy of international relations. That vision comprised a number of basic principles, most vividly articulated in his address to the United Nations in December 1988 but also in a number of speeches even before that, notably at the 19th party conference in June 1988. The most important of those principles were:
- an absolute rejection of the use or threat of force as instruments of foreign policy;
- freedom of choice as a universal principle, with no exceptions;
- the supremacy of common human values;
- reasonable sufficiency rather than strict parity in strategic armaments;
- the full integration of Eastern Europe and the USSR into the common European home.

These values were quite obvious to those in Gorbachev's immediate circle from the early years of *perestroika*, though not to most Politburo members.[31] And the link between those values and concrete changes in Soviet behavior was noticed in Eastern Europe and by Western observers as well. Chernyaev noted in his diary after Gorbachev's meeting with Helmut Kohl on October 28, 1988, that his boss behaved as if they were already entering a new world in which they shared basic values that comprised "his ideas—'freedom of choice,' 'mutual respect for each other's values,' 'renunciation of force in politics,' 'a common European home,' 'liquidation of nuclear weapons,' etc., etc."[32]

At home, this vision, in its practically complete form, was dramatically presented by Gorbachev in his main report to the 19th Party Conference at the end of June 1988. The theses for the conference were published in May, and struck like a lightning bolt for the Soviet public and attentive observers abroad. To hold that conference meant that Gorbachev would move ahead with a new momentum focusing this time directly on democratization of the Soviet regime. That this was a conscious decision on the part of the general secretary is clear from the long and detailed discussions of numerous drafts of the report by the Politburo, which preceded the conference. Gorbachev rejected several versions prepared by his speechwriters and insisted on including the language that he wanted himself.[33] The conference was

[31] Musgrove transcript, 113, 122.
[32] Document No. 30, Diary of Anatoly Chernyaev, October 28, 1988.
[33] Document No. 26, Notes of CC CPSU Politburo Session, June 20, 1988.

intended to be a powerful signal both domestically and internationally that *perestroika* was entering a new stage, featuring a serious opening up of the Soviet political system and even more radical changes in foreign policy, especially toward the socialist bloc. U.S. Ambassador Jack Matlock described the experience of first reading the theses and briefing Reagan on them in Helsinki on the way to the Moscow Summit in May 1988, realizing then that new thinking was "for real," and that "now we were in a completely new ballgame." As a result of that conference key characteristics of the Soviet state would be changed and with the advent of free, competitive elections it would cease to be a communist regime.[34]

The vision that the general secretary brought with him, and that was expanded and radicalized over time as a result of learning from his advisers and his international peers, had to be implemented by people who shared those ideas completely in order to be effective. In the tightly hierarchical Soviet system, where reform could only originate from the above, it made a great difference who was in charge of applying it. When Gorbachev started replacing the old guard with reformers, it sent a strong message to the allies and, as Archie Brown has pointed out, created a link between the new thinking and the new political actors, between the power of appointment and the power of ideas—a development that led to significant policy outcomes.[35]

The key appointments in the sphere of relations with socialist countries and in foreign policy in general were Eduard Shevardnadze as foreign minister, Vadim Medvedev as head of the Socialist Countries Department of the Central Committee (replacing Konstantin Rusakov) and then as ideology secretary and full member of the Politburo, Anatoly Chernyaev and later Georgy Shakhnazarov as foreign policy advisers, Alexander Yakovlev as a member of the Politburo and head of the International Commission, and Anatoly Dobrynin as head of the International Department (replacing Boris Ponomarev), who was later replaced by Valentin Falin in 1988. The political partnership for reform that Gorbachev gradually built (he liked to call it a "democratic coalition") was the crucial medium between the ideas and beliefs of the new thinkers and actual policy.

Gorbachev and the people he placed in charge of relations with Eastern Europe shared the view that it was unacceptable for the Soviet Union to interfere in the socialist countries' affairs, either by dictating policies or imposing judgments.[36] Medvedev emphasized this in his memoirs: "Gorbachev and all of us always stated in our meetings with leaders of the fraternal countries that the determination of a political course and the choice of direction and model of development were the exclusive right of the people and the party of every country. Any interference in this process from outside was impermissible."[37] Underlying this principle was a sense of great responsibility, not to say guilt, stemming from

---

[34] Musgrove transcript, 109-110.
[35] Brown, *The Gorbachev Factor*, 212.
[36] Musgrove transcript, 123, 147-149.
[37] Medvedev, *Raspad*, 34.

12

Moscow's crude domination of the region over the previous 40 years. The Gorbachev circle believed that they now had an obligation to find ways to help the socialist community escape the current crisis and democratize their systems following the new Soviet example.[38]

These two beliefs taken together provide an interesting dichotomy. Whereas the first prohibits any interference in the affairs of others, the second implies that the USSR still had an important role to play in the domestic developments of those countries. Gorbachev and his colleagues acknowledged this duality by exercising great care in their dealings with East European leaders, hoping to be able to support the reformers, and being reluctant to deal with conservative leaders. However, at the same time, they understood that the old leaders were the ones who could guarantee the stability needed to prevent anarchy and a rapid collapse of the system. This conundrum produced considerable ambiguity and indecisiveness in Soviet policy toward Eastern Europe, as noted by many scholars.[39]

Another common element among Kremlin reformers was the fact that none of them, at least in the first five years of *perestroika*, had questioned the choice of socialism as the desired system for the Soviet bloc. Their goal was to open up the system, to get rid of old and inefficient elements, and to build a democratic and even market-oriented brand of socialism, enriching their interpretation to include the earlier Eurocommunist thinking.[40] But the term "socialism" would remain in use, even though the content would evolve over time to embrace a social-democratic platform. This fact helps partially to answer the question why the Soviet leaders were not able to anticipate the avalanche-like developments that led to the collapse of the socialist commonwealth. Because socialist democracy had such powerful appeal in their eyes, it was hard for them to see that other socialist states might not want to emulate their reform. Leading the socialist alliance by purifying it and implementing true socialist ideals had been Gorbachev's aspiration for a long time, as he explained to Castro in April 1988.[41]

And last but not the least, Gorbachev's personal aversion to bloodshed and violence, also noted by many observers, played an important role in determining the choice of policies toward Eastern Europe.

Looking at the available evidence, one can say that even if Gorbachev did not have a well-defined strategy for dealing with the socialist bloc, all of the components of his thinking amounted to a clear vision, which he tried to apply while reacting to events in the region, and in fact did so rather consistently, relying on his reform coalition within the Central Committee.

[38] Author's interview with Vadim Medvedev, June 17, 1996. Moscow.
[39] Musgrove transcript, 141, 143.
[40] Musgrove transcript, 103-104.
[41] Conversation between Mikhail Gorbachev and Fidel Castro, April 5, 1988, Gorbachev Foundation Archive, Fond 1, Opis 1.

SOVIET REASSESSMENT OF EASTERN EUROPE:
FROM A CROWN JEWEL TO A BURDEN.

In 1985–1986, Gorbachev embarked on a thorough reform of intra-bloc social-ist economic relations. He was enthusiastic and optimistic about the prospects of economic cooperation and genuine integration within CMEA. The patroniz-ing was over; now the socialist countries could trade with each other on a mutu-ally beneficial basis. The need to change the relationship was felt acutely, and even falling fuel prices had not yet had the effect of undermining the chances for CMEA integration in the minds of the Soviet reformers. By early 1989, how-ever, the Kremlin had undertaken a comprehensive reassessment of CMEA and the prospects of close cooperation, leading Gorbachev to abandon the issue and instead to encourage East European leaders to pursue independent economic con-tacts with the European Economic Union (EEU). The focus thus shifted from intra-bloc engagement to all-European integration, in which the USSR would be-come an important partner. Along with that change, assessments of the strategic value of Eastern Europe had also been adjusted in the wake of progress on arms control and the development of greater trust in U.S.–Soviet relations.

The question of whether the Soviet leadership viewed the socialist common-wealth as a burden and how that perception contributed to the reformulation of Moscow's East European policy is often raised in the literature on the end of the Cold War. In *Enigma*, Jacques Levesque writes that the "cost" of Eastern Europe was not a significant factor in Gorbachev's thinking at the time, and he com-pares the region to nuclear weapons in terms of its value to the Soviet Union, noting that the fraternal allies were expensive but "essential attributes of Soviet power."[42] According to Levesque, the economic motivation is not the key to un-derstanding Kremlin policies. In other words, the Soviet reformers did not really see Eastern Europe as so great a burden in 1985–1989 that it would push them to abandon their partners. However, new evidence suggests that the answer to this question is a bit more nuanced.

In 1985 and 1986 Gorbachev was sanguine about revamping CMEA even while being aware of its economic deficiencies and lack of mutual engagement. After his first PCC session in Sofia on October 22–23, 1985, and a post-Geneva meeting with socialist leaders in Prague in November, the Soviet leader raised the issue of CMEA reform and integration at the Politburo. He spoke confidently and without alarm about progress in the "strengthening of the socialist commonwealth," stressed the scientific and technological revolution as the key to successful economic reform and emphasized that "responsibility in this issue rests with our country."[43] He spe-cifically mentioned the importance of intra-bloc integration as a way to prevent the allies from turning to the West in their search to satisfy their economic needs.

---

[42] Levesque, *Enigma*, 88.
[43] Politburo session November 26, 1985, Gorbachev Foundation Archive, Fond 2, Opis 1.

14

In June 1986, coming back from the PCC in Budapest, Gorbachev emphasized to his Politburo colleagues how important economic issues had been at the meeting and showed a deep understanding of the pressing problems the commonwealth faced. However, there still was an implicit consensus that CMEA was a net plus. Interestingly, especially in comparison with his later deliberations over Soviet–East European relations, energy and the Soviet role as a supplier of oil and gas at prices significantly below world market levels did not figure into the discussions.[44] The issue of Soviet subsidies to socialist countries was not a new one; it was repeatedly discussed by the Soviet leadership as early as the 1970s and later during the Solidarity crisis in Poland. The socialist countries' debt to the West was growing, reaching $163.9 billion in 1986.[45] Gorbachev was aware of the decline in oil prices but at the time apparently did not specifically connect that trend to the economic problems of Eastern Europe. The first discussion of the four-fold drop in oil prices took place at the Politburo on July 11, 1986.

Taking into account the general secretary's growing awareness of his country's economic plight, his evaluation of the prospects for CMEA and of the progress being made toward genuine integration throughout 1986 was surprisingly optimistic, especially as seen in his report to the Politburo immediately after the PCC meeting in Bucharest in mid-November 1986. Gorbachev at that gathering had encouraged Kádár not to listen to people "who are longing for a U.S. embrace" but to rely on the bloc partners, and he concluded his report by speaking about the "new stage in our collaboration with the socialist countries."[46]

However, the economic data from Eastern Europe combined with the oil price decline eventually began to generate apprehension. As early as January 1987, returning from a Warsaw meeting of the CMEA, Gorbachev spoke to his colleagues about the socialist countries' ties to the West as being a result of "our economic difficulties," and for the first time raised the notion of the Soviet oil and gas "spigot" as an instrument of foreign policy. The realization that the USSR could not provide the technologies the bloc needed, and that the partners could not pay for energy in hard currency, led the Soviet leader to emphasize the need for mutually beneficial trade and for a certain distancing from accountability for the allies: "It is in our interest not to be loaded with responsibility for what is happening, or could happen, there."[47] That discussion probably led to a report that is known to have been prepared by the CC CPSU socialist countries department on world oil prices. The document, usually a type that would be requested by the general secretary or other Politburo members, is not available, but there is a note about it in the Politburo records. That note mentions that world oil prices were discussed "outside the agenda" on February 26, 1987, on the basis of

---

[44] See Document Nos. 5, 6, 7.
[45] Gaidar, *Gibel' imperii*, 223–224.
[46] Document No. 8, Transcript of CC CPSU Politburo Session, November 13, 1986.
[47] Document No. 9, Notes of CC CPSU Politburo Session, January 29, 1987.

the report, and that its "quality of analysis was found lacking."[48] The Politburo discussion of this issue is not available either, but since the document was prepared by the socialist countries department, we may assume it must have dealt with the impact of the declining price of oil on the economies of the bloc and possible Soviet actions to redress the crisis. Eventually, along with the drastic drop in oil prices that began in 1986 came the slow realization that not only were the partners in fact a burden, but that the CMEA itself was unsustainable, in part because the Soviet Union was losing the economic leverage needed to keep the community tied together and to the USSR.

Thus, the new impetus to reform relations among the socialist countries in 1988 came from the realization by Gorbachev and those who were involved in policy-making toward the region that the socialist bloc had in fact become an economic drain rather than an advantage to the Soviet Union itself. Over the several years preceding the reform, the USSR continually faced an unfavorable trade balance with its partners, which it supplied with raw materials, including oil and gas, and from which it received in return manufactured goods that were generally of low quality. Besides this structure of trade, the Soviets gave substantial subsidies to the allies, especially when they perceived a threat of internal political instability. The last example of this practice was in Poland in 1980–1981.[49]

The real turnaround in Moscow's assessment of the cost of empire came in the first half of 1988. At a Politburo session on March 10, after describing the economic crisis in the Eastern bloc as based on "Western credits and our cheap raw materials," Gorbachev set out the Kremlin's main priority: "In our relations with the CMEA, we have to take care of our own [Soviet] people first." Prime Minister Nikolay Ryzhkov gave the real reason behind the trade problems: "The world price of oil has fallen from 180 to 54 rubles per ton." The USSR simply could not sustain the existing supply relationship any longer. Now the empire truly felt like a burden because "our foreign assistance alone takes 41 billion rubles annually from our budget," according to Gorbachev. The discussion was very frank and unyielding. No more glossing over the real problems would be accepted, trade issues would be discussed, and broad contacts with the West would be accepted as a fact of life. The general secretary drew the stark conclusion that "in the economic sense, socialism has not passed the test of practice."[50]

It is surprising in retrospect to realize how well Gorbachev's advisers understood the economic crisis facing the socialist system. In October 1988, Shakhnazarov drafted a very candid memo for his boss to use at a Politburo discussion, raising the realistic possibility that several East European countries could "go bankrupt at the same time," naming Poland, Hungary, Bulgaria and the GDR specifically. The memo posed a question about the existence of a Soviet general

[48] Politburo session, February 26, 1987, Gorbachev Foundation Archive, Fond 2, Opis 1.
[49] Musgrove transcript, 156.
[50] Document No. 19, Notes of CC CPSU Politburo Session, March 10, 1988.

strategy toward reform in Eastern Europe and whether the presence of Soviet troops in the allied countries was still warranted. The main recommendation was that "in the future, the possibility of extinguishing crisis situations with force should be completely excluded."[51] The note on the document on file at the Gorbachev Foundation shows that the Soviet leader actually spoke from the text prepared by Shakhnazarov at the Politburo session of October 6, 1988.

Thus, as far as Eastern Europe was concerned, the Soviets starting in early 1987 gradually perceived the economic costs of "empire" as exceeding the region's value, and came to accept this fully as a fact in 1989. There were several distinct factors accounting for the reassessment.

The first and decisive factor had to do with threat perceptions. Strategically, the territory of Eastern Europe had become less valuable with the arrival of long-range nuclear weapons. In the late 1980s, when the probability of a military conflict in Europe was seen as infinitesimal, its strategic worth diminished even more. The understanding reached between Gorbachev and Reagan in Geneva and especially Reykjavik played the main role in persuading the Soviet leader that an attack from the West was highly improbable. After Reykjavik and throughout 1987, U.S.–Soviet relations in general, but especially in the sphere of arms control, progressed in leaps and bounds, making a small but influential part of the Soviet leadership feel, in Chernyaev's words, that "no one will attack us even if we disarm totally."[52] The most striking evidence of the reassessment of the strategic value of the socialist camp came from a memorandum Chernyaev prepared in May 1990 on the unification of Germany. As he wrote to Gorbachev: "[Regarding] the discussions about the fact that, as a result of German unification and the possible entry of Poland into NATO, the borders of the bloc would move to the Soviet frontier—this [argument] is from yesterday; this is a strategy from World War II and the Cold War when our own security was measured not only in the military sphere, but also in the social and political spheres through the [socialist] commonwealth. [...] Our real security is being determined now at the Soviet–American [arms control] negotiations."[53]

The second factor was the declining price of oil and its effect on the balance of trade with the socialist countries and on the entire Soviet economic system, as discussed above. The Soviet leadership understood that they could not continue to support CMEA under conditions in which the USSR experienced trade deficits with such key members as Yugoslavia, Czechoslovakia, Hungary and Romania. "The objective reason" for the imbalance, according to a Central Committee International Commission session of March 28, 1989, was the drop in oil

---

[51] Shakhnazarov, *Tsena svobody*, 368.
[52] Diary of Anatoly Chernyaev, January 18, 1986,
http://www.gwu.edu/~nsarchiv/NSAEBB/NSAEBB220/Chernyaev_1986.pdf.
[53] Anatoly Chernyaev memorandum to Gorbachev, May 4, 1990, Gorbachev Foundation Archive, Fond 2, Opis 2.

prices from \$175 to \$45–50 per ton, on the basis of which "we have lost about 40 billion convertible rubles in this five-year period alone."[54]

The third factor in Moscow's reassessment was the development of Gorbachev's concept of the common European home and the need for economic integration with the West. Gradually, the Soviet leadership understood that if they did not allow the East European countries to reform their economies there would be no possibility for the USSR to "enter" the world economy—to integrate with the West. Research on integration and economic experimentation with market elements was gaining ground in Soviet academic circles, and Eastern Europe was often seen as a testing ground as well as a gateway to European integration. In 1989, Academician Andranik Migranyan wrote about the Soviet desire for a new type of international economic interaction: "No longer regarding ourselves as an alternative model of development for the whole world community, and having realized the fundamental weak points of our own economic and political system, we are deliberately trying not to hinder Western-style international economic contacts. On the contrary, we would like to integrate with that system and adapt ourselves to its existing structures. Significant in this respect is the change in our attitude toward the integration processes occurring in Europe and in the West as a whole. Recent Soviet foreign policy gives us grounds to outline a general path toward a single, transcontinental community."[55]

Notwithstanding Gorbachev's early calls for the development of a strategy toward the socialist commonwealth, policy recommendations were slow to come, and only in 1989 do we see a more or less coherent effort to deal conceptually with the changes in Eastern Europe. Two very important documents show the depth of analysis and recommendations that were on Gorbachev's desk by early 1989: a memorandum from the CC International Department, and another from the Institute of the Economy of the World Socialist System (the Bogomolov institute) of the Academy of Sciences.[56]

Both documents depicted the deep crisis underway in the socialist alliance, and emphasized the limited nature of Soviet leverage.

RETURN TO EUROPE: A COMMON EUROPEAN HOME

In the early years of *perestroika*, the new leadership waged an ongoing battle for the hearts and minds of West Europeans, both politicians and populations, with the goal of pulling them away from the more intransigent United States of the Reagan administration. The effort to split NATO was always at the heart of

---

[54] Gaidar, *Gibel' imperii*, 264.

[55] Migranyan at the time was based at the Institute of the Economy of the World Socialist System of the USSR Academy of Sciences. See his article, "For Discussion: An Epitaph to the Brezhnev Doctrine: The USSR and Other Socialist Countries in the Context of East–West Relations," *Moscow News,* no. 34, 6, cited in Chafetz, *Gorbachev,* 108.

[56] Document Nos. 41 and 42.

Soviet strategy during the Cold War years, and early Gorbachev-era Politburo discussions show that the reformers did not shy away from the same thinking. It was only later that the concept of a common European home developed into a more comprehensive vision and became not just an instrument but the ultimate goal of Gorbachev's foreign policy.

What did this new concept mean for Gorbachev? A common European home would be based on universal human values, collective security and economic integration. It incorporated a vision of a continent without borders, where people and ideas would move freely without fear of war or hunger. In this new Europe, both blocs would gradually dissolve their military organizations, and security functions would be taken over by the newly strengthened CSCE framework and the United Nations.

In 1985 and 1986, however, before the concept was fully developed, Soviet efforts aimed at Europe were more tactical in nature—designed to induce the United States to negotiate on arms reductions and to a lesser degree to satisfy Soviet economic aims. Gorbachev stressed this aspect of leveraging the United States with respect to Soviet European policy at the Politburo session following his return from the PCC meeting in Budapest in June 1986: "[T]he policy aimed at Europe is yielding great reserves. Everybody thinks so. Our work here is having an influence on the United States and on all world developments."[57]

As *perestroika* progressed, and especially as Gorbachev's contacts with West European leaders led him to see them as his primary peer group, his appreciation and understanding of Europe became richer and his approach less tactical. The reassessment of the socialist bloc as a burden rather than a strategic asset prompted Gorbachev to recognize the inevitability of becoming economically reliant on the West, and thus to see deep economic integration with Western Europe as a key imperative. Gorbachev himself was a convinced Westernizer whose views were influenced significantly by his travels in Europe when he was Central Committee secretary for agriculture. He was particularly impressed by the Italian communists and their Eurocommunist ideas. Therefore, his inclinations always lay in the European direction, even though it took some time for him to figure out exactly how Eastern Europe fit into Soviet designs.[58]

The vision of Europe and especially the idea of a common European home over time became central to Gorbachev's thinking about the future of the socialist community. He was concerned that in the eyes of West Europeans the image of the USSR was linked with invasions. Correcting this image was seen as a necessary condition for being accepted as one of the civilized nations of Europe. During Politburo discussions of the Warsaw Pact's new military doctrine, on May 8, 1987, Gorbachev brought up his conversation with Margaret Thatcher, which

---

[57] Document No. 5, Notes of CC CPSU Politburo Session, June 13, 1986.

[58] For the origins of the concept, see Marie-Pierre Rey, "Europe is Our Common Home': A Study of Gorbachev's Diplomatic Concept," *Cold War History*, Vol. 4, issue 2, January 2004, 33-65.

had left a lasting impression on him: "She said they were afraid of us; that we invaded Czechoslovakia, Hungary, and Afghanistan. This perception is widespread among the public there." Stating that the Soviet Union should stop lying about its conventional forces in the European theater, Gorbachev advocated troop reductions and directly tied this argument to the need to think "about Europe: from the Atlantic to the Urals."[59]

Europe, including the "return to Europe," was one of the earliest ideas of *perestroika*, always invoking Russia's identity as a European state and the implicit hope of pulling Europe away from the United States. The idea of a common European home was based to a large extent on Gorbachev's desire to turn the CSCE framework into the main structure of European security, which would mean a gradual dissolution of both the WTO and NATO. Seen mainly as an irritant by his predecessors because of its focus on human rights, the CSCE received renewed attention and support from the reformist leader almost as soon as he came to power. In fact, Shevardnadze's first trip abroad as foreign minister was to participate in the CSCE Vienna conference, at which the Soviet side made an unprecedented proposal to host a future CSCE meeting in Moscow on the humanitarian dimension of security. To make this possible, the Kremlin undertook significant changes in Soviet human rights practices, including releasing political prisoners and putting an end to the persecution of prominent dissidents.[60]

In early 1988, in an effort to invest the concept of the common European home with substance, according to its future Director Nikolay Shmelev,[61] and to shift the intellectual center of gravity in Moscow toward the study of Europe, the Institute of Europe was created within the USSR Academy of Sciences under Vitalii Zhurkin. The institute was involved heavily in preparations for the CSCE's Paris summit in November 1990, and provided detailed analyses to the Central Committee on the prospects for European integration and German unification.

Europe and "Europeanness" figured prominently in the Soviet attitude toward the socialist commonwealth in 1989. After the December 1988 U.N. speech, Gorbachev, encouraged by the enthusiastic European response and discouraged by the "reassessment pause" in Washington, decided to attempt a breakthrough on the continent. He asked his advisers to prepare a powerful speech for delivery in Strasbourg at the Council of Europe. The address was supposed to be drafted in secret, kept even from other members of the leadership. It was envisioned as "similar to the U.N. speech, only with a specifically European angle."[62] Gorbachev wanted to spell out his vision of Europe and of the common European home with all its constituent elements, as well as the process by which Europe could achieve that goal.

[59] Document No. 12, Notes of CC CPSU Politburo Session, May 8, 1987.
[60] Kashlev, *Helsinskii protsess*, 154–157, 172–175.
[61] Author's interview with Nikolay Shmelev, July 12, 2006, Moscow.
[62] Document No. 44, Anatoly Chernyaev Memorandum to Vadim Zagladin, February 4, 1989.

The Strasbourg address, delivered on July 6, 1989, was Gorbachev's passionate appeal to the West Europeans for Soviet entry into their community. Including such weighty terms as "European unification," he even quoted the great French writer Victor Hugo, who in the 19th century predicted that all European nations "without losing [their] distinguishing features and splendid distinctiveness [will] merge inseparably into a high-level society and form a European brotherhood." The common European home, Gorbachev explained, would combine four elements: collective security based on the doctrine of restraint rather than deterrence, full economic integration, environmental protection, and the humanitarian dimension—specifically, respect for human rights in every country. The entire edifice would be based on the new European identity rooted in universal human values and the rule of law: "what we have in mind is a restructuring of the international order in Europe that would put European common values in the forefront and make it possible to replace the traditional balance of forces with a balance of interests."[63]

Ambassador Yurii Kashlev, who was head of the Soviet delegation in Vienna, later explicitly tied Gorbachev's proposal to hold a summit of signatories of the original 1975 Helsinki Final Act in Paris in 1990 to the "stormy" events in Eastern Europe in 1989.[64] The summit, with its Charter on Europe from Vancouver to Vladivostok, would also be the culmination of Gorbachev's hope for integration on the model of the common European home. As events in the socialist camp were reaching their climax two weeks before the fall of the Berlin Wall, Gorbachev spoke approvingly about the changes with President of Finland Mauno Koivisto, emphasizing non-interference and proposing that representatives of the 35 states "get together and see what horizons of the European security and cooperation process are opening up now and what the possibilities of building the common European home are."[65] In a conversation with Zbigniew Brzezinski later that month, Yakovlev projected that "European countries will have a common parliament, common affairs and trade relations; the borders will be open," and he listed these as "components of the policies directed at building a Common European Home."[66]

Those policies were Gorbachev's priority for Europe, subsuming the revolutions in the USSR's "backyard" that were more evident at the time. In his conversation with Mitterrand in Kiev in December 1989, he outlined his main concerns in the following way: "First and foremost" among the priorities "should be European integration, the evolution of Eastern Europe and the all-European

[63] Document No. 73, Address by Mikhail Gorbachev to the Council of Europe, July 6, 1989.
[64] Kashlev, *Helsinskii protsess*, 182.
[65] Document No. 95, Mikhail Gorbachev and Mauno Koivisto Conversation, October 25, 1989.
[66] Document No. 96, Aleksandr Yakovlev and Zbigniew Brzezinski Conversation, October 31, 1989.

[security] process, and the establishment of a peaceful order in Europe."[67] Virtually all discussions of the socialist community in the Politburo placed the issue within the framework of the pan-European process. The emphasis on Europe also diminished the priority of the Warsaw Pact partners as such, which later came to be seen as no more than a vehicle for achieving the main goal. Sharing Gorbachev's thinking on Eastern Europe completely, Chernyaev believed that political integration of the Soviet Union into the family of civilized European nations was Gorbachev's dream and intention at the time, thus Eastern Europe was a sideshow, to which he had to turn again and again reluctantly.[68]

The idea that a common European home could be built on the basis of a mutual, gradual dissolution of both military-political blocs was quite persistent within the circle of Gorbachev's advisers and supporters, although it was not universally accepted within the Soviet establishment. Georgy Shakhnazarov was the strongest proponent of the idea of disbanding the alliances. He mentioned it repeatedly in his communications with Gorbachev, and prepared a long and detailed memorandum on the issue on October 14, 1989. The memo showed how Moscow's acceptance of the revolutions in Eastern Europe and the withdrawal of Soviet troops would logically lead to the ultimate goal of dissolving the blocs and strengthening the CSCE structures as the main framework of European security. The memo proposed to "put the process of relaxation of the military confrontation, which has already begun, onto a planned basis, and thus to envision the liquidation of the WTO and NATO by the end of the 20th century. Within the framework of this process, we should define a number of interim stages, the most important of which should be the elimination of the military organizations of the two blocs by 1995."[69] In this context, any use of force in Eastern Europe was seen as counterproductive. Rather than mourning the "loss" of a security zone, Soviet reformers closest to Gorbachev actually welcomed the transformation, as did Chernyaev in October 1989: "the total dismantling of socialism as a world phenomenon has been taking place [...] Perhaps it is inevitable and good. For this is a reunification of mankind on the basis of common sense."[70]

1989: EASTERN EUROPE AND THE SOVIET DOMESTIC CONTEXT

By early 1989, Eastern Europe was becoming international issue number one. The turmoil underway there was already being felt throughout Europe and in the United States. While the incoming George Bush administration was reassessing U.S.–Soviet policy in January 1989, Henry Kissinger, who was in Moscow

---

[67] Document No. 114, Mikhail Gorbachev and François Mitterrand Conversation, December 6, 1989.

[68] Author's interview with Anatoly Chernyaev, July 6, 2007.

[69] Document No. 93, Memorandum from Georgy Shakhnazarov to Mikhail Gorbachev, October 14, 1989.

[70] Document No. 87, Diary of Anatoly Chernyaev, October 5, 1989.

for a meeting of the Trilateral Commission, tried to reprise his role as statesman and negotiate an understanding with Gorbachev on Eastern Europe, somewhat along the lines of the Yalta accords of Stalin, Roosevelt and Churchill. Kissinger met with Yakovlev first and then with Gorbachev, to whom he brought a letter of introduction from the president-elect. It is apparent from both conversations that the former secretary of state was primarily concerned about the unfolding processes in the socialist camp: "the countries of Eastern Europe are now entering a [stage of] special evolution. As a result, after a period of time Europe could become explosive once again."[71] Kissinger was trying to carve a niche for himself in the new administration as an architect of post-Cold War Europe reminiscent of his role under President Richard Nixon, when he, Dobrynin and Brezhnev achieved a remarkable understanding on major issues of international politics within the secretive setting of the "back channel." His vision of postwar Europe—a gradual evolution overseen from above by a U.S.–Soviet condominium—must have appealed to Gorbachev. He was also concerned about the potential of rising German power and chauvinism outside NATO, and tried to impress the Soviet leader with that specter: the growth of nationalism in Germany, he warned, "will hurt us Americans in the next five years, but in 50 years it will hurt you." Gorbachev mentioned Kissinger's proposal to the Politburo on January 21: "Kisa hinted at the idea of a USSR–USA condominium over Europe. He was hinting that Japan, Germany, Spain and South Korea were on the rise, and so, let us make an agreement so that the 'Europeans do not misbehave.'"[72] However, the idea did not find support within the incoming U.S. administration and was never raised officially again.

For the next several months, the Bush administration continued to review its Soviet policy. Three of the president's most senior aides—National Security Adviser Brent Scowcroft, career CIA official Robert Gates who was deputy national security adviser at the time, and Secretary of Defense Richard Cheney—shared a hard-line view of the USSR. In their judgment, the Cold War was not over, Gorbachev had not passed all the tests required to prove that his reforms were serious, and even the U.N. speech was just a propaganda exercise. For this group, U.S. policy in Europe was seen through the prism of competition with Gorbachev, and aimed at preventing him from upstaging the new president.[73]

Because the Soviet leadership perceived the need to move very fast on arms control—specifically, to conclude the START treaty, which would require a 50 percent reduction in strategic offensive armaments—Bush's pause and seeming indecisiveness in the first months of 1989 were a source of huge frustration for Gorbachev and even rising suspicion that the United States was trying to undermine *perestroika*.[74] However, one result of this lack of progress in U.S.–Soviet

[71] Document No. 36, Aleksandr Yakovlev and Henry Kissinger Conversation, January 16, 1989.
[72] Document No. 39, Mikhail Gorbachev Report to the CC CPSU Politburo, January 21, 1989.
[73] Bush and Scowcroft, *A World Transformed*, 41–44.
[74] Grachev, *Gorbachev's Gamble*, 205–207.

relations was that it made the European process even more central to Gorbachev's project.

Nineteen-eighty-nine was supposed to be the year Gorbachev achieved a breakthrough in arms control, but it was also projected to be the year of Europe. After the U.N. speech, according to Chernyaev, Gorbachev's next priority was to "sort out what to do with our socialist friends."[75] In the fall of 1988, the Soviet leader held a series of meetings with his East European counterparts, culminating in a Politburo session devoted to the discussion of developments in the socialist camp. During a meeting with Józef Czyrek, secretary of the Polish Central Committee, former foreign minister and an especially trusted envoy of Jaruzelski, Gorbachev not only gave a green light but actually encouraged the process of Roundtable negotiations in Poland.[76] Academic institutes, the Ministry of Foreign Affairs and the International Department of the Central Committee were instructed to present reports with recommendations for a Soviet strategy for Eastern Europe, which they prepared by February 1989, and Vadim Zagladin, a top West European expert in the International Department was tasked to prepare a groundbreaking speech on Europe, modeled on the U.N. address, for Gorbachev to deliver that summer in Strasbourg.[77]

Gorbachev and his allies in the Soviet leadership knew well that the use of force in Eastern Europe was not an option, but they also understood that some ambiguity in this respect remained among East Europeans. To preserve such ambiguity was in fact one of the recommendations of the Bogomolov Institute memo. At the Politburo session on January 21 Gorbachev himself remarked on East European doubts about the extent of a possible Soviet response to unrest in the bloc. "The peoples of those countries will ask: what about the CPSU, what kind of leash will it use to hold our countries back? They simply do not know that if they pull this leash harder, it will break."[78] In March, just two days before the fateful Congress of People's Deputies elections, Gorbachev hinted at the boundaries of change to Hungarian party leader Károly Grósz: "the limit, however, is the safekeeping of socialism and assurance of stability."[79] And yet, earlier in the same month he tacitly allowed the Hungarians to open their borders when Prime Minister Miklós Németh informed him of the decision to "completely remove the electronic and technological defenses from the Western and Southern borders of Hungary." The Soviet leader did not disagree with Németh's characterization that the barrier had "outlived" its value.[80]

Reading Soviet Politburo discussions from most of 1989, one might be struck by a seeming paradox: it is almost as if Eastern Europe simply did not exist for

75 Chernyaev, *Shest let*, 267.
76 Document No. 28, Mikhail Gorbachev and Józef Czyrek Conversation, September 23, 1988.
77 Document No. 44, Anatoly Chernyaev Memorandum to Vadim Zagladin, February 4, 1989.
78 Document No. 39, Mikhail Gorbachev Report to the CC CPSU Politburo, January 21, 1989.
79 Document No. 52, Mikhail Gorbachev and Károly Grósz Conversation, March 23-24, 1989.
80 Document No. 50, Mikhail Gorbachev and Miklós Németh Conversation, March 3, 1989.

most of the year. Events taking place there occupy only a very small part of the dialogue. The issues that dominated the leadership's agenda included the first democratic elections to the Congress of People's Deputies, ethnic conflicts such as in Nagorno-Karabakh, the April 1989 events in Tbilisi,[81] economic reforms (especially in the agricultural sector), the miners' strikes, Baltic independence, troop withdrawal from Afghanistan, and Yeltsin's growing challenge to Gorbachev.

THE ECONOMY

Clearly, the overriding reason for the virtual "disappearance" of foreign policy issues from the Politburo discussions was that 1989 was the year when domestic economic problems came to the fore of both the leadership's agenda and society's concerns. Falling oil prices and the sharp drop in the "drunken" share of state revenues (as a result of the anti-alcohol campaign) undermined an already stagnated Soviet economy. This, combined with the expansion of *glasnost*, exacerbated the sensation of impending crisis. According to Vadim Medvedev: "The program of economic reforms of 1987 was in effect buried; people recalled it less and less. The main issue was that control over the money supply, over the monetary income of the population, was lost, and that gave a major push to the unwinding of an inflationary spiral, which became more difficult to stop day by day."[82]

The year began with intense preparations for the agricultural Plenum of the Central Committee, which took place in mid-March. Agricultural reform was another complex aspect of the economic challenge. Indeed, in some ways it was the hardest part of Gorbachev's agenda to press because of the prevalence of deeply traditional, conservative attitudes going back to the years of Stalin's collectivization. Aggravating the purely economic dimension of the problem was the fact that the CC Secretary for Agriculture was Yegor Ligachev—a powerful opponent of Gorbachev in the Politburo, who was intent on consolidating conservative opposition to the reforms. On March 2, 1989, Gorbachev spent his birthday, from morning to late evening, in discussions of "the most acute problems of the agro-industrial sector." Taking up agricultural reform meant confronting the truth about collectivization and early Stalinism, but the general secretary was willing to do that. According to Shakhnazarov, Gorbachev presented a "passionate speech" in favor of radical reform in agriculture, including allowing private rentals of plots of land, family teams, individual agricultural production—all of which Gorbachev still termed "returning to Lenin's respectful approach to the peasants."[83]

As mentioned above, energy also contributed directly to the crisis. According to Yegor Gaidar, at the time a radical economist and later prime minister in the

---

[81] Nationalist demonstrations in the capital demanding independence for Georgia and the annulment of Abkhazian autonomy took place early in the month, culminating in their harsh suppression by the authorities on April 9.

[82] Medvedev, *V Komande Gorbacheva*, 103.

[83] Politburo session March 2, 1989, Gorbachev Foundation Archive, Fond 2, Opis 1.

first Yeltsin government, the economy began to deteriorate very quickly starting at the end of 1988, and the critical factor was the drop in oil production due to crumbling infrastructure. Oil is an often overlooked chapter in the story of the end of the Cold War. Petroleum prices had already started to decline in 1986, but neither Soviet economists nor policy-makers were prepared for the effect it would have on the economy. Because central planning gave the illusion that the government could always control the economy by "emission" (printing as many rubles as it needed), the effect on real people was delayed, but then the cumulative blow turned out to be all the harder and more confusing when it came. From Politburo records it seems as though very few senior officials actually understood the depth of the economic crisis in the country. One person who sounded the alarm early and often, but was rarely heard, was Prime Minister Ryzhkov.

A critical Politburo session that finally shook the party leadership into reality and prompted them to find ways to deal with the crisis took place on February 16, 1989. Ryzhkov opened the meeting with a report on the state of the economy: "In three years of *perestroika*, government spending has exceeded budget revenues by 133 billion rubles. Losses due to the decline in oil prices constitute 40 billion rubles, and losses due to cuts in sales of vodka have reached 34 billion rubles. [...] In three years of *perestroika*, the industrial surplus has increased by 10 billion rubles. But in agriculture, we have lost 15 billion rubles. Chernobyl took away 8 billion rubles. In three years, the emission has amounted to 21 billion rubles. In 1988 alone the emission reached 11 billion, more that in any year since the war."[84]

As a result, over 40 billion rubles in currency not covered by consumer goods accumulated in the country producing an acute sense of deficits and shortages among the population. Only 11 percent of consumer goods (out of 989 items on the list at the time) were available in the Soviet Union without shortages by the end of 1989.[85] Popular discontent was brewing and assuming new, more assertive forms of expression. During Gorbachev's meetings with workers, he was subjected to open criticism. March 1989 erupted with the first miners' strikes on the eve of the elections to the Congress of People's Deputies. Throughout the year, the Central Committee received angry letters from workers complaining about acute shortages of food and basic consumer goods.

For Gorbachev and his circle, the answer more and more was seen in urgently expanding cooperation with industrial enterprises in the West, establishing and deepening direct relations between enterprises in the USSR and Eastern Europe, and especially in attracting Western investment and obtaining credits, which could be used to purchase consumer goods to redress shortages and to drain the excessive mass of money accumulated by the population.

---

[84] Politburo session February 16, 1989, Gorbachev Foundation Archive, Fond 2, Opis 1.
[85] Gaidar, *Gibel' imperii*, 248.

ELECTIONS TO THE CONGRESS OF PEOPLE'S DEPUTIES
AND THE EMERGING OPPOSITION

Nineteen-eighty-nine was also the year of the first democratic elections to the new Soviet legislature, the Congress of People's Deputies. The long-debated decision to hold a contested ballot was made at the 19th Party Conference in the summer of 1988. By the agreed-upon procedure, two-thirds of the deputies were to be elected from territorial constituencies, and one-third from public organizations; 100 of the latter seats were to be allocated to the Communist Party (Gorbachev personally selected many of the candidates for the party list from his supporters).[86] The coming vote and the process of selecting and nominating deputies were at the center of Politburo discussions through the end of March. Gorbachev's expectation was that with the new elections he would be able to get rid of the conservative majority in the Supreme Soviet and attract new reformers to his coalition, which would allow him to play off the more progressive parliament against the party bureaucracy, which by 1989 was becoming more and more intransigent.

Although Gorbachev and his supporters anticipated losses among the communists, the results came as a shock. Ironically, 85 percent of elected deputies were members of the CPSU, but not those who occupied positions of power and who expected to win. The Moscow and Leningrad party organizations suffered the heaviest losses—all top leaders and party bureaucrats were voted out even where they ran unopposed. The same was true for the *nomenklatura* throughout the country: 20 percent of party secretaries were defeated. On March 28, the Politburo held a long session devoted to the election results, which generated some extensive soul-searching by the Soviet leadership. Anatoly Lukyanov blamed the defeats on the economic crisis and the destructive influence of "informal" organizations like the human rights society Memorial. Yegor Ligachev pointed to the mass media and the way they had begun to cover the negative aspects of party history. He called on his colleagues to be cautious and pointed out that "in Czechoslovakia and in Hungary (1956 and 1968) everything began with the mass media.[87]

The results were not easy for Gorbachev to swallow. Even though the elections did clear out many conservatives from the Supreme Soviet, they gave an overwhelming victory to his main rival, Boris Yeltsin, who ran for the Moscow at-large seat, and brought many radicals to the legislature, such as prominent human rights activist and nuclear physicist Andrei Sakharov. Gorbachev now had a glimpse of the future. Concluding the session, he said "The Congress begins on May 25. Yeltsin says that he is already looking at which deputies he can include in his group." Indeed, the Congress began its work with an investigation of Gorbachev's involvement in the tragic events in Tbilisi on April 9.

---

[86] Shakhnazarov, *Tsena svobody*, 74.
[87] Document No. 53, Transcript of CC CPSU Politburo Session on Elections, March 28, 1989.

Another burning issue for the Soviet leadership in 1989 which carried direct implications for policy toward Eastern Europe was the growing discontent in the union republics and the movements for independence, which started in the Baltics and by the summer had also hit Georgia and Ukraine. The year began with Politburo discussions of the nationalist rallies in the Baltics and their demands for economic self-sufficiency. On January 30, the Politburo adopted a resolution on "extremist and anti-Soviet groups and organizations in the Baltics," and after rallies took place on February 15 and 16 in Lithuania demanding independence, the Politburo Commission on the Baltics held a special session on February 18. Gorbachev believed in persuasion and leverage. He was willing to allow the Baltics economic self-sufficiency as of January 1, 1990, but was convinced that even local nationalist leaders would realize that the region would not be able to survive economically without being integrated into the USSR.

The issue of nationalism, especially with respect to the Baltic republics, was a blind spot for Gorbachev and most members of the Politburo, having themselves grown up believing Soviet propaganda about the harmonious relations among nationalities in the USSR. In a poignant passage in his diary in December 1988, Chernyaev describes a conversation with his boss: "Gorbachev asked me [...] is it really true that the Baltic people really want to secede? I told him: I believe they do [...] And he told me (does he mock me or seriously think so?): they will perish when they cut themselves off from the rest of the Union." To this, Chernyaev could only respond by writing in his diary: "Self-delusion and naïveté."[88] Ironically, on November 9, as the Berlin Wall was about to fall, the Soviet Politburo was in the midst of deliberations over Baltic secession. In a comment at the session verging on panic, Ryzhkov prophetically warned of possible secessionist movements in Russia and Ukraine, concluding that "it smells of total collapse."[89]

Practically every month in 1989 brought more fires to put out in the republics. After the violence in Sumgait in 1988, Nagorno-Karabakh was now ruled directly from Moscow through a special envoy. In May and June, the Fergana Valley erupted in pogroms against the Meskhetian Turks whom Stalin had deported there from the Crimea. But the most politically damaging event for Gorbachev and his leadership was the suppression of the rallies in Tbilisi. On the night of April 8/9, first secretary of Georgia Jumber Patiashvili ordered troops to forcefully disperse the demonstrators, resulting in 19 dead and hundreds wounded. Gorbachev did not condemn the use of force decisively, which led to accusations of his complicity and dealt a serious blow to his reputation. At the same time, it was a lesson in acceptable methods. On May 11, during a Politburo discussion of the situation in

[88] Document No. 34, Diary of Anatoly Chernyaev, December 10, 1988.
[89] Document No. 99, Notes of CC CPSU Politburo Session, November 9, 1989.

the Baltics, Gorbachev made a very clear statement regarding coercive methods: "The use of force is out of the question. We have excluded it from our foreign policy, but especially against our own people it is out of the question."[90]

By September 1989, the wave of nationalism had rocked Ukraine with the first Congress of the Ukrainian nationalist movement *Rukh* pronouncing independence as its ultimate goal and with mass rallies of Ukrainian Catholics. First Secretary Vladimir Shcherbitsky resigned, and the second most populous republic of the Soviet Union was now voicing its grievances against the central government. Suddenly, the issue of the preservation of the Soviet Union as a federal entity assumed overriding priority, compared to which the cohesion of the external empire took a back seat. Gorbachev was faced with a dilemma—he could not keep the internal empire together without using force, but the use of force would doom his entire project both domestically and internationally. His only hope in resolving the nationalities problems lay in integrating his country into Europe as rapidly as possible and attracting foreign credits and investments along the way.

As follows from the above discussion, domestic political concerns, especially the looming threat of the dissolution of the USSR, lowered the priority of Eastern Europe in the thinking of the Soviet leadership and affected their calculations about the expediency of the use of force in the region. Meanwhile, tremors within the socialist commonwealth continued to build and the East Europeans readily availed themselves of the unique window for action afforded by Moscow's internal distractions and Washington's prolonged pause.

THE POLISH ELECTIONS AND THE LOSS OF EMPIRE.

When in June, as a result of the first free elections in Poland since the advent of communist rule, Solidarity took 99 out of 100 seats in the Senate and all 161 contested seats in the Sejm, it plunged the Polish party into the same soul-searching as the CPSU had gone through in late March–April, and the shock reverberated through the socialist system. One would have expected a reaction from the Soviet Politburo, but almost nothing was heard from Moscow. In fact, as seen from the documents, Gorbachev expressed only support for the reforms and elections in Poland. Moreover, later in the summer the Soviet leader gave his support to the coalition government in a telephone call with Rakowski—even though that meant Poland might make the momentous decision to leave the Warsaw Pact. Such a move, which now became imaginable, according to Gorbachev's press secretary, Andrei Grachev, would have had a major psychological as well as strategic effect on the socialist camp. As it was, Grachev wrote, "[t]he failure of the Polish communists represented a spectacular setback for the East European 'Gorbachevists' [and] a very tough first test for the principles of 'the new political thinking.'"[91]

---

[90] Document No. 60, Notes of CC CPSU Politburo Session, May 11, 1989.
[91] Grachev, *Gorbachev's Gamble*, 203.

And yet, coercion was not seen as an option, plus Gorbachev and his Polish allies, Jaruzelski and Mieczysław Rakowski, had been discussing similar possibilities since the fall of 1988, and especially during Jaruzelski's visit to Moscow in April 1989. The question was not whether the Soviet Union should try to reverse the Polish progress, it was how to preserve the influence of the reform communists in the new government, and to keep Poland in the Warsaw Pact.

Even though the elections in Poland dealt a blow to Gorbachev's hopes for reform communism throughout Eastern Europe, from his perspective, in the larger scheme of things, events were still under control. Coalition governments, even those led by non-communists, were acceptable as long as they were within the "all-European" framework and the overall trajectory was toward the common European home. This view is apparent in each of Gorbachev's conversations with Western leaders, in which he appeals to them to avoid an "uncontrolled course of events" in Eastern Europe, and calls for stability and a gradual transformation. He raises these concerns with Thatcher in April, Secretary of State James Baker in May, Kohl and West German President Richard von Weizsäcker in June, Mitterand in July and Thatcher again in September. Every time the need for stability in Eastern Europe is discussed, it is tied to progress on the common European home.

A similar Soviet reaction followed the reburial of Imre Nagy and the start of the Hungarian Roundtable negotiations on June 13. Gorbachev was privately concerned but outwardly supportive and encouraging of reform as long as it remained peaceful. On the same day as the Roundtable began, Gorbachev was in Bonn discussing with Kohl the situation in Eastern Europe, especially in Poland and Hungary. In those conversations one sees two allies and friends discussing a plan of joint action. This is how Kohl described Gorbachev's positions with respect to the East European countries, according to an American transcript of his telephone call to Bush immediately after Gorbachev departed West Germany: "The Chancellor emphasized Gorbachev's very close personal relationship with General Jaruzelski and their common approach toward developments in Poland. No such personal relationship exists with any one Hungarian leader, the Chancellor added, but Gorbachev also supports Hungary's reform efforts. By contrast, there is an enormous distance between Moscow and Bucharest, and also East Berlin."[92]

In another conversation during the same visit, on June 14, Kohl and Gorbachev discussed East Germany, and the level of communication and shared understanding is simply astonishing. Here is Kohl complaining to Gorbachev about Honecker and his wife: "Now a couple of words about our mutual friends. I will tell you directly that Erich Honecker concerns me a great deal. His wife has just made a statement, in which she called on the GDR youth to take up arms and, if necessary, defend the achievements of socialism from external enemies. It is clear that she implied that the socialist countries which implement reforms,

[92] Document No. 68, George H.W. Bush and Helmut Kohl Conversation, June 15, 1989.

stimulate democratic processes, and follow their own original road are the enemies. Primarily, she had Poland and Hungary in mind."[93]

The most symbolic event for the socialist bloc in 1989 took place in July. Right after his Strasbourg address, Gorbachev traveled to Bucharest for a PCC meeting. The speeches and conversations there have a surreal character as can be seen from available documents. The meeting was essentially a wake for the Warsaw Pact, taking place as two of its members negotiated the possibility of forming non-communist coalition governments, and after the paramount leader has just proclaimed the supremacy of common human and democratic values over class interests, and signaled to the allies that if their own populations vote them out or rise against them, Soviet "fraternal aid" would not be coming to the rescue. And yet, as Andrei Grachev confirms in his memoir, "behind the scene Ceaușescu and Honecker tried to raise the 'Polish question,' hoping to persuade their colleagues of the imperative need to render 'fraternal aid' to Poland."[94]

In this setting, the question arises—how did the East European leadership see developments in the region in the summer and fall of 1989, and how did they expect Gorbachev to react to them? From the evidence, it seems clear that the top ranks of the socialist states by the summer must have known that they could no longer count on Soviet protection against their own populations, that the solutions of 1956 and 1968 were no longer available to them. In remarks to the HSWP Central Committee as early as February 21, 1989, Foreign Minister Gyula Horn stated: "Today there is no question at all of an intervention within the Warsaw Pact—we have long surpassed the Brezhnev Doctrine."[95] This was even more obvious to Western leaders after Gorbachev's U.N. address, the Strasbourg speech, and numerous conversations the Soviet leader had with them in 1989. So the threat of force was not on the agenda in 1989.

However, the question becomes even more interesting: if the socialist leadership knew there would be no use of force by the Kremlin, would it not have been in their interest to behave as if such a threat existed in hopes of restraining their own domestic opposition? This was a strategy the Soviet and Polish authorities used during the Solidarity crisis, and the communist regimes could replicate their approach in 1989. Certainly the opposition, and especially the dissidents on the streets who were not engaged in direct interactions with Soviet reformers, had only the experience of previous attempts at reform to rely on, and those ended tragically in most cases. Thus, inhibited by their historical memory in which two factors held prevalence—the assumed strategic value of Eastern Europe for the USSR and the history of brutal suppression of reform movements—the opposition behaved very cautiously, moving tentatively so as not to provoke Moscow, and pledging allegiance to the Warsaw Pact along the way—as

---

[93] Document No. 67, Mikhail Gorbachev and Helmut Kohl Conversation, June 14, 1989.
[94] Grachev, *Gorbachev's Gamble*, 205.
[95] Békés, "Back to Europe," 255.

they did repeatedly during the Polish and the Hungarian Roundtable discussions. This self-restraint, induced in part by the "floating" of the Brezhnev doctrine,[96] resulted probably in the best possible course of events for the East Europeans— a "velvet," gradual and non-violent transformation that seemed to develop precisely along the lines envisioned by Gorbachev and his reformers. As long as there was no explicit, immediate threat of a dissolution of the Warsaw Pact and no major violence in the region, the Kremlin accepted very deep changes in the allied regimes that essentially transformed them into social democracies along the Scandinavian model.

THE FALL OF THE BERLIN WALL AND THE GERMAN UNIFICATION.

A key part of the end of the Cold War in Europe was the fast unification of Germany, which followed the fall of the Wall in Berlin on the night of November 9, 1989. The most vivid symbol of the division of Europe was taken apart by unarmed people without direction from either of the superpowers or even from their own leaders—becoming the symbol of the peaceful transformation of the European continent and international politics. The developments on the ground, the mood of the masses were far ahead of the imagination of the leaders, but to their credit, the Soviets stuck by the principles they proclaimed, the Americans kept engaged but cautious, and the West Germans moved ahead deliberately while reassuring the Soviets; thus by the fall of 1990 Germany was reunified in NATO.[97]

For Gorbachev and the Soviet leadership, the German unification was an issue that would come up at some point in the future, when the process of European integration, the building of the common European home would be well under way.[98] Germany was the most important trade partner for the Soviet Union in the capitalist world, and the relationship with Kohl was becoming especially important by 1989 in light of the Soviet economic troubles, yet Gorbachev kept to his vague line "history will decide" on the most crucial issue in that relationship.[99] Gorbachev was not opposed to German unification per se, but envisioned it as the culmination of a gradual process, including demilitarization, dissolution of the blocs, Soviet integration into Europe, Soviet trade benefits, and a new, far-reaching environmental regime.

---

[96] Ibid., 242.

[97] The Gorbachev Foundation published a comprehensive collection of Russian documents on German unification, Aleksandr Galkin and Anatoly Chernyaev, *Mikhail Gorbachev i germanskii vopros*, (Moscow: Ves' Mir, 2006).

[98] See Gorbachev, *Zhizn' i reformy*, vol. 2, 152. Grachev, *Gorbachev's Gamble*, 135.

[99] Gorbachev repeated variations of this line practically every time the issue of German unification came up, starting with his meeting with West German President Weizsäcker in July 1987, during his visit to Bonn in June 1989, and during the Malta summit with President Bush (see Document No. 110).

The Soviet leader's visit to Bonn in June 1989 brought a real breakthrough in Soviet–West German relations, and established Helmut Kohl as Gorbachev's close partner, especially at the time when the Bush administration was still stuck in its "pause" undermining the trust that had been built in U.S.–Soviet relations under Reagan. This new closeness between Gorbachev and Kohl went so far as to include a critical discussion of East German leader Erich Honecker, whom at that time Gorbachev saw as a major obstacle to reform in his country.[100] During the meetings, Kohl reassured Gorbachev that he would not do anything to destabilize the situation in the GDR and that economic cooperation between the two countries would expand. Nothing was said in the negotiations specifically about German unification, but the Bonn Declaration, which the leaders signed, laid out their shared vision of the all-European process which corresponded with Gorbachev's goal of the common European home.[101]

A major factor in Gorbachev's thinking about the German issue was his belief, based on his numerous conversations with Western leaders, that nobody in Europe wanted a united Germany, and that the historical memory of a strong militaristic Germany was still very much alive on the continent. Margaret Thatcher was quite outspoken in her opposition to unification. When she stopped in Moscow on the way back from Tokyo, on September 23, 1989, she asked that notes not be taken during a confidential part of the conversation, where she said in the strongest terms that Western Europe was not interested in unification of Germany even if publicly the NATO communiqué stated a different position. Moreover, the British Prime Minister promised that Britain would "not interfere and spur the decommunization of Eastern Europe. I can tell you that this is also the position of the U.S. President. He sent a telegram to me in Tokyo in which he asked me to tell you that the United States would not undertake anything that could threaten the security interests of the Soviet Union, or that could be perceived by the Soviet society as a threat. I am fulfilling his request."[102] British notes of the conversation confirm that Thatcher's intention was to make Western opposition to the unification clear to Gorbachev.[103]

Because of Britain's special relationship with the U.S., and because of the role Thatcher played in the relationship with the previous administration, Gorbachev was inclined to hear the above comment as evidence that the U.S. position on Germany was similar to the British. He had not met the U.S. President yet, but nothing in U.S.–Soviet communications at the time pointed to any substantive difference—Bush was emphasizing his prudence and intention not to destabilize Eastern Europe either. In fact, even in Malta, the U.S. president did not object to Gorbachev's statements about the long period it would take for Germany to

---

[100] Document No. 67, Mikhail Gorbachev and Helmut Kohl Conversation, June 14, 1989.

[101] Gorbachev, *Zhizn' i reformy*, vol. 2, 161.

[102] Document No. 85, Mikhail Gorbachev and Margaret Thatcher Conversation, September 23, 1989..

[103] Salmon, Hamilton, and Twigge, *German Unification*, 79.

become united. In one more seeming confirmation of the U.S. position against rapid unification, Zbigniew Brzezinski during his visit to Moscow in late October 1989 expressed his preference for the continuation of the existence of the two blocs: "[b]oth blocs should not be disbanded right now. I do not know what will happen if the GDR ceases to exist. There will be one Germany, united and strong. This does not correspond to either your or our interests."[104]

Mitterrand's position was probably closest to Gorbachev's own. He saw German unification as part of the pan-European process, which would take many years and possibly include the French model—membership in the political but not military structures of NATO. What mattered was that the European process should come first, and then German unification; and that European countries, France especially, should be included in all discussions of the future of Germany. This position was discussed repeatedly between Gorbachev and Mitterrand throughout 1989.[105]

Although the Western politicians were careful in their public statements on unification, the Soviet leadership believed that they only wanted to prevent German unification with Soviet hands.[106] This conviction along with more pressing troubles at home, mainly the unrest in the Baltics, explain Gorbachev's detached reaction to the fall of the Berlin Wall on November 9.

Actually, the first cracks in the Berlin Wall appeared much earlier, as far back as March 3, 1989, when Hungarian reform communist Prime Minister Miklós Németh informed the Soviet leader of the Hungarian decision to "completely remove the electronic and technological defenses from the western and southern borders of Hungary," and Gorbachev responded only that the Soviet Union was going to make its own borders more open—thus tacitly approving the Hungarian move. After the pan-European picnic on the Austria–Hungary border on August 19 and the final removal of the barbed wire and remaining electronic defenses on the Hungarian border on September 11, a flood of East Germans went through Hungary to Austria and to West Germany, essentially voting their socialist republic out of existence with their feet, as the popular saying went.[107]

In that tense atmosphere, Gorbachev decided reluctantly to accept Honecker's invitation to visit East Germany for the celebration of the 40th anniversary of the GDR. His intention was to meet face-to-face with the entire East German leadership and to encourage them in effect to remove their boss. In conversations with the SED Politburo, Gorbachev dispensed with his usual caution over non-interference in domestic affairs and told the East Germans that "life pun-

---

104 Document No. 96, Aleksandr Yakovlev and Zbigniew Brzezinski Conversation, October 31, 1989.
105 Document Nos. 71, 72, 74 and 104, Grachev, *Gorbachev's Gamble*, 151.
106 Document No. 89, Diary of Anatoly Chernyaev, October 9, 1989.
107 Document Nos. 79, 80, 81.

ishes those who come late," hinting at the need to invigorate their reforms.[108] Ten days later, Erich Honecker was sent into retirement, and replaced by Egon Krenz. Meanwhile, the demonstrations in Leipzig that started at the end of September culminated in a massive peaceful rally of about 70,000 marching around the historic center of the city. At that point the GDR leadership, knowing that Soviet troops were going to be of no help to them, made a seminal decision not to use the Tiananmen model of forcibly putting down the demonstrators. The process leading to the fall of the Wall thus became unstoppable.

As significant as the collapse of the Berlin Wall appears in retrospect, it was not seen as such by the Kremlin at the time. On the actual day the Wall was breached, the Soviet Politburo did not even raise the issue of developments in Germany: it was busy discussing the situation in the Baltics and the economic crisis in the Soviet Union.[109] When the news reached Moscow, the Foreign Ministry confirmed that the border regime was an internal German affair, and the leadership did not even call a special session of the Politburo. Instead, Gorbachev discussed the events in Berlin over the telephone with his most important partners at the time—Chancellor Kohl and President Mitterrand. These conversations, especially the one with Kohl, reassured the Soviet leader that all their understandings regarding Eastern Europe were still in force and that West Germany would act very carefully not to destabilize the situation in the GDR.[110] What mattered for Gorbachev was that his main priority—the European process—was still on track, and within that process the fall of the Wall appeared as a natural development. Chernyaev, however, sensed that the Wall's dismantling was more than just a symbol. He wrote in his diary, "[t]he Berlin Wall has fallen. An entire era in the history of the "socialist system" has come to an end."[111]

However, the vision of German unification as part of an all-European process, even as a development capable of speeding up European integration, was not given enough time to materialize. Under the pressure of the German events, Gorbachev at the end of November proposed that the CSCE summit be held earlier—in November 1990 in Paris. This proposal gives one a glimpse into Gorbachev's view of the timeline for possible German unification: a new European treaty was to come first and then, within the new Europe, Germany would be allowed to unify in a form that would not undermine the process of gradually dissolving the military blocs envisioned by the Soviet reformers. Looking at the situation in November 1989, there is enough evidence to argue that this view of German unification (perhaps without the dissolution of the blocs) was shared in all the main West European capitals, but not in Bonn.

---

[108] Document No. 88, Mikhail Gorbachev Conversation with Members of the CC SED Politburo, October 7, 1989.

[109] Document No. 99, Notes of CC CPSU Politburo Session, November 9, 1989.

[110] Document Nos. 103, 104.

[111] Document No. 101, Diary of Anatoly Chernyaev, November 10, 1989.

In November 1989, Kohl was probably the only politician in Europe who could feel the real pulse of events on the ground and the growing pressure for unification in East Germany. He decided to take the initiative and shape the process deliberately rather than wait for the European powers to define the conditions. However, in an ironic turn of events, his most decisive move was itself prompted by a remarkable and audacious independent overture by a senior Soviet official. Valentin Falin, the head of the CC International Department, who at the time was arguing for a German confederation, was sidelined and could not find a way to get through to Gorbachev with his ideas. As probably the most experienced Germanist among the Soviet leadership (he had served as ambassador to West Germany from 1971–1978), watching the events develop more and more rapidly, he decided that the best way to get Gorbachev's attention to his ideas was through Chancellor Kohl. He drafted two position papers, an official one, cleared with Chernyaev, that mostly reaffirmed the pledges made by Kohl to Gorbachev and stated that if they were kept, then "everything becomes possible;" and an unofficial one, which declared that the idea of confederation was something the Soviets were already discussing and were prepared to accept in principle. Nikolay Portugalov, who worked for Falin on the International Department staff, met with Kohl's national security adviser, Horst Teltschik, on November 21 and presented both positions to him. Teltschik's reaction was that if the Soviets were already discussing German unification and confederation was acceptable to them, it was time for the West Germans themselves to seize the initiative and propose the idea. That was the essence of the report he presented to Kohl on the Portugalov mission, and it formed part of the basis for Teltschik's draft of the 10-point speech.[112] Thus an adventurous Soviet initiative became a major push toward German unification, culminating in Kohl's presentation of his 10-point program to the Bundestag on November 28, which instantly made German unification the number one issue in Europe. However, Falin's gambit ultimately backfired because Gorbachev himself was not aware of it, and because at that time, contrary to Portugalov's assurances to Teltschik, he had not yet accepted the idea of confederation. To Gorbachev, then, the German initiative came across as an unexpected and unwarranted acceleration of the process.

It took the Soviet leadership some time to realize what the 10 points meant. In fact, their real meaning did not become clear until after the Malta summit and especially after the NATO summit in Brussels. Gorbachev, ironically, was particularly alarmed by the idea of confederation and by the fact that Bush gave the program his full support at Brussels. The Soviet leader's reaction to Kohl's speech was so emotional that it blinded him to the substance of the program, which

[112] Grachev, *Gorbachev's Gamble*, 146–147, The story of the Portugalov mission is confirmed in Kusters and Hofmann, *Deutsche Einheit*, 616; author's conversations with Teltschik and Grachev on October 2, 2009; Teltschik's remarks at the conference "Revolutions of 1989" in Vienna, Austria, October 1, 2009, organized by the Austrian Academy of Sciences and the Ministry of European and International Affairs.

essentially reflected real Soviet objectives at the time: it did not present a specific timetable for unification, mentioned the all-European process, and implicitly guaranteed the GDR's existence as a state for at least several years, which meant that the issue of Soviet troops on its soil would not have to be raised immediately.

In one respect, the Soviet leader had more grounds to object. In his conversation on December 5 with West German Foreign Minister Hans-Dietrich Genscher, Gorbachev accused Bonn of having "prepared a funeral for the European process" by rushing the idea of confederation and dictating conditions to East Germany.[113] While the 10-point program objectively did not contain a timetable for unification, it did alter the priorities, placing German unification above the building of the common European home. This meaning of the 10 points did not go unnoticed in other corners of Western Europe. Mitterrand raised this issue with concern in his conversation with Gorbachev on December 6: "We should not change the order of the processes. First and foremost among them should be European integration, the evolution of Eastern Europe, and the all-European process, the creation of a peaceful order in Europe .... Kohl's speech, his 10 points, has turned everything upside down."[114] From this time on, the idea of a common European home lost considerable ground in Europe.

After the Western allies accepted the 10-point program at the Brussels summit, the Soviet leadership finally focused on unification. At the end of January, Gorbachev accepted the idea of confederation but by that time even the Central Committee experts understood that in reality they could not rely on the SED any longer and that "all the state structures in the GDR have fallen apart."[115] The small group that Gorbachev convened to discuss the German issue agreed on the strategy of accepting confederation as a method simply to gain more time since, as Kryuchkov put it, "we need to start getting our people used to the idea of German unification." Also, looming over Gorbachev was the huge domestic problem of withdrawing 300,000 troops, including 100,000 officers with families. Gorbachev was very aware of the significance of Soviet troops leaving Germany— both symbolically in the context of the public memory of World War II and practically in terms of the logistical difficulties and the possible backlash within the army and society as a whole. Still, he ended the meeting by instructing Marshal Akhromeyev to "prepare the withdrawal of troops from the GDR."[116]

After settling on the strategy of buying more time and brooking no NATO membership for Germany, Gorbachev agreed to meet with Baker and then Kohl (the Germans had been asking for this meeting for almost two months). In the session with Baker on February 9, 1990, Gorbachev discussed various forms of German

[113] Document No. 113, Mikhail Gorbachev and Hans Dietrich Genscher Conversation, December 5, 1989.
[114] Document No. 114, Mikhail Gorbachev and Francois Mitterrand Conversation, December 6, 1989.
[115] Document No. 118, Diary of Anatoly Chernyaev, January 28, 1990.
[116] Ibid.

unification and association with NATO. Although he could not accept it publicly, he agreed with Baker's argument that the presence of U.S. troops in Europe was a factor in overall European stability, which implicitly meant accepting the idea of Germany's eventual membership in the Western alliance. It was during this conversation that Baker offered Gorbachev guarantees (that is the word used in the Russian memorandum of conversation—*garantii*) that NATO would not "spread an inch eastward," and the Soviet leader accepted the statement as sufficient on the basis of the trust he felt had been built between him and the U.S. leadership—never asking for a written pledge. Gorbachev's reasoning could partially be explained by the domestic dilemma he faced: how could he tell the Politburo that he had asked for written guarantees that NATO would not expand to the territories of the Warsaw Pact while the Pact was still in existence? That would have meant he had already accepted the idea that the socialist alliance was on its deathbed. In this conversation, Baker was not trying to mislead Gorbachev in any way; he was merely expressing the official position of the U.S. government at the time, which was fully shared by other Western leaders, talking specifically about the NATO presence on East German soil, but by implication also about any future expansion. However, the Bush administration would change that position very soon—without providing any notification to Gorbachev. Later, those assurances would be overtaken by events and ultimately overlooked by the Clinton administration, an unfortunate chain of circumstances that would lead to a persistent (and ongoing) debate in Russia on why Gorbachev failed to demand the guarantees in writing.

By the end of May 1990, Gorbachev accepted the right of the German people to choose alliances. This position was quite within his earlier pronouncements on freedom of choice, and was a strategically logical move for the Soviet Union because it was better to have a powerful and prosperous Germany as an ally and a friend.[117] This calculation proved to be correct: Germany became the USSR's most reliable creditor and trade partner and a source of direct aid in difficult moments; in fact, the FRG remains Russia's main ally in Europe today.

German unification finally was realized before the November 1990 CSCE meeting, which became the epilogue of Gorbachev's dream of the common European home. With Germany united in NATO, the Warsaw Pact soon lost the last reasons for its existence and was disbanded by its members in 1991. The Soviet Union followed suit soon thereafter. The European home was built but Yeltsin's new Russia never acquired an apartment in it.

THE QUESTION OF USE OF FORCE AND SOVIET TROOP WITHDRAWAL

Documents and oral testimony collected in this volume show that a rejection of use or threat of force was indeed one of the original ideas of the Gorbachev leadership. However, this issue was a major concern for U.S. policymakers and East

---

[117] Grachev, *Gorbachev's Gamble*, 158.

European public through late 1989. One of the most debated questions in the literature on the end of the Cold War has been to what extent was violent suppression by the Soviet Union ever a serious threat in response to instability or rapid reforms in the socialist countries? Related to this: what were the limits of change that the USSR would allow? The answers fall into two categories: how and when the issue of force was settled internally by the Soviet leadership, and how and when the East Europeans learned about it. The latter, of course, is most important for explaining actual developments in the region in 1989. Once the perceived threat of force had disappeared, all constraints were removed and the transformations assumed a revolutionary character culminating in the introduction of new political systems and the dissolution of the Warsaw Pact itself.

What we now know is that at no point, regardless of how unexpected or disturbing the news from Eastern Europe, was there any discussion at high levels of the Soviet party or government of using force against the opposition. Even with subsequently published memoirs of Soviet hardliners and Gorbachev's detractors, no signs of such deliberations have surfaced. Gorbachev himself in his memoirs made it clear that there were no doubts in his mind about the impossibility of using force in Eastern Europe from the day he was elected general secretary (and probably as early as his 1969 visit to Czechoslovakia). According to his own accounts and those provided by Grachev and Chernyaev, as early as the first meetings with socialist heads of state, Gorbachev's signal to them was "Do not count on our tanks to keep you and your regimes in power."[118] The earliest explicit documented statement to this effect by the Soviet leader to his own Politburo was made on July 3, 1986, for which he prepared a personal memorandum on June 26. At that meeting, the general secretary emphatically stated that "the methods that were used in Czechoslovakia and Hungary now are no good, they will not work!"[119] The way in which Gorbachev addressed his colleagues suggests that he intended to make a programmatic statement about a new stage in relations with the allies. From then on, it must have been clear to the rest of the leadership that violence was not an option. In the Soviet system, such a strong declaration by the general secretary would not be challenged. A similar statement was made to the socialist leaders during a CMEA session in November 1986 in Moscow.[120]

The emphasis on individual developments within each country and the renunciation of Soviet pressure became especially pronounced in Soviet internal discussions in 1989, as the Kremlin prepared itself for the coming changes in Eastern Europe. On January 21, 1989, after his meetings with the Trilateral Commission and later with Henry Kissinger, Gorbachev talked to the Politburo about the need to think about and prepare for attempts by the socialist countries to join

[118] Grachev, *Gorbachev*, 294.
[119] Document No. 7, Notes of CC CPSU Politburo Session, July 3, 1986.
[120] Archie Brown, *The Gorbachev Factor*, 249.

the EC. He was surprisingly optimistic about such possibilities, admitting that the East Europeans were not fully aware of Moscow's flexibility.

Internal analyses of Eastern Europe and policy suggestions from the International Department and the Bogomolov Institute in February 1989 strongly supported the idea that forceful repression would have "unacceptable consequences," but also suggested that some "vagueness" be retained "as far as our concrete actions are concerned [...] so that we do not stimulate anti-socialist forces to try to test the fundamentals of socialism in a given country."[121] In a crucial conclusion from the first memorandum, the authors point out that "it is very unlikely that we would be able to employ the methods of 1956 and 1968, both as a matter of principle and because of unacceptable consequences."[122] The Bogomolov Institute memorandum discussed above mentions those consequences more specifically and spells out the logic of why coercion would be the least rational decision for Gorbachev to take: "Direct interference with force by the USSR in the development of events on the side of conservative elements who are isolated from the people would absolutely clearly mean an end to *perestroika*, and the loss of the world community's trust toward us." At the same time, "it would not be able to prevent the collapse of the socio-economic and socio-political system that exists in these countries."[123]

Gorbachev himself repeated the same line widely in internal forums to make sure that all important layers of the Soviet bureaucracy implemented the new policy. One such layer, populated predominantly by conservative party holdovers, consisted of ambassadors to the socialist countries. In a meeting on March 3, 1989, Gorbachev explained to them the policy of non-interference and encouragement for reform, warned them not to be tempted to "reach for the stick and punish someone because of ideological or economic issues," and raised the issue of Soviet pressure in strong terms: "Do not impose anything on anybody! Every country is very specific. Considering this specificity, we are not playing with them. We reject force in everything, in all our policies."[124]

Another reason to remain vague about the limits of reforms might have been in order not to alarm domestic conservatives, the KGB, and especially the military, who felt strongly about "keeping" Eastern Europe, and who, even though they fell short of comprising an organized opposition, did make sure their preferences were known. There are some references to these concerns in the memoirs. According to Shevardnadze, in the fall of 1989 he and Gorbachev "were pressured to follow the scenarios of 1953, 1956 and 1968." From the available sources it seems that those pressures were mainly indirect—implied in discussions of the possible disastrous outcomes if Eastern Europe were to be "lost"—because so

---

[121] Document No. 41, Memorandum of the CC CPSU International Department, February 1989.
[122] Ibid.
[123] Document No. 42, Memorandum of the Bogomolov Institute, February 1989.
[124] Document No. 51, Gorbachev's Meeting with Soviet Ambassadors to Socialist Countries, March 3, 1989.

far no evidence has emerged suggesting that anyone in the leadership proposed to actually use force to keep Eastern Europe in the socialist camp. The price of doing so was certainly very clear to the foreign minister: it would mean sacrificing "freedom of choice, non-interference, and a common European home ... The very thought of it or of keeping a tight leash on the countries that some call 'buffer states' was insulting to us as well as to the people of those countries."[125]

What strikes one when reading Soviet documents from 1988–1989 on Eastern Europe is how many times Gorbachev was warned about the impending collapse of the socialist bloc, and how aware he must have been of the real state of affairs. And yet, during Politburo deliberations or in discussions with his closest personal assistants, on whom he relied more and more in 1989, the use or even threat of force was never proposed by anyone.[126]

While it is safe to argue that within the Soviet hierarchy, at least after July 1986, the issue of use of force in Eastern Europe was settled, the more interesting question remains: when did the leaders and opposition in the socialist countries become aware of this fact and how did that awareness alter their behavior? Did it affect each group's actions differently? One could argue that although the old guard did not sufficiently recognize the new signals at Gorbachev's first meetings with them in March, April and October 1985, once an understanding of the policy of non-interference dawned on them, it would have been in their self-interest to sustain the impression that the Brezhnev Doctrine was still in effect—to "float" it before their populations in order to constrain the actions of dissidents and to keep themselves in power. For the general public, it took until after the December 1988 U.N. speech for the belief to sink in that the Doctrine was no longer valid.[127]

Poland was an especially interesting case to consider in this respect because in a way it constituted Gorbachev's preferred testing ground for what was to happen in the Soviet bloc and in the USSR itself. The Soviet leader had a close and respectful relationship with Jaruzelski, probably his only true friend among the fraternal leaders. During their dinner in July 1988, after the 19th Party Conference, and in his speech to the Polish Sejm on July 11, Gorbachev was already speaking explicitly about freedom of choice and non-interference, and how these

---

[125] Eduard Shevardnadze, "No One Can Isolate Us, Save Ourselves. Self-Isolation Is the Ultimate Danger." *Slavic Review* 51, no.1 (Spring 1992), 118.

[126] Musgrove transcript, 168.

[127] Musgrove transcript, 203-205. Interestingly, concerns over Soviet intentions held longest in the United States. In February 1989 Ambassador Matlock mentioned the subject in his cables from Moscow; at the end of July Secretary of State Baker cautioned Shevardnadze not to resort to violence in Eastern Europe, (and Shevardnadze reassured him on the point); and even as late as September 22, NSDD-23 demanded that the USSR renounce the Brezhnev Doctrine and "refrain from the threat or use of force against the territorial integrity or political independence of any state." See Document Nos. 43, 45, and 47; Oberdorfer, *The Turn*, 360; and Document No. 84.

fit into his grand design for the common European home—almost as if he were rehearsing his forthcoming U.N. speech.[128]

The developments in Poland in August and September 1988 show that, in that country at least, the leadership was not at all worried about the possible use of force on the Soviets' part. The first Politburo discussion of the idea of Round-table negotiations, introduced by Józef Czyrek, took place on August 21, 1988. The objective was to engage the opposition constructively up to the point of free elections and participation in the government, and in doing so to co-opt Lech Wałęsa, Solidarity's leader. In the entire discussion, a record of which is available from the Polish archives, the Soviet factor was not raised once.[129] The exchange was surprisingly non-ideological and focused on the economic crisis. If the Polish Politburo at that time could envisage any punitive measures emanating from the USSR, one would expect that to have been a major issue in the conversation. A month after the initial discussion, on September 22, the Polish Politburo adopted a formal resolution on negotiations with the opposition, which was widely circulated to Central Committee members, associate Politburo members and regional secretaries. The Soviets were not consulted before those crucial decisions were made. They were informed only later.

To fulfill that task and to feel out the Soviets' reaction, the Poles sent an old friend of Jaruzelski who, as a Foreign Minister, was very familiar to the Kremlin—Czyrek. The day after the PUWP's decision on talks with the opposition, Gorbachev and Czyrek had a discussion that would set the stage for the developments of 1989 in Poland. The available record of conversation provides a glimpse of how willing the Soviet general secretary was to encourage internal political processes in Eastern Europe—more so than is generally believed—and how he genuinely tried to understand what was going on in Poland. After listening to the Polish envoy's discussion of the internal situation and particularly the strikes underway throughout the country, Gorbachev asked pointed questions about the role of the party and the reasons for its failure to obtain support among Polish workers. Here, he was not lecturing, but seeking information and listening to explanations. When Czyrek presented the Polish decisions to engage Solidarity and the Catholic Church, Gorbachev cautioned that the Polish authorities should act slowly so as not to appear panicked, but he did not try to exert pressure to change those decisions, let alone threaten punitive measures.[130] The two also discussed various candidates for the post of prime minister and agreed on Rakowski—an unusual step for Gorbachev who was generally not inclined to discuss allied personnel issues in such detail. He in effect gave the green light not

---

[128] Speech at dinner with Jaruzelski, the Gorbachev Foundation Archive, Fond 1; Gorbachev speech at the Sejm, *Pravda*, July 12, 1989, 2.

[129] Protocol from the meeting for the Political Bureau held on 21 August 1988 under chairmanship of the 1st Secretary of KC PZPR, comrade Wojciech Jaruzelski, Warsaw, Archiwum Akt Nowych.

[130] Document No. 28, Mikhail Gorbachev and Józef Czyrek Conversation, September 23, 1988.

only to the legalization of Solidarity but to the Roundtable negotiations and free elections, even to the possibility of forming a coalition government. This conversation provides even more reason to argue that by September 1988 the Polish leadership already believed that there was no threat of Soviet intervention. When asked if he was concerned about a possibility of Soviet use of force in the summer of 1989, the Tadeusz Mazowiecki said, "nobody in the leadership thought already in August 1988 that Gorbachev would intervene, but there were other serious concerns: economic pressure [from the Soviet Union], what Honecker and other allies might do, and what if Gorbachev would not survive."[131]

It would be logical to expect the Poles to discuss both the plans for initiating the Roundtable and their understanding of the Soviet position with other allied leaders, and to share their conviction that there would be no Soviet military response. One such meeting took place on the eve of the Roundtable in Poland. On February 1, 1989, Jaruzelski met with his Czechoslovak counterpart, Miloš Jakeš, to inform him of the talks that were due to start on February 6. The Polish leader explained how the process would work and his hope to be able to co-opt the opposition while staying within the framework of the new concept of socialism internally and within the WTO alliance in foreign policy. In the conversation, the socialist leaders never raised the possibility of a negative Soviet response, but rather emphasized that "an important change in relations toward the USSR has occurred. The earlier crises were always accompanied by an increase in antisocialism; now even the opposition says that it is trying to gain the friendship of the USSR."[132] It would be safe to conclude that by early 1989, at the latest, the top leadership of the socialist countries was no longer concerned about the threat of a Soviet intervention, and that the Kremlin was not only aware of that understanding but in fact promoted it actively for some time beginning in the summer of 1988.

A related issue of major importance that Gorbachev had to confront early on was the status of Soviet troops in Eastern Europe. If the Kremlin was serious about disarmament in Europe and about treating its allies as equals, what were Soviet forces doing on their territory? It is generally believed that the question of a pull-out was raised in the USSR in the fall of 1988, in preparation for the U.N. speech. However, at least one document from this collection shows that there was an attempt to initiate such withdrawals as early as spring 1987, in

---

[131] Conversation with the author at the conference "Revolutions of 1989" in Vienna, Austria, October 1, 2009, organized by the Austrian Academy of Sciences and the Ministry of European and International Affairs.

[132] Record of discussion led by General Secretary of the CC CPCz M. Jakeš and First Secretary of the CC PUWP and Chairman of the Council of State of the PPR W. Jaruzelski on February 1, 1989—a document presented at the International Conference "Poland 1986–1989: The End of the System," organized by the Institute for Political Studies of the Polish Academy of Sciences and the National Security Archive at The George Washington University, Warsaw-Miedzeszyn, October 21–23, 1999.

anticipation of Gorbachev's April visit to Prague.[133] In a memorandum prepared for his superior to discuss at the Politburo, Shakhnazarov proposed making an announcement that the Red Army would soon begin to pull out from Czechoslovakia. Shakhnazarov, who at that time was not even the general secretary's official adviser but merely the deputy head of the CC socialist countries department, argued strongly that such a step would allow Moscow to seize the initiative in the reform process and take steps voluntarily, which later it would be forced to do under pressure from the socialist countries. This enlightened reformer had foreseen the future quite accurately.

It is fascinating to see that even the radical Shakhnazarov at the time did not advocate redeployments from all socialist countries, and did not envision pulling out of Poland and East Germany at any point in the future. However, reducing troop levels in Czechoslovakia, he argued, would be seen as encouragement for local reformers and would raise the prestige of Gorbachev's *perestroika* among those populations. Implicitly, under Shakhnazarov's proposal, the interpretation of the events of 1968 would have to be changed too. At least, as he points out with reference to the Soviet–Czechoslovak documents signed that year, the conditions that purportedly demanded the original introduction of the Red Army into Czechoslovakia had ceased to exist, and therefore its continued deployment was no longer justified either by existing agreements or by the current situation. However, as far as we know, the memorandum was never discussed at the Politburo, and the failure to follow through on the concept in Prague represented an important missed opportunity, one that was not openly mentioned at the time and has rarely been noted since in studies of the end of the Cold War in Europe.

The fact that Shakhnazarov wrote that memo means that either Gorbachev requested it, or at the very least that Shakhnazarov was confident that the general secretary shared his views on this issue. Before he became Gorbachev's formal adviser in early 1988, he often served as an informal one, briefing him on Eastern Europe or drafting speeches and memoranda. Why would Gorbachev not follow up on this particular memorandum—at least with a Politburo discussion if not with the actual announcement? His failure to do so seems to confirm Mlynář's point that at the time he was still a hostage of the Brezhnev Doctrine himself. Had he acted on the idea, it would arguably have made the reform communists more decisive while they still had the advantage—before the non-communist opposition and the dissidents overtook them in the summer of 1989, as Shakhnazarov anticipated, and it would have been more of a piece with Gorbachev's own vision of "little *perestroikas*" taking root throughout the region.

As mentioned above, the question of troop withdrawals from Eastern Europe was repeatedly raised in discussions with advisers, and sometimes at the Politburo. Both the International Department and the Bogomolov institute memoranda suggested that a pull-out should be considered in the future. Fellow Warsaw Pact

---

[133] Document No. 10, Proposal from Georgy Shakhnazarov to the CC CPSU, March 1987.

representatives raised this in meetings with their Soviet counterparts, and Gorbachev was well aware of these suggestions. But he usually spoke in favor of very gradual reductions that fell short of complete withdrawal. Even on the eve of his December 1988 U.N. speech, he believed such a controlled turn of events was possible.[134] No specific timetable was ever discussed, however, which begs the question whether this was out of reluctance to provoke domestic opposition, or a function of Gorbachev's ambivalence toward the old guard in Eastern Europe. It seems most likely that his main focus was on the European process and that from his perspective progress on the core issue would then determine the timetable for withdrawal.

CONCLUSION

If any single event or series of events could be taken to signify the end of the Cold War, it probably was the wave of peaceful revolutions in Eastern Europe and the fall of the Berlin Wall in November 1989.

After 1985, the Soviet Union gradually abandoned the old pattern of intervention and tight control over internal developments in the socialist camp. It is important to note that during the second half of the 1980s the USSR still had the capability to dominate its allies militarily; even in 1990 several hundred thousand Soviet troops remained in Eastern Europe.

However, military intervention was seen as abhorrent and unacceptable to Gorbachev and his reformist coalition, who were at the peak of their power in 1989 and early 1990. The concept of security that the reformers shared had been transformed considerably from the traditional Soviet one to include such important elements as reasonable sufficiency in strategic weapons, universal human rights and values, and the common European home. In their view, the Soviet Union would not become less secure if it was surrounded by independent, friendly countries facing similar problems and united by a common process of democratic reform. Moreover, the country's security would, in fact, increase if democratization in the USSR and in Eastern Europe led them to participate "in the common European process and form together with Europe a unified economic, legal, humanitarian, cultural and ecological space."[135]

Although the reformers were aware of the possible repercussions of "losing Eastern Europe," especially among the military and the generation of World War II veterans, they made the crucial choice to abstain from using force and instead to encourage reform in Eastern Europe. The documents presented in this book make clear that the new leadership took this stand early on and stood by it to the end. As Gorbachev's interpreter-adviser Pavel Palazchenko stated in his memoir,

---

[134] Document No. 31, Meeting between Mikhail Gorbachev and Foreign Policy Advisers, October 31, 1988.
[135] Shevardnadze, "No One Can Isolate Us," 119.

the decision to "release Eastern Europe was made, and they did not go back on it when the full implications became clear ... I do not believe that the coming generation of leaders will ever have to make decisions of such magnitude or such agonizing difficulty."[136]

The transformation of Soviet policy toward the East European countries, therefore, can be explained by three main factors. Firstly, there was the influence of new norms and beliefs that determined the fundamental choices made by Gorbachev and his coalition. Secondly, the reassessment of the strategic and economic value of the socialist camp combined with internal political events in the Soviet Union in 1989 made Eastern Europe a lower priority for Moscow. Thirdly, Gorbachev's idea of a common European home made the use of force in one part of that home seem unacceptable and counterproductive.

Europe was at the heart of Gorbachev's vision for a new international order. Gradual mutual demilitarization and the eventual disbanding of NATO and the Warsaw Pact, along with economic integration between the CMEA and the EEC, were seen as the road to the common home. In that home, the use of force would be proscribed and all nations would have the freedom to choose their own socio-political system. Universal human values and not the balance of power would be the foundation of the new home. This new home would also require a new pan-European security structure free of Cold War associations and built, Gorbachev imagined, on the institutional basis of the CSCE, utilizing the remaining infrastructures from both NATO and the WTO.

Gorbachev's East European policy was an integral part of his ambitious effort to reform the Soviet domestic system, put an end to the arms race that was exhausting the economy, and integrate the USSR into the European democratic community of nations. Starting from these priorities and taking into account unfolding events, the peaceful outcome that transpired becomes perfectly logical even if it might have seemed unlikely at the time. In fact, the logic of that ultimate result was understood even by Western observers who followed the Soviet reform process closely.[137] The only imaginable scenario where force could have been used abroad was if a hard-line coup had been staged earlier than August 1991, when arguably the chances for its success were higher in the absence of a strong democratic movement in Russia.[138] However, even the hawkish defense minister, Dmitri Yazov, believed force should not be used beyond Soviet borders as late as 1990, and neither the military nor the KGB ever actually proposed to use it in Eastern Europe (as opposed to domestically, in order to keep the Soviet Union together, as in Vilnius in 1991).

Before Gorbachev's vision had a chance to be implemented, the Cold War ended in Eastern Europe, swept away by the rising tide of popular movements.

---

[136] Palazchenko, *My Years with Gorbachev and Shevardnadze*, 146.
[137] Musgrove transcript, 171-173.
[138] Brown, *Seven Years*, 205.

His hopes for a measured process controlled from above did not materialize. Instead, East Europeans took the initiative and were able to use the Bush administration's pause and the confusion on both sides of the Atlantic to their own advantage—holding free elections, tearing down the Wall, and eventually dissolving the Warsaw Pact. The Soviet leadership found itself behind the flow of events, reacting rather than directing them. Even though Gorbachev was shocked by Kohl's 10-point speech of November 28, 1989, and by Bush's apparent support for the German drive for quick reunification, he tried to salvage as much as possible of his vision of the common European home, hoping to achieve it at the Paris summit of the CSCE. According to his vision, Eastern Europe was part of the European process, the European scenario, which ruled out the use of force. All the evidence available today makes it clear that the Soviet reformers realized that a recourse to violence would mean the end of their entire experiment and the failure of Gorbachev's vision.

The end of the Cold War in Europe was a historic achievement, a true masterpiece of history, but it also contained an element of missed opportunity. Almost twenty years after the events discussed in this book, Russia remains in many respects separate from Europe, obviously not fully integrated economically and even less so politically. The common European home exists only within the boundaries of the European Union, which serves as a desired destination for former Soviet republics and therefore makes it a very sensitive issue for Russia. NATO has expanded beyond the former USSR's borders, incorporating the Baltic states, and Ukraine and Georgia have expressed interest in joining it. Tensions between Russia and the United States persist, with great power rhetoric gaining popularity among the Russian political elite and the population. Domestically, Russia is moving in a more authoritarian direction, successfully exploiting the notion of an external threat once again. What was clearly an opportunity used to the fullest by the East Europeans in 1989 could now be seen as an opportunity missed by both Washington and Moscow to integrate Russia into Europe both politically and economically, following Gorbachev's vision. In his conversation with British Foreign Secretary Douglas Hurd after the putsch of August 1991, the Soviet leader articulated this hope against the background of irreversible tendencies that were pulling his country apart. Still speaking of the Soviet Union, he said, "there is a chance, which we should exploit: to make permanent the integration of this enormous country into the international community. I don't know what the cost of achieving this goal will be, but I am confident that the price will not be comparable to what we all have paid for confrontation [during the Cold War]."[139]

---

[139] Gorbachev–Douglas Hurd Conversation, September 10, 1991, Gorbachev Foundation, Fond 1, Opis 1.

U.S. Policy and the Revolutions of 1989

By Thomas Blanton

The Cold War met a miraculous end during the late 1980s, with neither a bang nor a whimper. Instead, the lasting images of the Cold War's demise were almost all peaceful (except in Romania) yet incandescent. Hammers and chisels reduced the Berlin Wall to souvenir rocks while Beethoven's "Ode to Joy" blared out over the Brandenburg Gate. A demonstrator handed dandelions to armored police in front of signs that said "Havel to the Castle," and within days, indeed, the dissident playwright became President of Czechoslovakia. Grizzled union activists from Solidarity celebrated their 99-to-1 victory in Polish elections, as workers' ballots evicted the dictatorship of the proletariat. Goulash reformers took down the barbed wire on Hungary's borders and thousands of East Germans boarded trains to the West—the beginning of the end for the Berlin Wall. Even the Securitate's violent last stand in Bucharest and Timisoara—snipers on the rooftops and a rushed show trial for the last Stalinist standing (Ceauşescu)—provided the exception that proved the rule.[1] This all took place in the year of miracles, 1989; but hardly anyone predicted such an end for Stalin's empire, for the division of Europe, or for the Cold War.

Why did the Cold War end? And why did it end peacefully? How did it happen that an empire founded on conquest by Stalin's armies and repression by secret police chose not to strike back, not to use violence as the end approached?[2] Did the policies of the United States win the Cold War, or was the outcome the result of processes mostly internal to the Soviet Union? Was the growing disparity between the economies of West and East the key factor in the Soviet Union essentially giving up the fight, or was the "new thinking" of Soviet leaders more crucial to the end of the Cold War? Answers to these questions are as varied as the arguments about why the Cold War started. There is even debate over when exactly the Cold War did end, and confusion over the relationship between that ending and the subsequent dissolution of the Soviet Union.[3]

---

[1] For the images and sounds, see the TV documentary series CNN *Cold War*, Episode 23, "The Wall Comes Down" (www.CNN.com/ColdWar). For the liveliest first-hand reporting, see Garton Ash, *The Magic Lantern*, and Dobbs, *Down With Big Brother*.

[2] These questions, which shaped the Musgrove conference and our research agenda, were most usefully posed for us by Levesque, *Enigma*.

[3] See Blanton, "When Did the Cold War End?" Multiple participants in the Musgrove dialogue make the case that the Cold War ended well before the Soviet Union did, and that the proximate cause of the latter was the internal Soviet political competition between—in shorthand—the hardliners versus Gorbachev versus Yeltsin.

This essay seeks to analyze the actual role of the United States in the events leading up and culminating in 1989 in Eastern Europe. For the purposes of this book, the essay brings to the table some of the more useful memoir and secondary accounts on the U.S. side, providing context and a more analytical American perspective on the extraordinary documents and dialogue that are the heart of this volume. At the outset, it must be said that U.S. policy towards Eastern Europe did not substantially change in the 1980s, that U.S. assessments did not predict the revolutions of 1989, and that American documentation is not particularly explanatory for what happened in Eastern Europe in 1989—which is why the editors of this volume have not included here more than a sampling of U.S. primary sources. Yet because the secondary literature (so much of it written by Americans) makes such large claims for the U.S. role, and because the new Soviet evidence alters the received narratives in appreciable ways, this essay attempts to sort out what mattered and what really did not in the history of U.S. policy up to and including 1989.

The subject of the U.S. role in the end of the Cold War is certainly contested terrain, perhaps not as much among scholars as in the popular press and the public imagination. The death of former President Ronald Reagan in 2004, after a tragic decade suffering from Alzheimer's disease, brought an outpouring of encomiums that elaborated on the popular idea that Reagan should get the credit for winning the Cold War.[4] No few Reagan administration officials had already staked out this ground, aided and abetted by several prominent book authors primarily of a conservative orientation.[5] Leading the obituaries, the cover of *The Economist* magazine made the claim explicit as the headline on a formal photographic portrait of the late President: "The Man Who Beat Communism."[6] Few of the Reagan assessments at the time took a critical view of this notion, missing altogether the prevailing scholarly debate over the end of the Cold War, which pitted realists who saw the Soviet economic crisis and global market transformations as leaving the USSR with little choice but to retreat from empire, versus constructivists and liberals who emphasized the power of ideas and international norms, in effect Gorbachev's "new thinking" combined with his miscalculations, as ending the Cold War.[7] Notably, when asked directly if he deserved the credit

---

[4] *Time* magazine remarked that Reagan had been "a kind of living time capsule of the American Century, born before the phrase world war had been introduced, a child when the Russian Revolution gave birth to the empire whose defeat he would accomplish as President." Nancy Gibbs, "The All-American President," *Time*, June 14, 2004, accessed at *www.time. com/time/magazine/article/0,9171,994446,00.html*.

[5] The most prominent such accounts are by Schweizer, *Victory*; Schweizer, *The Fall of the Berlin Wall*; and Schweizer, *Reagan's War*. But a number of Reagan-era memoirs, notably by Caspar Weinberger and Robert McFarlane, make similar claims.

[6] *The Economist*, June 12, 2004.

[7] For the realists, see Brooks and Wohlforth, "Power, Globalization, and the End of the Cold War." The leading constructivists/liberals are English, *Russia and the Idea of the West*, and Evangelista, *Unarmed Forces*. For two insightful Reagan appreciations in 2004 from par-

for the changes in Soviet behavior, Reagan himself had remarked, in a Moscow summit press conference in May 1988, "Mr. Gorbachev deserves most of the credit, as the leader of this country."[8]

But the either/or debate about Reagan misunderestimates, as a later Bush might have said, a third possibility—that in fact it was the interaction between Reagan and Gorbachev, especially at the series of summits from Geneva in 1985 through Governors' Island in 1988, that constituted the primary U.S. contribution to the end of the Cold War, by reducing the sense of threat in Moscow and thus enabling Gorbachev in his efforts to change Soviet policy.[9] Specifically, Reagan's oft-repeated and evidently sincere abhorrence of nuclear weapons, his commitment to abolition, his understanding that there could be "no winners" in a nuclear war—all served to undercut the core Soviet Cold War insecurity, the fear of a Western first strike (like Hitler's *blitzkrieg*) or a Western invasion (such as the intervention on the side of the "Whites" in the Russian civil war).[10] Combined with a generational shift among the leaders in Moscow, Reagan's abolitionism encouraged Gorbachev's "new thinking" and undermined the Soviet military's unrelenting pressure for more spending. Combined with Gorbachev's increasing "peer group" interactions with other Western Europeans, in particular Margaret Thatcher (herself no abolitionist),[11] the summit encounters with Reagan gave the Soviet leader a new understanding of the Western sense of threat—and some ideas for reducing that sense, often unilaterally.

ticipants at the Musgrove conference who drew on some of the evidence now published in this book, see Vladislav Zubok, "Soft Power: Reagan the Dove," *The New Republic*, June 21, 2004, 32; and James Hershberg, "Just Who Did Smash Communism?" *Washington Post* "Outlook" section, June 27, 2004, B01. The author owes a particular intellectual debt, for extended conversations and cooperative scholarship over decades, to Professors Zubok and Hershberg, and to this book's lead editor, Dr. Savranskaya.

[8] Gorbachev, *Memoirs,* 457; quoted in Matlock, *Reagan and Gorbachev*, 302.

[9] For the texts of the summit memcons and a wide range of the preparatory and follow-up documents on both sides, see the forthcoming National Security Archive book, *The Last Superpower Summits: Gorbachev, Reagan and Bush* (Budapest/New York: Central European University Press, 2011), and the series of Web postings edited by Svetlana Savranskaya and Thomas Blanton at *www.nsarchive.org.*

[10] For a concise history of Soviet perception on this point, see Mastny, *The Cold War and Soviet Insecurity.* Or as French president François Mitterand told President George H.W. Bush on May 20, 1989: "Since 1917 the Soviets have had a major hang-up about encirclement. Since their Civil War, they have had a siege mentality." Quoted in Bush and Scowcroft, *A World Transformed* (New York: Alfred A. Knopf, 1998), 77. The most extensive treatment of Reagan's abolitionism, based on declassified documents and interviews, may be found in Lettow, *Ronald Reagan.* The most insightful account of the development of Reagan's nuclear thinking is in FitzGerald, *Way Out There in the Blue.*

[11] For an eloquent recent account of the Thatcher factor with Gorbachev, see Brown, "The Change to Engagement in Britain's Cold War Policy." The classic account of Gorbachev's instrumentality in ending the Cold War is Brown, *The Gorbachev Factor.*

Of course, Reagan's theological commitment to missile defense (the so-called Strategic Defense Initiative, colloquially known as "Star Wars") worked in the opposite direction, giving Gorbachev nightmares of what he kept calling "space-strike" weapons. Also threatening were the U.S. military buildup under Carter and Reagan (which looked to Moscow like the makings of a first-strike strategy), the periodic flare-ups of the spy wars between the KGB and the CIA, and the often-bellicose rhetoric produced by the White House speechwriters and many members of the Reagan administration.[12] Yet the face-to-face summit meetings palpably undercut the hard-line tendencies on both sides of the Cold War. In person, Reagan kept offering to share SDI, an offer Gorbachev could never quite trust, yet the underlying notion of cooperative security made its own contribution to the "new thinking."[13] Not until 1987 did Gorbachev exorcise for himself the "space-strike" nightmare, realizing that missile defenses likely would not work and could be overwhelmed by a much smaller expenditure on additional missiles. But the impasse on SDI, together with political developments on the U.S. side, created huge delays in completing much more extensive arms reductions. These missed opportunities suggest some evocative counterfactuals about the end of the Cold War. Likewise, the fact that U.S. policy towards Eastern Europe—the center of this book—did not appreciably change from the old-style "differentiation" all the way through 1988, sets the stage for Americans to remain in the wings through 1989 as well.

The documents and dialogue in this book suggest that the main contribution of the George H.W. Bush administration to the peaceful end of the Cold War was its passivity during 1989—the infamous "pause" in U.S.–Soviet relations—because this opened a kind of vacuum between the superpowers into which the East Europeans, both reform communists and opposition dissidents, could rush to make the revolutions of 1989. Contrary to Bush administration insiders who subsequently posited a "grand strategy" that put Eastern Europe at the center of U.S.–Soviet relations, the documentary record suggests that leadership actually came from the Eastern Europeans—ranging from the unprecedented mass movement of Solidarity in Poland, to the modest example when the reform communists in Hungary and Poland persuaded Bush during his July 1989 trip to the region to cease his pause and reach out to Gorbachev for a summit (ultimately held at Malta after the Berlin Wall had already fallen).[14] Similarly, the documents

---

[12] For examples of the dysfunctional internal workings of the Reagan administration with specific reference to the speechwriting shop, see Matlock, *Reagan and Gorbachev*, 163–164 and 292–293.

[13] For an insightful early appreciation of Reagan's interaction with Gorbachev, see Garthoff, *Détente and Confrontation*, 1175–1180, although Garthoff divides the schools of thought into "essentialists" (hardliners on the Soviet Union), "mechanists" (pragmatic negotiators), and "interactionists" (empathetic understanding of the other side as reactive), which is not the framework argued in this essay.

[14] The most eloquent argument for "grand strategy" may be found in Hutchings, *American Diplomacy*.

prove that the diplomatic initiative for the reunification of Germany came not from the U.S., but from West German chancellor Helmut Kohl, whose voluminous conversations with President Bush show the American almost always following, not leading, and even pleading for Kohl's guidance, while Kohl himself raced to keep up with events on the ground in Berlin and Leipzig, as East Germans drove toward unification.[15]

This essay argues that the hard-line skeptical view of Gorbachev that dominated the Bush White House in 1989 (contrary to Reagan's ultimate judgment, and even to the staff-level assessment in the CIA) cost the U.S. more than just that one year of missed opportunities for greater arms reductions. That missed year featured a continuous decline in Gorbachev's own capacity—given his domestic political situation—to deliver greater arms reductions and security increases, so that the opportunities missed were never to return. The U.S. record is shockingly replete with highest-level expressions of Bush's personal and political insecurity vis-à-vis Gorbachev—worries that the Soviet leader had the initiative, was more popular in Europe, kept coming up with surprises on arms control—without any apparent awareness, either in the White House or in the U.S. military, that all this Soviet initiative dramatically improved U.S. national security, or that even more dramatic disarmament in the U.S. national interest was possible. Ultimately, only in 1991, after the failed coup against Gorbachev, would George Bush make his own unilateral arms cuts—cuts the Soviets had offered as early as 1987, but now too little, too late for any parallel process that would leave the world more secure.

[15] The argument outlined in this paragraph and subsequently in this essay owes a particular intellectual debt to the papers and discussion in the Society for Historians of American Foreign Relations annual meeting panel, "Case Studies in Democratization? The United States and Eastern Europe in the 1980s," chaired by the author on June 21, 2007, and especially the papers by Mary Sarotte on the end of the division of Germany, and by Gregory Domber on the U.S. contribution to Poland's revolution. The conclusion about Kohl comes from Kohl's own initiative to publish in 1998 his most important memcons and telcons from 1989 and 1990 in a massive German-language volume, apparently without asking permission from the various heads of state (including Bush) whose conversations with Kohl provide at least half the text of the book. See Kusters and Hofmann, *Deutsche Einheit*. The larger point about East Germans driving the unification process is detailed in Noel D. Cary, "'Farewell without Tears': Diplomats, Dissidents, and the Demise of East Germany," *The Journal of Modern History*, 73 (September 2001), 617–651. Cary's excellent review essay of memoirs on all sides of German unification includes this comment (p. 642) about one of the leading American accounts, by former Bush aides Zelikow and Rice, *Germany Unified*: "[A]lthough Zelikow and Rice superbly analyze the diplomacy surrounding unification, there is something troubling about the seeming ease with which they can tell their story with such little reference to the streets of Berlin and Leipzig."

The pattern beginning in 1985 of Soviet breakthroughs in new thinking that went mostly uncredited, disbelieved, and disrespected in Washington would continue through the end of the Reagan administration, and well into the George H.W. Bush years. Left on the table were extraordinary possibilities for nuclear and conventional arms reduction and a safer world—potentials that left such unfinished business, even in 2009, that the American president Barack Obama would venture to a Moscow summit with Russian president Dmitri Medvedev (and Prime Minister Vladimir Putin) where the first two subjects concerned strategic weapons cuts (to levels not even as low as those discussed by Reagan and Gorbachev) and missile defense (the controversial U.S. plan for bases in Poland and the Czech Republic).[16] It is worth reprising some of that history to see what might have been, to cast some additional light on what U.S. policy achieved and missed achieving. As early as February 1987, according to Douglas MacEachin in the Musgrove transcript, the sequence of arms reduction proposals and concessions by the Soviets was nothing short of astounding. Geneva's 50 percent cuts in missiles followed by Reykjavik's abolition in 10 years then set the stage for success in abolishing intermediate range missiles (INF), the so-called "zero-zero option" originally proposed by U.S. hardliners primarily because they were sure the Soviets would never give up their weapons. "Even more damaging to those who thought the answer to zero-zero was going to be a forever 'no,' we also got a 'yes' to intrusive on-site inspections. This was a new era."[17]

Yet the INF Treaty was the most that Gorbachev would ever get until it was too late for him to really deliver from the Soviet side. Gorbachev wanted not just the zero option on INF in 1987 and 1988, but also the 50 percent across-the-board reductions that were contemplated in the START proposals, but Washington's poverty of imagination plus opposition from hardliners (especially the military services) prevented any progress. The new thinking was perhaps most evident when the Soviets proposed—to the shock of the Americans—far more intrusive on-site inspections and verifications than the U.S. military services would agree to: When Marshal Akhromeyev offered to allow on-site counting of the bombs deployed on each bomber, it was the American negotiator, Paul Nitze, who demurred.[18] Similarly, at the Washington summit, Gorbachev introduced the idea of major conventional cuts along with a mutual ban on chemical weapons

[16] For a sample of the coverage, see Michael A. Fletcher and Philip P. Pan, "U.S.–Russia Summit Brings Series of Advances," *The Washington Post*, July 8, 2009, A6.

[17] Douglas MacEachin, Musgrove transcript, 185.

[18] Record of Conversation Between S.F. Akhromeyev and P. Nitze at the U.S. State Department, December 8, 1987, Document No. 26 in Svetlana Savranskaya and Thomas Blanton, eds., "The INF Treaty and the Washington Summit: 20 Years Later," National Security Archive Electronic Briefing Book No. 238, posted December 10, 2007, at *www.gwu. edu/~nsarchiv/NSAEBB/NSAEBB238/*

and both sides ending their arms flows into Central America (supposedly a long-time goal of Reagan policy), but the "pragmatists" were completely unprepared, as was Reagan.[19] One reason why centered around the continuing suspicion in Washington about Gorbachev, the persisting disbelief that Gorbachev represented anything really new. The top U.S. intelligence analyst on the Soviet Union, Robert Gates (then deputy director of the CIA, who subsequently failed upwards to positions as high as Secretary of Defense), wrote a memo forwarded to the President and top Cabinet officials just before the Washington summit that described Gorbachev almost 180 degrees from the reality. Gates predicted that Gorbachev's reforms were merely "breathing space" before "further increase in Soviet military power and political influence," that Gorbachev would only agree to arms deals "that protect existing Soviet advantages" and undermine "Alliance cohesion," and that Gorbachev remained committed to Third World adventures (only three months later, the Soviets would announce the pullout from Afghanistan).[20] We can add this kind of blindered thinking to the list of reasons that Jack Matlock gave in the Musgrove transcript: "we could have gotten a START agreement and other things in 1988" had it not been for Iran–Contra and the replacement of top aides like Poindexter, who truly supported the arms reduction and nuclear abolition agenda of the President.[21]

Despite frustration on the larger goals of major arms reductions, the interaction with Reagan was exactly what Gorbachev saw in his takeaway from the Washington summit, where he praised Reagan to the Politburo for the "human factor":

> In Washington, probably for the first time we clearly realized how much the human factor means in international politics. Before… we treated such personal contacts as simply meetings between representatives of opposed and irreconcilable systems. Reagan for us was merely the spokesman of the most conservative part of American capitalism and its military-industrial complex. But it turns out that politicians, including leaders of governments if they are really responsible people, represent purely human concerns, interests, and the hopes of ordinary people—people who vote for them in elections and who associate their leaders' names and personal abilities with the country's image and patriotism. The people are guided by the most natural human motives and feelings. In our age, it turns out, this has the biggest impact on political decisions….[22]

[19] For a detailed account based on comparing and contrasting the various memoirs, see FitzGerald, *Way Out There in the Blue*, 427–439. For the summit transcripts, as well as the U.S. and Soviet preparation documents, see Svetlana Savranskaya and Thomas Blanton, eds., "The INF Treaty and the Washington Summit: 20 Years Later," National Security Archive Electronic Briefing Book No. 238, posted December 10, 2007.

[20] Document No. 17, [Robert M. Gates], Memorandum, Subject: Gorbachev's Gameplan: The Long View, November 24, 1987.

[21] Jack Matlock, Musgrove transcript, 187.

[22] Anatoly Chernyaev, notes from December 1987 Politburo session, quoted in Chernyaev, *My Six Years With Gorbachev*, 142–143.

The Moscow summit in May–June 1988 also made its major contribution on the spectrum of "the human factor." But the American side missed another opportunity in Gorbachev's proposed statement against the use of military force to address international problems—officials resisted old Soviet language like "peaceful coexistence" and probably also had in mind U.S. support for proxy wars such as in Nicaragua. The State Department's summary of the summit reported that "we had to bring the Soviets back down to earth" and "we were not going back to the kind of vague concepts we had seen in the 1970s that were subject to differing interpretations and could result in misunderstandings and recriminations."[23] Yet at the closing press conference, Gorbachev made clear that an American endorsement of the "new thinking" and rejection of "military means" would have helped him enormously in his efforts to restructure Soviet foreign and military policy, so he was disappointed that "the opportunity to take a big stride in shaping civilized international relations has been missed."[24]

Just as in arms control, U.S. policy towards Eastern Europe stayed the same in the late 1980s despite the evidence of change in Soviet policy. The decades-old notion of "differentiation" still drove American relations with the countries of the Soviet bloc, and within "differentiation" the degree of independence from Moscow of a country's foreign policies mattered more than that country's internal levels of repression.[25] Thus Romania's Nikolae Ceauşescu, the prickly Stalinist who denounced the 1968 Soviet invasion of Czechoslovakia (fearing he would be next), kept raising toasts with U.S. Presidents from Nixon to Reagan, despite running his country as a gulag. In the most authoritative statement of U.S. policy at the end of the Reagan tenure, the Deputy Secretary of State, John Whitehead, endorsed differentiation and pronounced in January 1988, "Let us be clear, the long-run Soviet interest in maintaining a hegemonic relationship with Eastern Europe has not changed."[26] In fact, as the evidence in this volume shows, that interest had long changed.

But even among analysts who saw the change in Soviet policy, there were blinders and missed opportunities. Douglas MacEachin in the Musgrove discussion described having received a draft CIA estimate in 1987 that said "obviously any government that accepts itself as communist will be permitted by Moscow, without being threatened with the use of force." MacEachin called the analyst who drafted the estimate and suggested taking up an additional question: "what

---

[23] State Department cable, "Moscow Summit Briefing Materials," June 8, 1988, Document No. 27 in Thomas Blanton and Svetlana Savranskaya, eds., "The Moscow Summit 20 Years Later," National Security Archive Electronic Briefing Book No. 251, posted May 31, 2008 at *http://www.gwu.edu/~nsarchiv/NSAEBB/NSAEBB251/index.htm*

[24] Garthoff, *The Great Transition*, 356.

[25] National Security Decision Directive 54, August 1982, spelled out the differentiation policy.

[26] Speech by Deputy Secretary of State John Whitehead, "The U.S. Approach to Eastern Europe: A Fresh Look," January 19, 1988, *Department of State Bulletin*.

is going to be the effect, if all East European governments believe what we have said we believe regarding the non-use of force?" But "I never did follow up on that question."[27] "The question that we did not ask in 1987 was: if it is true that national communism is now the best outcome, and is acceptable to the Soviet government, to Gorbachev, when will the Poles believe that? Now we understand that it might take them a little longer, and certainly the Czechs, and certainly the Hungarians, all having had some unhappy experience... And once they did believe that, why were they going to stop necessarily at national communism?"[28] When intervention was so costly in every measure, of course Moscow was not going to send in the tanks; the real question was when would the Eastern Europeans figure this out and act accordingly. In this light, Ronald Reagan was the only one in the U.S. government who got it: Evil empire? "No, that was another time, another era."[29]

The Moscow summit certainly reinforced the reform dynamics in Moscow and encouraged the progress that led to Gorbachev's U.N. speech, but produced no action on arms control, primarily because presidential nominee Bush didn't want anything negotiated during the campaign season of 1988 that could jeopardize his right flank. The pragmatists around Reagan, like defense secretary Frank Carlucci and national security adviser Colin Powell, were protecting that flank, plus Reagan's own abolitionist urges had been partially sated by the INF treaty. For Washington, also, nuclear arms reductions had gotten out ahead of conventional cuts, where there was significant Soviet advantage in Europe, so U.S. officials held up progress on the former, never anticipating in their pragmatic bias that Gorbachev would embrace major, even unilateral, reductions in Soviet conventional forces.[30] In retrospect, 1988 qualified as a lost year, but worse was to come.

While President Reagan strolled buoyantly through Moscow during his May 1988 summit with Soviet leader Mikhail Gorbachev, then-Vice President George H.W. Bush vacationed at the family summer house in Kennebunkport, Maine. On June 1, 1988, the newspapers featured the surreal photograph of the U.S. President walking in Red Square next to the Kremlin, with a U.S. military officer only a few feet away carrying the locked briefcase (the so-called "football") with the codes that would launch U.S. nuclear weapons—the largest single number

---

[27] Douglas MacEachin, Musgrove transcript, 140.

[28] Douglas MacEachin, Musgrove transcript, 172.

[29] Mikhail Gorbachev subsequently wrote that these words were the most important result of the Moscow summit: Gorbachev, *Ponyat' perestroiku*, 161.

[30] For further discussion of the reasons why Washington did not pursue what Gorbachev was ready to concede, see Jack Matlock, *Reagan and Gorbachev*, 306. For Gorbachev's own understanding, see Document No. 23, "Record of the Main Content of a Telephone Conversation between Gorbachev and Kadar," May 19, 1988, in which Kadar commented and Gorbachev agreed: "It seems they are following a policy of delaying the agreement for the reduction of offensive weapons. It looks like they do not want to give this issue to Reagan, they want to save it for the new president."

of which would land precisely where Reagan and the officer were standing.[31] Starved for news in Kennebunkport, reporters wrung a dour reaction from the Vice President to the euphoria in Moscow. Bush commented, "The Cold War's not over."[32] And indeed, this attitude would characterize the Bush administration's reactions to Gorbachev for a long time to come, and all through 1989.

THE IDEOLOGICAL END OF THE COLD WAR

The most astute observers of the Soviet Union saw the Cold War ending even before the Moscow summit. In the Musgrove transcript, Jack Matlock describes reading "the most convincing evidence" of Soviet change when he saw the theses for the CPSU 19th Party Conference, which were issued at the moment when Matlock and the Reagan party were in Helsinki, Finland, on their way to Moscow in May 1988. Matlock was "electrified" and found an equally excited reading from the scholar of Russia and Librarian of Congress James Billington, also part of the Reagan group, who said to Matlock, "this is world-shaking." The next morning, according to Matlock, he told President Reagan "we are in a new ball game" and "this is going to be a different country"—"when I saw a Communist Party document that borrowed more from the American Constitution than from Marxism-Leninism, I was impressed."[33]

For those who were less attentive to Party documents, the ideological end of the Cold War arrived at the end of 1988. On December 7, 1988, Mikhail Gorbachev made his famous speech at the United Nations, explicitly endorsing the "common interests of mankind" (no longer the class struggle) as the basis of Soviet foreign policy and, significantly for Eastern Europe, declaring "the compelling necessity of the principle of freedom of choice" as "a universal principle to which there should be no exceptions." Gorbachev particularly surprised CIA and NATO officials with his announcement of unilateral cuts in Soviet forces totaling 500,000 soldiers, and the withdrawal from Eastern Europe of thousands of tanks and tens of thousands of troops.[34] According to the internal Soviet evidence, Gorbachev sought to create a bookend for the Cold War that had been declared by Winston Churchill in Fulton, Missouri with his "Iron Curtain" speech of 1947: Gorbachev told his advisers the UN speech should be "an anti-Fulton, Fulton in reverse."[35]

---

[31] For the UPI/Corbis photo of the officer with the "football" in Red Square, see Schwartz, *Atomic Audit*, photo section between pages 458 and 459.

[32] Alessandra Stanley, "More Worldly Than Wise," *Time*, August 15, 1988, 18, quoted in Oberdorfer, *The Turn*, 329.

[33] Jack Matlock, Musgrove transcript, 110.

[34] For the full text of Gorbachev's speech, see FBIS-SOV-99-236, December 8, 1988, 11–19.

[35] "Gorbachev's Conference with Advisers on Drafting the U.N. Speech, October 31, 1988," Document No. 3 in Svetlana Savranskaya and Thomas Blanton, eds., "Reagan, Gorbachev, and Bush at Governor's Island," National Security Archive Electronic Briefing Book No. 261, posted December 8, 2008, *www.gwu.edu/~nsarchiv/NSAEBB/NSAEBB261/*.

Reaction in the West ranged from disbelief to astonishment. *The New York Times* editorialized:

> Perhaps not since Woodrow Wilson presented his Fourteen Points in 1918 or since Franklin Roosevelt and Winston Churchill promulgated the Atlantic Charter in 1941 has a world figure demonstrated the vision Mikhail Gorbachev displayed yesterday at the United Nations.[36]

Sen. Daniel P. Moynihan summed up as follows: "In December 1988, Gorbachev went to the General Assembly of the United Nations and declared, 'We in no way aspire to be the bearer of ultimate truth.' That has to have been the most astounding statement of surrender in the history of ideological struggle."[37] For other observers of Gorbachev's speech, it was not so much the ideological concessions as the unilateral military cutbacks that most impressed. Retired Gen. Andrew Goodpaster, a former NATO commander and top aide to President Dwight D. Eisenhower, called the cuts "the most significant step since NATO was founded" and said they opened the way to broad military reductions on both sides.[38] Longtime Soviet analyst and former U.S. ambassador to Bulgaria Raymond Garthoff noted that "the impact of this reduction was even greater than the numbers; it meant unilaterally giving up the preponderant armored striking capability of the Warsaw Pact for any attack on the West, as subsequent [CIA] estimates acknowledged."[39]

In the Musgrove transcript, Douglas MacEachin remarked that he was testifying before Congress at the exact moment Gorbachev delivered his United Nations speech, and the contrast made for one of the more dramatic moments in U.S. analysis of the Soviet Union—and explains much of the conflict that carried over into the incoming Bush administration. Behind closed doors at the Senate Intelligence Committee and accompanied by the CIA's other two most senior Soviet analysts, MacEachin opened his testimony by saying "in about 15 minutes or so we may find out if one of my analytical judgments is going to turn out to be correct," referring to his prediction that Gorbachev will have to cut the proportion of Soviet resources that go to the military. At the same time, MacEachin disparaged the "plausible but totally unfounded story of very large cuts." Later he said his colleague Bob "Blackwell just went down the hall to watch some" of the U.N. speech on television, and he mentions the "news bulletin" of the 500,000 troop cut, calling the discussion "analysis on the fly."[40]

---

[36] *The New York Times*, December 8, 1988, 34.

[37] Daniel Patrick Moynihan, "The CIA's Credibility," *The National Interest* (Winter 1995/96), 111.

[38] Goodpaster quoted in Oberdorfer, *The Turn*, 319.

[39] Garthoff, "Estimating Soviet Military Intentions and Capabilities," 28.

[40] Douglas MacEachin, Musgrove transcript, 171; also see Document No. 7 in Svetlana Savranskaya and Thomas Blanton, eds., "Reagan, Gorbachev and Bush at Governors Is-

MacEachin remarked that "if Gorbachev is successful he will cause major social displacement in the United States" because "[t]here are not many homes for old wizards of Armageddon, and it is kind of like old case officers trying to find employment." And MacEachin offered a true confession in another extraordinary passage, which demonstrates how prior assumptions about Soviet behavior, rather than actual intelligence data points, actually drove intelligence findings:

> Now, we spend megadollars studying political instability in various places around the world, but we never really looked at the Soviet Union as a political entity in which there were factors building which could lead to the kind of—at least the initiation of political transformation that we seem to see. It does not exist to my knowledge. Moreover, had it existed inside the government, we never would have been able to publish it anyway, quite frankly. And had we done so, people would have been calling for my head. And I wouldn't have published it. In all honesty, had we said a week ago that Gorbachev might come to the UN and offer a unilateral cut of 500,000 in the military, we would have been told we were crazy. We had a difficult enough time getting air space for the prospect of some unilateral cuts of 50 to 60,000.[41]

In fact, the National Intelligence Estimate issued just a week before the U.N. speech (and MacEachin's testimony) stated baldly: "to date... we have not detected changes under Gorbachev that clearly illustrate either new security concepts or new resource constraints are taking hold."[42] MacEachin's boss, Deputy CIA Director Robert Gates, was already on the record pushing an even harder line: In his speech to the American Association for the Advancement of Science in October 1988, Gates declared that "The Soviet leader's real purpose ... was to use détente to grab Western technology and improve the Soviet military machine: 'The dictatorship of the Communist Party remains untouched and untouchable.' Should the United States want to help revitalize the Soviet system? 'I think not.'"[43] Gates delivered this speech even after the 19th Party Conference, whose theses so impressed Matlock and Billington, and after the Central Committee restructuring and purge of Gorbachev opponents that occurred in September 1988, which MacEachin in the Musgrove transcript described as a "Rubicon"—"before that happened there was still room for those who wanted to disparage the implications of events in the USSR to make their arguments."[44]

land," National Security Archive Electronic Briefing Book No. 261, posted December 8, 2008. For the December 1988 quotations, see pages 3, 32, 36 and 37.

[41] Ibid., 37–38.

[42] NIE 4-3/8-88, quoted in Garthoff, "Estimating Soviet Military Intentions and Capabilities," 28.

[43] Quoted in Beschloss and Talbott, *At the Highest Levels*, 48.

[44] Douglas MacEachin, Musgrove transcript, 117. See also Document No. 33, CIA Intelligence Assessment, "Gorbachev's September Housecleaning: An Early Evaluation," December 1988.

Douglas MacEachin and his professionals would continue to have difficulty getting air space for any optimistic prognostications about Gorbachev's changes. Little of the rest of the world's amazement was evident in the highest-level U.S. government reaction to the U.N. speech. At the Governors Island meeting the next day, for example, President Reagan remarked to Gorbachev only that "he had had a brief report on it, and it all sounded good to him." President-elect Bush demurred when Gorbachev tried to jump-start arms control discussions—much to Gorbachev's frustration, since the Soviet leader intended his U.N. speech precisely to launch fast progress with the new administration and a new round of arms cuts. To the Soviet Politburo, Gorbachev described the moment this way: "[W]hen I managed to tear myself away from Reagan, I spoke to Bush about this indecisiveness. He snapped back: You must understand my position. I cannot, according to American tradition, come to the fore until a formal transfer of power has taken place."[45] According to the American memcon, Bush remarked that "he would need a little time to review the issues" (what had he been doing for eight years as Vice President?) but "wished to build on what President Reagan had accomplished, working with Gorbachev." Bush described the "theory" behind his "new team" as "to revitalize things by putting in new people." Ironically, Bush insisted "he had no intention of stalling things. He naturally wanted to formulate prudent national security policies, but he intended to go forward."[46]

But stalling was the defining characteristic of the early Bush administration. To a remarkable degree only obvious in hindsight, the transition from the Reagan administration to the Bush administration in January 1989 was one from doves to hawks. One insider commented later, "Indeed, the foreign policy shift under the Bush administration in 1989 was as stark in substance (though not in style or rhetoric) as the change from Carter to Reagan in 1981"; "[t]hough not quite the hostile takeover of government that characterized" that transition, "[a]n entirely new team came in, representing foreign policy approaches fundamentally at odds with those of the Reagan administration."[47] A key Reagan holdover, U.S. ambassador Matlock, was even more critical: "[W]hile I expected Bush to replace most Cabinet and sub-Cabinet appointees, I was not prepared for his tactics, which resembled a hostile takeover much more than a cooperative transition."[48]

---

[45] Document No. 35, Transcript of CPSU Politburo Meeting, December 27–28, 1988.

[46] Memorandum of Conversation, "The President's Private Meeting with Gorbachev," December 7, 1988, 1:05–1:30 p.m., Commandant's residence, Governors Island, New York—Document No. 9 in Svetlana Savranskaya and Thomas Blanton, eds., "Reagan, Gorbachev and Bush at Governors Island," National Security Archive Electronic Briefing Book No. 261, posted December 8, 2008.

[47] Hutchings, *American Diplomacy*, 6, 17.

[48] Matlock, *Autopsy on an Empire*, 185.

In contrast to Reagan and Shultz, especially, the top Bush officials were intensely skeptical of Gorbachev. National security adviser Brent Scowcroft wrote in his joint memoir with President Bush:

To oversimplify, I believed that Gorbachev's goal was to restore dynamism to a socialist political and economic system and revitalize the Soviet Union domestically and internationally to compete with the West. To me, especially before 1990, this made Gorbachev potentially more dangerous than his predecessors, each of whom, through some aggressive move, had saved the West from the dangers of its own wishful thinking about the Soviet Union before it was too late.[49]

Scowcroft specifically dismissed the U.N. speech when he described his staunch opposition to any early summit with Gorbachev in 1989:

Unless there were substantive accomplishments, such as in arms control, the Soviets would be able to capitalize on the one outcome left—the good feelings generated by the meeting. They would use the resulting euphoria to undermine Western resolve, and a sense of complacency would encourage some to believe the United States could relax its vigilance. The Soviets in general and Gorbachev in particular were masters at creating these enervating atmospheres. Gorbachev's UN speech had established, with a largely rhetorical flourish, a heady atmosphere of optimism. He could exploit an early meeting with a new president as evidence to declare the Cold War over without providing substantive actions from a 'new' Soviet Union. Under the circumstances which prevailed [in 1989], I believed an early summit would only abet the current Soviet propaganda campaign.[50]

The new Soviet evidence published in this book shows Scowcroft's analysis to be almost entirely wrong. Not only were substantive arms control accomplishments very much on the table right away, but Gorbachev was willing to address every American security concern, including going much further on conventional arms. Politburo member Alexander Yakovlev told the U.S. ambassador Jack Matlock during their December 26, 1988, meeting that Gorbachev was eager for "joint concrete forward movement on such important directions as reductions of strategic offensive weapons, chemical weapons, conventional armaments, and regional conflicts, without long pauses"! But Matlock could only tell Yakovlev that Bush's "approaches regarding continuation of U.S.–Soviet negotiations" on arms control would not be ready by February 15, 1989, because "the new President needs time necessary for an in-depth analysis." Perhaps anticipating the growing distrust and even paranoia in Moscow that would accompany the Bush "pause,"

---

[49] Bush and Scowcroft, *A World Transformed*, 13.
[50] Ibid., 46.

Matlock did assure Yakovlev that "we are not doing anything in the United States—openly or covertly—that would undermine your perestroika."[51]

In effect, top Soviet officials announced the end of the Cold War over and over in 1988 and 1989, but they did not hear the resonance they sought from Bush's Washington, and they had mixed feelings about the loud reverberations they heard in Eastern Europe. In January 1989 in Vienna, for example, Foreign Minister Eduard Shevardnadze greeted the opening of the Conventional Forces in Europe talks by saying that disarmament progress "has shaken the iron curtain, weakened its rusting foundations, pierced new openings, accelerated its corrosion," and proposed exactly the tactical nuclear withdrawal that the U.S. did not adopt until more than two years later.[52] But the new administration rejected this view; only three days after Shevardnadze's clarion call, the new American national security adviser pronounced on national television, "I think the Cold War is not over."[53]

THE KISSINGER CONDOMINIUM AND THE
BUSH SEARCH FOR "VISION"

As Gorbachev skeptics, the new President and his advisers were interested to hear from the premier Cold Warrior himself, former Secretary of State Henry Kissinger, who had played the "China card" among so many other moves to contain Soviet power. During the 1980s, Kissinger had worked to ingratiate himself with the hardliners of the Reagan administration, never quite understanding that the President himself was eager to go beyond détente, beyond freezing the arms race, to make a deal with the Soviet Union that would end nuclear weapons. Kissinger had denounced the Reykjavik proposals (only to embrace nuclear abolition when it became more fashionable in 2007), and even egregiously claimed that the INF Treaty in 1987 would weaken the NATO alliance and seriously damage American and European security.[54] Such views did not disqualify him with the new President-elect and his top adviser, Brent Scowcroft, who received Kissinger on December 18, 1988, a month before the inauguration.

Kissinger had planned a trip to Moscow, and hoped to become the senior player and essential "back channel" to Moscow that the Reagan administration had never allowed him to be. Brent Scowcroft had served under Kissinger in the

---

[51] Conversation between Alexander Yakovlev and Jack Matlock, December 26, 1988, State Archive of the Russian Federation, Fond 100063, opis 2, delo 148, translated by Svetlana Savranskaya, in Svetlana Savranskaya and Thomas Blanton, eds., "Reagan, Gorbachev and Bush at Governors Island," National Security Archive Electronic Briefing Book No. 261, posted December 8, 2008.

[52] Nation, *Black Earth, Red Star*, 308.

[53] Brent Scowcroft, statement on ABC television, January 22, 1989, quoted in Matlock, *Reagan and Gorbachev*, 313.

[54] Garthoff, *The Great Transition*, 320, 325.

Nixon National Security Council, replaced Kissinger as President Ford's top adviser, and then became the president of Kissinger Associates in private life (joining Kissinger in the 1987 opposition to the INF Treaty), while Bush had experienced a more complicated relationship with Kissinger, not infrequently marked by mutual disdain.[55] Yet, Kissinger's core concern about instability in Europe resonated with both Bush and Scowcroft, and they listened with real interest to Kissinger's idea of a cooperative superpower process, perhaps even a "condominium" (with Kissinger at its center, of course, engaged in secret diplomacy between Moscow and Washington) to maintain the balance of power and manage the pace of change in Eastern Europe.[56] The letter Bush gave Kissinger to take to Moscow did not include an endorsement of the idea;[57] in fact, Jack Matlock in the Musgrove dialogue dismissed the letter as nothing more than "a courtesy letter, the sort former Secretaries of State and former Presidents usually get from a sitting President, a sort of letter of introduction." But Matlock admitted that Bush's Secretary of State, James Baker, was actively considering Kissinger's proposals for a time, even though "[n]egotiating the future of Eastern Europe was, I thought, the last thing we needed to do"—calling up bad memories of the Yalta conference at the end of World War II.[58] In the absence of any developed strategy, and in the context of suspicion of Gorbachev, Kissinger's characteristic realpolitik had a certain real appeal; Bush, Baker, and Scowcroft were looking for "the vision thing" and did not reject the idea out of hand.

In Moscow, Gorbachev was happy to receive Kissinger as evidence that Washington was reaching out to him, even before the inauguration, and showed some interest in the condominium idea, if that was how Bush wanted to proceed. Kissinger's most substantive meeting, according to the documents, was with Politburo member Alexander Yakovlev, who heard Kissinger proclaim "his closeness to the new president... and to the people comprising his inner circle." Most strikingly, Kissinger warned that "[i]f the balance of military forces on the continent shifts drastically, 'a very complicated situation might emerge.'" A direct quote from Kissinger, according to Yakovlev's memcon, was the statement that "G. Bush, as president, would be willing to work on ensuring conditions in which a political evolution could be possible but a political explosion would not be allowed." Kissinger also argued that it was in the Soviets' interest to have

---

[55] For example, "weak" and "unsophisticated" were some of the adjectives used by Kissinger about Bush in conversation with President Nixon, see Tom Blanton, "Kissinger's Revenge: While Nixon was bugging Kissinger, guess who was bugging Nixon," *Slate*, posted February 18, 2002, accessed at *http://www.slate.com/id/2062229/*

[56] The most detailed account, given the continued classification of the Bush Library memcon of this meeting on December 18, 1988, is in Beschloss and Talbott, *At the Highest Levels*, 13–17.

[57] The original remains classified at the Bush Library, but this book publishes Anatoly Chernyaev's verbatim notes of the letter: see Document No. 38.

[58] Jack Matlock, Musgrove transcript, 178.

American troops in Europe, as "a guarantee against the adventurism of Europeans themselves" and that the goal of U.S.–Soviet dialogue should be to separate "issues of political evolution, which is impossible to stop, from those of security as such… to try to combine the continuation of political evolution with preservation of the status quo in the sphere of security."[59] Kissinger's subsequent meeting with Gorbachev focused less on the condominium idea, per se, than on Kissinger's continued effort to put himself in the "confidential channel" that would include his long-time counterpart Anatoly Dobrynin, as well as Scowcroft, as soon as the first days of March.[60] Gorbachev's foreign policy assistant, Anatoly Chernyaev, remarked in the Musgrove transcript that the Soviet leader was not impressed with Kissinger: "We were hoping Kissinger would bring some important message. But he came in with this idea of exchange of Eastern Europe for a 'good attitude' from the American side."[61]

When Gorbachev told the Politburo about the Kissinger conversations, the Soviet leader indicated some interest, and some caution. Interestingly, Gorbachev used the diminutive "Kisa" (cat) to refer to Kissinger, with connotations also of slinking around, as well as a movie reference to the pretentious deluded aristocrat in a classic Soviet film of the 1960s. Gorbachev said, "Kisa hinted at the idea of a USSR–USA condominium over Europe. He was hinting that Japan, Germany, Spain and South Korea were on the rise, and so, let us make an agreement so that the 'Europeans do not misbehave.'" Like Bush, Gorbachev did not reject the idea; in fact, Gorbachev said, "We should work on this range of issues also, but in such a way that it would not leak, because in Europe they are most afraid of what they understand the Reykjavik summit to mean… an attempt at conspiracy between the USSR and the USA over Europe."[62] But Secretary of State Baker would leak the concept and Kissinger's role as the messenger, clearly in order to kill the idea, and perhaps also just to show who was in charge, onto the front pages in late March 1989, to a predictable outcry from angry Europeans as well as most of the American diplomatic corps, who dubbed the plan "Yalta II."[63] Thus died the first hesitant step of the Bush administration towards a strategy and a vision, but perhaps having none was better than embracing this one.

[59] Document No. 36, Record of Conversation between Yakovlev and Kissinger, January 16, 1989.
[60] Document No. 37, Record of Conversation between Gorbachev and Kissinger, January 17, 1989.
[61] Anatoly Chernyaev, Musgrove transcript, 192.
[62] Document No. 39, Gorbachev's Report to the CPSU CC Politburo regarding his Meeting with the Trilateral Commission, January 21, 1989.
[63] For the details, including Thomas Friedman's front page story on March 28, 1989, planted by Baker, and Kissinger's "furious" reaction, see Beschloss and Talbott, *At the Highest Levels*, 45–46.

Instead of picking up where Reagan had left off, Bush decreed a thorough strategic review of U.S. policy that tied up the bureaucracy and the White House staff for months. The "pause" created a sort of vacuum in superpower relations and put off Bush's own first summit with Gorbachev for almost a year (December 1989 at Malta). Ambassador Matlock later described this period with a book chapter titled "Washington Fumbles"; while Gorbachev's national security adviser Anatoly Chernyaev used "The Lost Year" for his own chapter heading—not referring to the loss of Eastern Europe in 1989 but to the missed opportunities for major arms reductions like Reagan's.[64]

President Bush's orders for the review provide revealing evidence of the caution and limited vision prevailing in his administration. The defense review, only signed in early March because of difficulties getting a Secretary of Defense confirmed (John Tower fell victim to the airing of scandal in his personal life, leaving the job to Dick Cheney, who was even more skeptical about Gorbachev than Scowcroft), featured a major caveat on the first page: "Changes in Soviet domestic and foreign policies, including some announced but not yet implemented, are hopeful signs. But it would be reckless to dismantle our military strength and the policies that have helped make the world less dangerous, and foolish to assume that all dangers have disappeared or than any apparent diminution is irreversible."[65] Yet who was talking about dismantling? The offer on the table from Gorbachev included the Soviet Union going first with unilateral cuts, then engaging in a process of mutual reductions that would enhance both countries' security. The review order prefaced its nine pages of questions for the bureaucracy to study with the caution that Bush did "not expect this review to invent a new defense strategy for a new world" but rather "how, with limited resources, we can best maintain our strength, preserve our Alliances, and meet our commitments in this changing but still dangerous world." The largest change the review even contemplated was the possibility of bringing NATO and the Warsaw Pact into approximate parity. The review order also asked a question Ronald Reagan would never have posed in this way: "At what point do negotiated reductions in U.S. strategic force structure cease to be consistent with U.S. security requirements?"[66] So much for the idea of nuclear abolition.

Both Jack Matlock and Henry Kissinger in their respective meetings with Alexander Yakovlev in December 1988 and January 1989 attempted to explain Bush's intention to put relations on hold while he carried out a cross-the-board review of U.S. policy. Matlock tried to say the pause was only "natural" and

---

[64] Matlock, *Autopsy on an Empire*, 177; Chernyaev, *My Six Years with Gorbachev*, 201.

[65] National Security Review 12, "Review of National Defense Strategy," March 3, 1989, 1. Document No. 01789 in *Presidential Directives on National Security from Harry Truman to George W. Bush*, published by ProQuest in the Digital National Security Archive.

[66] Ibid., 2, 9.

"necessary... for a serious study," and that Bush "appreciates the fact that it is precisely the factor of the improvement of U.S.–Soviet relations that helped him score the victory in the electoral campaign."[67] In fact, the motivations were complicated. In the Musgrove dialogue, Douglas MacEachin commented that the new Bush administration "had to be constantly looking over their back, because everybody from the tougher line of their party was waiting for them to make their first capitulations... [T]hese politics delayed a lot of steps that could have been taken with more confidence by, for example, President Reagan...."[68] A State Department eyewitness to the pause, Richard Hermann, commented at the Musgrove conference that even the domestic politics had two dimensions, first that of protecting the new President's right flank, but also the "vision thing" and "Bush's lack of it" and "Bush's desire to create an image of himself as a leader coming out from under the shadow of Reagan ... " so that decisions "would be associated with him, rather than him as a junior to Reagan." Hermann noted other contributors to the pause, for example the drastic reduction in size of the National Security Council staff as the result of the Iran–Contra scandal, the resulting increased burden on the State Department, the preoccupation of the top State officials James Baker and Dennis Ross in the first months of the administration with personnel and appointments, as well as the ongoing "deep divisions in the intelligence community," and "to-ing and fro-ing" over whether Gorbachev would actually succeed.[69]

The "deep divisions" found unusual expression in the CIA's own estimate from April 1989 subtitled "The Gorbachev Challenge." The estimate actually included a section called "Disagreements" that summarized the opposing positions in Washington on Gorbachev. "Some analysts see current policy changes as largely tactical, driven by the need for breathing space from the competition.... They judge that there is a serious risk of Moscow returning to traditionally combative behavior when the hoped for gains in economic performance are achieved." In contrast, "Other analysts believe Gorbachev's policies reflect a fundamental re-thinking of national interests and ideology as well as more tactical considerations..." and amount to "historic shifts in the Soviet definition of national interest" and "lasting shifts in Soviet behavior."[70] The documentation in this volume, and in fact the evidence available to analysts at the time if their eyes were open, shows the latter group were correct. But the former group was in charge of the White House.

A more cautious ambassador than Jack Matlock might have waited for the results of the Bush policy review, but the veteran diplomat—one of the few survivors from the Reagan team—worried that the "mistaken ideas floating around

[67] Yakovlev–Matlock, December 26, 1988, op. cit.
[68] Musgrove transcript, 185.
[69] Musgrove transcript, 196–197.
[70] NIE 11-4-89, "Soviet Policy Toward the West: The Gorbachev Challenge," April 1989.

Washington" would prevent necessary progress with Gorbachev.[71] Matlock was clearly in the second camp described by the CIA estimate, but he was writing for superiors who were charter members of the first camp. So in February 1989, Matlock sent three cables back to Washington, implicitly forming a kind of bookend to George Kennan's famous "Long Telegram" at the beginning of the Cold War. Matlock's purpose was to convince the Bush officials not to delay dealing with Gorbachev, and that the Cold War was really over ideologically. Matlock's first cable took on the Bush administration's assumptions directly but carefully, arguing against the Scowcroft notion that the Cold War was "not over" by using a Chapter 11 metaphor, that "the Soviet Union has, in effect, declared the bankruptcy of its system, and ... there is no going back." Against the Gates notion that Gorbachev would not survive so the U.S. should wait to deal with a successor, Matlock predicted Gorbachev was likely to "remain the Soviet leader for a considerable time to come"—citing steps such as becoming the constitutional president that would help prevent a Central Committee coup against him. Against the prevailing Bush notion that Gorbachev only sought a breathing space in order to resume the competition later, Matlock tried to tell Washington that perestroika was compelled by objective necessity, and that intervention in Eastern Europe "would of course mean the end of reform in the Soviet Union" and therefore was unlikely; yet even the knowledgeable Matlock does not foresee the pace of change in Poland and elsewhere.[72]

The necessity of adjusting his language and arguments to the skeptical recipients in Washington had a certain cost, however, possibly even undermining Matlock's own engagement message. In particular, the second Matlock cable in February 1989 played to his audience with phrases about the Soviets sowing division within the NATO alliance and an entire passage that Scowcroft could have authored, centered around this statement: "If they [the Soviets] are lucky, they will induce the West to disarm as fast or faster than they do."[73] But if the Soviet Union disarmed as fast as the U.S., how would that conflict with the U.S. national interest?

Top Bush officials certainly read the Matlock cables—the Bush–Scowcroft memoir even mentions them,[74] perhaps the only embassy cables even referenced in the volume—but the ambassador's confidence about Gorbachev did not have a parallel in Washington. In fact, the internal commentaries of the Bush administration in this period of the pause betray an extraordinary sense of almost personal insecurity vis-à-vis Gorbachev. The retrospective memoir by Bush and Scowcroft in particular, drawing on their diaries and memos of the time, constantly refers to their concern about political competition with Gorbachev, and

---

[71] Jack Matlock, e-mail communication with the author, June 9, 2008.
[72] Jack Matlock cables, Document No. 43 (February 3, 1989), Document No. 45 (February 13, 1989), and Document No. 47 (February 22, 1989).
[73] Document No. 45, Jack Matlock cable, February 13, 1989.
[74] Bush and Scowcroft, *A World Transformed*, 39–40.

their worry that Gorbachev has the initiative. For example, the very first item in the "four-part approach for coping with Gorbachev" that was drafted by Condoleezza Rice for Scowcroft—taking the place of the "disappointing" strategic review document and hardly drawing on the Matlock cables either—focused not on any substance but on the need "to strengthen the image of America's foreign policy as driven by clear objectives" so the U.S. could "appear confident about our purposes and agenda."[75] The words "image" and "appear" speak for themselves. Or again, "Scowcroft pointed out that the United States was losing the battle with Gorbachev over influencing the direction of Europe... The President agreed that Gorbachev had undermined US leadership, and he wanted to go to the NATO summit in May with a series of bold proposals that would put us out in front."[76] But bold proposals to what end? If Gorbachev's proposals and actions were enhancing U.S. security, the internal White House process begins to sound more like a tennis match than geopolitics.

The classic demonstration of American insecurity occurred at the very first meeting between Secretary of State James Baker and Gorbachev in May 1989. In yet another bold initiative from the Soviet side, Gorbachev announced he was withdrawing 500 tactical nuclear weapons from Eastern Europe—the kind of step wished for by the United States for years—yet Bush and Scowcroft saw the event almost purely in terms of upstaging Baker and blindsiding him.[77] Baker's own take on Gorbachev's strategy was similarly blind: "Gorbachev's strategy, I believed, was premised on splitting the alliance and undercutting us in Western Europe, by appealing past Western governments to Western publics."[78] With this mindset, Baker mis-analyzed Gorbachev's proposal in the May 11 meeting for not only the "surprise" of 500 tactical nuclear weapons being withdrawn (hardly a surprise, the Soviets had tabled the idea before), but the even more striking offer for the USSR to withdraw all such tactical missiles from Eastern Europe by 1991. Baker wrote later, "It was a patently one-sided offer" because supposedly even after the Washington Treaty on Intermediate Range Nuclear Forces (INF) was implemented "the Soviets would have a huge tactical nuclear weapon advantage in Europe."[79] To the contrary, here Gorbachev made an offer that the Bush administration would actually take up only in the fall of 1991, when the United States pulled back all of its forward-deployed tactical nuclear weapons; but in 1989, one can only conclude that American insecurity created a major missed opportunity.

The new Soviet documentation shows that this American insecurity drove a policy focus in Washington in 1989 (and even after) that was blind to Gorbachev's domestic politics and the arms control progress that was necessary for

[75] Ibid., 40.
[76] Ibid., 43.
[77] Ibid., 71.
[78] Baker, *The Politics of Diplomacy*, 70.
[79] Ibid., 82.

him to keep his reforms cascading and his military-industrial complex in check. Instead, the new Bush administration decided to change the subject, in effect going 180 degrees from the Reagan vision at Geneva and Reykjavik that had such a profound effect on Gorbachev's thinking. The language that Bush administration officials subsequently used to justify their approaches had that mothball aroma of old clothes taken out of winter storage. For example, two senior NSC aides proposed a presidential speech on NATO that "may grab attention, particularly in Europe" because "[i]t marks various steps away from recent U.S. policy, e.g., a ringing endorsement of nuclear deterrence and a pledge, in effect, to avoid repetitions of Reykjavik."[80] The Bush assumption was that "[t]he greatest mistake would have been to accept the existing Soviet agenda as the starting point for our own approaches, which would have vindicated the view that nuclear arms reductions were the essential yardstick of East–West relations."[81] Therefore, "the main effort was to restore public support for the principle of nuclear deterrence" while "avoiding further denuclearization in Europe" and "focusing on the massive conventional imbalance in Europe."[82] The Americans apparently did not understand that for Gorbachev, the arms control agenda meant directly addressing the conventional weapons issue as well.

The disjuncture between Washington's shriveled strategic thinking and the actual possibilities already on the table from the Soviets about not only nuclear weapons but also the conventional imbalance was only equaled by the disjuncture between the Bush search for "vision" and the actual policy proposals that emerged from the U.S process. For example, President Bush sought "a bold initiative to reassert leadership" that he could take to the NATO summit in May 1989 and his staff came up with a proposed 25 percent cut in US troops in NATO to be matched by a Soviet decrease to an equal number (which would have been a disproportionate cut on the Soviet side).[83] But the Joint Chiefs of Staff headed by Admiral William Crowe "reacted with alarm" predicting a "drastic change in NATO strategy"; in fact, "[t]he JCS were unenthusiastic about cuts of any size" and pushed Bush back to a mere 10 percent cut.[84] Even then there was resistance among the NATO allies, and hard bargaining even to reach agreement on negotiating both conventional cuts and short-range nuclear weapons cuts with the Soviets[85]—this at a time when the Soviets would have happily matched any cuts,

---

[80] Peter W. Rodman and Robert D. Blackwill, Memorandum for Brent Scowcroft, April 11, 1989, Bush Presidential Library, NATO Summit File.

[81] Hutchings, *American Diplomacy*, 34.

[82] Ibid., 28.

[83] Bush and Scowcroft, *A World Transformed*, 78.

[84] Ibid., 73–74.

[85] Ibid., 80–85. Bush and Scowcroft described the blow-by-blow of the summit as a triumph for American diplomacy, yet they achieved only small cuts offered by NATO, and made any negotiations on short range nuclear weapons contingent on more conventional progress—all of which Gorbachev welcomed as a "serious and specific response" to his pro-

happily pulled all the tactical nuclear weapons out, would have been delighted with a "tit for tat" series of cuts; and European and U.S. security, as well as that of the USSR for that matter, would have been greatly enhanced. Not to mention the political benefits for Gorbachev at home, since actually delivering greater security would have enabled him to go further and faster on internal reforms as well. In his Strasbourg speech on July 6, 1989, that detailed his vision of the "common European home," Gorbachev would offer immediate cuts in short-range nuclear weapons as a step towards abolishing them; but the American side saw this only as "designed to create mischief within NATO" and thus "we were right in moving cautiously with respect to Gorbachev."[86]

The inadequacies of Bush administration policy found their most extraordinary expression in the text of National Security Directive 23, which was drafted and debated in April and May of 1989 but not issued until September. This highest-level document was supposed to lay out the conditions that would, in Robert Hutchings' phrase, "lead to a new cooperative relationship."[87] Such a relationship was already there on the Soviet side; the place it was missing was in Washington. Even while the NSD was in draft form, Gorbachev had already met every one of its major "conditions." For example, the NSD called for Soviet "deployment of a force posture that is smaller and less threatening" (which Gorbachev had already announced at the United Nations in December 1988), internal democratization to "establish a firm Soviet domestic base for a more productive and cooperative relationship with the free nations of the world" (the May 1988 theses for the Party Conference had rejected class struggle as the basis for international relations, while the March 1989 elections had ousted a series of Party bosses from the Congress of Peoples' Deputies and put dissidents on national television), and adherence to the principle of "self-determination for the countries of East-Central Europe" (the Poles had already agreed in their Roundtable on elections, and Gorbachev had already in September 1988 said go ahead to the Polish reformers, as he re-emphasized at the United Nations in December 1988).[88]

THE REACTIVITY OF AMERICAN POLICY

Events were in the saddle in the spring of 1989. With Washington stalled, into the superpower vacuum rushed the East Europeans. The Poles were first, as usual. The martial law of 1981 had only suppressed but not solved the underlying

---

posed cuts, yet the U.S. was ready to stop right there. Scowcroft later took credit for these cuts as "the first steps toward reducing the Soviet Army in Eastern Europe" (p. 85) as if Gorbachev had never spoken to the United Nations the previous December!

[86] Bush and Scowcroft, *A World Transformed*, Scowcroft section, 114.

[87] Hutchings, *American Diplomacy*, 35.

[88] Document No. 84, National Security Directive 23, "United States Relations with the Soviet Union," September 22, 1989; Document No. 28, Gorbachev–Czyrek memcon, September 23, 1988.

economic problems and the social protest (one of every six Poles had joined Solidarity, by far the largest mass movement against communism in Eastern Europe). Renewed strikes at the famous Gdansk shipyards in August 1988 had forced new negotiations, and by February 1989 the "round table" talks focused on how to hold elections and what kind of head start the communists would require even to deign to participate (guaranteed seats, lower house set-asides, etc.). One model came from the March 1989 elections in the Soviet Union for the Congress of Peoples' Deputies, in which Andrei Sakharov himself—the Nobel Prize-winning dissident, physicist, father of the Soviet H-bomb—took a seat and a microphone. In May 1989 the Hungarians began to take down the barbed wire on their border with Austria, and the opening started a trickle—subsequently a flood—of East Germans heading west. Some observers realized what they were seeing—in May 1989, these extraordinary developments led former national security adviser Zbigniew Brzezinski to tell *The Washington Post*'s Don Oberdorfer: "We are quite literally in the early phases of what might be called the post-communist era."[89]

Faced with the rush of change in Eastern Europe, the Bush administration, however, worried only that Gorbachev was somehow snatching the initiative away from the U.S., leaving Bush behind in the world's perception of leadership. Also much to Washington's dismay, neither were the East Europeans waiting for Bush to come up with policy. The language used by deputy national security adviser Robert Gates about the Polish events in his memoir betrayed the reality that gave rise to the world's perception: "We needed to respond to these developments."[90] The White House launched into a series of presidential speeches in April and May 1989 to address the image problem—some with quite prescient language about the events in Europe—but without much in the way of policy or actions to back up the rhetoric. Before a largely ethnic Polish–American audience in Hamtramck, Michigan, the President announced, "Democratic forces in Poland have asked for the moral, political and economic support of the West. And the West will respond. My administration is completing now a thorough review of our policies toward Poland and all of Eastern Europe."[91] So a cry for help was met with a review. The same handful of specific aid actions that Bush listed would show up in future speeches, a little debt rescheduling, some tariff relief, perhaps some investment insurance, support for the World Bank and IMF in whatever aid they came up with—but no real dollars for Poland, and this at a time when Solidarity was banking on Western aid as a political trump card for voters to pick the opposition over the communists.

[89] Oberdorfer, *The Turn*, 346.
[90] Gates, *From the Shadows*, 465.
[91] Remarks by the President to Citizens of Hamtramck, Hamtramck City Hall, Hamtramck, Michigan, April 17, 1989, (White House Office of the Press Secretary), Bush Library Photocopy, 3.

The point for Bush was to achieve "the vision thing," so the Hamtramck speech both soared and sputtered. On the one hand there was Bush's characteristic caution—"With prudence, realism and patience, we seek to promote the evolution of freedom"—but there was also the reach for the upper registers: "The West can now be bold in proposing a vision of the European future: We dream of the day when there will be no barriers to the free movement of peoples, goods, and ideas"—the Helsinki Final Act of 1975 had already committed all its signatories to this "dream." Bush said his vision included free elections, closer ties with Western Europe, and a renunciation by the Soviet Union of "military intervention as an instrument of its policy"—something that Gorbachev had already done at the U.N. speech.[92] Bush achieved more resonance with his speech in Mainz, West Germany, after the NATO summit. He specifically addressed Gorbachev's vision for Europe, drawing applause when he said, "There cannot be a common European home until all within it are free to move from room to room."[93] Instead of a common home, Bush argued for helping "Europe become whole and free"—a phrase that would become famous, but which started as a generic replacement for an earlier draft's specific mention of and encouragement for German unification, that Scowcroft took out because he was "concerned about unnecessarily stimulating German nationalism."[94] The Mainz speech tried to have it both ways, defending "our measured pace in arms reductions" while claiming "the Warsaw Pact has now accepted major elements of our Western approach to the new conventional arms negotiations"—as if Gorbachev had not catalyzed the whole conventional discussion with his unilateral cuts announced at the U.N. months earlier.

The Bush pause as well as portions of the ensuing rhetoric generated puzzlement, frustration, and ultimately real suspicion in Moscow. Gorbachev complained to Margaret Thatcher in April—quite accurately, as we now know—"there is a point of view emerging in the White House that the success of our perestroika, the development of the new image of the Soviet Union, is not beneficial for the West. Secretary of State James Baker returned from his trip to Western Europe on the verge of panic. Europe, according to him, is ready to respond to our invitation to build new relations in Europe and in the entire world. The West Germans, in this sense, have simply lost their minds." Thus, Gorbachev told Thatcher, the White House "desire[s] to undermine interest in perestroika, in our initiatives, and to present it all under the cover of general considerations—let's see where perestroika will lead, how will it end, whether it is associated with the person of Gorbachev only, and if so, whether we should make the future of the West dependent upon it. I tell you frankly, we are concerned about

[92] Ibid., 4.
[93] Remarks by the President at Rheingoldhalle, Mainz, Federal Republic of Germany, May 31, 1989, (White House Office of the Press Secretary), George Bush Presidential Library Photocopy.
[94] Bush and Scowcroft, *A World Transformed*, 83.

it."[95] Gorbachev did not have to wait to read the Bush and Scowcroft memoir to understand what was going on in Washington far more accurately than the Bush administration understood Moscow.

To Helmut Kohl, Gorbachev complained about the Bush speeches, especially the ones at Texas (May 12) and the Coast Guard Academy (May 24), featuring Bush rhetoric that reminded Gorbachev of the worst of the Reagan "crusade" statements from the early 1980s. Gorbachev said, "And all this at a time when we are calling for de-ideologization of relations. Unwillingly, the questions come to mind—where is Bush genuine, and where is Bush rhetorical? Where does he just play up the rhetoric, and where does he lay down the state line?"[96] More alarming for Gorbachev, his intelligence services were relaying reports that indicated hostility from Washington, not just caution. Gorbachev told Kohl in June 1989: "According to our information, there is a special group that was created in the National Security Council of the United States charged with discrediting perestroika and me personally…. We openly asked [Baker] about that. He and his colleagues were somewhat confused but did not give us a clear answer; they only tried to convince us that it was not so. However, I have some evidence that such a group does, in fact, exist."[97] One can hear in this discussion the rising influence of the KGB's Kryuchkov, himself mirror-imaging the suspicion that Washington had of Moscow. Kohl had not heard of such a group, and doubted "that it was charged with the tasks you have just formulated" but "if it exists it has some kind of monitoring functions, but not subversive ones."[98] Subsequent admissions by U.S. officials demonstrated that both Kohl and Gorbachev were correct: The NSC did create a special monitoring group, headed by Condoleezza Rice, to watch for the possibility Gorbachev would fail or be replaced, not so much to organize such an outcome, but certainly motivated by feelings of disbelief and discredit for Gorbachev.[99]

The West Europeans tried to reassure Gorbachev about Bush, but the Soviet leader had recognized the essential conservative caution that was characteristic

---

[95] Document No. 56, Gorbachev–Thatcher memcon, April 6, 1989.

[96] Document No. 63, Gorbachev–Kohl memcon, June 12, 1989.

[97] Document No. 67, Gorbachev–Kohl memcon, June 14, 1989. In Robert Gates' memoir, he describes being "embarrassed" by Gorbachev's discussion with Baker in May 1989: "In his introductory comments, he noted my presence and commented to Baker that he had heard that I was in charge of a 'cell' at the White House with the purpose of discrediting him. He made a few other comments and then told Baker that if they succeeded in their efforts to improve the relationship, then perhaps 'Mr. Gates would be put out of a job.'" Gates, *From the Shadows*, 477.

[98] Ibid.

[99] A number of former officials have described the contingency group, including former CIA director William Webster in his speech at the George H.W. Bush Presidential Library, November 1999 (author's notes); but there is some confusion over the timing. For example, Gates, *From the Shadows*, 526, says he commissioned the group in September 1989 to consider contingency plans under Condoleezza Rice's leadership.

of Bush and that would continue to restrain progress in U.S.–Soviet relations for the duration of Gorbachev's tenure in the Kremlin. Margaret Thatcher, wearing her own inimitable set of blinders, told Gorbachev in April 1989 she could "not see how [Bush and Baker] could make policy that would contradict President Reagan's course. Of course, Bush is a very different person from Reagan. Reagan was an idealist who firmly defended his convictions. But at the same time, it was very pleasant to deal with him, to have a dialogue, and to negotiate. Bush is a more balanced person, he gives more attention to detail than Reagan did. But as a whole, he will continue the Reagan line...."[100] The Kohl discussions with Gorbachev about Bush were even more intimate, in effect commiserating with the Soviet leader about Bush's caution, his lack of charisma, and his need to get out from under the shadow of Reagan, as well as the "Achilles heel" of the U.S. economy and stagnating living standards.[101] The most devastating assessment of Bush came—*quelle surprise!*—from the French: Only six weeks after being hosted at the Bush summer compound in Kennebunkport, French president François Mitterrand told Gorbachev that "George Bush would make very moderate policy even without the congressional constraint because he is a conservative. Not all conservatives are alike. Bush, as a president, has a very big drawback—he lacks original thinking altogether."[102]

THE BUSH TRIP TO POLAND AND HUNGARY IN 1989

Eastern Europe was hardly at the center of Bush policy making in 1989, despite later claims by Bush officials seeking some share of credit for the revolutions. The Bush and Scowcroft memoir is more honest: Between the narrative of the NATO summit-related meetings ending on June 1 and the one-paragraph mention of the June 4 electoral earthquake in Poland when Solidarity swept every open seat, the former president and his top adviser wrote a full chapter of 25 pages on the June 4 event that was most important to them—the Chinese massacre of demonstrators in Tienanmen Square and the U.S. scramble to maintain relations with Beijing.[103] Tienanmen was the road not taken by Gorbachev and the East European comrades, precisely because they knew the "methods of 1956 and 1968" could no longer work; and those ghosts helped keep change on both sides of the 1989 revolutions velvet and nonviolent. But while the White House worried about China, the Poles were peacefully changing the political landscape of Europe, accelerating the pace of history, and relying on workers' ballots to

---

[100] Document No. 56, Gorbachev–Thatcher memcon, April 6, 1989.

[101] Document No. 63, Gorbachev–Kohl memcon, June 12, 1989.

[102] Document No. 72, Gorbachev–Mitterrand memcon, July 5, 1989.

[103] Bush and Scowcroft, *A World Transformed*, Chapter 4, "Untying a Knot," 86–111, describes Bush's own stay in Beijing as the ambassador in the 1970s, Scowcroft's personal relationship with Chinese leaders, the secret mission of Scowcroft and Deputy Secretary of State Lawrence Eagleburger to Beijing in late June 1989, and the rather modest results.

abolish the supposed dictatorship of the proletariat.[104] At the first Central Committee Secretariat meeting after the election, the Polish communists complained of "a bitter lesson," "the party are not connected with the masses," and "we trusted the Church and they turned out to be Jesuits." The young comrade Aleksander Kwaśniewski commented, "it is well known that party members were also crossing out our candidates"[105] (he learned his electoral lessons well and in 1995 would beat Lech Wałęsa to become President of Poland).

After the Polish elections, the pace of change in Eastern Europe just sped up, and the White House went into reactive mode—again. Bush had already committed to attend the July G-7 summit in Paris, so a trip to Poland and Hungary was "tacked onto" the agenda, just before Paris—in part so that the Americans could defer East European requests for financial aid with the excuse of having to confer with the allies at the summit.[106] The timing worried the Americans, because Poland had entered a kind of political limbo: The communists did not have enough support to form a government, and few could yet imagine a Solidarity-led government. The American embassy focused on actually slowing down the change and ensuring that the communists, in the person of the former dictator turned reformer Wojciech Jaruzelski, at least retained the presidency, as implicitly agreed in the Roundtable negotiations of the spring.[107] Meanwhile, in Hungary, political liberalization had caught up with and was about to surpass the level of reform in the relatively liberal "goulash" economy. On June 16, the Hungarians held the ceremonial re-burial of Imre Nagy, the Stalinist informer turned leader of independent Hungary in 1956, executed as a counter-revolutionary after Moscow crushed the Hungarian uprising, and buried anonymously in a potters' field. The crowd in Budapest clapped loudest for the speech that blasted the communists' air-brushed history and called for Soviet troops to get out of Hungary.[108] For an American President whose mantra was "prudent foreign policy," this was all too much, too fast.

---

[104] The prescient U.S. ambassador in Poland, John Davis, had alerted Washington that the Solidarity victory would be overwhelming: Cable from Warsaw to SecState, "Election '89: Solidarity's Coming Victory: Big or Too Big?" June 2, 1989. Document No. 2 in Gregory Domber, ed., "Solidarity's Coming Victory: Big or Too Big? Poland's Revolution as Seen from the U.S. Embassy," National Security Archive Electronic Briefing Book No. 42, posted April 5, 2001, *http://www.gwu.edu/~nsarchiv/NSAEBB/NSAEBB42/*

[105] Document No. 61, Transcript of the CC Secretariat Meeting of the Polish United Workers Party, June 5, 1989.

[106] Bush and Scowcroft, *A World Transformed*, 112–113.

[107] See Gregory F. Domber, ed., "Solidarity's Coming Victory: Big or Too Big—Poland's Revolution as Seen from the U.S. Embassy," *http://www.gwu.edu/~nsarchiv/NSAEBB/NSAEBB42/*, op.cit.

[108] The speaker was Viktor Orbán of the youth group FIDESZ. Orbán would later become prime minister of Hungary as FIDESZ changed into the leading center-right political party.

The changes in Eastern Europe sparked calls in the American public debate for a "new Marshall Plan"—especially for Poland, where the heroic Solidarity activists expected no less, and used the prospect as part of their political platform. But a mild recession in the U.S. and a legacy of debt from the Reagan years had increased the federal budget deficit, and those economic constraints strongly reinforced President Bush's innate caution. He complained to West German chancellor Kohl in June 1989 after the elections: "[E]motions run high regarding Poland. While the President shared those emotions, he also felt it important to act carefully and to avoid pouring money down a rat-hole."[109] Instead of elaborating on his own government's analysis of events in Poland and Hungary, Bush kept asking Kohl for his advice—a constant refrain in the Bush–Kohl exchanges. Kohl ultimately responded with a detailed June 28 letter to Bush, highlighting the "paramount Polish interest i[n] the economic-financial cooperation," and boasting about the two billion marks' worth of "fresh money" that West Germany was extending to Hungary (the fine print showed that all this funding was loans and credits for buying German goods and services rather than direct aid, yet the totals dwarfed anything the U.S. was considering).[110] But Kohl's cautions about the Polish economic crisis—that the situation was "primarily the result of ... careless policies... of the 70s as well as the failed attempts by the West to provide aid...," and that funding should be coordinated by donor committees as in developing countries rather than through a Marshall Plan mechanism[111]—all undermined Kohl's own pleas for more U.S. aid and very much reinforced Washington's "rat-hole" thinking. Bush thus went to Poland and Hungary in early July 1989 with more rhetorical flourishes than actual deliverable dollars.

There was much to admire in the Bush speeches delivered before the newly-elected Sejm (Parliament) in Warsaw, and at the Karl Marx University in Budapest. Bush had eloquent praise for Hungarian and Polish culture (citing the Polish astronomer Copernicus and calling "the Budapest of memory" a "city that rivaled Paris in its splendor, Vienna in its music, London in its literature"), reassurance for Moscow ("let the Soviet leaders know they have everything to gain, and nothing to lose or fear, from peaceful change"), a "salute" for General Jaruzelski ("this regime is moving forward with a sense of realism and courage, at a time of great difficulty"), and even-handed praise for both reform communists and oppositionists for their courage.[112] Bush intended to lower the pulse rate of change, and both on television and in the records of the private meetings, the American President showed a greater comfort level with the reform communist officials than with the considerably more scruffy dissidents—particularly distressing

---

[109] Document No. 69, Bush–Kohl telcon, June 23, 1989.

[110] Document No. 70, Kohl letter to Bush, June 28, 1989.

[111] Ibid.

[112] Remarks by the President at Joint Session of Parliament, The Sejm, Warsaw, Poland, July 10, 1989, (White House Office of the Press Secretary), Bush Library Photocopy.

was the confrontational session in Budapest with opposition party leaders, now campaigning against the communists.[113]

The problem was that Bush had only his goodwill to offer. The speeches were most notable for the enormous gap between the effusive praise for Polish and Hungarian courage, and the tangible aid being extended by the United States. For Poland, Bush proposed better Western coordination of technical assistance, some rescheduling of debts and new World Bank loans, but only "a $100 million fund to capitalize and reinvigorate the Polish private sector" and a $15 million anti-pollution project in Krakow. The transcript of the Sejm speech conspicuously shows the audience did not applaud either amount, and even Brent Scowcroft subsequently described the package for Poland as "embarrassingly meager."[114] For Scowcroft, the Hungary presentation was the "best speech of the trip" yet "the audience did not seem to react to what I saw as the paucity of the assistance we could offer."[115] The laundry list for Budapest was slimmer even than for Warsaw: some changes in emigration restrictions, tariff relief, investment insurance, but in actual money, only a $25 million fund "as a source of new capital to invigorate the Hungarian private sector" (the transcript of the speech lists no applause at this item, in contrast to repeated applause for Bush's other flourishes).[116] Looking at the thinness of the offerings, combined with the President's obvious sympathy for the communist reformers rather than the opposition dissidents, one could well conclude that the real American role in the revolutions of 1989 was to slow them down, rather than catalyze them.[117]

The most important result of the Bush trip to Eastern Europe, the only major change in U.S. policy, was the conversion of the President himself—despite continuing opposition from his top advisers, particularly Scowcroft—to the belief that he needed to reach out to Gorbachev. Kohl and others had urged an end to the "pause" for some time, but not until the East European reformers explained how it helped them for the Americans and Soviets to be talking—and not until Bush became alarmed from his firsthand view of the pace of change in Poland and Hungary—did the President finally, on the airplane back from Europe, write a note to Gorbachev suggesting a summit. Kohl had said to Bush in June, "It would be a good idea for the president to send direct messages to Gorbachev

---

[113] Scowcroft remarked on the contrast between the "same tired old positions" of the "aging" Hungarian oppositionists as compared to "the progressive thinkers in the ranks of the Communists." Bush and Scowcroft, *A World Transformed*, 126.

[114] Remarks by the President at Joint Session of Parliament, The Sejm, Warsaw, Poland, July 10, 1989, (White House Office of the Press Secretary), Bush Library Photocopy, 5; Bush and Scowcroft, *A World Transformed*, 114.

[115] Ibid., 126.

[116] Remarks by the President at Karl Marx University of Economics, Budapest, Hungary, July 12, 1989, (White House Office of the Press Secretary), Bush Library Photocopy.

[117] This is the pioneering conclusion of Gregory F. Domber in his superb dissertation study of the Polish Solidarity revolution, "Supporting the Revolution: America, Democracy, and the End of the Cold War in Poland, 1981–1989," George Washington University, 2008.

from time to time. That would signal the president's confidence, which is a key word for Gorbachev, who places a high premium on 'personal chemistry.'"[118] Contrary to what Bush was hearing from his top advisers, Kohl reported that Gorbachev had "said emphatically that wedge-driving [among the NATO allies] was not his intention, and that the Soviet Union does not want destabilization in Europe, because this would mean disruption in the USSR as well." Kohl also told Bush there could be "rapid progress" on CFE just as there had been on INF in 1987, because the key was "real political determination" (which Gorbachev had, but was lacking in the U.S.).[119]

Jaruzelski had given much the same message to Bush in their discussions in Warsaw in July. "After Gen. Jaruzelski encouraged frequent contacts between leaders of both powers, Bush responded that they are thinking about that in Washington .... [Bush] worries, he added, that meeting with Gorbachev could create too great an expectation, particularly regarding arms reduction agreements which are still not ready."[120] But Bush's message overall was quite a change from the earlier skepticism about Gorbachev, or perhaps it reflected the President's own instincts rather than those of his advisers.[121] Bush told Jaruzelski, "It is not his goal to make Gorbachev's life more difficult and to trigger internal tensions in the socialist camp. He came to pay tribute to the reforms and changes and to encourage their intensification and expansion, to speak about how the United States could contribute to Poland's economic renewal, but not to interfere in any way in our internal affairs .... Also, he does not intend for the present visit to create a peculiar contest about who is more popular: Gorbachev in the West, in the FRG and France, or Bush in the East, in Poland and Hungary."[122] In a pronouncement that would be news to Brent Scowcroft and Robert Gates, Bush explained to Jaruzelski that as a result of the strategic review in the spring, "it was decided to unambiguously support Gorbachev and his perestroika policy. Bush personally values the candid dialogue with Gen. Jaruzelski and would be pleased if a similar one existed with Gorbachev."[123]

Encouragement for such dialogue from Kohl, Jaruzelski, and the Hungarian reform communists certainly helped, but what really affected George Bush

[118] Document No. 68, Kohl–Bush telcon, June 15, 1989.
[119] Ibid.
[120] Document No. 76, Information Note Regarding George H.W. Bush's Visit to Poland (July 9–11), July 18, 1989. *Notatka Informacyjna dot. Wizyty oficjalnej presydenta Stanów Zjednoczonych Ameryki George H. Bush (9–11 lipca 1989 r.)*, MSZ, 2/94, W-9, Dep III (1989), Ap 220-9-89. Document and translation courtesy of Gregory Domber.
[121] Scowcroft admitted in the joint memoir with Bush that "I had the definite impression that the President wanted to sit down with Gorbachev at an early date" but "He did not press the idea..." so Scowcroft was able to prevent it (p. 46). Bush himself wrote "I was probably less suspicious of Gorbachev than were others on my incoming team" (p. 9).
[122] Document No. 76, Information Note Regarding George H.W. Bush's Visit to Poland (July 9–11), July 18, 1989.
[123] Ibid.

was his sense from meeting the East European oppositionists that change was coming much too quickly. For example, after meeting Lech Wałęsa in Gdansk (an awkward meal in the electrician's apartment, a more successful public rally in front of the shipyard gates), Bush "wondered uneasily whether the Soviets might try to stop the changes in Poland after all, fearful that Poland would slip entirely from their grasp."[124] This was July 11, 1989, and Gorbachev had assured the Poles as early as September 1988 that he supported their negotiated process of coming to terms with Solidarity.[125] But the Americans could not believe their eyes. The lesson Bush took from those meetings with Polish and Hungarian dissidents was one that Kissinger had proposed back in December 1988. Stalling on the superpower relationship, out of an excess of caution, was no longer prudent, Bush concluded: "[T]o put off a meeting with Gorbachev was becoming dangerous. Too much was happening in the East—I had seen it myself—and if the superpowers did not begin to manage events, those very events could destabilize Eastern Europe and Soviet–American relations. We still did not know how much change Gorbachev would allow in the region, and I saw that the Eastern Europeans themselves would try to push matters as far as they could."[126] But managing events, Bush-style, meant another five months would elapse before Bush and Gorbachev would get together, and by then, revolutions—not stability—would be the norm in Eastern Europe.

The frustration in Moscow was palpable, not only with the pause, but also with the substance of what Bush was willing to discuss. The U.S. ambassador to Moscow, Jack Matlock, managed to see the Politburo member and leading "new thinker" Alexander Yakovlev at the end of July to find out how Moscow assessed the state of relations ("not bad" responded Yakovlev), and remarked that "we have not met for several months." Yakovlev repeatedly raised the issue of nuclear abolition, but Matlock each time demurred, saying in effect, that was the former President, not this one. "[W]e need to conduct negotiations on reducing both conventional and nuclear weapons more actively," Yakovlev urged. "The USSR and USA can achieve an agreement about liquidating nuclear weapons, but I am not absolutely sure that it would be possible to do that with all other countries. Today we can put nuclear weapons and their liquidation under strict international control. We could introduce a rule, according to which inspection visits could be arranged on the basis of any suspicion. In five years it will be too late." But the American had bad news: "Reagan believed in the possibility of liquidating nuclear weapons. Bush thinks that we need to reduce them to a minimum, but we should not liquidate them. He believes that without nuclear weapons the risk of war being unleashed would increase.... I personally believe that it would be premature now even to achieve an agreement in principle about the liquidation

---

[124] Bush and Scowcroft, *A World Transformed*, 122.
[125] Document No. 28, Gorbachev–Czyrek conversation, September 23, 1988.
[126] Bush and Scowcroft, *A World Transformed*, 130.

of nuclear weapons in the future."[127] With this epitaph, the superpowers buried the visions from Geneva and Reykjavik that had done so much to lift the Soviet sense of threat; and another two years would pass before Bush and Gorbachev even managed to sign the START treaty, with nuclear weapon numbers only reducing to about the level of 1982.

THE EAST EUROPEANS COLLAPSE COMMUNISM

Between the time that Bush reached out to Gorbachev in July 1989, and the actual meeting of the two superpowers at Malta in December, the East Europeans took apart the Stalinist system. After Bush left Poland in July, the Polish communists failed in their attempt to make a coalition government, and Solidarity voters made sure that former dictator Jaruzelski knew his election as president was due to them, but just barely. The U.S. ambassador John Davis deserved the credit for this maneuver, which was embraced by Solidarity (Adam Michnik's newspaper column on the subject was headlined "Your President, Our Prime Minister"), and for briefing Bush so well on the reassurances that would be in order for Jaruzelski himself to agree.[128] Bush had gone out of his way, both in his public speech to the Polish Sejm, and in his private meeting with Jaruzelski, to praise the general, telling him "the world is watching with bated breath and admiration," and emphasizing "that because of the course Gen. Jaruzelski has declared, and taken, his personal standing and popularity have never been as high in the United States as they are at present."[129] With those compromises, in August, long-time Solidarity activist Tadeusz Mazowiecki took the reins as prime minister of the first non-communist government in Poland since the Cold War started. Inspired by Poland, Hungary ran its own version of round table talks over the summer and early fall of 1989, settling the terms for elections in 1990. The process featured a delicious irony, in that had early elections been held, right there in the fall of 1989, the reform communists (the little Gorbachevs, so to speak) probably would have won; but the delay allowed the opposition space to make a case and dramatically shortened the reformers' time on the stage.

---

[127] Document No. 77, Record of Conversation between Aleksandr Yakovlev and Jack Matlock, July 20, 1989.

[128] Davis's role and Bush's reinforcement stands out in the copious documentary record on 1989 now available from Soviet, U.S., German, Polish, Hungarian, Czech and Slovak, Bulgarian, Baltic, and Romanian sources, as probably the only moment in that entire year where any U.S. official made any appreciable difference in the course of events. Cable from Warsaw to SecState, "How to Elect Jaruzelski without Voting for Him, and Will He Run," June 23, 1989; Document No. 4 in Gregory F. Domber, ed., "Solidarity's Coming Victory: Big or Too Big—Poland's Revolution as Seen from the U.S. Embassy," *http://www.gwu.edu/~nsarchiv/NSAEBB/NSAEBB42/*, op.cit. The Michnik column appeared in *Gazeta Wyborcza*, July 3, 1989.

[129] Document No. 76, Information Note Regarding George H.W. Bush's Visit to Poland (July 9–11), July 18, 1989.

The Berlin Wall actually cracked in May, and collapsed in September, as the Hungarian reform communists opened the Hungarian borders. The world witnessed a flood of East Germans come through, camping out in embassies and consulates, and finally embarrassing East German leader Erich Honecker so much that he allowed them to transit in sealed trains to the West—thus reversing the sealed train in which Lenin rode to the Finland Station in 1917. Recalling the snippet of barbed wire he received as a gift during his visit to Hungary in July, President Bush told British interviewer David Frost in early September that the "Berlin Wall will come down" before the end of the Bush term (January 1993), and that he trusted Gorbachev to keep his word—in contrast to his own defense secretary, Dick Cheney, who only weeks earlier told a veterans' group that the Soviet threat had not diminished and "if anything, the United States is facing a more formidable offensive strategic arsenal today."[130] (Persisting faith-based anti-Gorbachev attitudes like Cheney's would subsequently segue from "we can't trust him" to "he won't last" as the reasons not to conclude arms agreements.) On October 25, 1989, as mass demonstrations mounted against the East German government, Gorbachev's spokesman, Gennadii Gerasimov, coined the most memorable phrase of all, when he told reporters with Gorbachev in Helsinki, Finland, that the "Frank Sinatra Doctrine" had replaced the Brezhnev Doctrine for the Soviets, referring to the singer's signature ballad, "I did it my way."[131]

Behind the scenes, the Soviets seem to have provided a key piece of pressure on the East Germans against police repression, especially during the protests in Leipzig. Georgy Shakhnazarov remarked in the Musgrove transcript that the Moscow reaction to inquiries from the fraternal East European parties about repressing demonstrators—Shakhnazarov's example was from Prague in late November 1989—was "we do not support the use of force."[132] The East Europeans were also well aware of Moscow's policy: in fact, at the pivotal meeting of the Czechoslovak Communist Party on November 24, 1989, the premier Ladislav Adamec explicitly included in his list of reasons for not using force against the mass protests in Wenceslas Square the fact that "the international support of the socialist countries can no longer be counted on."[133] But even the most knowledgeable Americans continued to be surprised by Soviet policy: As Jack Matlock explained in the Musgrove transcript, "We could not believe that if it really came to letting political reform get out of control, [Gorbachev] would not clamp down

---

[130] Jack Nelson, "'Berlin Wall Will Come Down,' Bush Predicts; It Will Go During His Presidency, He Declares in Interview; Also Says He Trusts Gorbachev," *Los Angeles Times*, September 5, 1989, George Bush Presidential Library Photocopy.

[131] Beschloss and Talbott, *At the Highest Levels*, p.134.

[132] Georgy Shakhnazarov, Musgrove transcript, 204.

[133] Speech by Premier Ladislav Adamec at the Extraordinary Session of the Czechoslovak Communist Party Central Committee, November 24, 1989, Document No. 7 in Thomas Blanton, ed., "The Revolutions of 1989," National Security Archive Electronic Briefing Book No. 22, posted November 5, 1999, *http://www.gwu.edu/~nsarchiv/news/19991105/*

and use force. The surprise to us was, as he increasingly demonstrated, first in 1989 in Eastern Europe, and then in regard to the Soviet Union itself, that he was not willing to use force to keep the system in power, or even to keep himself in power. That was the big surprise, and the unpredictable part."[134]

The most public finale of the Cold War, of course, came with the fall of the Berlin Wall on November 9, 1989. In the words of then-deputy national security adviser and future CIA director Robert Gates: "No one who watched on television will ever forget the images of crowds of East and West Germans dancing on top of the Wall, hacking away bits of it for souvenirs, and finally dismantling whole sections with construction machinery. If there ever was a symbolic moment when most of the world thought the Cold War ended, it was that night in Berlin."[135] President Bush's own reaction was characteristically cautious and anxious about the effect on Moscow, saying only that he was "very pleased" and "not an emotional kind of guy," thereby seeming so reserved during an impromptu Oval Office press conference that reporters present could not believe what they were hearing.[136]

Bush's reticence, his determination not to "posture on the Wall," reflected not only the President's constant worry about the pace of change in Eastern Europe, but also the limited role that U.S. policy actually played, or could play, in the collapse of the Wall. President Reagan had stood at the Brandenburg Gate in 1987 and famously orated, "Mr. Gorbachev, tear down this wall."[137] Yet neither American exhortation nor Gorbachev's own hands actually brought the Wall down in November 1989; in fact, Gorbachev would have preferred the Wall to stand at least for a while as a negotiating chip in the difficult talks to come about the role of a confederated or united Germany in Europe. Instead, the deed was done by a combination of East German citizens taking matters into their own hands on

---

[134] Jack Matlock, Musgrove transcript, 117. Though it must be noted that Matlock himself, as early as August 1989, reassured Washington that the Soviets would not intervene in Poland: "In keeping with Soviet 'new thinking' in foreign policy, a strong reaction to Polish events does not seem to be appropriate.... [A]lthough Solidarity may be a bitter pill to swallow, our best guess is that the Soviets will do so, if it comes to that, after much gagging and gulping. Their essential interests in Poland will be satisfied by any regime, Solidarity-led or not, that can promote domestic stability and avoid anti-Soviet outbursts." Cable from Moscow to SecState, "If Solidarity Takes Charge, What Will the Soviets Do?" August 16, 1989, Document No. 8 in Gregory F. Domber, ed., "Solidarity's Coming Victory: Big or Too Big—Poland's Revolution as Seen from the U.S. Embassy," *http://www.gwu.edu/~nsarchiv/NSAEBB/NSAEBB42/*, op.cit.

[135] Robert Gates, *From the Shadows*, 468.

[136] "Remarks and a Question-and-Answer Session with Reporters on the Relaxation of East German Border Controls," November 9, 1989, *Public Papers of the Presidents of the United States, George Bush, 1989*, Book II: July 1 to December 31, 1989, (Washington D.C.: Government Printing Office, 1990), 1488–1490.

[137] For the fascinating back story on Reagan's speech, see James Mann, *The Rebellion of Ronald Reagan*, 117–219.

the evening of November 9, 1989, abetted by border guards who did not know what else to do. Earlier that day, an East German Politburo member, Günther Schabowski, had blundered so badly in a press conference that he implied the immediate end of border restrictions, instead of what the communists intended to be a palliative public relations move and only a gradual loosening of visa and travel limits over a period of months or years, in exchange for major financial aid from the West. So crowds gathered at the gates in East Berlin, and guards could get no instructions from higher-ups because the Politburo was in emergency session, so they finally let the crowds push through to West Berlin, in scenes broadcast live around the world.[138]

The West German chancellor, Helmut Kohl, happened to be in Warsaw on November 9 for what was supposed to be the beginning of a four-day trip, and had to rush back to Bonn and then West Berlin when the news broke—yet another sign of how unexpected was the Wall's collapse. Poland had been a major priority for Kohl earlier in 1989, and likely would have continued that way except for the collapse of the Wall. Kohl's conversations with Bush as late as October 23, in fact, centered around Poland and Hungary, not the prospects for the GDR; and even the phone call between Bush and Kohl on the morning of November 10 began with Kohl reporting on his Poland trip rather than the historic events of the night before.[139] In Kohl's discussions with Solidarity leader Lech Wałęsa on November 9, the latter almost plaintively complained that "events are moving too fast" in East Germany, "he wonders whether the Wall will still be standing in one or two weeks" (only hours later, the Wall fell), and if this continued nobody would pay attention to poor Poland—all of West Germany's help and money would focus on East Germany (as indeed it did).[140]

The fall of the Wall made obvious the end-of-the-Cold-War reality that the center of gravity no longer resided along the hot line between Washington and Moscow, but had moved to the very center of Europe. The conversations between President Bush and Chancellor Kohl both before and after November 9 showed the American leader practically pleading for the German to come visit and help prepare for the upcoming Malta meeting with Gorbachev, but Kohl had more important business than holding Bush's hand. On October 23, for example, Bush importuned Kohl: "We ought to get together for an informal session, perhaps

---

[138] For the most important documents on the events of November 9, 1989, including the press conference transcript of Schabowski's blunders, together with extensive analysis based on hundreds of interviews, see Hertle, "The Fall of the Wall;" for insightful analysis of East German and West German motives, see Sarotte, "Elite Intransigence and the End of the Berlin Wall;" for the most vivid television images, see the CNN *Cold War* series, Episode 23, "The Wall Comes Down" (*www.CNN.com/ColdWar*).

[139] See the West German and U.S. telcons for Bush–Kohl conversations on June 15, 1989; June 23, 1989; October 23, 1989, (Document No. 94); and November 10, 1989, (Document No. 102).

[140] Document No. 100, Kohl–Wałęsa memcon, November 9, 1989.

a few hours at Camp David." But Kohl responded diffidently, "I will think it over and find out when I can make it. It would have to fit into one day."[141] Then as events accelerated after the Wall fell, Kohl would not even offer a day trip. Bush said again, on November 17, "I would value your judgment and would like to get together." Kohl: "I have an enormous problem with freeing myself for two days. With the developing situation, I would like to stay here. There is also a budget debate in our parliament." Bush: "I will be available for as much time as possible. Input from the FRG, from Chancellor Kohl, to Gorbachev is more important than at any other time or for any other meeting."[142]

But Kohl did not need to talk to Gorbachev through Bush; the German could speak to Gorbachev directly, and he did so almost as quickly as he consulted with Washington after the Wall fell. On November 11 Kohl called the Kremlin and said exactly what the Soviet leader wanted to hear—"we did not want a destabilization of the situation in the GDR" and "we want the people of the GDR to stay home"—while complimenting Gorbachev on their "good personal contacts." At the very moment that crowds on both sides of the former Wall were calling for unification, the two leaders spoke in euphemisms about stability, as in Gorbachev's urging Kohl, "I hope that you will use your authority, your political weight and influence to keep others within limits that are adequate for the time being and for the requirements of our time."[143] And Gorbachev heard more than Kohl seems actually to have said, for instance, about the people of the GDR "staying home." Kohl was warning about refugee flows and the economic burden on West Germany, but to Gorbachev (as the Soviet leader subsequently told the French president François Mitterrand), Kohl "assured me in particular that he was going to abide strictly by the existing agreements..." and "I carefully noted his words that the Germans should live where they are living now."[144]

In effect, Kohl was busy reassuring both superpowers in such a way that would leave himself the greatest possible freedom of action. The rush of events on the ground in the Germanys, Kohl's own domestic politics versus the Greens and the Social Democrats, and the rapid collapse of the socialist leadership in the former GDR, led the Chancellor to prepare his own surprise package that he certainly did not want to be talking about beforehand, even to his own foreign minister and erstwhile coalition ally Hans-Dietrich Genscher, who heard Kohl's "10 Points" while sitting in the Bundestag with everybody else on November 28. Kohl's points were hardly prophetic—he proposed confederation and even he saw the process of unification in terms of years, not months as it actually happened—but the speech showed Kohl racing to put himself at the head of a crowd (East German public opinion) that was already moving towards unification more quickly than any of Kohl's peers from Washington to Moscow were comfortable

---

[141] Document No. 94, Bush–Kohl telcon, October 23, 1989.
[142] Document No. 105, Bush–Kohl telcon, November 17, 1989.
[143] Document No. 103, Gorbachev–Kohl telcon, November 11, 1989.
[144] Document No. 104, Gorbachev–Mitterrand memcon, November 14, 1989.

with. As Kohl's November 28, 1989, letter to Bush conveying the "10 Points" stated, "The events of the past summer have proven that they [the people of the GDR] do not feel or think as members of a separate nation," so Kohl's tenth point focused on "Organic development toward a situation in which the German people through free self-determination regain their unity..." while his sixth point emphasized the "pan-European process" and others spoke of "contractual association" and "confederative structures between the two states."[145]

Kohl claimed in his letter to Bush "The German government has in no way used the current situation in the GDR in order to single-handedly achieve its own goals." The Americans thought he was protesting too much. President Bush complained in his memoir, "Afraid of leaks, or perhaps of being talked out of it, Kohl informed none of the NATO allies—including us—of the speech beforehand..." and only had "a text delivered to me as the speech was given in Bonn." The comment from Bush's top adviser and co-author Scowcroft pointed to the bystander role of the Americans: "If he was prepared to go off on his own whenever he worried that we might object, we had very little influence." Bush called Kohl the next day after the "10 Points" speech, and Scowcroft commented, "Kohl over and over again expressed his solidarity with the United States and the allies and pledged that there would be no going it alone—only one day after he had, in fact, 'gone it alone.'"[146]

The Kohl–Bush letter did contain quite an endorsement of Gorbachev, worth repeating here in the context of American debates over winners and losers in the Cold War. Kohl wrote, "Regarding the reform process in Poland, Hungary, Bulgaria, the CSR, and not least the GDR, we have General Secretary Gorbachev's policies to thank. His *perestroika* has let loose, made easier, or accelerated these reforms. He pushed governments unwilling to make reforms towards openness and towards acceptance of the people's wishes; and he accepted developments that in some instances far surpassed the Soviet Union's own standards." Kohl warned Bush that "western help is coming much too slowly" for the East Europeans, and urged "strong stimulus to the arms control negotiations" that have such "significant meaning for us Europeans."[147] But neither admonition had much effect.

Seven days before the "10 Points" surprise, the Americans had hosted foreign minister Genscher in the Oval Office. President Bush specifically asked, "Is there a likelihood that the rapidity of change that has come to Eastern Europe will result in an instant demand in Germany for reunification? We know in the long run this is for the German people to decide, based on self-determination. But will reunification move faster than any of us think?" Genscher responded, "No one can

---

[145] Document No. 109, Letter from Helmut Kohl to George H.W. Bush, Bonn, November 28, 1989, (first published in German in Kusters and Hofmann, *Deutsche Einheit*, op. cit.).

[146] Bush and Scowcroft, *A World Transformed*, 194–196.

[147] Document No. 109, See Savranskaya and Blanton, "The Soviet Origins of Helmut Kohl's 10 Points," National Security Archive Electronic Briefing Book No. 296, posted November 18, 2009.

foresee... It is important for all to know that we will stick to our obligations in NATO and the EC... But all of this must be done in a way that does not alarm the Soviet Union. That is why we must stick to our current borders... German re-unification is discussed more outside Germany than inside Germany" (that would change with Kohl's speech). The German diplomat encouraged Bush to "focus more on the arms control process" because "The more arms control in Europe, the less likely Soviet military, or even political, intervention in Eastern Europe. Second, the philosophy of the Russians has changed." But Bush told Genscher that the Malta summit would not be "an arms control meeting. If Gorbachev tries to make it an arms control meeting, I will say we have our allies and we will make no unilateral deals. He might propose the total withdrawal of all U.S. and Soviet troops from Europe"—to which Genscher responded, "I do not think he will play the German card. He is very much satisfied with a U.S. presence on German soil."[148]

THE LAST COLD WAR SUMMIT

It took George Bush practically the entire first year of his presidency to manage a face-to-face meeting with Gorbachev, and the American president would not come around to the value of unilateral arms reductions until the fall of 1991, well after such gestures could do much good for Gorbachev's reform agenda. Despite what Bush had told David Frost, his preparations for the Malta meeting reflected continuing suspicion and sense of competitiveness (as Bush had told Genscher), rather than any recognition of the arms race in reverse which Gorbachev was offering—and which key Soviets (like Yakovlev and Shevardnadze) were detailing for the Americans at the time. The actual Malta proceedings seem almost poignant in retrospect, starting with the terrible weather that prevented the stage-managers' notion of alternating U.S. and Soviet ships as the venue—and provided a rather-too-neat metaphor for the way in which revolutionary events in Eastern Europe had already outrun both superpowers' control. Bush confessed to Gorbachev, "First of all, I admit that we were shocked by the swiftness of the changes that unfolded. We regard highly your personal reaction and the reaction of the Soviet Union as a whole to these dynamic, and at the same time fundamental, changes." Gorbachev told Bush, "Sometimes I hear that in the current situation we are not fulfilling our mission with regard to our friends. I always respond in such cases: first, nobody asked us to help; second, the changes are proceeding according to the constitution." Bush responded: "I would say more—that it is thanks to you that they are proceeding peacefully."[149]

---

[148] Memorandum of Conversation, Meeting with Foreign Minister Hans-Dietrich Genscher of the Federal Republic of Germany, November 21, 1989, 10:10–10:45 a.m., George Bush Presidential Library, 2007-0051-MR. Present on the American side were President Bush, Secretary of State Baker, chief of staff Sununu, adviser Scowcroft, and other aides.

[149] Document No. 110, The Malta Summit, Excerpts from the Soviet Record, December 2–3, 1989, one-on-one session, December 2, 1989.

At Malta, a consummation so devoutly wished by Gorbachev throughout 1989 now was too little, too late, not least because the Americans were insistent on no unilateral arms cuts, but also because Gorbachev's own freedom of maneuver was rapidly constricting given his domestic politics. And the Soviets continued to be amazed at the way Bush ducked the strategic weapons opportunities and instead focused on what Moscow saw as side issues, at best, such as Soviet support for the Nicaraguan Sandinistas, or the imputed Moscow hand behind Castro's geopolitical moves.[150] Here was evidence, yet again, for the way in which domestic politics drove international affairs, since Bush had to protect his right flank in the Republican Party, for whom Castro was the devil, the Sandinistas were a communist beachhead pointing at Texas, and Gorbachev himself was merely a new glove around the iron fist. Gorbachev told Bush, "It is not quite clear to us what you want from Nicaragua. There is political pluralism in that country, there are more parties than in the United States. And the Sandinistas—what kind of Marxists are they? This is laughable. Where are the roots of the problem? At the core are economic and social issues." Likewise on Cuba, "The issue now is how to improve the current situation. There is a simple and well-proven method: one has to speak directly to Castro. You must learn: nobody can lord it over Castro."[151]

The only substantial outcome of the Malta meeting occurred on the psychological level, the establishment of a new level of personal trust between the two leaders. On the American side, this still was not enough to overcome the obduracy of the Pentagon against rapid arms cuts[152] and especially of the U.S. Navy against the on-site verification procedures that the Soviets had agreed to (a Cold War irony in that the tables turned at the end and the Americans were the closed suspicious actors on verification negotiations). On the Soviet side, trust did not do much for Gorbachev in the absence of tangible deliverables such as aid or arms cuts; the personal relationship only reduced any remaining sense of threat on both sides—yet Gorbachev still felt it necessary in the Malta meeting to assure Bush that the USSR did not consider the U.S. to be the enemy and would never attack. Gorbachev complained that the Soviets had "approved and implemented a purely defensive doctrine," while "the U.S. continues to be guided by

---

[150] Anatoly Chernyaev, Musgrove transcript, 192.

[151] Document No. 110, The Malta Summit, opening session, December 2, 1989. Gorbachev even brought with him to Malta a direct message from Castro to Bush: "During your contacts with the president, we request that you find the ways and means to convey Cuba's interest in normalizing relations with the United States."

[152] Even after Malta, Secretary of Defense Richard Cheney resisted any proposals for arms control, believing the Soviets had not really changed, and saying at a January 16, 1990, White House meeting, "Arms control is in the way of arms reductions.... Why negotiate for further reductions? It just creates problems for the allies." Bush and Scowcroft, *A World Transformed*, 208–209. Meanwhile, the window was closing in Moscow: Bush and Scowcroft described in retrospect the hard-line opposition to Gorbachev coalescing in March and April 1990, 218, 220, 222.

a rapid reaction strategy that was adopted over 20 years ago" so "why is the U.S. being so slow in enacting perestroika within its own armed forces?"[153]

The sessions at Malta included fascinating exchanges on "the question of reunification of Germany, which is making both you and us nervous, as well as many Europeans," as Secretary of State Baker said in the final session.[154] In the one-on-one discussion, Gorbachev complained about Kohl, who "fusses and bustles around too much. He does not act seriously and responsibly. We are afraid that the topic of reunification may be exploited for electoral gain, that it will not be strategic factors but the mood of the moment that will take the upper hand." Gorbachev even asked Bush, "Would a unified Germany be neutral, not a member of any military-political alliances, or would it be a member of NATO? I believe we should let everyone understand that it is still too early to discuss either of these options. Let the process take its course without artificial acceleration." Bush agreed: "I believe that in his actions Helmut Kohl was greatly influenced by the emotional reaction to events…. They [meaning the West Germans] speak about this topic with tears in their eyes." And Bush reassured Gorbachev, "We will not take any rash steps; we will not try to accelerate the outcome of the debate on reunification."[155] In the final plenary session, Bush told Gorbachev with a somewhat characteristic double-negative, "I hope that you understand that you cannot expect us not to approve of German reunification. At the same time, we realize the extent to which this is a delicate, sensitive issue. We are trying to act with a certain reserve…. I will not elaborate on each East European country but will stress the thought that we understand very well the meaning of the section of the Helsinki Act governing national boundaries in Europe."[156] The implication here of commitment to existing borders was clear to Gorbachev, but Bush's reserve would diminish once he saw Kohl right after Malta.

In retrospect, the American president's dinner with the German chancellor on December 3 in Brussels carried more significance for the sequence of events in 1990 leading to German unification than anything Bush and Gorbachev said to each other at Malta. Bush briefed Kohl on the summit discussion: "We spent much time on the German question. Gorbachev said you are in too much of a hurry…. I don't want to say he went 'ballistic' about it—he was just uneasy." Kohl responded by pointing to the expanding crisis in the GDR, in effect saying that those events were driving his approach, but also assuring Bush "I will not do anything reckless." The candor about their peers in Europe was also striking. Kohl said, "Everyone in Europe is afraid of two things: (1) that Germany would drift to the East—this is nonsense; (2) the real reason is that Germany is developing economically faster than my colleagues. Frankly, 62 million prosperous Germans are difficult to tolerate—add 17 million more and they have big

---

[153] Document No. 110, The Malta Summit, plenary session, December 3, 1989.
[154] Ibid.
[155] Ibid.
[156] Ibid.

problems." Bush asked, "Are any of the EC leaders opposed to your 10 points?" Kohl described most of the EC attitudes as "fine" with Mitterrand against but too "wise" to oppose the process, and "Great Britain is rather reticent." Bush interjected, "That is the understatement of the year." Kohl said Thatcher "thinks history is not just. Germany is so rich and Great Britain is struggling. They won a war but lost an empire and their economy. She does the wrong thing. She should try to bind the Germans into the EC." A turning point in the conversation occurred when Kohl corrected Bush on what the Helsinki Final Act said about changing borders, that it can be done "by peaceful means." And Kohl warned Bush that unless they moved towards unification, Kohl's own domestic politics could trend towards neutrality, exactly Bush's fear. Yet neither leader foresaw the speed of events, and Kohl even dismissed the idea of unification within "two years. It is not possible; the economic imbalance is too great."[157] Bush recalled in his memoir, "I think Kohl was hoping for the earliest possible reunification, but he wanted to do or say nothing that would imperil it.... I probably conveyed to Kohl that I had no objections to reunification, and in a sense gave him a green light."[158] Kohl went on the next day in public comments to cite Bush's support for the confederative ideas in the "10 Points"; so this meeting with Kohl marked the point that Chernyaev was describing, when he said, "Even the Americans jumped into the first car when they saw that the train was moving ahead" on unification.[159]

Gorbachev did go "ballistic" when next he saw West German foreign minister Genscher, on December 5. Gorbachev's harsh rhetoric, even to the point of summoning up the ghost of Hitler—"You have to remember what mindless politics has led to in the past"—exceeded anything before or after in his dealings with his European peers. The "10 Points" had been bad enough—"ultimatums" and "crude interference in the internal affairs of a sovereign state"—but what really rankled Gorbachev was Kohl's public commentary citing Bush's approval. Just at the moment the Soviet leader had finally gotten the Americans engaged, it just did not matter anymore; events on the ground in Germany were driving the process and Kohl was proving the most adroit politician on the scene. The net effect was to destroy Gorbachev's plans: "Judging from all this, you [the Germans] have prepared a funeral for the European process."[160] Here is Gorbachev's recognition of the way that the collapse of the Wall, the collapse of GDR legitimacy, the rapid democratization of East Germany—all this had become the central dynamic of the end of the Cold War, brought about by East Germans, with Helmut Kohl surfing the wave.

---

[157] Document No. 111, Memorandum of Conversation between Bush, Sununu, Scowcroft, and Kohl, December 3, 1989, Brussels.

[158] Bush and Scowcroft, *A World Transformed*, 199.

[159] Anatoly Chernyaev, Musgrove transcript, 200.

[160] Document No. 113, Record of Conversation between Gorbachev and Genscher, Moscow, December 5, 1989.

But at least after Malta the Americans had finally realized Gorbachev was for real, and that the Cold War was over. When a popular uprising in Romania just before Christmas 1989 met violent repression from the state security forces and turned into a coup d'état against communist dictator Ceauşescu, first the French foreign minister Roland Dumas and then the American Secretary of State James Baker mentioned with approval the possibility of Soviet intervention to settle the situation. Baker actually tasked his ambassador to Moscow, Jack Matlock, to query the Soviets on an urgent basis; and the records of that conversation from the Soviet Foreign Ministry contain a remarkable back and forth between the American side and Moscow's "new thinkers." Matlock "let us know that under the present circumstances the military involvement of the Soviet Union in Romanian affairs might not be regarded in the context of 'the Brezhnev doctrine.'" In response, Deputy Foreign Minister Aboimov told Matlock "we did not visualize, even theoretically, such a scenario" and so—in a clear reference to the invasion of Panama that the Bush administration had just launched—"the American side may consider that 'the Brezhnev doctrine' is now theirs as our gift."[161] Interestingly, during the Malta summit, after Gorbachev complained about various American interventions around the world (helping Philippine president Corazon Aquino against a mutiny, sending military aid to Colombia, pressuring Noriega in Panama), he said, "Europe is changing; governments are falling—governments that were also elected on a legitimate basis. One wonders if during this power struggle someone were to ask the Soviet Union to intervene, what should we do? Should we follow the example of President Bush?" To which Bush responded, "I see."[162]

THE GERMAN UNIFICATION END GAME

The rapid unification of Germany in 1990 offers an instructive epilogue to the analysis presented in this essay about the limited impact of U.S. policymaking on the revolutions in Eastern Europe. Chancellor Kohl subsequently praised U.S. support as essential for his success in pursuing unification, citing specifically the letter sent by President Bush on February 9, 1990, in which the American wrote, "If events are moving faster than we expected, it just means that our common goal for all these years of German unity will be realized even sooner than we hoped."[163] But the key word here is "events," in the same meaning given by the

---

[161] Document No. 116, Aboimov–Matlock memcon, December 25, 1989, Soviet Foreign Ministry. See the discussion in Blanton, "When Did the Cold War End?" including Ambassador Matlock's commentary on the meeting.

[162] Document No. 110, The Malta Summit, one-on-one session, December 2, 1989.

[163] Bush–Kohl letter, February 9, 1990, Document No. 170 in Kusters and Hofmann, *Deutsche Einheit*. Kohl told Bush in his phone call of February 13, 1990, that "the letter you sent to me before I left for Moscow will one day be considered one of the great documents in German–American history."

American philosopher Ralph Waldo Emerson when he wrote, "Events are in the saddle and ride mankind." From November 1989 to March 1990, public opinion in the GDR moved dramatically away from any notion of "stability" and towards radical notions of capitalist prosperity, helped along by the lure of the deutschmark (a metaphor for West Germany's superior economic performance), Kohl's adroit announcement of proposals like rapid monetary union, the cascading leadership collapse of the GDR reform communists from Krenz to Modrow including multiple corruption cases, and popular revolts against the persisting security structures such as the Stasi (including occupations of Stasi offices in January 1990 when chimneys signaled the burning of files). Even the accelerated schedule for parliamentary elections in the GDR, moved up by the reform communists to help them or their Social Democratic allies prevail, backfired on March 18, when a turnout of more than 90 percent gave an unprecedented 48 percent victory to Kohl's coalition, the pro-unification Christian Democrats and their allies.[164]

Read in this context, the documentary record of highest-level exchanges leaves a sense of leaders scrambling rather than deciding. On the Soviet side, there was a grudging realization that even the NATO allies most opposed to German unification, such as Britain and France, would not go public but rather, as Chernyaev noted after a Thatcher meeting with Gorbachev: she wants to prevent unification "with our hands," without taking on the fight herself.[165] By January 28, 1990, as Chernyaev wrote, the KGB chief Kryuchkov remarked that the GDR "is not a real state anymore" and Gorbachev's closest advisers more or less agreed that "the process of German unification cannot be stopped. But we need to keep the process going with our presence and not against us."[166] In other words, Gorbachev did not fear the strategic implications of a unified Germany (hardly a security threat, but rather a major source for trade and economic assistance); his real concerns were for his own domestic politics. Top Gorbachev adviser Andrei Grachev subsequently described this period (the first half of 1990) of back-and-forth on various formulas on Germany and NATO as Gorbachev simply "trying to gain needed time in order to let public opinion at home adjust to the new real-

---

[164] For the Bush and Scowcroft commentary on their surprise, see *A World Transformed*, 233 and 258.

[165] Document No. 85, Thatcher–Gorbachev memcon, September 23, 1989, and Document 89, Chernyaev's diary, October 9, 1989.

[166] Document No. 118, Excerpt from Chernyaev's Diary, January 28, 1990. The meeting included Gorbachev, Yakovlev, Shakhnazarov, Chernyaev, Shevardnadze, Ryzhkov, Kryuchkov, Falin, Federov and Akhromeyev. Chernyaev was most shocked at the ignorance of the supposed expert on Germany, Rafail Federov, who claimed "nobody wants unification, especially in the FRG." But Gorbachev, just as he would in the Soviet Union, vastly underestimated the degree to which the communists had lost legitimacy, remarking about the SED (even after Kryuchkov said the SED "ceased to exist") that "it cannot be that among 2.5 million party members there is nobody to constitute a real force." The SED's successor party would win only 16 percent of the vote in the March 18 elections.

ity," while "hoping to get at least partial political compensation from his Western partners…"[167]

On the U.S. side, the scramble to keep up with events produced some formulations offered to Gorbachev in early 1990 that have become the subject of enormous controversy, both in the scholarly literature and more importantly, in Russian political discourse (rising chauvinism, anti-Gorbachev backlash, nostalgia for empire). The key discussions took place in Moscow in February 1990, between Secretary of State Baker and Gorbachev (as well as Shevardnadze), and are published in this volume. The prime U.S. concern focused on the possibility that a unified German state would choose neutrality, and "could very well decide to create its own nuclear potential instead of relying on American nuclear deterrent forces," Baker told the Soviets. He argued, "NATO is the mechanism for securing the U.S. presence in Europe. And if NATO is liquidated, there will be no such mechanism in Europe. We understand that, not only for the Soviet Union but for other European countries as well, it is important to have guarantees that if the United States keeps its presence in Germany within the framework of NATO, not an inch of NATO's military present jurisdiction will spread in an eastern direction."[168]

Baker framed the question this way, after warning Gorbachev that "the process is going much faster [toward unification] than anyone would have expected last year": "Supposing unification takes place, what would you prefer: a united Germany outside of NATO, absolutely independent and without American troops; or a united Germany keeping its connections with NATO, but with the guarantee that NATO's jurisprudence of troops will not spread east of the present boundary?" Gorbachev responded: "We will think everything over. We intend to discuss all these questions in depth at the leadership level. It goes without saying that a broadening of the NATO zone is not acceptable." Baker said: "We agree with that." Gorbachev took Baker's point: "It is quite possible that in the situation as it is forming right now, the presence of American troops can play a containing role…."[169] Earlier in the same conversation, Gorbachev had quoted the Polish president Jaruzelski, "that the presence of American and Soviet troops in Europe is an element of stability."[170]

Baker's phrase—"not an inch" eastward—had its predecessor in discussions with Genscher on February 2, in which the German foreign minister had proposed a combination of Germany in NATO with East German territory remaining outside the alliance.[171] The awkwardness of such arrangements would doom them, but their ghost would remain in the final treaties around German unification, decreeing a "special military status" to the GDR territory with limits on

---

[167] See Grachev, *Gorbachev's Gamble*, 157–158.
[168] Document No. 119, Record of Conversation between Gorbachev and Baker, February 9, 1990.
[169] Ibid.
[170] Ibid.
[171] Bush and Scowcroft, *A World Transformed*, 236–237.

NATO deployments and the like. But Gorbachev's response in Moscow was a position in transition—his German expert Valentin Falin had argued for confederation, yet the GDR state was losing every day the capacity to serve as an equal confederate—and neutrality seemed for a moment at least a fallback that would limit the domestic political damage. But Baker was convincing on the notion of NATO restraining Germany, especially in the context that Gorbachev had already outlined to Bush at Malta: "What to do with institutions created in another age? ... They must be utilized to strengthen security and stability and improve relations between states. Let NATO and the Warsaw Treaty Organization become to an even greater degree political, but not only as military organizations; and let there be a change in their confrontational nature."[172] So "not an inch" amounted to a global commitment, not just an immediate tactical ploy about the territory of the GDR. Yet Gorbachev did not ask Baker for any written or formal version of this commitment—never thinking such a formality was necessary (he did not envision the collapse of the Warsaw Pact at this point, since even the Solidarity government in Poland had signed up), and thus he left the field open to subsequent events, including ultimately the successful appeal from East European leaders Lech Wałęsa and Václav Havel to President Bill Clinton in 1993 for NATO expansion.[173]

On Baker's heels came Helmut Kohl, reinforcing the same message to Gorbachev. Baker wrote Kohl a concise briefing letter immediately after his own Gorbachev meeting. The Baker phrasing became even more precise: "I told him that the FRG's leadership was strongly in favor of a unified Germany remaining in NATO and not being neutral. I explained that we agreed with this, and thought the Soviets should not reject such an outcome. In this regard, I mentioned that it was unrealistic to assume that a big, economically significant country like Germany could be neutral. And then I put the following question to him. Would you prefer to see a unified Germany outside of NATO, independent and with no U.S. forces or would you prefer a unified Germany to be tied to NATO, with assurances that NATO's jurisdiction would not shift one inch eastward from its present position. He answered: ... Certainly any extension of the zone of NATO would be unacceptable. (By implication, NATO in its current zone might be acceptable)."[174] Kohl reported to Bush in a phone call on February 13 that "I told Gorbachev again that the neutralization of Germany is out of the question for me," and when Bush asked "Did he acquiesce or just listen?" Kohl said, "My impression is that this is a subject about which they want to negotiate, but that we can win that point in negotiations."[175] Indeed, it would take some very ex-

---

[172] Document No. 110, The Malta Summit, plenary session, December 3, 1989.

[173] See Goldgeier, *Not Whether but When.*

[174] Document No. 120, Letter from Baker to Kohl, February 10, 1990.

[175] Memorandum of Telephone Conversation, Telephone Call from Chancellor Helmut Kohl of the Federal Republic of Germany, February 13, 1990, 1:49–2:00 p.m., The Oval Office. George Bush Presidential Library photocopy.

pensive phone calls from Kohl to Gorbachev in September 1990, amounting to billions of deutschmarks in German aid and credits to the USSR, to complete the deal.[176] Subsequent scholars (not least the American foreign policy aides who participated in these arrangements) have pointed to those February meetings with Gorbachev as decisive: "The mask had slipped. Gorbachev had allowed both the Americans and the Germans to leave Moscow believing that he was not willing—or perhaps not able—to offer decisive opposition to their plans. In fact that was true."[177] But the real turning point in German unification was not February, but the March 18, 1990, elections, which took away any possibility of decisive opposition.

The scholarly literature has developed two extreme versions of the discussion Baker had with Gorbachev, and perhaps they deserve each other. Michael MccGwire's version contains the clearest expression of the subsequent Russian sense of betrayal from NATO expansion, claiming an ironclad commitment from the West against any expansion of NATO. Mark Kramer's rebuttal argues the predominant Central European attitude towards NATO expansion, both summarizing the critics and explicating the newly-available documentary record that MccGwire did not or could not consult.[178] Both advocates overstate their cases. Kramer fundamentally argues that no one in early 1990 even foresaw the possibility of NATO admitting Poland or the other new democracies; therefore, no one could possibly give assurances against such inclusion. This is true enough, as far as it goes, but Kramer leaves out the entire Gorbachev vision for the withering away of both NATO and the Warsaw Pact. Regrettably, Kramer edits one of the documentary quotations from the February 9, 1990, Gorbachev–Baker meeting by adding brackets that distort, even contradict, Gorbachev's actual meaning (see above): "Of course it is clear that an expansion of NATO's zone [to the GDR] would be undesirable."[179] This is the phrase to which Baker said, "We agree with this." Read with a modicum of understanding of Gorbachev's vision, this exchange and the repeated U.S. use of the word "guarantee" explain why Gorbachev and his aides believed then and believe today that they received "assurances" against NATO expansion. Jack Matlock, who was present at the Baker meeting and subsequently described the U.S. formulation as a "clear commitment,"[180] suggested in the Musgrove transcript that a written assurance against NATO expansion was the only "better deal" that Gorbachev might possibly have gotten

[176] Brown, *The Gorbachev Factor*, 246–247.

[177] Zelikow and Rice, *Germany Unified*, 190.

[178] MccGwire, "NATO Expansion;" and Kramer, "The Myth of a No-NATO-Enlargement Pledge to Russia."

[179] Kramer, "The Myth of a No-NATO-Enlargement Pledge to Russia," 48. Kramer also undercuts Gorbachev's emphatic use of the Russian word *nepriemlemyi* by translating it as "undesirable" when the actual meaning is "unacceptable" (even Baker's subsequent letter to Kohl renders the word as "unacceptable"). See Document No. 120.

[180] Quoted in Kramer, 39.

from the Americans: "During German unification, if he had pressed, and if it had been important to him, he could have probably gotten better assurances that there would be no further expansion of NATO. He did not press that issue, and therefore, it was left sort of unclear."[181] The end of the Soviet Union in December 1991, followed by Bush's own failure to win re-election in 1992, completed the devaluation of any such bilateral assurances.

CONCLUSION

American policymaking might qualify at best for a supporting actor award in the extraordinary drama that was the end of the Cold War, and particularly for the revolutions of 1989. Ronald Reagan deserves credit not for his military buildup and "Star Wars" fantasies, but for the way his interaction with Gorbachev around their mutual dream of the abolition of nuclear weapons helped relieve the Soviet sense of threat and ultimately helped Gorbachev end Cold War thinking in Moscow. George Bush deserves credit for his caution, his prudence, his inability to posture—all reassuring in its way to Moscow, even though the cost of all that caution included a series of missed opportunities for dramatic arms reductions that would have left the U.S. and the world much safer. Gorbachev himself was less a "best actor" of 1989 than the producer of the whole spectacle, having set the stage, encouraged the reformers, agreed to a theater workshop, packed the house, and turned loose the talented thespians. But the leading roles in 1989 all featured East Europeans, with some West Germans also in the mix at least for the unification end game. The Poles led the way, created the most experimental theater, pushed the limits, and opened the space. Hungarians and Czechs provided thrilling second acts of their own, reprising and restaging their respective tragedies of 1956 and 1968. And Germans on both sides of the Wall brought the division of Europe to an end, first by plunging through those Hungarian fences and Czech embassies in September, then taking over the main squares of Leipzig and other Eastern cities in October, ultimately pushing through the Wall itself in November, and then voting overwhelmingly in March 1990 for a union with the West that brought the curtains down on Gorbachev's concept of the "common European home."

That concept initially had drawn a defensive reaction from the Americans, who saw the "common home" as just a stalking horse for getting rid of NATO, undermining alliance cohesion, and pushing the U.S. out of Europe. But once Gorbachev explicitly stated that the Americans belonged in Europe too, criticisms of the common home idea fell back on ideological arguments. The astute British scholar Timothy Garton Ash noted, "Gorbachev did not say there were many social systems in Europe… He said there were just two, East and West, 'socialist' and not. By implication, the common European home should

---

[181] Jack Matlock, Musgrove transcript, 208.

be built around, and in spite of, this central difference."[182] So Europe would exist as a semi-attached house, so to speak, with a wall down the middle, perhaps a common front porch for receiving visitors and a common back yard for barbeques and a garden, but you live on your side and we'll live on ours. General Jaruzelski maintained a somewhat different view than Gorbachev, when he said to President Bush in July 1989, "if the West is interested in success of our reforms, they should see them not only in a Polish context but also in terms of spreading conditions. In Bucharest [the Warsaw Pact summit] we spoke in favor of arms control, détente, the development of East–West relations, and a common European home. At the same time, if you are dealing with Poland we support the American concept, that it should be a house with free corridors between the respective rooms."[183] The Solidarity prime minister Tadeusz Mazowiecki put it more circumspectly when he talked directly to Gorbachev, "In connection with your idea of a Common European Home, I would like to note that in this home our apartments share the same landing" (in other words, they were the closest of neighbors).[184] The Bush administration's view was more harsh: "The 'common home' was flawed not because it excluded the United States—this Gorbachev quickly corrected—but because it proposed to validate and stabilize a status quo that was inherently unacceptable and unstable…a vision that would have eased Europe's divisions superficially without addressing any of its root causes."[185]

Yet that status quo rapidly changed in 1989, clearly as a result of Gorbachev's vision that turned out not so superficial after all. The miracles of 1989 showed that exactly the common home vision allowed for root causes and divisions to be overcome by the divided peoples themselves. Gorbachev himself would move in his own conceptions of socialism very far from the Leninist or Marxist notion, until he was for all practical purposes a social democrat, attempting to achieve a demilitarized Soviet Union. At this point, after 1989, it was the West that kept the Wall up, in the sense of preventing the integration of the USSR into Europe, with lasting consequences for today's Russia and its retreat into chauvinism and authoritarianism. What if the integration of the Soviet Union with the West had been the goal of U.S. policy (without any Gulf War diversion in 1990–1991 where Gorbachev's partnership brought him so little benefit either on economic aid or arms reductions), perhaps starting with the energy sector, in the context of massive reductions in military-industrial investment? But perhaps the integration of Russia with the West was simply too much to ask in the new Europe, with Central Europe just out from under the bear, hardly eager to look east, or to allow Russia to be integrated together with its former vassals. As the Hungarian scholar András Bozóki has commented, the last thing the Eastern Europeans wanted was

[182] Garton Ash, *In Europe's Name*, 123.
[183] Document No. 76, Bush–Jaruzelski Information Note, July 18, 1989.
[184] Document No. 107, Gorbachev–Mazowiecki memcon, November 24, 1989.
[185] Hutchings, *American Diplomacy*, 11.

to build yet another house with the Soviet Union in it.[186] As the CIA estimates show, the Americans and the Europeans shared the worry that you could let Gorbachev into the house, a fine roommate, even let him read your kids to sleep, but what if the next roommate that Moscow sends is one of the tough guys, what if Gorbachev does not last, how long will Gorbachev last? You might not want to be integrated with the next leadership group—this was certainly the prediction Eduard Shevardnadze made in his resignation message on December 20, 1990.[187]

So a more realistic counterfactual would be to ask, what if there had been no Bush "pause" (a pause that actually began during the presidential campaign in 1988)? Gorbachev was at his peak of political power in 1988 and the first half of 1989; the evidence shows he was ready and eager to deliver previously unthinkable cuts in nuclear and conventional weapons. That clout only dissipated as his domestic politics degenerated, as he let the Soviet empire go, as the Russian economy continued in crisis, and as he had nothing to show for his "new thinking" but standing ovations in foreign cities and breadlines at home. What if instead the superpowers had quickly achieved 50 percent or more reductions in strategic weapons (instead of the 30 percent in START) and the tactical nuclear withdrawals that only happened in the fall of 1991, too late to buttress Gorbachev's standing? Most likely, the revolutions in Eastern Europe would have proceeded more or less as they did—the evidence in this volume shows for example, that the Poles already had Gorbachev's approval in 1988 for making a deal with Solidarity. Gorbachev might have had more staying power, more ability to make the reforms that advisers like Yakovlev were pushing, more political clout to keep the hard-liners at bay. Thus one can envision a very different relationship between today's Russia and the world, and between today's world and nuclear weapons, which Presidents Obama and Medvedev are still talking about trying to reduce in 2009, 20 years after the Cold War ended.

---

[186] András Bozóki, panel commentary, University of Pavia conference, "Britain and Europe in the 1980s: East and West," October 2, 2007, notes by the author who served on the same panel.

[187] "Dictatorship is coming," he warned the Congress of People's Deputies. See Shevardnadze, *The Future Belongs to Freedom*, 212; Dobbs, *Down with Big Brother*, 325.

Dialogue: The Musgrove Conference, May 1–3, 1998

*Transcribed and translated by Svetlana Savranskaya,
edited by Thomas Blanton*

PARTICIPANTS:

*Former
Officials:*

Anatoly Chernyaev
Douglas MacEachin
Jack Matlock
Georgy Shakhnazarov
Sergei Tarasenko

Scholars:

Csaba Békés
Thomas Blanton
Malcolm Byrne
Chen Jian
Karen Dawisha
Ilya Gaiduk
Richard Hermann
James Hershberg
Jacques Levesque

Pawel Machcewicz
Andrzej Paczkowski
Vilém Prečan
János Rainer
Svetlana Savranskaya
Oleg Skvortsov
William Wohlforth
David Wolff
Vladislav Zubok

CHAPTER 1: INTRODUCTION

Thomas Blanton (moderator): Welcome. We have three goals for this conference. The first is simply to enjoy this place. Musgrove was built by Nancy Reynolds Bagley as a vacation retreat and a nature preserve for a beautiful section of St. Simons Island. This is where President Carter first gathered his Cabinet after the election of 1976 and before the inauguration. Thanks to the generosity of Smith Bagley, the Brenn Foundation, and the Arca Foundation, we are meeting like presidents. I have found that the biggest challenge at Musgrove is to bring to the table the conversations that take place away from the table as people do, shall we say, conferencing with a human face.

The second goal is to contribute to the ongoing multinational effort to grapple with the history of those revolutionary events of the late 1980s, and the way the world changed, and the Cold War ended, in 1989. Next year, in 1999, our partners in East and Central Europe will recreate some of that history, bringing veterans and witnesses to the table, with their own documents, from Politburoș, from oppositions, from U.S. and Soviet sources, so that they can relive and learn from their own histories. So the point of these three days is to put on the table the key questions that you really want answered in this larger process. What are the mysteries that remain to you, as experts, as veterans, as researchers? What are the mysteries that need to be answered? What would you tell us to do if you were commissioning our research?

The third goal is to grapple with some remarkable new evidence. This thick briefing book of documents exists in very large part because of the generosity of Anatoly Chernyaev, and the Gorbachev Foundation, which is committed to the process of scholarly enquiry and has set, I believe, a new standard for openness in these matters. Included here are multiple selections from Anatoly's daily diaries from his tenure as Gorbachev's personal aide for foreign policy from 1986 through 1991, including notes of Politburo sessions and meetings with foreign leaders. I plan to use these materials as a crowbar to help wedge open the American files on these subjects. So thanks to Anatoly and to Georgy Shakhnazarov, and everyone who contributed to this documentary encyclopedia.

Now I will ask Vlad Zubok to give you what we Americans would call the "greatest hits," the highlights of this new evidence, the likes of which many of us, as students of these events, hardly expected to see in our lifetimes. Vlad has carried so much of the research load for this project and for the documents in front of you, that I would like to give him the first word on the documentary findings.

Vladislav Zubok: Now the pressure is on me to be really brief in describing this briefing book. The word "brief" fails, I guess, to describe what is inside there. Now, I believe, when you deal with documents, each of them was remarkable by itself, but when you put them together, you create a quality in itself, because the combination is amazing. Putting them together, the documents became more and more revealing to me.

Several things I would like to mention. The majority of the documents are from the Gorbachev Archive, Russian documents, although there are some amazing American documents. In particular, I would like to mention the CIA reports, and Jack Matlock's cables from Moscow in February 1989, which sort of correlate nicely with Kennan's "long telegram" that marked the beginning of the Cold War, as Jack's cables mark the end of the Cold War in Europe. To me, one highlight of this briefing book is how much was spoken within the narrow inside circle of Gorbachev's about the possibility of collapse in Eastern Europe.

We find in the documents that it was discussed in Georgy Shakhnazarov's memorandum to Gorbachev—what would happen if there was a general collapse in Eastern Europe? And still [...] We put here Vadim Zagladin's notes to Gorbachev, his personal notes to Gorbachev about his trip to Europe, including Czechoslovakia, where he had many friends, in May 1989, and there are serious warnings about a collapse that might be in the making. Yet the question that we should discuss is why all this happened without Gorbachev actually acting on those warnings, or not really acting in a serious way.

Again, I must mention, one of the highlights of the book is the report by the Bogomolov institute[1] to the International Commission of the Politburo, headed

---

[1] Document No. 42. The Institute of the Economy of the World socialist System, directed by Oleg Bogomolov, was part of the USSR Academy of Sciences.

at that time by [Alexander] Yakovlev, and we have these documents thanks to Professor [Jacques] Levesque, who obtained them in Moscow from, I guess, the authors of these documents. There are several reports, but the Bogomolov institute report is perhaps the most revealing of the extent of how far Russian analysts went in predicting what might happen in Eastern Europe. Another thing that sort of struck me as important as I looked at, as I selected documents for this briefing book, is the relevance of debates on what to do with the Baltic republics, with the Transcaucasian republics, to the secession crises that have already flared up inside the Soviet Union.

So for me, what was striking was to find at that time, from the end of 1988, that the Politburo spent much time debating how to preserve the core of the empire, not to mention its periphery in Eastern Europe—and one key phrase that Gorbachev used at some point: that if we go too far we might undermine the Slavic core of the empire. He used the word "empire," actually, which was kind of unusual for a debate among communist leaders, "socialist empire."

I found it also interesting to what extent Gorbachev relied on the international audience, on world leaders, as his reference group to test his ideas, to sound his ideas out—as he used the term: "to roll out the ideas," and that is why there are so many, to the extent possible, many memcons—Gorbachev talking to [François] Mitterrand, Gorbachev talking to [Margaret] Thatcher, and so on and so forth.

So at some point I felt that those leaders became his most important reference group. And he took it very seriously when he found signs of mistrust. For instance, if you look at the additional documents, here at the end of the briefing book, you will find some reports from the Deputy Director of the U.S. and Canada institute on his meetings with some prominent Americans. And those prominent Americans told him that there was a group in the National Security Council, with Robert Gates and others, plotting to compromise Gorbachev and his *perestroika*. What is amazing is that Gorbachev took those rumors very seriously, because he repeated that line in his conversations with Western European leaders. He complained about it to [Helmut] Kohl, he complained about it to Mitterrand. He took it very seriously.

On the collapse, I think that my favorite documents—there are many documents here on the collapse, and how it took the Soviet leadership by surprise, as well as everyone else, and we have documents from the Malta summit, we have official documents. But the most important things were said unofficially, not in official documents. We can compare, for instance, two documents here in this briefing book: a cable—a document that I got, actually, from Tom, a cable[2] from the U.S. Embassy in Sofia on November 9, the day when the Berlin wall collapsed, the Embassy reported that "no major changes are expected," "little prospect for changes." The next day, Zhivkov was gone. And on November 9, when

---

[2] Document No. 98.

we look into Chernyaev's diaries, we find an amazing line, that the whole thing is collapsing, the Yalta system is collapsing, and that is, probably, for the good. This is probably the most amazing highlight from the whole briefing book—a personal assistant to the general secretary of the Communist Party of the USSR, whose external empire was in the process of collapse, comments: "Perhaps it is inevitable and good," and welcomes this change.

CHAPTER 2: THE EMERGENCE OF SOVIET "NEW THINKING" AND EASTERN EUROPE

Blanton: Our first session is called The Emergence of Soviet "New Thinking" and Eastern Europe. That means, in relation to Eastern Europe, or as it applied to Eastern Europe. The second session will focus on Moscow's reaction to the events of 1989, for which we borrowed the adjective "enigmatic" from Professor Levesque. The third session will be on the domestic context of the new thinking and the events in Eastern Europe, which often went in parallel. Tomorrow, our fourth session is on the superpower context, particularly the relationships in 1989, and in the final session, into lunch tomorrow, we will try to draw some of the conclusions and reflections, and put down on paper some of the key questions that we want to make sure are asked at the conferences next year, in 1999, and throughout our multinational research project.

For each session we have asked a particular scholar-participant to lead off with a few minutes, four or five minutes, of questions. Some of these questions will simply be informative ones, mysteries that are still left, some are intended to be provocative, and to stimulate argument and debate. For this morning session, Professor Levesque will lead off with a few minutes of questions. Jacques?

Jacques Levesque: OK, thank you. I will start with a couple of questions to our Russian colleagues on the topic of this morning's session. What strikes me when looking at the place of Eastern Europe in Soviet new thinking is the extraordinary similarity between the Soviet approach and the concept of European reconciliation that was developed ten years earlier by the Italian Communist Party at the time of Eurocommunism. In two words only, what the Italian communists proposed at the time was a gradual de-antagonization of the two military blocs, through not only disarmament and economic intercourse, but with a significant degree of democratization of Eastern Europe, as being an absolutely necessary component of the process. A significant, but undefined degree of democratism was seen by them not only as desirable in itself, but as necessary for substantial advances in the field of disarmament, and economic intercourse.

At the same time, the Italian communists conceived that the democratization should take place in a context that respected the security interests of the Soviet Union, and the continued existence of the two de-antagonized blocs for a very long period of time. To me, this striking similarity between the Soviet thinking of Eastern Europe is not simply a matter of chance. There are two different, but compatible ways of explaining this similarity. One is the influence of the ideas through networks. So, my first question to our Russian colleagues is: Do you consider that your relations and exchange of ideas with the Italian communists, for instance, had a significant influence in shaping your views on European politics? I was telling Mr. Chernyaev yesterday that I was in Rome in the mid-1980s, conducting research on the Italian Communist Party at the Central Committee there. And I talked with Italian intellectuals and leaders in the Communist Party. And when you were nominated as special assistant to Gorbachev for foreign affairs, they were all excited. They said, "we know this man very well, we are on the same wavelength, so he will certainly contribute to bringing significant change in the Soviet approach to world politics." I asked so many persons, advisers of Gorbachev, this question about their intellectual relationships with the Italian Communist Party, and also the Social Democrats in Europe, and did not get a very conclusive answer.

Therefore, I would consider another explanation, a structural explanation. Namely, that the process of democratization of a communist party, be it the Italian, the Czech in 1968, or the Soviet in the late 1980s, generates similar patterns of thinking and of politics, more or less independently from the circulation of ideas. One of these unmistakable patterns is, to put it in a nutshell, a highly idealistic search for universal reconciliation, which supersedes the central concept of struggle. So, my question to you is: What is your preferred explanation for these similarities?

Anatoly Chernyaev: Indeed, there were some parallels, perhaps connected with the changes that emerged even before the Prague events, and they accelerated after those events, in the minds not only of free-thinking intelligentsia, meaning those who did not hold official positions, but also in the minds of intelligentsia that found themselves in the apparatus of the party and the state. I suppose that because we represent not researchers but a living historical source here, then it would be more interesting to speak about my personal experience. I met with Italian communists in 1967, and even earlier, when I was working on the journal *Problems of Peace and Socialism*. And I found a commonality of approaches with them, as well as with other intelligent communists, on the basis of simple common sense, on the basis of the feeling that the ideology had stopped working long ago. The ideology no longer served as a formative element in the development of our society, nor as a justification for the existence of our society, because it was so much behind the real processes.

When Eurocommunism emerged, even though we sometimes had to speak against it, working in the apparatus of the Central Committee, in the *nomenklatura*, and carrying out certain directives, in our hearts I and some of my colleagues from the International Department of the Central Committee agreed with the Eurocommunists. We were very discouraged by the fact that those new approaches you have mentioned, which we considered fruitful, and which, we thought, were based on a more serious and deeper understanding of the processes that were underway in Europe and in the world, in the world economy, and so on—they were rejected by our leadership.

103

And we had a dilemma between feeling personal sympathy toward those people, with whom we had been in contact for many years, and our career situation. When we met with them in Moscow, or in Rome, or in Bologna, or in Milan, we spoke the same language. They did not understand certain things, did not take some things into account, for example the cumbersomeness and the inertia of our society's development, which had accumulated so many stereotypes, so many factors of internal development that were based on Soviet dogmatism. They thought that it would be easy and simple to transform our society. By the way, we also had similar illusions when we began *perestroika*, that it would be easy to do. But the outcome of *perestroika* has now shown how it was in reality.

In short, we had arguments but we remained friends, because we thought that they were basically right. We already had the same sources for understanding the situation that they had, and of course we fed on their achievements, their understanding of the problems. Here you would ask: What about your bosses, what about [Mikhail] Suslov, or [Boris] Ponomarev, for example, for whom I worked in the International Department? How could they tolerate it? They must have known that behind the curtain, in our private conversations, we were following a different line, and were not behaving as apparatchiks should. They knew—not everything, but they knew a lot. Things happened, sometimes not just in our personal meetings, but during international meetings, meetings of International Departments.

There was the following practice—apparatchiks from socialist countries would gather together, and with the French and the Italians, and we talked not only at the tables; it was boring at the tables. We talked also over some spirits, in cafes, bars, etc. Sometimes we learned later from our bosses that we had not behaved correctly, and said wrong things to those same Eurocommunists. It turns out that our colleagues from the socialist countries, especially the Germans, by virtue of being very disciplined people, reported to their superiors what their "Soviet comrades" were saying. [Laughter] And this is the way we learned about it.

So why did the leadership tolerate it? Our leadership wanted to preserve the peace and well-being of the International Communist Movement. To allow a split, a rupture in the communist movement meant to discredit ourselves among not only communists, but among the Western publics. It was highly valued. And that is why we were a kind of a link, a connecting unit between our leadership and the European fraternal communist parties, which were deviating ideologically, even criticized us, and sometimes harshly, on some issues. And therefore, such officials as me, and Georgy [Shakhnazarov]—and there were others like us, if not dozens, still many, in our two International Departments—were needed by the Central Committee of the Communist Party in order to hold the communist movement approximately within the framework of what was necessary for influencing international public opinion.

I would perhaps end my answer here. If you have any additional questions, I will answer them later. I think I have answered the main question of why and how we were similar to the Eurocommunists, and different from them, and why they were tolerated in Moscow.

Georgy Shakhnazarov: Anatoly spoke from a personal level. Those were the personal impressions of the people like us, who were, in his words, the connecting link between the leaderships of the parties, and who, perhaps, were allowed more freedom than others. Besides, it might be that they did not know about everything, about what we were discussing over drinks, in secluded corners of all kinds of international conferences. I would like to answer Professor Levesque's questions in more conceptual terms.

To what extent did the Italian Communist Party, their findings, and the Eurocommunists in general, of course including the legacy of Gramsci, have an impact on the reforms that took place in our country, and on the emergence of new thinking? I personally think that that influence is extremely exaggerated in various books and articles, because, after all, we were ripe for new thinking, and came to it on our own. The Italians did not slip it in from outside, neither did the Eurocommunists. You can judge it by many indicators. This is from my personal point of view, and from the point of view of the people with whom I was in touch, those whom they now call "dissidents within the Central Committee, within the central party apparatus."

Those people understood long ago, even in the post-war years, and you can see it in Anatoly Sergeyevich's war and post-war diaries, that the processes that were unfolding in our country were calling for serious corrections. We did not call them *perestroika*, but we thought that we needed a shake-up of the whole system. We could not part with the system in general. We were true socialists and communists, and we believed, indeed, that a just and prosperous society could be built, but still we could see all the defects of the system, including the aggressive behavior in the international arena, and also the direct participation in the arms race, and everything that would push the world toward the precipice. We could see it with our own eyes.

As far as the official side of the business was concerned, I will add this observation. Long before the Italians were ripe to criticize what we then called "real socialism," long before they began to attack it in Togliatti's memos, and so on—those processes had already begun in our own party. Take for example the changes that were introduced under Khrushchev. Besides, if we take the Warsaw Treaty Organization (WTO), it was during the meetings of the Political Consultative Committee of the WTO that the ideas came up about a simultaneous dissolution of the two military-political blocs, and every session reflected certain debates over this idea; it was written in every communiqué. To what degree it was hypocrisy or a real proposal, now it is hard to tell. And then we did not think about it: Was it a propaganda step, or not? But I am convinced—if there had been the slightest response from the West to that idea—some process of disarmament would have begun much earlier than it actually happened.

In particular, the ideas and the proposals that were coming from Khrushchev were not heard in the West. Our readiness to go further was greater than it was perceived and known in the West, as it happened later when Gorbachev emerged. And even then it did not happen at once; acceptance came slowly and gradually.

Therefore, I think that the Italian influence is very exaggerated. Anatoly Sergeyevich is right, we spoke with them as with equals. We had no substantial differences, rather we had national differences, because from the Russian side many things looked different than from the Italian side. But in essence—to be in favor of democracy, peace and progress, to work for disarmament, for closer relations between peoples—we shared all those ideas. Thank you.

Sergey Tarasenko: I completely agree with my senior colleagues, but I would like to present the position of the Ministry of Foreign Affairs. Relations with socialist countries and with the communist movement as a whole, especially at the most recent stage, were never in the zone of the Ministry's priorities. The Ministry was not directly involved in all those issues, and in principle the Ministry was left to deal with less favorable tasks, such as damage control operations. It would only get involved if something happened, in order to smooth out or to settle something. But we had to deal with some practical aspects of international politics, because the socialist countries represented one front, more or less, presented similar positions, held consultations to work out a common position for the General Assembly of the United Nations, for all kinds of international fora, and so on.

But by the time we get to the period of *perestroika*, even before, we felt that the organizational structure itself of the so-called socialist camp was not very good, that it did not fit with world standards. We operated with a mirror image, and we compared [ourselves to] NATO, NATO structures, the way it worked, how relations among allies in that bloc were built. At the same time, we saw the WTO. And we saw that within the WTO the organizational side looked very weak. In practice there was a complete monopoly of power by our side. This was only exacerbated with time, when our partners began to make their own international policy. It became more and more apparent. It is well known that it went together with many tragedies and conflict situations, for example, when our military killed civilians, when some tank crashed into some bus. People were killed. There were a large number of negative aspects that caused extremely negative reactions in those countries. We simply could not let that go on without trying to do something to improve the situation. Again, a practical aspect of the situation— our propaganda always utilized every case of protest rallies anywhere around American bases, like in Greece, in the Philippines—"Look how people are outraged because of the presence of the American troops; everybody is protesting."

In our inner circle we spoke about the fact that one needed to understand that the presence of our troops in Hungary, or Czechoslovakia, or in Poland, or in the GDR was not welcome either. The people were not very glad and happy about the presence of our troops there. And that presence in most cases was very visible and not very pleasant, when many bad things transpired. And we then attempted, in a very cautious form, to raise the question about the need for some kind of reform inside the WTO, even if only of the organizational structure, because the situation was such that our base in any of the fraternal countries at that time meant tens of kilometers of fence, beyond which even the local authorities were

106

not allowed. As far as I understood, even the prime minister of Hungary could not freely enter the territory of a Soviet military base.

We thought that it would have been nice to have a rotation of the leadership, at least to have two flags over the base, one flag should be other than Soviet, for example, the flag of the WTO. In other words, we thought we should at least formally improve the facade of that building. We spoke with the military about it, but we always encountered a lack of understanding and resistance—that we should not change anything, that everything was all right, everything was normal. However, when *perestroika* began, we in the Foreign Ministry wrote a memo, addressed it to Gorbachev, via [Eduard] Shevardnadze of course, but he was going to show it to Gorbachev. We submitted our ideas regarding the need to reform the WTO—both in terms of organization, and also that we should scale down our presence and make it less visible, and less provocative for those countries. Such a memo was written, and I still have a copy of it somewhere at home. I left it at home. There was nothing extraordinary in it. It was designed after NATO, and proposed some things that we borrowed from NATO practice in order to make that facade look better. We wrote that memo, gave it to Shevardnadze. He took it. And I do not know what happened next.

Sometime later he returned the memo to us with a resolution saying that it would be better to return to this issue later on. Whether he showed it to Gorbachev or not I personally do not know. But normally, knowing his practice, I think he did. They probably decided that that was not a priority, and that we should not deal with it. But the situation continued to deteriorate in this respect. I remember, we mentioned our German friends here who were very disciplined—when [Erich] Honecker told us, via the ambassador, "Please fix your barracks, at least, because they look terrible. Try to put your soldiers into a better uniform" because the soldiers were seen in the city in very unsightly uniforms, and made a poor impression on the people. And the issue was put to us almost in the following form: Either keep your people behind the fence, and do not let them in the city, or dress them better, or dress them in civilian clothes. The issue reached a very unpleasant level. And unfortunately for this issue—I do not know how they felt about it in the Central Committee—we dealt mostly with our military, and our military were absolutely unresponsive on this issue.

I think if we had chosen that road at the beginning of *perestroika*, in 1986, for example, if we had given a new appearance to our defense union—for example, there was a proposal to separate the Soviet troops from the WTO troops, put those under the WTO flag, let our troops be present not as Soviet troops, but as WTO troops, subordinated to the command of the WTO, not to the Soviet Defense Ministry in Moscow, but to the United Command. But if you remember, at the final stage, when the WTO was already doomed and was falling apart, the military were forced to make some changes, propose some reforms, but it was so shallow—practically nothing. They took the position: to preserve everything as it was; to change nothing with the exception of some insignificant, cosmetic changes. Even if we could do some of these things, the changes early on, in 1986 for example, I do not think that it would have made a big difference in the course of events, in the development that was underway. But we still would have found ourselves in a better situation, especially in terms of our withdrawal, a more peaceful withdrawal from Central Europe. That issue could have been less controversial. Still, in my opinion, it could not have changed what happened. But it would have been useful, and would have played its role.

Chernyaev: I have several lively episodes for you, related to Jacques Levesque's question. The Soviet leadership of the 1970s consisted of very different people. There was Suslov—and they rightly called him the "Soviet Savonarola."[3] For him ideology was always first; he was very suspicious and very cruel regarding any ideological deviations. And then there were people like [Andrey] Kirilenko, who was Suslov's rival for the position of number two in the party. [Leonid] Brezhnev also belonged to the latter category. Those are people who, if they ever read Lenin in their higher party school, I am sure they never read Marx or Engels. For them ideology [laughs] was at best a secondary influence. For them the most important part was to preserve the power of the state and the leadership of the Soviet Union. And it was from that point of view that they approached the Italian Communist Party and Eurocommunism.

Here is one of the episodes. It happened in 1975 or in 1976. Kirilenko led the CPSU delegation to a Congress of the Italian Communist Party. It was precisely during the peak of Eurocommunism. I was not a member of that delegation, but Zagladin was. He told me about it in detail. And later I heard Kirilenko speak about it in person when he called Ponomarev, and they discussed the results of the trip. And he even said at the Politburo later, "Why do our guys pick on the Italians, criticize them in articles? They are good guys, what's the problem? So what if they are talking too much, if they say some things that we do not understand, for God's sake! The important thing is that we feel good with them, and they gave me a good reception." I am saying this to emphasize that for the people who considered Soviet state power the most important, not ideology, they wanted to keep the Italians, as well as the others, as our friends, as one of the factors of our international influence.

One more point. When they were deciding whether to send Gorbachev to [Enrico] Berlinguer's funeral, there was a big discussion in the Politburo. Initially they did not want to send him because they understood that he was a person with democratic leanings. Berlinguer did a lot of harm to us ideologically. But still, they decided to send him because they understood that Gorbachev could find a common language with them, that he could speak like a normal human being, non-confrontationally. And that hunch was supported by the events: Gorbachev had discussions with them, but carried them out on friendly terms. They saw what Thatcher would see later—that you can do business with this man.

---

[3] Girolamo Savonarola (1452–1498) was a Dominican friar based in Florence and a religious reformer devoted to asceticism and the renunciation of paganism and vice.

And here you are right—the Italians' ideas, their discussions in the framework of Eurocommunism, their view of the world, and of the direction of global and European development, all this had a great influence on him. He remembers it, and he mentioned it in his memoirs. Therefore, this was a factor of certain influence, but Georgy is also right, if Gorbachev had not been mentally and intellectually prepared by all his previous development for this understanding of the Italian point of view, then nothing would have happened.

These are the two episodes that I wanted to relate to you. This is also very important for our explanation of why they later decided to choose Gorbachev after Chernenko's death and not somebody else. Because those old men understood that the time had come to change things. And it was not so much their fear of losing their positions and privileges of power, but even with all caveats and their personal differences, their duty to the people and to the country was ingrained in them—by Marxism-Leninism, and the party, by the way.

Blanton: Thanks. I would like to ask Jack Matlock to comment on your understanding of the origins of new thinking, the influences, the Khrushchev possibilities, the Eurocommunist ideas, the underpinnings of new thinking. How did you explain it to yourself, and to your peers and policy makers, particularly as Gorbachev was developing these ideas in the early part of his years in power? But particularly the origins, as you saw them.

Jack Matlock: First, I have never studied in detail the origins, and I would not presume to speak with any authority or particular insight. As we Americans saw the new thinking developing, attitudes within our government differed greatly. Doug [MacEachin] probably knows better than I some of the differences that people had. My own feeling was that the Soviets were reacting to the situation as they saw it and that their analysis of some of their internal problems was not that different from ours. I certainly did not detect a strong foreign influence, from the communist movement or elsewhere on that.

Obviously, there were people in the Soviet Union, just as there were here, who knew what these problems were. Some of our specialists probably studied them in greater detail than did the political leadership in the Soviet Union. But most of our leaders were not ideologically inclined. Most of them did not pay much attention to ideology in a direct sense. Basically, as we watched "new thinking" being developed, the question was: How sincere is it, and what does it mean concretely? When Gorbachev started talking about defense sufficiency, for example, our reaction was: "OK, what does that mean? That is different rhetoric, yes. And maybe it is meaningful. But we have heard words that sounded different before, and the policies did not change." It was only when "new thinking" became embodied in policies that those of us who were attentive—which is not everybody—began to say, "Hey, this is real." For me the most convincing evidence came with the theses for the Party Conference in 1988.

When these theses were issued, we were sitting in Helsinki, briefing [Ronald] Reagan on his trip to Moscow, which was just a few days off. The text came in fairly late in the evening, and I went to my room, thankful for having something

I could read that was unclassified. Most of our books were classified and had to be read in special rooms. I began to skim through the theses, and I was electrified. Jim Billington had come with the first lady (actually, because Nancy Reagan wanted to be tutored on Russian art so that she could one-up Raisa Maximovna [Gorbacheva]). I went to him and said, "Jim, read this, and see if you are as excited as I am." And he called me about 4:00 in the morning, and said, "You are right, this is world-shaking." The next morning I told Reagan: you know, we are in a new ball game. I could not find any references to Marxism-Leninism in the theses, and it was clear that if the theses were adopted by the Conference—and since they were being proposed by the general secretary, presumably they would be—this is going to be a different country. So, our understanding of "new thinking" developed step-by-step—first it was "let us wait and see," and different people had different criteria on what they considered important. For me, ideology was important and when I saw a Communist Party document that borrowed more from the American Constitution than from Marxism-Leninism, I was impressed.

Blanton: Thank you very much. Doug MacEachin, could you illuminate for us a little bit the struggles, the very different perceptions that Jack just referred to inside the U.S. government from your point of view at the [Central Intelligence] Agency, as the head of SOVA, the Soviet Analysis Office, during those years, 1984–1989?

Douglas MacEachin: I do not think the conference will be long enough for me [...] [laughter] to describe for you all the different views. I think I would parallel what Jack has said, but let me go back to the late 1970s to give you some background.

This is very important, because what you are trying to do in this kind of situation is look at the intentions of other people. There is no empirical proof, there is nothing that says, "this will happen." You can sense that something is going on, that there are some changing views [...] But if you think the analysis is difficult, try to present that kind of spectral analysis to someone who has a deeply held different view, and persuade them that major change may be occurring. So, in the earlier stages it was more a sense that—for example, I remember, in 1979, I think, there was a statement at a Soviet Party Congress that, as I recollect, a committee would be formed to look into some problems [...] little things that spawned a belief in a lot of us who were observing—I must confess that at that time I was doing more military than politics—that maybe there is a groundwork developing for some change.

I will also tell you quite frankly that in the early 1980s we were hearing all kinds of gossip that Gorbachev was a rising star. That was in 1980–1981–1982. In fact, as evidence that seemed to confirm this, there seemed to be a reaction developing against him in some Soviet political circles.

So, this was the setting as we got to 1985. I will give you a little anecdote. When Brezhnev died, Vice President [George H.W.] Bush was, I think, in Africa, and he was the senior U.S. person designated to go to the funeral. He wanted someone with Soviet expertise to go with him. I was the guy who gave him his

110

morning intelligence papers, so his office asked if I knew somebody with the appropriate expertise. So we sent a colleague of mine, one of my friends. At another funeral one year later the Vice President's Office called for my friend again; another funeral one year later, and they called for my friend again. And so he was there for [Konstantin] Chernenko's funeral with James Baker (at that time the White House chief of staff). According to my friend, Baker told him that in his view "This guy (Gorbachev) is a real astute politician." And Baker was there with Gorbachev in a room for only one day, I think. So, there was a sense of something happening, but nothing specific.

That is all I can say about views up to that point. And, as Jack says, we did not see anything being driven by external factors. Maybe particular discussions, formulation of the ideas, but the motivations, we thought, were all internal.

And then, I would say, by 1986, the division of views about Gorbachev in Washington had become fairly clear, I thought. Because you could not argue any more over whether the government, the leadership of the Soviet Union believed they had serious problems. The chairman of the Party said they had problems. So that argument, despite what you read today, was not really what the contention was all about. Instead it was the two views that we have talked about at breakfast.

One view said: all of the foreign policy and arms control was merely an effort to buy time to make the existing system's problems go away, thereby building up a more robust and threatening opponent. And I have copies of speeches in my file, which I'll send to you. They are not speeches I made—

Blanton: [William] Casey?

MacEachin: Yes, and others close to him [referring to Robert Gates].

The other view, for most of us who had grown up reading Russian literature in college, was this feeling that this effort toward change was for real. And the change was not merely doctoring, but would become of a significant, fundamental, systemic nature. That it would be different.

Now, that said, and it is all on record, I was one of those who did not believe that Gorbachev's economic policies were going to succeed. So that was in some respects bad news. But it was also good news, because we believed that bigger steps were going to have to be made, and that those bigger steps were going to have to be of a fundamental nature. And what ultimately convinced me, and most of my colleagues, were the events of September 30, 1988.[4] I thought that was where the line was crossed. I could not foresee the future from that point on, but I was pretty sure that whatever it was, it was not going to be like the past.

Karen Dawisha: I have a couple of questions. My own feeling is that it would be a mistake for us to look back and say that Gorbachev's new thinking can be

---

[4] At the September 1988 Central Committee Plenum, Gorbachev engineered a major restructuring of the Central Committee apparatus, which among other things created the International Commission headed by Alexander Yakovlev and produced a radical leadership shake-up, removing several hard-liners from their posts, including Andrey Gromyko, Yegor Ligachev, and Viktor Chebrikov.

traced to Khrushchev, to the Prague Spring, etc. I mean, my concern with that is that while it is true that there were reformist elements in all of those regimes, that to say that would be to forget the essential nature of the Brezhnev leadership, which was a highly oppressive external force, and a highly energized ideological force in the Third World. And my question is: If Anatoly's and even Georgy's statement is right, that all of these things can be traced, that we were talking in the corridors, that we were having these conferences with the Italians, that the Germans were reporting on us, then why wasn't the International Department of the Central Committee cleaned out? Why didn't the military take more robust measures to prevent Gorbachev from coming to power? My own feeling is that they could not possibly have realized what they were getting themselves into. They could not possibly have thought that Gorbachev was—this is a question to you, it is my own feeling, but I am wondering, why wasn't there a more robust effort to prevent Gorbachev from coming to power? Because he moved so quickly [...]

Levesque: Or to stop him afterwards.

Dawisha: Yes, he moved really very quickly once he came to power. I do not think it was only in September 1988 that it was clear. I think, you know, the "bleeding wound of Afghanistan," it was there in 1985. The words that he was saying about military spending, it was a hit to the military, to the real ideological state, right-wing core of that regime in the very first five or six months. The question that I have really is: Did the—if I can call you this—the reformers, the liberals in the party, know themselves about Gorbachev? Did you have meetings with Gorbachev? Did he seek you out, or did he keep his own counsel? I ask this because in the documents that we had for previous conferences, on Afghanistan, for example, Gorbachev is pretty silent. I mean, it seems to me that he bided his time and he did not show his hand before he came to power. So what was your assessment of Gorbachev?

Chernyaev: I will try to clarify the situation with Gorbachev. When Gorbachev turned up in Moscow as the secretary for agriculture, and as soon as he made himself known to some degree as a new member of the leadership, the people in the apparatus of the Central Committee noticed him immediately. Georgy and I were present at sessions of the Secretariat, sometimes at Politburo sessions. At the Secretariat sessions we were present as deputies of the heads of the international departments. And we saw how great was the difference in conducting the Secretariat sessions between Suslov, or Kirilenko, and when Gorbachev took the reins when they were absent. It was a completely different style. There was a desire to consult, to discuss issues, to invite experts, to make decisions on the basis of some elementary analysis. And there was a very strict lack of tolerance toward disorderliness, idleness, toward irresponsibility in regard to the implementation of the decisions that had been made—a very tough attitude. It was surprising that the toughness was in the words, but no "organizational conclusions," as we used to say, were made. That weakness of Gorbachev came out later, when Gorbachev became the chief—the general secretary.

Now, as soon as Gorbachev turned up in Moscow he began to gather around himself people who were capable of independent thinking. Mostly these were people from the Institute of the World Economy and International Relations: [Nikolay] Inozemtsev, [Georgy] Arbatov, Yakovlev, of course, [Vadim] Medvedev in the first stage, who now is considered a retrograde by our public opinion, but he played a big, positive role at certain times. We can name several other people. In short, Gorbachev wanted a real analysis of the situation, both the internal and international situation. Inozemtsev, we should give him his due, sometimes even took risks in his courage and directness—he took risks even under Brezhnev, and of course later when he joined the Gorbachev team. He dared to speak up even at a Plenum of the Central Committee. He gave them a realistic picture of what was happening in the West, and how we, the Soviet Union, really looked in comparison with the West. And his audience, the members of the Central Committee were blindfolded by the ideology, absolutely conservative people. They did not want to hear his report. Inozemtsev was driven off the podium. Gorbachev gave him the floor on purpose; he told him earlier that he would have to speak. It was very rare that a scholar was given the floor at a Plenum of the Central Committee. As a rule, the speakers were secretaries of regional committees, and here they had a scholar on the podium who dared to lecture them, telling them how to live, telling them about what is happening in the world, and in our country, as if they did not know better! That was outrageous.

Gorbachev not only demonstrated that he wanted to associate with new people who were capable of independent thinking, he really wanted to know what was going on in the world, and in our country. So Gorbachev had an internal impulse. He came from Stavropol already convinced that we could not live like that any longer. That was his famous phrase. Even as a secretary of the Regional Committee, he understood that. When he attempted to do some unusual things in his region, some innovations, and was immediately rebuffed from Moscow, either his financing was removed or he was reprimanded. He understood that the system did not allow innovations or changes even at the local level. He was ready for changes. That is why he acted like this. Sometimes our guys would come from the Politburo sessions and say, "He is quite impudent, he says such things that one gets sick from hearing them!"— from their point of view, the *nomenklatura*.

In short, it was clear that he was a new person in the CPSU leadership, and he raised hopes among us, in the apparatus, among the Moscow intelligentsia, even before he became general secretary. This is undoubtedly so. Now, did his colleagues—and you mentioned the military—see the danger that such a person would come and start changing everything and that we would be in trouble, and the country, as they understood it, would be in trouble? As far as the military was concerned, gentlemen, I have to tell you this. There was no opposition, at least more or less organized, even at the tables with drinks. On the part of generals and colonels, there was no opposition, and there could not have been any in the Soviet system.

The general secretary for the generals was God, the Czar, the Chief, and the highest authority. The party was master of the situation. If any general dared to say anything like what Chernyaev or Shakhnazarov discussed with the Italians, or among themselves, he would lose his post the very next day—and they all knew it very well. It was a strictly disciplined cohort of people who were brought up in the party spirit. However, tradition was at work here also: in the Czarist Army officers and generals, even if they did not agree with something, kept it to themselves—the oath of allegiance was above everything else. Therefore, until *glasnost* did its work, until the really crucial changes had begun and the society felt that it was now allowed to organize opposition and to criticize the general secretary and to do it publicly—up until that time the generals were silent and stood at attention.

They soon began to grumble among themselves, to vent their dissatisfaction. But to think that generals could have any influence on any kind of changes in the party leadership, not to allow somebody, or to recommend somebody else instead of Gorbachev—it would have been a completely senseless business. It was absolutely impossible in our system up until a certain moment, approximately before 1989, when the socialist system began to fall apart, and when the issue of troop withdrawal was raised. I think I have responded to all your questions and doubts.

Shakhnazarov: I would like to add to the response to Karen's question. This question represents the essence of our entire meeting because we want to find the roots of the new thinking. To the question about the Italians, I responded that the roots were in our country, not in Italy, not elsewhere. I would say the same to Karen's question. We came to these reforms through our suffering, ourselves. There was a growing understanding in our society that we could not live like this any longer, that it was abnormal. And, therefore, that understanding went through several stages. When I said that it began with Khrushchev—yes, it did begin with Khrushchev—but it began even before Khrushchev. Professor Liberman, before he had the opportunity to publish in a newspaper, wrote letters to the Central Committee proposing a reform of the economic system, because all literate, intelligent economists saw that the system was not competitive. Not that it was bad in principle—it is capable of producing good results with large effort, but it is simply not competitive. They saw that. They moved by the method of trial and failure.

If the West had given a better response to Khrushchev's proposals, then the process probably could have begun then. And then later, as you know, there were several attempts to undertake reforms. [Alexey] Kosygin was nurturing the idea of reforms, even Brezhnev was ready for them. I remember, one time we were sitting in Zavidovo discussing international affairs, and along with that, on Brezhnev's initiative, discussing the need to hold a Plenum on economic reform. Then later Brezhnev changed his mind. He was no reformer in this sense, he did not want to change anything, he did not want any complications, and he rejected the idea. Therefore, Gorbachev grew on this wave of reforms, of reform ideas, which had been maturing for a long time in our society.

Now let me say about Gorbachev as a person. I would like to remind you, if we put the purely political issues aside for a moment, that there are a number of well-known novels in which authors present perspectives of emergence and consolidation of totalitarian societies in our world. One of these novels is [Evgenii] Zamyatin's *We*, another—Orwell's *1984*. In all these novels totalitarian society breaks down only when there emerges a man who is capable of standing up against that society, that system. Gorbachev became such a person for us because our system could only be reformed from the top down. Only Emperor Alexander II could reform the system of serfdom. Only the general secretary of the Central Committee could reform our system because he had the resources that nobody else had. The system would have broken anybody else. But he broke the system down.

Therefore, what do we have? We had many people who understood very well that something had to be done, that we could not carry on like this any longer. They wrote memos, they wrote letters, they published in the press, they used Aesopian language. Writers wrote novels, in which they concealed all this. Everything was clear. But nothing could be done before he emerged—the savior, who snuck through, or maybe life itself led him through to the very top. He became general secretary, and he began to reform the system from the top down. This is how I see all this.

And the last point. When he found himself in that position—Karen, you asked a fair question—why there was no resistance on the part of the conservatives? Did they just keep their mouths shut, and accepted everything? At first, everybody wanted change, and everybody thought that it would be the strengthening of socialism, improvement, democratization, but in principle, the Soviet Union would continue to be a great power. Therefore, the Politburo, science, public opinion, the military, directors of enterprises—everybody supported Gorbachev, unanimously. Everybody thought that he would do what was necessary. Ligachev, who was invited to this conference, but who unfortunately did not come, writes about it in his book. He said that up until 1989 we all supported Gorbachev, we all thought that everything was going as it should. This is true.

And then there emerged Nina Andreyeva, others emerged too, who began to see that the process was not just about an improvement of the system, but it might be moving toward undermining the system as it existed. And from that time on, we saw fears and direct obstructionism. Then what happens later? When you say that there was no resistance on the part of the conservative forces—this is not true. It was precisely that resistance that knocked Gorbachev down after the 19th Party Conference.[5] Because he would make a decision, we would meet in sessions every day, work on documents week after week, design some very important measures—and nothing got done. Days come and go, and nothing changes in real life. Obstruction. The party that was losing power did not want to

---

[5] June 28–July 1, 1988.

implement those measures. And the apparatchiks could not think about anything else other than saving their own skin, and about where to find a place for themselves. The military began to express their dissatisfaction, but they were afraid.

As a result, all this led to the outcome where the general secretary found himself powerless. And the last blow against him was delivered by the democrats led by Yeltsin, who turned Russia against the Soviet Union. This is how I see it. Therefore, I share the opinion that has been expressed here, that the 19th Party Conference was the decisive turning point, because for the first time it clearly outlined our goals of civil society, a lawful state, democratization of the country, economic reform [...]

Chernyaev: [And getting rid of the] Party monopoly.

Shakhnazarov: Political reform, just short of the word "private property;" the Conference had just about everything else. And why did the Conference pass that? Because many people simply did not understand what they were talking about. Let us take "civil society." What is civil society? Even if we started to discuss this issue right now at this table, we would not be able to come to any definition. Lawful state, what is that?— A state where one is supposed to abide by the law. Didn't we have that before? My lawyers were saying all the time, "socialist legality, legitimacy." It means there must be law there. Therefore, first of all, they did not understand what it was all about, and then, secondly, in the beginning everybody was afraid. Anatoly Sergeyevich was right: the general secretary occupied a position like that of the Russian emperor. The emperor is a person who is given to the country by God. Therefore, everybody must listen to him, no questions permitted. I think, Karen, you are absolutely right in asking this question. The key here is that our society nurtured the need for reform inside itself. And this is very good, because it proves that no totalitarian society can last forever, that sooner or later it will be undermined from the inside. Although external influences, of course, are important also, they help internal forces in some way. But if there are no internal forces, nothing will happen.

Blanton: Doug, did you want to add something here?

MacEachin: Just a bit of clarification. What I was describing earlier [the debate in Washington over whether Gorbachev's changes were real] began to be prominent about 1986, by April, which was almost exactly one year after Gorbachev took over the party leadership. The argument about the implications of the new thinking was of sufficient intensity to have been the subject of written "bullets" that were exchanged. This was one of those cases where the existence of an argument that says "it is not significant" is probably the most powerful argument that it is significant. And I think you know what I am saying. There was enough of an argument that said "it is really just a process that in the end would not change anything," to indicate that everybody, or at least a lot of people, saw that it had potentially major implications for the whole security and geostrategic picture.

When I talked about 1988, it was after the 19th Party Conference, and then in the period after that, in September, when the major restructuring took place. The

116

difference then was, I think, that before that happened there was still room for those who wanted to disparage the implications of events in the USSR to make their arguments. Whether you believed it or not, they had room to argue that "that's all right, it will eventually drift back to the Brezhnev-style system." But I think that after the end of 1988, no matter what your slant, you could not very well argue that some major lines had not been crossed, or that the future did not look like it was going to be a very tumultuous few years. You could not very well argue that it was just talk and political rhetoric, which could easily erode back to what it had been before. So that is the distinction that I was making with 1988. If there was a Rubicon, I would argue that it was about at that time.

Matlock: Among senior American officials, I probably recognized earlier than most how serious the potential was for change in Soviet policies. What we could not predict, and I suspect Soviet officials could not either at that time, was how Gorbachev would react when the inevitable difficulties began to develop. It was very clear to us that *perestroika* was not going to be an easy process, and the more serious Gorbachev was about political reform, the more opposition there would be.

Second, most of us, even the ones who were convinced that this was a very serious change, were doubtful that one could change the Soviet economic system incrementally. The whole system was designed to avoid market relations, to make them impossible. Now, how one changes that incrementally, we could not see. Therefore, we were in a position of saying: look, we do not think this is going to improve economic performance. If Gorbachev persists, it will mean that he believes he can control this process. But if he proceeds the way he says, he probably cannot control the process. When he realizes he cannot control it, will he revert to the old methods? Or will he let matters pass beyond the point that the old methods will no longer be effective?

That was the big question in our minds, at least in the minds of those who were convinced that *perestroika* was genuine and dedicated to profound change. We knew that Gorbachev was a forceful person and very bright. We could not believe that if it really came to letting political reform get out of control, he would not clamp down and use force. The surprise to us was, as he increasingly demonstrated, first in 1989 in Eastern Europe, and then in regard to the Soviet Union itself, that he was not willing to use force to keep the system in power, or even to keep himself in power. That was the big surprise, and the unpredictable part. I would be interested in the comments of our Russian colleagues regarding their thoughts at the time and whether it was valid for us to keep a question in our minds as to how far Gorbachev would let the reform process go.

Levesque: I think this is a very central question, indeed. When *perestroika* developed, everyone was convinced that there would be a limit to change at a certain point in time, but not only in the United States, and the U.S. government, but in Eastern Europe, for instance. Those reformist leaders were convinced that there were limits to change that could be introduced, but that these limits were never clarified, and they seemed to be expanding all the time. And finally, we all discovered that there was no limit at all, to the great surprise of everyone. But even those reformers in Eastern Europe were saying that if there were these limits, they were not quite clear about them, and they were always trying to identify them. And each time we set a given limit, in a hypothetical way, it kept withdrawing. So, that is one of the big mysteries of the whole process.

My follow-up question to Jack: Is it your belief that in Gorbachev's mind, at some point in time, there were some limits, but that he had to withdraw them progressively? And in your own mind, from the beginning, were there some limits that you saw in the process that was going on?

Chernyaev: I will try to give you some logic of the evolution of Gorbachev's ideas, and, subsequently, the policy. It is an absolute mistake to think that the new thinking of 1985 and the new thinking of 1990 were the same thing. It was not like the new thinking emerged in Gorbachev's head, and then he just followed that scheme moving the society along, and building his policy. Nothing like that. Elements of new thinking had been accumulating, and each element had been developing internally. Everything began with the idea of improvement of socialism, from appealing back to Lenin's NEP [New Economic Policy], from the efforts to understand what Lenin had said before he died, and that which was interpreted incorrectly and subsequently smothered by Stalin. And had he not smothered it, everything would have been different in our country.

He [Gorbachev] thoroughly read all the Congresses and the Plenums of Lenin's time, of the end of 1919, 1920, and 1921. And he was not doing it just to preserve the image of a Marxist-Leninist leader, of a leader loyal to the ideology. In his heart, he wanted to understand the capacity of Soviet society, the possibility of reforming it. You probably know from his memoirs, he said, "Why did Khrushchev's reforms fail? Why did Kosygin's reforms fail? Because they did not touch the system. They were doomed to failure." And for the first three or four years he was convinced that we should not touch the system, that we would not go beyond the limits of socialism.

Twice—in 1989 and in 1990 (I wrote about it in my books)—when we went to Foros[6] on vacation, he called me up on the very first day and said, "Tolya, let us write an article on 'socialism and the Market'." He was saying that the opposition was growing from the basis that he was abandoning socialism. "I have to prove to them that socialism includes the Market." Similar to what Jack was saying here, "Market yes, private property no."

He spoke about some approaches, some approximations, like cooperation and leasing, but to state that private property was sacred—that he could not allow himself to do because of ideological considerations. And, by the way, it was also his personal conviction, i.e. he stood on this position not only because he was

---

[6] A village on the southern tip of the Crimean peninsula where a government dacha was located. The Soviet leader was vacationing in Foros on August 19, 1991, when hard-liners instigated the coup against him.

afraid that they would tear him to pieces for, essentially, returning capitalism into the Soviet system.

These two elements were constantly struggling inside him. He believed in the possibility of reforming socialism up until the very end, until everything began to fall apart. He believed that socialism could be improved, that it could be made socialism with a human face, even better than Dubček's in 1968. This is just one side of the issue.

There was also another side. It shows that he genuinely counted on an internal reform of socialism. That is why he held on to the party, counting on Lenin's famous idea that in our situation only the party could be the leader, only the party could direct everything, and change society.

He was trying to turn the party into a vanguard of *perestroika*. That was an absolutely dumb, excuse me, idea, from the very beginning. I was deeply convinced that it was—maybe my colleagues will not agree with me—because the party did not exist as a public or even as a political organization for a long time. There were 20 million party members, but in essence it was represented by the *nomenklatura*, comprising maybe several hundred thousand members—the party bureaucrats.

That party was designed for the administration and management of Soviet society. But such a party was not capable of changing the system, under which it enjoyed at least some negligible privileges, if you compare them now with the privileges that the "democrats" enjoy. It was incapable, but Gorbachev held on to it until the last moment.

Yakovlev and others suggested that he should have split the party already in 1988, even at the beginning of 1988. Gorbachev understood long ago that something was wrong with the party. This is why the famous Plenum of January 1987 was designed as an internal stimulus to start the party reform, to move it. He understood that it was the source of resistance, the *nomenklatura*. That is why he put the issue about reform of the political system so sharply.

And Jack is quite right about it—the economy could not turn into a market economy within the framework of our socialism. And when they began to introduce market elements, when they began to cut off pieces from our planned economic system, which was built according to a scheme, piece by piece—a system where, as Gorbachev liked to say, when they needed to build a latrine in a village 100 kilometers from Orenburg they had to ask Moscow for permission—once that system was slightly pricked, it immediately began to fall to pieces. It was a monolith that was built and then ossified over the decades. It was impossible to build a real market within that framework. And the party held that system together, it played the role of a carcass, of a binding force.

Gorbachev understood that the party needed change. But he still believed that it was possible to turn at least a part of that party into his base. And I think that this, along with the nationalities issue, was Gorbachev's major mistake that led to the failure—precisely that he held on to the party up to the very last moment. He was trying to change it, but still he was holding on to it. Moreover, even when he understood that it had already turned into an opposition force, he held on to the position of general secretary. We were telling him, "Why are you holding on to this business? Quit the party, and then some healthy part of it will pull itself toward you, and then you will have a public organization of your own, your base. Otherwise you will find yourself alone. The intelligentsia is beginning to feel disillusioned, they think that you are slowing down." And it was the major force.

Shakhnazarov: He had a chance to take the position that was later taken by Yeltsin.

Chernyaev: Yes, that is true. We were telling him to resign, to leave his position. But he said no. He told me directly, "If I release the chain by which I am holding this monster, using the position of general secretary—the influence of the image of general secretary, the inertia of it—if I break this chain, this monster will overthrow me the very next day. I control it by this chain." It was a puzzle for us.

We think it was a mistake. However, he thinks that we did not understand anything, and that that was the only way. Such was the logic of developments. It was present in those articles about socialism and the market that he attempted to write three times (one of them was published)—and, by the way, he was preparing to write another one on the same topic right before the putsch, in Foros, along with the draft of the Union Treaty that Georgy was in charge of. However, I have to mention that, essentially, by that time in his conception of socialism, all the main elements of it had been emasculated, and only the form remained. There was nothing left there from our classic Soviet socialism, to which we were accustomed, and which we, excuse me, had built [laughter]. These were the limits.

Blanton: Were there limits?

Shakhnazarov: I would like to state that I completely agree with everything that Anatoly Sergeyevich has just said. I would not even take the floor to add anything to it, except for his last phrase. Why? Because when we are talking about socialism we need to define what we have in mind. Gorbachev meant everything good and healthy that was in our system. And there were elements that are now present in many countries and that are not called socialism. I think that here, in the United States, there are may social elements that are very visible. Another example—[Yasuhiro] Nakasone, a well-known prime minister, thought that Japan was half-socialist, and he wrote about it.

In other words, if you do not take the stiff model that developed in our country as the example, but if you take what we have now lost, or are in the process of losing—free health care, free public education, the large network of institutions that were designed to take care of people, and which are being missed now, including the resort facilities, sanatoriums, day care facilities, nurseries, and so on—we are longing for these now. We should have preserved all of them. That is also socialism. You do not have to use the word "socialism," you can call it "public capitalism," or you can call it anything else. This is what Gorbachev wanted to preserve.

Roughly speaking, the main task was to ennoble that society, and to link the social benefits with genuine democracy. And I believe that it was our blunder that

120

we thought that it would be rather easy to do. All rights and political freedoms were written down in our Constitution. Therefore, we should have just brought real life into alignment with the Constitution.

When somebody asks, what was Gorbachev's main mistake, I have a standard answer: I say that he made two mistakes, or that he can be blamed for two things. First of all, that he brought political freedom to our country. And second, that he did not abandon that freedom when they began to use it to destroy the state.

On other issues I completely agree with Anatoly Sergeyevich. But I would emphasize that the idea of socialism is alive, it will live forever, and moreover, I believe that the future belongs to socialism. The open question is whether we will be able to combine the idea of equality with the idea of freedom. During the time of the French Revolution they had an easy solution—they just proclaimed equality and freedom. You and I, however, live in a century when it became clear that those two ideas were mutually exclusive, and that it was very difficult to implement them both. One can say that we broke our necks when we tried to do it the easy way.

Zubok: I would like to ask you, our Russian participants, to return to the question that was posed. It seems that Gorbachev never raised the issue of limits—that we cannot go any further, otherwise we will die as a great power, otherwise we will lose our spheres of influence in Eastern Europe: those issues that Professor Levesque has called the limits, the line that could not have been crossed. Sometimes Gorbachev spoke at Politburo sessions like a statist. But did you have the impression that he did not even think about that, that if the Soviet Union undertook those reforms it could cease to be a great power, it would lose its geostrategic, geopolitical sphere of influence in Europe?

Chernyaev: Gorbachev developed ideas that were completely different from his predecessors about what the Soviet Union was as a great power. Our previous leaders associated that primarily with military might, with political and military influence over a great territory, not only of Eastern Europe, but of other continents as well, in opposition to another great power, which you represent here.

And if you presented Gorbachev with the question: would you sacrifice the freedom that you had given to the countries of Eastern Europe, to your colleagues—in Poland, in Czechoslovakia, and elsewhere—in the name of preserving the imperial image, and of great power status in the old Soviet meaning of the word, he would say that the question for him was absurd. He would say that he told the general secretaries from the very beginning that they were responsible for their policy only to their own peoples, to their parties. That conversation happened right after [Konstantin] Chernenko's funeral. Literally, on the next day, he gathered all of them in his office in the Kremlin, and told them that from then on there was no more Brezhnev Doctrine, that kindergarten was over. "Where you go, how you get there—that is your business, I will not interfere. I will not interfere even when you ask me for it." And he carried it through to the end. They made efforts to ask for it. Not directly, but sometimes through his colleagues, through the apparatus, through the *nomenklatura*. They tried to appeal when they understood that the Soviet props to their regime had disappeared, when they got scared for their seats. Therefore, he did not have a problem there.

However, he did have some illusions. He believed that if he gave freedom to the countries of Eastern Europe, then they would choose to follow *perestroika* and socialism with a human face. There we see the illusions, or a lack of understanding, maybe even a lack of knowledge about the depth of all the processes that were underway in our relations. They had chosen something completely different—not socialism with a human face. Moreover, they turned away from us. Somewhere in his heart, he had some instinctive understanding of that turn of events.

I remember one conversation with him when we were in Kiev on the occasion of Gorbachev's meeting with Helmut Kohl, it was in the summer of 1990.[7] On the way back [Yuli] Kvitsinsky, [Vitaly] Ignatenko, and I were in Mikhail Sergeyevich's cabin on the plane. We touched upon Eastern Europe, and he said, "We are pretty tired of them, and they are tired of us. So let us be patient. Some people constantly push me, demand that I give them orders, advice—to Honecker, for example." It was after the conversation with Kohl, who complained about Honecker to Gorbachev, that he did not want to undertake anything, that he was hurting himself. Gorbachev said, "I said no! Let them deal with each other independently."

And even as far as the economy was concerned—nothing like that. They switched to hard currency. That undermined our economic relations. We immediately turned from being creditors to being debtors of our allies. I would not say that it was a conscious policy of the "dismissal of the empire," as Gorbachev sometimes used to say. It was a natural and logical consequence of his position— since we were introducing freedom in our country, we would hold to the same principle as far as our allies and all other states were concerned. We will not interfere in their internal affairs. Let them decide how to build relations with us in the future.

Gorbachev underestimated the fact that the forces of good were not very strong in the world yet. The geopolitical conceptions, and the rules of the game were still being built on the basis of evil, on the basis of a crude egoistic model of development. He had some illusions and some romanticism about that. But he never regretted doing it that way. When he is asked: how come you gave away Bulgaria, East Germany, etc., he responds: "Gave away? To whom? Poland—to the Poles. Bulgaria—to the Bulgarians. Czechoslovakia—to the Czechs and the Slovaks. Who did I give it away to? You have no right even to pose this question." I hope, Vlad Zubok, that I have clarified some things. He had absolutely no problems with it. And no regrets. There was some frustration because they turned away from us.

---

[7] The meeting in question was almost certainly June 14, 1989, in Bonn; see Document No. 67.

Shakhnazarov: I would like to add from documents to what Anatoly Sergeyevich has just said. When I became his assistant, we traveled to all the socialist countries beginning in March [1988]. First of all, we went to Yugoslavia. There, on the plane, I informed him about Nina Andreyeva's article. He did not know about it yet. It was on March 14.[8] [...]

I traveled with him to all the countries except for Poland. I was sick then, and Anatoly Sergeyevich went to Poland. And we had our first conversation in Belgrade, with the chairman of the Presidium of Yugoslavia, [Lazar] Mojsov. Gorbachev told him, "No one can impose anything on anyone. We have common socialist ideals, a common heritage in the classics of Marxism, but each party develops this heritage through its own experience, its traditions, and the consideration of its international position. As for big and small states, I said in my talk with Reagan: today neither the USSR nor the U.S. can impose its will on any country."—I would question that—"They could pressure them, but not impose their will." The world is different now, each state strives to determine its fate independently, and we must take that into account. Of course, the major powers carry more responsibility than the smaller countries. But they must not crush the rights of others. I can tell you that this was his absolute conviction from the very beginning. That was clear on the second day, or within a couple of days after he was elected general secretary.

In our Department,[9] where I was deputy director and in charge of relations with Poland, Czechoslovakia, and the GDR, there was First Deputy [Oleg] Rakhmanin. He was an expert on China, and a very good, knowledgeable, expert. He translated Khrushchev's conversation with Mao Zedong. He was a very conservative person, a very strong fundamentalist. He decided, like many other people, that Gorbachev's coming to power meant the end to stagnation—when we had our weak, old, senile general secretaries—that now we had a strong young man who would discipline the socialist camp because it had become very disorderly: [János] Kádár was doing whatever he wanted; Honecker was hiding some things from us, making deals with West Germany, trading with them, accepting loans, letting people travel; [Nicolae] Ceauşescu was doing nobody-knew-what; the Poles flirted with the Americans and planned to purchase Boeings instead of our airplanes.

In other words, he thought, it was time to call them to order. So he published two articles in *Pravda*, and they were received as a reinstatement of the Brezhnev Doctrine. (Even though the Brezhnev Doctrine had never been published anywhere, we thought that there was such a doctrine.) We immediately began to receive a huge number of responses to those articles. First of all, our

[8] Nina Andreyeva, a teacher from Leningrad, wrote a letter critical of Gorbachev's educational reform program that became a focal point for public and internal party debates after it was published in the conservative newspaper *Sovetskaya Rossiya* on March 13, 1988.
[9] The CC CPSU's Department of Relations with the Communist and Workers' Parties of Socialist Countries was known internally simply as *Otdel,* "the Department."

liberal-minded friends called us, followed by official phone calls—"Is this really the official point of view of the new leadership? If so, it is a scandal. Where are we going?"

When Gorbachev found out about it, he was mad.[10] I was told—I was not his assistant yet at that time—that he was throwing papers around in a style very uncharacteristic of him, and saying, "What is happening here? Why are they portraying me as some kind of monster who has come to power?" He gave instructions to send out telegrams with explanations of our position, that the article was wrong, that we respected the rights of the socialist countries, that there would be more freedom and democracy, mutual consultation. Some time after that Rakhmanin was sacked, removed from the apparatus. Therefore, from this point of view, there could not be any doubts regarding his position, from the very beginning, that there should be normal relations, and there was no thought at all about keeping that conglomerate which we called the socialist commonwealth together by any means.

At the same time, it would be a mistake, and even an underestimation of Gorbachev if we think that this man, to whom destiny had given the reins of this huge empire, had an attitude of "you can go now, we do not need you any more." Of course not. In his own way, he wanted to preserve that big commonwealth, which would be built anew on a new basis. As a statist, he understood that the Soviet Union needed a belt of friendly states along its borders. He believed that an alliance was necessary, a military and a political alliance, as long as international relations were like they were at the time. He was a statist. But at the same time, it was not his main priority, he did not want to hold it together by violent means, just as he did not want to hold the Soviet Union together by violent means. This is very important.

And now regarding the issue of how far he could go, as Vlad asked. This is what I can say: on some issues he is still undecided. For instance, let us take the issue of private property on land, up to and including buying and selling land. I can tell you that I belong to a group of people who think that under our [current] Russian conditions, it would lead to big trouble if land could be bought and sold freely now because many agricultural enterprises which might not be the most profitable are going under before our eyes, and the land is falling into the hands of speculators. This means that our peasants could go bankrupt very quickly, lose that land, and subsequently that a multi-million-person crowd would flood the job market. That would create great pressure on the political system, up to peasant riots, a "Vendée,"[11] revolutions, you name it.

Therefore, one has to be very careful with this. Our current leaders do not understand it. Russia is not like Poland with stable farming traditions, and private

---

[10] Rakhmanin published the articles under the pseudonym "Vladimirov." See Document No. 2 for a related Politburo discussion.

[11] The Vendée was an area of major counter-revolutionary activity in France in the 1790s.

farms. Gorbachev once told me personally—and I think he said the same thing to Anatoly many times—he said, "You know, Georgy, you all think that I have some sort of ideological brakes that would stop me at some point. Nothing like that. I can go as far as the situation demands." And his goal was to let the country, the people, live better. "So, if they prove that private property would help, we will introduce private property." But he had to be convinced that it was so.

Chernyaev: On Gorbachev and ideology. He even managed to quote Lenin in his attitude toward ideology. He used to say "Remember what Lenin said, that he would not stop before any ideological taboos, that he would discard them and decide the issues on the basis of common sense." He managed to find those quotes. And he actually acted on them.

Now, as an illustration of what Georgy was talking about, about his attitude to our allies, here is a Politburo discussion of [Nikolay] Ryzhkov's conversation with [Lubomír] Štrougal—he was prime minister of Czechoslovakia then. It was November 19, 1987.[12]

Ryzhkov was sharing his impressions [...] He said that Czechoslovakia was pregnant with change, according to Štrougal. Štrougal said to Ryzhkov that we should have begun the reform in the 1970s. He also said that if they started *perestroika* in their country the results would be visible faster than in any other country. Gorbachev comments, "Yes, it is a cultured country. And that means a lot. That is what we are lacking here."

Ryzhkov informs the Politburo about Štrougal's anxiety about the forthcoming Plenum of the Central Committee, that he expects some serious struggle, and that such struggle could be very dangerous in the situation of transition. Gorbachev says, "We should meet this cultured government halfway. Our line will be: to participate in the discussion of everything in a friendly manner. But only they must make the decisions. If the question of distributing posts there arises, let them think through everything themselves and decide [...] God forbid we go to them with our own jumble of thoughts on the theme of their *perestroika*. It could destroy everything."

Ryzhkov reminds the audience that we had a cautious attitude to Štrougal in our leadership, who was not very pure ideologically. Gorbachev comments, "Štrougal is a good prime minister, but it is unlikely that he would be able to unite the leadership as a general secretary. The split there is coming from [Vasil] Bil'ak. I hinted at this to him." Then Ryzhkov said, "Against the background of the other socialist countries' prime ministers, Štrougal stands above everyone." Gorbachev again says, "Make sure you do not interfere in their affairs under any conditions, even if they ask you about it." [Laughter]

Oleg Skvortsov: I would like to move back to the agenda, because during the first session we discussed issues that were quite removed from what we mentioned in the agenda. I would like to go to some specific issues that Gorbachev

---

[12] This is the date of the Politburo's discussion. See Document No. 16.

had to face when he came to power in 1985. I believe there was a complex of problems that we can mention now. To start with, it should be noted that by the mid-1980s we had a coalition of all the most developed industrial countries against the Soviet Union, and also, we lost China. So we saw a ring of enemies around the country.

The second factor that influenced Gorbachev's decisions in 1985 was the technological backwardness of the Soviet Union. We were lagging behind all the industrialized countries of the West. As you know, starting in the 1970s, there was a microchip-computer revolution in the West, new technologies.

The third set of problems, and we are going to touch upon that later, consisted of the internal policy issues in the Soviet Union. Those were also very difficult, sometimes intractable, issues for the new leadership. Subsequently, when I am through with this thought, I will have a follow-up question to our veterans: do you believe that the situation in place in 1985, by the time Gorbachev came to power, do you think it was intractable, and the fall of the Soviet Union six years later was inevitable? Because, in my opinion, there were more difficult situations in the history of Russia, and Russia was able to overcome those previous crises with better results, or at least it remained intact. That would be my question to you.

But before that, I would like to go back to Eastern Europe. Of course, we are thinking about the impact of the new ideas on Eastern Europe, but we forget the issue of how Eastern European parties were formed. The leaders of those countries had to become more nationalistic in their behavior to ensure that they remained in power in the Eastern European countries. The next step after that—after they would become more nationalistic, more independent of the CPSU, would be to push for liberalization. And that was a step toward their own fall. So for them it was a vicious circle. Was the Soviet Union in a position to influence these policies, in this situation? [...]

As for the election of Gorbachev in 1985, in my opinion this was forced on the Politburo by the situation, because there was no alternative. Here our Western participants tend to forget about it, and do not ask this question. I think that when [Yurii] Andropov died, Gorbachev had a chance to become general secretary. But he was not elected, and that was not because the Brezhnev–Chernenko clan had won, but because they wanted more time to make a judgment about whether Gorbachev would be appropriate for them, or whether they could find somebody else to reform the country differently. Because they saw both his strengths and his weaknesses, which you know very well—the fact that he came from Stavropol, that it was not the most difficult region, that he did not know the economy very well, did not know other problems. That made them extremely cautious. Therefore, they needed a pause, in my view. That year, and then a year-and-a-half passed, and there were no other candidates.

Therefore, Gorbachev was chosen as a matter of necessity. In my view, we should not underestimate this, because it is a very important factor. And to conclude, I would like to return to my question: Were those problems so unsolvable that from March 1985 to December 1991, in just six years, we lost everything that we had? Like a company that went bankrupt instead of selling some of its assets and making a profit while preserving the rest, we had totally liquidated our company. Mr. Matlock put it very well in his cable about the procedure "Chapter 11," about bankruptcy in the United States which the Soviet Union had now declared.[13]

Vilém Prečan: Only one remark. When Gorbachev told the Czechoslovak leadership, "it is up to you," in 1987, it meant a message to the Czechoslovak society that there is no hope, because the Soviet Union under Brezhnev gave all the power to [Gustáv] Husák, Bil'ak, and others, who were so powerful. So, in 1987, it was like cynicism, this message. But later, two years later, in 1989, they did not get any help from Gorbachev when the people turned their back to the leadership under [Miloš] Jakeš. So, it developed positively. But I remember in the summer of 1989, there was the big question—how far? Where is Gorbachev's limit? How far can we go without Soviet interference? Because the memory of 1968 was deep in everybody who was over 30.

Andrzej Paczkowski: I have some questions to Mr. Chernyaev only. The first is: if I understand correctly, you were with Gorbachev in Poland in July 1988. And many Polish analysts, of the opposition bloc of today, thought that during Gorbachev–[Wojciech] Jaruzelski meetings, Gorbachev pushed Jaruzelski to reform Poland. But until now, we have no evidence from those meetings, only very formal information given by Jaruzelski to the members of the [Polish] Politburo. But very general. My question is: Are those analysts correct that Gorbachev pushed Jaruzelski to reform Poland? And my second question is: Was there any influence from the Polish events on the Soviet political elite in the mid-1980s? Especially, I am thinking about the debate which took place in the Polish Communist Party in the autumn of 1987. There was a very long memorandum from [Mieczysław] Rakowski to Jaruzelski in which Rakowski wrote that real socialism had lost all creative possibilities; it is necessary to recognize the opposition in Poland. And a big part for the free market in Poland is necessary. My question is: Were those thoughts known by the Soviet elite—that memorandum, and other papers—or did they exist only in Polish political circles?

Chernyaev: Georgy will respond to the second question, because he was involved in those issues in the Central Committee. But because I substituted for him during Gorbachev's visit to Poland, that you mentioned, I can give you my testimony that there were no attempts to teach Jaruzelski what he should do in Poland, whether he should accelerate the reforms, what kind of reforms, and how to do it—there was not even a hint. Gorbachev would not allow himself to act like that even with Honecker.

One has to say that Jaruzelski enjoyed Gorbachev's almost absolute trust and respect, as everybody knows. He thought that Jaruzelski was a man who was

---

[13] See Document No. 43.

capable of gradually leading Poland out of a crisis and to normalcy, to preserve it as an ally, as a friendly state. And Gorbachev had no concerns about that as long as Jaruzelski was in power.

Georgy can correct me, but I think that in his conversations with other Polish figures, Gorbachev always followed precisely the same line as far as Jaruzelski was concerned: the USSR approves of Jaruzelski, and we believe that you should approve of him too.

To Rakowski he related with some doubt, but with great respect. Rakowski also was attracted to Gorbachev, and they had several conversations—Georgy can tell you about them. But also, there exist transcripts of those conversations, notes were taken by the interpreter, and sometimes they spoke Russian. It was written down in Polish, but there is also a Russian version, and we have it in our archive in the [Gorbachev] Foundation. There is not a hint, not a single line about it. So it is quite natural that you do not know anything about it—because there was nothing like that. [Laughter]

Shakhnazarov: In our *nomenklatura*, in our apparatus of the Central Committee, Poland was seen as the pearl in the crown of the Russian empire. It always occupied the first place in all respects, and even at the party Congresses, when somebody needed to open the discussion, the floor usually went to Poland. During sessions of the Political Consultative Committee of the Warsaw Treaty Organization, a speech by our general secretary was always followed by a speech by a Pole. As far as the Polish leadership was concerned, you probably know that [Edward] Gierek was not chosen in Moscow. He was chosen by the Polish leadership. Moscow wanted to elect Jaruzelski, already then, ten years before everything happened.

We had a head of a sector, whose name was Kustikov. He can testify that our leadership, especially our apparatus, believed that Jaruzelski was the most talented reform-minded representative of the Polish leadership. Later, I would like to join Anatoly Sergeyevich in saying, Jaruzelski enjoyed absolute respect and trust from our leadership as a cultured person, good leader, genuine Pole, and at the same time—a big friend of the Soviet Union. His unusual biography is proof to that. His father was killed in the Soviet Union. Jaruzelski himself defended Poland with the Soviet Army.

Now, as far as Rakowski is concerned: of course, we knew about all the documents that were written by your leadership, there were a sufficient number of ways of getting them from Poland. Special services did their work, the intelligence, and there were also Poles who considered it their duty to pass along certain materials. Then it was not considered some kind of a betrayal of national interests, because we were a kind of single unit. We had a contradictory attitude towards Rakowski. In the Department (*Otdel*) of the Central Committee, where I worked and was in charge of Poland, in particular, there was a group of people, not a big one, who sympathized with Rakowski, and supported him from the very beginning. They tried to persuade others that he was the man on whom we should place our bets, or one of those on whom we can place our bets, who

128

understands the real situation in Poland, and the dangers that popular movements represent, in particular, [the trade union] Solidarity.

At the same time, there were many people opposed to him, who thought that even if he was not a straight-out traitor, then he still was from the liberal intelligentsia who could do great harm to our relations, and to the cause of socialism in Poland with his views. That was the prevailing attitude towards Rakowski in the Soviet leadership. I attended all the sessions of the special Commission on Poland of the Politburo, and I do not recall a single instance when Rakowski, or [Andrzej] Werblan, or any others like them—dissidents within the apparatus—were not criticized. We believed that those were the people who spoiled everything in Poland.

That particular memorandum which you have mentioned met with expressed disapproval on our side. Our leadership was also very disturbed by Rakowski's frequent and long statements in the press. He wrote long articles in which he deliberated about the future of socialism, Russian–Polish relations, and the like. Very often he expressed unorthodox ideas. Therefore, he was criticized in all respects, and there were even efforts, in the Brezhnev times, to put pressure on him in order to prevent him from making further statements. But later there was a turning point—sometime around the Polish crisis [of 1980–1981], our leadership understood that even such people could be useful, that we should not push them away. And then there was a breakthrough, and for the first time Rakowski became a member of the Central Committee, as you remember.

Therefore, when you consider the situation as a whole, as we have done numerous times, with some of the people present here, and as we discussed it in Poland, I can only reiterate that of course we wanted to preserve Poland in the socialist commonwealth up until the time when its future itself was in question. We did everything that we could. But in the Commission on Poland all the discussions were concluded by statements to the effect that we should not put pressure on Poland, and that it was impossible to resolve anything there with force, that we had to reject that option once and forever—Beginning from Suslov, who was the first chairman of the Commission, then Andropov replaced him, then Chernenko, and then Gorbachev, under whom it was dissolved. All four chairmen began their work with the following statement: let us do everything possible to preserve Poland as an ally, but let us never allow even a thought of using force there, as it was in Hungary or Czechoslovakia.

Suslov said openly, and he was the harshest person, the ideologue: "In the worst case, we will give up Poland; what can we do? We cannot fight for it, it is out of consideration." But he also said that precisely because we could not fight for it we should create an impression, as much as possible, that we could do it. Because that was the only possibility for our side to keep the Poles from undertaking extreme steps, like leaving the Soviet bloc. That is why we undertook all kinds of propaganda actions and the like. And I can tell you honestly, I could even take an oath on the Bible, truth, only the truth, that our leadership excluded the possibility of, and would have never taken a decision to introduce, troops.

129

Although of course, God directs us, nobody knows what could have happened in the end, if there were confrontations, provocations, if the troops had been pulled into the events automatically, and so on, and so forth.

Paczkowski: Excuse me, when did that Commission of Poland finish its work? What year?

Shakhnazarov: It was sometime in 1988, or even in 1989. It was formally disbanded but in reality it had ceased to exist before that; it did not convene for almost two years before that. Then they recalled that such a Commission existed, and the Central Committee made the decision to dissolve it. But I cannot tell you the exact date of that decision. It was some time in 1988. May be even in 1987.

James Hershberg: Jack Matlock has conducted what he calls "an autopsy on an empire." I am wondering if we are now almost in a position to complete the death certificate of the Brezhnev Doctrine, which until now has had an empty space next to the line for "time of death," because there is an ongoing debate over whether the Brezhnev Doctrine was, as Georgy has suggested, already dead by the time of the Polish crisis of 1980 to 1981, or, as certainly most Americans did not believe it was dead, until the events of 1989 actually took place. And I would be interested if our Russian colleagues could inform us about how they saw the attitudes on the admissibility of forcible intervention in the allies develop. I want to point to a couple of documents.

Georgy Shakhnazarov's notes for Gorbachev, for the Politburo meeting of October 6, 1988,[14] include the passage that "When it came to a crisis in any of [the East European countries], we had to come to the rescue at the cost of huge material, political, and even human sacrifice. We should clearly see, moreover, that in the future any possibility to extinguish crises by military means must be fully excluded. Even the old leadership seems to have already realized this, at least with regard to Poland." Mr. Chernyaev suggested that at the time of Chernenko's funeral, Gorbachev told the East European communist leaders that kindergarten is over. Their countries' fates are their responsibilities—implying that in the beginning of Gorbachev's term already it was commonly understood that the Brezhnev Doctrine was dead.

And yet on the American side, even in Jack Matlock's cable of February 1989,[15] he had advanced so far as to say that the Soviet Union "might well refrain" from using force in Eastern Europe, so long as there was no serious attempt to leave the Warsaw Pact.

So I am wondering, first, where do you see a commonly understood consensus in Moscow emerging that force cannot be used? Second, was this even in a case where a country might seriously attempt to leave the Warsaw Pact, or was that something that, as Jacques Levesque's book suggested, was only conceded after the events of November 1989, or even possibly March 1990, when the

---

[14] Document No. 29.
[15] Document No. 45.

130

GDR made clear its choice to join West Germany, and not maintain a separate existence. Third, how do you disentangle the sources for this evolution? Do you see it as, essentially, a moral, principled decision by Gorbachev that force is inadmissible? To what extent was it a pragmatic decision—that it would destroy *perestroika* internally? And different pragmatic reasons that it would destroy possibilities for relations with the West, from a positive standpoint.

And also, to what extent did the fear of American sanctions, or Western sanctions, in the case of an intervention, and in particular, what effect if any did the Reagan administration sanctions, such as the limitations of the pipeline deal, aid to the Mujaheddin in Afghanistan—to what extent did they influence considerations as to the pragmatic costs of continuing the Brezhnev Doctrine? And I will just leave it there with one small addition to put on the table. Doug MacEachin mentioned April 1986. I have always wondered whether another event of April 1986—Chernobyl—was the first contingent, or unanticipated, event that forced Gorbachev to change his timetable, the first event that forced him to begin to lose control over the entire process of new thinking, reform, in many different aspects. And really, until that moment it was a process that he could control. From then on he progressively began to lose control.

William Wohlforth: This is a pure addendum to Jim Hershberg's question. I wish to add nothing of my own. I want only to clarify what we mean by the use of force. If by the use of force we mean the sending in of troops, their occupation of the country, their use of weapons, directly against demonstrators—that is one thing. But force is used if you deploy military forces, and you act as if you are willing to use it even if you, in your heart of hearts, are not. So that in effect the Soviet Union did use force in Poland in the Polish crisis of 1980–81 by having maneuvers. I just want to make sure that the distinction is clear between how Gorbachev acted in the Polish crisis of 1989—namely, not even a hint of the willingness to use force—as compared to the earlier policy. In other words, the distinction is clear.

Pawel Machcewicz: I would also like to refer to the Brezhnev Doctrine and to Jim's question. In July 1988, when Gorbachev was in Warsaw, he had a meeting with Polish intellectuals at the Royal Castle in Warsaw. It was supposed to be the meeting that would prove how democratic and how open a leader Gorbachev was, and that he was able to face all, even the most difficult, questions. But there was one question he could not, he did not want to answer, raised by one of Polish intellectuals, Marcin Król, who openly asked whether Gorbachev could say that the Brezhnev Doctrine was not valid any more.

And Gorbachev, according to the testimony, seemed very perplexed, and he said that he would think it over, and that he would send back a written answer. But no answer came back, as far as we know. And my question is whether you remember the situation and whether, really, any thoughts were given to this question whether the Soviet leadership thought it would be appropriate to address this question openly, or was it too sensitive a topic to raise in such an official way? Or were you still not ready to say that the doctrine was simply a matter of the past? And only a year later, during 1989, you somehow came to the conclusion that it was a dead doctrine.

David Wolff: While we are throwing out possible dates for the end of the Brezhnev Doctrine, I was just going through the chronology. On page 5 of the chronology prepared by the National Security Archive—November 6, 1987—we have a meeting between [George] Shultz, William Webster, Robert Gates, and CIA analysts, at which Shultz disagrees with Gates, pointing to the renunciation of the Brezhnev Doctrine. I am not quite sure where he is referring to a renunciation [...] previously too. But that is in there without anything further. The date on that is November 6, 1987. It is on page 5 of the chronology.

János Rainer: Just two brief comments for the afternoon session, on the topic that is on the floor now. The first is that the development of this new thinking of Gorbachev and his inner circle concerning what has to be changed within the system and international relationships, especially in the socialist camp, shows a striking similarity to the development of the mid-1950s revisionists. First of all—the thinking of Imre Nagy in Hungary.

The second is that the minutes, the lengthy protocol of the first official meeting between Kádár and Gorbachev in September 1985, I think, provides a very interesting insight into the thinking of Gorbachev being in power in this early stage. As far as I know, this protocol has been only published in Hungarian, and maybe it was not published either in Russian or in English. And from this picture one can have a little bit of a different impression of Gorbachev's attitude from what was described in the morning. First of all, during the conversation, Gorbachev was talking a lot about the change, but mainly in very general terms.

For example, "The system had not changed for decades, it is high time for a shake-up." But only in general. As for definite questions, the attitude to change was rather technical. For example, he was talking about how to change the management of the large socialist enterprises. And that was all. But concerning the issues that Kádár touched on, for example, he behaved more like the first secretary of an empire. Just two brief examples. He suspiciously asked Kádár, "What about your very close and wide contacts with the West? What are your purposes? For example, in conducting 50 percent of your foreign trade with the West. Why don't you turn to us?" And Kádár answered in short, "Because we requested loans from the Soviet Union, but we were refused. That is why we had to turn to the West."

The second example. Kádár reflected on the 1985 electoral reform in Hungary. The sense was that it was necessary to nominate at least two candidates in each electoral district. But some thought that it was not enough. So he turned to Gorbachev and told him, "I had a rough Hungarian thought that our system had no proper tools to let the steam out of the engine when the tension is higher than optimal." And Gorbachev's remark was, "What do you think? We have a strong sword of criticism and self-criticism. Isn't that enough?" So the question is whether Gorbachev's thinking, Gorbachev's attitude was different within the inner circle of aides, and different while in official negotiations with reform-minded partners—communist leaders, like Kádár?

132

Chernyaev: I will try to respond to some of the questions. On Poland and the crisis of the beginning of the 1980s. I know about publications, and not only calculations of our analysts and scholars, but also publications of the Central Committee apparatus officials who express a different opinion. Some of them think that there was a question about an invasion, of a repetition of 1968, others think that it was absolutely excluded. My position is based on certain facts, and I think that at that moment, in 1980–81—it was absolutely excluded, impossible.

And again, the general secretary decided everything, even though they discussed the issues in the Commission and in the Politburo. Here is one episode. Brezhnev was on vacation with his assistant [Anatoly] Blatov and an official of the Propaganda Department, who was very close to Brezhnev, who always took part in preparing materials for Brezhnev—Nikolay Shishlin, unfortunately deceased. He was a very intelligent and educated person. We were friends, and I also had very good relations with Blatov. When they returned from the South, and we had a friendly talk, as we often had, Shishlin said, "Anatoly, Brezhnev had all kinds of proposals from Moscow on that issue. And he said in front of us without any doubt, 'Forget it. Nothing like this will ever happen. It is impossible. Forget about the possibility of an invasion.'"

I am relaying his words to you approximately as he told me about that conversation with Brezhnev. And if one uses some common sense, first of all, we had already been pulled into Afghanistan, we had already understood what that meant, and we had no idea how to get out. And then Poland. Everybody understood the difference very well: when the situation in Czechoslovakia [in 1968] was discussed, and when finally the decision to introduce troops was made, our main concern was to persuade President [Ludvík] Svoboda that the Czechoslovak army should not resist, so that there would have been no bloodshed. He gave us his word. And he delivered on it. He was against the invasion but he was able to guarantee that the army would not resist.

However, we understood very well—we have a long history with the Poles—that if we introduced troops there, it would have been a bloody mess, terrible bloody mess. All our leadership understood that very well. Therefore, those two circumstances—Afghanistan, and the fact that we were dealing with the Poles, knowing all our mutual history—absolutely excluded an invasion. And there was no discussion of it.

Now, you put the question correctly—what were our guidelines? The Brezhnev Doctrine was in force. There was no moral factor then that emerged under Gorbachev later. And that factor excluded use of force. It was not there under Brezhnev, or under Chernenko, or under Andropov. And the doctrine was implemented in its forceful version.

As far as all kinds of doubts are concerned, which you expressed here, that Gorbachev was speaking differently with his aides, Politburo colleagues, inside the inner circle, and with others. That is true. I remember very well that several times Gorbachev expressed his dissatisfaction at the Politburo sessions with the fact that Hungary fell into the arms of the West, and he was supported by many of his colleagues. That it accumulated a huge debt to the International Monetary Fond, that it was becoming dependent. Those doubts came from the ideology. However, at the same time there also was the understanding that the camp was beginning to unravel, and that we could not do anything. And then a little later—in 1988 or 1989, I cannot recall now, but I have the document, and I will give it to you—Gorbachev said, "There is information from various sources, and from intelligence, that Poland is crawling away from us, and we, in Moscow, are doing nothing. And what can we do? Poland has a $56 billion debt. Can we take Poland on our account in our current economic situation? No. And if we cannot—that is it. We have no influence."

It never came to Gorbachev's or his colleagues' minds that we could use some kind of force. And we could not have kept it up with economic means. The question of our relations with our allies had been raised at the Politburo repeatedly: we had to develop new technologies, machine-building, we had to reach the highest technological levels, we had to re-orient our military-industrial complex. Because that was the key issue in preserving the socialist camp, our friendship, and our friends. They needed new technologies, new materials. The Germans wanted that, the Czechs wanted that, and the Hungarians too. We could not give that to them, and so they went to the West. There was the problem. It was our internal problem. So let us develop the machine-building industry.

You probably know that this was the main issue of the Plenums in 1985 and in 1986. All those Plenums demanded: let us develop the machine-building industry, new technologies, conversion. Let us use our high technologies from the military-industrial complex. That was a good lever for keeping our friends together. This is how the question was defined.

Of course, Gorbachev was a very emotional person. And sometimes he could say something, in his own circle, that could be interpreted as if he was holding on to the Brezhnev Doctrine. But we knew him very well as a person. As far as morality was concerned, and as far as his policy, which was oriented toward democratic reforms, the use of force against our friends was absolutely excluded. When he became general secretary, and when he developed his agenda, his number two priority, in this sense, was the withdrawal of troops from Afghanistan.

Now regarding Chernobyl, in response to your question. I think that in the West the political and even ideological importance of Chernobyl for the course of *perestroika* is exaggerated. They believe that it was a test of *glasnost*, that Gorbachev wanted to hide something, and his *glasnost* did not work, and as a result the population suffered great harm, the image of the Soviet Union was hurt too, and that it had a great impact on the further course of *perestroika*. I do not think that this point of view had grounds in reality. Of course, Chernobyl was a terrible shock to all of us—moral, political, and economic, first of all, because it required colossal expenses. Not only expenses for aid, but there was a question about the future of the nuclear power industry as such.

The Greens had already emerged by that time, and they demanded that the station be closed down, and not only the station in Chernobyl, but other stations also. We lost a lot of money in re-orienting systems of power supply. And we had to close down some things, or stop reactors at existing stations. We suffered colossal losses. And in that sense Chernobyl had an impact on the course of *perestroika* because it limited our economic resources even more. But as far as our conviction that we should persist, that *perestroika* should continue, that Chernobyl had not stopped us in that respect, I think there should be no doubts.

I have one of the Politburo sessions on Chernobyl. It is a very long document; I will not read from it, but I am passing it on to you, so that everybody can read it. Here Gorbachev is saying openly and sharply that we have nothing to hide. We have no right to hide anything. That would be a crime not only before our own people, but before the international public. You have it all here.

I would like to add one more thing regarding the Poles. Not only had we great respect for Jaruzelski in our government, in our elite, but there is a very respectful, warm and good attitude toward the Poles among our people. Unfortunately, it is not reciprocal. It might be that we bear some sort of historical responsibility before them.

We understand it. Individuals who know history in all its detail, beginning from the Time of Troubles, from Catherine the Second, the divisions of Poland, and Polish riots understand all that. But somebody who does not know about all this would not understand why the Poles dislike us so much. In our people, in all strata, there is no contempt, let alone hate, toward Poles. There are no bad feelings. This is just one more argument about why an intervention in Poland would not have been supported. The intervention in Czechoslovakia had not been supported by the people either. But Czechoslovakia still was farther away.

Zubok: A very small question. You promised to tell us about Gorbachev's weaknesses. You said that sometimes he used very harsh words but no "organizational conclusions" followed them. Some of his aides, and Archie Brown cited some of them in his book *The Gorbachev Factor*, said that the general secretary was by nature incapable of spilling blood, that he was a weakling. Do you agree with such an evaluation? That it could have an impact? That he could have tried to conceal it as a moral factor, presented it as his high moral standard, but in reality it was a simple human weakness? Statesmen have to spill blood.

Chernyaev: This is not a weakness, precisely. You are quite right, you cited Archie Brown, and now you can cite us also—the use of force was naturally disgusting for Gorbachev, and especially of bloody force. Therefore, when he is accused of Tbilisi, and of Vilnius, we are very surprised, and outraged. We were next to him. Yes, he made a tactical mistake, a political mistake after the events in Vilnius. He should have spoken out, condemned, fired those responsible, filed criminal charges against them. He had not done that because he was unsure: they mistreated the military in Lithuania; it had been provoked by the local communists. He behaved incorrectly in the political sense. But he was not an initiator, not an organizer—he carries no moral blame for the Vilnius events. And he accepts the political responsibility for that. As president, he was responsible for everything that was happening in the country. You are absolutely right.

Shakhnazarov: I would like to add that if Gorbachev decided to use force, everything would have been over in a matter of hours, and we would be representing the Soviet Union, not Russia, at this table.

Zubok: But not Gorbachev. (Laughter)

Shakhnazarov: Not Gorbachev. This is my response to Oleg Skvortsov. (Laughter)

And I would like to add something. I would like to speak conceptually about the Brezhnev Doctrine since people talk about it a lot. First of all, what is that doctrine? Did it exist? No. Such a doctrine never existed. There was no document that conceptually defined that the Soviet Union had special rights in that zone, and that it had a right to use force to defend its allies, or to defend the regimes that were in power there, from any kind of attack. There was no doctrine in the sense that the Monroe Doctrine was formulated. The Brezhnev Doctrine is similar to the Truman Doctrine, which he formulated after the war developing the idea that the Yalta system and the results of World War II meant that the United States and their allies had a right to defend themselves using any means against an aggression on one of them.

Therefore, what Western propaganda called the Brezhnev Doctrine was really the Stalin Doctrine, if you will, the doctrine of Yalta. It was a parallel response to the Truman Doctrine, which stated the same: that the U.S. had a moral right to be involved in those regions, that those regions were under the U.S. indirect control, and that that was the result of World War II. This is what the Brezhnev Doctrine is all about. You will not find a single document where Brezhnev himself stated it. It is a different issue that Brezhnev had applied it in 1968 in practice, and that is why they named it after him. However, Khrushchev had applied it before him. So we might as well call it the Khrushchev Doctrine. And then the next question—if Gorbachev had used it, we could have called it the Gorbachev Doctrine. But he had not applied it.

Now, Jim [Hershberg] asked, why did the Soviet leadership refuse to go into Poland? And as a good scholar, he answers his question himself. Quite right—first of all, because of Afghanistan. Secondly—because there was no money. Thirdly, because they were afraid of the Western reaction. Fourth, because the people did not want to fight, and so on, and so forth. You are right. But of all these factors it is principally important that the Brezhnev leadership did not want to interfere in Poland because they believed that the Soviet Union would not be able to do it. But for Gorbachev such issues were associated with the moral factor. He spoke not just about the fact that we "cannot," he said "we do not want to interfere." And that is his principal difference from all his predecessors. That was the second question.

Now the third question. Bill [Wohlforth] made a comment about the introduction of troops. Then the question becomes: how do you introduce troops? Our troops were already there. We did not need to introduce them. Or we needed a secondary introduction of troops. I recall a joke about when there was a popular uprising in Florence, under Medici. So they came to the [Piazza della] Signoria, and shouted, "Republic! Republic!" Modesto came out and said, "What is wrong? What do you want—we already have a republic." The people thought for a minute and replied, "Then give us one more." The same with those troops. The troops were stationed there. The question was whether to use them or not. They had strictest orders not to get involved in anything. Let the Poles do whatever they wanted. Even if they started fighting among themselves, do not leave the barracks. This is how the question was posed.

János spoke about the Hungarian experience, very interesting. He asked whether the Soviet leaders had ever thought about an official renunciation of the Brezhnev Doctrine. Let me repeat: not only had they thought about it, but essentially they already began to abandon it, and had abandoned it. But to say about it publicly, to say, "you know, friends, beginning tomorrow, if you wanted to leave us, and to join NATO, do not be afraid"—of course, they could not do that. One would have to be a complete idiot to do that. Not a single state leader would allow himself to do such things. To the contrary—they would try to scare the allies, to say, "keep in mind, we have solidarity among allies, we are all together, the camp is strong, we will not allow [...]" and so on. That is what they were supposed to do, and they did it. But in essence, they had abandoned it long ago.

And the last question was asked by Oleg Skvortsov. A very interesting question. Were the results of *perestroika* reversible? Why did we lose everything that we had in those six years? First of all, it is difficult to agree that we have lost everything that we had. Maybe we have lost one half, but not everything.

Levesque: A better half? (Laughter)

Shakhnazarov: That's a good question. I, personally, believe that the dissolution of the Soviet Union was, in the end, unavoidable, as well as the dissolution of the socialist camp. This is my opinion. Because those states, and those people, that were parts of the Soviet Union—whether you call it an empire or not—in essence they were ripe for independence. They might have done it ten years later, twenty years later, but I believe it was unavoidable. The same question relates to the socialist commonwealth. It is very clear to me, and I can tell you honestly, as a Bolshevik, that already twenty years ago, in our internal discussions, in the apparatus, I, for example, was absolutely convinced that the time would come when the GDR would unite with the FRG. We argued about it with Kvitsinsky, with [Vladimir] Semenov—all thinking people, all rational people thought that it was inevitable. As it was inevitable that other countries of Eastern Europe would become independent, would be more attracted to the West—all this was more or less clear. The question was—when, and at what price?

Our trouble, and if you will, our tragedy, was that we paid a much higher price for that than we wanted to pay. When German unification began, we were hoping that we would be able to get a united Germany outside NATO, and even that maybe both blocs would be dissolved, and replaced by a common European security system. I am not even speaking about the economic and material losses, and so on. But unfortunately, events unfolded in such a fashion that we were not able to do it in an optimal way, and maybe there is our fault in it. But what was predetermined by history happened with the worst possible scenario for the Soviet Union. Therefore, our losses were huge.

Chernyaev: I would like to respond to your question regarding what happened during Gorbachev's visit to Warsaw. Allegedly, somebody there asked him a question about the Brezhnev Doctrine, and instead of giving a direct response that it was over with, he began to go in circles, and did not say anything definite. I do not remember such an episode, and I do not remember such a question. He was asked a question about Katyń,[16] and there he began to go in circles. He said that the Commission was working, let it sort things out. He included the issue of Katyń among all the difficult problems of Soviet–Polish relations beginning from 1918–1920, and avoided that concrete issue altogether. But as far as the Brezhnev Doctrine was concerned, I was present at all of those meetings, and I do not remember that. Maybe there is a mistake here.

Machcewicz: Just one remark. I remember there must have been such a question because public opinion had quite an interest in this question, because it was a kind of attempt to find out what are the public limits of the autonomy given to socialist states.

Hershberg: I want to close with a joke because one of the only negative results of the end of the Soviet Union, and the end of the Soviet empire in Eastern Europe, was the collapse of political humor since people did not need to make subversive jokes any more. I think everyone is familiar with the joke that was made when Gorbachev visited Prague in 1987, and people asked, "what is the difference between you and Dubček?" And one of his aides said, "19 years." Shakhnazarov said, maybe in an alternative future he would have come here as a Soviet representative, but not as Gorbachev's representative, and that reminded me of the second joke that I heard in 1987, which did not receive any attention. Someone asked, "what is the difference between Gorbachev and Dubček?" And the answer was, "none, but Gorbachev does not know it yet." (Laughter)

CHAPTER 3: MOSCOW'S "ENIGMATIC" REACTION TO EVENTS IN 1989

Blanton: The title of this session is "Moscow's Enigmatic Reaction to the Events in 1989," and I think a large part of the discussion we had before lunch actually makes a nice transition to that enigmatic reaction, because it is precisely around this threat of the use of force implied, implicit, understood by East Europeans, expressed, or not expressed, on very different levels. As Bill Wohlforth laid it out, it is not only the intervention of Soviet troops, it is the threat of intervention by Soviet troops. It is also the Soviets urging Czech authorities to use force, or simply Soviets giving permission to Czech authorities to use force. So, there

---

[16] A reference to the mass execution of several thousand by the Soviet NKVD in the Katyń Forest near Smolensk in 1940. In all, some 15,000 Polish officers were known to have disappeared after their internment in Soviet camps in September 1939, but it was not until April 1990 that the Soviet Union finally admitted the NKVD's responsibility.

138

are many different levels of this threat, and it seems to me that the ambiguity of which Georgy spoke—precisely because we could not use force in Poland is the reason why we needed to threaten to use force in Poland in 1980–81—brings us into this discussion.

MacEachin: I promised that I would be as brief as I could, but since we are on the record I will be speaking carefully so that I do not hear later from the people I used to work for about what I have said.

There is a standing U.S. conventional wisdom about the use of force that revolves around the Polish crisis of 1980–81, repeated even two days ago in the *Boston Globe*. It asserts that the U.S. learned about the Soviet "intention" to invade Poland, made strong public and diplomatic interventions, and thereby helped deter the invasion. That is the conventional picture, and it has been presented in books by at least three people who held senior positions at the time. I am going to use this occasion as an opportunity to give an alternative view of that picture, because what is now the conventional wisdom was not the unanimous opinion at that time. [....]

The picture that was seen in late 1980 was interpreted as an exploration of military force options and preparations. But nothing remotely in size or scope compared to what, in our view, took place in July of 1968. Nowhere near that scope. And compared to 1968, the target, if Poland was going to be a target, was twice the size, in both geography and population, and in military force. I am giving you very simplified data, but that kind of data led any person who was a military analyst to conclude we were seeing signs of Soviet leadership that may be looking at the option of military intervention, considering that they may have to resort to it, and seeking to scope it out. But for whatever reason, by the first week in December 1980—I hate to put it in terms of a decision—but at least somebody said "not now." And then there were discussions.

I will also go further to say that I think that there is a heck of a lot of evidence that a few months after the December 1980 events, it did look like opinions had formed on "we are not going to do it." I think that Afghanistan by that time started to really carry weight, for whatever reason, in the discussion that went on after that and in all the actions that took place. Which brings me to my main point here: I will offer as a hypothesis, that it was about that time that that experience began to affect the people who were going to hold key positions in the decision making process in the next several years. Whether the Brezhnev Doctrine was officially declared dead or not, I think the corpse might have been in the bed about then.

Last point. I have to tell this a little bit anecdotally. We all have things in our lives that we wish we had done differently. It was, I think, in 1987 that an assessment was being made as to what would be the impact of Gorbachev's policies on Eastern Europe. And in this discussion I have to be careful. At the time I was trying to leave my job because it was [...] I had enough of the stress of it. And so I was taking secret German lessons—not secret from my boss. So, I had to leave at 6 o'clock for the lessons. Late one day I received a draft of an estimate that described the important impact of Gorbachev's policy in Eastern Europe, and said that obviously any government that presents itself as communist will be permitted by Moscow, without being threatened with the use of force. I called the author and said "I have to go to my lesson, but I really think we should take up one more question, and that is: what is going to be the effect if all East European governments believe what we have said we believe regarding the non-use of force?" And then I said, "well, I will see you tomorrow," and then I went off, and I never did follow up on that question. I always regretted to this day that we did not stop that project and take on the next question, because that is where, I think, things really had a major impact. I think you saw the impact in 1988–89.

Tarasenko: This discussion should not leave another idea out, another, I should say, pole of our policy of that time. It is the principle of freedom of choice, that every country has complete freedom of choice. That is partly an answer to the question about the Brezhnev Doctrine. If you do not take into account the fact that at that time we spoke about freedom of choice very frequently, and emphasized it in every way as one of the fundamental principles regulating relations between states, then we would get an incomplete picture. I would also like to remind you that when Shevardnadze gave an interview to *Time* in May 1987—it is in this chronology—there was a direct question: what degree of freedom of choice do you allow your allies?

The question is not an easy one for the minister to answer. They found a solution by saying that the Soviet Union allows the allies the same degree of freedom of choice that exists among the countries-members of NATO. In other words, that a member of the socialist commonwealth has the same freedom of choice that a NATO member has. The same freedom of choice, and the same freedom of action. This way we did not renounce our capability to do something, if there was a need, and at the same time it looked like we behaved just like the other. Therefore, if NATO would use force, the Soviet Union could do the same.

Shakhnazarov: That was a good answer.

Levesque: On this point of use of force, and on the Brezhnev Doctrine, I think it is clear that Gorbachev never contemplated the use of force, but this being said, I think it shows clearly here from the documents that we have, for instance, in the memorandum of the Central Committee of 1989 to Yakovlev,[17] and also in the memorandum of the Foreign Ministry—Gorbachev was strongly advised to maintain some degree of uncertainty about what the USSR would do to protect its interest in given circumstances. And I think that it is not a matter of chance, as our Polish colleague said, that Gorbachev refused to address directly the issue of the Brezhnev Doctrine. It is not an accident that he declined to answer it. As a matter of fact, he was asked very often by foreign journalists about the Brezhnev Doctrine, and he answered the way Shakhnazarov has answered, by saying that there is no such thing as the Brezhnev Doctrine.

---

[17] Document No. 41.

Well, I am sorry to say, there was such a thing as the Brezhnev Doctrine. Of course, it was not a document signed by Brezhnev, it dated before Brezhnev. But it meant something concrete, and when Gorbachev was asked about it, he refused to answer in a very clear-cut manner. The freedom of choice was a way of answering indirectly with the ambiguities that you tried to maintain about it. So it is very slowly that he dispelled that Brezhnev Doctrine, in a very implicit manner, which became more and more explicit. And the turning point to me was the speech that he made in France in the summer of 1989.

It was not a complete repudiation, but it was clear enough. And it had a direct impact on the acceleration of the events in Poland. I would like also to stress that Gorbachev's policy toward Eastern Europe was fundamentally ambiguous, and ambivalent, in the sense that on the one hand, he sincerely wanted reform in Eastern Europe, but at the same time, as the documents show, he insisted on political stability. He wanted political stability in Eastern Europe because the absence of stability would disturb the process of *perestroika* within the USSR. So it is at least partially contradictory to have stability and to have a reform in Eastern Europe, with all the uncertainties that would have come up. So there is, I think, a basic element of ambiguity in Gorbachev's approach to change in Eastern Europe. And to come to my first point again, if he never contemplated force, he yielded to this advice, at least for a certain period, up to 1989—not to dispel and dismiss openly and clearly, in a non-ambiguous manner, the Brezhnev Doctrine.

Matlock: Regarding the situation and our perceptions in 1981, and Poland, I would recall that I was at that time, from January until early September, in charge of our Embassy in Moscow. And by March 1981, I had concluded personally that the Soviet Union would not intervene militarily in Poland. I sent a cable to that effect, which, I was told, had a considerable effect, particularly on Secretary [Alexander] Haig. But the reasons, it seemed to me, were precisely the ones cited here, particularly the fact that Afghanistan was already a problem. It was clear that these interventions were no longer necessarily as quick and decisive as, say, 1968 in Prague had been. It also seemed to me that the overall rhetoric regarding Poland was simply not such as would provide a sort of political cover.

That having been said, there is something else to take into account regarding the United States and its warnings. Many of us felt that our warnings were important mainly to make a record for our own people, that is, politically, at home. My judgment at that time would have been: I do not think they are going to intervene in Poland militarily, but if they decide they have to, they would do it regardless of what we say. They know *we* are not going to intervene militarily. We cannot threaten that. And the other ties we have with the Soviet Union, particularly after Afghanistan, were so tenuous, the Soviets did not have much to lose.

However, politically, in the United States, it was extremely important to make the case that we were giving warnings, because many, especially Republicans, ridiculed Carter when he was surprised by Afghanistan. In fact, he said that he was surprised and that he did not really understand the Soviet Union until that happened. We could not allow Reagan to be put in that position. So, whatever happened, he had to be in a position to say that the Soviets were acting just like they usually act. This, among other things, would have prevented an overreaction. We generally thought that Carter had not only overreacted to Afghanistan, but had ineffectually reacted. Such things as the Olympics boycott, and the grain boycott—which, of course, was one of the first things that Reagan reversed.

Although we might have taken such steps under the same conditions, we were under no illusion that they had much effect. My own advice in the administration, along with that of others, was that some of these things were idiotic. I have in mind in particular closing the Consulate in Kiev, and then sending their consul out of New York but leaving all the U.N. people there. It was as if we were shooting ourselves in the foot. I believed that the only thing we needed to do in Afghanistan was to make sure that the Mujaheddin were well-supplied, particularly with better anti-aircraft weapons, so that the Soviets cannot use close air support.

Eventually, the resistance was going to wear them down. We did not create the Mujaheddin, but we could supply them. The other "sanctions" were nonsense. I recommended opening up communications, and stopping the other things.

We had many different opinions in the administration, and in the first couple of years, 1981 and 1982, there were those who really did want to use Afghanistan and the imposition of martial law in Poland to break all economic ties. We saw that in the pipeline dispute, and in other things. But basically, by 1983, the predominant opinion in the White House, particularly with the president, was that the sanctions were not working and therefore we would have to find other measures. But we had to protect the president against seeming either soft or surprised, regardless of whatever the outrage was. So, part of this was setting us up politically so that if something happened, we did not have to overreact.

Zubok: We are forgetting that Eastern Europe was not the main area of Gorbachev's foreign policy in 1988, far from it. He wanted to end the Cold War by achieving a relaxation of tensions, a détente, and a partnership with the United States and Western Europe. When one reads documents showing the preparation of Gorbachev's speech at the U.N. in December 1988, this is what we see.[18] Gorbachev says that the speech should be "anti-Fulton—Fulton in reverse." And he instructed the assistants, including you, Anatoly Sergeyevich, to write this speech at the "world level," as ambitious as possible.

In particular, one part of those ambitions was the renunciation of the use of force in any circumstances and any conditions. The right to choose. And when, as we can see in the document, Shevardnadze timidly raises the question whether it was time to withdraw troops from Hungary, Gorbachev responds, No, no, we should cut the number of troops, but we should not withdraw at once. There is a clear contradiction here: he is giving the Hungarians the freedom of choice,

---

[18] See Document No. 31.

but does not want to withdraw the troops now, he wants to do it at some future date, apparently hoping that he would be able to negotiate with Western Europe and the United States, and to end the Cold War on an equal ground, and to build a common European home. Don't you think that while Gorbachev was dealing with the higher plane of policy—ending the Cold War—he had lost the lower, and more practical, level of policy—his East European policy?

Skvortsov: Vlad has just stated the thought that I also wanted to mention regarding the duplicity of Gorbachev's policy toward Eastern Europe. Our main topic of this session is still Gorbachev's policy toward Eastern Europe. Therefore, I have the following question to our respected veterans. In 1986, as it is described in many memoirs and statements of many well-known figures, Member of the Politburo and First Deputy Chairman of the Council of Ministers of the GDR [Werner] Krolikowski, and other people who were behind him—there was a significant group in the GDR leadership—sent a message to Gorbachev via Ambassador [Vyacheslav] Kochemassov, and that message was delivered personally. Later, when Krolikowski came to Moscow, they had a conversation on the same topic. They asked Gorbachev to give his support to change the GDR leader, Erich Honecker. Those requests were made two or three times. There was no reaction on Gorbachev's part. Of course, I have my own opinion, but I would like to ask you, and to hear your response: how do you explain such inconsistency in Gorbachev? At that time Honecker's replacement would have been less painful than it was in October 1989, especially because the major part of the Politburo members supported the request, the healthy part.

Chernyaev: Regarding the duplicity of Gorbachev's policy. I wrote about it many times, both in my book and in my articles, especially on the issue of German unification. There you can find Gorbachev's statements that are quite contradictory. For example, one day he would be meeting and speaking with Helmut Kohl, or with [Hans-Dietrich] Genscher. Then in a couple of days he would be meeting and speaking with [Egon] Krenz and [Hans] Modrow. In the first case, they would be speaking about how to manage the peaceful and smooth process of all-European reconciliation. They would be talking about it still in the framework of reconciliation of two German states. But to the new German leaders, who replaced Honecker, he would say, "Hold on! The main thing is to preserve sovereignty, to preserve law and order, so that you avoid riots, so that your state does not decompose."

I would like to object to those who accuse Gorbachev of duplicity. Had he been linear, had he been unable to adjust to the circumstances and to his interlocutors, everything would have turned out much worse than it actually did. For him, it was most important to contain that process within some kind of acceptable, peaceful limits, to avoid an explosion, and the destruction of all the things he had built on the main plane of his policy, which Vlad has just reminded us about in his remarks. The main goal for Gorbachev was to preserve the process of disarmament, of the liquidation of the Cold War. From that point of view, from that context, the events in Germany, in the Warsaw Treaty Organization, were secondary for Gorbachev. They were subordinated to the main events. If you want to use this term, "duplicity," this is what caused it. But he was not duplicitous in terms of trying to keep Eastern Europe in the sphere of interest of the Soviet Union. He was not undermining his principles of new thinking and freedom of choice by doing that.

Somebody reminded me here—and we did not pay attention to it at the time—when he spoke at the United Nations—it was the end of 1988—everybody was excited about his concrete proposals on unilateral troop reductions. But that was not the most important part. The most important was that he rejected the Marxist-Leninist analysis of the international situation, and analyzed it from the point of view of existing realities. And secondly, that he announced the main principles of his new thinking: freedom of choice and non-use of force in international relations. That is what it was. And it was done absolutely sincerely and consciously. And it was not just an accident, as you have just reminded us; there were many versions of that speech, but he decided to take it in this direction when we worked on the draft.

Now regarding the statement that had we replaced Honecker earlier everything would have been much better, would have turned out smoother. The formulation of the question itself is inadequate to the situation, to put it mildly. It was impossible for Gorbachev in principle to raise the question of removing a leader of a friendly state. He could not have done that. He avoided those questions, even when they hinted at them and even when they demanded it. When the events leading to the fall of the Wall began unfolding, [Todor] Zhivkov, let alone Ceauşescu, directly demanded that Gorbachev use force. In his conversation with Ceauşescu—I do not know whether you have this document —when he began to insist, "what are you doing, why are you just watching idly while everything is falling apart?" Gorbachev responded, "Do you want to send the troops in? Well, send them, and we will see how you do it. I will not do that."

So, the issue of replacement, even of Honecker who really disliked Gorbachev and to whom Gorbachev related with irony but did not give much respect, did not exist for Gorbachev. Replacing him from Moscow was impossible for Gorbachev. It contradicted all his philosophy, and went against the essence of his policy of *perestroika* and new thinking. Georgy, did I miss something from those questions?

Shakhnazarov: I would like to ask you to look at this issue from another angle. When I am asked whether Gorbachev's policy was two-sided, I respond that all policy is two-sided. Let us take, for example, how France and Britain acted toward German unification. Neither Thatcher nor Mitterrand wanted that to happen, especially to happen so quickly. As allies they assured the Germans that they were with them in their heart of hearts, while at the same time giving hints to Gorbachev that he should prevent it from happening. Is that a duplicitous policy or not?

Or let us take the United States. When all these processes began in our country, first they doubted us, then when they realized that Gorbachev was doing something good from their point of view they supported him, and then, while still supporting Gorbachev in rhetoric, shifted their support to Yeltsin and helped him to come to power. By the way, I would like to ask Jack at some point to speak about this issue that interests me very much, because I am strongly convinced that if the Group of Seven in London had given its support to Gorbachev, and if they had given Gorbachev the money that it repeatedly gave Yeltsin later, it is very possible that events might have taken a completely different turn.

As a matter of fact, Washington had abandoned Gorbachev, regardless of the fact that in their hearts they liked Gorbachev and respected him in many ways. But they saw in Washington that Yeltsin was willing to go farther in some respects, and therefore we see the duplicity of policy here also. That is why I think that we should be clear about duplicity. For Gorbachev, as for any other statesman, politics was the art of the possible. And he, on the one hand, promoted certain views and tried to implement them in policy, but on the other hand he was always forced to take reality into account, as a leader of the party, the state, and the alliance. As the leading figure of an empire, of one of the two military-political blocs, he was obligated, by his position, to try to preserve his bloc as much as he could. But when he could not, he had to make concessions. The major issue was: to use force to the end, or not?

The same problem existed inside the country. Take the Baltics. Was it possible to preserve the Baltics by force? Of course it was. Instead of dealing with a small uprising of local communists, he should have given an order—we had two divisions there, two days would have been enough to put an end to it. After that—and I have written about this in my book—the U.S. would have been offended, the West would have staged a boycott for a year against the Soviet Union, and China would have been forgiven. And everything would have returned to normal. But he did not use force, because he did not consider it personally acceptable. That is why we should measure those things not from the standpoint of contradictions in his policy, but to remember that every time he was faced with something that was unacceptable for him, he did not do it. He did not violate his principles.

Of course, this is all philosophical discussion but I think that it is essential to helping us understand the situation as a whole. If it was possible to preserve the Soviet Union, of course we should have preserved it. Gorbachev should have done it. If it was possible to preserve the alliance in a different form, even if it was a group of neutral states, he should have done that. We still want it now. We do not want Eastern Europe as a whole to become a part of NATO. We do not want it—neither the politicians, nor the people—because we think it would mean isolation for Russia, that it would be unfair to Russia, that it promotes xenophobic and nationalist forces in Russia itself. It pushes Russia toward some sort of militarist revival.

Chernyaev: I would again return to what Vlad has mentioned, when Shevardnadze told Gorbachev that it was time to withdraw the troops from Hungary and Czechoslovakia, and he responded, in principle, yes, but we will do it slowly and gradually. There is a lot that is hidden behind those words. It was a signal that withdrawal is necessary, showing that we do abide by the principle, that we renounce physical presence as a means of keeping countries together. On the other hand, for us it was an internal problem. It was not merely an economic problem. We did not know what to do with those divisions, and where to station them. We paid a heavy price for it later, when we moved all the troops home *en masse*. But there was also a psychological problem. Once we start to withdraw troops, the howling starts: what did we fight for, what did 27 million of our soldiers die for in World War II? Are we renouncing all that? For Gorbachev at that time, when they began to accuse him of everything, when we had already heard the words "traitor," and "agent of influence," those issues were very sensitive; he had to take them into account.

There is one more issue that Vlad has mentioned, and I would like to expand on it a little. I think that I told some of you that last year I set myself a goal that I would type up all my notes from the Politburo sessions, and from all closed meetings with Gorbachev. Politburo sessions were held every week, if you remember. So it was from 1986, when I became assistant to the general secretary, up to the beginning of 1990, when the Politburo had lost any weight, and when I stopped being assistant to the general secretary and became assistant to the president, and so I was no longer invited to Politburo sessions. And now I have typed up almost all of my notes, and I have a full transcript of them. I am still in 1989—I have not finished all of them yet—and I have 800 computer pages, which is more than 1,000 typewritten pages, maybe 1,200 pages altogether. There is a lot of material there, both on foreign and domestic policy. But I am talking about it now because foreign policy, even in the most dramatic moments, even in the period of German unification, took up only five or six percent of the considerations of Gorbachev and the Politburo, of their time and their nerves.

You have to take this fact into consideration, in this context. His main goal was to put an end to the Cold War, to the arms race. Malta was coming. Therefore, such "details," as Eastern Europe, and even the process of unification that had begun, were really secondary. Of course, when a scholar begins to research a certain topic, a bias emerges because he tends to think that his topic is the center of the universe. But if you look at it in the context of all of Gorbachev's work, even the issue of German unification becomes just another issue. And besides, we should constantly see this internal political aspect of foreign policy, this domestic background against which Gorbachev made all of his foreign policy decisions.

Ilya Gaiduk: I would like to return to the question about a possible replacement of Honecker, because Gorbachev's position on that issue is characteristic of his position on many other issues of foreign, and even domestic, policy; that is apparent from many documents that were included in the briefing book. His desire to avoid making decisions at the time when those decisions could have been made easily and painlessly. Maybe not easily, but at least with less pain than had to be incurred when the decision was made later. As a matter of fact, I can accept the explanation that Anatoly Sergeyevich has just given us—that Mikhail Sergeyevich did not want to interfere in the internal affairs of East European states.

But on this issue, with Honecker, the situation was somewhat different. Here, the initiative did not originate in Moscow. Moscow had not decided that they had to replace Honecker. The initiative originated with the members of the Politburo of the Socialist Unity Party of Germany [SED]. And I would emphasize that it was the initiative of the majority of the Politburo members. And at that time, in 1986, the Soviet positions in the countries of Eastern Europe were sufficiently strong—I mean, among the leaders, they listened to Moscow's opinion. Then Gorbachev could have played the critical role. And it would not even have been considered interference on the part of the Soviet Union, or of the Soviet leadership in the affairs of the GDR because there was no interference. But that tight link that existed between the East European leaders and the Soviet Union explains the fact that the members of the SED asked Gorbachev, in order to receive his approval at least, and to act on their own. They were not talking about interference. And there would have been no direct interference. Looking at the situation as it was at the time, it was completely normal.

Shakhnazarov: I wanted to take the floor to respond to this question. It seems like my young colleague does not fully take into account the situation that existed between the Soviet Union and the socialist countries. The West called them "satellites." Of course, they were dependent, of course they were in our bloc. There was strict discipline on some principal issues that had to deal with the overall relations between this bloc and the other bloc. On other issues the leaders of those countries were completely independent. The personality of a leader played a great role.

Therefore, whether Gorbachev wanted to replace Honecker or not, the issue was whether he could do that at all. I have already mentioned that Gierek had not been elected in Moscow, he had been elected by the Poles, as had Gomułka, because Gomułka was a respected leader who was capable of taking the steering wheel in that situation, after the events that had happened [in 1956]. The same with other leaders. We did not even talk about Ceauşescu—he did whatever he liked, and nobody could do anything about it, especially on personnel issues. I will give you an example.

Take the Poles again. We had been receiving signals, and our intelligence services, and other "well-wishers" were telling us that we had to remove [Edward] Babiuch, that he was against the Soviet Union, that he was pro-Western, and so on. There were two groups in the Department. One group was saying, "Leave him alone, he is a normal person and does good work." Others picked up those intelligence reports and insisted that we had to remove Babiuch. Babiuch was a secretary of the Central Committee. Brezhnev mentioned him in his conversation with Gierek, that he was not behaving properly. Several days later Gierek returned to Poland and made Babiuch prime minister.[19] Then our services reported again that there were some intrigues against [Stefan] Olszowski, who was our

[19] Babiuch served in the post from February to August 1980.

great friend and overall pro-Soviet. By the way, there was an argument about it in the Department. I said, "Do not mention it at all in the memo to Brezhnev." But they decided to mention it, to tell Gierek that he should support Olszowski. Brezhnev told Gierek, "You know, Gierek, you need to support Olszowski." Gierek leaves the Soviet Union, returns to Poland, and two days later removes Olszowski from the Politburo and sends him to the GDR as ambassador.[20]

This is what the real situation was like. Oleg thinks that it was so simple, just tell them to "remove Honecker." It was nothing like that. First of all, there was no clear division in the German leadership, there was no clear majority that was confident that Honecker had to be removed. He held very strong positions. He had his political base, as our leader [Russian Federation President Boris Yeltsin] does now, primarily in the military institutions. And the power institutions were very loyal. Secondly, he had a number of strong allies within the Politburo. Such people as [Kurt] Hager, [Hermann] Axen and others were not at all inclined to support the younger ones and to overthrow Honecker. Krenz was behaving ambivalently because he was Honecker's man himself. Honecker made him a "Krenz-prince," as we used to joke, initially, and then began to push him away because he did not like his ambition. This was the real situation.

The same thing in Czechoslovakia. We did not want Jakeš to be elected. There was a very negative attitude to him in the Soviet leadership. But the Czechs elected Jakeš nonetheless.[21] We had no other choice—it was not our choice. We were more inclined to see such people as Štrougal elected. But I would like to emphasize once again that as a matter of principle, as Anatoly Sergeyevich said, Gorbachev was against imposing his choice of leaders. And that is why he did not respond to all requests from Krolikowski. And there was not only Krolikowski—long before Gorbachev, during Brezhnev's times, there was a constant internal struggle going on within the German leadership between the [Willi] Stoph group and the Honecker group. Stoph did not like many things that Honecker did. He represented approximately the same positions that Kosygin did in our country in his dispute with Brezhnev. He spoke from more of a practical, economics standpoint. Honecker was more of an ideologue, more of a politician. Nonetheless, even Brezhnev never made any attempts to interfere in those internal German petty quarrels. He used to say, "Leave me out of this, let them sort it out on their own, and let them decide."

As far as Honecker was concerned, when we discussed it with Gorbachev, he used to say, "Let those Germans decide this themselves. It is their business." The only thing that Gorbachev did in this respect was that in his conversation with Honecker, and then with the German leadership, when he explained our view of the problems to them, he put it in such a perspective as if to suggest to the

---

[20] Olszowski lost his Politburo seat at the VIII PUWP Congress in February 1980, and was appointed envoy to East Berlin the following month.

[21] Jakeš was named head of the CPCz in December 1987.

German leadership that they should change, that they should make many changes, otherwise they could be too late. I can give you this document if you do not have it, because I personally took notes during those conversations. Maybe that thought gave them a push. And it was also important that the public gave Gorbachev a great reception, that they shouted, "Gorby! Gorby! We need our own Gorby!" That pushed the reform-minded part of the German leadership toward the idea that Honecker had to be replaced. But it was too late.

Levesque: Again, about Gorbachev's ambivalence. What you said about his behavior with Honecker is a clear pattern of behavior, not only in this case but also in general. Gorbachev behaved exactly the same way with Czechoslovakia. If in 1987 he could have said a hint about his preferences to Husák, then things would have been very different. And again, the pattern is the same also with Bulgaria. I was told by Petr Mladenov that he, during the meeting of the Warsaw Pact summit in 1989, in the summer of 1989, succeeded in taking Gorbachev away from Zhivkov for a couple of minutes. And he told me that he told Gorbachev, "We are preparing something in Bulgaria to change the leadership." And the only answer he got from Gorbachev was, "It is your business." So, Mladenov told me that he was dismayed. He expected more concrete words of support. And that made all of the difference, because he was so dismayed that he waited months before doing something. And it happened only in November, while if he had received not some sort of meddling or a strong push to do something, but some explicit encouragement to do something, things would have changed more rapidly in Bulgaria.

So, to me, it is a clear example of Gorbachev's ambivalence. It is not simply a matter of principle, of not meddling, it is a matter of refusal to take responsibility for what would have happened. I think that is also a point. It is also a matter of principle, of course, but also a way of avoiding a difficult responsibility at a given point in time. And I think in Czechoslovakia in 1987 a slight hint to Husák would have made the difference. And a different message than the noncommittal one that he gave to Mladenov in the summer of 1989 would also have changed things rapidly.

Shakhnazarov: But this was not his ambivalence. This was his position of principle. It is a question of your assessment.

Dawisha: Just a small point. When Jacques quotes Gorbachev as telling Mladenov, "It is your business." To use such words, which were exactly the same words that Brezhnev used in telling [Antonín] Novotný that the Russians were not going to intervene in Czechoslovakia [in 1968], is in itself highly ambiguous, because any East European leader would know that to say this means nothing. Let them do it. If they make a mess of it, they have the ability to sort it out by any means. I mean, this is the problem with this period: without a clear unified statement to the entire East European leadership that they are free, and that they would suffer the consequences, each East European leader individually had to figure out what was the limit of their freedom, and it was not possible.

Chernyaev: I would like to comment on your statement that Brezhnev and Gorbachev sometimes used the same words. Let me address you to distant history. Let us take the beginning of 1968. We, a group of officials of the apparatus of the Central Committee, are sitting in Zavidovo, which is now called Rus', where Yeltsin receives all his high guests. We are putting together a big speech for Brezhnev to deliver at the International Conference of Communist and Working Parties, which took place in 1969. Brezhnev was leading the effort—how he was leading it is not of any interest to us now, it is a different question, and it would lead us far away from our topic.

Suddenly we learned that Brezhnev was going to Prague, to Czechoslovakia. We were left behind in Zavidovo. It was expected that he would stay there for 10 days or so. However, three days later he turns up in Zavidovo. We sat together at breakfast. There was a round table, a huge one like this. Brezhnev sat in the middle. We asked questions. Arbatov, who was quite an obnoxious man among us, and who always sat directly across from him, asked, "Leonid Ilych, what happened, you were going to stay there for a week, or ten days, and instead, you came back to us?"

Brezhnev expressed himself in expletives, because there were no women there. He said, "I got into such a stew—one [person] comes and says one thing, another says a completely different thing. Novotný does not understand anything." He said, "I understood that I was being pulled into something that I never, under any conditions, want to be involved in, not for anything! Let them sort it out themselves, between themselves." That was January 1968. In May the position had changed, and the troops had been introduced in August. Why did Brezhnev change his mind? Six months earlier Brezhnev's attitude was: "I do not want to be involved in this dirty porridge under any conditions, let them sort it out themselves." Brezhnev was a very different person then. So, if you want to compare the Brezhnev of that time with Gorbachev, you can do it in this episode, but not more than that.

Shakhnazarov: I would like to return once again to that very interesting phrase that Jacques mentioned regarding what Mladenov told him. Because if a general secretary of the CC CPSU [responded] to a statement that they, essentially, wanted to undertake a coup d'état —from the point of view that was prevalent at that time, to remove Zhivkov—if in response to that he did not say "Don't do that," and just said, "It is your business," then by saying that he lets them know that we were not against it. What else do you think he could have said? "Yes, do it, do it quickly?" Do you think a politician could have done otherwise? The issue is in interpretation.

Zubok: I would like to focus our attention a little bit. —We are already dealing with 1989, when East European outposts were beginning to crumble, and I completely agree with Anatoly Sergeyevich—and it is reflected in this briefing book—that the leadership was already dealing with more burning issues at that moment, like the Baltics and political reform. The question is different. I am interested in the procedural, bureaucratic aspect of this—why was there no "emergency team" on Eastern Europe, no headquarters, which would concentrate only on East European affairs?

150

There was a practice of setting up Politburo commissions. We have a document here from a Politburo session from January 21, 1989,[22] at which Gorbachev says that we should discuss this question at the Central Committee Commission on Eastern Europe. "Let Yakovlev, with scholars, look at it [a number of problems in Eastern Europe]. We are facing a serious problem there." As a result, there emerged a number of interesting memoranda, some of which were given to us by Professor Levesque: a memo from Bogomolov's institute, a memo from the International Department of the Central Committee, from the KGB, although we do not have that document. In other words, some work had begun. But ultimately, no headquarters emerged. First of all, who was in charge? It is clear that Gorbachev could not have been in charge of everything, which leaves us with his assistants. Who was in charge of Eastern Europe?

Shakhnazarov: I was.

Zubok: You were. (Laughter) And what role did Yakovlev play in that process?

Shakhnazarov: I would like to say that you are absolutely right—there was anxiety. I personally had written several memos, and one of them has been published in my book. There were memos from institutes, we received them, studied them, reported some things to Gorbachev. But you have to keep in mind that in 1989 all our thoughts were focused on the internal situation. I, for example, was in charge of political reform along with Eastern Europe. Therefore, most of my time was devoted to memos and reports, to Gorbachev's speeches at the Congress of People's Deputies; in the Supreme Soviet we worked on drafts of laws on openness, on public organizations, and so on.

And it is not an issue of who was in charge, but [the fact that] the attention of the entire leadership was switched to internal problems, and so Eastern Europe was on the back burner. We felt that, and sometimes we regretted that fact, and said to each other that it would lead to no good if we did not pay attention to Eastern Europe. But we still believed that if our internal situation improved, if our *perestroika* moved ahead with democracy and political reforms then those countries also would be able to pass through that difficult stage faster and easier, and that would bring them closer to our country. If, however, our domestic situation deteriorated, then we would not be able to do, or salvage, anything, and in that case they would run away from us anyway, and to the West. A very simple explanation. Gorbachev really did not have time, and so that issue was for us of secondary importance. It was more important to preserve the Soviet Union and to win the battle that was unfolding inside with the forces that were trying to put Russia alongside other republics in opposition to the Union center. That was our sole concentration. That is all.

Csaba Békés: First let me make my personal comment on the Brezhnev Doctrine, which I wanted to make earlier. I completely agree with Shakhnazarov, that

[22] Document No. 39.

if there was such a thing as the Brezhnev Doctrine, that was the Stalin Doctrine. As far as the documentation is concerned, my opinion is that it is connected to the name of Khrushchev. I am not talking about secret Politburo meetings signed by Khrushchev to this effect. However, he was in Hungary in 1958, and made a public speech, in which [he expressed] the essence of the Brezhnev Doctrine, which is known: in case socialism is in danger in one of our friendly countries, we will help. This was practically verbatim included in the speech. So, if something can be considered as documentation of this doctrine, this Soviet doctrine, I think that speech can be such a thing.

Now, first of all, I would like to draw attention to the similarity of these two very important, crucial periods in the post-war history, namely, 1955–56, and 1985–89–90. You understand why they are very important, so I do not have to go into detail. As far as Third World policy issues, the development of East–West relations in these two different periods shows very much similarity, at least to me. And also, more importantly, the Soviet Union's special relationship with Eastern Europe, and with the satellites, in both periods was a crucial issue—the reorganization and resettlement of the existing structure of relations with the satellites. In 1955–56, it was a more modest development, and, of course, it did not include very big concessions up to a point. But the events of 1955–56 in Poland and Hungary resulted, actually, in a situation where the Soviets had to tolerate concessions, which they did not mean to make before. In Poland it was the victory, or the acceptance, of national communism, whereas it was still in essence communism, but a national one, which can be very divergent from the actual Soviet Bolshevik type.

And we have a very good record of the Presidium meetings, from the Malin[23] notes, you know, on October 30, 1956, where the whole Presidium decides to accept the solution that if it is needed, the last concession can be that the Soviet troops could be withdrawn from Hungary, not only from Budapest, but from the whole country, which was the unanimous demand of Hungarian society, of course. This had been out of the question even two days earlier. But partly under Chinese pressure, it was then accepted unanimously. And the important thing here is what [Dmitri] Shepilov, the foreign minister then, says. He says, as an explanation of the decision—and everybody actually accepts this—at least there was no objection, "We have to prepare for a long struggle with national communism." That is what he said. What does that mean? For me, it means that for the Soviets at that time, accepting national communism, at least in these two countries when there were just Hungary and Poland, was the worst option, but still could be accepted if there was nothing else—what can you do?

---

[23] CC CPSU Presidium member Vladimir Malin took handwritten notes of meetings during this period. This document from October 30, 1956, appears in Csaba, *The Hungarian Revolution*, Document No. 49.

In the 1980s, from 1985 to 1989, it is the same issue: accepting national communism is the worst option for the Soviet leaders, which by 1989 becomes wishful thinking. This should be the worst that could happen to us. But these countries stopped developing in national communism, stopped at the limits of communism, whatever communism it should be—a modernized one, a more democratic one, or a national one—but still within the communist framework, and actually for them it was now the best option by 1989. And this also includes the potential idea, that if not [communism], then of course beyond these limits is already capitalism. And then the question becomes: what to tolerate, and what not to tolerate?

And here for me is the big question. They were accepting national communism in the region, but it was not a big deal. Under the circumstances in the 1980s, it was not really a big concession by then. The big question was whether the Soviet Union now, in very different conditions, was willing to go beyond this limit and give up the empire as such, by letting go of these countries and have them become capitalist even, as the very worst option. So the big question for me, which I would like to ask here is: when was this psychological turn, or change, in policy making, in Gorbachev's and your own thinking at the time—what year, what month, what event (it could be one or two)—when can we accept that they [the East Europeans] can go, even if they go capitalist? (Not only that they would go national communist, because that was quite normal already.) This is my big question.

And as far as the use of force is concerned, which has been extensively discussed here. I was asked to be provocative, and I promised to be provocative. My question is: why did you not use force? Of course, I am not complaining that you did not. (Laughter) But there were many arguments here trying to explain why, what factors contributed to not intervening. But none of these convinced me, if I am trying to think as a Soviet decision maker. Because none of the facts, like spoiling East–West relations, whatever, all these things that were mentioned, nothing like this happened when in 1956 Khrushchev decided, and the Khrushchev leadership decided, to intervene in such a case. Nothing bad happened to East–West relations—actually, to the contrary. He was not deposed—to the contrary, he could have been deposed had he not intervened in Hungary. And letting Hungary go—that would have created the danger that he might lose his position.

So I do not see that in this case, for Gorbachev, it was an obvious and logical step to declare that he would not use force. Also, the ambiguity that was mentioned many times by Professor Levesque is a very important factor, because even here, in February 1989, in the document of the International Department of the Soviet Communist Party,[24] it is not ruled out at all. There is one opinion, but there are several others saying, generally, it is a principle that we should not intervene in settling crises in Eastern Europe. But there is one opinion, at least,

[24] Document No. 41.

in the case of an external intervention, which practically speaking means Western external intervention in events, or in the developments of East European countries. Such an eventuality is considered, even in February 1989. So, I still would like to have more—and more convincing—arguments to see why it was so easily accepted, and that the countries of Eastern Europe were quite easily abandoned in this sense, without much force and much fighting for them. I am not complaining of our devaluation here. But still, it is a historical problem, it interests me.

And the last comment, or question, is a more practical and actual question. There were two major issues which were basic in the development of the forthcoming events: first, the Polish elections, and the Polish government in the summer of 1989, which was the first non-communist government in the whole region, which meant that from this time on this wishful thinking, this hope that national communism could be an option, actually was gone, at least for one country. So actually the system was already not the same. Was there any communication or consultation with the Communist Party, first of all, with leaders in Moscow before these events, and also possibly with the Western partners, from the Polish side. Was there any kind of intervention, or any kind of looking around *to see* what they would say?

And the other such event was allowing the Germans to go through Hungary.[25] Another question is whether this very important event, which actually was the first step towards the unification of Germany, was consulted with the Soviet leaders or not? It is very important to know, because the Hungarian communist leaders claim that they did not.

Machcewicz: Just a short question that somehow relates to Csaba's question. Very recently, Mieczysław Rakowski visited Washington DC, and he gave a speech at George Washington University, and he mentioned a telephone conversation which he had with Gorbachev in June 1989, after the election of the 4th of June.

Levesque: August.

Machcewicz: August 1989. It was after the election, but before the Mazowiecki government was created, formally and finally created. And according to Rakowski, Gorbachev really did not know what was going on in Poland. He did not realize how serious the situation was. He did not realize that the communist system was about to collapse. And my question is: what was your real assessment in Moscow of developments in Poland? Were you aware of where those developments were leading? And another question that relates to the first one: what was your strategy, if you had one, towards developments in Poland and in other countries? Did you hope, did you think that it would be possible to preserve the socialist system led by open-minded reformist leaders, which would recognize

---

[25] In September 1989, Hungary began allowing East Germans to transit the country and cross the border freely into Austria, despite the GDR's long-standing prohibition against travel by its citizens to the West.

the opposition, introduce market reforms, but still hold a political monopoly over the Communist Party? Was there any strategy at all? Or was it just reacting to events?

Zubok: A very quick question to Sergey Petrovich [Tarasenko]. Can you tell us what Shevardnadze was doing when the crisis of German refugees was developing first in Hungary, and then in Czechoslovakia? Did he have any discussions at a high level, and if he did, what was the content of those discussions? And if he did, what did the East Germans know about that?

Levesque: During the 10th Plenum of the Polish Communist Party, of the Central Committee of the Polish Communist Party, in the end of January 1989, between the plenary session and the start of roundtable talks, General Jaruzelski was in Moscow. What do you know about this visit?

Dawisha: I have a comment, but it is a question in terms of interpretation. Following on what Csaba has asked us to think about—about why the Soviets did not use force. I was very impressed from the documents, and from what has been said this morning about the extent to which Eastern Europe diminished in concern, in terms of the amount of time spent on the issue by the Politburo. I was very taken in looking at the documents we have, which is, of course, a minute proportion of the total documents, with the amount of time that could be spent discussing whether or not two departments of the Central Committee should be merged, which was a much greater amount of time than was spent discussing what was going to be the change of leadership in East Germany.

From the documents that we have, it seems to me that this question is a very important conclusion that it is not that the Soviets necessarily changed their assessment of what was possible or desirable in Eastern Europe. It was that the total amount of time and priorities of the Soviet leadership shifted. And it shifted in two directions: it shifted internally, that when Gorbachev came to power, clearly, his number one concern was with the possibility of internal collapse, political collapse, a complete loss of authority of the Communist Party, complete loss of morale within the Communist Party, complete economic collapse.

And secondly, he had new thinking, which was extremely revolutionary on the international stage. If one accepts that the positions in Eastern Europe could only be maintained if you kept imperial thinking, then the moment imperial thinking is thrown overboard, what in the hell is your position in Eastern Europe? It becomes a complete drag on new thinking.

And you can imagine all these poor little East European leaders, who spent all their time thinking about nothing except what was going on in Moscow, trying to get the problems of their country onto the agenda of the Politburo. And if only five to seven *percent* of all the time in the top body was being taken up with this issue, then even if they were only looking for one sentence from the top leadership, it must have been very difficult for them to even get this one sentence. So for me, this is a very important aspect of the reason why they did not use force. However, we do not have all the documents, we have by no means all the documents on Eastern Europe.

155

We do not have military documents. And surely, the military were highly involved in the discussion of their positions in Eastern Europe. And I wanted to ask Georgy, you were sent to the "lion's den" many times as a representative of the International Department to negotiate with or to listen to what was going on in the high command, in terms of their reaction to new thinking, and their new military doctrine. And we have some of the documents here. So, how much time did they spend talking about and thinking about what was going on in Eastern Europe? Was it only five to seven *percent*? Did they also react in the same way that Gorbachev did?

And also, of course, in the KGB? We do not have these documents. So, what is your impression about whether there were other organs that were spending much more time on this issue?

Shakhnazarov: I will try to respond in a most laconic way, because it is a very broad question. First of all, I would like to say that we are underestimating the economic factor. We practically have not spoken about it. I am trying to respond to the first question. When did our leadership become ready to drop some of the burden of the relations with the allies, and, crudely speaking, to release the leash by which Moscow held its satellites? One has to keep in mind that, ideology and Soviet military forces stationed in those countries notwithstanding, our influence was based 90 percent on economic ties. And at a certain time that burden became too much for the Soviet Union; we could not carry it any more.

And then the process began. Initially we changed the system of payments for oil deliveries. We used to sell oil to them four or six times cheaper than on the world market, and that way we were able to support all socialist countries more or less. And we delivered approximately 100 million tons in one five-year term. Such countries as the GDR received 17 million tons, Poland—14 million tons, Czechoslovakia—16 million, Romania—even though it had its own oil reserves, it always insisted that we sell our oil, and they always got some. We began from reconsidering the pricing system. That was a substantial blow to the socialist countries.

Another issue is that when the Polish events began [in 1980], we had to put a lot of our money there, and to redirect resources from other countries. Altogether it cost the Soviet Union approximately 10 to 15 billion dollars, not counting increases in oil deliveries, and other goods. That is why when Gorbachev just began to approach the positions of power, he had to deal with these problems. When he became Number Two in the party hierarchy, he made his first trip to Bulgaria where he had to tell Zhivkov that we were not able to give them their annual loan on the order of 400 million rubles any more. The Bulgarians pressured Brezhnev into granting them that annual loan, and they used it to subsidize their agricultural production. This is how it worked.

In Hungary, approximately 50 percent of their gross national product came from foreign trade operations. We saw the country as if it was already halfway out of the socialist camp. And the impossibility of carrying that burden any longer, in my opinion, played the decisive role, in that from a certain time we began

156

to say: let them be more free, but they should not ask so much from us in the economic sense; we cannot drag this imperial burden any more. It was over with the historic words of Suslov, which he spoke at a meeting of the Commission on Poland. You have to understand the context, because Suslov in our system was like the Pope for the Catholic church. So, he said once, we had already quoted him during our conference in Poland, "It is okay even if Poland becomes capitalist, as long as they do not join NATO." If Suslov admitted that possibility, it means that the Soviet leadership as a whole had already accepted that. By the way, I would like to remind you that in 1968 all the events in Czechoslovakia, the Prague spring, were received with indignation, with anger and disapproval, but they did not talk about introducing troops. They began to speak about the introduction of troops only after the head of the International Department, Koberko, published his article to feel out the reaction. The essence of the article was that Czechoslovakia should leave the Warsaw Treaty organization and join NATO. Only when that transpired, that was seen as the final attack [...] The leadership could not allow that to happen.

Now, as far as Mazowiecki is concerned, I have a transcript of a conversation between Gorbachev and Mazowiecki. It is a very interesting document because from the very beginning of it Mazowiecki tells Gorbachev that he is very grateful for the Soviet leadership's positive attitude toward the new Polish government, and at one point he says, "We understand that there are ideological ties that exist between the CPSU and the PUWP, but from my point of view the state-to-state union is more important. And that can be guaranteed by various forces representing a wide political spectrum of the Polish public."

Gorbachev responds to him, "We recognize the right of every nation to determine its future independently. And, of course, it is the Poles' business to decide what kind of government they want to have. Since we have a good relationship with the Polish people, we are ready to work with any government that they elect. I believe that good neighborly relations between our two countries are in Poland's strategic interests." Here for the first time, Gorbachev admitted, openly and unequivocally, that we accepted any scenario of development for the political regime in Poland. What was important for us was the strategic union with Poland. In the same conversation, Mazowiecki raised the issue of a possible visit by Lech Wałęsa, and Gorbachev agreed to meet with him. It was November 24, 1989. I am passing this document to you, and you can make a copy, and use it.[26]

Another question that Professor Dawisha asked was about the military. Of course, we always had disagreements with the military. And it is natural, because the military, everywhere in the world, does what they are supposed to do, namely think mostly about security. Therefore, I think in the United States also, there are certain tensions between the military and the politicians. In our Warsaw Treaty Organization we had the following procedure: the General Staff

[26] See Document No. 107.

would prepare a report to Marshal [Viktor] Kulikov, who was the commander-in-chief of the Unified Forces of the Warsaw Treaty Organization. That document was presented to the Central Committee. We studied it in the Department and began to work on it.

Initially we would make comments, and they would change certain things in the report, and after that they would come to the Central Committee and we would sit together as a team to finalize that document. Of course, we tried to make it more political, to lift it up, and the military pressured for more money in order to persuade our friends that we invest a lot of money, buy more military technology, and so on and so forth.

Arguably the most interesting meeting was the session of the Committee of Defense Ministers of the WTO, which took place immediately after the Party Conference, if I remember correctly, in July 1988. At that meeting Gorbachev spoke about our goals, what our plans were, why *perestroika* took its current shape, and so on. That is not interesting. What is interesting is that before the session, as usual, they presented the plan of work for the Committee of Defense Ministers to the Central Committee. And our military also presented their draft of Marshal [Dmitri] Yazov's speech. The text was quite pacifist, I would say. In the first part of the speech, our military spoke about the need for *perestroika*, reconciliation, the movement toward peace, and the like. And the rest of the draft said that in order to do that we needed to strengthen such-and-such flank, add such-and-such military technology, and so on; in other words, they requested more spending for armaments.

We had great debates with them. And Marshal [Sergey] Akhromeev at that time was already Gorbachev's assistant. He was a military officer, a respected leader, and an intelligent person. We did have arguments with him, but those were rational arguments, and we were always able to reach common conclusions. We were able then to find formulas that said that we needed to reduce our military muscle, not increase it. Therefore, there was that problem. But it was not an acute problem for us because, as Anatoly Sergeyevich has already said, there was no opposition in the Army, and there could not have been. There were some people who were extremely negative, like General [Albert] Makashov, who is now the main hawk in the Duma, on the left.

Chernyaev: [Vitaly] Varennikov.

Shakhnazarov: Varennikov was more moderate then. But to think that they rose against the general secretary, against the Central Committee—that was absolutely unimaginable up until the very end, up until the putsch of 1991. Am I right?

Chernyaev: Approximately.

Tarasenko: Petrushenko, Alksnis.[27]

---

[27] Col. Nikolay Petrushenko and Col. Viktor Alksnis were outspoken members of the hardline *Soyuz* (Union) bloc in the Soviet Duma who publicly attacked Gorbachev's reform

Shakhnazarov: I think that I have answered all the questions.

Tarasenko: I would like to make a short comment about that dramatic moment when there was the "running away after the summer vacation," so to speak, when the citizens of the GDR began to vote for another system with their feet. It so happened that at that time Shevardnadze was already at the session of the General Assembly, it was mid-September 1989, when all the ministers gather in New York. Genscher, and the GDR foreign minister,[28] I do not recall his name now, were already there too. And because that issue by that time had become like a fast-progressing illness, I know that Shevardnadze met with both ministers sometimes several times a day. I was not there, but I know. They had additional contacts through [James] Baker. In principle, the decision had been found in New York, and the urgency of the issue was removed. They came to an agreement, and sent instructions to their relative capitals on how to act: to let those East Germans, who had already left, go. And the West Germans promised that they would not provoke the East Germans. In other words, they were able to resolve the issue temporarily, for a short time only. Later it emerged in its full force and urgency.

CHAPTER 4: THE DOMESTIC CONTEXT

Blanton: This session has been titled "Domestic Context" where we will get into some of the issues that Georgy has raised about these limitations: economics and so forth. But there is one major issue still hanging over from the previous session, and that is, it seems to me, the role of Shevardnadze. And I would say, particularly after the events in Tbilisi in April 1989, when the Soviet Union did use force against the Georgians, among Eastern Europeans you can hardly blame them for seeing the possibility of use of force against them in that same way.

And some of the evidence that we have, but it is limited, suggests that at least after those events in Tbilisi, Shevardnadze began exercising a somewhat independent role. In fact, by November of 1989, we actually have a declassified U.S. cable from Baker to the Sofia Embassy saying that, according to a report from an unimpeachable source, which could only be Shevardnadze, Shevardnadze personally intervened to support Mladenov, to boot Zhivkov in November. Now, it is not an ambiguous answer, "it is your business," it is a cable that says that Shevardnadze intervened and booted the guy. So, this is a different kind of Soviet role vis-à-vis the countries of Eastern Europe, and I wanted to ask Sergey about Shevardnadze's reaction, starting from the events in Tbilisi in April 1989. In the Shevardnadze–Gorbachev relationship, to what degree in those subsequent months did Shevardnadze play an independent role? And then I want to give Jacques Levesque a chance to ask Sergey a follow-up question on the refugee issues.

program in 1990 and helped prompt Shevardnadze's resignation.
[28] Oskar Fischer.

Tarasenko: The events in Tbilisi, of course, were a big surprise. Gorbachev and Shevardnadze were returning home from a trip to London. There had been demonstrations there for several days, a crowd gathered in front of the Government Palace. I would like to explain some context to you so that you understand our mentality. When our leader returns home from a foreign trip, and there are demonstrations in front of a republican Central Committee, one has to do something. That is why, I think, the local government forced the events—to disperse the rally. They did it in an unfortunate way. They calculated that there would have been no people in the street at that time, but to the contrary, most people had gathered in the square by that time. As a result, 20 people were dead. When we arrived, Gorbachev received a telephone call—I understand that he was informed about the situation. He spoke with the Georgian leader. And then he ordered Shevardnadze to take charge of that problem, and to fly to Tbilisi immediately.

Shevardnadze was not excited about going there because of his past position in Georgia. It was a delicate issue for him to interfere in the affairs of his successor. He called them and received some comforting information, that everything was all right, that the situation was under control, and that he did not need to go. In several days, as was the practice after such foreign trips, we convened the Committee of Ministers of the WTO, and our foreign minister reported about the negotiations with our Western counterparts. We sat down to prepare documents for the Committee of Ministers, and suddenly we got a telephone call—and it was a Saturday—that we had to fly to Georgia immediately. The minister was flying at 10 a.m. I and another assistant packed our suitcases and flew to Tbilisi.

The situation there was very difficult. It was very difficult to relieve the consequences of that action. Our recent Defense Minister [Igor] Rodionov was the commander of the Caucasus military district. He was in charge of that operation. I am not going to tell you how it all happened. But it was a very unpleasant moment that had an impact on my attitude toward this general. They used gas. Next day there were several hundred people in the hospitals with respiratory problems. Doctors made requests to General Rodionov to tell them what exactly they used, what kind of gas, so that they could treat the people. The response was: this is a provocation, we did not use any gas, there was nothing like this. One day later they admitted that they did use gas, and they named the kind that was used.

That lie, especially when people were in the hospitals, was terrible. One thing is that they carried out their primary task poorly, but they could have dealt with the consequences better. The minister stayed there for 10 days to calm the situation. There was the following moment: they had a Plenum of the Central Committee at which he made a speech. Georgia was very suspicious of the center at the time. We sent the speech to Moscow through the TASS channels, and requested that it be published. We knew our practice: they could cut or censor the speech. We called them on the telephone and sent a telegram telling them not to change a comma, not a single character. We said: You either publish it in full, or do not publish it at all; but if you change a single word, it will ruin everything. At that time, such a request was not an easy thing. I do not know who, and at what level, made the decision—it was the newspapers' business, our internal propaganda. But eventually the speech was published in full, and reconciliation was achieved.

You probably understood from what my senior colleagues said that we had less and less time left for international affairs. And therefore, Shevardnadze's role became more prominent—not because he wanted to do more, or because he wanted to show himself off more. It was simply because many problems needed to be solved, and he often had to make decisions without any directives, without consultations with the center. He had to make decisions on the spot, often during his trips.

I think that Anatoly Sergeyevich can speak as a witness, because he was very helpful in resolving issues, because Shevardnadze often sent telegrams to Gorbachev which stated that they had achieved such-and-such a compromise, such-and-such a package deal, especially on missiles, on disarmament—and if he could not get an affirmative response until, let us say, 10 p.m. Moscow time, he would do this and this. It is a diplomatic trick—to state a deadline. That forced the center to either make a decision or to let us pass our decision. Usually our proposals were approved. Usually the center gave their approval. Rarely, it would pass automatically.

However, there were some brave decisions that our military did not like. The military generally did not like a great deal of the disarmament process. This is just a general rule. Therefore, it was not a voluntary power takeover. It was a result of a vacuum of power, a vacuum of attention to specific issues. Traditional coordination on issues of disarmament requires substantial effort and energy. You have to convene representatives of five or six different ministries or organizations. It is practically impossible to come to a common denominator. In that case one has to make a forceful decision. And the minister took such forceful breakthroughs onto his shoulders. He took the responsibility.

I can tell you about the Mladenov case. I did not attend their meeting. They spoke Russian, and they met one-on-one. I know that at that time U.S.–Bulgarian relations were very tense; I do not remember why.

Shakhnazarov: Because of the Turks.

Tarasenko: Yes, because of the Turkish issue. So, the secretary of state did not even want to meet with the Bulgarian minister, he did not want to have anything in common—some kind of sanctions were in force. I was always present at Shevardnadze's meetings with the secretary of state. And I was present at that meeting. They had already got to such a level of personal trust that Shevardnadze said: "Do me a favor. I know your position, but it is very important and it is necessary. And I want you to know about it." In response, the secretary of state said, "Then you can also do me a favor—meet with [Jonas] Savimbi. We know your position toward this Angolan separatist. But do it in the interests of the cause of peace. It would help if you met with him."

This is how they decided that: the secretary of state met with Mladenov, and our minister met with Savimbi. Later it became a routine practice: even on disarmament issues, when it involved their positions, sometimes important positions, they were very open with each other, and often said, "I need your help, I need your help to deal with my domestic problems—to get approval I have to get something from you. Some concession. Give me this, and then it will be easier for me to get that." And that was reciprocal: the secretary of state asked Shevardnadze, and Shevardnadze asked the secretary of state. And that way they were able to move ahead, because often they found themselves at a complete dead end, when it looked like there was no way out. But they had to move somewhere. And they moved by taking side roads, and moved the negotiations ahead.

Returning to new thinking. It mostly related to foreign policy; domestic policy was involved indirectly. *Perestroika* and *glasnost*, and all other terms related to internal policy; new thinking was in the realm of foreign policy. And in my view, of all that was accomplished under Gorbachev, most of the progress had been made in foreign policy. I think it was not only because there were conceptual ideas presented by the general secretary, but also because Gorbachev made the right choice when he picked Shevardnadze as foreign minister. He turned out to be a natural-born diplomat.

This can easily be explained because in the Soviet practice a regional secretary, a secretary of a republic, had to be a diplomat in order to have a normal relationship with the center. Georgia always was the most liberal republic—they had no problems with dissidents or with emigrants. They dealt with their problems in a calm way. Already at that time Shevardnadze was able to find ways to resolve all those urgent problems. And in Soviet times to get credits, or to get oil, also required some diplomatic skill. To get anything, one had to have diplomatic skills.

So, he played a more and more independent role out of necessity. And at the final stage, during the conflict with Saddam Hussein, during the Persian Gulf War, he had to do many things all by himself, informing the leadership after the fact.

Levesque: I have a tentative answer to your question concerning the opening of the Western border of Hungary to East German refugees. At the same time, I would like to know whether this answer makes sense to Sergey Tarasenko from what he knows. I discussed this issue in Budapest with László Kovács. He was in 1989 a deputy to Foreign Minister [Gyula] Horn. At first, he told me their official position was made by the Hungarians independently. But afterwards, what he said qualified this to a considerable extent. He first told me that before making that decision they were extremely concerned about the Soviet reaction.

He said, "We knew what to expect from the East Germans, but we did not know what to expect from the Soviets." In other words, they were extremely concerned about what would the Soviet reaction be. So he did not say, "We asked for permission," but he said, "We sent some feelers to Moscow, to Shevardnadze's office, informing Shevardnadze of our intention to decide along the lines of opening the border. And after a few days," he said, "we received an answer from Shevardnadze, which was extremely short—there were very few words: it is an issue that concerns Hungary, East Germany, and West Germany." He told me, "We were extremely relieved to receive such a message from Shevardnadze. And we interpreted it as a green light." And he said, "Of course, when we did that, we knew that it would be a terrible blow for Honecker. And we certainly knew that they knew in Moscow that their message was a terrible blow for Honecker." Because Honecker at the time was exerting pressure on Moscow so that Moscow would press the Hungarians not to open the border.

So, again, Georgy, the Soviet Union played a very significant indirect role. I would like, maybe Sergey Tarasenko, to confirm this story that I was told in Budapest. Does it make sense to you?

Tarasenko: That is right. Shevardnadze sided with the Hungarians on this issue. Not only in this message, in this wording, but generally.

Levesque: I was told by [Károly] Grósz in Budapest that they decided at the top level of the party that that issue would have to be resolved at the level of the Foreign Ministry, that the party leadership would not take care of that. So apparently Horn had some autonomy in making this decision, but they consulted the Soviet side before making the decision.

Chernyaev: First of all, I would like to react to what Jacques Levesque has just said. I think that it would be extremely interesting from a linguistic point of view to compare Gorbachev's conversations with Western leaders and his conversations with East European leaders. If, in the first case, they talked at the level of common sense, practical realism, and sometimes even pragmatism, even down-to-earth pragmatism sometimes, a feeling of mutual trust emerged at that level, and they were able to make serious policy. In the second case, with allies and friends, conversations were still saturated with ideology to a large extent.

That played a negative role, judging from the historical perspective. It convinced the interlocutors that Gorbachev would not give up his ideological principles, that he would come to their rescue whatever they were doing, that he would not abandon them, any perturbations notwithstanding. This fact is very important to keep in mind.

Why did Gorbachev act this way? Unfortunately, with the exception of Jaruzelski, he did not feel that other East European leaders were his equals (*Kádár* had been gradually deteriorating). He did not think that they were at the level of modern international relations. He could not allow himself to speak openly with them because he understood that they were locked in ideologically, and that they would misunderstand him even worse if he was to speak with them as he spoke with Western leaders. This is the first question.

Now I would like to react—not to answer, but precisely to react—to the questions posed by Mr. Békés. Because there are no answers to such questions, they do not exist in nature. I was asked dozens of times, and Gorbachev was asked also: Tell us, on what day, in what month, in what year, did you agree to German unification? There is no such date. The same with regard to the whole of Eastern Europe and to other questions that you posed; for example, when did he decide that he would not try to save communism? From the time—you are absolutely right on this—when communist ideology disappeared from his foreign policy, from the time he understood, first instinctively and then consciously, that it was not a tool for resolving modern practical issues of international development; from that time on he could not care less whether a communist regime in Poland or in Hungary would survive or not.

Georgy cited the conversation with Mazowiecki. I was also present at that conversation. The first new non-communist leader of a socialist country came to Moscow. The conversation was absolutely normal—no skittishness or suspicions, no tensions regarding the fact that the visitor was representing a socialist country, and no special acting toward him.

Gorbachev talked to him like he talked to Genscher, Baker, and others. He talked with him as with a person who had reached the level of modern understanding of international affairs. He did not have a problem with the fact that here was a new man who would lead Poland away from the Soviet Union. For him it was important how to work practically on economic issues, cultural issues, and so on. In other words, he was talking with a man who represented his state, statesman-like. The Poles decided what they wanted to do, and he would deal with the representative whom they elected. That logic, that transition from the ideological mentality to the mentality of common sense in Gorbachev is impossible to date.

I cannot answer this question, I cannot tell you when Gorbachev gave up the communist approach to international affairs. I understand my scholarly colleagues. In order to conduct scholarly analysis, one needs some kind of logical framework. Unfortunately, it does not work like this in politics. This is why I was very impressed by Jacques Levesque's book: because he is not trying to fit the events and peoples' positions into schemes. He analyzes real events, real processes, not schemes. I disagree with some of his conclusions, but it does not matter. The strength of the book is in the fact, as ironic as it sounds here, that he rejected the "Soviet approach" toward analyzing schemes.

For example, the socialist camp began to shatter. Was there any conception of how to react, any scenarios, alternatives? If it goes this way—what are you going to do? And if it goes that way—what are you going to do? There was nothing like that. No commissions, and no committees had discussions about alternatives. This is what the Kremlinologists were doing in the West. No conceptions were prepared. And if such conversations arose at some Politburo sessions, we focused on very concrete problems: for example, how to react to the Germans running across the border to Hungary. What did we decide? Let them run, let them decide themselves. It is not our business to hold them, or to turn them back to the GDR. Telling you about all this, I wanted to draw your attention to this point: That we cannot answer some of the questions that science poses to us, because these are different planes of objective logic.

Hershberg: On the concrete questions about Gorbachev's response to concrete events in 1989, there are two mysteries that always puzzled me, and I think are also relevant to the question that Vilém Prečan raised earlier trying to figure out

164

what are the limits. The issue has already been raised. Two questions that I am wondering about: can you illuminate for us Gorbachev's reaction to the Chinese crackdown at Tiananmen, because I know, for many reformers, who in the West and probably in Eastern Europe looked to Gorbachev for a new standard of morality, there was great disappointment when Gorbachev, for whatever reason, refused to condemn the crackdown in Beijing, and even criticized Andrey Sakharov when he tried to do so at the Congress of People's Deputies.

Was that purely a pragmatic calculation from Gorbachev, whereas he in his heart was opposed and horrified by the use of force? Or did he see it as a rational response of a leader to control his own people? That is the first mystery.

The second concerns the statement issued by the Central Committee on August 26, 1989, while Gorbachev was on vacation, three days after the 2 million-people human chain in the Baltics took place, from Vilnius to Riga to Tallinn. And I just think I remember reading about this in *The New York Times* in the United States. The statement from the Central Committee sounded like it was issued from the Politburo of Joseph Stalin. It used the language of accusing the Baltics of being Fascist, nationalist, saying they were risking their very existence, a blatant threat to use force.

And interestingly, Ambassador Matlock in his book wrote that it was inconceivable that this statement was issued without Gorbachev's approval, even though he was not in Moscow when it was released to the press. And yet, it certainly went against the entire thrust, and the entire language of Gorbachev. Can you clarify, was this Gorbachev trying to draw a line between the internal empire and the external empire in Eastern Europe? That within the Soviet Union there was a different code of conduct? Or was this an early sign of the kind of independent action that can happen when Gorbachev goes on vacation in August?

Zubok: My question is a follow-up question on this point. Valentin Falin is not present here, we tried to invite him, but he could not come even though he was interested. As far as I remember, in his memoirs, he said that while the socialist bloc was crumbling, he was running around the Central Committee, knocking on doors, to Yakovlev and to others, and suggesting various measures. But nobody was willing to listen to him, and all his suggestions were in vain. I have a question in this respect: what could he propose? Were there any proponents of the use of force in some versions in that period? Can you name anybody who proposed to use force?

Chen Jian: Actually, you know, in history, sometimes the result was determined by the order. One example was in 1989, while in Eastern Europe there was a lack of force—use of force—but on the other side, there was an extreme case of use of force, especially in Beijing. And actually, in 1989, it should have been a kind of turning point for the international communist movement, because for the first time in three decades it seemed that a unification of the international communist movement was in order with Gorbachev's visit to Beijing. And actually, Gorbachev's new thinking in foreign policy was comprehensive, and included major adjustments in the Soviet position toward China, including a commitment to changing Soviet policy toward the Vietnamese occupation, or invasion, of Cambodia, which was something Brezhnev refused even to talk about for almost five or six years. Actually, even after Brezhnev. And also, a new commitment to changing Soviet policy toward Afghanistan.

And these were exactly Deng Xiaoping's preconditions for meeting with Soviet leaders. And not until 1988 was the foundation created. So, exactly, what were Gorbachev's aims in visiting Beijing? This is one question.

And then his visit to Beijing created a kind of stage for the already existing pro-democracy movement in Beijing. Because of his visit to Beijing, you find that the entire world paid attention to it. Somehow, however, the focus of his visit was shifted from him to the daily developing student movement. But without his visit, the whole 1989 Beijing crackdown story could have been completely different, without that kind of international attention.

So then comes Jim's question about why Moscow refused to openly condemn the Beijing massacre. Of course, another question is, really, the hidden meaning of it—what exactly was the role of the Beijing massacre for the future, not just decision making, but also mentality of leaders in Moscow and in the Eastern European countries? Actually, if it had not been for the Beijing massacre in the early summer of 1989, what would their whole understanding be about the necessity of using force, and the consequences? And as a result, practical policy making would have been completely different.

Wolff: There has been a lot of talk in the course of the afternoon about Gorbachev's ambiguity in a general sense, but not in the sense of him being a divided character, who divides his time and his character, in a way, between internal matters and external matters, and how each time he goes on a trip all kinds of things happen, and he has to return and somehow pick up the pieces—whether we are starting with the Nina Andreyeva letter back in 1988, where he is off in Yugoslavia and he comes back in the middle of a crisis, or if we are looking at 1989, where he goes off to China and comes back to face that Havel has come out of prison, and the Polish church has been legalized, and Lithuania has declared its sovereignty. Or we can produce a whole set of these things.

This goes back to Vlad's question about what is Gorbachev's reference group in different periods? Does his reference group switch somehow, or is he somehow continuing to have this very complex life between the two places? It is sort of a general question about how he's managing to live between these two sets of ideals, and I guess, the very specific question you could ask is how did the communications work when he was traveling? Did he know everything that was piling up on his plate at home when he was off traveling? Did he get that level of detail, or did he come back to surprises every time?

Chernyaev: First, regarding Tiananmen Square, and that terrible murder. Several days later, Gorbachev and I were in the FRG. That was a famous visit that became a turning point in Gorbachev's understanding of the German issue, but that is a separate topic. At the press conference, which was extensive, very sincere, and sometimes harsh, Gorbachev was at his best, and they interrogated him about the events that had just happened. "Such events happened, you are a person of new thinking, you are against violence, for democracy, and human rights. You proclaimed those principles at home, and you abide by them. Look what happened."

Gorbachev responded in the following way, "I would advise you not to make rush judgments about China, about that great state, in which very serious processes are underway right now. I was there. I saw it. It is very easy to condemn it, but what's next? What serious politician can allow himself not to take the Chinese factor into account in the perspective of development? Who would make a witches' Sabbath out of it? Of course, it could be done at the level of Sakharov, but not at the level of state leaders. I cannot make such statements." This is how he answered that question. He was asked again, but he did not change his position. When we got back on the plane, he was saying, "What did they want from me? To condemn China? I do not like what happened there, but I am a statesman, I am a leader of a great power. And we are talking about another great power. Why would I do such things!"

This was his attitude. You may say that it was ambivalence again. No, it was the position of a statesman. I never liked that, I was emotionally upset. But I also recognized his right to do so. And sometimes, when I was too insistent with my opinions regarding duplicity, he used to tell me, "That is for you to do, that is your position, and I have other responsibilities, and I have my own position. You report to me, and I have huge responsibilities." Georgy can add something here, because he was in China with Gorbachev, if I remember correctly.

Now regarding the demonstration with candles in the Baltics. We learned about that when we were in Foros. Gorbachev was on vacation, and I was with him in charge of all the papers. He received phone calls from the KGB, from the Central Committee, I do not remember who exactly called, but they demanded that there should be a response, that we could not let it stand—that there should be a very harsh reaction. They sent us several drafts of statements from the Central Committee. I am not bragging about myself, but at the level of my responsibility, only to Gorbachev, and to nobody else, I told him that we could not do that—meaning that we could not make such a statement, that we would not have changed anything, but would only have made those people angrier, and thus made our own situation worse.

So I can admit that I was categorically opposed to that statement. But he disagreed with me: "We have to show them that we have the Constitution, the law. They are demanding secession from the Union. We will deal with this issue within the framework of our Constitution, of the integrity of our state." Stepping a little bit ahead of myself, I can give you my personal opinion—I am not hiding it, I wrote about it in my books. I think that Gorbachev made a very serious mistake with the Baltics. Had he let them go earlier, had he agreed with their independence and not tried to stop them with economic sanctions and other pressures, all the future problems related to the preservation of the Union as a new democratic confederate state on the basis of the New Union Treaty would have been easier. I am absolutely convinced. Because the Baltics always were an alien formation within the Soviet Union. And not only many politicians, but even common people perceived it as such.

When our Russian people traveled to Latvian or Estonian resorts, they thought they were going abroad. They had a different way of life there, and a different standard of living. I can cite my personal experience. I fought in the war in the Baltics in 1944–1945, took part in the liberation of Riga. When we crossed the former border (of 1934), we had the feeling that we had entered a foreign country. And that was the people's attitude toward us too. Of course, there were different attitudes. There were negative feelings, there were the "greens," the guerillas, but there also were people who related to us positively. Those who saw us as liberators thought that after we liberated them from the Germans, after the war was over, they would return to 1939, and we would leave.

And if we had done that, history would have been completely different. But in the late 1980s, when all the processes began, we had to let the Baltics go immediately, and then the tumor that later metastasized with separatism to all the republics would have been removed, cut off. This is my story, I was present at that statement's origin. You did not believe that Gorbachev could have signed it, but unfortunately he did, he approved that very harsh document of the Central Committee.

Now regarding Falin who went door-to-door in the Central Committee. I do not know about that. What could he have achieved with that? I do not know. I do not know anybody, except maybe several generals, who wanted it, but they kept it to themselves. But to propose the use of force, or introduction of troops, or anything like that—they did not. What could we do? Everybody was saying we need to do something, but what exactly? Nobody seriously proposed to use force.

Now, regarding the trips to China, and what Gorbachev's goal was there. The goal was very natural—we had to put an end to that abnormal situation where we were waging a Cold War not only with the West but also with China. The second one was even harsher—that the Cold War could have a very bad ending. That situation with China did not give anybody any benefits—economic, political, or psychological. He went there to normalize our relations. Moreover, we did not even think about the kind of relations we had in the early 1950s, the great friendship, or that the two great powers would revitalize the international communist movement together—that never even came to Gorbachev's mind, let alone the Chinese. Gorbachev's task was just the opposite—to remove the ideological aspect of the relationship with China, to free it from ideological nostalgia. This is what I can tell you.

Shakhnazarov: I would like to begin by stating my disagreement, for the first time, with Anatoly Sergeyevich. Mao Zedong called it "contradictions within the people." It concerns his position on the Baltics. The statement was primitive, and very dumb indeed, but in principle Gorbachev was right in reacting harshly in the beginning. He could not have done otherwise, it was his duty as head of the Soviet state. Yesterday I read in *The Washington Post* that there was a small group of people in Texas who are in favor of the secession of Texas. There was a commentary that Texas had joined the United States forever, I think in 1844, and that the issue was not a real one. But there is still that group.

Now what is the U.S. president supposed to do—just let that develop? Or when the Lombardian separatists raised those issues? The Baltics were a part of the Soviet Union, and the Soviet president had to do everything possible to preserve it as such. I categorically disagree with the opinion that if we had let them secede earlier that would have made preservation of the rest of the Soviet Union easier. Nothing of the sort. Such an action, once it starts, inevitably leads to subsequent actions. If the Baltics can do it, then the Uzbeks can do it, and then the Ukrainians can do it too. That is why he had to undertake those measures. And he tried to do it. We had written a law, set a five-year timetable, with a necessary referendum, and the resolution of all economic and other issues, including territorial issues. If the breakup of the Soviet Union had happened on that basis, then at least Russia would have kept the Crimea.

Therefore, I leave the question of justice aside for now. We are not talking about right and wrong. There are some laws of state life that no country would break. Take Yugoslavia for example, Kosovo. It is a very complex problem. The West is completely on the Albanian side, but it does not take into account the simple fact that the territory of Kosovo is the core of the Yugoslavian territory, and the Serbs were in the great majority in that area. It is their historic mistake that they let the Albanians become a majority there. Should they now give that territory away to the Albanians without any resistance? Therefore, I strongly doubt that.

As far as China is concerned, I was there with Gorbachev , and took part in the discussions. There was a man who was very close to Gorbachev, Zhao Ziyang, then [general] secretary of the Central Committee of the Chinese Communist Party. Their discussions were almost at the same level as Gorbachev's conversations with Jaruzelski, and with other people who were close to him. And that is why Gorbachev believed that there was a chance that China would choose their road. Unfortunately, it did not happen. But when Gorbachev talked with Deng Xiaoping, he understood that that man personified a very big trend in political thought, and that we should let China choose its own way, without forcing them to do anything.

By the way, he explained it best in his lecture at the Sorbonne, if anybody remembers that episode.[29] The French were insistently asking the question, how he, a democrat, a thinking person, could refrain from condemning China. And he told them, "What should I condemn? You have to understand, it is a completely unique society, in which the issues of democracy are not yet raised the way they are in your country, and now in my country too. They have to be ripe for that. We should not force them, but rather give them a chance to resolve those issues on

[29] July 5, 1989.

their own." Therefore, I believe that he was absolutely right on China, especially because in less than a year the Americans also had to normalize relations with China. Even more so now.

Now, I would like to add on the issues that have already been discussed here. I would like to add to what Sergey Petrovich said about Shevardnadze. I think that when a painter works on his painting, he does not start with details, like a boot, or a woman's foot, or curtains. He starts with thinking about the composition of the painting. It's the same with what was happening in our country—we have to look at it in its entirety, at the whole picture. In the beginning, all the secretaries of the republics—Shevardnadze, Aliyev, Nazarbaev, Karimov[30]—all presidents today—felt themselves as parts of one large system, and acted accordingly. And Shevardnadze felt that way too.

But at a certain point in time they all realized that the national liberation movement for the independence of the republics was beginning. Then they were faced with the question whether they should remain a part of that system, or whether they should turn from communists into nationalists. And they have done that, one after another, some earlier, some later. Shevardnadze also followed that path. And from the moment when the thought about the possibility of Georgian independence crossed his mind, he stopped being a member of the Communist Party of the Soviet Union and a Politburo member, and became a Georgian. All the rest of them experienced that. As far as the events in Tbilisi are concerned, you have to look at them from the perspective that I just mentioned. It was one of the bursts of the liberation movement, which eventually led to the breakup of the Soviet Union.

Falin did go door-to-door. And he visited me too. He was angry, he wrote memos to the effect that we need to take harsh measures, we should not just sit and observe it. But Anatoly is right, there was nothing concrete in those memos. He was just making noise, saying that it was no good that we were giving everything away without a fight. But he could not propose anything concrete. The same with Kvitsinsky, and with some of our other German experts who are now writing their memoirs, their articles, where they pour dirt on Gorbachev, and accuse him of every mortal sin. But at the time, they could not propose anything of substance.

And the final comment. You repeatedly posed the question of whether Gorbachev knew, whether he understood. What did he think when he acted one way but not another? Gorbachev's influence as a deity in charge of the entire process had great significance. But you have to take into account the fact that as Gorbachev influenced events, the events influenced him too. He developed himself, moving to a large extent by trial and error. Life pushed him ahead and sometimes submerged him into some unpleasant situations. Every time he was forced to find answers.

---

[30] Geidar Aliyev of Azerbaijan, Nursultan Nazarbaev of Kazakhstan, and Islam Karimov of Uzbekistan.

We do not have to look for a thought-out system. He did not do his reforms like other great reformers, like Luther, who nailed his 102 [sic] Points to the wall of the Wittenberg church, who knew far in advance what they were supposed to do; everything was planned out. No. He chose his direction correctly. The non-violent method was also correct. The rest depended on God, and on the people, and on other politicians, and on the United States. And unfortunately, we did not hear much about the latter here.

This is my final comment. To tell you honestly, I would like to hear more from your side. You see, we come, we bring the documents, we give them to you, and we are glad to do it because we see that there are people here who write history in a good sense, who preserve it for the future. But for our part, we would like to know: what did the Americans think about? Is it true what some of our politicians on the left are saying, that it was the Americans who had planned everything, who pushed Wałęsa ahead, who provoked everything?

[....]

MacEachin: I am puzzled by the description of the [Soviet] 1989 response as an enigma. I will explain why I do not see it as an enigma.

But let me offer some related information. I just checked this record of testimony I have here, which, if you do not have a copy I will get you one. This was testimony which by a coincidence occurred when I was asked to appear before the Senate Select Committee on Intelligence (actually it was a Task Force of the Committee) on the 7th of December of 1988. While I was sitting in front of the Senate Committee Task Force, Gorbachev was up in New York before the U.N. General Assembly announcing unilateral military force cuts. As I was giving this testimony, I kept sending my colleagues out of the room to check the television broadcast. You will see if you read the testimony record that at that particular time, as late in the game as that was, this was something that had been forecast earlier. We all like to brag about when we were right and forget about when we were wrong, but it was nonetheless considered a very radical estimate, judgment, and had not been accepted even by the senator to whom I was talking that day. You can see this because I opened the briefing by saying that I won my bets, Senator, and then his staff started to denigrate the implications of the force cuts. You can see in the record how this conversation played out.

What I am saying is that the developments at that particular time should be looked at in the context of what we have said here about 1987; we have agreed that by then national communism was the best outcome—it was acceptable, and was the best outcome—and that there would be almost certainly no intervention under circumstances where a government identified itself as national communist.

I teach a course in analysis, and part of what we emphasize in the course is always asking the next question. If you come up with an answer, sometimes the answer itself turns over into another question. As I mentioned earlier, the question that we did not ask in 1987 was: if it is true that national communism is now the best outcome, and is acceptable to the Soviet government, to Gorbachev, when will the Poles believe that? Now we understand that it might take them

171

a little longer, and certainly the Czechs, and certainly the Hungarians, all having had some unhappy experience. But when would they believe that national communism was acceptable?

And once they did believe that, why were they going to stop necessarily at national communism? In other words, it was the case of once you let the tiger out of the box, how do you get the tiger back under control? As those of you who own cats know, when you open the cat's box the cat would not jump out right away, it would check, sniff the air, and if it looks okay, then you cannot catch it, it is out and it's running. This was the kind of picture that we thought might come about.

Now, let me explain a part of the analysis. We did not have special knowledge; I wish we were half as good at that as people thought we were, but we were not. We did not have all the knowledge of all the discussions that necessarily must have been taking place, but we had seen Shevardnadze's statement earlier in the year, saying that communism was not the basis for foreign policy. I think Medvedev had done a piece, something along those lines, about the same time. More importantly, again we had to take a look at what we were talking about. Somebody here today asked some of these questions: What do you mean when you say you will not "tolerate" something? If you will not tolerate it, what are you going to do besides calling it dirty names? What are you going to do to change it? Maybe you can get somebody in the country to pull off a coup. This can be very risky—at times these things get off track, and do not go the way they were planned. Maybe you can get the military there to do something. If you are going to use military force [...] could the Soviet Union have used its own military forces exclusively, without cooperation or at least token participation by all the other Warsaw Pact countries?

Now let us put ourselves in 1988 moving toward 1989 with these questions on the table. So you have to ask yourself: How big a military force could carry out a military intervention? And remember, if you are going to undertake military intervention of this nature, you want to be sure that it is the kind of military intervention that does not invite the "host" to fight back. So, how big an intervention force are we talking about? In my recollection, it was twenty-some divisions in 1968. And if we are talking about Poland, we are talking about a country twice as big as Czechoslovakia.

What is the political setting in the USSR in 1988? Let us look at the events: a conference in June and July which put major developments in train for domestic purposes; the events of September 30th with even more major domestic political activities put in train, which I still think was one of the most important sets of actions taken; in December Gorbachev announces a cut of 50,000 in the Soviet forces based in Eastern Europe, a significant reduction; a 500,000-person reduction in overall Soviet military forces.[31] All these things are in train. And getting

---

[31] In his U.N. speech, Gorbachev announced overall reductions of Soviet armed forces by 500,000 men, 10,000 tanks and 800 aircraft. Out of this number, 50,000 men, 5,000 tanks,

out of the Afghan entanglement is still underway at this time. So you have to ask yourself the question: under those circumstances, is the USSR going to put together a huge military force for intervening into another country?

So, military intervention not only ran counter to what the Soviet leadership was saying [...] I agree there was ambiguity, but it was a calculated ambiguity, and while there was ambiguity there were reasonably forthright statements made by Foreign Ministry and other senior officials. There also was the question: What is the cost in 1989, with all these domestic issues on the plate—the political reorganizations, the reduction of overall military forces, the pullback of some forces from Eastern Europe—of putting together a military intervention in an East European country, which could very well result in a pretty awful outcome, which could make the repercussions of Tienanmen Square look fairly tame?

So, I guess my point is that by 1989 the box lid was open, the cat was sniffing the air, and once it got out no one knew what would happen. But none of us where we were, rightly or wrongly, believed there was any potential for the leadership of the Soviet Union to sacrifice all the things that it had been attempting to achieve for the last three-and-a-half years, and all the challenges it had given itself for the next few years, to pay that price. We thought instead that the Soviet leaders would attempt to work out some kind of acceptable relationship based on economic interest and common interests in the politics of the region.

So I keep coming back and saying: everyone that I talked to was always scratching their head, and affirming that [...] we agreed that once the use of force was not an obvious penalty, a lot of things could happen. Nonetheless, it also always surprises me that so many people have so much trouble figuring out—Gee, why did the sudden developments in East Europe happen?—when it seems consistent both with what the leadership was saying and with the realities of the costs. I would have thought that to have made a case, to have made an argument, in 1989, that the USSR would intervene militarily to suppress something in Hungary or Poland or Czechoslovakia would have been a major credibility hurdle. I would have said to someone trying to make that case that the burden is on you to make that argument. If you had been working in Washington making estimates, I would have said you've got a tough case to make because it just does not stand up to every piece of evidence we have.

[....]

Zubok: I would follow the example of my colleague, Mr. Hershberg, and I would just tell you a couple of jokes and general things, because I am really not the person to draw conclusions from this very interesting discussion. This reminds me of a phrase from De Tocqueville, from his famous book, *The Old Regime and the French Revolution*: The counterrevolution was already rising, but nobody was able to see it. Big events always come as a surprise.

and other combat equipment would be withdrawn from Eastern Europe.

And a second idea. It was mentioned here many times, and it is also obvious. We are dealing with systemic processes, the process of destroying everything that was created under Stalin and after Stalin. And the collapse of Eastern Europe was simply insignificant in that context. And the third idea that I have, as a historian, is that we need to look at it from the perspective of the ability to defend oneself, to remain viable. And the system was unable to react adequately to the crisis. If we go back to the Kronstadt uprising [of 1921], there were no important movements that would arise along the entire perimeter of the Soviet Union since then. There were certain localized attempts at uprising and it was very easy for the system to put those down, so the system did not learn anything. It was just like Honecker was not ready to confront people in the streets [...] The same in our country—our local leaders and even our central leaders were not prepared to deal with events on that scale. That is all I wanted to say.

CHAPTER 5: THE SUPERPOWER CONTEXT

Blanton: [...] We are going to begin this session on the superpower context, and I have asked Karen Dawisha to lead off with some provocative questions and mysteries, as she sees them [....]

Dawisha: [T]his book of documents is absolutely fascinating. We really owe a great debt of gratitude to those like Anatoly who provided them, and those who translated them. They are truly unique. One of two major conclusions that I reached from reading the documents, was that, I do not think we can underestimate the extent to which Gorbachev trusted the counsel of Western leaders. I would say he trusted Western leaders more than he trusted East European leaders. And to me it is very striking, the extent to which he was willing and felt free to talk in very negative terms with Western leaders about the failings of his East European colleagues.

This is very striking, and of course it is something that the West European leaders would never do to Gorbachev. They would hint sometimes about the slowness with which the new Bush administration was reacting to events in the Soviet Union, but always counseled that it is a good administration, it is going to follow the same general line, and that they would carry the message to Washington. I think it is very striking because it does show the extent to which there was a complete revolution in thinking of this man, and the closest people around him.

And in his thinking, I think, we see the emergence of two very important ideas and assumptions. And I would suggest, in the end, both of them proved to be wrong. One was—he assumed that Western leaders would support and would be able to deliver on the entry of the Soviet Union into Europe, and the transformation of European politics into a unified, open state—onto a non-militarized basis. His discussions with [Finnish President Mauno] Koivisto about reconvening the Helsinki process. His discussions with Thatcher, with Mitterrand, and, of course, most of all with Kohl indicate that he believed they supported this. And they, I think, gave him ample signals that this would, in fact, happen.

The revolution in his thinking, although this document is not in the book, but I know all of you are familiar with it, was to me most amply demonstrated in his speech before the Sorbonne, where you have, basically, the embrace by Gorbachev of the ideas of the French Revolution—the liberal ideas of individual rights, and the rejection of class analysis, first of all. The first German idea and the second German idea, which was rejected, was a kind of Bismarckian geopolitics. So, the question is: Were those two German ideas thrown over too soon, particularly the second one? Was it unrealistic, and even naive, and hugely romantic of Gorbachev to reject the notion that geopolitics could be somehow transformed?

The second aspect of his policy, which I think proves not to be the case was that he believed, and it is supported clearly in the documents, that the Western leaders would not take advantage of the transitions taking place in Eastern Europe, that they would not promote the collapse of the USSR itself. And, most importantly, that they did not even want the unification of Germany. And this is clearly there in the documents of his numerous discussions with Kohl, where although clearly Kohl does not say, "We do not want unification of Germany," Gorbachev comes away with that; but Thatcher certainly says that they do not seek the unification of Germany. Mitterrand says the same, and it is reported that Italian Foreign Minister Attali [sic], also says that we do not want the unification of Germany, we do not want just one Germany.

He is also led to believe, I think, quite clearly by a back channel, and I would like to hear from Jack on this, back channels with Kissinger and with Brzezinski, including discussions with Brzezinski in November 1989, that the United States was willing to, in Kissinger's description, enter into some kind of condominium arrangement with the Soviet Union in Europe. Brzezinski also says in November 1989 that a complete collapse in Germany could disrupt and lead to a collapse of European institutions [...] this is not quite the way that he put it but the implication, I think, for Gorbachev was that the United States would itself not seek the unification of Germany.[32]

I think that both of these assessments were incorrect, and profoundly flawed. And clearly, while Gorbachev could not have known everything in advance, we need to find out from our colleagues here today the extent to which this perception was wishful thinking on Gorbachev's part, and to what extent it was based either on a complete misreading of the nature of Western politics or on a correct reading of signals that were given to him as a part of a campaign to get him to provide concessions that were favorable to the West. On the first question—the misreading of Western politics—did Gorbachev appreciate the extent of resistance to cooperation with the Soviet Union, which still existed in the United States up to November 1989? I was very struck reading National Security

---

[32] See Document Nos. 36 and 37 for discussions on this topic with Kissinger, and Document No. 96 for discussions with Brzezinski (in October 1989).

Directive 23[33], which was issued in the end of September 1989, where even in September 1989 it was the view of the U.S. government that we had to wait to see what Gorbachev was going to do, and we needed concrete actions, including the demilitarization of Soviet foreign policy.

This is, I think, very striking that over four years after Gorbachev had come to power—and we have, I think, by then a major turnover in Eastern Europe—that the United States is still waiting for concrete actions. So, I would like to ask Doug MacEachin a question in this regard. Clearly, from his perspective in the CIA, he had gone through a decade of pretty hard times, infighting and so forth, in the CIA. And I know that many of the people in the CIA deeply resisted the politicization of intelligence, including, I am sure, Doug. To what extent was it still a real uphill battle in 1989 to put out into political circles a kind of very strong support for what Gorbachev was doing? What was the extent of self-censorship even among the analysts?

I know that when I was working in policy planning and then in the Politico-Military Bureau in the State Department in 1986 and 1987, it was still strongly the view in State that the battle for the de-politicization of intelligence had not been entirely won, and I wonder what his view of that is, from the perspective of 1989? Also, I wonder if Jack could tell us something about the extent to which the struggle over the lifting of the Jackson–Vanik Amendment[34] was very much constraining the extent to which we could really open up to the Soviet Union, and recognize the real changes that were taking place there, particularly since obviously the Soviet Union was still supporting radical Arab regimes, even if the arms flow had declined.

And finally, to our American colleagues, perhaps particularly to Jack, what was his view of the back-channeling that was going on? How much was there? And what was put into that channeling, for what purpose? Gorbachev is obviously worried in 1989 about cautiousness and resistance in Washington, and even speaks very directly about the rumor that there had been an NSC group set up to shape a more negative view of Gorbachev in the policy community. And it seems to me, reading your three memoranda from Moscow[35], which were excellent, that without saying you are addressing the debate in Washington, you clearly do. You speak very openly about all of the problems, all of the resistance, and all of the potential real reasons why one should not, or one might not, support Gorbachev for this reason, and then try your best to shape a more positive view.

So I wonder if you could help us out with what was going into the back channel, how did you know about it, what was your reaction to it, and how could you combat it—particularly, I think, Kissinger's role?

---

[33] Document No. 84.

[34] A part of the 1974 Trade Act, the amendment restricted trade relations with the Soviet Union and other non-market economies that denied emigration rights to Jews and other citizens.

[35] Document Nos. 43, 45, 47.

Matlock: There are also a couple of questions that Georgy raised yesterday, that I will try to cover, but taking Karen's first, which are at the heart of the subject this morning. The first question: Was it unrealistic for Gorbachev to think that Bismarckian geopolitics could be transformed? I do not think it was unrealistic at all. As a matter of fact, I think Bismarckian geopolitics have been transformed, and not as a result of what any leader has done, but rather because the world has changed. I think that sort of analysis, that sort of thinking is no longer relevant.

It still persists, and we see it on our side on such issues as NATO expansion. I would call that "*perezhitki*" [remnants] of old attitudes. I think the world has changed, and perhaps Gorbachev understood this better than some of the other leaders. One can say, perhaps, that he was premature in adapting his policies to it, but I do not think so. I think that the situation in the Soviet Union would have been much worse if he had not made these adjustments. And his difficulties really stem not so much from the unresponsiveness of the Western leaders as the structural difficulties he faced as a leader of the Soviet Union, which was essentially a system which was no longer capable of functioning as a fully efficient state. I think that is the fact of the matter. In dealing with these various things, he probably got the best deals with Western leaders that were objectively possible, particularly given the fact that the Western leaders each had his or her own concerns that tended to distract them.

So, I do think that the Western leaders were absolutely sincere when in general terms they pledged their support. Now what Gorbachev understood by that we will have to ask our Russian colleagues. They did not mean at that point direct financial support, clearly. That was not what was on their minds. They meant a sort of political support, endorsement, certainly refraining from creating additional difficulties. So far as back channels, there were not any. Kissinger's visit in January 1989 may have been perceived as such. I would be very interested in hearing our Russian colleagues' understanding of this visit.

He brought a letter from the president, but it was not a letter which in any way authorized him to deal with issues. It was a courtesy letter, the sort former secretaries of state and former presidents usually get from a sitting president, a sort of a letter of introduction: please see the guy. Presidents do it as a courtesy, understanding, and perhaps wrongly, that the other government knows that this person speaks only for himself. Otherwise, the letter would state explicitly that the visitor would discuss a certain subject on the president's behalf. The letter Kissinger had was not such a letter.

Kissinger wanted to go to Moscow and the president gave him the letter, simply a letter of introduction. Meanwhile, we tried to let it be known that he was not speaking for the president. Meanwhile, Kissinger had made certain proposals which Baker was considering—he did not reject them out of hand but after consideration Baker decided that what Kissinger wanted to do was not a good idea. And that was to enter in some sort of negotiation with the Soviet leadership about the future of Eastern Europe. That was the proposal I strongly opposed, not because it was Kissinger's idea and it was outside the system, though that will always give the official representative in another country some problem, but because it was a bad idea. I explained in my book why. It was clear that what was going to happen in Eastern Europe was going to happen. And if we were seen in active negotiations, no matter how well-meaning, with the Soviet Union, this would be viewed by the East Europeans as somehow trying to settle their fate.

We had gone through decades of misunderstanding about what had happened in Yalta. And Yalta had been a political issue at home. Roosevelt never intended to agree to Soviet domination of Eastern Europe. The question was where our armies would stop, and who would occupy which territory as the war ended. And, of course, Roosevelt thought he had an agreement that the Polish government would be democratic. Stalin's understanding and his were quite different on these things, as we know.

Negotiating the future of Eastern Europe was, I thought, the last thing we needed to do. This was finally the administration's position, aside from the sort of discussion we had later at Malta where we made clear that any military intervention would destroy the growing relationship. And we also made clear that we did not intend to make use of changes in Eastern Europe against them; we did not attempt to discuss the future of the area. To negotiate how far the East Europeans could go without a Soviet intervention was not our business. Eventually Baker and Bush agreed.

So that was never a back channel. As far as Brzezinski's visit, that was even less of a back channel. He did not even have a letter from the president. He made some very interesting public statements and he made the same ones in private, and they perhaps got some people thinking. I was present when he gave the address at MGIMO [Moscow State Institute of International Relations], and you could see that his audience was shocked when he pointed out that you can have a divided Germany in a divided Europe, but if your policy is a common European home and a united Europe, you cannot have a divided Germany in a united Europe. He posed the question: Have you thought about that? Have you thought about the implications? He posed the question without answering it, other than saying that it was impossible to think of a united Europe without a united Germany. I do not know what impact it had. He was not speaking for the administration. He was speaking what I think was an obvious truth.

He had a personal reason for that visit, and it was one that had been arranged for him, I think, directly through the Soviet Embassy in Washington, to visit Katyń. I went with him, and Strobe Talbott, who was then with *Time* magazine, also came along. The visit to Katyń took place a couple of months before it was officially admitted what had actually happened.

We read this as a signal that the Soviet government was going to own up to that, and actually Brzezinski made some very conciliatory statements, that the truth about Katyń could be the basis for future Polish–Soviet friendship and accord, because both had suffered from Stalin and Hitler. Admitting the truth, he argued, could put the issue behind us. It was an eloquent statement, made to the public. It was not a "back channel." Neither Kissinger nor Brzezinski was speaking for the administration.

In general, I would say regarding back channels, if it is of any interest, that there were attempts in the Reagan administration, in 1983, '84, and '85, to get some going. Largely because of bureaucratic conflicts on our side in the first instance, and secondarily, bureaucratic problems on the Soviet side, none materialized. But there was a time, particularly when there were no arms control negotiations, that we genuinely thought that maybe the best thing to do would be to get some sort of authorized back channel going.

Part of the reason on our side was to have a negotiation which the president and the secretary of State could control but would not involve in the early stages elements in the bureaucracy that would try to torpedo it. That was our problem in the administration, and though we could not cut out any Cabinet member, we could have cut out people lower down until we got something that the president was comfortable with, and then opponents could not torpedo it. In the early stages they could, by leaking, by developing a lot of public pressure. And they were doing that. So, on our side, it was an honest attempt to try to get negotiations going which would not formally violate the Soviet policy of not negotiating. We hoped to get some informal talks going and bring them at least far enough that we could go public and be somewhere close to agreement. The way it was, once early negotiating positions were publicized, it became like a sporting contest, with the media keeping score.

Those of us who wanted to move toward an agreement needed a way to avoid a destructive internal debate in the United States. The Soviets, at that point, had a much easier time controlling their public statements than we did. Later they, too, had trouble keeping them under control. But in, say, 1983, '84, '85, this was a real problem for us. The special channel did not work. There were several reasons. We don't have time to go into detail.

We had no back channels, effective back channels, at any time during the Reagan and the Bush administrations. We did all business through the official representatives and the principals. Actually, that was preferable when it is possible. Once trust developed, there was no need for a back channel. There was not anything that Kissinger could have said that I could not have said, or somebody else from the administration. There was no point in using outsiders. Obviously, our society and others too have a number of self-promoters who try to leave the impression that they are speaking for the president. And maybe sometimes this created some confusion, though I suspect that the Soviet leaders at that point were familiar enough with us that they were able to sort this out and understood that for what it was.

Now on Jackson–Vanik. This was a constraining factor on the whole economic side, but not only Jackson–Vanik. Frankly, we wanted to get the damn thing off, and for that we needed the emigration legislation passed by the Supreme Soviet, but it kept being delayed. Those who tried to push it, like Fedor Burlatsky, would come to me and say, "Look, Gorbachev is not doing anything, and until he weighs in with the Supreme Soviet, it is probably not going to pass." And finally, in 1990, I called Gorbachev's attention to the issue a couple of times, and the legislation finally passed before Gorbachev went to Washington. I believe it was in the spring of 1990, but it may have been later, but that was still an issue when Gorbachev visited Washington in June 1990.

But a bigger issue by that time was the economic sanctions on Lithuania, which were imposed, I think, in April 1990. And as long as these were on, it was politically out of the question in the States to remove trade barriers. The whole Baltic issue began to play a greater role in the Soviet Union after the Lithuanian independence declaration, and what started out to be an economic boycott actually turned out to be very little. To what degree this was the result of our pressure, or of other things, I cannot say.

In Washington, these factors militated against lifting Jackson–Vanik restrictions. There is no question about that. But in general, on Eastern Europe, until the discussion at Malta, we really refrained from any detailed discussions with the Soviet authorities, other than making it very, very clear that any Soviet military intervention would bring to an end whatever cooperation was developing between us. And that was simply a political fact, not a matter of saying: that is our policy. Our president's hands would have been totally tied politically.

By then, it was pretty clear to us that there would be no Soviet intervention in Eastern Europe. We did not have to be shrill about our position, and we did not have to repeat warnings in every conversation. Earlier in 1981, when the question was whether the Soviet Union would invade Poland almost every official conversation had to start with a statement on that topic. In 1989, we let events develop largely without comment. Some in Washington doubted that this was wise, but I think the events proved the position that I had set forth in the cables in February. Developments were confirming what those of us had said who thought *perestroika* was real.

Now, just briefly to Georgy's question yesterday. Why was there no economic aid to Gorbachev in June 1991? The short answer is: because there was nothing to aid, to be quite honest. There were other reasons. None of the Western leaders were particularly well-positioned at that time. George Bush was piling up the largest deficits in our budgetary history in the United States; he was being attacked in his own party for agreeing to a tax increase. And by then he was beginning to say that that was a mistake. We were going into a recession, which was going to cost him his reelection the following year. To come up with a lot of money was not something that was going to be easy to do. Some of the allies were better off, but the thing is, in order to get major economic assistance, the United States is key.

There really was no possibility then of major government-to-government assistance, if by major one means a hundred billion dollars, the sort of magnitude Gorbachev was talking about. That amount of funds could have come only from private investment. And for that there had to be a Soviet policy that was credible to private investors. If the United States failed in any way, it was by not pushing harder in 1989 and '90 for some multinational structure to deal with the transition in Eastern Europe and the USSR. [....]

When I proposed in my February 1989 cable to expand our agenda to include economic matters, it was specifically discarded, and the idea reemerged only in December at the Malta summit. [....]

When I was asked about the prospects of aid by Soviet journalists at the time [1990–91], I said, pouring money into the Soviet economy now would be like pouring water onto a sandy beach. It is one thing to prime a pump; it is another thing if the pump does not work, or there is no pump. And as yet, we did not see a pump. [....]

Now, on the other question that Georgy raised: did the CIA work on undermining the Union? Absolutely not. I am absolutely convinced, and I was informed of every covert operation we had in the Soviet Union from the time when I worked in the White House in 1983, and while I was ambassador. We had no covert action designed to destabilize or undermine the Soviet Union. There were some covert actions, and most of these had been written about, in Eastern Europe, particularly in support of Solidarity, in ways such as providing some printing facilities, and so on. That would have been totally insignificant under most circumstances: help in getting things printed, and information distributed. That happened. But there were no such activities on Soviet territory, even resembling it. Our trade unions were criticized for providing fax machines to some of the independent unions that developed during the strike of the miners, but government was not involved in that. That was done entirely by the unions, and also, it was entirely open. There was nothing covert about it.

Everybody had intelligence collection—this is the point I tried to make to [KGB Chairman Vladimir] Kryuchkov, when he was accusing us of these things—sure, everybody was looking for information on all sides. But covert action to destabilize—absolutely not. And as a matter of fact, there was always a great hesitance in our government because there was a certain ambiguity regarding the whole national question.

On the one hand, we were unambiguous in our attitude toward the Baltic states. We had never recognized them as a part of the Soviet Union, and we could not act legally as if they were a part of it. But we recognized *de jure* the transfer of all the other territory that had occurred after World War II. After all, Czechoslovakia conceded Subcarpathian Ukraine voluntarily to the Soviet Union. The lands in Western Ukraine were conveyed by the peace treaty; Moldova was conveyed by the peace treaty with Romania, which the United States also signed. So, we did not call into question all these other territories.

We recognized the twelve republics. We did not recognize the Baltic states as part of the Soviet Union. So, there was no way we could take any position other than that they should be given the freedom of choice. But, it stopped there. And clearly, we would have preferred, much preferred to see a voluntary Union and, I think, Bush made it very clear. We were not trying to stir up, and certainly not to the point of violence, because we did not see it in our interest then. Many people now in retrospect say it is in our interest to keep Ukraine independent. But at the time, most people did not consider independence a feasible alternative, and when we thought about it we were not sure we wanted it anyway. Obviously, it is much easier to deal with one nuclear power than with twelve.

We were not so stupid that we did not see by the middle of 1991 that the reform was coming from Moscow, and for the most part not from the regional capitals with maybe the exception of the Baltic states. So, if there was going to be reform and democratization, it was going to come because of *perestroika* and Gorbachev, and not because of the breakup of the Soviet Union. The very cause of democracy, which was important to us, though not always at the very top of the list, was served, we thought, by supporting the Union Treaty. We did everything we could—which was not very much—to support it, and that was shown mostly in Bush's speech in Kiev on August 1st, 1991, when he said very clearly that independence is not the same as freedom, and urged that they make a choice for freedom. His speech was meant not just for Ukraine but for all the other republics, Georgia in particular, which was falling apart with this crazy Gamsakhurdia.[36]

MacEachin: I cannot address Karen's question about "politicization" of intelligence without first calling attention to the fact that as regards the USSR, ideological or philosophical splits between U.S. political factions did not begin in 1980. If you look at the political platforms in the United States, there were two fundamental subheadings. One was the role of the government in the well-being of a citizen—more active, less active. And the other was policy with regard to the Soviet Union. We can start with the Nixon–Kennedy debates in 1960 on the missile gap that did not exist; go to Johnson–Goldwater in 1964; go to 1968, again with Nixon, this time versus Humphrey; go to Carter–Ford in 1976, and obviously Carter–Reagan in 1980. [....]

Th[e] Team B exercise[37] criticized the analysis in the National Intelligence Estimates as being too soft on the Soviet threat. Its principal criticism was that too much attention was devoted in these estimates to the physical aspects of the force developments, and not enough attention was given to the evil intentions and goals, which this particular group had cast in a certain light. If you read those estimates on Soviet military forces and goals that were written in the subsequent four or five years, 1977 through 1981, they are among the most strident and ideologically slanted estimates in my entire experience. [....]

---

[36] Zviad Gamsakhurdia, a long-time political dissident and nationalist during the Soviet era, became president of Georgia in May 1991 but his brief rule was criticized as dictatorial and he was toppled from power in January 1992. In September 1993, he undertook an unsuccessful armed rebellion from his base in western Georgia against the successor government of Eduard Shevardnadze.

[37] In 1976, then-CIA Director George H.W. Bush authorized an alternative analysis of the Soviet threat to be undertaken by hard-liners who were sharply critical of CIA assessments. The exercise became known as "Team B."

You have to understand, what I am trying to describe is the atmosphere. But it was poisoned. Different personalities take on these philosophical arguments differently, and the atmosphere in the mid-1980s was poisoned by the way this philosophical argument was conducted. I will tell you that I hated this and was prepared to resign in the mid-1980s because of this.

In hindsight you will find that the written CIA products gave a pretty accurate portrayal. I have done my best to get as many of these products released as I can, and I will try to get some more. The truth of the matter was that there seldom was a problem with somebody at a senior level seeking to force a major change in the written product, it is just that they, in effect, threw it in the wastebasket by denigrating it in denial.

Another way to do it I can illustrate with a specific empirical example—an issue that was partially declassified in the Gates hearings[38] having to do with chemical weapons. A paper done by the CIA which said, "We do not believe the Soviet Union is planning to use chemical weapons in Europe," was the second-most-hated paper we did in my tenure in the Soviet office. I will tell you later what the most hated was. So, one way to deal with that was to call for a National Intelligence Estimate. Get all the agencies to the table, and you will have a vote of ten to one, and so what a policy person will see is this estimate and not the CIA paper.

This acrimonious atmosphere was flourishing at a critical time in history, an absolutely critical time in history, because here we have these indications of potentially momentous changes taking place. And at this time the most heavily debated, and the mostly loaded, issue which I am not going to get into in much detail, dealt with "Was there a Soviet plot in the Third World?" If you check the ratification hearings of the incoming Cabinet members, such as Secretary Haig, you will see it was a central issue from the start. Go get the videotapes of his confirmation hearings and see what he was talking about, for example about the threat in Central America, moving practically to the Mexican border. So, a lot of the emotion that you hear about, Karen, is in that area, having to do with the Soviet Union and the Warsaw Pact.

There was no challenge to a whole series of papers done openly, given to Congress, and published by the government Printing Office in the 1970s and into the early 1980s that described the assessment of the economic problems being faced by the Soviet Union and the bloc and the Warsaw Pact, and the likelihood that sooner or later those things were going to result in some sort of major political development. When and how remained open questions. That is on the record.

But this became the one issue on which I took the most [...] I am trying to find a polite word with more than four letters to use for it [...] heat—that is only four—the CIA estimate in the early and mid 1980s about the sad state of the economy in the Soviet Union, and that this meant that there was not going to be

[38] The Senate hearings in 1991 to confirm Robert Gates as director of CIA.

an increase in defense spending, and that there had not been, in fact, too much growth in defense spending since at least the late 1970s. [....]

At one meeting, I had given a draft assessment of the Soviet economic situation to a person who was supposed to read it to Congress, that person threw the draft at least as far as that pool table. It is a true story, and I have four witnesses to it, all of whom would testify under oath. It was always rather shocking to me that later we heard that nobody saw the Soviet economic problems.

By 1985, and this is when you get into a different argument that I want to describe, by 1985 you cannot really argue that issue any more because the new first secretary has said, "We have an economic problem, and we have to do something about it." And he starts a program. And then the issue is, what is his effort going to mean? And I will try to describe the debate that ensued on this question: there was a political and an economic aspect to it. And it related to a lot of things that happened in the late 1980s.

There was one view that said, Gorbachev is just trying to buy time, hold down the arms race with new arms control proposals because the economy is in trouble, until he can fix the economy and then, boy, watch out. The other view said—and both of these views are in writing, you can read them—that Gorbachev is really serious and he will not back off. That was directly connected to the economic [...] Is there an economist in the room? One, I am sorry to say. So I will try to keep this arcane economic language simple. The basic analysis was [that] the problem was productivity. Productivity is a certain function of capital and labor, and the problem with declining productivity is that it feeds on itself like a nuclear breeder reactor. Declining productivity affects the consumer, the consumer is also a laborer, that affects productivity, and it was a spiral.

Brezhnev had been cheating, because faced with declining economic performance he had been shaving capital investment since the late 1970s into the early 1980s. And apparently, Gorbachev's economists agreed with this analysis because one of the very first things he did with the economic program was to turn this around, or try to. And that confronted Gorbachev with the problem: where is the increased capital investment going to come from? If you did your analysis carefully you would conclude that it could only come from one place, ultimately, and it was the defense sector because it could not come out of the consumer sector, and that was not going to come from foreign investment.

We told that to Secretary Shultz at a meeting a few of us had with him in March of 1986. It was a very pleasant meeting. It was the last pleasant meeting I ever had with Secretary Shultz, because when he saw me it was not the CIA but someone who worked for Bob Gates and Bill Casey, and anybody who was associated with them was dead on arrival when he walked into the room. I am using a little bit too colorful language, but it was a very emotional time.

Matlock: He respected you and [Robert] Blackwill.

MacEachin: Well, we were the only ones then, (Laughter) and unfortunately he may have leaked it back to our headquarters, in which case we were shot back there, too. (Laughter)

184

Okay. So, the backdrop I have tried to paint contained philosophical confrontation, and then there was the economic reality. And there was our assessment that the reforms and cutting down alcohol and all those kinds of things were not going to produce the results Gorbachev hoped for; and that he would, sooner or later, more likely in a very short time, run into this decision on the need for more dramatic steps; that probably about 1987 or '88, in preparing for the next five-year plan, the defense spending issue was going to have to come up. That was our prediction, and that was the prediction that we gave to Secretary Shultz, and he agreed with it. That is when we had figured the time would come, that is, when we were looking for the defense spending cut, and we were clearly believing that Gorbachev's arms control effort was not just going to be breathing space, that it was a serious, fundamental change.

The opposing side of that argument in U.S. circles was: "Gorbachev does not need to go as far as you CIA analysts are saying. You are underestimating the potential for fixing the Soviet economy without making a fundamental change. That gets to the point Jack raised, whether this was going to be just a new and stronger threatening opponent, or was in fact the opponent going to be gone. And those were heated debates, very heated debates.

[....]

March of 1985, Gorbachev comes in. I do not know if it is open or not, but we understood there was a discussion with the military leadership about a month later. Interestingly enough, we had noted in the Soviet media that Brezhnev had had a meeting with the military leadership about two weeks before he died. To us it signaled that the issue of resources and military strength was clearly on the table.

Somebody asked me when did I think the Cold War was over. Intellectually, for me, it was November of 1985 in Geneva, when Gorbachev made his first 50 percent proposal. That was serious stuff.

Matlock: Fifty percent was in Reykjavik, in 1986.

MacEachin: No, I remember this one. Fifty percent was in Geneva, 1985. Reykjavik was when we went all the way up to the brink of a comprehensive arms control agreement, and then it broke on the Star Wars issue. And that was 1986. By February of 1987 we had "yes" to zero-zero on INF. Even more damaging to those who thought the answer to zero-zero was going to be a forever "no," we also got a "yes" to intrusive on-site inspections. This was a new era.

That said, I think Jack Matlock is exactly right, the momentum for that broke a bit in the 1989 transition. It broke because the new administration was seen, even though it was the same party as the outgoing administration, as bringing in some people who were viewed as a part of the "softies" from the earlier era. And they had to be constantly looking over their back, because everybody from the tougher line of their party was waiting for them to make their first capitulations. All politics is local. I think that these politics delayed a lot of steps that could have been taken with more confidence by, for example, President Reagan, who did not have to look over his back—assuming that the Reagan administration would have taken them.

One more example, which I talked about yesterday that we have discussed many times was the question of what was going to be the impact of Gorbachev's policies on Eastern Europe. By the end of 1988 the analysis was that it is now just a matter of when do the East Europeans begin to see the opportunity that is available for them. And once they start, you have no way of hoping it is going to stop at national communism. It might, but there is no reason to believe it will. And there is no reason to believe that there is going to be a military action. [...]

Two other quick things. I was asked and promised to address this Schweizer book,[39] which I now understand is getting wide readership, but I cannot understand why, because I will go on record saying it belongs in the dust bin. There may have been people who thought they were running some kind of a plot to break the bank in the Soviet Union. [To Matlock] Have you read the book?

Matlock: I have not read it, but I know the thesis, and it is absolute nonsense.

MacEachin: Yes, it is utter nonsense, and I can even, with mathematics, demonstrate that it is absolutely dead wrong. There may have been some people who deluded themselves with thinking that that was what they were doing.

The other thing that I was going to say is I have always looked back at that critical period—1986–87–88—and realized how much the Iran–Contra affair disrupted the efficient functioning of the foreign policy network, because the key players in it were all fighting for their lives in a major scandal, and there were a number of changes in key positions, and that was a very bad bit of timing. And it kind of left the secretary of state on his own when it would have been far better to have had cohesion among the foreign policy players.

Matlock: Just a very quick one or two points. First of all, I think, Doug has given us a wonderful insight into the various disputes that went on in the intelligence analysis. However, an outsider sometimes has the impression that the president is somehow bound by these National [Intelligence] Estimates, and the thing is that those of us working on the NSC staff and in the State Department, we knew very well what the disputes were. I do not know of a case that Reagan ever read an NIE, a National Intelligence Estimate. We would send them to him, but our cover would say, "these things are highly controversial, and they were not able to get agreement because the military representatives do not want to undermine their budgetary proposals in Congress." We can understand that. And the president is not stupid; he is going to support the things in Congress, but when he makes foreign policy, and also, particularly if it is a judgment over intentions, he makes up his own mind. Once Reagan met Gorbachev, he did not need an intelligence officer to tell him whether he was a guy he could deal with. He felt it instinctively.

And so, you know, Doug was fighting the great battles, and they were important, and I am not saying they had no influence, but I am saying that you should not worry that the NIEs were watered down because, frankly, most of us did not

[39] Schweizer, *Victory*.

read them. We knew what they were, but we were closer to the president, and we would send brief memos. We were always honest with the president. We never misrepresented what the intelligence community thought, but we put in our opinions, and they tended to be more persuasive than the watered down negotiated things.

And then the final point. I think you are absolutely right about something most people do not recognize, and that is that probably we could have gotten a START agreement and other things in 1988, if it not had been for the Iran–Contra affair. Both Poindexter and MacFarlane had the whole game plan in mind to complete it then. They were highly supportive, something Shultz did not always understand. And clearly, in his memoirs, he did not understand to what degree these guys were supporting him. When Carlucci and Colin Powell came in, they were good people, but they did not know the game plan and they were not pushing. If it had not been for Iran–Contra, we would have accomplished much more in 1988; you are quite right.

MacEachin: I would like to say just one more thing. Jack, on these NIEs, you are so right. In fact, I recently read an essay by someone who said that nobody ever—not just the president—nobody reads the NIEs. This essay was written in 1968 by a guy named Sherman Kent.

Hershberg: Author of many of them.

MacEachin: Yes. The fact of the matter is, the NIEs—this is the unfortunate part of it—are a sort of doctrinal showcase. This is what we "declare" we believe. For all those of you who want to get a leak of intelligence, it will be leaked from this authoritative document. I could not agree with you more. The only intelligence that counts is the stuff that you take in to the boss and put on his desk and talk to him about. That is the only stuff that ever affects anything.

Shakhnazarov: Just very briefly. First of all, I would like to thank you for that most interesting presentation. I covered two pages with notes, and also it was very nice to learn that the CIA was supporting the USSR. But as for the fact that the president did not read the NIE, that is clear for us because our president does not read anything either. But if we talk about the substance of the comments, they did clarify a lot for me.

I will tell you, we have people who believe that whatever happened was a direct result of a plot planned and operated by the CIA, by Washington, and by Western intelligence agencies, Israel; and in the long run that Gorbachev was a CIA agent, or an agent of influence, as they say. Gorbachev and Yakovlev are agents of influence.

And this is the point of view represented not just by certain uneducated people—it is substantial. There are articles published. And I believe that for our historiography this is a very substantial theme that will continue to develop. Of course, to think that the United States did not play any role in the process is impossible, in spite of all that Jack has told us [...] I believe him, I think that as ambassador he did his best to help a positive process. Still, some element of orchestrating on the part of Washington and Western leaders was there. Perhaps 10 percent maybe 20 percent, but we would be disrespectful of ourselves if we were to think that what happened in Russia was a direct result of simply Western influence and Western plotting, plotting of the enemy. Of course, there were a lot of mistakes and realizations on our part, etc.

Still, I would like to ask my last question, which I still have some problems with. The question is: When was this break, the change of attitude in the U.S. leadership towards Gorbachev from the opinion about him as an intelligent and outstanding enemy that you can work with, from that position to assessing him as a human being, a partner, and perhaps even a future friend? And my second question: When did the United States leadership change from supporting Gorbachev to supporting Yeltsin? That is an issue of principal importance. And when Jack was telling us why it was impossible to help Gorbachev economically, I understand—funds are always short.

You did not have the funds, but during times of catastrophe or calamity, countries usually can find enough in their purses to support the troubled country, as they supported Mexico, Korea, and others—you know, tens of billions of dollars. As Gorbachev said at the time, they found almost a hundred billion dollars to hit Iraq, but they did not find anything to support us. I still think that if a massive aid plan had been put together, maybe not like the Marshall Plan but, you know, just substantial help to cover the deficit of goods in the market and appease the people, the situation might have taken a totally different turn and development.

I would like to simplify my questions again, and ask two questions. First: When did the United States start seeing a friend in Gorbachev, or rather, when did they stop viewing him as an enemy? Question number one. And the second question is: When did they stop viewing him as a friend, in the political dimension, not in the moral dimension? Morally, I know, the Americans, both the government and the people, like him a lot. He still enjoys appreciation, but they stopped supporting him as someone to bet on in our country. Thank you.

Blanton: The part of the answer to that question which extends beyond 1989 I would like to put off to the next conference that we manage to put together, because I want to bring this discussion back to the superpower context for 1989, just to keep it useful for the development of agendas for the next year, which we are really focusing on. With that caveat, I want to call on Anatoly, and then I will come back to you, Jack, for a brief response.

Chernyaev: I would like to go back somewhat to the problems that were put forth by Karen in her first remarks. Whether Gorbachev was not too quick in his reforms, was he not naïve, was he not too hasty to renounce or to retire Bismarckian geopolitics? Perhaps that was his final mistake. Well, you see, we are running the risk of following a pattern that is not realistic. Gorbachev came to power with a very serious intent to reform the country, and reform it in a fairly brief time, because based on experience, on our history, he knew that if you take too long in reforming, then the reforms can rot before they develop.

But in order to start economic and social reform, and then later political reforms, he had to deal with the arms race first. He had to stop the arms race. That was his priority. And he could only stop the arms race, and what I am saying might sound trite, but I just want to give a logical insight into what we were thinking at the time [...] Gorbachev could only end the arms race if he was successful in changing relations with the United States. What was our interpretation of the United States and Reagan in the mid-1980s? Reagan was the leader of imperialism, of an aggressive superpower, and that was absolutely beyond doubt, that was absolutely clear for the leadership of our country.

But Gorbachev also based his thinking on the fact that there were some reasonably thinking people in Washington, that they could see where the arms race was leading humankind, that it was already verging on a catastrophe, and doing major damage to the U.S. economy too, and that common sense could be a foundation for common process for Gorbachev. So Gorbachev based his thinking on that. And then he added universal human values to it. Then, when he met with Reagan *tête-à-tête* in Geneva, face to face, the mistrust was still there, but a sparkle of trust twinkled between them—human trust. And then what happened—it turned out that the mistrust had a real foundation.

Of course, they rolled back, but the real ground for trust was there, and he could see it with his own eyes. Jack Matlock recently brought some documents to Moscow, and showed them to me. They impressed me greatly. Those were the speeches that Reagan made in 1983–84, long before Gorbachev came to power. It was under Andropov. When I was reading through those documents, I could see almost all the elements of the new thinking already, both in the actual proposals and in the philosophy. There was no intent to destroy the Soviet Union, there was an intent to set up a normal relationship.

Then Reagan, of course, says that we are going to fight for human rights, that communism is unacceptable, and that some people blame him for calling the Soviet Union the "evil empire," and the Soviet Union called him the imperialist aggressor; so what? Besides this, there is simple human interest—real people, and let us think about them and find a common language, let us come to negotiations, not only about arms but about relations in general, let us normalize them. We did not know about this in the Central Committee. *Pravda* was ordered to publish articles calling those Reagan statements "rhetoric" that cannot be trusted. Now it clear to us that he did mean those things, they were not just rhetoric. It was his actual sincere belief in the possibility of dealing with the Soviet Union. This is why when Gorbachev and Reagan met, when this sparkle of trust emerged between them, it had a basis in reality on both sides. That was the first issue I wanted to raise.

Now, the problem of threat. From what has been said here, I could feel, and I have known it for a long time, that the Americans were even more blindfolded by the Cold War than we were in the Soviet Union. It was easier for us to pull out of the dogma, get rid of the stereotypes of the Cold War period in spite of the fact that we lived in an ideological state, and we had the party, and so on and so forth. I am reacting to your statements that Gorbachev was acting too fast. Gorbachev wanted to play fair. He genuinely wanted to establish trust. He realized that he had to make not only the first step—he used to say that everybody had to travel their part of the road—he also realized that, and he spoke about it at Politburo sessions many times, we would have to go further than the other guys because we had to earn trust, people had to believe us; until they started believing us, we would not get any support. I can see, and I was aware of it then, that the problem of the Soviet threat was developed in detail and in all directions in the United States. At the same time, the problem of the American threat was never even seriously considered in the USSR because by the time Gorbachev came to power nobody believed that the Americans would ever attack us or try to invade us, and so on. Propaganda was another issue—it continued to repeat the same things about the threat over and over again! Based on that, Gorbachev could be absolutely free on this issue. Nobody in the Politburo believed that the Americans were going to attack us. But the logic of the Cold War brought us to that difficult situation. Now we had to deal with that mess. So, these were the facts that he based his thinking on, and that is why he made concessions that he was blamed for later.

Later, when he met with Shultz and held negotiations with him twice, he was very impressed. He saw a great statesman who considered not only American interests but also the full scope of global development. In Shultz, Gorbachev saw a man who did not come to destroy or undermine the Soviet Union. In a friendly way, he mentioned to Shultz a few times, "Let us not play games, it will not work, we know everything about one another. We know who the main spies are—Shevardnadze and Shultz are the main spooks, and your ambassador, sure. Let us not play games with one another. Let us play fair and straight." So these were Gorbachev's motives when he was beginning his dialogue with America.

A lot of various issues have been raised during our discussion here. Perhaps I could take the floor again later to address some of them. For now, let us talk about Germany. When the issue of our attitude to the all-European process was raised, and the theme of the European home emerged, the German issue followed naturally—what to do with Germany? Can you have a divided Germany in a united Europe? Gorbachev talked about that with [German President Richard Von] Weizsäcker in 1987. Weizsäcker told him, "Well, of course, the European home is great, everybody has a room, and you can walk from room to room, but then there is a wall right in the middle of the house, right in the center of Europe." He hinted delicately! Gorbachev then still supported the position of two states, the GDR and the FRG, that would both be members of the U.N. He said that there was the Moscow agreement. Let us start from here. Let history be our judge. Well, we did not have to wait long for that judgment.

But still, it remains a mystery to me, an enigma. I do not know if you can answer this question: When, and whether at all, there was a change in the U.S. leadership's position toward the unification of Germany?

Gorbachev's original idea was that, just as the British, Mitterrand and the Italians, the United States was not interested in the unification of Germany. He thought that if that huge state in the middle of Europe was to emerge, in a Europe that is being united, for geopolitical and economic reasons it would not be in the interests of the United States. Later on he thought that Bush and Baker joined the process of unification so actively, pushing Kohl towards unification at some point because they wanted to be the godfathers of unification, so that the historic credit for unification would go to them—Bush and Baker—not to Gorbachev. That is why they acted so fast. And they wanted to get Germany closer to the United States because they would have played a positive role in the unification.

But again, going beyond 1989, I must tell you what happened. The present German leadership indeed believes that Germany was primarily unified through the effort of the United States. Last year, on October 3, when they celebrated the anniversary of unification, in Stuttgart this time, Gorbachev happened to be in Germany. He was not even invited to the celebration. Bush was invited—from the United States to Stuttgart. And the burgermeister [mayor] of the city, speaking at the opening ceremony, said something that shocked many Germans. He said, "Some people believe that we owe a lot to President Bush for the unification of Germany. No. We owe everything to President Bush, everything, 100 percent." And what about Gorbachev? What was his role? I repeat, he was not even invited to Stuttgart.

Returning to 1989, I would like to pose this question again: When (or whether) did the United States change its position towards unification?

As to the comment about economic aid, you are quite right in your reasoning. At that time giving money to us would have been like pouring water on a sandy beach. Georgy already said that we were not talking about any kind of Marshall Plan. The money had to go not to the economy at the time, but to Gorbachev. If he were to have come back from London, from the meeting of the Big Seven, at least with some promises; if he were to have received at least the 14 billion that was approved later, not on December 3 but earlier, when [Rodric] Braithwaite, the British ambassador, brought a letter from [Prime Minister John] Major, which said that the G-7 decided to give us $14 billion—if that happened [...] events in the Soviet Union could have taken a different turn.

However that assistance arrived when the object of the assistance—the Soviet Union—was already disappearing. There were just five days left until the Belovezhsky agreement.[40] If Gorbachev had that money—not even $100 billion—indeed, he was asking the Americans from time to time, "Did you find the hundred billion to support this country?"—which became a new one, a peace-loving country, a democratic country, which you wanted to have as a partner, but you could not find this money. We were not talking about helping our economy, we were talking about helping Gorbachev as a state leader, in order to give him support and to keep the country together.

---

[40] The agreement to dissolve the USSR signed by Boris Yeltsin, Ukraine President Nikolay Kravchuk and Belarus leader Stanislau Shushkevich in the Belovezhsky Forest region of the former Soviet Union (present-day Belarus) on December 8, 1991.

So Gorbachev held a grudge about that. And when he became real friends with Baker, Baker was giving him advice on how to calculate interest, what to do with prices, and stuff like that. It started in Malta. At the breakfast in Malta, Jack, we were there together. The president and the secretary of state had shown a surprisingly high degree of interest in our purely practical problems; they were trying to give Gorbachev advice on how to make the market work better. I do not know what form the assistance might have had. But as I have said already, if Gorbachev had received that money, then he probably would have been able to keep the republics on this dollar leash. Of course, this is just my hunch.

You also touched on Kissinger, his visit in January 1989.[41] Now people put too much emphasis on this story. Gorbachev was not impressed by Kissinger at all, by his statement. Of course, he invited him, and talked to him in all seriousness, because he thought that there was a pause because of the change in the administration, and Gorbachev was really frustrated with that. He was afraid that everything he had achieved with Reagan, when they met on Governors Island[42]—Bush was there also; he nodded while Reagan was turning the job over to him—might have been lost. Reagan was convinced that Bush would pick up where he left off, that he would carry on with everything that Reagan was dreaming about, and that had just begun—the disarmament. Therefore, we were hoping that Kissinger would bring some important message. But he came in with this idea of an exchange of Eastern Europe for a "good attitude" from the American side. And then the pause continued until May, basically. And again, there was some misunderstanding of our relations between Moscow and Eastern Europe. Some people must have thought that they were our pocket satellites, and that they would do anything we would tell them to do. This was not so.

This misperception became evident at first in Malta. Remember, Jack, they had a private conversation. Gorbachev thought that Bush would immediately raise some important questions so that they could then be addressed in detail at the meeting of delegations. And Bush started talking about Nicaragua and El Salvador. Gorbachev was very forthcoming. He promised to stop all the shipments of weapons to Cuba and Nicaragua. Then Bush raised the Cuban problem: Why are you still supporting Cuba? And Gorbachev took time to explain: "You overestimate my influence over Castro. He is not my puppet. He is an independent political figure. You should not think that I can tell Castro what kind of policies to pursue. I am not in a position to do that."

But that is, of course, a separate issue. But there was this pause in the relations. And it was very frustrating for Moscow for many reasons. We were not sure about the course that Bush was mapping out. We were concerned that the process could have been rolled back. There were opponents, and very serious opponents who thought that Reagan was too liberal, [moving] too fast in relations

---

[41] See Document No. 37.
[42] December 7, 1988.

192

with us. That was Reagan! And by the way, Reagan expressed his concern about the pause in March and April of 1989, am I right?

Regarding the question of when the breakthrough happened—when they started to believe Gorbachev, and when they became disillusioned in him and stopped believing him? I cannot answer the second question, but the first question has several stages. First they believed Gorbachev as a person—that he was honest and sincerely wanted to reform the Soviet Union, turn it into a democratic state. But there was a limit—they believed Gorbachev, but for a long time they did not believe that he would be capable of accomplishing what he wanted. And that mistrust regarding his ability to accomplish what he had decided lasted a long time.

I always categorically disagree with the opinion that Bush and Baker were trying to undermine the Soviet Union, or that they were taking their time so that it would fall apart on its own. No, they did not have those intentions. They sincerely considered Gorbachev their partner, and they thought their policy was an accomplishment on the American side. Maybe I am mistaken. Later, when both Bush and Baker retired, some arrogant statements appeared in their memoirs where they praised themselves for being able to put an end to communism. But I never felt that in their real policy, and Gorbachev did not either. He believed in the sincerity of the trust that was established between them.

I might ask for the floor later, but this is how I wanted to react. In sum, there was no rushing on Gorbachev's part. There was no naïveté. But there was not only the desire but an objective need to act assertively, a willingness to make concessions, an understanding that if we did not give something to the Americans during negotiations, and if we did not make concessions, they would never move to meet us halfway. This is how I explain his assertiveness.

Matlock: On the question, when did the U.S. see Gorbachev as a friend in the full sense, that is as hard to answer as when the Cold War ended, and it depends, because this was a gradual process. I would say in the final sense, with Reagan, probably it would be when he came to Moscow in 1988. After that, I do not think there was any doubt on his part. With Bush, probably from Malta, the first full meeting at Malta in 1989. The question when did we transfer support to Yeltsin, I do not think we ever really transferred support, and I think that probably the whole thing was exaggerated. Washington was much less eager to deal with Yeltsin in any form than I was, and we had a few disputes over that. [...] I felt that, with Yeltsin increasing in his political influence we had to maintain contact with him, and I had maintained contact personally, as ambassador, with him, even when he was out, and I felt this was important.

Number one, to know what he was thinking, and after all, it was supposed to be a pluralistic political system. It was very clear to me that Yeltsin was incapable of somehow staging an unconstitutional takeover from Gorbachev. That was not his threat. I did think that Gorbachev had terribly mishandled the situation, that he should have kept him on the team from the very beginning, but, you know, that was his problem. But Washington was very cautious, and did not give him a very good reception.

On the other hand, Yeltsin, in dealing with us, was always totally correct in his references to Gorbachev, and particularly at that time, in June 1991, when [Gavriil] Popov[43] came to me, for example, it was to send a message to Yeltsin about the conspiracy against Gorbachev. And when Bush delivered it and said, "What shall we do?" the first thing Yeltsin says, "You've got to warn Gorbachev." And that is why I came in. It was not only Bush's, but also Yeltsin's desire that he know this. But this was not support for him, and the transfer only occurred after I left, when it was clear that the Soviet Union was not going to continue, and I would say, after the coup, and even long after the coup—not really until November. And it was clear after the referendum in Ukraine that Ukraine was going to leave. We had to recognize that. There was no way that we could avoid it any more.

So, yes, when it was clear that that was where the power was, of course, we had to start dealing with him. But until then, there was a great reluctance in Washington to think that he was an alternative. One thing—they really did not like him that much, to be quite frank.

Blanton: A quick question for you, just on that point, though. You said that for Bush the turning point was at Malta. Separately you have said to me that from your perspective they could have held Malta in April and that it might have made some difference. The title of that chapter in your book for that period is "Washington Fumbles." It is an interesting parallel because Anatoly's [chapter] title is "The Lost Year."

Matlock: I think that is right. But the reason was not that he did not have a certain confidence in Gorbachev. They had hit it off. The problem was his right wing. And I think, also, the baggage they brought. After all, Scowcroft, who is a fine person, had been head of the commission to find a basing mode for the MX [missile], and this is still at the front of his mind—how he convinces the Congress to agree to MX basing. Now he was not going to do that if the Cold War was over. Now OK, they came around, they understood eventually, but it took a little time.

Even though in a certain sense Bush was a part of everything we did in the Reagan administration, and at times when things were tough, early on, he was the most consistent one pushing the President to negotiate, and negotiate on a good basis—but his own political position was not as strong, and I think his political instincts were that the right wing of the Republican Party would do him in if he did not beat his chest a little bit. But beating his chest does not come naturally to George Bush, and he did not handle it very well. We did try to convey the whole time that this was domestic, and did not really have anything to do with our long-term policy.

---

[43] Chairman of the Moscow City Council and a reform-oriented economist.

I had a long lunch without instructions with [Aleksandr] Bessmertnykh explaining to him that domestic politics was causing the pause, and please explain this to Gorbachev, just be patient, things are going to come back together. I could not predict just when. And I think Sasha [Bessmertnykh] understood it; he had been in Washington, and I think he understood our politics. But I think it was hard for Gorbachev to understand. No, objectively speaking, if we had not had that political problem, we should have been able to just pick up. But the Reagan group and the Bush group were two entirely different groups, and politically they did not trust each other that much. It was almost an unnatural alliance. Even when Jim Baker was chief of staff of the White House, his crowd was basically a different one from the Shultz group and the ones that were, say, original Reaganites. After all, they had campaigned against Reagan almost up until he became his partner in the campaign. This was the root of the problem; it was not anything substantive in the relationship.

Tarasenko: I will take very little time. Because I was with Shevardnadze, I will tell you about his role. We cannot speak about Soviet foreign policy and about the U.S. perception of the Soviet Union without speaking about what Shevardnadze was doing. After all, the first contacts we had in the beginning of *perestroika* began with Shevardnadze. There was the first meeting between Shultz and Shevardnadze in Helsinki.[44] There was some taking the measure of each other and their views on what was happening, and what could happen; some element of attention on Shultz's part. It is not an accident that Shultz bet $10 against Gates that Shevardnadze was telling the truth. He won that bet on Afghanistan. In other words, we cannot say that Gorbachev acted independently, and that there was nothing else beside him.

And I would also like to say a word for the Ministry of Foreign Affairs, to which I belong. The American experts and the American school at the Ministry were quite strong. We had Kornienko, Komplektov, Dobrynin[45]—there were many good people there. From the point of view of the Ministry, and the American experts of the Ministry, the processes that were underway during the pause were absolutely clear to us, and we could easily explain them. Especially when a vice president becomes president he has to distinguish himself from the policies of his predecessor. He has to formulate his own policy. It is simply a law of politics. And we did not see anything tragic in it, and we had to make efforts to persuade our leadership that it was a normal process, that they were just sorting things out among themselves. Therefore, it would be incorrect to say that we were surprised, and that we did not understand. At some levels it probably was true, but not at others.

Chernyaev: It was we who did not understand.

[44] July 31, 1985.
[45] Deputy Foreign Minister Georgy Kornienko, Ambassador to the U.S. Viktor Komplektov (1991–1992), Ambassador to the U.S. and later head of the CC International Department Anatoly Dobrynin.

Tarasenko: You had the entire world as the focus of your attention. I was only looking at the United States. American experts had their America. We did not deal with the whole world, for better or worse, but we did know something. When you study the same problem for 30 years, even the last idiot learns something. (Laughter) There was at least some understanding. Therefore, I would like to testify, as somebody who was present at all ministerial meetings with the American side, that Shevardnadze always made efforts to present Gorbachev and his policy and his intentions in the best possible light during all his meetings with the American side.

He did not speak from a personal point of view, he always cited the general secretary, "Here is the general secretary's line. I am telling this to you confidentially, trust me, this is serious, this is for the long term, this is a genuine, conscious choice." Therefore, that was the preparation of the soil. You have to plow before you can plant anything. That is exactly what the Foreign Ministry in general and Shevardnadze in particular were doing—preparing the soil. And if it was not for this preparatory work, the Geneva summit would not have taken place. It was the ministerial-level preparation for everything that later transpired at the highest level. It would not have happened if there had been no understanding between Shultz and Shevardnadze.

Blanton: I would like to ask Rick Hermann to start off with a couple of minutes right now with the perspective that was seen from Policy Planning at State, and Jim Baker's perspective on the pause, and these other subjects, and on the German question as well.

Richard Hermann: I will make a couple of comments on this pause. I hope they are not defensive, but explanatory, as best I can remember it. I agree very much with the argument that was made earlier that it was domestic politics, and I would say there were two dimensions to that. I arrived there [at the Office of Policy Planning] in April of 1989, and one of the buzzwords at the time was "the vision thing," it was called, and Bush's lack of it, and that we needed some kind of vision of where things would be going. So, there was a lot of to-ing and fro-ing to see. But what I really thought was related to that was Bush's desire to create an image of himself as a leader coming out from under the shadow of Reagan.

And he certainly sensed that in the Republican Party Reagan would be a hard act to follow in terms of a leader—the personality, and all that. And it was important that he declare the notion that there would be an assessment of where we were, and then decisions would start to get taken by him, Bush, and Baker. And that would be associated with him, rather than him as a junior to Reagan. And I think that was important to him. A part of the domestic politics, I thought, was already talked about by both Ambassador Matlock and Doug MacEachin, and it was the right wing. This was sporadic.

There were places, there were pockets of the Republican right that were really powerful on some issues. And they were on the Hill, for example, on Afghanistan, and on Nicaragua. Some of these policies had established not just inertia,

196

but strong political supporters, and they were not ready to do battle with them right off the bat. And some of the issues that were on the immediate lot, like Nicaragua and Afghanistan, would create a constraint. And they did not want to fight with those people right away. That is one set of ideas.

There is a second, more mundane one. That is that the National Security Council was being reformed. Brent Scowcroft had authored, or co-authored the Tower Commission Report investigating Iran–Contra. And several very important players in the Bush transition team had either been scathed or close to it by Iran–Contra. The result of the Scowcroft commission, or the Tower Commission, of course, was to put not only checks and balances on the National Security Council [staff], but to reduce its size, and the initial decision was to reduce its size almost by half in the early period of the Bush administration.

Now, it is never a very large staff, but now we talking about numbers below fifty. And the decision was taken, at least as it was related to me, that a lot of decision making in foreign policy would move over to Baker, and that it would be run out of Dennis Ross's shop with Bob Kimmitt his undersecretary, and [Robert] Zoellick,[46] and that there would be policy staff, and so on. But running, of course, the State Department, is different than running the NSC: it is not an organization of less than a hundred, but thousands. And I think that this reform of the NSC slowed some things down, and, of course, as someone mentioned earlier, Brent Scowcroft was more skeptical about—I do not think the intentions of Gorbachev—but the prospects that he would be successful.

And that leads me to another point I want to make. There were still, as Doug MacEachin suggests, deep divisions within the intelligence community, and—we were just talking at the break—I think it was evolving. It was not the old "dove"–"hawk" debate, as we all knew it for twenty years. It was sort of that. It was much more complicated. It was: Gorbachev's for real, but given he is for real, can he in fact be successful? Or is what he is proposing to do impossible? And will he be blocked by other forces in the Soviet Union? And if he is, how should we position ourselves, given these now very difficult to predict eventualities. And there was back and forth, put our cards on Gorbachev and hope for him, and I think that was ultimately where most people came up. But it was not the consensus view by any matter of means, and once that assessment had begun, then a lot of to-ing and fro-ing went on over the spring and summer of 1989, as the intelligence community made all these assessments.

Another item I would like to point out. Baker and his chief of staff, Dennis Ross, had very important roles in the campaign. They ended up, therefore, playing a very large role in the transition, and a very large role in appointments. Much of the early couple of months of the administration was making

---

[46] In 1989, James Baker had become secretary of state, Dennis Ross was director of the Office of Policy Planning, Robert Kimmitt was undersecretary for political affairs, and Robert Zoellick was counselor to the Department.

appointments, much of which was happening through their office, and they were busy, essentially, creating a foreign policy bureaucracy as they wanted it. Well, not bureaucracy, but appointments as they wanted to set it up. And related to that, I will just throw it on the table although it is a minor issue—well, not so minor—there were other issues that were really important to Baker and Bush.

One was the Middle East, which commanded a lot of time in the summer of 1989, and was of particularly great interest to Dennis Ross, who had a lot of influence with Secretary Baker. And there was a lot of complaining about that, whether or not so much time should be devoted to the Middle East as opposed to larger strategic issues, but nevertheless, that was it. I thought, on the two points on Germany, that one real breakthrough came in [...] I forgot if that was October or November [1989], when [Chairman of the Joint Chiefs of Staff] General [Colin] Powell went to Europe and came back, and people from our staff and his staff had concluded that we were way behind the power curve on arms control, and we needed to move a lot more quickly. And I think the JCS became supporters of change [...]

With regard to Germany, and I will finish here, because it is illustrative of the early part of the administration we were working with, I think that Mr. Chernyaev is exactly right, although I do not know if there was so much of a change. I think, initially, on the German question, there was a lot of discussion about whether this was good or not good for U.S. interests. And there was some hesitancy about whether or not this would be a good thing or not. But surely by late October, I cannot remember, I could look it up, I remember very specifically the secretary tasking Frank Fukuyama and me and a few others to write some points for him to take to a Sunday morning television show that would be four ideas about how the unification of Germany should proceed.

And it is indicative for this administrative problem of moving from the NSC to State that I do not think in the early period, maybe not even in the later period, that the relationship between the secretary and some of the assistant secretaries, and in particular people in the bureaus, was everything it should have been. And that there was a lot of action occurring in the secretary's office, sometimes with the rest of the building in the loop, sometimes not—and when not, then resentful that they were not, and back and forth, and back and forth. But the notion that the secretary, on Friday afternoon, would say, "On Sunday I want to make a statement that is important, draft me something," and then he would say it, or say it from a plane somewhere in Moscow, and then the fight in the building would be: this is policy, the secretary said this. And then it would proceed like this.

And it allowed both Zoellick and Ross to have a lot of influence, and I think, they decided on the German question that this was going to happen, and that we would be in a much better position to be in the front of the train trying to steer a little, than try to jump on the back of the train later on. And I think, by early November of 1989, the decision was taken—this train has left the station, it is not entirely clear just how the tracks are going to go, but this is the way it is going to be, and we will be better off up at the engine, not in the caboose. [....]

Gaiduk: I will try to be brief, and to state my opinion regarding Gorbachev's foreign policy, and the Soviet international situation at the time Gorbachev came to power in comparison to what transpired by 1989. And my opinion on this is not just a personal opinion, it is substantiated by my conversations with veterans of Soviet foreign policy, for instance with Anatoly Fedorovich Dobrynin, and I also talked with a number of officials of the International Department of the Central Committee, who participated in developing this policy. And I would like to follow up on the point that in 1985, in contrast to the internal situation, Soviet international standing was quite solid.

There were elements that Gorbachev could have used in his foreign policy, for example the fact that nuclear parity had existed, and that was a very important element of the strength of the Soviet Union—I would say its trump card—that Gorbachev could have used in his foreign policy. Therefore, Mikhail Sergeyevich had [an] alternative: to bargain—and then his genuine call for building qualitatively new international relations could only be applauded. But how do you build those relations?

Gorbachev as a state leader should have based his policy not only on universal human values. He should have pursued universal human values, at the same time taking his country's national interests into account. And that alternative was available for Gorbachev: either give up all the strengths that we had in the name of the highest goal of building qualitatively new international relations—or he could bargain. And the second alternative would have taken Soviet national interests into account. He could have bargained in order to preserve Soviet positions as much as possible. [...]

Anatoly Fedorovich Dobrynin writes in his memoir on page 636: "At that critical, final moment of the Cold War, Gorbachev and Shevardnadze had no coherent, balanced, and firm foreign policy to end it in a fitting and dignified way on the basis of equality. As the Cold War had begun to wind down in the second part of the 1980s, this balance of power with the West was widely recognized and could have created a base upon which to transform international relations into a new and non-confrontational era. With an inexplicable rush, they actually gave away vital geopolitical and military positions which we had, instead of using them to achieve a new era of stability and equal cooperation."[47] This is the essence of what I wanted to say. I would like to hear from our veterans of Russian foreign policy what their reaction is to this opinion, which I share. Thank you.

Chernyaev: Now you have heard both the positions of the new thinking and of the old thinking here. It is precisely the position of old thinking to present national interests as contrary to universal human values. If we had taken the position presented by Dobrynin, it would have meant prolonging the final stage of the Cold War for many more years. One has to use a global yardstick to measure the effectiveness of Gorbachev's foreign policy. First of all, the result is that we

---

[47] Dobrynin, *In Confidence*.

managed to put an end to the Cold War, to the confrontation. We managed to begin a genuine process of nuclear disarmament, and later of conventional disarmament. This is the result. It is a historic, global result of the policy of new thinking.

If we took the bargaining position—as Falin recommended then, and is still defending on the issue of German unification—if we had followed Falin's logic, we would have failed with unification and provoked an unimaginable European crisis, or maybe even a global crisis. Because the "process has really started," using the famous expression. Even the Americans jumped into the first car when they saw that the train was moving ahead. What was Gorbachev supposed to do? He was trying to find a middle-of-the-road position, but then he realized that it might turn against our own Soviet interests because it would put unified Germany in opposition to the Soviet Union, and we would not get the results that we counted on from a unified Germany.

And we got those results—we got a unified Germany as a friendly state that values what had been done by Gorbachev, regardless of all the diplomatic moves by Kohl and others. But that is a different issue.

I would like to make one more comment. You have cited the document of the National Security Council. There are other documents that are no less important, for example two public statements by Baker in October 1989[48] in which he openly stated that we are looking for points of mutual interest. Neither Gorbachev nor anybody else expected America to give us presents out of some kind of sympathy. It [the United States] moves according to its own national interests. It negotiates with Gorbachev and reaches certain agreements. Baker formulated it very well in his two famous statements: We are going to meet Gorbachev halfway because it is in our own interest.

And Gorbachev understood this very well. When he made concessions, they were justified from a moral and political standpoint. When somebody argued with him from the standpoint of the balance at the Politburo, in the Central Committee, etc., when the military tried to defend its positions, as they were supposed to do, he used to say to them, "Are you going to fight a war? I am not going to fight. Is anybody from my colleagues in the Politburo going to fight? No? Then let us start from here." Our concessions were the result of that logic: we were not going to fight a war, we wanted to put an end to the Cold War, we wanted nuclear disarmament and the liquidation of nuclear arms. That was new thinking, which led to quite specific global historic results.

Tarasenko: I would like to briefly comment on this particular issue because I worked with Dobrynin in the Embassy in Washington. I deeply respect him, and I owe him very much. He is a great ambassador, a great diplomat; there could not be two opinions about it. But the problem with memoirs in general is that

---

[48] Speeches before the Foreign Policy Association in New York on October 17, and the Commonwealth Club in San Francisco on October 23, 1989.

a person always wants to be smarter with hindsight than he was at the time, when things were happening. It seems like we have this particular case here. If you recall the period of *perestroika*, Dobrynin had moved to the International Department of the Central Committee. As far as I know, he tried to create a counterbalance to the Foreign Ministry, in other words to transfer the Foreign Ministry to the Central Committee. He took several good experts with him to the Central Committee. And we practically had a competition between Dobrynin and Shevardnadze for influence in foreign policy. He lost due to purely physical factors, because the Foreign Ministry had a much better organized team than *Staraya Ploshchad'*[49] in Moscow. I do not want to offend my colleagues.

Chernyaev: That is absolutely correct.

Tarasenko: We had better access to information. We could decide whether to disseminate that information or not, to inform a particular person or not. And that gave us substantial superiority over other internal agencies. I think that his statement that you quoted is completely divorced from reality. I have worked in the Foreign Ministry for 30 years, and I worked with good people—with Dobrynin, with Kornienko, next to Gromyko. In other words, I was lucky. I had a chance to learn from them. And I can tell you very honestly that in no other period except this period of *perestroika* did our foreign policy deal so much with our real national interests.

Nothing was done that was outside a pragmatic approach: what is good for the country, what is necessary for the country at this moment, what would help the country. All foreign policy was based on those assumptions. I am a little bit baffled by all these discussions about national interests in our Russian context. I have never seen any papers or any conceptual statements as to what the national interests of Russia are. Or the Soviet Union. It was clear with respect to ideological interests—socialism should win and so on. But to speak about Russian national interests?

I was in charge of the Middle East and I tried to understand: our "vital interests in the Middle East"—what were they? In general, we needed to have influence, we needed to have our presence there. But how? What do we get from that? There is nothing beyond this formal and general statement, which has no substance to it. Probably for the first time during the *perestroika* period, and my senior colleagues would probably agree with me, this was the first time we acted very pragmatically with specific interests in mind to help solve our domestic problems. That was our priority at the time—to remove, to shake off that huge burden that had accumulated on our shoulders. And we were quite expeditious in doing so.

I remember the first time I came to Washington with Shevardnadze. You know, there were constant rallies, there was a group of protesters across the street

---

[49] *Staraya Ploshchad'* or "Old Square," was the site of Central Committee headquarters in the capital.

from the Embassy. The very next time, the group was gone because Shevard-nadze stepped out of the Embassy, walked toward the protesters, and asked them what was the problem. "Let us go inside the Embassy, let us talk. Send in your representatives. We will talk about the issue and find a solution. We are ready to find solutions." And they were gone. Then there were the Baltic émigrés, and the Afghanis came over. There were a number of demonstrations.

But it was a change of image for the Soviet Union that we were trying to achieve from the very start, and it was our priority after the Korean airplane,[50] after some other acts. We tried to get everybody to treat us like normal people. And I think that the fact that we were successful dates back to the very early days of *perestroika*. People started looking at the Soviet Union with different eyes, and the respect that Gorbachev enjoyed was a direct result of the fact that his policy was viewed in a certain light.

Shakhnazarov: I would like to disagree with one of the statements made by one of our young colleagues. They said that the Soviet Union had an advantage in foreign policy, in a situation of domestic weakness. This is not a logical comparison, because a country that is weak economically and unstable politically and also has internal conflicts would manifest it in foreign policy. Foreign policy, whatever your starting point is, regardless of whether you read Marx or Weber, foreign policy is an integral part of the general political course of a country, and it reflects all the difficulties and all the specifics of the situation in the country. What kind of advantages do nuclear weapons give foreign policy? What do you do with them? Quite often nuclear weapons can be a disadvantage. This is on the first issue.

The second issue concerns bargaining. Of course Gorbachev was bargaining, as Sergey Petrovich has justly put it. He specifically considered the national interests of Russia more than anyone else. [....]

Gorbachev did bargain. Ilya, I think you are making one substantial mistake. You do not take into account the fact that the collapse of the Soviet Union and everything else voided any bargaining that Gorbachev was involved in. What we are blamed for, including us—the assistants—is that we did not have a document spelling out German obligations regarding property issues as well as others that should have been reflected in the agreement. People forget that should the Soviet Union have remained intact, then many obligations on the German and on the American part would have been carried out in full. But since the Soviet Union collapsed they all lost their value, they were voided.

You are saying that we have lost everything. But the decisive factor in it was not Gorbachev's foreign policy or those mythical concessions, because he got compensation for each concession that he made. Yeltsin was the major factor,

---

[50] On September 1, 1983, Soviet fighter aircraft shot down Korean Air Lines flight 007, which had drifted into Soviet airspace near Sakhalin Island. Soviet officials later claimed they did not know the airliner was civilian.

the emergence of a new political power, starting from the Declaration of Independence of Russia on June 12, 1990. It practically voided the center as the old power. The center could no longer control or govern the country, and after that time all its energies were directed toward trying to help the Soviet Union by any means possible, including the agreement. That was the major problem, and not at all the fact that he would not fight for the national interests in his policy. Thank you.

Hershberg: One quick point, and then one quick question coming out of that comment. The paragraph from Dobrynin's memoirs that my friend Ilya read also appeared in the English edition, and it was the paragraph I most disagreed with, and thought it was the most wrong-headed, if not the most ridiculous, because it reminded me so much of the "who lost China" debate in the United States in the 1950s, as if China was the Americans' to lose. It reflected, to my mind, a mindset that in 1989 the future of Eastern Europe could be decided by people in Moscow and Washington, and completely ignored the forces that were coming up from the ground in Eastern Europe.

This leads me to my question, which is directed to the Central and East European guests that we have here, and especially to Andrzej [Paczkowski], and Vilém [Prečan], who were old enough to be witnesses not only in 1989 but to the earlier crises in East-Central Europe. At what point in the events—in 1989, or maybe you would say even earlier—did you stop believing that this was going be a repetition of past crises that would be decided by decisions in Moscow, and perhaps Washington, but would in fact be decided by people in Warsaw and Prague and Budapest? If our younger witnesses would like to also chime in, please. At what point did you realize that you were breaking out of this superpower narrative of the Cold War, and that you could actually determine your own fate? When in 1989 did that realization strike you? Thank you.

Blanton: Vilém, do you want to address that?

Prečan: Only in late November of 1989 did I start to believe that the Soviet Union would not interfere. The question was not only what kind of interference by the Soviet Union, but whether Gorbachev or Moscow gave a free hand to the domestic leadership. That means that if Jakeš decides to use weapons in Prague against demonstrators, what would Moscow's reaction be? And there was one single hope on the 21st and 22nd of November 1989—that Gorbachev was very interested in his meeting in Malta, and he would not allow—this was my opinion at the time—Jakeš to spit into his (Gorbachev's) soup.

Hershberg: Let me clarify. Vilém, did you ever find evidence whether Jakeš communicated with Moscow, or considered this option and sought Soviet approval?

Prečan: No, but I know that it was Thursday night, the night of November 23. I knew, or I learned later, that there was a telephone call between Jakeš and Štrougal. And Jakeš told—as I heard it—he told Štrougal that there was no hope for him to take over the leadership because he, Jakeš, would not give it up. But in the evening of Friday the 24th of November Jakeš gave up and resigned. So,

I asked, why? Why this change of mind? And I thought that there must have been some message from the Czechoslovak Embassy in Moscow, information on how Moscow newspapers reported on the demonstrations; and it was my belief that this was what had changed Jakeš' mind.

Shakhnazarov: I will tell you how it happened because I was working on Czechoslovakia. Our ambassador called, and he sent a cable, and he said that the Czech leadership was thinking of using force against the demonstrators, and most probably after their Politburo meeting they would ask me what the reaction from Moscow would be. And he was asked: What do you think? Of course, our position was that it should not be done. And he was told, "If they ask you, that is what you need to tell them, that we do not support the use of force." But then there was another communication from him—that he was not consulted, because the Czech leadership themselves decided not to use force, and Jakeš resigned.

Prečan: Do you have any evidence of that? Any documents?[51]

Shakhnazarov: I do not know right now, but I think there must be something like cables, or something like that.

Blanton: Well, that is a good segue to the final session, which is "Mysteries and Evidence That We Need to Pursue." Let me just call on Andrzej Paczkowski, perhaps, to respond to Jim Hershberg's question in the Polish context that is very, very different than the Czechoslovak context.

Paczkowski: This is not possible because the process in Poland was very long, and very, very complicated. I see that next year we will have an occasion to debate it for three days.

Dawisha: Only three?

Paczkowski: Only three (Laughter). If we need more—why not? I would add only a very general vision. This final period started in Poland in 1986. Maybe the precise day was September 11, when the minister of interior declared that all political prisoners were free. And at this moment processes started, which in the first stage would be very similar to the other reforms in Poland. [The goal] was to find some social body to co-opt into the political elite, but to stay within the political structure governed by the Communist Party. And this first stage was finished at the roundtable talks.

But starting in the summer of 1988 there was a second current in Jaruzelski's thinking and of his crowd, that it maybe was necessary to include another form in these processes—not co-optation, but negotiations. Negotiations with such social structures as Solidarity. And for me, the crucial period for Polish changes was between September 1988 and January 1989 because there was one group in the leadership of the Polish Communist Party, which tried to do all changes in the Chinese way, namely only economic reform without political change. And the creation of the Rakowski government, and the first decisions, economic decisions—a free market, liberalization of the *zloty*, free internal conversion of

---

[51] See Document No. 108.

zlotys into dollars—it was possible that the Chinese way would be repeated in Poland. But in China there was no structural political opposition to battle against this current. In Poland the situation was different. And the existence of Solidarity, I think, protected all the people in the Communist Party who tried to do the two reforms in parallel—political and economic.

This stage was marked, I think, by a conversation, a TV debate, between Wałęsa and the leader of the Syndicate [communist labor union federation], [Alfred] Miodowicz, and when Gorbachev was at the U.N. in December. The first ten days of December 1988 made the decision for the Polish leadership to try to move in two parallel ways. And this all happened only after their realization of this situation.

Rainer: Jim's question was when did we feel that we were free? I think, as it was in Poland, it was a long process in Hungary as well. From the point below, from the side of the opposition forces, there were three main steps, or three crucial events. In 1988 we definitely did not feel ourselves to be free. Not even in late 1988. It was quite characteristic that nearly all the main leaders of the democratic opposition traveled to the United States for long-term fellowships. It was worse to stay in Hungary where the domestic political situation was quite interesting, even at that time.

The first main step was in February–March of 1989. It can be described by two events. One was the reassessment of the 1956 events. Why did certain circles of the party, the reformist [Imre] Pozsgay, for example, [do this?] [...] And the acceptance of the principle of a multi-party system. And there was no official reaction from Moscow. Then came June of 1989. June the 16th, and I have to correct the movie, which we watched two days ago. It was not a state organized event, the state only accepted it under pressure from society. It was organized by the opposition forces. This is only a minor mistake, but it is quite important for us. And it was all the more crucial [...] because it was only a few days after the Tiananmen Square events.

And when we stood in our square in Budapest, watching hundreds of thousands—I personally was involved in the organization of this event—I thought, okay, we have done it, because there was still no reaction from Moscow. And the realization was full in September 1989. There were also two or three main events: letting the East Germans leave through Hungary, and just after they began to leave the so-called National Roundtable finished its work with an agreement between the party and the opposition—an agreement on certain changes in the Constitution, free elections for March of the next year, and so on. From the two or three points, I think, the crucial one was, both politically and morally, June 16.

CHAPTER 6: MYSTERIES, QUESTIONS, CONCLUSIONS

Blanton: In this final session, what I am asking for is your commission to us, in the broader sense, of a large cooperative multinational enterprise: what would be the research agenda that you would give us over the next year? As Andrzej pointed out, for just the events in Poland we are going to have a substantive discussion over three days or longer, and each revolution will be the center of a conference with its own briefing book. And so this session is simply a starting point for a baseline. I would like to start with Jack Matlock, and then Doug MacEachin, and then Anatoly Chernyaev and Georgy Shakhnazarov and Sergey Tarasenko to get their suggestions to us, commissions to us on the top three mysteries of the end of the Cold War to them—even now—and the three pieces of evidence that they would commission us to go get, if we can.

Matlock: I will start. I am not sure that I can fulfill your task, and I do not want to seem arrogant or a know-it-all because this is not my attitude, but frankly, I do not see any deep mysteries here. There are a lot of unanswered questions, perhaps, of detail. But I honestly do not see a mystery. I think what happened was that maybe we had in our systems unique individuals at a crucial time in history who were able to look at things in a new way, and not be bound by the sort of stereotypes—some of which clearly even very capable people of the previous period, like Anatoly Dobrynin, continued to be bound by in their thinking.

And I think it is important to understand why it is that Dobrynin's view, which has also been expressed by others, is also, in my opinion, an invalid one. It is invalid because of one thing they never cite—of course, there are some exceptions: what precise agreements could have been reached in the Soviet interest which would have been different from those reached? They just say, "He could have made better deals." I cannot think of a single issue on which a better deal was possible from the standpoint of the Soviet interest.

Is one arguing, for example, that an attempt, even if it had been agreed to by the United States, to limit the sovereignty of East European countries would have been an asset to the Soviet Union? Oh, it would have been a problem. In fact, their previous policies had saddled them with so many liabilities. The real task was getting rid of those liabilities. And increasingly, the way we saw it in the United States, we were helping them to get rid of those liabilities because we too wanted stability, and we wanted peace. Obviously, arguing with our own people, we would use a certain rhetoric for that, sure.

We wanted to use what influence we had to change the internal structure. We wanted to change it the same way that Gorbachev himself had said he wanted to change it. But that was not because we wanted to make the Soviet Union weaker. We wanted to see someone there who could be a partner, and could be a healthy economy, meeting the needs of its people, and therefore not a threat to its neighbors. You know, that was really our goal. It sounds very idealistic, but that was what we really believed. Now, in arguing with people you use all sorts of arguments, and some of them, if you take them out of context, may even sound somewhat aggressive, but that is only possible if you take them out of context, and lose the entire context.

Now, I do not think it is a mystery, I think it is interesting to know, to go back to one of the questions raised earlier, and that is: why was there not more economic assistance? And to me, the answer is clear, and I gave it before, but

I think it needs more amplification on both sides. On the one hand, it was very clear—the difficulty that Gorbachev had in finding a roadmap to the future. He was trying to change the system in effect—he may have not realized it—almost 180 degrees, from one of total centralized control over the economy to one that basically was a market economy, which the government would use in various ways—maybe not market ways, but on the basis of principles that were consistent with the market. He would not have put it in those terms. He was looking for a democratic socialism. And yet, put in our terms, it was a way to fundamentally create a free enterprise economy, but one that would be productive enough that would support a lot of social services. I think that is really what eventually was meant by socialism.

Nobody—and I stress, nobody—knew how to do that, and anybody who says they did, and is sure about it, is simply talking through their hat. There was no roadmap. We did not know, they did not know. If the question from Georgy and others is why you did not want to put more money into supporting our socialist enterprises, the answer is very clear. And I gave it several times then. I would tell my Soviet interlocutors: if you want us to help you keep viable state-owned socialist enterprises, there is no way we can do it. We do not know how to do it. We cannot even run an efficient post office by the government.

The only way we know how to run efficient enterprises is to privatize and create competition. De-monopolize, privatize, create competition. If you want to do that, we have some experience that is relevant, but it has to be fitted to your conditions. It is not a roadmap. If you do not want to do that, what we do is totally irrelevant, and throwing money into doomed state enterprises is not going to help one bit. And that was the problem. And yet I think there was a lack of action in 1989 and 1990, when something might have been started on both sides in talking frankly about the problem. Because by then, after Malta, there was a personal relationship, and if in private Gorbachev had gone to Bush and said, "Look, I've got a big problem ahead of me, which is also your problem. Let us put our heads together, and maybe get our experts very quietly to start looking at it. What can we do to get over this, and by the way, this is something that not only affects us, it affects our friends in Eastern Europe, it affects other economies. There is a big transition ahead of us, none of us knows how to do it. Let us see if we can do it in a supportive way." Well, that was not really said. And then on Bush's side, although it was increasingly apparent what the problem was, he was waiting for Gorbachev to come up with something. And maybe it was something that Gorbachev was unable to come up with. So, I do not see it as a mystery, but that is still a question that needs to be examined.

And I will just give one example. I know we do not have much time. But I will give one example, and that is when Bush sent the businessmen to Moscow in 1990. And that was just after the September meeting in Helsinki. And actually, that was an attempt to send people who potentially could bring billions. Each individual could probably command, with the right projects, ten billion or more, in investment. And okay, they were given a lecture by the Chief of Gosplan with almost no mention of reforms but a mention of "we will let you invest in our things." And they said "fine." There was a guy interested in communications, telecommunications, the head of Sprint, there were people in the oil business.

These were titans of American industry. They were also Bush's political supporters. And so we said, "Fine, give us a list where you want your investment. Let us set up a committee. Fine, we will set up a committee." We never received that list, that committee was never named. Our Embassy followed up. We were told we would get it in ten days. Our Embassy followed up a week later, two weeks later, six weeks later, three months later. Nothing happened. And meanwhile, how were they going to invest? What were the conditions? So, in a sense we were groping for ways without really focusing on it. Granted, they were focusing on the Gulf War and other things. My point is, I think we probably need more [...]

Shakhnazarov: When did that happen?

Matlock: September 1990. It was just after the Helsinki meeting, which dealt mainly with the Gulf War and Iraq, and then from Helsinki they came directly to Moscow, met with Gorbachev, and at that time he told them: "The Chairman of Gosplan is going to brief you on what we are going to do." And I thought at the time, good heavens, you know, it is like putting the fox in charge of your chicken coop. The problem was breaking up Gosplan for crying out loud. And how were you going to do that if you were not going to break it up? But that is not for us to say. But my point is, we really could not find a way to be helpful, and it would have taken a long time, and somehow our leaders did not focus on it—I think this is crucial—on the lack of support.

But also, and I would just conclude by saying if those who say that Gorbachev could have gotten better deals, which would have gone down with the West, I would like to hear what they were, because I can think of none. Or, I can only think of one exception, and that is: during German unification, if he had pressed, and if it had been important to him, he could have probably gotten better assurances that there would be no further expansion of NATO. He did not press that issue, and therefore it was left sort of unclear. And people can argue that inasmuch as he agreed to allow East German territory to become a part of NATO, that there was no agreement really not to expand NATO eastward. My own view is that the expansion eastward is going to weaken NATO, and if it continues it will weaken it even more, and NATO will simply become irrelevant. Therefore, I do not see this as a huge geopolitical problem. I regret that it is happening.

Blanton: That will be our second conference from now.

Matlock: That is right. But my point here is, I think you've got to get out of the mindset that the previous positions on either side were necessarily in their interest. The zero option is a good example. That was in the Soviet strategic interest, more so than in the Western, if you are looking strictly in those terms. They just did not see it for a while. Therefore, it was not a concession. And this is true of many of the others. These agreements really were in our mutual interest, given the circumstances and given the alternatives.

Blanton: Thank you very much. [...] I am going to resume, and perhaps ask Anatoly to try to deal with the following: are there mysteries, or even just unanswered questions? Because we got at least two from Jack. We got these: What were the deals that could have been gotten that were better than what Gorbachev got? And what was the problem with economic assistance? So we've got at least two. But I want to ask Anatoly to give your unanswered questions or mysteries.

Chernyaev: Because you set a goal to define only three problems, I will propose the following. Maybe it is not for a single meeting like this. First, let us synthesize the results and the outcomes of the end of the Cold War in the context of those negative developments that subsequently unfolded after the end of the Cold War. This is a big, synthetic task. Second, there is an element of mystery: Helmut Kohl's Ten Points, November 28, 1989.[52] I do not think that anybody would doubt that they played a very important role in the further process of German unification. But what happened here, what went into this phenomenon? Was that the result of Kohl's ambition to be the father of the nation, the Unifier? What came from his electoral considerations? And what represented a real need to hurry to do certain things to keep the process under control? Was there a realistic threat of being late? This is the second point.

Now, the third point. Let us try to extract perceptions on the part of Soviet people from various strata—the former leadership, the elite, the common people—of the American threat by the mid-1980s. What did the American threat consist of in their perception? Then it would be easier to understand why Gorbachev's policy was received with support. In order not to take the floor again, I would like to say just the following. We are eternally grateful to you for the work that you have undertaken because this is important not only for scholarly purposes, not only for the future. First of all, it is of assistance to us, because we cannot undertake such a project in Russia now. That is why we are thanking you personally, because you visit us all the time, you use us, you invite us all the time, but also we want to thank you in a more general—national, if you will—sense. Thank you very much.

Blanton: Thank you very, very much. Now Georgy, please. You have five minutes. Three mysteries, three questions, and three pieces of evidence that you want us to find.

Shakhnazarov: At Tom's request, I am going to formulate three problems that in my opinion need to be studied. We more or less know why Gorbachev acted this way and not the other, what he wanted, what did not work. In other words, Gorbachev's line has been more or less studied. But there have been no studies of the role played by Western Europe. It seems that it was all done in Washington. However, we know that maybe up to 40 percent of the international factors came from those meetings with West European leaders, like Thatcher, Mitterrand, Gonzalez, and others, what they said, the positions of the leading West

---

[52] See Document Nos. 111, 113.

European states. Anatoly Sergeyevich has his tremendous experience, his notes of meetings, his documents, his recollections. I think he can, as we say, dig out his closets, and find something interesting for us.

The second issue is the role of our internal opposition, our internal processes. I believe that our young colleagues, historians, took a very critical position in assessing the policies of *perestroika* to a large extent because they underestimate what was happening inside the country. They underestimate the role of those explosive processes which occurred unexpectedly and broke up many of our intentions, plans, and calculations, including Gorbachev's calculations. I think that this factor should be included in our analysis: the factor of internal processes.

Third, even though Jack and Doug gave interesting presentations today, I am still not very satisfied by how we discussed the U.S. role. Not because I want some kind of new revelations like the document that Oleg has read to us. We should learn about this in more detail, with documents. We should know how the Americans acted in those situations? Not because we want to accuse anybody, or justify ourselves—just because we are writing history. As Balzac said, "History is most often forged while it is being made." If we do not determine exactly how everything happened now, then the wrong information will go down to the next generations.

I agree with Jack, and I understand it when he says that they could not give the money because it was like throwing it down the drain. Then I ask: how come you found 25 billion dollars to give to Yeltsin, the money that is being spent on patching up the budget, for the New Russians to steal and take out of the country? Why is there money available for this, but it was not available then? Just several billion to support Gorbachev? Let us try to explain this for ourselves. Maybe because Yeltsin in response began to sell out Russian resources? Maybe this is the answer? Aluminum is being exported, other things too. This is not to blame anybody, especially because we are not involved in real policy now, we are looking at it as old men, as historians. But we must have clarity as to the role played by the United States, by the American factor in all these events.

And I would like to conclude by saying that I have several documents that I will pass on to you, including the document of the meeting of the general secretaries that took place in Bucharest in July 1989, some German documents, discussions that I have mentioned. We will give all these materials to Vlad. I would also like to add to what Anatoly Sergeyevich has said regarding the organizers of this project, that we are very grateful to the owner of this beautiful plantation for the opportunity to be here, to work, and to relax here, although it is not enough, of course. (Laughter)

Blanton: It is never enough.

Shakhnazarov: And thank to all of you who helped us.

Tarasenko: I would like to join my colleagues in expressing our deep gratitude, and to say that we appreciate such events very much. This conference was very well organized, and it is very useful for history, and useful in every other sense because the question is about mysteries and evidence related to the mysteries. You know, for me the question that is not clear is whether the Cold War has really ended? For a couple of years I have been confident that the Cold War is over. When exactly it ended—under Shultz or under Baker—is a different question. But recently I found a quote from the [Cheshire] Cat, who said, "The war did not end, it just fell asleep." And I started thinking—maybe the Cold War has just fallen asleep?

If you want evidence—in March of last year the U.S. Embassy in Moscow refused to give me a visa to visit the United States to take part in a Hofstra University conference. I took it as a computer glitch. That was the only explanation: you know, things like this happen. My visa for this particular trip was only issued twenty hours before my departure, after you intervened. I have never, during the Cold War, experienced such a situation. My visa was always guaranteed at all times. Something is happening apparently between the two countries, and moreover, when my visa was denied, I was still the holder of a diplomatic passport […] I think that events like this are extremely useful, and we need to continue them, and we need to give everybody a chance to speak, we need to cover the picture from different angles. I cannot see any magic lens: you know, we need to do this, we need to do that. Just the process of communication—we talk, we share opinions, we look at things. Some of them make sense, some do not; it is a dialogue. We need to continue with the dialogue as best we can, continue developing the dialogue. I do not have a problem at all here. Thank you.

Blanton: Thank you very much, Sergey. Let me just ask Doug MacEachin to do one of his famous bullet-point briefings, the way he used to do them for Ronald Reagan: *punto, punto, punto, punto.*

MacEachin: I no longer have a diplomatic passport, and I no longer do that, but I will try. And I may not be contributing anything because this is my first session, and I do not know necessarily what you have already done.

First, I thought the key question at the very end of our discussions was: what was the perception in the East European capitals, and when was what perceived? I would really like to be present some time where we go into that in great depth—

Blanton: Come next year.

MacEachin: —with views from different domestic factions, because I think that is critical.

Number two, I have always been curious in great detail about what went on in the Brezhnev period from about 1978 to the end of it, in terms of the perceptions then about economic and social problems. How much concern was there—I know there was at least some, I read about some—and what kind of stage setting was done then for what would happen later under Gorbachev? It just seems to me that the world did not suddenly get invented under Gorbachev.

Number three, a proposition: by 1989, the impact of the previous three or four years was roughly, as I would describe it, that Gorbachev had shown his commitment to reform, had moved beyond just economic adjustments to really make major political change in the society, and the political system had opened. That, however, created an enormous problem, and everything I have read from my own files, and from the files of the academics with whom I am now associated, shows we were all writing then about tremendous change, all kinds of social turmoil, [...] ethnic uprisings in various places, the economy has not delivered. We wrote that in many ways people now have more freedom to express their dissatisfaction, and there is a backlash coming. Everybody I knew was saying that, and I would be very interested to know in as much detail as possible what was the perception on the other side, because I tell you we were saying that here, and the State Department was rejecting it. And a lot of people were saying that was wrong. You were seeing it in Moscow, but many people in Washington did not have your vantage point. And I really am interested to know: why was our perception that different from those in Moscow? It was a perception on this side of the Atlantic that caused people to say: whether Gorbachev is still in office in the next two to three years is a great question. And yet we did not seem to get any kind of sense of that from our interlocutors. Those are the three mysteries to me.

Blanton: Thank you, Doug. I would like to give the floor to Jacques Levesque, and then Vlad has the last two questions here.

Levesque: About Eastern Europe. We now know well enough that Gorbachev himself, personally, stood aloof and exerted very little pressure for change in Eastern Europe. When he did, he did it in a very indirect and a very prudent manner. However, you did send much stronger signs to Eastern Europe. The fact that your signs were not backed by Gorbachev, of course, limited their impact. For instance, I was surprised to see in Vadim Medvedev's book, *Raspad*, how he was able to speak to Zhivkov in a much tougher manner than Gorbachev himself did, and he was much stronger in what he said to Zhivkov. I am talking now about the reformers.

There were harder signals sent to Eastern Europe by other Soviet circles: the military, the KGB, for instance, and on these we know nothing. What were the signals those people were sending? Of course, they had a limited impact because also Gorbachev was not backing these signals personally. But some signals were certainly sent by the KGB, by the military, all over Eastern Europe. For instance, I would be very interested to know what is the part that the KGB played in Romania in December 1989? The KGB was there. It is unbelievable that it could have been entirely inactive and done nothing. So, what were the signals that the KGB was giving there? We know nothing. I would like to see some documents coming not from the reformers, because we know—well, if there is something else, the more the better—but we have had quite a few documents from the reformist side, but very little from the other circles that exerted their limited influence in the area.

And my main question then, in terms of [an] enigma, the big enigma for me—maybe the answer is not to be found in documents—it is hard for me to understand how Gorbachev could stay so long in power before the putsch took place. After having lost the whole of Eastern Europe, and having lost the whole of Germany to NATO, after having begun to lose the Baltic states, it is only in the Summer of 1991 that the putsch took place. To me it is a big mystery how could he

212

stay in power so long with what had happened before. I think you gave us a very interesting insight when you talked about the power of the function of the general secretary in traditional Russian and Soviet terms, how powerful his office was. It is a very important element of an answer. But to me, the enigma remains: how is it possible that he could have stayed in power so long after having lost not only Eastern Europe, but a part of the Soviet Union?

Zubok: As a historian, I would like to point out that we have just started the study and research of all sides of the process, and all the factors that resulted in what started in 1989 and brought about what we have now. First of all, I would like to give my support to those who were speaking about the economic factor. And when Doug MacEachin asked who is an economist here, it turned out that we did not have an economist around the table. That is a major fault. Economic as well as internal factors were immensely important in 1989 for the Soviet Union. And Gorbachev admits that in this regard *perestroika* failed totally. That was clear by 1989.

Looking at the excerpts from documents that we have, from the Politburo records, we may ask ourselves: what did he read, what was reported to him, especially after Chernobyl in 1986, about the deteriorating state of the Soviet economy, about the inevitable financial collapse of the country? There are some signs of this awareness of the ever-deteriorating situation when he was stating more and more seriously that we could not afford another round of the arms race. And he was doing it at the Politburo level, and he linked it to the actual economic crisis.

Everybody knows that in 1985, when Gorbachev came to power, the country was not in the best shape. But many reformers admit that the policy of reform turned the gradual economic deterioration into a total collapse, and how much that influenced the tactics of the time. That, I think, has not been studied at all. We tried to invite people like Batsanov, who was Kosygin's aide and for a while an aide of Ryzhkov, but that did not work out. I think we need to do better next time. We do not have the information—we have some general ideas, none of them specific—[about] how the drop in oil prices in 1986 influenced the situation. If you read our materials, we did look at that issue, we gave the chronology of oil price decreases.

Second issue. We need to find out how, and to what degree, the U.S administration, and precisely the administration of George Bush, reacted when they realized that the Soviet economy was not just in bad shape, but was in a state of collapse. Nikolay Shmelev mentioned in his memoirs about going to Jackson Hole with Baker and Shevardnadze, when he actually, basically, overwhelmed Baker with his analysis of the Soviet economy, and Baker was shocked, according to Shmelev. Then Baker realized finally that he was dealing with a superpower about to collapse economically. Whether that is true—or maybe he had realized that before—there are a lot of specific questions and they bring us to the issue of the economy. The rest really does not matter. There are problems all around. We know very little about the military other than that they behaved. We really do not have any documents, we do not have any records of the Defense Council sessions, none of their proposals. The same goes for the KGB.

213

My mystery, my enigma, as a scholar, is why, in your personal files, Anatoly Sergeyevich, there are basically no military- or KGB-related notes. You were Gorbachev's aide on foreign policy. Did they not send you those materials, or maybe you did not keep them? There is testimony to the fact that Gorbachev, actually, worked directly with the KGB. They would bring him their briefings, and then they would take them back without showing them to anybody else. And also those power structures—the military, the KGB—this issue has not really been developed in our discussions of 1989, nor actually of 1988.

And I would like to say that I believe that at this conference we realized that it all started before 1989. All this mess started before 1989, and if there were any options to re-organize the East European policy, those opportunities existed only before 1989. And we have to study the events of 1988 in order to understand how it all developed. We need to find out what Gorbachev was thinking at the time.

And also, an issue of concern for me [is] the cause of the inevitable continuing politicization of the subject of 1989 [...] It is quite inevitable that *perestroika* suffers from the shadow of the collapse of the Soviet Union, and the fact that we all, Soviet citizens, could see what was happening to Russia at the time. To what degree do we, as historians, honest historians, need to get rid of this shadow? It is a matter of personal choice, personal ethics.

I would like to call for a closer study of documents rather than relying on the memoirs of our hard-liners, which I went through very earnestly. All these memoirs, perhaps with the exception of Kornienko and Akhromeev, *Through the Eyes of a Marshal and a Diplomat*, actually were met with no interest among the public. At least in this book they tried to prove that they were right in their certain views. All the other memoirs say something like, "We cannot say anything about it. We did go to Berlin in October 1988, but we cannot tell you anything about what we did there." They only blame the policies of Gorbachev and Shevardnadze. This is an unfair position. That they are reluctant even to discuss this subject, even to participate in the discussion is a very sad symptom for me. I believe that we will need to make a lot of effort before we can hope to pull something from those people that can realistically be judged by history. Thank you.

Blanton: I would just end with two thoughts. One of them is rather famous, for historians at least, concerning whoever it was who asked Mao Zedong at one point, "Well, Chairman Mao, what is your opinion now about the French revolution?" And Chairman Mao said, "It is a little too early to tell." And this is a caution, I think, to all of us.

The final comment, I think, should be the last word for this particular conference. And it really comes from Svetlana's ten-year old daughter, Natasha. And I do think this was the ultimate compliment to any conference I have ever been a part of. Natasha last night said two things. When she saw us dancing, she said, "I want to be like them." (Laughter). And then the second thing she said was, "This is better than a sleepover!" (Laughter) And indeed it is. And it is all due to you. Thank you very much.

214

Documents

Document No. 1: Transcript of Mikhail Gorbachev's Conference with CC CPSU Secretaries

March 15, 1985

These minutes, which are as close to an official transcript as can be found in the Soviet archives, provide Gorbachev's report to and discussion with top CPSU officials about his first meeting as Soviet leader with the East European allies. That encounter occurred immediately following the funeral of General Secretary Konstantin Chernenko, Gorbachev's predecessor. Interesting hints emerge here about Gorbachev's attitude to the various leaders. For example, he is very positive about Poland's Wojciech Jaruzelski, Hungary's János Kádár, and Czechoslovakia's Gustáv Husák, but negative to the point of sarcasm about Romania's Nicolae Ceauşescu. Ironically, the meeting also discussed renewal of the Warsaw Pact for another 20 years. In his memoirs, Gorbachev describes this meeting as a watershed, as the moment when he talked to each of his counterparts about the need to "revitalize" relations and to take full responsibility for their own countries. In this retrospective view, his statement to his fellow leaders signified no less than "a shift to new realities, a rejection of the Brezhnev Doctrine." Similarly, Anatoly Chernyaev would later comment at the Musgrove conference that the meeting was a turning point. Yet the document below does not entirely bear the weight of such a claim, and one wonders whether the East European leaders heard Gorbachev's message quite so clearly.

Gorbachev: I think that we gave a fitting farewell to Konstantin Ustinovich Chernenko. It was well received by the party and the people. I spoke with Konstantin Ustinovich's family yesterday. The family is very grateful. Now we have to think through all the questions related to memorializing K. U. Chernenko's legacy. Let us entrust comrades [Yegor K.] Ligachev and [Mikhail V.] Zimyanin to work these issues through. At the same time, we should make decisions on all the issues regarding material support for K. U. Chernenko's family. We already have a draft of this decision. Today, the flow of condolences in connection with the death of Konstantin Ustinovich continues, and many of these condolences have important content.

The people and the party as a whole received the decisions of the March Plenum of the CC CPSU with high approval. Responses and greetings are coming from all parts of the country and from abroad.

Dolgikh: Very positive responses.

Gorbachev: The people support the party's policy and are expressing their satisfaction with the unanimity that was exhibited at the Politburo session and the CC CPSU Plenum. This undermines completely the slanderous allegations of the Western press, which in recent months has expended rivers of ink to prove that there was a rivalry, a struggle for power and so on, within the Soviet leadership.

Zimyanin: Now they have bitten their tongues.

Gorbachev: The overall reaction of working people to the decisions of the Plenum is positive. The Soviet people support actively the thoughts expressed at the Plenum about the need to concentrate on practical work, on discipline and order, and on the continuation of our Leninist party line.

Zimyanin: Yesterday, the scholars who took part in the USSR Academy of Sciences session were talking about it very actively.

Gorbachev: Such support from the working people gives us strength and places many obligations upon us.

As far as the international resonance of the decisions of the Plenum is concerned, I felt it especially during conversations with the foreign leaders who arrived for Konstantin Ustinovich Chernenko's funeral. Almost all of them tried to meet with our leadership and spoke about the need to develop contacts and cooperation.

The meeting of the leaders of the member-states of the Warsaw Treaty Organization took place in an exceptionally warm, comradely, and business-like atmosphere.

Romanov: Comrade [János] Kádár spoke very positively about that meeting and its business-like, constructive character.

Gorbachev: Kádár was the first to speak at the meeting. He gave a very good, I would say internationalist, speech. [Erich] Honecker supported him actively. Comrade [Gustáv] Husák's speech at the meeting was exceptionally important.

Rusakov: Husák's speech was the best.

Gorbachev: The leaders of all the fraternal countries spoke about the need to hold regular meetings at the level of first secretaries of the communist and workers' parties of the socialist commonwealth. Comrade [Wojciech] Jaruzelski said directly that we should meet much more often, maybe even without preparing for such meetings, without reading speeches in front of one another.

As a whole, the meeting was conducted in a spirit of great unity and mutual understanding. Comrade Husák, touching upon the question of the renewal of the Warsaw Treaty, proposed to renew this Treaty up to the celebration of the 40th [*sic*] anniversary of the victory over Hitler's Germany. Other leaders of the fraternal countries supported him. When it came to [Nicolae] Ceauşescu's turn, he started vacillating, stating that the term for which we renew the Treaty is not all that important. He said that we could renew it for 10 years, not for 20 years. Therefore, we had to respond to him quite decisively, saying that we were all united on the issue of signing the protocol of the Warsaw Treaty's renewal, and that this was our common point of view. One has to say that Ceauşescu swallowed those words and remained silent.

Rusakov: However, upon leaving the room, he said that this issue would be decided finally after the conversations Chairman of the Romanian Council of Ministers Dăscălescu will have in Moscow.

Gorbachev: But in general, I responded to him quite firmly. Summing up the results of this conference of the fraternal countries, I believe the time has come to

218

think seriously about how we can develop a system for meeting with the leadership of the states of the socialist commonwealth. We have to think through this issue very well. [...]

[Source: Volkogonov Collection, Reel 17, Container 25. On file at the National Security Archive. Translated by Svetlana Savranskaya.]

Document No. 2: Diary of Anatoly Chernyaev regarding the "Vladimirov" Article

July 5, 1985

Anatoly Chernyaev's diaries, one of the most important documentary sources to come out of the late Soviet period, include almost daily notes of unusual candor, combining quotes gleaned from other officials with Chernyaev's own observations. This excerpt relates to the domestic politics Gorbachev was forced to deal with, and points up the way in which Gorbachev's personnel choices drove change. The context for this entry was the publication in Pravda on June 21, 1985, of an article under the pseudonym "Vladimirov." In reality, the author was Oleg Rakhmanin, the hard-line deputy head of the Central Committee's Socialist Countries Department Rakhmanin criticized the pursuit of independence and innovation in the socialist community, especially in Hungary and Romania, making particular mention of nationalist sentiments and unnecessary reforms. Western and East European press coverage immediately noted the contradiction between these views and the new Gorbachev course toward the socialist countries. According to Chernyaev's diary, Gorbachev used the occasion of the next Politburo meeting to blast Rakhmanin's boss, Konstantin Rusakov, commenting that he had been obliged to make telephone calls to the socialist leaders to dissociate himself from the article. Rusakov lost his position soon after this incident, and was replaced by Vadim Medvedev. Rakhmanin was eventually replaced by Georgy Shakhnazarov.

And this is what happened: on July [sic] 21, *Pravda* published an article by "Vladimirov" on the socialist commonwealth; an edifying article and with obvious critical implications for Hungary and the GDR, not to mention Romania. It mentioned the "nationalistic movements," and even "Russophobia," and the "models" and "reforms," and even "discipline," not to mention proletarian internationalism in its classic form!

The article was immediately noticed by the American, English, FRG, French, and Italian press. What, they said, could this mean? Are these Gorbachev's true thoughts, or opposition to Gorbachev? He allows himself reforms, but for his vassals—no way, [they must] toe the line. The feeling of bewilderment was felt also coming from Berlin and Budapest [...]

And so on Saturday (July [sic] 29) Gorbachev said at the PB: what is this turning out to be! We say that the consolidation of the socialist commonwealth is our first priority, we display maximum resourcefulness and tact in order to consolidate this orientation, to eliminate misunderstandings, to strengthen trust, etc.; and all of a sudden all this comes to nothing. I have already had to come up with excuses—I made up a pretext to call Kádár and Honecker, and among other things let them know that "this article does not reflect the opinion of the leadership." That is how I have to extricate myself.

– Did you know about this article, M.S. [Mikhail Sergeyevich] asks [Konstantin V.] Rusakov, about the fact that it was being prepared in your department? Do you know that its author, "Vladimirov," is your first deputy, CC member [Oleg B.] Rakhmanin?!

– No, replies Rusakov.

– And did you, M.S. addresses [Mikhail V.] Zimyanin, know that the central CC organ—*Pravda*—was given such an article?

– No, replies another CC Secretary responsible for the press.

– And you, he says to [Viktor G.] Afanas'ev, did you not understand what you were doing? Why didn't you send this article around the PB, or at least around to the secretaries?

The editor-in-chief of *Pravda* mumbles something, referring to Rakhmanin's go-ahead power and to the fact that he is first deputy of the Socialist Countries Department and that he should understand what he is doing.

– So, Gorbachev counters. [...] Firstly, it is an absolute disgrace that the department deputy (Rusakov) does not know what is going on in his department. Secondly, why do we need such workers in the CC apparatus who act as they wish on the most important political questions, and we have to clean up the mess for them afterwards. Such behavior deserves immediate dismissal from the CC. [...] However, since this is the first time (here M.S. wasn't telling the truth [...] he cannot fail to know that Rakhmanin runs "his own" policy on, for example, issues with China—countering the CC and harming state interests!) [...] we will limit the measures to a strict warning.

I think if it was anyone else but Rakhmanin, he would have been dismissed immediately. Something, somebody is backing him. [...]

Still, one thing is clear: now there is no chance for Oleg Borisovich [Rakhmanin] to become not only a CC Secretary, which, judging by his actions, he clearly aimed to do, but even a department deputy in place of his ailing chief, Rusakov.

[Source: Anatoly Chernyaev's Diary, Manuscript. On file at the National Security Archive. Translated by Anna Melyakova.]

Document No. 3: Memorandum from Anatoly Chernyaev to Aleksandr Yakovlev on Germany and Eastern Europe

March 10, 1986

This memorandum—one of Chernyaev's very first formal memos after his appointment as Gorbachev's foreign policy adviser—illustrates both the daring and the caution that characterized the new thinking. The substance of the memo outlines Chernyaev's vision of Europe as the center of the new Soviet foreign policy and Germany as the key issue in Europe. Remarkably, after calling Erich Honecker "somewhat uncontrollable," a novel characterization of the hard-line East German leader by a Soviet official, Chernyaev suggests that Gorbachev should take the initiative in resolving the issue of German unification himself, which would serve as a "trump card" in drawing the Federal Republic closer to Moscow. At the same time, however, the memo maintains a rather cautious and traditional tone—warning of "many underwater rocks;" quoting Lenin on bringing Germany and Russia closer together; and falling back on great power rhetoric rather than invoking a demilitarized "common European home"—a notion which would only take hold somewhat later.

On relations with Thatcher. It seems like we turn to Great Britain as an important factor in European policy only from time to time. Obviously we don't have the necessary systematic and persistent [approach in place] yet. McLennan[1] and the Labour [Party] both told us that there was an opportunity to "encourage" England to pursue a more independent policy, "to distance" itself somewhat from Reagan. We should urgently think about that, especially in connection with [Eduard] Shevardnadze's forthcoming visit there. Gradually, Labour's positions are getting stronger. One should not exclude their coming to power in a year-and-a-half or two. We should energize our relations with them, and give them something for the elections.

And still, it is not England that can serve us as the key power in European affairs. It appears expedient to pay more attention to the FRG, in the most comprehensive terms. If we succeed in drawing it closer to us—and there would be more opportunities for that under the Social Democrats—that would be the greatest achievement of our European and global policy. Everyone would begin to stir instantly—from Washington to Paris to other capitals. "The spirit of Rapallo"[2] is still alive and still terrifies some people. One should also not forget Lenin's

---

[1] General Secretary of the Communist Party of Great Britain (1976–1989).

[2] The Treaty of Rapallo of 1922 was an agreement between Soviet Russia and Germany, which dealt with pre-war and World War I debts and claims. The agreement enabled Germany to circumvent certain clauses of the Treaty of Versailles and represented the first time the Soviet regime was recognized *de jure* as a state.

instructions about the importance of a rapprochement between Germany and Russia.

It is well known that Comrade Honecker is somewhat uncontrollable on the so-called "German–German question." Here we require a certain caution. Our position regarding his visit to the FRG a year-and-a-half ago was absolutely correct. However, now it would hardly be appropriate to repeat it. We should start thinking seriously—maybe we should just saddle this entire "German–German question" in such a way that it would benefit the socialist commonwealth, socialism, and our policy. Because the most important trump card here—resolution of the so-called question of "German unification"—is in our hands. And we could use this fact as the basis of our entire effort to pull the Federal Republic in our direction. There are many underwater rocks here.

[*Source: Archive of the Gorbachev Foundation, Fond 2. Opis 1. On file at the National Security Archive. Translated by Svetlana Savranskaya.*]

Document No. 4: Speech by Mikhail Gorbachev
to Ministry of Foreign Affairs

May 28, 1986

This speech to a large gathering of Foreign Ministry officials was intended to send a powerful signal to the bureaucrats directly responsible for day-to-day foreign policy that Moscow would begin to treat Eastern Europe very differently from now on. Aimed at an internal audience, the remarks show that the coming change was genuine and that Gorbachev expected his new policies to be enforced. As early as October 1985, according to memoirs by Chernyaev and by Medvedev, Gorbachev had discussed with the Politburo the idea of a non-interventionist approach, saying that the USSR would now reject the "policing" of its socialist allies. The document below is further evidence of this new thinking, and features the striking phrase: "It is impermissible to think that we can teach everyone. No one gave us that right."

We have to understand that relations with the socialist countries have entered a new historical era. The time when we helped them to form their economy, their parties, and their political institutions is past. Countries and states that have 40 years of independent development have their own parties, their own political institutions, their own way of life, and they have achievements—in many areas greater than our own. These are full-fledged states, and we cannot lead them by the hand to kindergarten as we would little children. We need a different type of relationship now. If we understand this then it will become clear what our relationship with them should be.

There are objective interests, which require the socialist countries to be united and consolidated. But they are not fulfilled on their own, automatically. More and more, their fulfillment comes by means of economic interests. Our friends' situations largely depend on the state of our affairs. This means that we need the convincing power of example and mutual economic gain to strengthen our cooperation, consolidation, and unity.

We are building our relations with the countries of the socialist community on the basis of respect for their experience, understanding of national specifics, and trust in the search for national approaches, even though some of the steps that our friends take may be detrimental to the common cause.

Our friends should feel that they are walking alongside us, rather than being towed behind. Regrettably, a well-known gap has formed between what is said on this matter and the real character and quality of the work. This does not allow us to draw our allies most effectively toward our common cause. In order for the relationship with our friends to truly be a high priority our contacts with them need to be efficient and informal. It seems that we have been able to achieve

224

this at the highest level. Political collaboration and an institution for multilateral working meetings for the leaders of fraternal parties are forming. But we must go further [and reach] a preliminary agreement on the essence of our foreign policy actions.

What is preventing us from coordinating our foreign policy plans, and from sharing the foreign policy efforts of the fraternal parties? Why do we have to come forward with all the initiatives? Sometimes it is better if they bring something forward. This would stimulate our friends' foreign policy activity.

After all, they know that if we do not support their initiative and it has not been coordinated with us it will not play out; it is doomed. Such an understanding exists. And this opens up an opportunity for new approaches. We should consider our allies' sense of self-worth—even if we are talking about the smallest countries—and not ignore their interests. It is impermissible to think that we can teach everyone. No one gave us that right.

On the contrary, as the most powerful country in the socialist community we should show modesty, respect for the experience of others and for their striving to find resolutions to problems on their own. The new quality of our work requires us to overcome the preconceptions, smugness and inertness that still exist in our consciousness.

One should have an interest in one's host country. *A priori* plans are harmful; before our eyes they turn into spurs. There are no uninteresting countries. There are uninteresting people, who do not know how to see and hear what is going on in another country, but who think that they know everything anyway and can give advice to everyone. This is the source of the uninteresting information that is sent to Headquarters [...]

[*Source: Mikhail Gorbachev,* Gody trudnykh reshenii, izbrannoe 1985–1992. [*The Years of Difficult Decisions, Selected 1985–1992*], Alfa-Print: 1993, pp. 50–51. Translated by Anna Melyakova.]

No more.
Policing of
Socialist States

Closed session (internal
audience)

Document No. 5: Notes of CC CPSU Politburo Session

June 13, 1986

These notes taken by Chernyaev at the Soviet Politburo provide a detailed assessment from Gorbachev of the economic problems and dependencies that exist within the Warsaw Pact. The meeting takes place just after Gorbachev's return from the Budapest meeting of the WTO's Political Consultative Committee. After dismissing Ceaușescu's speech to the allies ("to hell with him"), the Soviet leader remarks that economic issues took up a third of the session and that the Pact's relations need to be organized more on the basis of mutual benefit than on one-sided support from Moscow. Although his presentation shows a profound awareness of existing problems, Gorbachev is optimistic about the prospects of reform and genuine integration within the CMEA. There is not yet a sense that the East European countries have become a burden on the USSR that outweighs their benefit. Gorbachev even recounts a conversation with János Kádár in which he told the Hungarian leader to "lean on our shoulder..."—advice that would change completely within a year. Also remarkable is Gorbachev's comment that the Chernobyl nuclear disaster had "a silver lining" in that it raised the question: "what if a nuclear war were to happen?" Immediately offering his own answer, he exclaims: "That would be it!" Compared to subsequent discussions following the 1986 decline in the price of oil, there is little talk here of fuel issues or the role of the Soviet Union as a "spigot" for the socialist community.

Gorbachev: On the outcomes of the PCC in Budapest. It is important that this agency has started to really function in parallel with bilateral communication, which must not be underestimated. It is a good forum for coming to agreement on our foreign policy.

The recent meeting left a good impression: the speeches were more interesting, with a broader scope. Our friends value independence very much, but this does not make the situation worse, it makes it better. They are still drawn to us.

The significance of the XXVII Congress is becoming clearer to everybody. With time, its significance for the fate of socialism, for the victory of a new way of thinking will come to light. The response to the XXVII Congress continues to grow. As Jaruzelski[3] said, "the phantom of the XXVII Congress is making its way around the capitalist world."

At the Congress in the GDR, Honecker did not have much on our Congress. I asked him: what bothers you about our Congress? He even blushed. But that was in Berlin at their Party Congress. Now he is already using our terminology and is demonstrating very friendly relations.

---

[3] First secretary of the PUWP CC, chairman of the PPR State Council. [Footnote in the original.]

226

There is a lot of confusion and running ahead in Ceaușescu's[4] speech. In relation to us he is always trying to steal the march, as if he has already done everything before us.

Well, to hell with him! We are talking about the fate of humanity here! Don't we have enough problems with America? And he keeps trying to teach us. It's a mess in his head, a jumble. Nevertheless, in general the atmosphere was productive.

It seems like everybody agrees that we need to maintain a dialogue with the West, that we need to expand the channels of communication, that we should not interrupt the negotiations, and keep a hold on the situation, especially when positions critical of the United States surface in Western Europe.

What do we need in essence: the policy of dialogue is objectively isolating the United States in Europe.

Relations with the socialist countries have come to the point where connections need to be made exclusively on mutually beneficial grounds. The leaders of the socialist countries strongly agreed on the necessity for new forms of relations within the framework of our community.

On the FRG. There is general agreement at meetings with friendly nations that we need to work with the FRG. They are strongly connected with the FRG, economically above all. Husák is especially close to our position. Everyone agreed when we said that we taught Kohl a lesson. But we must not drive it to extremes. Kohl has already begun to get nervous, and that is good. Honecker said this, and Kádár did as well. But on no account should we ruin our relations.

However, everyone wants to get closer to the FRG, and as a result everyone rushed to the window we created by saying that we "need to work [with the FRG]." [...]

Our policy aimed at Europe is yielding great reserves. Everybody thinks so. Our work here is having an influence on the United States and on all world developments.

On the PRC. There was nothing new at the conference. I reminded them of Deng Xiaoping's statement on the "incompatibility of core interests." Deng Xiaoping's position is well known: national interests are the most important. But I feel something will be changing. Cunhal[5] will be going there; he asked me for advice. That could be a possible approach. But we should not wait until it comes to the stage of normalization along party lines.

We would like each side (in the WTO) to come forward with initiatives. We need to act on a coordinated basis, but everyone has the right to propose initiatives and to act independently. The centrifugal processes in our community also come from weak agreements. We must overcome artificial unity in the PCC and create comradely cooperation.

---

[4] General secretary of the RCP CC, president of Romania. [Footnote in the original.]
[5] Álvaro Cunhal, general secretary of the Portuguese Communist Party from 1961–1992.

Everyone is very concerned with the economy and our relations in this sphere. In all the speeches this theme took up a third of the time.

They are looking for new solutions. Many new aspects of the issue were brought out. This is the strongest element in the pressure they are putting on us. And it is understandable. Our relations are bureaucratic, when they should be dynamic. Everything right now is slack, slow, and gets lost in all kinds of committees and departments. We have reached the point where we need to build connections on mutually beneficial grounds, and where we need to press our friends on the quality of the goods they are supplying us.

This is what the basis for diplomatic work and for propaganda should be. Propaganda support for our foreign policy is very weak.

How do the Americans do it? As soon as they accept some resolution or think of something, messengers go to all ends of the country to explain and convince people. We need to develop a similar operational mechanism.

(*To [Aleksandr N.] Yakovlev and [Anatoly] Dobrynin*): Propaganda support is your work. The journalists did a good job in Budapest. Consider that 500 journalists came from the West to cover the PCC.

At a separate meeting of general secretaries I spoke about Chernobyl. They were dumbfounded by the losses: 3 billion [rubles] as of now. And with Europe's population concentration, what if a nuclear war were to happen? That would be it! So, my friends, every cloud has a silver lining.

I told them about my meeting with the MFA diplomatic staff. They told me that they hold similar conferences annually. The content of our conference interested them a great deal. In a word, everybody is for collaboration. We developed closer relations with many people.

Husák thanked me for changing the atmosphere in his country. But everyone has one question: as soon as the matter of summit talks within the framework of CMEA comes up, people's faces change. Better to do it within the framework of the Warsaw Treaty, they say. The nature of relations is different there. Why? Because in the framework of the Warsaw Treaty we see something resembling integration; outside of it, it's whoever gives more.

Nevertheless, we agreed to liven up our work within the framework of CMEA as well. We could, for example, convene a special CMEA forum. However, everyone prefers to make agreements on a bilateral basis. They avoid questions of integration. But we need to try to clear this CMEA-level conference of bilateral problems. Only the most important issues should be brought before this general conference.

On the International Communist Movement. Honecker supports a conference of communist parties on questions of peace. His idea is that whoever does not want to come does not have to. We should first work through this problem within the framework of the socialist countries in preparation for the 70th anniversary of the October Revolution, since then we will have to organize some general activities for the delegations anyway. Grand rallies alone will not be enough.

We could do it this way: let them know that we are in favor of a frank discussion. Let them think about it and propose their formula.

Ryzhkov: Right now everybody is speaking resolutely about the new format of relations within the International Communist Movement.

Gorbachev: The situation in Hungary is very critical. They are taking their cue from the West. Is this a political choice, or are they forced to do this? Kádár is a deep and complex person, and he is devoted to us and to socialism. There is no doubt about that. That is why it was important to give him moral support, so that the government does not split up.

There are two wings in their government. One is practically in favor of abandoning the framework of socialism. The other is for real socialism together with the USSR. Kádár is getting weaker physically. We need to support him politically. In that way we will support the healthy powers that are in the majority. But we can't say to him: Kádár, dear, here is the situation and here is the course, and here is the April 1985 CC CPSU Plenum's example. The Romanian way represents a decrease in the standard of living. Kádár will not go that way. The Hungarians could not bear it. On the outside, they have plenty of goods in their stores. But in reality Hungary is in a dangerous position. Their prices are at the same level as our cooperative ones.

I told him: lean on our shoulder, it will be easier with the West as well. Their economic mechanism works pretty well in certain directions, but it is directed at distribution, not production. It is not imbued with a general strategy, it is not closely tied to the STR [scientific and technological revolution]. Depending on how relations develop with us, they will adjust their course; otherwise they will just have to halt production.

[*Source: Archive of the Gorbachev Foundation, Fond 2. Opis 2. On file at the National Security Archive. Translated by Anna Melyakova.*]

Document No. 6: Memorandum from Mikhail Gorbachev to the CC CPSU Politburo on Topical Questions regarding Collaboration with Socialist Countries

June 26, 1986

This very rare personal memo from Gorbachev to the Politburo goes much fur-ther—and adopts a much more negative tone—than the leadership discussion held only 13 days earlier (see previous document). Drafted by Shakhnazarov and Vadim Medvedev,[6] the document candidly admits that "Moscow was viewed as a kind of conservative power that hindered reforms;" that the Pact's integration is "sharply behind" that of Western Europe; and that "we continue to be at the commodity ex-change stage" in economic relations. "A genuine turning point in the entire system of collaboration with our allies is needed," Gorbachev writes, including "a radical perestroika of the economic cooperation mechanism." An important point is Gor-bachev's statement that the USSR should use the force of example rather than the example of force: "[W]e must fulfill this role not through exhortation and especially not through directives, but through ideological-political influence, constructive ini-tiatives to deepen collaboration, [and] the power of our example."

In an interesting case of cognitive dissonance, Gorbachev writes that the social-ist countries should be the main priority for Soviet policy—even though in his own mind they clearly are not. His priorities at the moment are Europe and arms control. As Chernyaev points out in his book, My Six Years with Gorbachev, the Soviet leader relegated Eastern Europe to the very bottom of his agenda. However, in a formal communication such as this he evidently felt the need to follow the traditional ideo-logical hierarchy of priorities and place the socialist community first. At the end of the memo, Gorbachev calls for the Central Committee, the Foreign Ministry and the KGB to prepare a strategy document outlining concrete measures to take. But no such paper would ever appear.

As of late, I have often had to deal with questions concerning relations between the USSR and the fraternal countries and the condition of the world socialist sys-tem. These questions were prominent at the XXVII Congress. Certain practical steps were taken.

However, right now, as we are developing on a broad front the work of solidi-fying and implementing the Congress' resolutions, the need arises to exchange opinions on this issue more thoroughly, and to develop a conception that would allow us to speed up this process. It is important to eliminate everything that

---

[6] The document comes from the Shakhnazarov file at the Gorbachev Foundation, but has no signature and precedes the date Shakhnazarov became either a Gorbachev aide (February 1988) or deputy director of the Socialist Countries Department of the CC.

impedes the development of interactions with our friends; we need to provide a new impetus to that development in order to take a major move forward and release socialism's potential on an international scale. During the meeting of fraternal countries' leaders in Budapest we were convinced once again of the necessity of holding a broad discussion of questions related to this.

Over the last four decades, world socialism has turned into a powerful international formation. There are solid foundations for the new system in the majority of socialist countries, the leading role of the party has been consolidated, and maturity and national self-awareness have grown. The socialist countries have withstood serious internal and external trials and not one of them has returned to the old order. Bilateral and multilateral communications among socialist states have developed broadly, and the countries have formed international organizations—the Warsaw Treaty and the Council for Mutual Economic Assistance.

All of these are our strengths. But we cannot deny the fact that in recent years, as the scientific-technological revolution has opened new vistas for developing the socialist system, that development has instead slowed down. Regrettably, it must be said that to a certain degree centrifugal forces have become evident within the framework of world socialism. There is a real danger of a weakening of its influence on the overall trend of international affairs.

What is the cause of all this? This is not a simple question; it cannot be disposed of with a one-word answer. However, undoubtedly one of the main causes is that the nature of relations established during the period of world socialist formation is coming into conflict with the necessities of life.

In the beginning, the Soviet Union, the largest and most experienced socialist state, led the fraternal countries by the hand, as it were. And they thought it necessary to follow our example, recommendations, and advice in everything. Economic relations developed with an accent on the USSR providing resource support through raw materials and fuel, and developing primary industries.

Such a system of political and economic cooperation was reasonable for the beginning stages of the formation of the world socialist system. But it became less and less justified as the fraternal countries gained power, as their economic strength and political stability increased and their international authority grew.

All of the Politburo members have a good deal of experience in communicating with the leadership of the fraternal parties and know well that over time there was less sincerity, frankness, and trust in our relations.

The regularity of contacts with fraternal party leaders was disrupted, and the meetings that took place often bore the stamp of showiness and formalities. The necessity of such contacts is especially urgent under present circumstances, when for objective reasons a period of change in leadership is taking place in the majority of countries.

We should admit honestly that Moscow has been viewed as a kind of conservative power that hindered reforms that were ripe for implementation. Some of our allies, afraid of a domineering reproach, cautiously introduced certain correctives into the practice of building socialism. Instead of jointly discussing topical issues of socialist development we often assumed the function of sole custodian of Marxist-Leninist teachings; at the same time we judged everything from our own standpoint, inadequately considering the novelty of the issues and the specific character of the fraternal countries. We did not very seriously and respectfully take into consideration their own searches [for solutions].

All of these shortcomings have built up over the years and have done real damage. Take this fact, for example: it has been 15 years since we agreed to embark on the path of socialist economic integration, but this process is sharply behind the integration process in Western Europe. In essence, in many aspects we continue to be at the commodity exchange stage. At the same time, since the CMEA countries were not able to make a collective technological leap forward and the Soviet side was not able to meet our friends' demands for up-to-date technology and equipment, those countries developed a tendency to resolve pressing social-economic problems by switching to the track of intensive management through credits from the West. It is well known what difficult consequences this has had for Poland, and to some extent for other countries of the community.

Our interactions on questions of foreign policy also leave much to be desired. Even the information from our allies, including on major issues of sovereignty and security, has been neither sufficiently complete nor timely. Almost all of the initiatives of recent years originated in the Soviet Union; the fraternal countries were left only to show support and approval. This led some of them to tend toward taking discrete actions [*separatnym deistviyam*] in order to provide for certain concrete interests and national ambitions (Romania, the GDR to an extent, Hungary). The potential for adopting a concerted foreign policy by the allied states was not fully exploited.

This conclusion suggests itself: a genuine turning point in the entire system of collaboration with our allies is needed. This would completely correspond to the ideas, purposes, and spirit of the XXVII CPSU Congress' decisions. As is now evident, this [idea] met with a sympathetic response—even satisfaction—from the leadership and *aktiv* of the fraternal parties.

With good reason, relations with the socialist countries were identified as the priority for the Soviet Union's foreign policy. First of all, we need to ensure that this general formula is filled with real content. We understand that the situation places a special responsibility for the fate of world socialism on the CPSU, and we cannot escape it. Our country was objectively placed into the leadership role in the socialist world as a guarantor of security for the fraternal countries and their social achievements. But we must fulfill this role not through exhortation and especially not through directives, but through ideological-political influence, constructive initiatives to deepen collaboration, the power of our example, and creative and effective resolutions for problems in social development.

What do the practical tasks of *perestroika* in our collaboration with the fraternal countries look like?

First of all, [our task] is to consolidate the socialist countries' unity, counteract centrifugal tendencies on the basis of truly deep, scientific-technological and economic integration, and transition from purely commercial relations to broad cooperation in production. A radical *perestroika* of the economic cooperation mechanism must be realized, which should result in concentrating CMEA work on the coordination of economic policies and the creation of organizational, monetary and financial, and legal conditions for the broad development of direct connections among associations, enterprises, scientific and development organizations, and joint firms. This sort of shift in economic relations requires a display of political will by all sides, and increased party control over these processes.

Secondly, a fundamentally different approach toward the evaluation and study of the fraternal parties' experiences is needed, and the implementation of this knowledge in our country. The highest judge can only be socio-political practice, and the main criteria are the acceleration of development and the consolidation of socialism in practice. This kind of attitude toward the collective experience will not only bring us great benefits, but will contribute to an increase in our country's authority and the respect of our friends and allies for our party.

Thirdly, cooperation, the exchange of experiences, and communications between collectives and the broad working masses should become the norm of our people's lives.

We need to decisively eliminate backward, bureaucratic practices in this area; remove obstacles that hinder people from traveling on business to fraternal countries; and develop economic, administrative, and legal rules. This would liberate the process of communications rather than fetter it, and allow the general collection of such problems to be resolved locally.

Fourthly, it is necessary seriously to improve and sharply stimulate the socialist countries' foreign policy collaboration mechanism. Despite the importance of relations with the U.S. and the major West European states, relations with our allies must occupy first place. We must strictly observe equality of rights; we must act in full correspondence with Lenin's instruction that we want a truly voluntary union. It is important to consider our friends' opinions, their interests in all our policies not only in form but in practice as well. Give [them] a broader field for their foreign policy initiatives and actions on a coordinated basis.

The considerations stated here do not encompass the full diversity of issues relating to interactions with the fraternal countries under present-day circumstances. But it is necessary first of all to decide on the principal policy approach toward these issues.

It seems to me that after exchanging opinions at the Politburo, the CC CPSU, the MFA, and the KGB departments could be assigned to prepare a document, which would develop concrete measures on the basis of political evaluations for *perestroika* regarding our relations with the socialist countries, overcoming negative phenomena, and providing the necessary acceleration on this exceptionally important matter.

Gorbachev, June 26, 1986

[*Source: Archive of the Gorbachev Foundation. Shakhnazarov Collection. On file at the National Security Archive. Translated by Anna Melyakova.*]

Document No. 7: Notes of CC CPSU Politburo Session

July 3, 1986

Gorbachev intentionally provokes this discussion at the very beginning of the Polit-buro's regular Thursday meeting—even before the scheduled discussion of Cherno-byl—in order to set his line on Eastern Europe and make sure it is taken seriously by the top leadership, which is still dominated by "old thinkers." (See also the previous document.) Chernyaev's notes contain a blunt repudiation of past Soviet policy—Gorbachev's first explicit articulation to the Politburo that there will be no military intervention in Eastern Europe. The Soviet leader also repeats his earlier complaints about the lack of economic integration and rejects the old "administrative methods of leadership." Anatoly Dobrynin, recently appointed head of the CC's International Department, adds the further interesting suggestion to remake the WTO in NATO's image, incorporating "constant daily integration of foreign policy work" and "dis-cussion of all international events and actions."

―――――――――

[...]

Gorbachev: We all became aware that we had entered a new stage with the so-cialist countries. What went on before could not continue. The methods that were used in Czechoslovakia and Hungary now are no good; they will not work![7]

Dobrynin: We need to act like NATO: constant, daily integration of foreign policy work through different mechanisms, discussion of all international events and actions.

Gorbachev: A new society is forming, which will develop on its own founda-tion [...] the mechanisms of bilateral relations are becoming more complex. [...] What was in the past is now causing discontent, encouraging centrifugal forc-es. [...] Nothing will work out if we work within the old framework. We cannot use the remnants of the Comintern [...] "administrative methods of leadership" with our friends. Fidel was right: the CPSU's influence can only be ideological, only through example! Everything else is an illusion. And we don't need it, this kind of "leadership." It would mean carrying them on our back.

The economy is the most important [factor]. Here there is a major lag in coor-dination and integration. And this hinders, and will continue to hinder, all other aspects of relations. From the conception of *perestroika* to its realization is still a long way. We are behind. The central question is—what are the main issues?

―――――――――

[7] This refers to the Soviet-led armed interventions to crush opposition movements in Hun-gary in 1956 and Czechoslovakia in 1968.

234

Exactly so. The country is abuzz, it is waiting. This is serious, intense work. It is here that the weak links are making themselves felt.

[*Source:* V Politburo TsK KPSS ... Po zapisyam Anatoliya Chernyaeva, Vadima Medvedeva, Georgiya Shakhnazarova *(1985–1991) (Moscow: Alpina Business Books, 2006), p. 61. Translated by Anna Melyakova.*]

Document No. 8: Transcript of CC CPSU Politburo Session

November 13, 1986

In this record of the Soviet Politburo meeting immediately following the Political Consultative Committee meeting in Bucharest, Gorbachev gives a markedly positive assessment of the socialist countries' willingness to reform. He reports that "our friends" have now accepted perestroika, self-reliance, and the changes in relations he argued for in June, and recounts positive conversations with Husák, Kádár, Zhivkov, and even an approving comment by Ceauşescu, whom he describes as running a "dictatorship" and "dynastic socialism." But a disquieting note sounds in Gorbachev's report of his private conversation with the ally he most respects—Jaruzelski. The Polish leader warns, "I look at my colleagues [and know] that nothing will come of them. Ceauşescu will do none of what we agreed to. And others simply will not be able to: they are old and have fallen behind. Let the two of us ... pull the load together." Despite this, Gorbachev goes on below to express his "sense of confidence that the problems can be solved, in the USSR and in the Community." And his Politburo colleagues duly chime in, including Prime Minister Nikolay Ryzhkov, who declares: "I believe this to be a historic change." Absent in this discussion is any mention of the precipitous decline in oil prices during 1986, which would ultimately undercut whatever economic leverage Gorbachev still had with the socialist allies.

ON THE RESULTS OF THE MEETING BETWEEN LEADERS OF THE FRATERNAL
PARTIES OF THE SOCIALIST CMEA MEMBER-STATES
(MOSCOW, NOVEMBER 10–11, 1986)

Gorbachev: The meeting was unprecedented in the scope of the problems discussed, in its composition and atmosphere. It will help in bringing the fraternal parties together and developing the collaboration of the socialist countries. One could say that during this meeting we achieved more results than ever before. These results wholly and completely correspond to our party's policies.

First point: the meeting marked the ratification of the XXVII Party Congress within the framework of the socialist community. If until now this line was adopted only at separate congresses, and even then not entirely, now in essence the conceptions of acceleration, *perestroika*, and energizing the human factor are accepted by our friends as the general line. This is the most important political outcome of the meeting.

It is true that this process is not yet complete. But it is a difficult process. Now we can say that our friends have understood all the Congress' ideas and the approaches to policies. By the way, they adopted the XXVII Congress under pressure from the workers and the party masses. In this way, under different

236

circumstances, the CPSU ensures its vanguard position on the basis of equality of rights and independence.

Second point: the principles of relations within the community were announced, and were supported by everyone. Ceaușescu was especially pleased: finally, he said, "his conception" was adopted.

Our friends thankfully acknowledged the fact that we self-critically evaluated our past and took responsibility for it. Zhivkov[8] said: "The USSR is speaking of itself in this way for the first time."

Third point: the practical outcome is that we opened the way for the radical reconstruction of collaboration within the community. Everything will be based on self-reliance.

Fourth point: we were right to invite non-European members of the community. But it also became clear that the issue of less-developed countries within CMEA has not been worked through. The passivity toward this problem is evident. They look at it this way: let the USSR help. And some (*the GDR, Hungary*) even want to squeeze out something for themselves from the others' underdevelopment.

But there are also signs that the "underdeveloped" countries are changing. Fidel, for example, seems to have understood that he made a mess of things. Vietnam is setting realistic goals for its forthcoming Congress. They are inclined toward counting on a resolution of the food products problem, counting on the manufacturing goods, and counting on the individual. In a word, the re-evaluation is beginning.

We froze [*zamorozili*] so much money there! I propose to create a separate program for the less-developed CMEA members. And we should discuss it at one of the next meetings with the leaders of the socialist countries.

Fifth point: the question of collaboration in the sphere of (*ideological*) fine tuning had a special place. [...] There was more criticism about this sphere than about the economy. Here, as well, Jaruzelski was the most substantive [speaker].

Ceaușescu is aiming to isolate himself within CMEA.

In general many thoughts were expressed. This is particularly important in the context of fine tuning. We do not have a serious conceptualization of the last 70 years since [the] October [Revolution], or of the last 40 years that we have worked together with our friends.

There were proposals to have CC secretaries who deal with international issues meet regularly for purposes of strategic cooperation. Why don't the CC secretaries of agriculture, or the economy in general, also convene?

Issues of coordination and information-sharing should be solved simply: meet without any kind of strict schedule—leave in the morning and come back in the evening. It would be a quick, concrete, and direct exchange of opinions. [...]

---

[8] General Secretary (1954–1981 First Secretary) of the Bulgarian Communist Party CC, chairman of the People's Republic of Bulgaria Council of State. [Footnote in the original.]

We have never heard such evaluations of Soviet foreign policy. Our colleagues did not restrain themselves in their praise. It was even uncomfortable to sit and listen to all of it.

We have truly made large-scale advances. It has become easier for them to act [...] and to coordinate their actions with us. [...]

Ceaușescu proposed removing intermediate-range missiles from the "package." But he was too late [...]

The CC Departments are to go over all the ideas proposed at the meeting. Each department is to make a selection according to their specialization and to create a plan to carry out or to respond to the suggestions.

I am not sure what we are proposing to do for the 70th anniversary of October. [...] An informal meeting of delegations that will arrive for the celebrations? The general secretaries of the socialist countries support this idea. But I think we should invite not only communists but everyone who is interested. Let the monolith of the International Communist Movement unite all sides.

Themes? There can be a variety. For example, "October and the World," "Marx and the World," "Lenin and the World." [...] Whichever one we choose, we will still be talking about socialism. We have to think everything through. Let the CC Secretariat propose something.

What else should we mention about the meeting of the general secretaries?

Ceaușescu kept repeating his own thing, and worse than before, especially on international issues. He spoke excessively, with much demagoguery. For example: "we should speak about communism in a tactical sense, and our strategy is—'Toward Communism'!" He cast a shadow over *perestroika* with these words. And—"What is the point of going through *perestroika*? In Romania we went through it a long time ago!" It's as if he should get a decoration for democracy, while Romania is really under a Ceaușescu dictatorship. [...] He is for "socialism by inheritance," for a "dynastic socialism." He said: "there is no need for new forms of collaboration, but Romania will not be against using the new forms."

Fidel is happy. We saw and heard it with our own eyes and ears. He considers Africa to be the "weakest link" in the chain of imperialist domination, and the place where this chain should be broken. He complained of the poor arming of Cuban troops in Angola. He asked for General [Konstantin] Kurochkin to be returned to Angola. He asked me: why is the Pope coming to Latin America, but Gorbachev is not coming?

Jaruzelski made the most energetic contribution. He has many problems, but I am sure that he will deal with them. When we were alone he said to me—I look at my colleagues [and know] that nothing will come of them. Ceaușescu will do none of what we agreed to. And others simply will not be able to: they are old and have fallen behind. Let the two of us, he said, pull the load together.

Kádár—I would not say that he really enriched us with ideas this time. But he is a wise and flexible politician. He is unconditionally on our side. He does not really understand what is waiting for him at home. He does not have a feeling of concern.

238

I told him: you need to take a political position. You are surrounded by some people who are longing for the USA's embrace, and some who are sticking with the socialist countries. The latter are competent comrades, but they lack the political conceptualization for the necessary next steps.

The American specialists and our [Abel] Aganbegyan (*academician, economist*) are giving you two years to find a solution. It would be good to create reserves in this period of time. We are concerned about you. I told him about our assignment to Ryzhkov about buying meat and grain. He reacted. It seems the Hungarians do not have anything to trade with the West. I told him that for now the USSR cannot really help. But you must use (*at the upcoming HSWP Plenum*) all of your authority to make the principal policy decision (*vote*).

Nikolay Ivanovich [Ryzhkov], take everything into your own hands, invite the people, decide what you want to do, and how.

In general, I encouraged Kádár.

I had a good conversation with Husák. We discussed everything. He understood and appreciated our support, and asked us to help him realize the change. He left me a draft of his CC CPCz Plenum report. […]

Vietnam is a large country, the people are strong. They are a reliable base in our strategic plans. […]

Ryzhkov: I believe this to be a historic change. How formalistic we made our relations, what stereotypes and dogmas we collected over 30 years! We saw that life was moving forward, that everything was changing and we just kept repeating the same thing over and over again.

Your concluding words at the meeting were impromptu, but they added a great deal to the main speech, which was important not only for them, but for us as well.

Gorbachev: I felt that perhaps the CPSU was limiting the consequences of *perestroika* too much—for technology, the economy, etc. […]

Ryzhkov: […] The issue of prices. We will have to make our way here as in a jungle. These past two years in CMEA we have only been doing cosmetic work, and now we see that the situation there does not correspond to the needs of its members.

Shevardnadze: The most important thing is that people do not become disappointed. […] After all, the MFA is not really ready to change the way they work.

On the question of economic advisers in embassies—are we going to take people from the highest posts for these positions again?

Gorbachev: Make sure that everything that was said here and at the meeting is noted at Dobrynin's [International Department]. […]

All of the participants at the working meeting responded positively to our positions on the issue of relations among the fraternal parties, and to our ideas on the necessity for the entire system. […]

In general it can be said that it is quite difficult to work with them, but this shows once again that our efforts must be balanced and persistent. […]

Gorbachev: The session was rich in content. Our delegation did a good job. Now we need to act toward the goal of entering a new stage in the development of our collaboration with the CMEA countries. I would support Nikolay Ivanovich's thought that we ourselves need to show more persistence in making decisions on the issues that are coming up. We need to look for partners with whom to establish direct connections more actively, and to involve the USSR Council of Ministers more broadly so that it can listen to the department heads on these issues and keep issues of economic collaboration under its control. Right now, on the other hand, our departments obtain capital investment from the government but do not use the options of resolving these issues through cooperation and direct connections, because that is more bothersome for them. If we are not active in this area, everything will remain as it used to be.

Do we approve the draft regulations?

Politburo members: Approve.

The CC CPSU draft regulations on these issues are adopted.

[*Source: Archive of the Gorbachev Foundation, Fond 2. Opis 2. On file at the National Security Archive. Translated by Anna Melyakova.*]

Document No. 9: Notes of CC CPSU Politburo Session

January 29, 1987

At Gorbachev's first meeting as general secretary with the leaders of the East European fraternal parties in 1985, his new language was already remarkable (even if his audience did not hear it clearly); but this Politburo session at the beginning of 1987 represents the fullest expression of Gorbachev's principle of non-interference in Eastern Europe—beyond the repudiation of military intervention. Gorbachev tells his colleagues, "And we should hold more firmly to the principle of each communist party being responsible for what happens in its country. We need this. It is in our interest not to be loaded down with responsibility for what is happening, or could happen, there." The motive here seems to stem from a growing sense of Eastern Europe as a drain on the USSR, rather than a net asset—its benefit as an essential security buffer, in the Stalinist conception, was beginning to be outweighed by the costs of its economic upkeep. Increasingly, the Soviet Union's own "economic difficulties" at this stage mean that the West is the only possible source of "state-of-the-art equipment and technology" while the USSR is simply a "spigot" for gas and oil.

These notes also reveal some of the character of the internal Soviet leadership debate. Yakovlev notes how Soviet reform processes are creating political problems for the East European "friends," and Dobrynin tries to defend Honecker, and in so doing, may be seen as implicitly criticizing perestroika ("our friends do not know the positive" in it). Gorbachev sees leadership change as inevitable and imminent in Eastern Europe, describing the fraternal leaders there practically as "little Brezhnevs," but he is not willing to interfere directly to replace them with "little Gorbachevs:" "We cannot assume the position of giving political evaluations or snubbing people. We can have only one kind of influence: through the example of our own actions." There is no defined strategy in his presentation, however, just a call for "[m]ore contacts, more information" and continued friendship.

ON THE OUTCOME OF THE WARSAW MEETING OF CC SECRETARIES
FROM CMEA COUNTRIES REGARDING INTERNATIONAL AND IDEOLOGICAL
QUESTIONS

Yakovlev: Our friends are having political troubles because of our XXVII Congress and now because of our Plenum: they don't know what to do and how to behave with us.

Dobrynin (he went to Berlin before the meeting—A.Ch.) We should not dramatize nuances in Honecker's and the SED's behavior. We have the same position on international issues as they do, except for German–German relations. We should broaden our relationship with the GDR as a counterbalance. Our friends do not know the positive in *perestroika* very well.

Gorbachev: We have disagreements with him [Honecker] in the sphere of *perestroika*. He compares our self-government with Yugoslavia's: how poorly we know each other, after all! He sees [Mikhail] Shatrov's play about Lenin as a deviation from the traditions of October. He is unhappy with our treatment of Sakharov.

(*Chernyaev's note: Aliyev fell asleep a long time ago!*)

Medvedev (*he was in Berlin as well—A.Ch.*): The SED rejected the slogan "Learn from the Soviet Union How to Win." The Delhi Declaration was not printed in the GDR. Criticism of the U.S. has been toned down. We should not speak of a separate SED line because there is no SED CC resolution on that. We are talking about divergences and deviations.

Gorbachev: So far, nothing unexpected is happening. We could have expected this. Those roots go beyond our April Plenum.

Honecker, Kádár, and Zhivkov—they all have deviations from us. Economic ties with the West have gone very far. That is the result of our economic difficulties. We could not provide them with state-of-the-art equipment and technology, so they got into debt with the West.

On the political side, our relations on the highest level have slackened while relations between them have become broader. Our approach should be:

a) To develop the attractiveness of Soviet processes, to show the dynamism of our development and our foreign policy. We cannot respond to their actions by starting down the path of shutting off spigots (gas, oil).

   To pay in currency, if they insisted on it, would be catastrophic for them. It is pointless to shout that we are wrong to give it to them so cheaply. We need to shift to mutually beneficial trade. And we should hold more firmly to the principle of each communist party being responsible for what happens in its country. We need this. It is in our interest not to be loaded down with responsibility for what is happening, or could happen, there.

b) But we also cannot ignore the other side of the issue. It is ripe for change. They are approaching the moment of changing the leadership. Some leaders have been in power for 35–25–17 years. There is a ton of problems piled up, but at that age it is just physically difficult to deal with those problems. In essence, a struggle is going on in the highest echelons. A process of renewal is underway, and it is happening one way for some and another way for others. We cannot assume the position of giving political evaluations or snubbing people. We can have only one kind of influence: through the example of our own actions. And as we see, the society in these countries has the right reaction toward us. There are nuances in evaluations, they are noticeable. Kádár and Honecker do not believe that our process is irreversible. Husák pays us many compliments, but is against everything new in his country. A caricature appeared on the streets of Prague, which reads "Misha [Mikhail] should deal with them all!" They mean Husák, Štrougal, Bil'ak. Zhivkov said about the preoccupation with campaigns [*kampaneishchina*]: your Khrushchev caused

242

1956 in Hungary by his reforms. And now Gorbachev is destabilizing the socialist community. The situation in Bulgaria is tense.

But we should not be too dramatic. We should not think that they are not our friends anymore. We should remain friends. And we need to react calmly, regardless of what Honecker says. We need to see everything. We should not oversimplify things. We should work in a friendly mode and not aggravate the situation. More contacts, more information.

[*Source: Archive of the Gorbachev Foundation, Fond 2. Opis 2. On file at the National Security Archive. Translated by Anna Melyakova.*]

Document No. 10: Proposal from Georgy Shakhnazarov to the CPSU for a Partial Soviet Troop Withdrawal from the ČSSR

March 1987

This provocative memorandum shows the essential role played by key reformers—top aides to Gorbachev—in thinking beyond conventional notions and ultimately (but not immediately) seeing their ideas put into action. Here, Shakhnazarov urges Gorbachev to announce unilateral Soviet troop withdrawals from Czechoslovakia during his upcoming April 1987 trip to Prague. The memo reads like a debater's brief, taking each possible point of objection and arguing against it, finding every distinction between the Czechoslovak case and those of East Germany or Poland where force reductions at this time are unthinkable. The proposal also emphasizes the public relations and political gains to be had from such an action, and uses remarkable phrases such as: "Soviet troops are being kept in the ČSSR, for the most part, as a remnant of an empire and out of habit." However, Gorbachev was not yet ready to accept this advice from Shakhnazarov, who at the time was not a formal adviser to the party leader (he was promoted to that position in early 1988), but a first deputy head of the CC Socialist Countries Department.

What is new here is the notion of Moscow taking unilateral action to lower its military profile at a time when back-and-forth proposals for mutual NATO and Warsaw Pact troop reductions (including a Gorbachev speech in April 1986, a Warsaw Pact appeal in June 1986 for a 25 percent decrease on both sides, and NATO's acceptance in December 1986 of specific talks) are producing only negotiations, not progress. Shakhnazarov's own concern is how to advance reform in Czechoslovakia and strengthen the progressives in the party there. Gorbachev's speech in Czechoslovak capital on April 10, 1987, would ultimately propose no such withdrawals, and would avoid any reinterpretation of the Prague Spring of 1968. Shakhnazarov's idea of unilateral cuts—and not only in Czechoslovakia—would have to wait until the Soviet leader's December 1988 United Nations speech.

It seems advisable to assign the USSR Ministry of Defense to look into the question of withdrawing a substantial number of Soviet troops from the ČSSR and to generate proposals concerning M.S. Gorbachev's visit to that country, which is being planned for spring 1987.

By announcing a withdrawal agreement with our Czechoslovak colleagues during that visit, we would be investing this matter with major political significance. The political weight of the visit and the decision to withdraw troops would each increase the other's impact on the world community.

The desirability of such a serious political act at precisely this moment is dictated by a range of broad considerations.

Firstly, it would substantiate M.S. Gorbachev's statement at the X PUWP Congress in summer 1986 in which he said that Soviet troops stationed in other countries are not there indefinitely. This could fundamentally undermine attempts by Western reactionary circles to present that statement, which signaled a major turning point in the approach to the military-strategic situation in Europe, as a propaganda trick. The seriousness of our desire to achieve a breakthrough in new thinking in European politics would be significantly emphasized by a decision to withdraw troops from the ČSSR.

The current political phase is marked by increasing pressures on the European track of our policies. Those Western circles which oppose disarmament are trying to play the disparity card on issues of weapons and armed forces between the Warsaw Treaty and NATO; they are building up resistance to our nuclear arms reductions program on that basis. Considering these conditions, the proposed troop withdrawal would undermine the validity of their tactics.

Judging by an array of signs it is possible to say that Western reactionary forces are seriously apprehensive about the Soviet Union taking any such steps. Specific evidence of this is the concept they propagate that any withdrawal of Soviet troops from European socialist countries is called "the ousting of the Soviet Union" from those countries.

In the political sense, the decision to withdraw troops would to some extent make up for our above-mentioned refusal to extend the unilateral moratorium on nuclear testing. The peace movement in Western Europe would have a new, persuasive argument.

From the point of view of Soviet–Czechoslovak relations, the proposed act would be very important and timely. In the country itself, the withdrawal of a segment of Soviet troops would be seen as a sign of greater trust in their leadership and the communist party, whose policies have provided a high level of political stability in society. At the same time, this step would express our confidence in the new leadership's ability to consolidate the situation in the country; it would be a serious [expression of] preliminary support for the leadership. It would also serve to rectify the latent feeling of our Czechoslovak colleagues that their deep and sincere dedication to the Soviet Union and the CPSU is little noticed here.

For its part, the Czechoslovak leadership has never, not even as a hint, mentioned the issue of withdrawing Soviet troops. That is why our initiative would have unique significance for them and would create political and emotional connections of a special kind.

It is important to emphasize the point that a considerable decrease in the number of Soviet troops on Czechoslovak territory would significantly reduce the expenses associated with their presence and would be well-received by the general population.

Before making a decision, it is necessary to weigh the possible or expected negative effects of this action.

It is possible that the withdrawal of troops from Czechoslovakia would encourage the leadership of the HPR, the GDR, and the PPR to try to arrive at a similar adjustment for the Soviet troops stationed on their territories.

Without completely excluding the several possibilities that exist for such attempts, we should emphasize that stationing our troops in the ČSSR has encompassed (and still does) special foundations, causes, and agreements, which differ from the status of our military forces in other East European socialist countries.

When we brought Unified forces into Czechoslovakia in August 1968 we made the statement that they would leave the country once the threat to its freedom and independence had been eliminated. In the agreement on conditions for the temporary presence of Soviet troops on ČSSR territory of October 16, 1968, it was stated that they were to remain "in order to ensure the protection of the Socialist Commonwealth from the growing revanchist aims of West German military forces."

Both these conditions have to some extent run their course. Soviet troops are being kept in the ČSSR, for the most part, as a remnant of an empire and out of habit.

There is a totally different situation in the GDR. There, Soviet forces are in a key sector of the European theater of operations, in a state that does not have the capability to withstand the NATO bloc with its own forces. Also, GDR territory does not provide sufficient defensive depth, and the republic does not share a common border with the USSR.

The stationing of Soviet forces in Poland and Hungary, as in the GDR, is radically different from the situation in the ČSSR because its foundation goes back to the defeat of Nazi Germany in 1945.

The military-strategic correlation of forces in Central Europe, considering the relative importance of nuclear missiles in the balance, allows us to withdraw a segment of our forces—tanks and infantry, without touching tactical-operational air-defense and missile complexes—without sustaining any losses. A shared border between Czechoslovakia and the USSR and the preservation of the corresponding infrastructures would allow us to return the withdrawn troops in case of a deterioration in the military-strategic situation. By the way, when preparing documentation for a withdrawal, this point should be discussed specifically. It would seem that the balance of plusses and minuses argues unequivocally in favor of the proposed step.

A draft CC CPSU resolution is attached.

[*Source: Archive of the Gorbachev Foundation. Donated by G.Kh. Shakhnazarov. On file at the National Security Archive. Translated by Anna Melyakova.*]

Document No. 11: Notes of CC CPSU Politburo Session. Report on Mikhail Gorbachev's Visit to Czechoslovakia

April 16, 1987

Here Chernyaev captures Gorbachev's report to the Soviet Politburo about his recent trip to Czechoslovakia and the popular adulation he encountered there. The Soviet leader compares the Czechoslovaks' newly-positive attitude toward the USSR to that of May 1945, after the defeat of the Nazis. But the downside of Gorbachev's popularity is the sharp contrast with attitudes toward the current Czechoslovak communist leadership: "[T]here was always awkwardness when we appeared before the public. The people chanted 'Gorbachev, Gorbachev.' Husák was next to me but it was as if he wasn't there."

During the trip, Gorbachev had declined to change the Soviet interpretation of the events of 1968 (that the Prague Spring was a counterrevolution that had to be stopped with Soviet force), which both internal and external critics saw as a major missed opportunity. For example, a January 5, 1990, assessment by the Soviet CC International Department described the failure to admit the 1968 mistake as having led "to a most serious disenchantment of the population of that country who expected that this visit would bring about changes" (see Document No. 117). But a leading figure of the Prague Spring, Zdeněk Mlynář, who had been Gorbachev's law school classmate, wrote in 1987 that Gorbachev had little choice but to support the dependent Czechoslovak leaders on 1968; to do otherwise would have demolished their credibility and aligned Gorbachev with the opposition. Characteristically, Gorbachev left it up to the Czechoslovak communists to decide whether and how to rehabilitate the Prague Spring participants.

Chernyaev's notes include Gorbachev's remark that his Prague oration was the first public speech in which he put forward the concept of the "common European home;" but in his speech to the British parliament (published in Pravda on December 19, 1984), Gorbachev proposed making Europe a "common home" rather than "a theater of military operations."

The main outcome is the turning point in the people's attitude toward the USSR. The atmosphere reminds one of May 1945. Especially the young people—their behavior makes a very powerful impression. It would have been impossible to organize this enthusiasm. There was breath-taking fraternization with us. But there is also another side to this phenomenon—the people's attitude toward their leadership. The issue is not with Gorbachev, whom they welcomed. Here I saw an evaluation of our work, the attitude toward our *perestroika*.

They called out to me: stay here, at least for a year! In essence this is a criticism of the present Czechoslovak leadership. And this is very serious. We are seeing a similar [phenomenon] in the GDR. Here as well, people are ahead of the political views and the level of the leadership. This is dangerous. The leaders feel that they are falling behind and are losing the people's confidence, especially since their political opposition is hanging onto our *perestroika*.

In Prague they compare *perestroika* with their 1968. They had the right idea then, but the figure—Dubček—was wrong. This was used by outsiders.

The leadership may feel that they are losing. And this puts a certain responsibility on us. We cannot allow doubts and uncertainty about our *perestroika* to arise in the leadership circles. But they themselves have to form an efficient governing body. We have to influence our friends' public opinion in all directions within the framework of our morals, our attitude toward the past and the present. Then we will get real support from the people there.

We are embarrassed. Wherever you go in the West there is a whole gallery of statesmen from the distant and the recent past. But we have nobody. We lived and worked for 20-30 years, but who was in the leadership—nobody knows.

Criteria? The criteria must be academic, Marxist, Leninist. We must tell the truth. And this truth elevates our history. We have already felt a growing responsibility before our friends.

Everywhere we hear thoughts and hopes turned toward us. We need to deepen our understanding of our role in the world right now. Many aspects here have not been thought through.

In Czechoslovakia I said candidly that we will not conduct our *perestroika* at their expense. But you, too, do you expect to live at our expense? If you are for integration, let us do it honestly, let us get through this process as well. There is a difference in prices, in wages. We will adjust. In the economy, Czechoslovakia can be our most reliable partner of all the socialist countries. It enjoys a considerable level of technology, and it is prepared to collaborate with us.

I told them that right now we are moving from formulating the concept of *perestroika* to practicing it. If there is something that works for you, take it. The only thing we are counting on is solidarity. In the international arena we will firmly hold to equality, even though we are big and you are small.

[About] the attitude toward 1968. How do we regard this event? Half a million were "crossed off" their party rolls. That was a third of the party. What should we do with them? With Dubček everything is clear—a betrayal of socialism. But what to do with ordinary communists? I told them that it is their decision what to do with these people. I let it be understood that we have no intention of reconsidering our position on 1968. But I also emphasized that we cannot stop.

There was always awkwardness when we appeared before the public. The people chanted "Gorbachev, Gorbachev." Husák was next to me, but it was as if he wasn't there. I kept trying to push him forward, and always used the phrase "Comrade Husák and I ..." But the people did not respond to it.

As far as my speech there, in which I first put forward the idea of a common European home, the West noticed it even though they are trying to keep it quiet.

[*Source: Archive of the Gorbachev Foundation, Fond 2, Opis 2. On file at the National Security Archive. Translated by Anna Melyakova.*]

248

Document No. 12: Notes of CC CPSU Politburo Session

May 8, 1987

This Politburo discussion about the Warsaw Pact's doctrine features a notable level of internal disagreement, debate, and substantive argument—quite different from the usual Politburo style of call-and-response and preaching-to-the-choir. Here, Defense Minister Sergey Sokolov and other old guard run headlong into the new thinking on military affairs. The deliberations also include the first open admission in available Politburo records of the imbalance of forces in Europe, the first acknowledgment that Soviet troops will have to be withdrawn from Eastern Europe, and the first explicit recognition, insisted upon by Gorbachev, that a new doctrine of "sufficiency" needs to replace the traditional Soviet insistence on "parity." If matching weapon for weapon continues, Gorbachev says, "we can forget about building socialism."— "[W]ill we keep turning the country into a military camp?" Bolstering his argument, he refers to an earlier meeting with Margaret Thatcher, at which the British leader explained the West's threat perception ("they were afraid of us; that we invaded Czechoslovakia, Hungary, and Afghanistan") and tutored him in the concept that real deterrence requires only a credible retaliatory capacity, not an equal number of weapons.

Here we also find a cautious early version of the 1988 United Nations speech: the ideas about a troop withdrawal are tentative—"Let us say we keep 170,000"— yet there is an explicit recognition that it is "not so important how many troops there are" although their presence in any numbers is important as a "political matter." Only 20 days after this discussion, the young German pilot Matthias Rust lands his small plane near Red Square after evading Soviet warning systems, thus giving Gorbachev the opportunity to fire Sokolov and an array of top military leaders who could not accept the new doctrines.

ON THE DOCTRINE OF THE WARSAW TREATY ORGANIZATION

Gromyko: We have always had a defensive doctrine, both in the political and the military sense.

Shevardnadze: I am for publishing the truth about the number of our troops in central Europe. […] Not for withdrawal, but for the truth [about numbers] and argumentation.

Yakovlev (supporting Shevardnadze): We should say something about the imbalance. Otherwise we will come not only to a propaganda dead end, but a political one as well.

Gorbachev (to Marshal Sokolov): When you enter a place, think about how you will leave. […]

Sokolov: Our (*Warsaw Treaty Organization*) military personnel levels are right now higher than NATO's by 170,000. Out of that, 70,000 are Soviet troops, the rest are allied troops. There is no imbalance. And then, how would we reduce them? How do we keep what we've won? Withdrawing troops would be a political mistake.

Chebrikov: The issue of an imbalance deserves serious attention. But we are taking into account the territory from the Atlantic to the Urals. In that case, there is no imbalance.

Dobrynin: The essence of the issue is whether to say that we have more troops in the center of Europe than NATO has, or not. We need to close down Vienna[9] somehow. If we want to be honest, we have to say that. We have been cunning for 13 years, and we have to admit it now.[10]

Medvedev: There is a phrase in the doctrine: "we will respond with all available means." Does this mean with nuclear weapons as well? It is necessary for every formula to be precise, not "in general."

Vienna will not be "resolved" if the sore point (*imbalance*) is not resolved.

We cannot continue with lies. […] We cannot ignore public opinion. And we need to speak openly about the territory of Europe as being from the Atlantic to the Urals.

Zaikov: It would be better to speak about imbalance in Mikhail Sergeyevich's speech.

Gorbachev: They (*in the West*) know about it anyway …

Zaikov: They know, but it is a different matter when you say it. We need to acknowledge it openly. The question of control arises next. So far we have been trying to avoid control ourselves.

Gorbachev: How the imbalances were formed—the skewed proportions in different types of weapons, here arguments must be used as well.

Akhromeyev: I think that we should try to find a solution to the issue of the imbalance in armaments in Europe, and we should state it openly.

Gorbachev: Firstly. I disagree that there is "nothing new" in the document. Our understanding of the problems has deepened. Policy is the main issue here. Speculation continues. Remember, I told you about my meeting with Thatcher. She said they were afraid of us; that we invaded Czechoslovakia, Hungary, and Afghanistan. This perception is widespread among the public there. It persists in the minds of many people. Anti-Soviet propaganda is based on it. We should strengthen our policy for the humanization of international relations with our actions.

There were public statements by our generals in military journals, for example Marshal Grechko's article. They put the West on guard and reinforce their distrust.

---

[9] Negotiations on conventional arms forces in Europe (CFE) were being held in Vienna.

[10] Since the mid-1970s, when the negotiations began, the Soviet Union had been unwilling to admit its superiority in conventional forces in Europe, especially in numbers of tanks. The figures were never published and were kept secret as late as Gorbachev's U.N. speech in December 1988 when he announced deep unilateral reductions in conventional forces in the European theater.

That is why politically it makes sense for me to give a speech and publicly state the new doctrine.

Secondly. What should the character of this doctrine be? We are not just "sitting" or "lying" on our military doctrine, we are trying to find a way to make the world more stable. Now even parity has ceased to be a guarantee. Therefore, we propose to act in an appropriate fashion. And we will not be stubborn about having 27,000 tanks and almost 3.5 million soldiers there.

I would like to support Vadim Andreyevich [Medvedev] on the issue of implementing "all appropriate means." This is too ambiguous.

We overlooked a very important question—the question of sufficiency. Many scholars and the public have responded to this idea. And we need to make a statement that we are striving to keep armaments at the lowest level.

About the imbalance. I must say: nobody in the Defense Council[11] could explain clearly what strategic parity is. This is not a question of statistics, it is a question of military policy. Strategic parity means that we have a reliable guarantee of the defense of our country. And the enemy will not attack us because in that case it would receive an unacceptable retaliatory strike. If we anticipate such a result, then we have parity. But if we start counting—they have a rifle, we have a rifle—then we can forget about building socialism. They have 6 billion [sic] people working on armaments. So should we try to catch up with that number? We should put an end to such an approach. I ask the question: will we keep turning the country into a military camp in the future as well? They clearly want to pull us into another round of the arms race. They are counting on our military exhaustion. And they will portray us as militarists. They are pulling us into SDI.

These are the positions from which we should formulate our military doctrine.

And when we speak about the number of our troops in Europe, and if we state the numbers honestly, then we will have to come to the decision to withdraw them at an appropriate time. It is important for the leadership of our allies that we maintain our military presence there. And it is not so important how many troops there are. We also need a presence; it is a political matter—so that others know: if they touch our allies, they will have to deal with our power.

Somewhere in here lies the fruit of long contemplation. This must be the only direction of our thinking. [...] We need to approach Eastern Europe from these positions. We have defenses there, we have strong powers.

What is the difference whether there are 380,000 there or 300,000 there? What is important is the matter itself, and the positioning of the troops.

Therefore, the approach of one soldier there, one soldier here, they have a bullet we have a bullet, is not our approach.

---

[11] The Defense Council was formally the highest Soviet decision-making body on defense and national security policy (including arms control negotiations), subordinated to the Presidium of the Supreme Soviet. The chairman of the Presidium of the Supreme Soviet was also chairman of the Defense Council.

We need to find a way to resolve Vienna. The numbers are important here, we need to make that clear. Let us say we keep 170,000. But there should be no rush, as if we were going to withdraw the rest immediately. We should tell the government heads about this at the PCC in the context of the Budapest initiative. We must not allow it to look like a retreat. We need to think this through, discuss it with our allies, and then make a proposal to the West during negotiations. Let them react. Maybe they will tell us that we do not need to do it. It is important for us to give free rein to a policy of trust, trust and more trust. The West talks about it all the time, and we are just dancing around it.

And if we are talking about Europe as between the Atlantic and the Urals, then you (NATO members) should go ahead and withdraw troops. We will have to deal with their troop numbers. Here they are afraid, because they would have to ship the Americans across the ocean.

[*Source:* V Politburo TsK KPSS ... Po zapisyam Anatoliya Chernyaeva, Vadima Medvedeva, Georgiya Shakhnazarova *(1985–1991) (Moscow: Alpina Business Books, 2006), pp. 180–183. Translated by Svetlana Savranskaya and Anna Melyakova.*]

Document No. 13: Report on Mikhail Gorbachev's Visit to Romania

June 4, 1987

Gorbachev's report to the Politburo about his trip to Romania describes a very different experience from the popular reception he received in April in Prague. Chernyaev's notes show Gorbachev's clear discomfort with Ceauşescu, the overall oppressive feeling he found in a country where "human dignity has absolutely no value," where the robotic chanting by the crowds "makes one's head burst," and where there are shortages of virtually everything. Still, Gorbachev believes he must show support for all the allied leaders, even though in this case he "feel[s] like a fool." Unlike in Czechoslovakia where the cheers for Gorbachev were for reform and against the existing communist leadership, in Romania Ceauşescu made sure the orchestrated chants wrapped the Soviet leader tightly together with the dictator—and Gorbachev did not like it.

Gorbachev: Our patience and adherence to principles in relation to Ceauşescu in particular and the country in general have paid off.

I was impressed by the construction in Bucharest. Ambitious architecture. Ceauşescu said that by 1990 housing construction will be completed. But the people's situation is very difficult. The consumption of meat per capita is 10 kilograms per year. Foreign debt is around 3 billion dollars. There are constant shortages of power, heat, food products, consumer goods. And Ceauşescu has been telling me all this time that he has already achieved everything.

I look at him and feel like a fool. He already has everything decided in terms of democracy, free elections, and the cooperation of free labor collectives.

When Ceauşescu and I went out to the people, their reaction was like a wound-up music box: "Ceauşescu—Gorbachev!" "Ceauşescu—peace!" When I came closer to the people I would ask them: do you know any other words? Later I was told that these criers were brought there on a bus for this purpose. All of this produces an oppressive feeling.

Human dignity has absolutely no value. I was not able to have a normal conversation with people anywhere: neither on the street, nor at the factory I visited. They just kept yelling "Ceauşescu—Gorbachev!" "Gorbachev—Ceauşescu!" It makes one's head burst. [I] was taken to a store and a market. There is window dressing everywhere. People say that after I left, masses of people rushed to get the goods.

Ceauşescu was terribly offended when I spoke publicly about *glasnost*, about *perestroika*, when I allowed myself to speak concretely about what we are doing in the USSR. He was put out of temper by that.

Therefore we need to act carefully, step by step, without rushing and overestimating our possibilities. At the same time we need to consider that the Romanian leadership wants very much to get closer to us.

Ceauşescu tried to blame us for punishing him economically for his independent policies. In return I also asked him a question: you went to the West for help and support and wanted to get its sympathies at our expense. So what claims can you have of us now? And what is stopping you from making contacts with us, the USSR, at least through social and district organizations?

He is unbelievably impudent. His self-assurance and self-praise are simply monumental, comparable only with his attempts to teach and admonish everybody. On international issues he exhibits chaos and confusion [*krutezh*]. By the way, he spoke sharply against the idea of "sufficiency" in our military doctrine.[12]

The question might arise whether it was necessary to visit him at all. I think that specifically in this situation it was necessary.

[*Source:* V Politburo TsK KPSS ... Po zapisyam Anatoliya Chernyaeva, Vadima Medvedeva, Georgiya Shakhnazarova *(1985–1991) (Moscow: Alpina Business Books, 2006), pp. 194–195 Translated by Anna Melyakova.*]

---

[12] The Gorbachev leadership tried to replace the concept in Soviet military doctrine of strict numerical balancing of armaments with the West with the concept of reasonable sufficiency based on the minimum level of armaments required for basic nuclear deterrence.

Document No. 14: Report on Eduard Shevardnadze's Visits to Bulgaria, Hungary, and Yugoslavia

July 9, 1987

Here Foreign Minister Eduard Shevardnadze tells the Politburo about his travels to Eastern Europe, and hints of distress sound throughout the report. Bulgaria is "outwardly" all right but inwardly "uncertain." Hungary faces the possibility of "social turmoil." Yes, perestroika *is popular in Yugoslavia, but new problems accumulate daily in the area of economic collaboration. Yet again Gorbachev calls for a "general assessment of economic relations" between Moscow and its allies because "the deciding moment is approaching." A strategy is needed, but once again none is forthcoming.*

Gorbachev: Our relations with the socialist countries remind one of inter-ethnic relations in the Caucasus: the smaller the nation the more rights and respect it demands for itself, the more importance it attaches to its language and different governmental portfolios.

Shevardnadze: *Bulgaria*. Outwardly everything looks good. But there is an element of indecision and uncertainty. Mladenov (minister of foreign affairs) says: somehow we will make it. The most important thing is for the USSR's *perestroika* to be successful.

Zhivkov spoke about the "Bulgarian phenomenon." He had a mentor's tone, he was teaching us. He began almost every phrase with the words "take into consideration ..." He visited the FRG and he "teaches:" all socialist countries must work out a general conception in relation to the FRG.

Bulgarian nationalism is clearly evident, not only in relation to Turks, but also in relation to Russians.

He raises the question of the Balkans as a nuclear-free zone. The Yugoslavs are for it. It is aimed at Greece's position, which has American bases. We need to speed up the resolution of this issue.

Hungary. I do not exclude the possibility of social turmoil there. The economic reform has affected the entire population.

Yugoslavia. Our *perestroika* is very popular there. The leadership and society think that a new stage of relations with the USSR is needed, and a new Declaration (the previous was adopted in 1956 [sic] during Khrushchev's visit)[13] as well. They link its adoption with Gorbachev's visit.

---

[13] The Belgrade Declaration of June 3, 1955, was adopted during Khrushchev's trip to Yugoslavia in May–June of that year. The Declaration proclaimed that various roads to socialism were possible, and the effect of the visit was to help heal the Soviet–Yugoslav split, which had been caused by Stalin's alienation of Yugoslavian leader Josip Broz Tito.

In contrast to the past, the Yugoslavs avoided sensitive issues, [they] even left Kampuchea alone. They are prepared to mediate there.

The question of economic collaboration was raised in a sharp manner. New problems accumulate daily.

Gorbachev: We need to make a general assessment of economic relations with the socialist countries. The deciding moment is approaching. Perhaps we, in the government, should summarize everything we have on that up till now [...]

[*Source: Archive of the Gorbachev Foundation. Fond 2. Opis 2. On file at the National Security Archive. Translated by Anna Melyakova.*]

Document No. 15: State Department Intelligence and Research Report: "Economic Reform in the USSR and Eastern Europe"

September 16, 1987

This succinct assessment from the State Department's Bureau of Intelligence and Research reviews the progress of economic reform in the socialist countries and notes surprisingly that "[t]here is no apparent organized opposition in the USSR to Gorbachev's reform" although "vested interests" will constrain reform in Eastern Europe. There, Bulgaria is the best prospect, according to the analysis, but the Poles could also "achieve some liberalization." Missing in particular is a sense of the trade union Solidarity's strength: within a year of this assessment, a renascent union would compel the Polish government to negotiate; within two years, Solidarity would run the government.

KEY JUDGMENTS

Economic reform has proceeded at widely varying rates in the USSR and Eastern Europe. Prospects are uncertain given the political dynamics working in the individual countries. The systemic changes so far adopted by Yugoslavia and Hungary—with emphasis on decentralization and a role for market forces in decision making—have pushed those economies far away from the traditional Stalinist command economy. Other countries in the region have been less ambitious, content to streamline or otherwise tinker with the system in an effort to promote efficiency.

The Soviet Union. Gorbachev is pushing the USSR into giving serious attention to systemic reform. Measures actually implemented have been minor, barely keeping the USSR apace with Poland and Bulgaria, the other bloc countries advocating limited systemic change. But prospects for reform in the USSR are greater, including a role for market forces. Meaningful reform of prices will be crucial to the success of Gorbachev's efforts to restructure the economy.

There is no apparent organized opposition in the USSR to Gorbachev's reform. But reform threatens the interests of many bureaucrats and party apparatchiki and gives ordinary workers cause to worry about job security. These same vested interests constrain reform in Eastern Europe.

Eastern Europe. Near-term prospects for further reform are best in Bulgaria (where obedience to Moscow coincides with genuine interest in reform). The Poles are receptive to reformist ideas; with prodding from Moscow and perhaps the International Monetary Fund—and luck with the domestic political situation—they could achieve some liberalization.

Leadership resistance to reform is greatest in Romania—Ceauşescu clings to Stalinist methods of control—and among the East Germans, who believe that the German Democratic Republic has demonstrated that central planning does work. *Glasnost* is encouraging the reform-minded in Czechoslovakia, but hardliners fear they will be undermined by another "Prague Spring."

[*Source: U.S. Department of State, Bureau of Intelligence and Research. Obtained through FOIA. On file at the National Security Archive.*]

Document No. 16: Notes of CC CPSU Politburo Session

November 19, 1987

At this meeting of the Politburo, Chairman of the Council of Ministers Nikolay Ryzhkov discusses his talks with the Czechoslovak prime minister, Lubomír Štrougal, the most reform-minded member of the leadership there who in 1988 would be forced into retirement by the hard-line Miloš Jakeš. Ryzhkov says Štrougal "stands above" all the other socialist prime ministers, while Gorbachev speaks approvingly of the "cultured government" in Prague. These notes provide further inside evidence of Gorbachev's consistent refusal to interfere with the allies, even as they faced political challenges to implementing reforms, allowing them instead to decide their own personnel matters. As Gorbachev puts it here, "God forbid we go to them with our own jumble of thoughts on the theme of their perestroika.*" To the extent there was a Gorbachev vision for Eastern Europe, it seems to have been simply that of encouraging "little Gorbachevs" (like Štrougal) in place of the "little Brezhnevs" (like Honecker).*

ON RYZHKOV'S TALKS WITH ŠTROUGAL (CZECHOSLOVAK PRIME MINISTER)

Ryzhkov: Czechoslovakia is heavy with *perestroika*. Štrougal said that the reforms should have been started in the 1970s. And if *perestroika* begins for them results will appear sooner than in any other country.

Gorbachev: Yes, culture means a great deal.

Ryzhkov: Štrougal said to me: What did we do? We took your Congress resolution, and took the prepared formulas. (*Ryzhkov goes on to read what he said to Štrougal*). Štrougal told me that the CPCz Plenum is coming up soon. But one cannot go to the Plenum without a ready conception of *perestroika*, with only a draft plan for reforms, especially in this time of struggle for power; it would be risky. I cannot imagine the Czechoslovak leadership without Štrougal.

Gorbachev: We should meet this cultured government halfway. Our line will be: to participate in the discussion of everything in a friendly manner. But only they must make the decisions. If the question of distributing posts there arises, let them think through everything themselves and decide [...] God forbid we go to them with our own jumble of thoughts on the theme of their *perestroika*. It could destroy everything.

Ryzhkov: We were careful in speaking with Štrougal.

Gorbachev: Štrougal is a good prime minister, but it is unlikely that he would be able to unite the leadership as a general secretary. The split there is coming from Bil'ak.[14] I hinted at this to him.

Ryzhkov: Against the background of the other socialist countries' prime ministers, Štrougal stands above everyone. But the struggle for power consumes everything and distracts from important affairs. And the ethnic question has come up as well. Before, Slovakia was the periphery, now it is in command. They come to us for advice. This is very important. But now we must not tell them who goes where. Let them decide everything for themselves.

[Source: Archive of the Gorbachev Foundation. Fond 2, Opis 2. On file at the National Security Archive. Translated by Anna Melyakova.]

---

[14] Vasíl Bil'ak, a hard-line Slovak communist politician and party ideologist, was a member of the CPCz CC Presidium from April 1968 until he resigned in December 1988. After the communists fell out of power in 1989, he was expelled from the party and later faced charges for his role in the 1968 Soviet-led invasion of Czechoslovakia and its aftermath.

Document No. 17: Memorandum from Robert Gates, "Gorbachev's Gameplan: The Long View"

November 24, 1987

Two years into the changed relationship between Moscow and its Eastern Europe-an allies, the top U.S. intelligence analyst on the Soviet Union—Robert M. Gates, then the deputy director of CIA—reads Gorbachev almost completely wrong. In this memo for President Reagan (who was about to sign with Gorbachev the treaty that eliminated intermediate-range nuclear forces), Gates predicts that the Soviet re-forms are merely a "breathing space" before the resumption of the "further increase in Soviet military power and political influence." Gates misses the Soviet recogni-tion that the Stalinist economic system has failed; he incorrectly predicts that Gor-bachev will only agree to arms reductions that "protect existing Soviet advantag-es;" he claims the Soviets are still committed to the protection of their Third World clients, whereas only three months later, Gorbachev would announce the pullout from Afghanistan; furthermore, Gates sees any Soviet force reductions as a threat to "Alliance cohesion" rather than a gain for security in Europe. This hard-line as-sessment of Gorbachev is not shared by President Reagan, however, who would re-scind his "evil empire" rhetoric while standing in Red Square in May 1988; but this analysis would become the dominant view in the U.S. government with George H.W. Bush's inauguration in early 1989. Gates himself would move to the White House as deputy national security adviser—in effect, failing upwards.

SUBJECT: GORBACHEV'S GAMEPLAN: THE LONG VIEW

The December Summit and INF Treaty are important achievements for the Ad-ministration and for Gorbachev. Yet, while there is substantial uncertainty about the U.S. strategy toward the USSR beyond 1988, Gorbachev's gameplan poten-tially can be played out over a prolonged period—thus giving him and the USSR a significant advantage. His long range strategy is an important backdrop for the Summit. Understanding it is essential to maintaining perspective during and after the meeting and to identifying both pitfalls and opportunities.

Domestic Imperatives

There is general agreement among the Soviet leaders on the need to modernize their economy—not so much for its own sake or to make Soviet citizens more prosperous but to strengthen the USSR at home, to further their own personal power, and to permit the further consolidation and expansion of Soviet power abroad. They differ as to the pace of change and whether economic modernization also requires a loosening of political controls. Gorbachev thinks so; many on the Politburo either disagree or harbor serious reservations.

There is also general agreement in the Politburo that economic modernization requires a benign international environment. The Soviets' need to relax tensions is critical because only thus can massive new expenditures for defense be avoided and Western help in economic development be obtained. The roots of Gorbachev's dynamic foreign policy are to be found at home and in the need for a prolonged breathing space.

Foreign Policy Consequences

The elements of foreign policy that spring from domestic economic weakness are a mix of new initiatives and longstanding policies.

1. Gorbachev wants to establish a new and far-reaching détente in the late 1980s to obtain technology, investment, trade and, above all, to avoid major new military expenditures while the Soviet economy is revived. Gorbachev must slow or stop American military modernization, especially SDI, that threatens not only Soviet strategic gains of the last generation but which also, if continued, will force the USSR to devote huge new resources to the military in a high technology competition for which they are ill-equipped. The Soviets know that détente in the early 1970s contributed significantly to downward pressure on Western defense budgets, nearly halted military modernization, weakened resolve to counter Soviet advances in the Third World, and opened to the USSR new opportunities for Western technology and economic relations.

2. A less visible but enduring element of foreign policy—even under Gorbachev—is the continuing extraordinary scope and sweep of Soviet military modernization and weapons research and development. Despite Soviet rhetoric, we still see *no* lessening of their weapons production. And, further, Soviet research on new, exotic weapons such as lasers and their own version of SDI continues apace. Virtually all of their principal strategic weapons will be replaced with new, more sophisticated systems by the mid-1990s, and a new bomber is being added to their arsenal for the first time in decades. Their defenses against U.S. weapons are being steadily improved, as are their capabilities for war-fighting—command, control, communications and leadership protection. As our defense budget declines again, theirs continues to grow, slowly but steadily. Gorbachev is prepared to explore—and, I think, reach—significant reductions in weapons, but only in ways that protect existing Soviet advantages, leave open alternative avenues of weapons development, offer commensurate political gains, or take maximum advantage of U.S. unilateral restrain or constraints (such as our unwillingness in the 1970s to build a limited ABM as permitted by the treaty).

3. The third element of Gorbachev's foreign policy is continued protection of Soviet clients in the Third World. Under Gorbachev, the Soviets and Cubans are now providing more than a billion dollars a year in economic and military assistance to Nicaragua; more than a billion dollars worth of military equipment was sent to Vietnam, Laos, and Cambodia in the first six months of this year; more than four billion dollars in military equipment has been sent to Angola since 1984. And, of course, Cuba gets about five billion dollars in Soviet support each year. At a time of economic stress at home, these commitments speak volumes about Soviet priorities.

4. The fourth element of Gorbachev's foreign policy is new and dynamic diplomatic initiatives to weaken ties between the U.S. and its Western allies, China, Japan, and the Third World; to portray the Soviet government as committed to arms control and peace; and to suggest Moscow's interest in diplomatic solutions to Afghanistan and Cambodia. In Europe, Gorbachev through INF is trading a modest military capability for what he sees as a significant political gain. We can and should expect new and bolder initiatives including conventional force reductions—possibly unilateral—that will severely test Alliance cohesion. Similarly, new initiatives with China and Japan will be attempted to overcome bilateral obstacles to improved relations and to exploit problems between them and the U.S. And, in the Third World, they will seek to take advantage of any relaxation of U.S. vigilance or constancy.

CONCLUSIONS

There clearly are great changes underway inside the Soviet Union and in Soviet diplomacy. Yet, it is hard to detect fundamental changes, currently or in prospect, in the way the Soviets govern at home or in their principal objectives abroad. The Party certainly will retain its monopoly of power and the basic structures of the Stalinist economy will remain. A major purpose of economic modernization—as in Russia in those days of Peter the Great—remains the further increase in Soviet military power and political influence.

These enduring characteristics of Soviet governance at home and policy abroad make it clear that—while the changes underway offer opportunities for the United States in arms control, Afghanistan and other areas—Gorbachev intends improved Soviet economic performance, greater political vitality at home, and more dynamic diplomacy to make the USSR a more competitive and stronger adversary in the years ahead.

Robert M. Gates

[*Source: Reagan Presidential Library. Obtained through FOIA. On file at the National Security Archive.*]

263

Document No. 18: Telegram from Rozanne Ridgeway to All European Diplomatic Posts, "Eastern Europe: Invitation to the Dance"

December 1987

The CIA's Robert Gates was not alone in his reluctance to advocate a reassessment of U.S. strategy in response to Gorbachev's new initiatives. In this cable from the State Department to European posts, Assistant Secretary Rozanne Ridgeway coins an attention-getting title—"invitation to the dance"—but includes little substance other than a mention of Vice President Bush's earlier trip to Poland. Similarly, the various cables and discussions mentioned here apparently produced few changes in actual U.S. policy. In a January 19, 1988, speech entitled "The U.S. Approach to Eastern Europe: A Fresh Look," Deputy Secretary of State John Whitehead would simply restate the old policy of differentiation (treating each socialist country according to its maverick tendencies, meaning Stalinist Romania became the U.S. favorite), and would assert, "Let us be clear, the long-run Soviet interest in maintaining a hegemonic relationship with Eastern Europe has not changed."

[...]

1. (S[ecret]- Entire Text).
2. This is to invite you to the discussion of Eastern Europe by cable which [Deputy Assistant Secretary of State] Tom Simons suggested at the end of his presentation in Oslo December 14.
3. The focus is the prospects of change in Eastern Europe and the implications for U.S. policy over the near and middle term. The purpose is to clarify our thinking about the issues preparatory to discussion within NATO as early as mid-February. As some of you will recall, when the vice president reported to NATO on his late-September visit to Poland, he suggested a ministerial-level exchange as early as December. The Washington summit made this impracticable, but we continue to believe such an exchange would be useful to us and other allies, and we are pursuing options for scheduling it.
4. By now you will have received both ambassador [to the GDR Francis J.] Meehan's very thoughtful cable (refer), and embassy Oslo's record of Tom Simons' remarks in Oslo. While I regret not having been able to attend the session, I understand that his presentation was well received, and produced solid, stimulating discussion. So you may wish to take these two cables. [...]

[*Source: U.S. Department of State. Obtained through FOIA. On file at the National Security Archive.*]

Document No. 19: Notes of CC CPSU Politburo Session

March 10, 1988

This Politburo discussion memorialized by Chernyaev marks a conspicuous change of tone among the Soviet leadership about their socialist allies. No longer are the Eastern European countries seen on the credit side of the ledger and about to reform, but as significant debits, absorbing Soviet raw materials as well as billions of rubles of foreign assistance. During the discussion, Gorbachev points up the failure of the CMEA, the bloc economic organization founded by Stalin in 1949 as an alternative to the Marshall Plan and western European cooperation. He also makes a stark acknowledgement: "In the economic sense, socialism has not passed the test of practice."

A key complicating factor in this period is the falling price of oil, which Ryzhkov notes has plummeted from 180 to 54 rubles per ton. Gorbachev remarks that "we cannot remain a provider of cheap resources for [the allies] forever." After Yegor Ligachev warns of "political upheavals" in the socialist countries, Gorbachev laments: "If the situation begins to crack, the very idea of socialism will be discredited." Yet the only strategy the Soviet leader proposes for dealing with the yawning crisis is his already-failing "acceleration" policy of investing in machine-building and technology.

About CMEA

Gorbachev: [Take for example] the "Ball Bearing" plant. We make a single unit for 60 rubles, while it costs 400 dollars on the world market. But we cannot sell it to our friends for 400 dollars.

I went to this plant. You walk through the departments and feel like you are continually stepping from the Stone Age into modernity and back. And people's moods are different in different departments. In one, young people are eager to work, others are empty. Some departments are pure scrap metal, built in the '50s or even '30s. We should let the plants earn hard currency.

Hungary and Poland have three times as much differentiated trade with the West as we do. We look at them askance when they walk away toward the West, but we cannot replace [Western goods] with anything.

In CMEA we almost have no trade, only primitive exchange. Oil is the main item. And our representatives feel no need to trade with them. And they do not feel it either. In the European Union there is a market, but not in CMEA. They [Eastern Europeans] even sell us food for currency now.

Our [foreign] assistance alone takes 41 billion rubles annually from our budget. Cuba takes 27 billion. In [our] relations with CMEA, we must take care of our own people first of all. It has become unbearably hard for us to conduct business as we have been doing in previous decades. The comprehensive program is dead. This is a very important issue.

Those who conclude that the economic situation in the socialist system has a tendency to worsen are right. And that leads to socio-political aggravation. Since we are making this judgment, we have to have a precise analysis of where we stand while conducting a calm discussion. We need to look into everything.

For instance, Poland, [First Secretary Edward] Gierek. What was it all based on? On credits from the West and on our cheap fuel. The same goes for Hungary. There are specific features in Yugoslavia. But even Yugoslavia is on the brink of collapse. We should draw lessons from all this.

What is our approach? Our priority is political stability in the socialist countries. This is our vital interest, from the point of view of security as well.

We need the goods from the socialist countries. And we bear our own responsibility for socialism. In the economic sense, socialism has not passed the test of practice. Therefore we should hang on even though the situation is strangling us. This is the first thing we should keep in mind. We cannot isolate ourselves from CMEA. But what is to be done? The main objective in our approach is what we are trying to do today—to step up the application of the STR results, machine-building, technological reconstruction. This will liberate [the socialist camp] from the need to purchase technology from the West. Consequently, this will free up hard currency. And it will have great significance from the point of view of quality and increasing prosperity. There is nothing more important than the STR. Through the STR we will get our friends interested in trading with us.

We should raise the question in the CMEA candidly: should we become integrated or not? And they must make up their mind, because we cannot remain a provider of cheap resources for them forever. If they tell us "no," then our hands are free. Phrase it exactly like that: either-or. And it is time to stop releasing triumphant information about the relationships in the CMEA. Everyone knows what the situation is really like.

* * *

ON THE SOCIALIST COUNTRIES' COMMUNIST PARTY MEETING IN HAVANA

Gorbachev: Medvedev was there, his report provides evidence of new trends. Energy and independent thought are growing. We have encouraged this and called for this, and now we are witnessing it. The approach is correct: relying on the collaboration of friends and on equality rather than on a monopoly. We will keep the initiative not due to power but due to intellectual leadership and business-like, comradely dialogue. Of course it was simpler before. But it can no longer be done as it was before. Our friends are already thinking about what is happening here, assimilating it. And by far not everyone understands everything in our approaches and new thinking. There are nuances in our friends' reaction to *perestroika*. This is why the processes are dramatic. [...]

ON THE ECONOMIC SITUATION IN SOCIALIST COUNTRIES.

Ryzhkov: [There are] two difficult questions—the financial and the currency ones. The world price of oil has fallen from 180 to 54 rubles per ton. In five years we have given 40 billion rubles of assistance to other countries. We have no real trade with the socialist countries. We need a real market and currency convertibility. [...]

Ligachev: Some socialist countries are facing political upheavals. In Poland everything is moving in the direction of renunciation of the party. South Yemen needs assistance.

Gorbachev: We receive much troubling information about the situation in the socialist countries. The situation is worsening, which threatens an aggravation of the socio-economic state. We need a balanced analysis of the roots of the events. It seems that the answer here is not simple. The entire world is going through a period of serious changes. It is true that the developed countries are going through this period more quickly and painlessly. We, on the other hand, are behind in scientific-technological progress. Our foreign economic setting is changing. The countries that are more connected to the foreign markets are feeling this especially strongly.

Many mistakes are being made in economic policies. A number of socialist countries have gone into debt; they live off loans at the expense of our oil. We should draw lessons from all this. The stability of the socialist countries is our vital interest from the perspective of both security and our economic interests, because our trade volume with the socialist countries is 80 billion rubles. If the situation begins to crack, the very idea of socialism will be discredited. The socialist countries are a kind of forward defensive position for us.

The key question is what is going on in our country, in particular with the reconstruction of the engineering industry, which needs to be given broad access to the foreign market? Why shouldn't we, for example, sell ball bearings? We should rethink the 13th five-year plan from this perspective. We should not waste our national income on the Afghan war, for example. When we give to somebody we should look at where the money is going. We should not be shy about it. Of course, it would be a mistake to free ourselves from assistance to Cuba or Vietnam. But we should not get involved further, and we should take everything we can from our economic relations with them.

Regarding CMEA: we need to finally clarify the issue of whether we want integration or not. We should prepare a conversation about this at the top level, maybe a meeting at the level of general secretaries.

[Source: Archive of the Gorbachev Foundation. Fond 2. Opis 2. On file at the National Security Archive. Translated by Anna Melyakova.]

Document No. 20: Record of Conversation between Mikhail Gorbachev and Lazar Moisov

March 14, 1988

This excerpt from Chernyaev's notes of a Gorbachev meeting with Yugoslav Communist leader Lazar Moisov in Belgrade provides one of the clearest expressions of Gorbachev's renunciation of intervention in Eastern Europe. Gorbachev says both the United States and the USSR have learned that neither "can impose its will on any country. They could pressure them, but not impose their will." Of course, Yugoslavia had long maintained its independence of Soviet policy. On March 19, Pravda would publish a joint Soviet–Yugoslav declaration from the Belgrade trip that represented perhaps the most authoritative public disavowal of the Brezhnev Doctrine to date, referring to "the impermissibility of interference in internal affairs irrespective of the pretext." However, in conversations with the more dependent Hungarians and Poles, Gorbachev as late as spring 1989 would maintain some ambiguity about just how far autonomous change could go without the Soviets taking some action.

No one can impose anything on anyone. We have common socialist ideals, a common heritage in the classics of Marxism, but each party develops this heritage through its own experience, its traditions, and the consideration of its international position. As for big and small states, I said in my talk with Reagan: today neither the USSR nor the U.S. can impose its will on any country. They could pressure them, but not impose their will. The world is different now, each state strives to determine its fate independently, and we must take that into account. Of course, the major powers carry more responsibility than the smaller countries. But they must not crush the rights of others.

[Source: Archive of the Gorbachev Foundation, Fond 2. Opis 1. On file at the National Security Archive. Translated by Anna Melyakova.]

Document No. 21: Notes of CC CPSU Politburo Session

March 24–25, 1988

This document is fascinating proof that the Soviet leadership was aware of the "spillover" effect of Gorbachev's liberalization, particularly the "glasnost" publications about Stalin and Soviet history, on the countries of Eastern Europe. By this time there were plenty of signals from the communist leadership and Soviet informers in these countries that the East European populations had begun to see Gorbachev as a possible "liberator" from their local regimes. Referring to secrets that might damage Soviet prestige, the KGB's Viktor Chebrikov tells his Politburo colleagues there are some documents that should stay confidential forever. Noteworthy is the outburst of Foreign Minister Shevardnadze that reveals the growing impatience of Soviet reformers with the seemingly immutable conservatism of these regimes. Yegor Ligachev's words betray the fundamental Soviet dilemma: how to reform the USSR without losing "socialism" in Eastern Europe.

DISCUSSION OF THE "NINA ANDREYEVA AFFAIR" [15]

[...] *Ligachev*: Arguably we will muddle through, and survive the attacks [by radical, anti-Stalinist forces in the Soviet mass media], but there are the socialist countries, the world communist movement—what to do about them? Would we risk breaking apart this powerful support that has always existed side-by-side with our socialist countries? History has become politics and, when we deal with it, we should think not only about the past but also about the future.

Chebrikov: I would like to touch upon an unusual question. There are things that should remain secret. I would use this expression: There should be Kremlin secrets. Nobody should learn about them. A man dies and his secret dies with him. Do you understand what I mean? Should we turn inside-out the secret that should pass away? Incidentally, we should look at the experience of other states; they take a strict approach to similar affairs. They have established time-limits: which material should be published after 30 years, which after 50 years; some materials are sent to the archives with the classification "not for publication." [...]

---

[15] In early March 1988, the newspaper *Sovietskaya Rossiya* published a feature article by "a professor from Leningrad," Nina Andreyeva, under the title "I cannot forsake my principles." It quickly became a manifesto of the forces opposed to the radicalization of *perestroika*. Some Politburo members, including Ligachev, encouraged this process. Gorbachev was abroad at the time, but when he returned he used the "Andreyeva affair" as an occasion to root out the conservative forces.

Some time ago I was in charge of the [KGB] archive. Even today I have access to it. I had to read many documents from the 1930's, even before the rehabilitation and even before the post-war years. Those materials had a terrifying effect on me regarding the crimes that had taken place in those years. And of course my perception and understanding underwent a painful transformation, my consciousness was changed. A similar transformation is happening in millions of people right now. It is not a simple process: it happens one way for some people and differently for others; some may disagree with it or refuse it, etc.

Gorbachev: I have been receiving letters in which the authors write: You have set out to destroy what had been built by Stalin—a great state, national order. Of course I understand that if I am called a reactionary it is not just in society. What I am receiving I would not wish any of you to get. But I think that there are goals you believe in, [of which] you are convinced and [for which you are] prepared to go all the way; otherwise what kind of a character are you, what are you doing here? Behind you is the country, the world; and if you, like a petty soul, like a small fry, panic, cry "wolf" and crouch down to save your own skin—then it is all over. […]

Shevardnadze: Primitivism and intellectual narrow-mindedness prevented N.S. Khrushchev from implementing to the end the line of the Twentieth Party Congress [in 1956]. Primitivism and narrow-mindedness, I am deeply convinced, are leading many socialist countries into deadlock. Take, for instance, Bulgaria; take the old leadership of Poland; take the current situation in the German Democratic Republic, in Romania. Is that socialism?

I will be frank: The communist and working class movement today is in a profound crisis, in a most profound crisis. Pick any party. Therefore all the things that we have been doing over here—*perestroika*, renewal, improvement— are revolutionary processes. In essence, they promise the rescue of socialism. And any primitive approach can kill our enlightened cause.

[*Source: Archive of the Gorbachev Foundation. Fond 2. Opis 2. On file at the National Security Archive. Translated by Vladislav Zubok.*]

Document No. 22: Record of the Main Content of Conversation between Mikhail Gorbachev and Gustáv Husák

April 12, 1988

Gorbachev is committed to leading by example rather than telling the East Europeans what to do, but he is not above lubricating the process of change with his personal diplomacy. Here he commiserates with the former Czechoslovak communist leader, Gustáv Husák, who was replaced in December 1987 by the marginally less hardline Miloš Jakeš, about the "difficult but timely step" of leadership transition. "Our support was simple," Gorbachev says, "we just told you to make the decision yourself." Husák remarks that the Czechoslovaks are lagging "by a stage or half a stage" on perestroika *(leaving unmentioned his own resistance to reform), while Gorbachev comments quite candidly that "[g]lasnost is rubbing some people painfully, and some are panicking and getting lost."*

Gorbachev: I welcome you, Cde. Husák, our old and good friend, on behalf of the entire Soviet leadership. A great deal connects us; our relations have been tested by history. We value your enormous contribution to socialism and we are glad that today you are in good health and actively participating in the work of your party.

Here, in our close circle, we can say that you did a great thing and took a difficult but timely step, which has ensured the continuity of the leadership. We know that M. Jakeš values you and consults with you.

G. Husák expresses thanks for the support during "that difficult time."

Gorbachev: Our support was simple: we just told you to make the decision yourself.

Husák: I do not regret the decision I made, it was the right one. At the CC CPCz Presidium and at the Plenum everything went smoothly. Now I fully support Jakeš, he needs it. After all, authority is not acquired overnight.

Gorbachev: M. Jakeš should be supported. He is a diligent, honest person; he was by your side during a difficult time of crisis.

Husák: Yes, his actions are energetic, even better than I expected.

Gorbachev: What are the attitudes in the party and in society?

Husák: Overall they are not bad. People support the direction of the leadership, and they understand the slogans of *perestroika* and democratization. But these ideas have not seeped into people's souls yet.

Gorbachev: From our personal experience we know that it is a long process. It won't happen that you fall asleep before *perestroika* and wake up after it.

Husák: At the April Plenum Jakeš said that we should not expect quick results. The Plenum has become the mobilizing factor for all party organs. In April we will have regional party conferences, and in May *oblast* party conferences.

Gorbachev: At the June Plenum the CC decided to prepare reports by party organs at the end of the year, where the party organs would report to communists on the progress of *perestroika*. In some places such meetings began to revert to the old ways, so we had to stop. We unfurled a program in the press, stirred up the party, and then a real, serious conversation started.

Husák: We can say that we are behind you by a stage or half a stage, but our people are accepting the *perestroika* slogans.

Gorbachev: The nature of stages, of course, is very relative. But right now is just such a moment when the difference between them is clear. During the first stage everyone here actively made speeches for this or that aim of *perestroika*, although by far not everybody understood exactly what they were talking about. Now the time has come to introduce directly a self-supporting basis for the economy and elections for the leadership. *Glasnost* is rubbing some people painfully, and some are panicking and getting lost.

Husák: I am following your work very carefully.

[...]

[*Source: Archive of the Gorbachev Foundation, Fond 1. Opis 1. On file at the National Security Archive. Translated by Anna Melyakova.*]

Document No. 23: Record of the Main Content of a Telephone Conversation between Mikhail Gorbachev and János Kádár

May 19, 1988

This transcript offers a fascinating view into Moscow's relations with the fraternal allies during the Gorbachev era. Three days before the Hungarian party conference at which long-time communist leader János Kádár is to be replaced by the reform-minded premier, Károly Grósz, Kádár checks in with the Kremlin: "I deemed it my duty to make sure you did not find out about our changes through the newspapers." According to this transcript, the Hungarians first relay word through KGB chief Vladimir Kryuchkov, then Kádár speaks with Gorbachev directly, who says "I welcome your decision." Gorbachev's role in the telephone call, again, is not to dictate but to reinforce, offer reassurance, and leave the responsibility with the Hungarians; but "welcome" is very much the appropriate word. Kádár works on face-saving measures, presenting the changes as largely his own idea. Most striking in retrospect is the illusion both men held that leadership changes and a little perestroika *would allow the party (both in Budapest and in Moscow) to "consolidate" its position and stay out in front of popular demands for reform.*

Gorbachev: Hello, Comrade Kádár! I received the information you sent me. As I understand it, you are coming to the party conference with a conception that has been thought through and that takes into account the situation in Hungary and in the party.

Kádár: That's right. This conception was discussed at the Politburo and my colleagues agreed with it completely.

Gorbachev: It is very important that Comrade Kádár will be keeping his position in the party and that he will stay and direct all the changes during this transition stage. That is how I understood the information relayed to me through Comrade Kryuchkov. I welcome your decision.

Kádár: Yes, that is so. At first we thought about greater changes, but my colleagues at the Politburo convinced me that it would be in the interests of the party to arrange everything as it is right now.

Gorbachev: I understand that you had to make a very difficult decision. The process must not have been easy. This is evidence of the political wisdom of Hungary's leader and of my friend, János Kádár. The most important thing is that the interests of the country and the party were taken into account. I will be frank—I did not expect any other outcome. I was sure that the decision would be made when it was ripe and necessary.

Kádár: I thought about it for a long time.

273

Gorbachev: Of course, our work together has not come to an end; we are going to keep our political and personal connections. That is what I would really like to do. I would be glad to meet with you and exchange opinions on any issue.

Kádár: Thank you. I am touched by your words.

Gorbachev: Your situation and ours are not simple. But the most important thing is that we see a way out of these situations. Particular responsibility lies with our parties.

I would like to repeat once again, Comrade Kádár, that we will continue to work together. I am ready to help Hungary on specific issues as much as I can. For our part, we are counting on the solidarity of our Hungarian comrades in the struggle for *perestroika*.

Kádár: Thank you. That is how it will be. As for our personal contacts, I think that we have found a good form of direct and reliable communications, including the one right now (*laughs*). You have received accurate information. This time the conversation was difficult. It was not the personal aspect that was important to me. Remembering your concern about the Hungarian state of affairs, I deemed it my duty to make sure you did not find out about our changes through the newspapers. That is what I said at the Politburo session, and my comrades supported me. We have always appreciated your interest in Hungary and your understanding of our problems.

Now about some issues concerning me personally. Firstly, I believe that an appropriate form of change in the top leadership has been found. All the Politburo members have supported it. I think that this form is significant domestically and internationally. It is true that lately in Hungary sentiments against my leaving have been getting stronger, our "worst [*zakliatye*] friends" have started talking about it. But I had to make a decision.

Secondly, I will not remain a member of the Politburo. At the conference we will submit a proposal to change the Charter and to establish the new position of Chairman of the HSWP. While he would not be a part of the Politburo, the chairman could still attend any meetings of the leadership and express his opinion. What were our reasons for this? It was the fact that matters do not progress very well when both the old and the new leaders are part of the governing body. Members of the Politburo look in both directions, and nothing good comes out of that. If it is necessary, I could always speak with any member of the leadership privately or be present at any meeting.

Thirdly, the need to lessen my personal physical load was another reason that led me to this decision. It had become burdensome to me.

I want to assure you that our relations will remain the same.

Gorbachev: Thank you for that message.

Kádár: I think that the conference will be useful and will provide an opportunity to clarify important questions. Most importantly, the party's course for the socialist development of our country will be defined more exactly. We think that the conference will allow us to consolidate the party's position as well.

We had a problem with the question of whether a change of leadership was appropriate at a conference. At the last CC Plenum we had at first submitted a proposal to change about one-third of the leadership, but the feelings were such that we had to go beyond what is outlined in the Charter. It was decided at the Plenum to propose at the conference to re-elect the entire membership of the CC and the CCC [Central Control Committee]. Therefore, the CC will not resign, and its mandate will be in effect until the next congress.

There will not be a report at the conference. I will only make an introduction and comment on the draft of the resolution. The CC Plenum fully supported such an approach to the conference.

The HSWP has the post of Deputy General Secretary, but this time we will bypass that provision of the Charter and will leave the position vacant. There is one argument for that: if a leader is 70 or older he needs a deputy. But if the general secretary is 57 he does not need one.

Moreover, with the agreement of Politburo members at the CC organizational Plenum, after the conference I will make a proposal to elect CC secretaries rather than a CC Secretariat. That way, we will eliminate a link in the leadership chain. If this passes, in the future the party will sanction a governing body—the Politburo—which has direct access to all party organizations, down to the primary ones.

CC secretaries will oversee designated sections and direct the apparatus, but it must be clear that there is only one governing body in the party.

Gorbachev: That is a very interesting and important proposal.

Kádár: I have had this idea for a long time and I thought that now would be a good time to implement it. Even before this, we had the principle that elective bodies would lead the party, but in practice it was always distorted in favor of the apparatus. Now all the major questions will be decided in the Politburo. At the same time we eliminate the problem of dividing the *nomenklatura* between the Politburo and the Secretariat.

I thank you for the phone call and for your attention to our affairs. In the spirit of what has been said, I will try to continue working, and implementing what will be decided at the conference.

We know that you have a conference coming up. Plus, Reagan will be visiting you in a week. The U.S. Senate's position on the issue of ratification seems to be changing for the positive; the senators even voted that you and Reagan have the authority to sign the document. As I heard it, 91 senators expressed this view.

Gorbachev (*laughing*): Yes, yes, at the meeting we presented our powers.

Kádár: It seems they are following a policy of delaying the agreement for the reduction of offensive weapons. It looks like they do not want to give this issue to Reagan, they want to save it for the new president.

Of course, the U.S. president's visit is very important, but the main thing is the conference. We are all rooting for you. I wish you good health and send my greetings to your colleagues in the CPSU leadership. Also say hello to Raisa Maksimovna [Gorbachev].

Gorbachev: I can only express my complete agreement and understanding. I have neither questions nor doubts about this.

Briefly about our affairs. Today a Politburo session took place. We discussed and approved theses for the party conference. We feel that it is an interesting document, one that provides a good platform for discussion and for work at the conference. The expectations the people and the party have for this conference are enormous. This obliges us to be at our best.

After the meeting with Reagan I will devote all my time to preparing the report. The party and the entire country are mobilized right now. We are living in a difficult but great time; we must make sure that *perestroika* succeeds. It has to work.

Once again, I emphasize that we are on the threshold of major events. I am glad to speak with you. I embrace you and wish you good health and success. Please give my heartfelt hello to all the colleagues in your leadership.

[*Source:* Mikhail Gorbachev: Zhizn' i reformy [*Mikhail Gorbachev: Life and Reforms*], *Novosti: 1995, pp. 331–333. Translated by Anna Melyakova.*]

Document No. 24: Comments from Georgy Shakhnazarov on Viktor Kulikov's Report at the Warsaw Treaty PCC

May 25, 1988

This biting and often sarcastic memo by top Gorbachev aide Georgy Shakhnazarov deconstructs the inertia and old thinking demonstrated by the Soviet commander of Warsaw Treaty Organization forces, Marshal Viktor Kulikov, and by implication, the entire Soviet military establishment. A year after Gorbachev insisted to the Politburo that a doctrine of sufficiency should replace the old commitment to parity with NATO (see Document No. 12), Kulikov insists to the WTO's Political Coordinating Committee that the danger of war in Europe is actually increasing and that stockpiles, airstrips, "chemical support" and airborne troops all need to be expanded. Shakhnazarov comments that the economies in almost every East European country are in a pre-crisis state, in part due to the military burden. He also informs Gorbachev that the military, through their plans, could undermine the international credibility of new disarmament initiatives by interpreting "the concept of a defensive doctrine in a highly bizarre way." Gorbachev's response in the document unfortunately does not specify what kind of instructions Defense Minister Marshal Dmitri Yazov actually received from the Soviet leader. Yazov himself later would deny that there was "any new doctrine" adopted for the WTO. William Odom's 1998 study[16] of the Soviet military shows that they only paid lip service to the formulas presented by Gorbachev and his civilian advisers.

---

1. I get the impression that, despite many assurances of loyalty to a defensive military doctrine, a genuine reappraisal of strategic conceptions in this direction has not even begun in our country.

   On page 3 of the report [Viktor Kulikov] attempts to prove a thesis that, despite the INF Agreement, the danger of war in Europe will not decrease, but in fact will increase. Arguments used to prove this notion are not convincing. Meanwhile it effectively justifies a program of reciprocal increases in our military power. When planning the rearmament of all branches of the armed forces, [the military] does not provide data about the resources this would require, although the list alone makes it clear that military expenditures would not go down, but would go up significantly. And this is being proposed when the process of disarmament has begun and, in particular, the prospect of talks and the achievement of an agreement on conventional arms reductions and military forces in Europe is becoming brighter.

---

[16] Odom, *The Collapse of the Soviet Military.*

2. It has been known for a long time that the Romanians have been bluntly rejecting our programs for a military build-up, and the leaderships of other [East European] countries accept them without enthusiasm, united by Alliance discipline. Nevertheless, the report includes a rebuke to the fraternal countries which are more frequently refusing to purchase [Soviet] armaments (p. 6).

Military expenditures in Eastern Europe (albeit according to Western data) are twice as high per capita as in the majority of NATO countries. Our friends understandably cannot afford to carry this burden any further, particularly under pre-crisis economic conditions in almost every [East European] country. Which is more profitable for us: that they continue their arms build-up and march towards economic disaster or, on the other hand, that they save on military expenditures and improve their economic situation, reinforcing *de facto* the security of the commonwealth?

3. The thesis that the role of "chemical support of troop combat actions" has increased (p. 5) is doubtful. The report also says that chemical troops will be reinforced with flame-throwers and camouflage (p. 11). How does this correspond to our declarations of readiness for a complete ban on and liquidation of chemical weapons?

4. The document contains a declaration about the need to support military-strategic parity with NATO (p. 7).

This thesis under current conditions should be spelled out to avoid its "verbatim" implementation.

5. It is not clear what is meant [when it is said] that the combat and numerical strength of each allied army "is intended to be preserved on the level prescribed by the Protocols by the end of 1999." Does this mean a planned over-fulfillment, building up a larger military force ahead of time?

6. An example showing that [the military] understands the concept of a defensive doctrine in a highly bizarre way can be found in the thesis concerning the intention to devote more attention in the next five-year plan to shock-assault detachments (p. 9). Until now this arm of the service has not predominantly existed for defensive tasks.

Another example: on page 11 the report recommends increasing the stockpile of fuel and ammunition, creating these stockpiles on the territory of Hungary and Bulgaria, and creating stockpiles of armaments and equipment for the deployment of reserve formations, etc.

On p. 12 the report points out the need to expand the network of airstrips, and to continue equipping protective hangars for military aircraft.

In general the report admits that implementation of the prescribed tasks, which should maintain military-strategic parity, would require large-scale efforts by the Allied Command and the Ministry of Defense to equip troops, and large-scale mobilization of the scientific and industrial potential of the socialist countries.

In other words, overall the report speaks not about a reduction of military efforts, but, on the contrary, their intensification. It would not be at all surprising that even if the report of the commander-in-chief does not leak to the West (and under present circumstances in the WTO such leaks cannot be excluded), the West would easily be able to conclude, on the basis of the facts and of those measures for a build-up that would be implemented, that in reality we do not want to disarm—moreover, we do not even want to lower the level of armed confrontation.

In essence, the document presented does not indicate that any attempt is pending to reassess the real military-strategic situation in Europe. The key component of this situation is the continuing Western intention to preserve nuclear arsenals at a certain level. The focus is still on nuclear deterrence but not on the task of waging an offensive war by conventional means. With this in mind, we should rethink our strategy. Existing nuclear means protect us from direct aggression and thereby make a further increase in conventional armaments and military forces redundant.

On the other hand, as many politicians from the Left are telling us, with some justice, only our concrete steps to reduce armaments will trigger corresponding measures in the West. This will provoke such a wave of popular movement there that governments will have to move towards us.

Then should we provide bourgeois militarists with arguments to continue and intensify the arms race?

Resolution of M.S. Gorbachev: "Cde. D.T. Yazov received instructions."

[Source: Published in G.Kh. Shakhnazarov's Tsena svobody *[The Price of Freedom] (Moscow: Rossika-Zeus, 1993) Translated by Vladislav Zubok.]*

Document No. 25: National Intelligence Estimate 11/12-9-88, "Soviet Policy toward Eastern Europe under Gorbachev"

May 1988

At the end of May 1988, Ronald Reagan would walk through Red Square in Moscow and pronounce that the "evil empire" was from "another time, another era." Judging by this National Intelligence Estimate, the president at this stage is well ahead of his own intelligence community. Because NIEs emerge from a painstaking bureaucratic process involving all intelligence agencies in a search for consensus, sharp language and pointed findings are usually lacking. This was especially the case with Soviet estimates during this period when hardliners in the U.S. Defense Department and at the top of the CIA suspected Gorbachev's motives. In this context, this NIE (based on information available to analysts as of May 26) makes a fairly bold conclusion—that almost any government in Eastern Europe would be acceptable to Moscow as long as it called itself communist. The USSR would invade only "in extremis," the analysis states, because Gorbachev is facing "greater constraints than did his predecessors against intervening militarily in Eastern Europe." Yet it is Gorbachev's own attempts to bring perestroika *to the other communist countries that "have increased the potential for instability in Eastern Europe." The NIE envisions three "extreme" scenarios, each of which would in fact materialize over the coming months, and in far more dramatic and sweeping forms than the NIE imagined: (1) a backlash in East Germany and Romania against Gorbachev's reform policies, (2) a popular upheaval in Poland, Hungary or Romania against the party and the Soviets, and (3) sweeping reform in Poland or Hungary, even beyond* perestroika.

KEY JUDGMENTS[17]

General Secretary Gorbachev's policies have increased the potential for instability in Eastern Europe. But they have also expanded the scope for diversity and experimentation, affording new possibilities for evolutionary reform in the region.

Gorbachev has set an ambitious agenda for Eastern Europe. His aims are to secure East European support for the Soviet modernization drive, promote broader Soviet foreign policy objectives through closer Warsaw Pact coordination, and stimulate a deeper process of economic and political regeneration in the region. Aware of the region's diversity, he has set general guidelines for reform rather than detailed plans. But he faces East European realities—severe economic problems, aging leaderships, and mounting social discontent—that conflict with Soviet objectives.

---

[17] Information available as of May 26, 1988 [as indicated in original document].

Soviet policy under Gorbachev has sought to balance the competing objectives of encouraging change and promoting stability. Although Gorbachev has avoided a high-risk strategy of forcing change on these fragile political systems, continuing Soviet pressure, as well as the example of the Soviet reform program, has introduced new tensions into the region.

Growing Diversity, Sharper Conflict

For the next three to five years, Eastern Europe's outlook is for growing diversity—in responding to reform pressures, crafting approaches to the West, and managing relations with Moscow.

– Economically, Eastern Europe cannot deliver what Gorbachev wants. As the gap between goals and results grows more acute, Gorbachev is likely to exert stronger pressure on his allies to forge closer economic ties, upgrade performance, and implement domestic economic reforms.

– While the recent leadership change in Hungary probably comes close to Gorbachev's preferences for Eastern Europe, prospective successions elsewhere are not likely to yield the dynamic, innovative leaders Gorbachev needs to achieve his more ambitious goals in the region. Consequently, his pressures for change will continue to be aimed at regimes ill-equipped and, in some cases, unwilling to respond.

Thus, at best, Gorbachev's approach can achieve only evolutionary progress toward political rejuvenation and improved economic performance in Eastern Europe. Continued, and probably heightened, Soviet pressure will lead to sharper conflicts, and both with Eastern European societies and between Moscow and its allies.

Potential Challenges to Soviet Control

Cross-pressures emanating from Moscow, coupled with severe economic and political dilemmas in Eastern Europe, could yield more serious challenges to Soviet interests. Three extreme scenarios are possible:

– *Popular upheaval* in Poland, Romania, Hungary, involving a broad-based challenge to party supremacy and ultimately to Soviet control.

– *Sweeping reform* in Hungary or Poland, going well beyond Gorbachev's agenda and eventually threatening to erode party control.

– *Conservative backlash*, involving open repudiation of Soviet policies by orthodox leaders in East Germany, Romania, or elsewhere.

Of these, popular upheaval is the most likely contingency. Gorbachev will expect his allies to act decisively to end any political violence or major unrest. Indeed, East European leaders are at least as aware of the need for vigilance as Gorbachev is, and they have at their disposal powerful security forces that have proved effective in containing unrest. Should events spin out of their control and beyond the limits of Soviet tolerance, the ultimate controlling factor on change in Eastern Europe will be Soviet force:

– Gorbachev faces greater constraints than did his predecessors against intervening militarily in Eastern Europe; his foreign policy and arms control agenda, and much of his domestic program as well, would be threatened.

– A Dubček-like regime would have much greater latitude to pursue reforms now than in 1968, and Soviet intervention to stop it would be more problematic.

– In extremis, however, there is no reason to doubt his willingness to intervene to preserve party rule and decisive Soviet influence in the region. [...]

DISCUSSION

[...] *Outlook: Growing Diversity, Sharper Conflict*

26. Soviet policy toward Eastern Europe is likely to continue along the lines already established under Gorbachev. Its key elements will be:

– Within the framework of firm party control, *sanctioning of diversity and experimentation* as the keys to economic and political viability.

– Continued *pressure for reform* without dictating specific measures or demanding slavish emulation of Soviet practices.

– Insistence on *foreign policy coordination*, whereby the East Europeans are afforded greater room for tactical maneuver but are expected to hew closely to the broad lines set in Moscow.

– Mounting pressure for *improved East European economic performance* and increased cooperation in high-technology areas.

– Longer term efforts toward *strengthened institutional ties*, coupled with alliance management techniques that facilitate Soviet control and influence through a more participatory system of give-and-take.

27. These broad contours of Soviet policy will remain in place so long as Gorbachev's domestic position is secure and Eastern Europe remains quiescent. A major change in Moscow would obviously alter the equation:

– *Gorbachev's ouster* would curtail the Soviet reform drive and heighten uncertainties in Eastern Europe as the new regime sorted itself out. His removal on political grounds would send another new signal to the divided East European regimes—this time a sharply antireformist one—and undercut Soviet authority, at least temporarily.

– *Retrenchment in Moscow* (with Gorbachev still in office) would strengthen the existing orthodox leaders in Eastern Europe without fully arresting the pressures for change. Perceived lack of unity in the Kremlin would further polarize Eastern Europe, with conservatives seeking to restore the status quo ante and reformists continuing to push for change.

– *More daring Soviet reforms*—a result, perhaps, of Gorbachev's need to overcome bureaucratic resistance through radical policy and personnel changes—would further destabilize Eastern Europe and strain relations with Moscow. Rising pressures within the East European regimes might prompt some of them to implement sweeping reforms or force out existing leaders.

28. Gorbachev has played a skillful political game so far, pulling back when necessary while gathering support for the next push forward. Although the chances of a domestic showdown have increased, Gorbachev seems to have the upper hand and appears inclined to push his reform agenda further and more forcefully.

29. *Growing Diversity.* For the next three to five years, the outlook in Eastern Europe is for growing diversity—in responding to reform pressures, crafting approaches to the West, and managing relations with Moscow. Diverse East European arms control proposals and economic approaches to the West will facilitate some Soviet objectives, but they will also complicate the tasks of alliance management and run counter to the joint action needed for scientific-technological cooperation. In Gorbachev's broader view, moreover, diversity is no end in itself but rather a vehicle for economic and political regeneration. These goals are nowhere in sight in Eastern Europe. Except perhaps in Hungary, they are not likely even to be seriously pursued.

30. *Glasnost* and *perestroika* will continue to yield mixed results. Barring leadership changes, Romania and East Germany will continue to resist reform pressures; Bulgaria will continue to experiment at the margins but will proceed only haltingly toward real "restructuring." The new Czechoslovak leadership under [Miloš] Jakeš will push more forcefully for economic change, but serious movement toward economic and political reform remains a distant prospect. Hungary and Poland could be more interesting:

– The appointment of Károly Grósz—a tough, self-confident risk taker in the Gorbachev mold—as General Secretary of the Hungarian party and the promotion into the leadership of outspoken reform advocates marks an important turning point. The new leadership is likely to be much more aggressive in pressing economic and political reforms, but it faces severe problems—including workers unhappy with austerity, intellectuals demanding more freedom, and an economy that is stagnating and burdened with a heavy foreign debt. Failure to develop a more radical and effective reform program would further contribute to a rise in tensions.

– Evidently with Soviet blessings, General Jaruzelski has already consolidated a rather unorthodox pattern of party-military rule, moved toward granting the Catholic Church new legal status, and proposed economic reforms that, on paper at least, go well beyond Moscow's. The disastrous economic situation and social discontent—as shown by the recent wave of strikes—make successful realization of the reforms unlikely, but the urgency of domestic problems may also push the regime toward the social dialogue it has rejected up to now.

31. In foreign policy, the East European regimes have reason to be satisfied with Gorbachev's skillful engagement of the West and their own increased room for maneuver. So long as Moscow maintains a conciliatory approach to the West, Soviet and East European policies will remain generally congruent. At the same time, Gorbachev's encouragement of a more active role for the East Europeans will increase the chances for open conflicts of interest at CSCE (Conference on Security and Cooperation in Europe) talks and in other Pan-European

forums. There will also be increased risk of further embarrassments to Moscow arising from Hungarian–Romanian polemics or the public airing of East European human rights violations. Hence, foreign policy coordination will require more skillful management, and Gorbachev will need to prod the Czechoslovak and Bulgarian regimes toward more active diplomacy while restraining the occasional independent-mindedness of the Romanians, Hungarians, Poles, and East Germans.

32. At the same time, East European realities will limit the parameters of possible Soviet initiatives. Not only must Gorbachev weigh the consequences of Soviet policies on political stability in Eastern Europe, but he must also take into account the perceptions and likely reactions of East European leaders. Their views are not likely to deter him from policies he considers vital to Soviet interests; but, on matters as potentially destabilizing as inter-German relations, his options are limited. Indeed, Gorbachev's campaign for a common "European house" of growing intra-European cooperation implies a degree of national autonomy in Eastern Europe far beyond what he or any other Soviet leader would countenance. Moscow will find it increasingly difficult to promote this line in the West without introducing new divisions into Eastern Europe as well. (The Berlin Wall will stay, whatever tactical advantages Gorbachev might see in its removal.) [...]

Potential Challenges to Soviet Control

45. There are at least three more extreme scenarios that could lead to serious challenges to Soviet control over Eastern Europe.

46. The Hungarian Revolution of 1956, the 1968 Prague Spring, and the Polish social revolution of 1980–1 (along with numerous other lesser upheavals) provide ample evidence of the inherent instability of Moscow's East European empire. Each of these had its own dynamic, but each led ultimately to a broad-based challenge to party supremacy and Soviet control in the region. And each led to crisis—meaning in the East European context the actuality or imminent likelihood of Soviet military intervention.

47. However, Gorbachev's sanctioning of reform and experimentation implies a more liberal Soviet definition of "crisis." Liberalizing reform (of the kind espoused by the 1968 Czechoslovak leadership) may no longer lead so swiftly and automatically to a "crisis situation" in Moscow's eyes.

48. *Popular upheaval.* Several of the usual instability indicators—discontent over living standards, weak and divided leadership, social unrest—are evident in several countries, and all face pressures emanating from Moscow. New shocks—severe austerity measures, the death or ouster of a top party leader, or the emergence of an organized and emboldened opposition—could bring about serious instability almost anywhere, with Poland, Romania, and Hungary the most likely candidates for trouble:

– The likelihood of multiple, simultaneous upheavals is higher than it has been in more than 30 years. In the late 1980s and into the early 1990s, virtually

all the East European countries face analogous sets of problems: stagnant economies, leadership successions and reformist pressures from Moscow.

– As in the past, however, possible scenarios would be highly country-spe-
cific. Only in Romania is there a significant possibility of widespread violence;
elsewhere, the greater likelihood would be a broad-based, organized challenge
to regime authority. (In Poland, however, this latter scenario could also lead to
a cycle of repression and violence.)

49. For Gorbachev, a possible upheaval in Eastern Europe constitutes the
greatest external threat to the Soviet reform program and his own continued tenure. Despite the greater tolerance he has shown for experimentation, he will expect his allies to take swift, decisive action to end any political violence or major
unrest. Indeed, the East European leaderships are at least as aware as Gorbachev
is of the need for vigilance, and they have at their disposal large security forces
that have been effective thus far in containing disturbances. Should events over-
whelm the capacity of local leaders, there is no reason to doubt that he would
take whatever action was required, including military intervention, to preserve
party rule and Soviet authority in the region. Like his predecessors, Gorbachev
would exhaust all other options before undertaking Soviet military intervention.
Indeed, he faces even greater constraints:

– A Soviet invasion of an allied country would do irreparable damage to his
image in the West and undermine the entire edifice of his foreign policy.

– An upheaval in Eastern Europe, particularly one attributable to Gorbachev's
reform pressures, could also threaten his domestic standing. It would add domestic political pressures for his removal from power and the curtailment of his reform program.

[*Source: Central Intelligence Agency:* At Cold War's End: US Intelligence on the
Soviet Union and Eastern Europe, 1989–1991. *Ed: Benjamin B. Fischer, 1999.*]

Document No. 26: Notes of CC CPSU Politburo Session

June 20, 1988

In the Musgrove dialogue, Ambassador Jack Matlock comments that he reached a turning point in his opinion of the Gorbachev reforms—that they were fundamental, not just tactical or public relations moves—when he read in the May 27, 1988, edition of Pravda the texts of the theses for the upcoming XIX Party Conference of the CPSU. At the time, Matlock was in Helsinki briefing President Reagan for his imminent trip to Moscow. These Chernyaev notes provide an exclamation mark on the dramatic change Matlock had detected. They cover one of the many Politburo discussions held in June 1988 concerning the statement the general secretary planned to deliver to the Party Conference, which took place June 28 through July 1. (Multiple staff groups had been working at the Central Committee and at the leadership's dachas to produce drafts for the speech.)

Chernyaev's notes do not mention Eastern Europe, but they illustrate the zenith of Gorbachev's revolution from above. Even the conservative stalwart, Andrei Gromyko, then chairman of the Presidium of the USSR Supreme Soviet, feels obliged to join the chorus of "new thinking" and support unilateral reductions of arms. Gorbachev's hands-off attitude toward the mass media brings to mind the policies of Alexander Dubček 20 years earlier, at the outbreak of the "Prague Spring" in Czechoslovakia. At the same time, the discussion reveals omens of the future radical reforms that doomed the Soviet Union. Gorbachev proposes the election of communists to state bodies (soviets) "by the free vote of the people. In other words, communists would be in power legally for the first time." This is not only a startling admission about the illegal past, but a revealing statement of Gorbachev's belief that a free vote would sustain the leading role of the party.

POLITBURO DISCUSSION OF GORBACHEV'S DRAFT REPORT TO THE XIX PARTY CONFERENCE.

From Gromyko's remarks: Could the Soviet Union afford to convert all resources to civilian objectives? Hundreds of billions went for military [purposes]. There is one big "but." They wanted to bend us to their will. In the U.N. Security Council we proposed to the United States that we cease the arms race. They rejected our proposals. That is why we could not halt our production of nuclear weapons and did not want to reduce the number of our military bases. They had thousands of those. And we could not do otherwise in the name of the country's independence.

During Khrushchev's time we built 600 bombs (nuclear). He said then: how long are we going to do it? Under Brezhnev we could have taken a more rational position. But we continued to stick to the principle: they are in a race and we are in a race, as in sports.

286

Science and intelligent people had already arrived at a conclusion about the senselessness of this race. But both they and we continued it. We approached this issue in a primitive way. And our high command proceeded from the assumption that if a war was started, we would win it. And so we made more and more nuclear weapons. That was our mistaken position, absolutely mistaken. And the political leadership bears the entire blame for it.

Tens of billions were spent on production of those toys; we did not have enough brains. But you all know how those issues were decided then. We should strengthen this point in the theses. I believe that it would make the report a contribution to policy and theory in this sphere.

Ligachev: How do we admit people to the Party now? Here are the statistics. Every 16th worker gets admitted, and every second-to-fourth person from among scientists, writers, and the like.

Gorbachev: This issue is unresolved indeed. We cannot admit everybody who wants to [join] the Party, and at the same time, we cannot alter the nature of our workers' party. We also admit very few young people. We need some criteria.

The mass media are doing a great job with *perestroika*. We would not have moved anywhere without them. However, we would have to say that group-think dominates the media. We need to say that in the process of criticizing, the press puts a person in a position where he has no rights. As Lenin said, what comes out is "literary jockeying." *Glasnost* should be healing. And how would you heal if a person cannot respond to what has been written about him? The framework of *glasnost*, the framework of democracy, the framework of socialism—we need to think these through and speak about them openly. [...]

It has been proposed that we should emphasize even more strongly that we managed to remove the threat of nuclear war; we should stress this even more. Yegor Kuzmich [Ligachev] has proposed that. However, I would not get too excited about it. We came to a correct understanding of the situation, and we should give it a dispassionate assessment.

It says in the first draft "thanks to our power." No—thanks to new thinking. If we do not stress realism and do not propose realistic things nobody on the other side will meet us halfway, and nothing good will happen. This is a collective process, even though the conclusion that the threat of war has been removed is very important. It is very important that the world has woken up and is taking its fate into its own hands [...]

About the Komsomol. We used to have this phrase: "in partnership with the CPSU." I do not insist on the term "under the leadership," but we should somehow state it so that relations with public organizations are understood in a democratic way. But not in such a way that everybody would read it as they want: what it means to lead, but not to order about. I understand it as ideological and political influence on the youth. In other words, I am in favor of leadership, but in a correct form.

The question is how to combine democracy and *glasnost* with the strong central power that is necessary for our big country and a multinational state.

287

Therefore, we proposed this formula: "in conjunction with the party leadership." There were many doubts. Still, I think, we should not propose anything else here—yet. We said: "at this stage," i.e. the present political culture does not allow anything more significant. Among the Novo-Ogarevo team,[18] many people were not excited about this phrase. But I am deeply convinced, and I have thought this way all my life, that Lenin's idea of "soviets [councils] with communists" is a promising and correct idea. If we want to ensure the success of *perestroika*, we cannot do it without the party. If we do not find appropriate organizational solutions for its implementation, it will not work. We need to strengthen the executive committees, but only by strengthening the soviets themselves, assuming that communists would be elected to them by the free vote of the people. In other words, communists would be in power legally for the first time. And that way we would have a check on the general secretary, not so that he can do anything: he can do anything, but only within the law.

In short, we should think about the country, not about our seats. And if somebody has been trying to adjust their work to be liked by Gorbachev, or Shcherbitsky, or Gromyko—we are against it. We initiated a process of a kind that requires us to think and think about the country. And in the future, when we have led the country to a more open state, many things will become clearer.

Shevardnadze: Emphasized the thesis on human rights: how well we expanded it; it is a great cause.

Gorbachev: This section is still raw here. Human rights came from our revolution. And what did it lead to? In short, it will not work in our theses yet.

Shevardnadze is saying that *perestroika* should eliminate the distortions in ethnic relations, and that the section on seceding from the USSR is simplified in our Constitution.

Gorbachev: What are you saying? Under the command-administrative system you can write anything into the Constitution. Under conditions of democracy you need to be careful about it.

We should state honestly that the party will lead, but it will lead exclusively on a legal basis, on the basis of a free mandate from the people.

In the Politburo we were talking about opposition parties. We believe that here we need to develop a firm policy. Only when we present this policy, when it gives results, will we then resolve our doubts about other parties; then everything will fall into place. Now the issue is not multi-party systems, the issue is the correct road for all of society. The soil in which extremism grows is the same we want to leave behind ourselves. And today we are only planning many things.

Comrade Dolgikh was saying here that the people demand that we be on our guard. This is not the issue. Not "on our guard," but we should do our work, so that we have results. For me there is no question about it—socialism, as we see

---

[18] Novo-Ogarevo was a state house (dacha) near Moscow where advisers and speechwriters gathered to draft Gorbachev's speeches and other documents.

it now, fits the principles of democracy. But we will not achieve such socialism without the party, and we should reform the party.

Regarding the mass media. Everybody seems to support the thesis that democracy and *glasnost* do not mean anarchy. Many of us are inclined to press them down a little. But I would say that now we have accumulated some experience, and now we are already in a position to write a law on the mass media. We could not do it before now. We were rightly afraid that we could strangle them [the media] to death.

I would say the same about the KGB. Let the country live, and let the KGB work in the new situation. Later, we will see.

Vorotnikov gives a high appraisal of the international section of the theses. He notes that we did indeed let ourselves get pulled into the arms race. We found ourselves on the brink of a catastrophe.

Gorbachev: This is the softest term. [We] could use stronger words.

Vorotnikov: It is not imperialism; we are the ones to blame. We failed to use all [available] means for peace. We were pulled into somebody else's logic.

Gorbachev: There is a stupid dialectic here: if they do it, we will also. There were opportunities, yes, but we got sucked into it. If you look closely, we were always catching up, and we did not use political methods to achieve our objectives in a proper manner. This admission can alleviate our guilt to some degree. We wanted to ensure strategic parity. That is a good concept, strategic parity. But we were pursuing simply parity, mechanical parity. Did we want to have parity with all of NATO? To race the entire world regarding the levels of armaments: cannon by cannon, plane by plane? Then let us introduce ration cards for food, turn the country into a military camp, and just race and race onwards.

The situation has been changing, and now it is completely different. And we still have not used what we possess. We are not changing direction. But we were not capable of using our peace-loving capabilities in a reasonable way. Originally, we wrote in our theses that we found ourselves on the brink of war. That was how it was in the original draft, but then we decided to soften the wording so that we did not scare anybody.

[Source: Archive of the Gorbachev Foundation. Fond 2. Opis 2. On file at the National Security Archive. Translated by Svetlana Savranskaya.]

Document No. 27: Speech by Mikhail Gorbachev at a Dinner with Wojciech Jaruzelski

July 11, 1988

In remarks drafted by Georgy Shakhnazarov, Gorbachev toasts his hosts at a private state dinner in Warsaw, then goes beyond the usual thanks for hospitality to provide a detailed explanation of his concept of the common European home. First mentioned by Gorbachev in London in 1984, publicly announced in Prague in April 1987 (see Document No. 11) and most fully detailed in Strasbourg in July 1989, the idea of the common European home provides the foundation of Gorbachev's strategy to end the Cold War. For many Westerners (often referred to in these documents as the "reactionary circles") this rhetoric sounds too much like the traditional Soviet effort to split Europe from the United States under the guise of "peaceful coexistence"; and it would not be until the end of 1989 that Washington's leadership, to take one prominent group, would comprehend that Gorbachev was truly pursuing something very new. Here, to an insider communist audience of Poles and Russians, the Soviet leader ties the idea directly to the Helsinki process, underway since 1975, and proposes (not for the first or the last time) that concrete steps are needed not only to transform the military blocs with the goal of liquidating them but also to build an economically-integrated Europe. Perhaps most important is Gorbachev's endorsement of "socialist pluralism." This concept would give Moscow's advance blessing to events just two months away—the renewed Solidarity protests in August which would bring the Polish authorities back into a dialogue with the opposition in September and lead to the negotiated revolution of 1989.

I will start by expressing my sincere gratitude for the heartfelt welcome. Everywhere we went today we were greeted by open, friendly people. Everywhere we saw something more than mere hospitality. Sincere interest in our country, sympathy, human kindness—that is what distinguished our meetings today. We see the great interest of the Polish public in the developments of Soviet *perestroika* as a factor of great political importance. [...]

My participation in the work of the Sejm left an unforgettable impression. The meeting with the elected representatives of the Polish people confirmed that the robust Soviet–Polish union is a mighty tree, which has deep roots, a wide crown, and many new strong branches. [...]

I think that the concept of socialist pluralism is also applicable to relations between the parties and countries of the socialist world. A respectful attitude to each other's interests, and numerous, often diverging views and experiences—this is not only the basis of mutual understanding and healthy, genuinely friendly ties, it is also a source of acceleration for our movement forward. [...]

I will allow myself in this connection to talk about what content we invest in the concept of a common European home

Both historically and politically this idea is a direct continuation of those ideas that were included in the All-European Conference in its time. The Helsinki process was a great achievement; its potential is far from exhausted, and unquestionably it should be continued. However, the course of European politics shows that a number of problems extend beyond the framework of this process. We have to go further, to rethink the entire situation in Europe from the standpoint of the new political thinking.

A breakthrough is necessary first of all in European security. We can solve this problem in a big, radical way only if we follow a course toward a continuous process of disarmament—nuclear, chemical, and conventional. Lately some reassuring signs have appeared in this area. Now there are contacts not only between political figures and societies, but also between military figures. Naturally, the public feels safer when generals meet at negotiating tables rather than sitting in shelters.

In this manner, a kind of "peaceful coexistence of military blocs" is forming. And if we succeed in continuing to move toward increasing levels of trust, we will be able, as athletes say, to raise the bar of politics in Europe by aiming at the liquidation of military blocs. If the resolution of this issue becomes a reality, then is there any point in postponing it till the 21st century?

We also need a breakthrough in developing economic collaboration between the two sides of the continent. We have been speaking out in favor of this for a long time and we are glad that things have started to move [forward]. With time, the benefits of trade, exchanges of ideas, and cooperation will become more and more obvious for both sides. But politics, in order to be ahead of commerce, as it should be, must present an inspiring goal. That goal could be all-European economic integration. [...]

Now it would be important to move from this general idea to creating something that could be called a working draft; and then move step-by-step toward erecting the edifice of a new Europe.

[*Source: Archive of the Gorbachev Foundation. Shakhnazarov Collection. On file at the National Security Archive. Translated by Svetlana Savranskaya and Anna Melyakova.*]

Document No. 28: Record of Conversation between Mikhail Gorbachev and Józef Czyrek

September 23, 1988

This extraordinary conversation provides additional evidence that Gorbachev had changed Moscow's relationship with Eastern Europeans much earlier than usually assumed. Here, Polish Politburo member and former Foreign Minister Józef Czyrek has a lengthy discussion with the Soviet leader in Moscow, not asking for his permission but informing him that the Polish communists have decided to start the process of Roundtable negotiations with the opposition, including the Catholic Church and Solidarity. The Polish Politburo discussed opening such negotiations at Czyrek's initiative on August 21, and passed the formal resolution on September 2. According to the Polish transcripts, these discussions did not even mention the Soviet factor, which indicates that by August, probably as the result of Gorbachev's visit to Poland in July, the Polish leadership was not concerned about the possibility that the USSR would resort to force or other outright pressure. .

Here, Czyrek respectfully informs Gorbachev about a decision that has already been made. In turn, the Soviet leader treats his visitor not as a supplicant but as a peer. Gorbachev is mainly listening and learning about the situation in Poland. But he also gets involved in the discussion of personnel issues—something he usually avoided— in this case, the consideration of candidates for the position of prime minister. Despite the vice of excessive ambition, Rakowski seems to be the best candidate, both agree. (The pattern of this conversation would repeat in Rakowski's own phone call to Gorbachev on August 22, 1989. Contrary to press reports of the time, which would claim that Rakowski had to ask for the Soviet leader's permission to allow a Solidarity-led government, the actual discussion would consist of Rakowski informing Gorbachev and the latter agreeing.)[19]

In the conversation below, Czyrek tells Gorbachev that the Polish leadership hopes to split the opposition by "co-opt[ing] the banner of Solidarity along with Wałęsa." Thus, the June 1989 elections to the Sejm will allow for opposition candidates while preserving 40 percent of the seats for the PUWP, with the result that the government will be formed with representatives from the opposition. (In fact, after an overwhelming victory, the opposition would form the government). Gorbachev expresses his full approval for the Roundtable approach and the program of Polish reforms. Czyrek thanks him with the telling phrase, "Poland is your testing ground."

---

[19] Foreign Minister Genscher's Notes of the Conversation between Chancellor Kohl and Minister President Németh and Foreign Minister Horn, Palais Gymnych, August 25, 1989, published in Kuster, *Deutsche Einheit*, 377–380.

Gorbachev: asks the Polish guest to what extent the outbreak of strikes reflects deep processes in the country and to what extent it represents the result of subversive actions of the opposition.

Czyrek: These events have several causes. The first is our weakness. In Katowice, where the strikes started, the administration dragged out the introduction of the "Miner's Charter" for too long, even though the miners had demanded it for a long time. We should have started negotiations with them to establish fair wages. Now, as a result of shrinking rates for work on Saturdays and Sundays, they lost more than 30 percent of their salaries.

Another reason—during the reorganization implemented last fall, we preserved the old system of management in the coal industry, and multi-thousand strong collectives did not have their own self-government. The bureaucracy, which works like an army organization, allowed a gap to form between the collectives and the managerial apparatus. The mines were not granted the same rights that were given to the industrial enterprises, but instead agglomerations were created in the coal industry, which creates a concentration of a lot of bureaucrats, whom the workers see as free-loaders who live on their account. In addition, Katowice became something like a closed zone; the flow of information to the center was extremely poor.

Thirdly and finally, we saw the weakness of the party and state structures, and that many pressing problems were still unresolved. Secretaries of the party committees at the mines receive their salaries where they work, and so they are dependent on the local bosses. They could be paid 150,000 zlotys, or they could be paid 70,000 zlotys. There was no workers' self-government, and therefore there was nobody to criticize them, make demands, and thus to ward off the worst. As far as Solidarity is concerned, its positions are not that strong in that region.

Gorbachev: This means that here we are seeing the expression of workers' discontent.

Czyrek: Yes, recently we sent party journalists there and the miners told them very openly about everything. They did not feel any workers' pride, they saw themselves as objects of manipulation. In the north, in Gdansk, the situation is entirely different; there they had a political strike.

Gorbachev: Why is Solidarity able to preserve its positions along the coast?

Czyrek: It has become a kind of tradition: the workers on the docks in a way are proud that they are an independent political force, initiators of the struggle for workers' rights. Many young people who work on the docks live in dormitories; the atmosphere there is quite overheated. Party organizations are essentially not involved with them.

Gorbachev: Would it be possible to create some targeted programs and try to remove the problems that have accumulated in the most vulnerable areas? Or does the government today, under conditions of the reform, simply not have a capacity to do that?

Czyrek: It is difficult to decide everything from the center, and the local party organizations, the local administrations are not very mobile. That is why the memory of Solidarity still lives among the people—not about Solidarity as it was in reality, but about an [imaginary] organization that would stand up and fight against indifference, the bureaucracy, and so on. At the Plenum, we posed the issue this way: we have to immediately start solving problems that worry people, and to inform them about the measures being undertaken.

Gorbachev: During my trip to the Krasnoyarsk *krai* I had an additional opportunity to see that the people understand that there are problems that require time to be resolved, that we need to accumulate resources. But they are concerned that basic daily issues are not being resolved, for which one does not need millions, only simple human attention. There a bathhouse has not been built, here a roof is leaking, water pipes are not working. [...] And then they start to express their anger—where are the authorities? They should be all fired!

Czyrek: Yes, we got used to seeing those as "little things;" we spoke about grand causes and did not notice the most important things. Our enemies exploited that.

Gorbachev: Now new secretaries have come to several of the *oblasts* and started working with new energy. For instance, in Orel, Tula and Kursk. And the situation is changing fast. Even though they have not done much yet, the workers have started praising them already.

Czyrek: Today the number of demands in our society has grown rapidly, but the majority understands that they should not try to fulfill them through strikes. There is a societal need for a force that would uncover deficiencies, fight against bureaucratic inertia, and defend the interests of the workers. To our regret, we were unable to make the party organizations, labor unions into such an instrument. We were not able to make the PUWP simultaneously the ruling party and the opposition party.

Gorbachev: [...] In the past, we made appointments from above, and even if they were not bad people, they felt accountable only to the center. Now the situation is changing. Half of the party secretaries have already been changed, and the same will happen with the soviets [councils].

I would like to ask the following question—could it happen that the change to the new system that you are now working on will be seen as a demonstration of the PUWP's inability to carry on its work? If that happened, the consequences could be dangerous.

Czyrek: This is a real problem for us. I suspect that our wise and experienced political opponent is trying to push the development of events in the country precisely in this direction.

Gorbachev: And this political opponent of yours, as you call it, how do you see it?

Czyrek: It is diverse—it is the anarcho-syndicalists, simple anti-communists, and an element of the Church. [Józef Cardinal] Glemp is not a part of it. Opposition sentiments are especially prevalent among the intelligentsia. First of all, it is those who left the party, the renegades, such as [Jacek] Kuroń and [Adam] Michnik. They used to be members of the PUWP, even left-wingers, created a youth organization of the so-called Red Khazars.[20] Then they got into a confrontation with the leadership, were subjected to repressive measures, and changed their banners.

Gorbachev: Anarcho-syndicalism is the rejection of the existing order. Do they have any positive program?

Czyrek: This is their weakness: they don't have one, just plain rejection. They switched to the other side of the barricades, but kept the radicalism of their views, and now they are waging the main attack against the party.

Gorbachev: Are they able to influence the workers because of the weakness of the party organizations?

Czyrek: They have some decent propagandists, but not enough forces for any fundamental actions. That is why they are constantly trying to ingratiate themselves with something else. In the past, they toadied to the Solidarity movement, and now they are trying to hook up with what is left of it. If we assess their influence now, we could say that this extremist wing was unable to capture the leadership of the opposition. By the way, they were the only ones who argued against the negotiations underway now.

Gorbachev: I would like to understand this better—is your method of resolving the situation really commensurate with the scale of events, or maybe you—please don't be offended—are starting to panic a little bit? Maybe you should try to resolve concrete problems without undertaking major steps effectively legitimizing the opposition?

Czyrek: This is how the situation developed. We made a decision—to preserve the government until the end of the year, then to evaluate its performance and decide what to do with it in the future. Events speeded up this scenario, not even due to the strikes so much, but rather because of the deterioration of the economic situation. Inflation rose, market supplies worsened, people got worried, and the basis of social stability was undermined. Against this background, our trade unions have moved forward into battle. They are not very strong *per se*, but their leadership is very dynamic, such as the OPZZ [All-Poland Alliance of Trade Unions] and Chairman [Alfred] Miodowicz. They used the opportunity to express the public mood and by doing that to strengthen their positions. And because we have always tried to give them greater weight, we decided not to interfere with it.

Gorbachev: Obviously this is the right thing to do. Otherwise, Solidarity would win.

Czyrek: Yes, the party ranks have become smaller recently, but the labor unions have kept their positions among the working class. They include 52 percent of working people. But the price of that gain was the government crisis.

---

[20] The original Khazars were a semi-nomadic people of Turkic origin; between the 7th and 10th centuries they lived in what is today southern Russia, eastern Ukraine, and parts of the Caucasus.

Medvedev: At least the labor unions won.

Czyrek: They are our first barrier against Solidarity. Importantly, public opinion maintains too that the government was toppled not by the strikes, but by the labor unions. They even say that the party did it with its own hands.

Gorbachev: In other words, let the critical voice exist, if it is not directed against socialism and the party leadership. Is that true, however, in reality?

Czyrek: It is hard to say; there are different views [among the opposition], but the wing we are negotiating with—Wałęsa and a part of the Church—seem to accept the realities existing in Poland.

Gorbachev: And what is their philosophy?

Czyrek: They think approximately as follows: there should be a ruling party in every society, and since Poland has a socialist regime, therefore the party should be socialist too. But [the party] itself should be very different.

Gorbachev: So they are not questioning the socialist choice?

Czyrek: Moreover, they are even saying that the Church in general has now moved to a position equidistant from capitalism and socialism. John Paul II criticizes both this regime and that regime in order to show that the only wise choice is the Church. In the past, Church figures claimed that socialism was the devil's invention. Now they have understood the irreversibility of the social changes, and even though the bourgeois order is closer to Wojtyła's[21] heart, he has to accept the reality. Many prominent figures of the Church, including Professor Stelmachowski,[22] are saying that the Christian doctrine is closer to socialism than to capitalism, but as far as freedom of religion is concerned, here they give preference to the West.

Essentially, we have a great task before us—to reconcile the Church with socialism. We took this road with a full understanding of how high the stakes were. If the Polish experiment succeeds, it will have great importance for all countries with strong religious beliefs. We don't have any [selfish] ambitions, we are not doing it to be the first [...]

Gorbachev: The majority of your population are believers; one has to take that into account.

Czyrek: As a whole, the Polish Church is in favor of national conciliation, but of course it is trying to realize some gains from it, first of all by strengthening its influence in education and in the mass media. The position and the mood of the bishops is not clear-cut. The conservative faction of the bishops argues for recognition and the full legalization of Solidarity. That faction enjoys the Pope's support. Another part, represented by Glemp, considers a revival of Solidarity in its present form impossible.

---

[21] Karol Wojtyła was John Paul II's name before he became pope.

[22] Andrzej Stelmachowski was an academic and Solidarity activist who became marshal of the Polish Senate in 1989 and later minister of education.

Now I will talk about the party, and about its leading role. Here we are working on several directions. If we don't resolve the economic and social problems, it will be difficult for the PUWP to justify its right to be the leader. Will the party succeed in becoming the vanguard force in the Polish *perestroika*? Here is a paradox, one could say, an unfairness [in the party situation]: The party is promoting novel methods, notwithstanding resistance in its own ranks, but society nonetheless sees it as a conservative force, which is defending its interests and its officials. This is the tragedy of our party.

Gorbachev: This is a very important issue. In the assessment, in the analysis of the past, in our country too, there are statements that the party is to blame for many things. There are not many, but such voices come through. They say that what happened under Stalin and under Khrushchev and under Brezhnev—these are all the deeds of the communists. They complain that today *perestroika* is proceeding slowly. In order to prevent the spread of such sentiments we have to transform the party, and make its policies and the cadres more dynamic. In our country, not all party officials understood the essence of the moment. From this fact comes the need to have a turnover of personnel, especially locally. The entire trip to the Krasnoyarsk *krai* was essentially devoted to these issues. People do not doubt *perestroika*, but believe that [local] leadership, local bureaucrats are blocking it.

Now the situation is gradually changing. In that same Krasnoyarsk *krai*, they have already replaced half of their leading cadres, and they were choosing from several candidates. I have to admit, initially we had different plans. However, when we approved the course to democratize the party, including the apparatus, then we understood that we could not drag it out, and at the conference[23] we made the appropriate decision—not to wait for the congress, [but] to begin the process of renewing the party.

Coming back to your affairs, I want to ask—does the working class understand that it needs such a party? Does it associate its interests with the PUWP?

Czyrek: What I just said about the weakness of the party primarily concerns the attitude of the working class toward [the party]. In the intelligentsia circles, our innovating policy is seen more clearly. The working class looks at it as if from below—[as something that] has been done by the bosses, by the party secretaries, in practice. And because there is a lot of ugliness and inaction there, many people do not consider the PUWP their own, workers' party. Often one hears expressions that nobody listens to the workers, that they don't have any influence in the party.

Gorbachev: Could it be that the leadership focused on improving contacts with the intelligentsia, which in itself is important and difficult, and somewhat dropped the work with the "class base"?

---

[23] The XIX Party Conference.

Czyrek: You see, we tried, we went to the factories, held meetings of worker activists, a plenum with worker participation. But the trouble is that the economic situation is hurting their interests. They see that life is easier for the peasants, not even mentioning the private sector. They say, "you are creating conditions for multimillionaires, but what are workers left to do?" In short, the key to correcting the situation is in the economy.

Gorbachev: In short, you need to solve concrete problems, without forcing the creation of new institutions and arrangements too much. You have already done a lot in this direction, and we are looking closely at your experience [as we] reform our own political system. But still the main thing now is the [existence of] concrete problems, and the lack of a resolution could undermine any political regulation, even the smartest kind. And how are the peasants behaving?

Czyrek: They are not going on strike, because peasants never strike anyway. However, there is discontent about the fact that the prices for industrial products are rising faster than the prices for food. In the last two years the profitability of agriculture has fallen by 18 percent. But this discontent is not taking on a political character, it is spilling over into economic demands. The village also is trying to achieve greater freedom in the organization of economic life. Now our local organs do whatever they want.

I am recounting everything that worries us, but there are no grounds for panic. Nobody is demanding that we transfer the factories to private hands. They say: yes to socialism, no to drawbacks! As I already said, they do not support the strikes. They demand more effective action by the party and the state. They say: we will support you if you work energetically, and do not permit decreases in living standards.

Our strategic line remains the same—it is to rely on the broad coalition of social forces. And our tactic is to split the opposition, and to pull the more realistic segment into negotiations, to co-opt the banner of Solidarity along with Wałęsa, to isolate the extremists, and start a fight with them. The Church is also afraid of anarcho-syndicalism and in the worst case will keep their neutrality. They do not want confrontation, and they do not want to share influence with Kuroń and Michnik. We think that there is now a chance to employ this tactic, and that is why we decided to negotiate. We received signals from the Church and from Wałęsa about their readiness for compromise. We got "whispers" from the West along the same lines. There was of course, the choice—to start this ourselves, or to let them take the initiative. We thought for a long time and then Jaruzelski decided to take it upon himself. It was not easy to persuade the Central Committee.

Gorbachev: But when you, in your expression, co-opt the Solidarity banner along with Wałęsa, wouldn't that be interpreted as your agreeing to its revival?

Czyrek: Those concerns exist in the party. There will be no return to Solidarity. At the same time, however, we admitted that there is a problem with the Polish model of a labor movement. The closed model, which we created, is imperfect. Where is our thinking taking us? We need unity in the labor movement, but a unity based on pluralistic principles. In other words, we reject the Italo-French form of labor movement, and adopt the Austrian and West German [version] as our basis. There, every enterprise has one labor union, with one council, but within it various clubs are represented—socialists, communists, and Christian Democrats.

Gorbachev: So, one enterprise could have two labor organizations, but they would have a joint council?

Czyrek: Wałęsa and others agree to hold negotiations on the basis of the provisions of the Law on Labor Unions, which was adopted in 1981. It says: one labor union at each enterprise. We want to act on that basis. One labor union, and a joint council, which could be constituted from various groups and clubs. Of course, Wałęsa and his supporters will fight for going beyond that framework, but, as Stelmachowski tried to convince me, ultimately they will agree to the type of pluralism that we are offering. They also are showing signs of weariness, because at most enterprises they are not supported, but on the contrary are criticized.

It is hard for me to say what is the influence of the international factor on the actions of the opposition. One thing is clear—they have no choice but to praise *perestroika*. The positive attitude toward the changes is so great [in Poland] that the opposition cannot allow itself to speak against it. Sometimes our people even praise us for it, even though we are lagging behind you and need to learn more from you.

Gorbachev: But first of all you should think about solving concrete problems, taking into account the situation in the country.

Czyrek: Yes, of course. I want to say that smart people "from the other side" understand the need for agreement under the present conditions. There the international factor also has a direct influence. I suspect that the Americans and West Germans are not pushing the Polish opposition toward confrontation, but rather to the opposite—advising it to accept the dialog. How much of it is due to your influence? I don't know. But the overall situation, the new thinking are doing their share. Representatives of the White House kept beating on us like a drum in the past, and now they are saying that we should strive for conciliation.

Gorbachev: But the main thing is the mood of the masses. They are also sick and tired of confrontations, which are still promoted by some people like Kissinger and Brzezinski. [...] And what is the government going to be like?

Czyrek: We came to the conclusion that in the present conditions we should not establish relations between the party and government based on the old principles. It is necessary that political forces take part in a coalition and determine the direction of the policy, and that its implementation be the business of the government. And it should not be the case that the government would point a finger at the party, but the party would not be able to criticize it [in return], because it is, so to speak, "our government." The party cannot be a guarantor of everything, and cannot cover every stupid [action] and mistake made in the course of governing. Jaruzelski will speak about this explicitly from the podium of the Sejm. If the government does not carry out the political line consistently, it should bear the responsibility. The party will not interfere in concrete decisions. The people should know that we are not deciding who should get what salary.

Of course the party cannot completely avoid responsibility for the government. Messner[24] is a good person, he has done everything he could. But if mistakes were made, it was not because the Politburo bound his hands. And such efforts—to shift the blame from the government onto the party—do take place.

Gorbachev: But the party, obviously, cannot limit its functions, and the first among them is to appoint the government and to determine state policy.

Czyrek: Of course not, but we will not work out the details. There are experts for that. As far as the new government is concerned, there is no decision yet. Some people believed that it should be primarily a collegium of experts, but we did not agree with that. It would look like the party was unable to form a full-fledged cabinet. Therefore, we will argue that it should be headed by a politician. We are looking at several people. There was the candidacy of [Roman] Malinowski, the chair of the OKP [Citizens' Parliamentary Group] but we rejected it. It would seem like the PUWP was hiding around the corner, and within the party there would be dissatisfaction with the fact that we were giving away such a serious position. Malinowski himself, however, entertained such ambitions; he wanted to become head of the government of national unity.

Gorbachev: Some kind of Piłsudski? Father of the nation?

Czyrek: Something like that. He is a capable person, but he has some weaknesses. The second candidate is Baka[25], a hard-working person. But here in Poland, they are afraid of professors. Besides, he could be criticized as one of the authors of the reform, which so far has not brought any major results. And we think that it would be good for him to work on deepening the reform without being prime minister.

Kiszczak's[26] candidacy was put forward. He is a good organizer, a disciplined person, and has a lot of experience from the martial law period.[27] But it would not be very good if there was one more general. At this point, Kiszczak will be kept in reserve, just in case he is needed.

The next figure is Rakowski, an experienced, capable person. However, he is not an economist. But that is not necessary with a well-constituted government. He had some breakouts before, but in the end he became strongly engaged in the policy of renewal. His nomination would be a signal to the Church and to

---

[24] Zbigniew Messner, the prime minister since November 1985, was forced to relinquish his post just a few days after this conversation, following an unprecedented no-confidence vote in the Sejm.

[25] Władysław Baka, a professor of economics, was government plenipotentiary for economic reform from 1981–1985, president of the National Bank of Poland from 1985–1988 and 1989–1991, and a Politburo member in 1989.

[26] General Czesław Kiszczak was minister of the interior from 1981–1990 and briefly served as prime minister in August 1989. He was a close associate of Jaruzelski.

[27] Martial law was declared on December 13, 1981, to deal with the Solidarity crisis.

Solidarity, who take him seriously. On the other hand, the labor union would treat him positively, and a favorable attitude from journalists and the intelligentsia would be assured. Recently he has done some good work in the party, and gained a reputation as a creative person, and even those people whom you might call our fundamentalists have come to support him.

Gorbachev: Does he have far-reaching ambitions?

Czyrek: He does have ambitions, but because they would be covered by our common interests, this is not dangerous. The main thing is to make sure that the personal does not prevail over the public. Jaruzelski knows him better; he sees his weaknesses but believes that we can overcome them. To what extent this assessment is accurate—you should speak to Jaruzelski himself.

Gorbachev: My task is to ask questions. We feel okay [*neplokho*] about Rakowski. You said it right—that he has drawn certain lessons, gained experience, turned from a journalist into a politician, and undoubtedly possesses the intellect and the capabilities. But we heard—this is a completely confidential conversation, just for you and for Comrade Jaruzelski—that behind the aggravation of the situation in Poland are attempts to take shots at Wojciech Władysławowicz [Jaruzelski]. Some people are interested in this, and it is connected with the behavior of Rakowski. I decided not to mention it to Jaruzelski during my conversation with him.

Czyrek: I have no grounds to say whether that is so, but many of my friends mention Rakowski's ambitious nature. [...] I value his intellect and I know that he would be afraid to be the prime minister for long because a person in that position exhausts himself very quickly, burns up. It might be that he would start fighting to become first secretary by transferring Jaruzelski to the presidency. I told Jaruzelski about that, just like I am telling you now, so my conscience is clean.

Gorbachev: Poland needs Jaruzelski. He not only has not exhausted his capabilities, but on the contrary is playing the key role. You should not allow a split in the PUWP at this stage of Poland's development under any conditions.

Czyrek: So far, it is [Tadeusz] Porębski[28] who has mainly been acting in this direction. He has been actively inciting the club (faction) of the PUWP in the Sejm against the party leadership. Recently, he wrote a letter to Jaruzelski agreeing with the change of government, but pointing out that none of the above-mentioned persons could be prime minister. He says that if any of them is nominated, he will retain his right to speak against him publicly. Jaruzelski was going to talk to him, but I said that a person who is opposed to the policy of the first secretary should not be the leader of our deputies' club in the Sejm.

Gorbachev: Your position is very important.

---

[28] Tadeusz Porębski, a professor, was chairman of the PUWP Parliamentary Club from November 1985–June 1989, a Politburo member until December 1988, and deputy speaker of the Sejm from June 1988–June 1989.

Czyrek: My position is to help Jaruzelski. I believe that he should lead Poland onto a straight and stable road. We do not have any other person with his capabilities. A split in the party would be deadly. However, I do not see such a danger right now. Most likely, somebody will be waiting for the all-Polish conference of delegates to the X Congress of the PUWP (March 1989) and will try to replicate the Hungarian example. But we do not have the same situation. Those forces that are against Jaruzelski are also against the policy of *perestroika*. There are not too many of them.

Briefly about some other issues. We have entered the path of dialog. It has already produced some fruits. For example, the opposition has stopped threatening a wave of strikes. A split is discernible in the opposition camp; some are already calling Wałęsa a collaborator. If we succeed in co-opting Wałęsa, who still remains a symbol both in the country and abroad, the opposition will be weakened substantially.

Gorbachev: Just do not forget about the time interval, so that the shift from treating Wałęsa as anathema to integrating him into the renewal process is not too sudden. Otherwise that could create the impression that you have panicked.

Czyrek: We have considered that. In practice, the changes will not be instantaneous; the elections to the Sejm will take place in a year. And now the conditions for negotiations consist of an atmosphere of calm and reasonableness. One more thing—not to reinstitute Solidarity; that would be hard to achieve, but we will be striving for it. And thirdly—to look for conciliation at the main intersections of the societal model, to try to work out a joint electoral platform and an agreement on the distribution of seats in the Sejm. We are thinking along these lines: to keep 40 percent for the PUWP, to give 20 percent to the Council of Trade Unions and DP, 10 percent to the independents, and 20 percent to the constructive opposition, which acts on the basis of the agreement. If the issue is resolved this way, then after the elections we could form a government of national unity that includes representatives of the constructive opposition. But in this case, there will be problems with Rakowski's candidacy. The opposition has big problems with him. However, it might be that by that time he would be able to improve the situation, if the elections don't lead him too far.

On Saturday, we will have a Politburo session, and after that a meeting of the conciliatory commission with the participation of allied parties. On Monday, a Plenum of the Central Committee, and in the evening the deputies club in the Sejm. At the Sejm session, Jaruzelski, on behalf of all political forces will introduce a proposal for Rakowski's candidacy for the premiership. It will take several days to form the government—to consult with the parties, trade unions, and independent figures. This is a question of political culture, and one should not regard it as [simply] theater.

Gorbachev: Are you going to continue negotiations with the so-called constructive opposition?

Czyrek: First of all, the Roundtable will convene. It will be truly round—because we do not want Wałęsa sitting alone across from Kiszczak; there will be allied parties, trade unions.

In the process of establishing contacts on the eve of the "Roundtable" we have encountered a number of concrete problems. We are considering offering the post of deputy prime minister, and a number of ministers' and deputy ministers' portfolios to the opposition. In general, they agree that the structure of the Sejm should be decided not at the elections, but on the basis of the proposed agreement at the center. In any case, at the negotiations we will emphasize—and this also seems not to cause objections—that we are not talking about creating a political party but about representing opposition groups in the Sejm and in the [upper house of the] parliament. So far the issue of creating new political parties has not come up. The Church does not raise this issue either, because, in the opinion of the Polish leadership, they do not see it in their interests. There have been no statements to this effect from Solidarity either, although naturally it would be hard to give guarantees for the future.

In terms of societal structure, it would be reasonable to envisage creating some new institutions through which the ambitions of society could be satisfied. Experience with the catholic clubs shows that they remain [just] clubs, without turning into political parties. With the help of similar steps we are hoping to split the political opposition away from the trade union [opposition]. We are not afraid of the latter, and their political activities would be placed within a defined framework, although naturally one should not close one's eyes to the possibility of certain shifts.

As far as economic reform is concerned, we have no substantial discussions or differences with the opposition. They do not have their own program, and so the discussion of pluses and minuses is being conducted around proposals originating from the PUWP. In the final analysis, coordination on political, economic and social problems could lead to the creation of a joint electoral program of a national coalition.

As our positions move closer toward one another, a council of national conciliation, which would develop a joint electoral program, could be created on the basis of the "Roundtable." [...]

In the forthcoming period, we envisage that in addition to the big "Roundtable," with many people around it, we will organize five "little Roundtables" on separate issues (political reform, social reform, economic reform, problems of the village and agriculture, and the trade union model), and to conduct further work within those frameworks. All of this work is being conducted under the direct leadership of the Politburo, and of W. Jaruzelski. Members of the Central Committee and the leaders of regional PUWP committees are regularly being informed about it.

Gorbachev: Will Jaruzelski mention these negotiations?

Czyrek: In a general form, in the context of unity and conciliation. We will continue our stance for conciliation, regardless of whether it is with Wałęsa or without him.

Gorbachev: Thank you for deciding to inform the CPSU leadership. Everything that happens in Poland is very important to us. The choice you and I made is difficult, but necessary. In essence, we both strive to solve an important task, which is to develop the potential of a socialist system. This brings us even closer together as friends and colleagues. Our parties require collaboration and the preservation and strengthening of Soviet–Polish relations. This is necessary for the strategic interests of our country.

We are in solidarity with your actions, we understand the challenges facing Poland, and the significance of the period you are going through. This is what I think: if [your actions] were characterized by a hasty forfeiting of positions, then we might have some doubts. But you are following political channels that were defined ahead of time, and your methods of overcoming difficulties seem reasonable. I asked you some tough questions. All the possibilities need to be accounted for, including the worst-case scenario. The West could once again paint everything in this light: The leadership yields and Solidarity wins. We have to try to ensure there is no impression that this is a defeat of the PUWP. You have all you need to conduct this matter with confidence, calmly, and prudently. You rightly see the risk that an opposition political party might create. The trade unions also have to stay united, so there is no threat of opposition forming under the roof of Solidarity.

This is how we understand the situation in Poland. Of course, these are your issues and you will be solving them. As we understand it, the question of Rakowski as the head of the government is decided

Czyrek: This is Cde. Jaruzelski's choice, which I support under the circumstances. The Politburo does not know about this yet.

Medvedev: There are ambiguous feelings about him.

Czyrek: Everybody knows about his ambitions.

Gorbachev: Perhaps this is good. I think his political experience could be useful if he does not see this post as a trampoline to fight for a higher one. This could complicate the situation, and Jaruzelski should be protected.

Czyrek says that he is planning a proposal that would require Jaruzelski to take a vacation.

Gorbachev: We are waiting for him [to come].

Czyrek says a heartfelt thank-you for the conversation.

The understanding and good relations with our Soviet friends means a great deal to us. Jaruzelski asked me to convey warm greetings and to assure you that we will act in the spirit of your conversation with him. He felt much better after a long conversation with you over the phone.

We are fully aware that both parties want to infuse socialism with a new dynamism, so that our people can develop their creative forces. We understand the significance of what is happening in the USSR. In this sense, Poland is your testing ground. We have a feeling of responsibility before our own people, and before the common goal.

I have two requests. The development of joint enterprises is stuck right now because of pricing trends. Your representatives make calculations based on internal prices without taking into consideration governmental subsidies, while our representatives calculate based on our prices.

Gorbachev: The same problem persists in all the [socialist] countries.

Czyrek: Maybe we should adopt the principle of world prices? And one more question. We would be grateful for your support of the PUWP in its relations with the United Trade Union Committee. We have high regard for the position you presented in Warsaw, and the telegram for the United Trade Union Committee congress.

Gorbachev: We should include this in the program for inter-party contacts.

Czyrek: We also thank you for your support of our policies in regard to the Church. Glemp's visit to Byelorussia consolidated his position in the Vatican, and he is behaving decently. It might seem strange, but we would also like to ask for help with the opposition. There are differing views [among the opposition], and certain confrontational forces; but in general they have to acknowledge that socialism is the core of the country's development.

Gorbachev: If you have specific proposals, let us know so that the MFA and the International Department can take some action.

Czyrek: The last point concerns the forthcoming meeting between you and Kohl. The West Germans and the Americans hold the key to our debt; they are our major creditors. You could help to exert some influence on them.

Gorbachev: Perhaps you have specific proposals about this, as well? As for general support in principle, there is no question about that.

[*Source: Gorbachev Foundation, Fond 1, Opis 1. On File at the National Security Archive Translated by Svetlana Savranskaya.*]

Document No. 29: Preparatory Notes from Georgy Shakhnazarov for Mikhail Gorbachev for CC CPSU Politburo Meeting

October 6, 1988

This document reveals some of the reasons for Gorbachev's "non-policy" in Eastern Europe. The USSR "transferred" its own system failure (brought on by "factors rooted in the very economic and political model of socialism") to Eastern Europe after World War II. After that experience, the Kremlin leadership now appears to want above all "to avoid criticism for trying to impose" Soviet-style reforms through force "on our friends." In this memo, Shakhnazarov thus repeats the taboo expressed by Gorbachev in conversations with his advisers and at Politburo meetings: no more military interventions. Shakhnazarov reminds Gorbachev that "even the old leadership" renounced the use of military force towards Poland in 1980–1981. But Gorbachev, as a member of the Politburo at that time, remembers it well.

At the same time, Shakhnazarov points to the dangers of a "non-policy" and compares the Kremlin attitude towards Eastern Europe to "bury[ing] our heads in the sand like an ostrich." He suggests that the Kremlin should carefully consider its options, particularly for an economic and financial bailout of the bankrupt Eastern European regimes. Clearly lacking political stature for the task himself, Shakhnazarov proposes that the Politburo's International Commission, headed by Aleksandr Yakovlev, tackle this "huge problem." In January 1989 the Yakovlev Commission, indeed, would order analyses of the situation of Eastern Europe (see below), but the Soviet leadership never manages to identify any specific policy options.

Why did Shakhnazarov never follow up this memo to convene an expert group— in effect, joining the ostrich in the sand? In the Musgrove dialogue, he explains that during these months more than 90 percent of his time was devoted to political reform, such as preparations for the March 1989 elections to the Soviet Congress of People's Deputies. As a result, Eastern Europe fell off even his radar screen. Into this vacuum of inattention rushed the Eastern European opposition movements.

Mikhail Sergeyevich!

Perhaps you will find these thoughts useful.

Today we are discussing the results of our talks with leaders or prominent figures from a number of socialist countries—K. Phomvihan, Vo Chi Cong, E. Honecker, N. Ceaușescu, [J.] Czyrek. Now Zh. Batmunkh is asking for a meeting.

Each country has its unique situation, and we would be correct not to approach them as one bloc; we are trying to figure out specifics regarding each of them and to build our policy on the basis of such an analysis.

At the same time, today's exchange and broadly speaking everything that we know, all the information we are receiving, encourages us to make a multi-faceted evaluation of the situation in the socialist commonwealth. With all the differences and nuances, there are multiple signs that certain similar problems are increasingly plaguing the fraternal countries. The very similarity of the symptoms of the disease testifies to the fact that its catalyst is not some kind of malignant germ that has managed to penetrate their lowered defenses, but factors rooted in the very economic and political model of socialism as it has evolved over here and has been transferred with minor modifications to the soil of the countries that embarked on the path of socialism in the post-war period.

We have already laid bare the weaknesses of this model and are beginning to remove them in a systematic way. This is actually the super-task of *perestroika*— to give socialism a new quality. A number of countries have followed us and begun, even ahead of us, the process of deep reforms. Some of them—the GDR, Romania, the DPRK [North Korea]—still do not admit the need [for reform] but do it instead for political reasons, because their current political leadership does not want to change anything. In reality all of them need changes, although we do not say this to them publicly in order to avoid being criticized for trying to impose *perestroika* on our friends.

But the fact is that obvious signs of a crisis require radical reforms everywhere in the socialist world. And subjective factors play a huge role. For instance, in more-than-backward Laos, Phomvihan is acting skillfully, and there are some good results. But those who stubbornly turn a deaf ear to the call of the times are driving the malaise ever deeper and aggravating its future manifestations.

This concerns us directly. Although we set aside our rights as "elder brother" in the socialist world, we cannot renounce the role of leader, the role that will always objectively belong to the Soviet Union as the most powerful socialist country, the motherland of the October Revolution. Whenever any of them was in crisis, we had to come to the rescue at the cost of huge material, political and even human sacrifice.

We should clearly see, moreover, that in the future any option to "extinguish" crises by military means must be fully excluded. Even the old [pre-Gorbachev] leadership seems to have already realized this, at least with regard to Poland.

Now we must reflect on how we will act if one or even several countries simultaneously become bankrupt? This is a realistic prospect, for some of them are on the brink of monetary insolvency (Poland, Hungary, Bulgaria, Vietnam, Cuba, the GDR). Even Czechoslovakia, which has so far stayed afloat, now finds its external debt rising rapidly.

What shall we do if the social instability that is now assuming an increasingly threatening character in Hungary coincides with another round of trouble-making in Poland, demonstrations of "Charter-77" in Czechoslovakia, etc.? In other words, do we have a plan in case of a crisis that might encompass the entire socialist world, or a large part of it?

We are worried by this. When we receive alarmist cables from time to time, we do what we can; but all this is at best like applying a lotion to a sore— not a systematic, thoughtful treatment strategy for the disease, not to mention a preventive measure.

It is high time to discuss these issues at the Politburo in the presence of experts. We should not bury our heads in the sand like an ostrich, but should look to the future with eyes open and ask ourselves the most precise questions:

- Could the socialist countries escape a pre-crisis situation without Western assistance?
- What price would they have to pay for this assistance?
- To what extent should we encourage such a course of events or put up with it?
- To what degree are we interested in the continued presence of Soviet troops on the territory of a number of allied countries (excluding the GDR)?

We should assign the newly established International Commission of the CC the task of preparing materials for this discussion. This is a huge problem, in scope as well as in significance; we should tackle it continuously, but the first exchange should take place as soon as late December—early January 1989. There will be a working conference of the leadership of the commonwealth in Prague in February and that gives us a chance to share some of our conclusions with our friends. They are already expecting it although each of them, of course, sees the situation from "his own angle."

[Source: Published in G.Kh. Shakhnazarov's Tsena svobody *[The Price of Freedom] (Moscow: Rossika-Zeus, 1993) Translated by Vladislav Zubok.]*

A lighthearted President Mikhail Gorbachev at an undated event with Georgy Shakhnazarov, one of his closest aides and a key figure in the development of *perestroika*. Shakhnazarov participated in the 1998 Musgrove conference, the transcript of which appears in this volume. (Courtesy of Andrey Morozov, http://amorozov.ru.)

Mikhail Gorbachev (third from left) attends his first Warsaw Treaty Organization meeting as Soviet leader in May 1985. At the session in the Polish capital, bloc leaders (from left) Nicolae Ceauşescu, János Kádár, Gorbachev, Wojciech Jaruzelski, Todor Zhivkov, Erich Honecker and Gustáv Husák agreed to renew the alliance for 20 years, but it would dissolve from within by 1991. (http://www.geocities.com/wojciech_jaruzelski/zyciorys4.html)

The final press conference after the Reykjavik summit, October 12, 1986. Seated in front row, from left: Anatoly Chernyaev, Anatoly Dobrynin, Eduard Shevardnadze, Mikhail Gorbachev, Alexander Yakovlev and Sergei Akhromeyev. (Courtesy of Anatoly Chernyaev)

Ronald Reagan and Mikhail Gorbachev in animated conversation at the Washington summit in December 1987. The summit culminated in the signing of the historic INF treaty, the first to call for an actual reduction in the number of existing nuclear delivery vehicles. (Courtesy of the Ronald Reagan Library)

Ronald Reagan receives a warm Muscovite welcome on the famed Arbat during the Moscow summit in May 1988. (Courtesy of the Ronald Reagan Library)

Mikhail Gorbachev and Alexander Yakovlev on board the Soviet leader's airplane. Yakovlev, a former chief of ideology for the CPSU, was a prime mover behind *glasnost'* and *perestroika*. (http://www.lebed.com/2005/4364-2.jpg)

Mikhail Gorbachev and Margaret Thatcher are joined by their spouses (seated opposite) during a break in talks at 10 Downing Street, April 6, 1989. The two leaders developed a strong bond during the late 1980s, as Gorbachev did with his West German and French counterparts. In the left foreground of this photo is Gorbachev's foreign policy adviser, Anatoly Chernyaev, who played a central role in the 1998 Musgrove conference. (Courtesy of Anatoly Chernyaev)

The Polish roundtable talks involving the regime, Solidarity and the Church took place at the Namiestnikowski Palace in Warsaw beginning on February 6, 1989. Although the ruling PUWP tried to use the process to control the direction of political developments, the April 4 agreement ultimately helped topple the communist system in Poland, and spurred similar momentous changes elsewhere in Eastern Europe. (http://www.tiger.edu.pl/aktualnosci/okragly_stol.jpg)

George Bush and Lech Wałęsa relax in the White House, November 14, 1989. Wałęsa received the Medal of Freedom during the visit but his real goal was to urge Washington to free up millions of dollars in aid for Poland. (Courtesy of the George Bush Presidential Library and Museum)

The U.S. and Soviet presidents meet on board a U.S. naval vessel off Malta. On the left side of the table are Mikhail Gorbachev, Alexander Yakovlev and Sergei Akhromeyev. On the right side: George Bush and Brent Scowcroft. The summit of December 2–3, 1989, was the last between the superpowers during the Cold War and marked the end of the Bush administration's policy "pause" over Soviet relations. (Courtesy of the George Bush Presidential Library and Museum)

James Baker, Brent Scowcroft, Raisa Gorbachev, Anatoly Chernyaev and Mikhail Gorbachev at the Novo-Ogarevo estate outside Moscow after the signing of the START Treaty, August 1991. (Courtesy of Anatoly Chernyaev)

Gorbachev policy adviser Anatoly Chernyaev and U.S. Ambassador Jack Matlock meet face-to-face. Both men made important contributions to their government's policies in the 1980s—and later at the Musgrove conference in 1998. (Courtesy of Anatoly Chernyaev)

Former U.S. and Soviet officials, accompanied by East European, Russian, American and Canadian scholars, gather to revisit the ground-breaking events of 1989 at the Musgrove conference center, St. Simons Island, Georgia, in May 1998. (Photographer unknown)

Conversation at Musgrove: Georgy Shakhnazarov, Anatoly Chernyaev and Svetlana Savranskaya consult during a break in the conference, May 1998. (Courtesy of Thomas Blanton)

Jack Matlock, Georgy Shakhnazarov, Malcolm Byrne, Douglas MacEachin, and Vladislav Zubok during the Musgrove conference. (Courtesy of Thomas Blanton)

Thomas Blanton and Anatoly Chernyaev celebrate Chernyaev's agreement to donate his original diaries to the National Security Archive. The inset page from November 10, 1989, notes: "The Berlin Wall has fallen ..." (Courtesy of Svetlana Savranskaya)

Document No. 30: Diary of Anatoly Chernyaev regarding a Meeting between Mikhail Gorbachev and Helmut Kohl

October 28, 1988

This remarkable diary entry by Chernyaev gives his impressions of Gorbachev's meeting with Kohl, little more than a month before the seminal U.N. speech. Kohl's trip to Moscow marks a distinct warming of German–Soviet relations after the chill of the early 1980s, and in particular the establishment of a candid personal relationship between the two leaders. (Kohl would later become the direct intermediary between Gorbachev and Bush in 1989). At the political level, these notes provide more evidence of the way Gorbachev adopted a new peer group—composed of Western leaders such as Thatcher, Mitterrand, and Kohl—outside his own Politburo. At the personal level, Chernyaev gives a fascinating summary of Gorbachev's ideas: "'freedom of choice,' 'mutual respect for each other's values,' 'renunciation of force in politics,' 'a common European home,' 'liquidation of nuclear weapons.'" Chernyaev comments: "you physically feel that we are entering a new world." We also see a crucial element of Gorbachev's diplomatic style—his eagerness to please and to compromise—when he chooses not to use the sharp words planned for Kohl.

Kohl met one-on-one with Gorbachev (plus me and Teltschik—assistant to the chancellor). When you watch this striving "at the highest level" to speak as one human being to another (mutually), you physically feel that we are entering a new world where the determinant is no longer class struggle, ideology, and polarity in general, but something all-human. And you realize how brave and far-sighted M.S. is. He declared the new thinking "without any theoretical preparation," and began to act according to common sense.

After all, his ideas—"freedom of choice," "mutual respect for each other's values," "renunciation of force in politics," "a common European home," "liquidation of nuclear weapons," etc., etc.—all of this is by no means new. What is new is that a person who came out of Soviet Marxism-Leninism, from a Soviet society conditioned from top to bottom by Stalinism, began to carry out these ideas with all earnestness and sincerity when he became head of state. No wonder the world is stunned and full of admiration. But our public still cannot appreciate that he has already led them from one state to another.

Sometimes he is still caught in the old clichés. For example, after the "embrace" with Kohl during the first meeting, Kohl gave a speech several hours later in which he again and again spoke about a "unified Germany" and about "Berlin, ..." The next morning M.S. consulted [with us] on what sharp words he should use with him at the start of the negotiations. He even made [Valentin] Falin and me write a "page" so that he would not forget the severity of everything he wanted to say. But he did not use any of it. [...] Later it was as if he "made excuses," saying that Kohl needed [to speak] about unity in order to fight off his allies and the overly-enthusiastic public at home!

[*Source: Anatoly Chernyaev's Diary, Manuscript. On file at the National Security Archive. Translated by Vladislav Zubok and Anna Melyakova.*]

Document No. 31: Notes of a Meeting between Mikhail Gorbachev and Foreign Policy Advisers

October 31, 1988

In this document Gorbachev in effect brainstorms with a narrow circle of foreign policy experts on the content of his upcoming speech to the U.N. General Assembly. In addition to Shevardnadze and Chernyaev, the group includes Yakovlev, Dobrynin, and Dobrynin's deputy, Valentin Falin. The major thrust of Gorbachev's initiative, as he envisions it, relates to disarmament and the gradual withdrawal of Soviet troops from Eastern Europe. But its spirit is less pragmatic than messianic. He visualizes himself as a world figure who will not only assuage the security fears of Western countries, but will outline an entirely new cooperative global order. When he says, "In general this speech should be anti-Fulton—a Fulton in reverse," he means nothing less than to undo the Cold War, declared most famously by Winston Churchill in his "Iron Curtain" speech in Fulton, Missouri, in March 1946.

Indeed, Gorbachev's U.N. address on December 7, 1988, would endorse the "common interests of mankind" as the basis of Soviet foreign policy and—most significantly for Eastern Europe—declare "the compelling necessity of the principle of freedom of choice" as "a universal principle to which there should be no exceptions." Reaction in the West would range from disbelief to astonishment. U.S. Sen. Daniel Patrick Moynihan would call this speech "the most astounding statement of surrender in the history of ideological struggle," while retired Gen. Andrew Goodpaster, a former NATO commander and top aide to President Eisenhower, would describe Gorbachev's announcement of unilateral troop cuts as "the most significant step since NATO was founded."[29]

WHAT ARE WE GOING TO TAKE TO THE UNITED NATIONS? ATTENDED: SHEVARDNADZE, YAKOVLEV, DOBRYNIN, FALIN, CHERNYAEV.

Gorbachev: This is what I think. First of all, we need to define new thinking—how our policy is reflected in the minds of the people, politicians, and the military. Single out significant, permanent factors.

We should present "the new us," show them how we are changing, how we comprehend the changing world, and how we are developing along with it. This is the first part of the speech.

The second part—and the main one—is to affirm that the new thinking, our new foreign policy, is fully connected with *perestroika* and with objective processes within the country. Tell them what we are going to do next at home.

Present the basic principles of our new military-political doctrine, as concretely as possible, and what it means for the international situation.

---

[29] Blanton, "When did the Cold War End?" 184.

Show them our new military thinking as a part of the new political thinking and emphasize the military-technological side of our doctrine. In the speech we should make public the figures regarding our armed forces. Identify the reductions we are going to make unilaterally. It would be better if we could unburden ourselves of weapons in two years and then publish how much we had and how much we have left.

Recently, I met with Komsomol members at their exhibition on science and creativity. They overwhelmed me with questions: What do we need such an army for, Mikhail Sergeyevich? Why do we need so many tanks, so many missiles? In short, the people will accept the idea of unilateral disarmament in the event that the international situation changes. However, we are already working in this direction. We have just given 6 billion rubles for public health—precisely by cutting military expenditures.

Shevardnadze raises the issue of whether it is time to withdraw our troops from Hungary.

Gorbachev: Yes, but first we need to reduce the numbers, not withdraw all at once. By the way, Khrushchev had all the right intentions in the military sphere. But look how he implemented them.

The third part—about the United Nations. Describe what it has lived through during the Cold War. Emphasize that it was created for purposes of cooperation and coordination, and therefore it was only natural that its role diminished during the Cold War; its role "decreased."

This organization is called the United Nations for a reason. In this context it should have a universally accepted doctrine, which would reflect the rights of the peoples, their right of free choice, human rights. Show the U.N. role as an instrument of the new world.

The fourth part: How do we see our contribution to the creation of the new world? We are not just calling for it, we are going to act. In the speech, we should present a set of responses to Western anxieties.

In general, this speech should be anti-Fulton—a Fulton in reverse. And we can already lean on some of our experience with work we have done according to the new thinking; we can show movement in the right direction. But they will believe us only when they see that we are making clearly evident, real steps.

The American theme should be present in the speech, i.e. our look at Soviet–American relations now and in the future.

We should present our worldview based on the results of the last three years. We should stress the process of demilitarization in our thinking, and the humanization of our thinking.

We should point to the fact that today international politics and contacts are expanding not only to the ranks of the people and politicians, but to the generals as well.

[*Source: Archive of the Gorbachev Foundation. Fond 2. Opis 1. On file at the National Security Archive. Translated by Svetlana Savranskaya.*]

Document No. 32: Summary of Conversations between Károly Grósz, János Berecz, Miklós Németh, Mátyás Szűrös and Aleksandr Yakovlev

November 10–11, 1988

This extensive document is one of a series of important records from the personal files of Aleksandr Yakovlev which provide extraordinary detail on the relationship between Gorbachev's regime and the East Europeans—in this case, Hungary. In May 1988, the reformer Károly Grósz had replaced the aged and ailing János Kádár as general secretary of the Hungarian party; here, Grósz is meeting one-on-one with Yakovlev, the Politburo's second-ranking member and a leading new thinker. Subsequently, the talks would include other members of the Hungarian party delegation (the economic planner and future Prime Minister, Miklós Németh, former ambassador to Moscow Mátyás Szűrös, and ideology secretary János Berecz).

The Big Brother dynamics in these talks are striking; the East Europeans are supplicants, looking to the Soviets for approval—a revealing insight into how the top levels of the socialist commonwealth actually interacted. Grósz tells Yakovlev all the details of the Hungarians' internal political discussions and provides candid assessments of individual personalities in the party. He warns that the party might split apart even before the next congress. He also goes so far as to suggest cutting Soviet troop levels in Hungary by 20 percent, a move which "could be used very well in a political sense, in the domestic and in the international spheres." Grósz comments that at two recent sessions of the CMEA he was shocked by the "flow of prayers and mutual entreaties ... We need to seriously change our collaboration." Yet he restates the Hungarian need to keep Soviet oil coming at the usual rate at least through 1995. He further describes a meeting of the bloc's general secretaries where there was a "dialogue of the deaf" with leaders such as Ceaușescu claiming that "history has confirmed the correctness of his course." For his own part, Grósz says, "I know that nothing is in order in Hungary, everything needs to be changed, and history has made our mistakes visible."

The talks took place one-on-one. At the start, *K. Grósz*, who had agreed to the general meeting the day before, emphasized that he would like to add to what he said at that meeting several questions which he would like M.S. Gorbachev to consider.

Regarding leadership. We are not very united on this. It is not a matter of different political views, although there is some of that as well. The main issue is with the difference in human qualities.

It is becoming clearer that the personnel decisions that had to be accepted at the conference in May were hasty, not thought-through and justified. If we can overcome these differences by the XIV Congress of 1991, then they will become just an episode of the past. But if we cannot, they could lead us a very long way, up to and including the possibility of the Party splitting into several parts during the Congress or before.

We are all one generation—we grew up together, have been working together for many years, and know each other well. This is one side of the issue. But there is another side. Some of our colleagues have too many ambitions, which are often not tied to the work and its substance, but to securing posts.

Where is the way out? In November I intend to reject the post of chairman of the HPR Council of Ministers. Many of my colleagues are against such a step, but I physically cannot work more than I am working now, and I feel that continuing to labor at two posts will be detrimental to the quality of work.

I would like, *K. Grósz* continues, for Nyers to be appointed to the post of prime minister. It is true that he has a social-democratic bias, and that he keeps old and close ties with the Western European social democrats. But Nyers is an honest man and he does not have personal ambitions.

Why would I like to see him in particular in this position? People say there are two or three younger candidates who are capable and talented. This is true. But we are worried that today and especially in the forthcoming situation they might not be able to withstand the pressure of problems and might ruin their life as a result. Nyers is 66 right now, he could work for two or three years, while the younger colleagues could build up more power during this time.

Other than Nyers, Németh is being promoted as a possible candidate for this post. But I am worried that an appointment to the post of chairman of the Council of Ministers might be harmful for him right now. He should wait for two to three more years.

Pál Ivani, the current chairman of the Budapest City Council, is also being named as a possible candidate. But at 45, he is also relatively young. Németh has experience primarily in executive work, Ivani in political work.

Kádár is strongly against Nyers' candidacy. The issue is that the current Parliament chairman is not nonpartisan, and Kádár is worried that if a person with a social-democratic bias becomes chairman of the Council of Ministers then on the whole it could give rise to incorrect perceptions of the real situation.

Besides the comrades named, we also have two self-appointed candidates. They are Pozsgay and Szűrös. The difficulties with them are not on political issues. We anticipate that when the economy enters a pre-crisis condition they might not have the firmness, steadfastness and resolve. The world is difficult right now, the situation inside and outside the country is not simple, and problems cannot be solved with pretty words.

Why do I myself reject this position? Because I hold the party and the situation within the party to be the most critical element in the developing situation. Right now the party is not strong in spirit, is beginning to weaken in terms of organization, and is showing indecisiveness in the labor movement.

I think it would be good if we could hold elections before 1990. The head of the government will be 76 in two years, and he promised me he would retire; I have already spoken with him about this. If Pozsgay's actions until that time show him to possess enough maturity, then his candidacy may be advanced for the post of president. And by 1990 I will have to find candidates to succeed Nyers and myself.

I, *K. Grósz* said, feel uncomfortable and personally responsible before Szűrös. He is talented, but he is too full of ambition.

Twenty years of friendship connect me with Berecz, *K. Grósz* went on, but there are also problems here. He considers himself to have been passed over for the posts of general secretary and Council of Ministers chairman.

It is unpleasant for me to speak about all of this. But I would like you to understand that in the next two-to-three years these human factors, which are not very serious from the point of view of major goals, may play a very big role in all of domestic policy life in determining the progression of our affairs and in our party.

Further, *K. Grósz* stopped at the question of the Soviet troop presence in Hungary. He said that when E.A. Shevardnadze was here some time ago, he asked a question about this, saying that the Soviet leadership was troubled by the public protests on this issue. I said to him then and I want to repeat it now: do not worry. But in the course of time this question could become political

I said this to Comrade E.A. Shevardnadze: if in the purely military sense you do not see any obstacle to reducing the number of troops even by 20 percent, then this step, if it were taken, could be used very well in a political sense, in the domestic and in the international spheres.

Regarding supplies of special equipment. I already raised this question during the discussions in Moscow. In this area we have built good factories and created large capacities. Our products are going to the Soviet Union and other countries in the socialist community, including 94 percent of the export going to the USSR. In the past five-year period the total shipment of special equipment to the Soviet Union amounted to 1.56 billion rubles, for an average of 350 million rubles per year. The reciprocal imports of special equipment over the same period of time amounted to 1.7 billion rubles.

We would like to reduce those imports right now by about 360 million rubles, including imports for the remaining two years of the five-year-plan period. The corresponding Soviet organizations agree to this, but with the same reduction in supplies of Hungarian special equipment to the USSR. Meanwhile, your military says that they need Hungarian special equipment.

At the same time, the balance of trade in consumer goods favors Hungary. But we cannot transfer this to the sphere of trade in special equipment. I do not understand, continued *K. Grósz*, what is the logic? Why is such a situation created that would force us to re-profile part of our military facilities? Of course, we can scale down these facilities; we can switch them to production of television sets and household electronics or some other civilian manufacture. But then they will be lost for military production.

Should we do this now, only in order to find some short-term, immediate way out of a temporary situation? Or is it more rational to find a way to hold out for two or three years and work out temporary solutions? We could lose world-class factories, workers of the highest qualifications, and smoothly-running production. And if we need it again in a couple of years, we will have to start from nothing.

Our countries' Gosplans cannot come to an agreement, saying that such a pattern of mutual supplies of special equipment was established a long time ago and must remain unchanged. But perhaps it would be appropriate to reconsider this pattern, think about whether it is right and justified? In other words, it would be beneficial to study the mechanism of mutual relations in this sphere in general, to re-check and re-think all of its sides under current conditions.

Regarding bilateral economic relations. We had a good discussion of these problems with N.I. Ryzhkov in April of this year, *K. Grósz* continued. A mutual understanding was reached then that we will not be able to increase the level of production output, but we will work to preserve what has been achieved so far. We agreed that for the period up to 1995 the USSR will continue to supply Hungary with energy products at the current level. But as of now, it cannot confirm such a commitment after 1995.

I respect this position, said *K. Grósz* further. It is clear, frank, and it gives us six years to prepare for new conditions. But after the discussion, practical matters developed in such a way that this year we expect about a 20 percent fall in output. And the reductions will not be for export, but for import.

The USSR's Gosplan proposes to reduce the import of products of the machine-building group, but to maintain the current level of supplies of agricultural and consumer industry products. I understand your needs related to the necessity of saturating the domestic market with goods. But a unit of export in machine-building is cheaper for us because in the production of agricultural and especially consumer industry goods the fraction of initial Hungarian imports from the West is relatively high, making the production of goods for export possible.

If we are forced to reduce output, if there is no other solution, then let us do it proportionally to the structure that has developed. We consider such an approach to be correct and fair, and we do not think that we are taking advantage of anybody when we propose such an approach.

Also we cannot understand where the Soviet leadership stands on this and where the collaboration mechanism and the apparatus are having an impact. But this is a crucial question for us, and it should be decided on the basis of reciprocity.

Further, *K. Grósz* raised some questions unrelated to each other, dealing with the collaboration between fraternal parties and different international problems.

Regarding multilateral meetings of general and first secretaries.

I first took part in such a meeting in Warsaw, he said, and I was struck by the depth of differences in approach and position of the leaders of the fraternal parties and countries.

M.S. Gorbachev opened his soul, and what took place afterwards? One of the leaders stood and said that he had been building socialism for 40 years, he has

316

solved all the problems, and history has confirmed the correctness of his course. The person speaking after him says that he too "stood at the cradle of the revolution" and everything is in order in his country. But I know that nothing is in order in Hungary, everything needs to be changed, and history has made our mistakes visible. That is why I essentially did not speak.

Is this a criterion for renewal? For how many years has a leader stood at the wheel of the party?! It was a dialogue of the deaf. People spoke at different "frequencies" and could not understand each other. The current approaches of a number of socialist country leaders make it impossible for one to really count on the renewal of our collaboration.

About the Iranian leadership's request. The chairman of Iran's administration and the chairman of Iran's parliament have addressed us with a request, *K. Grósz* said, to let you know that they would like to see an improvement in USSR–Iranian relations. While blaming the USSR for offering military help to Iraq in the course of the Iran–Iraq war, they pose the following question:

For Iran, one of the consequences of the end of the war is the necessity to carry out a re-equipment of the country's armed forces. Iran stands before a decision: should it carry out a post-war rearmament of its army orienting itself toward the FRG's help in this, or counting on the USSR's help? They would prefer to rely on the help of the Soviet Union.

Iran understands, they said, the reasons why the USSR most likely will not be able to provide this kind of aid directly. However, if they are in principle willing it could be organized through intermediaries.

If, *K. Grósz* added on his part, the Soviet Union makes a positive decision in this matter, we would appreciate it if you would send us a preliminary notification about this. This question troubles me, he continued, because we have already raised it in Moscow. The Iranians assert that they already have agreements with the USSR about this, reached through Y.M. Vorontsov and K.F. Katushev. We would be thankful to the Soviet side for information on this question, because we are expecting the president of Iran to visit Hungary in the near future.

Regarding *Israel*—sooner or later we will have to restore diplomatic relations with Israel. We must acknowledge that the decision made 20 years ago cannot be considered normal; history has not justified us in this. We supported the decision at the time; but we have always thought that it is impossible to play the game while off the field. The paradox is also in the fact that at the time we broke relations with Israel because of Egypt, as a sign of support. But today Israel and Egypt have been developing mutual relations for a long time.

Relations with Israel for us are not a matter of money; reciprocal trade amounts to about 20 million dollars per year for both sides. But about 160,000 Jews live in Budapest right now, and about 250 Hungarian Jews live in Israel. Of course family and human contacts exist between them, but broad intergovernmental relations do not. I do not see any point in such a situation; we need to resolve this problem. I would like, *K. Grósz* emphasized, for our Soviet colleagues to understand our reasoning here.

In conclusion, *K. Grósz* said, [there] is the personal question about S. Gaspar, the current chairman of the World Federation of Trade Unions. In May of this year at the party conference he was not elected to be a Politburo member, not even a CC HSWP member. An uncomfortable situation has resulted. In the leadership of a world organization stands a person who has lost the national political ground from under his feet.

A.N. Yakovlev thanks K. Grósz for his straightforward and frank presentation of questions, and emphasizes that he will make everything known to the CC CPSU Politburo. I think for both our parties, he says, it is important to concentrate on political matters. The human factor in politics is extremely important and the role of the party here is key. He briefly comments on some of the questions brought up by K. Grósz.

* * *

The day before, on November 10, 1988, the first talk between HSWP General Secretary and Chairman of the HPR Council of Ministers K. Grósz took place in a larger group in the CC HSWP. Also present from the Hungarian side were Politburo member and CC HSWP Secretary J. Berecz and CC HSWP Secretary M. Szűrös.

K. Grósz emphasized at the beginning of the conversation that the Hungarian leadership views the present visit as a show of support from the CPSU, which has special significance during this period. The opportunity to consult with the Soviet colleagues and learn about their opinion of the situation in Hungary is important to the HSWP leadership; perhaps it is possible to judge the situation more objectively from Moscow.

Speaking of the internal situation in Hungary, *K. Grósz* noted that the country is going through a very difficult moment of crisis. The cause for this lies in the long decades during which the HSWP fell behind reality and soothed itself with illusions. The XIII Party Congress resolutions (1985) turned out to be political improvisation; life quickly proved their inadequacy. Problems that we had been trying for a long time to "sweep under the rug" came to the surface.

The last years' quantitative changes led to a negative qualitative outburst and this does not concern the economy alone. The entire system of the country's political institutions turned out to be lagging behind real life. We will have to pay a heavy price today for the fact that the party dealt with surface phenomena without trying to examine their causes, the roots of the problems. There were pseudo-actions, which were presented, and accepted by many, as real action. We, *K. Grósz* stressed, somehow believed in the idea that we have enormous potential for renewal, but when this idea was tested it turned out to be self-delusion.

Subjectivism seriously damaged the work of the staff. During the last 30 years the country was led by a big personality—we grew up under his leadership, we are his students, we are personally much indebted to him. But with all due respect, we must clearly say that the big tree cast a big shadow. We are all guilty that our deep respect for this person prevented us from holding him back from subjectivism in deciding questions of personnel.

We, the leaders, ourselves proved to be unready either politically or spiritually for such a rapid change of circumstances as took place at the conference. We still have to work at achieving harmony on matters of political approach, as well as work style. The people who are now in the leadership have known each other for a very long time, but now they find themselves together in different capacities, and we will have to adjust to this psychological factor.

It is clear that right now the HSWP needs a long-term program for the next 20 years. But we have to prepare it under conditions in which everyday life makes demands, and when everyday problems are extremely difficult. That is why it was decided to make an inventory of the most relevant problems and to work out a plan of concrete actions for the next three-four years, so that during this period we could elaborate our long-term goals.

In this context, right now we have the greatest clarity on economic issues: we have a stabilization program until the year 1990. Concepts are forming as to how and in which direction to rebuild the political structures. A plan for legislative work has been developed; it aims at filling the substantial gaps from past decades and at creating the basis for a socialist legal state.

A question arises: will we be able to maintain control of the processes of change that have begun? The answer is yes; in general we have the power to do this. But undesired moments arise which are difficult to neutralize. Tensions arose between the party and the youth (including the working youth), who do not see promising prospects for themselves; there were tensions as well with the humanitarian intelligentsia.

However, the worker and peasant masses' trust in the party in general still remains. They believe that the HSWP will be able to deal with the situation, but they would like to understand its essence; they would like the leadership to act with more confidence in its power and more decisiveness, to define its plans more clearly.

What have we been able to achieve lately? The first reassuring tendencies have appeared in the economy. They signify the presence of solid reserves, since the results were reached not through serious changes but through superficial measures. But these results are not sufficient from the point of view of social needs, of solving the problem of debt. Net indebtedness is 13.7 billion dollars; interest for 1988 alone totaled 1.3 billion dollars. For the normal functioning of the Hungarian national economy, imports must reach 5–5.5 billion dollars per year; exports barely exceed this sum, so the debt problem cannot be solved through the assets of foreign trade.

According to the stabilization program mechanism, we plan to halt the growth of the debt by the year 1990. Of course, with a very large effort, we could meet this goal in the given timeframe. But wouldn't this strain lead to a crash of the Hungarian economy after a certain period? After careful consideration, we decided to "stretch" this period somewhat, during which time the increase in the debt can grow, in order to avoid unnecessary turmoil.

In order to maintain Hungary's solvency, we need to receive 3–3.5 billion dollars of new credits per year. It is not difficult to "obtain" them on the exchange market. But a further escalation of debt would mean a burden for future generations, which they will not be able to manage.

There is only one way out: to increase the economy's export potential in both directions—in the dollar and ruble markets. We need to save ourselves from crisis, but by running forward, not backward.

Regrettably, a large proportion of economic executives proved incapable of managing the economic processes. Before it seemed that this happened because they were not paid enough. Now they are paid much more, but the effect is the opposite. It seems the problems are deeper than that: in the mindsets, in the understanding of ethics and morals. The incentive system is not sufficiently developed; people do not feel they are masters of the workplace; egoism is the ideal.

Unusual trends have appeared against this background. A wave of mass demands for wage hikes has come up. Strikes have become a widespread phenomenon. Some strata of the population feel the leadership's uncertainty and are subjecting the leadership to straight-out blackmail in order to snatch some more material benefits for themselves. The leadership is under enormous pressure right now. Much, if not everything, depends on the leadership's ability to win over support of the rational forces to its side, and turn them into allies for the next three or four years in the struggle against extremist material demands.

The party is the key in this situation. While the danger in society comes from the Right, both deviations have appeared in the party. For some in the HSWP the current changes are too radical, for others they are half-measures and insufficient. Some think that a state of great chaos has developed in the country, and the reason for it is the rejection of the previous work methods which had proven their value before. The leadership in these situations must hold firmly to the initial conception; it must withstand the pressure and mobilize party members to bring the policy into life consistently, to fight and agitate for it.

Issues that have existed in latent form but were never the subject of broad discussions have come to the surface. First among them is the question of a multiparty system. It seems we can no longer avoid the emergence of new parties, but we are not interested in forcing this process. It will be necessary to rethink the substance of the party's leading role, so that it stops being paternalistic toward other organizations, and does not answer for "all" and "everything," but only for the key issues. Otherwise it will not be able to be at the forefront of society.

The most difficult situation right now is with youth organizations. The Hungarian Komsomol has lost its influence on the youth. It must be created anew, but with a new foundation. In the trade unions it seems the party will be able to maintain its influence for a long time. There is no real danger of repeating the Polish syndrome, but we must have a realistic view of the emergence of a multifaceted, pluralistic trade union structure.

Switching to bilateral relations, *K. Grósz* emphasized the HPR's enormous interest and sympathy for the changes in the USSR. A paradoxical situation has developed, where the Soviet example is cited by both the HSWP's friends and the opposition. But this is much better than the time when people were not interested in the affairs of the USSR.

Hungary is interested in closer and more effective cooperation with the USSR, with not only economic affairs in mind, but also political, ideological, cultural, and other relations. We are not satisfied with the effectiveness of our cooperation, but we understand that it is not due to a lack of good intentions. It seems the deficiencies are related to the two countries' structural differences, to routine problems, and to the fact that, objectively, our possibilities are not limitless.

As the head of the Hungarian government I took part in two sessions of the CMEA, and was shocked by the flow of prayers and mutual supplications. People with experience reassured me: it has always been like this, and it will go on like this. But I could not be reassured. We badly need to change our [means of] collaboration.

Despite our efforts, it seems that next year a reduction in the volume of Soviet–Hungarian trade will be inevitable. We can accept this as a temporary solution, but this cannot be the long-term prospect.

There is one way out—to transfer the focal point of cooperation from the intergovernmental level to the level of enterprises. Intergovernmental regulation should extend only to the largest projects, which fit into the general set of interests of the socialist countries. Tengiz[30] cannot be subject to enterprise collaboration due to the scale of the transaction, but determining who will supply whom with what kind of tires should not be the prerogative of Gosplan.

We need once again to reconsider many aspects of our relations, and to overcome the formalism we still face sometimes. It is necessary for the secretaries and CC department heads one day to take inventory and decide what we need in our relations and what should be thrown out as incidental and obsolete.

K. Grósz expressed his gratitude for the USSR's policy towards Hungarians in the Transcarpathian region. This was a big boost for the HSWP as it faced the difficult problem of the Transcarpathian region.

There were also talks with J. Berecz, M. Németh, and M. Szűrös.

J. Berecz noted as he characterized the situation in the party and the country that it cannot be regarded as normal, that difficulties are growing. Elements of crisis are present, negative attitudes predominate in the population. But the process of change has started in the country. At the same time, the party is late in responding to the new questions of social development. It does not explain to the people that the country is going through a period of permanent reforms, that there is no going back to the past.

---

[30] A major oil field in western Kazakhstan.

There are radical attitudes in the party itself, which have primarily been expressed through the change of leadership at the pan-Hungarian Party Conference, and keep manifesting themselves in the demands to speed up the fulfillment of adopted resolutions. A segment of the party membership does not understand the new developments; a certain confusion is present. The process of switching to political methods of work is going painfully. Discussions in the party have become aggravated, including discussions assessing the past.

The most important task right now is for the HSWP to mobilize, to be able to control social processes rather than just putting out fires. It is necessary to immediately find opportunities for contacts and dialogue with the new social organizations and unions, which have developed through democratization; we need to influence their positions.

The reorganization of the CC HSWP apparatus has started in the provinces as well. It has become necessary to strengthen party organizations at places of residence, where the alternative and opposition organizations mostly operate, while the party is presented mostly to pensioners. This detail is especially important in relation to the forthcoming elections. We should promote the work of the primary organizations, building them on the basis of both production and territorial principles.

Making up for lost ground, the HSWP is paying attention to the formation of a socialist legal state, and the creation of legal guarantees of law and order. The program in the area of legislation contains 29 laws.

We will have to change the Constitution. There are strong opinions among the intelligentsia in favor of introducing a multi-party system. While not rejecting this in principle, the HSWP right now is conducting a policy aimed at holding out the resolution of this question, although the law on unions and assemblies that is to be adopted in January does not preclude a multi-party system. But in circumstances where the HSWP is in a weakened condition we will have to clarify, in addition to this law, that the question of creating political parties will be regulated by other normative acts.

In the economic sphere the Hungarian colleagues are placing great hope in the impact of the law passed in October on economic associations. In the opinion of *M. Németh*, this law will allow more effective use of government, as well as public, property. Possibilities for mixed forms of property are being created, free enterprise will be more widespread, as will broader incentives for foreign capital.

However, the adoption of this law has come up against ideological stereotypes, making a portion of the party membership fear the return to capitalism. Naturally the HSWP does not want a return to capitalism, *M. Németh* noted, but it intends to strengthen the entrepreneurial attitude toward using government and cooperative property. The need to service foreign debt is a great hardship for the Hungarian economy; the interest alone is 1.3 billion dollars. This inhibits the rate of structural change in the economy. The process of economic stabilization entails the inevitable liquidation of unprofitable enterprises; it entails the emergence of unemployment.

M. Szűrös noted that at the stage of socialism that has unfolded in the majority of the socialist countries, there is a growing need for a friendly exchange of opinions on foreign policy. Touching upon the question of improving the work of the Warsaw Treaty, the CC HSWP expressed the opinion that striving for monolithic unity and a consensus on all issues, characteristic of the previous period, right now hinders us from moving forward, and this was evident at the last PCC meeting in Warsaw. It is clear that similar to the CMEA, in some cases we need to act on the basis of individual countries' interests.

M. Szűrös repeated Hungary's well-known position regarding the desire to take part in immediate measures to reduce the armed forces and regular armaments in Central Europe, including unilateral steps. Hungary's readiness to be a distinctive testing ground for such measures was emphasized—to take on the role of a coordinator for steps toward reducing regular arms inside the WTO.

The Hungarian colleagues also have the intention of creating an international center for human rights in Hungary. In connection with this, a proposal was put forward to conduct a meeting of expert-representatives from the CSCE member-states in Budapest, in order to discuss establishing such a center with coordination and research functions. In M. Szűrös' opinion, it would be possible to conduct a preparatory conference on one of the human rights issues in Hungary's capital before the Moscow conference on humanitarian issues.

Having stated the HSWP's support of the "common European home" concept, M. Szűrös confirmed the Hungarian comrades' readiness to continue the work of preparing a pan-European "Roundtable" for parties and movements. In accordance with the USSR agreement, the HSWP recently proposed to the CDU/CSU and the Italian Socialist Workers Party that they put forward an initiative on this issue, and they are waiting for a response from those parties.

M. Szűrös informed us that the HSWP, which in 1987 together with the Social-Democratic Party of Finland and the Italian Socialist Party advanced the idea of conducting a conference of non-nuclear European countries, is planning to develop its initiative by holding a new meeting of experts in Rome in 1989, with the addition of three more countries (from the WTO, NATO, and the neutrals).

Speaking in favor of conducting a "European Reykjavik," the CC HSWP secretary [Szűrös] at the same time expressed the opinion that this useful idea should be given time to mature. Forcing the implementation of this idea, which could alienate the partners, should not be allowed. Emphasizing the importance of broad preparatory work, M. Szűrös noted that in the course of this work it would be necessary to expose the Americans' attempts to devalue the idea of a "European Reykjavik" by referencing the USSR's efforts to distance Western Europe from the USA and Canada.

A.N. Yakovlev gave a detailed account of the major direction of the CPSU's work in implementing the XIX Union Party Conference resolutions, including conducting political reform, forming the socialist legal state, and solving pressing practical issues of economics and national welfare.

The Hungarian colleagues were informed about our assessment of international problems, and about the Soviet Union's point of view regarding improved cooperation among socialist countries within the framework of the WTO and CMEA. Special attention was given to our countries' and parties' cooperation in the European region.

The conversations were recorded by N. Kosolapov, V. Musatov, V. Dorokhin.

[*Source: State Archive of the Russian Federation [GARF], Moscow. Yakovlev Collection. Fond 10063. Opis 1. Delo 256. On file at the National Security Archive. Translated by Anna Melyakova.*]

Document No. 33: CIA Intelligence Assessment, "Gorbachev's September Housecleaning: An Early Evaluation"

December 1988

This document provides the CIA's evaluation—prior to Gorbachev's U.N. speech—of the radical personnel changes the Soviet leader made at the September Party Plenum. There, Gorbachev consolidated the two Central Committee international departments (covering socialist and non-socialist countries) into a single body; created a supervisory International Commission with Yakovlev at the head; and completely rearranged the party's power structure. The CIA's analysis is detailed and informative but typically cautious in its "lowest common denominator" view of the dramatic changes inside the Soviet Union. No doubt the writers understood that senior echelons of the U.S. intelligence community such as then-Deputy Director Robert Gates—as well as the incoming Bush administration—still regarded Gorbachev's initiatives and their growing popularity as a threat to the stability of the Western alliance system and a formidable challenge to U.S. foreign policy. Thus the assessment uses language such as, "The West is likely to face greater Soviet foreign policy activism"—as if such activism by definition could not be in the interest of the United States.

This was an intelligence failure. Eastern Europe remained relatively calm, but in the Baltic republics and the Caucasus forces of national independence, and ethnic and social centrifugal dynamics were already beginning to destabilize the Soviet Union. Only after his retirement as CIA director did Gates declare that the effects of Soviet political reforms and glasnost were "unforeseen by Gorbachev, and unforeseen by CIA." [31] Perhaps the most notable statement in the assessment is the following: "Given the realities of the system, Gorbachev can only hope to lay the groundwork for a process of change that could take decades." However, the assessment continues, if he fails to improve the quality of life of Soviet citizens, "the political gains of September 1988 could be short lived."

KEY JUDGMENTS:[32]

General Secretary Gorbachev has moved rapidly to capitalize on his strengthened political position. Since his dramatic leadership shakeup in September, Gorbachev and his new leadership team have been active on almost all policy fronts, issuing statements and taking actions that reflect a new, more favorable political balance for him at the top.

---

[31] Gates, *From the Shadows*, 439.

[32] Information available as of December 1, 1988 [as indicated in original document].

There are still significant constraints on Gorbachev's power, but he is in a better position than ever to advance his reform agenda. Although we cannot confidently predict specific policy moves, we identify below the areas that are likely to be or are being affected:

- *As both President and head of the party, Gorbachev now directly supervises the process of strengthening the legislative institutions and transferring some executive powers from conservative and resistant party bodies to the presidency.* In Early December, the Supreme Soviet approved legislation outlining a restructured Supreme Soviet and electoral system, giving the General Secretary much of what he wanted. Gorbachev's concomitant reorganization of the party Secretariat not only diminishes the authority of Yegor Ligachev—widely perceived as leader of the party's conservative wing—but also makes it easier for him to cut back the size of the party apparatus. The reorganization and the creation of commissions that report directly to the Politburo virtually remove the Secretariat from its traditional role as a major power entity. The arrest for bribe taking of former top Uzbek officials who are members of the Central Committee suggests that the leadership changes have enabled Gorbachev to penetrate the protective walls of the party apparatus in prosecuting his war on corruption.

- *The leadership shakeup has apparently helped Gorbachev's effort to give greater priority to consumer goods and services and may lead to an increased diversion of resources from military to domestic economic needs.* Gorbachev acted before final decisions had to be made on the 1989 economic plan and before preparations of the 13th Five-Year Plan had gone too far. The leadership has adjusted the 1989 plan to benefit the consumer and social sphere, bolstered efforts to increase food production, and taken new steps to commit resources of defense industries to the production of consumer goods. The personnel changes are likely to facilitate the expansion of controversial economic programs, such as cooperative activity and land leasing. Ligachev's continued responsibility for agriculture could pose a problem on the latter issue, but, as indicated by his public actions in October, Gorbachev now appears to be setting the agenda for agricultural reform. This agenda will continue to move in the direction of private leasing.

- *The new leadership team appears to be more tolerant of national assertiveness.* Since the leadership shakeup, the drive for greater political and economic autonomy in the Baltic Republics has gathered strength. Moscow has not cracked down on this activity—and has even encouraged some of it—apparently hoping to co-opt nationalist organizations that generally support Gorbachev's reform goals. But even the more radical reformers in the leadership are not prepared to allow independence for national republics, and, if Moscow and republic leaders cannot successfully co-opt nationalist organizations, they will probably have to rein them in, using force if necessary.

- *Gorbachev's political shakeup tilts the balance even further in favor of a more pragmatic, non-ideological approach to foreign affairs.* Gorbachev's two closest Politburo allies, Aleksandr Yakovlev and Eduard Shevardnadze, are now formally in charge of managing the party and government foreign policy decision-making bodies. The West is likely to face greater Soviet foreign policy activism, including bold—possibly unilateral—moves designed to generate international support for Soviet positions. The leadership's efforts to pursue more pragmatic policies in the Third World are likely to be invigorated by the changes as well.
- *The prospects for advancing "new thinking" on national security issues have increased.* The composition of the Defense Council has probably changed, reducing the representation of traditionalists who might constrain Gorbachev's room for maneuver on arms control and oppose unilateral cuts in military force levels. In addition, Gorbachev is now in a better position to reform the national security decision making process to allow inputs from a wider array of interests and thereby avoid ill-considered uses of military force. As with foreign policy, the United States is likely to face accelerated Soviet activity on national security issues, particularly with respect to bilateral and multilateral arms control.

Gorbachev has not achieved a decisive consolidation of power at the top. But he has probably strengthened his position in the leadership sufficiently to buy additional time to see if he can make *perestroika* work. Moreover, he has begun to build a political base outside of the party that could enhance his ability to exercise power for some time to come. Gorbachev's display of political muscle sent a powerful signal throughout the system that foot-dragging and fence-sitting are no longer options. This should help him in the battle with the bureaucracy to implement policies that the leadership has agreed to.

At the same time, Gorbachev's power play may have raised public expectations of change beyond what the new leadership is willing or able to deliver. Indeed, the regime is facing new pressure from those who feel the proposed political reforms do not go far enough to promote democratization or increase regional autonomy. CIA doesn't believe he can do it

Political strength alone is not sufficient to guarantee the success of Gorbachev's policies. The Soviet system is highly resistant to change, and political consensus at the top cannot overcome all the social and economic obstacles to successful reform. Given the realities of the system, Gorbachev can only hope to lay the groundwork for a process of change that could take decades.

Gorbachev will be held increasingly accountable for any future failures of *perestroika*. Recognizing this, he is trying to use his strengthened position to push through policies designed to improve the economy and the quality of life of Soviet citizens. If he fails to achieve this goal, the political gains of September 1988 could be short lived. [...]

We do not believe that foreign policy was a major factor in Gorbachev's personnel shakeup. Conflict over political and economic reform initiatives almost certainly precipitated Gorbachev's decision to make sweeping changes in his leadership team. No current foreign policy issue is as pressing or seems to have generated as much controversy as the problems the regime faces on the domestic front. Nevertheless, the changes come at a time of sharpening debate over the historical and ideological roots of contemporary Soviet foreign policy, issues over which the leadership itself has been divided. The leadership changes have increased Gorbachev's control over the foreign policy making process and tilted the balance decisively in favor of those who advocate breaking with the past and taking a more pragmatic, flexible, and non-ideological approach to foreign affairs. The pattern of recent positive Soviet moves toward China, Taiwan, South Korea, and the ASEAN countries, for example, will probably be reinforced by the new leadership team, as will Moscow's less disruptive behavior at the United Nations and more evenhanded policy in the Middle East. Moscow's efforts to sway Western public opinion can be expected to continue along the same track. In addition, Medvedev's role in shaping recent Soviet policy toward the Communist Bloc suggests that tolerance for diversity in Eastern Europe will continue.

The leadership shakeup represents a victory for those who have sought a revision of the ideological underpinnings of Soviet foreign policy to allow for greater operational flexibility. In a major speech to a conference at the Ministry of Foreign Affairs this summer, Shevardnadze virtually called for taking ideology out of international relations and said that peaceful coexistence can no longer be considered a specific tactical form of "class struggle." This was a major break with a central ideological tenet of the Brezhnev era in which vigorous international competition and conflict with the West—especially in the Third World—were portrayed as consistent with a policy of detente.

While Gorbachev was on vacation in August, Ligachev implicitly but unmistakably attacked Shevardnadze's position, asserting publicly that "class interests" must predominate in international relations and that "raising the question in another way" only causes confusion among the forces of "social and national liberation," a reference to Moscow's traditional left-wing allies. Chebrikov later echoed Ligachev's views, although in more subdued tones.

Perhaps the most important personnel change affecting foreign policy was the removal of President Gromyko. Foreign Minister Shevardnadze and Central Committee secretary Yakovlev, Gorbachev's closest Politburo allies, are now clearly in control of the management of foreign policy:

- Although he was no longer playing a direct role in foreign affairs, President Gromyko almost certainly maintained his status in the Politburo and Defense Council, where, by virtue of his unrivaled experience in dealing with the West, he probably was an influential spokesman for those in the party skeptical of Gorbachev's "new thinking."

- Yakovlev, as head of the Central Committee's new International Policy Commission, oversees the work of the restructured International Department. This department, which now incorporates the former Bloc Relations Department, is headed by Valentin Falin, who appears to be a Yakovlev protégé. In recent months, Shevardnadze has emerged as the leading advocate of change in the international debates over both the form and substance of foreign policy.
- Medvedev, who as ideology secretary will probably keep a hand in inter-Communist relations, also is a new thinker—he sided with Shevardnadze and Yakovlev on the issue of deemphasizing the class content of Soviet foreign policy. However, his ties to Gorbachev are less clear.

Anatoly Dobrynin's appointment as a special assistant to Gorbachev in the Supreme Soviet Presidium will keep him involved in foreign affairs, but it is unclear how much influence he will have without the resources of the International Department to draw on. [7 lines excised] Although he seemed well on his way to becoming Gorbachev's top foreign policy adviser when he moved to the Secretariat in 1986, he has since been increasingly overshadowed by Shevardnadze and Yakovlev.

NATIONAL SECURITY POLICY

Like foreign policy, national security policy was not a key factor precipitating the leadership changes, but it is likely to be affected by the reconfigured power balance. As mentioned above, the leadership now appears willing to divert at least some resources from the military in order to achieve domestic economic goals. At a minimum, the prospect of military cutbacks should reinforce the leadership's commitment to continuing—or even expanding—the arms control process. In addition, the new leadership team appears receptive to demands from reformers that, in order to avoid repeating what are now viewed by many Soviets as mistakes—such as committing Soviet troops to Afghanistan and deploying SS-20s in Europe—national security decisions must be made more judiciously, with input from a wider circle of specialists and, to some extent, from the public at large.

The leadership changes should create a more favorable environment for "new thinking" in the Defense Council, where important decisions on arms control and military commitments abroad are made. Although the exact composition of the Defense Council is not clear, it is likely that it included Gromyko as President, Ligachev as "Second Secretary," and Chebrikov as head of the KGB. Direct evidence of conflict over national security issues is sparse, but the public statements of these three men and some reporting suggests that they hold comparatively traditional views on national security issues and may have acted as brakes on some

329

aspects of Gorbachev's drive to implement "new thinking." Gromyko is now out of the Defense Council and the other two may be forced to relinquish their seats because of the change in their responsibilities as Central Committee secretaries. It is not clear whether the new KGB chief, Vladimir Kryuchkov, will sit on the Defense Council without being a member of the Politburo.

Besides removing potential obstacles to the reform of national security policy, Gorbachev may have added potential allies to the Defense Council. If Yakovlev was not already a member, he almost certainly is now by virtue of his new position as head of the Central Committee commission on international affairs. Medvedev may also be a member as ideology secretary, although his claim to a seat is less certain as he does not hold the "second secretary" position. Both men may be more likely than the traditionalists to support bold new arms control proposals and unilateral troop reductions abroad.

In addition to changing the composition of the Defense Council, the leadership changes have probably improved the prospects for change in the national security decision making process. In particular, by taking over the presidency, Gorbachev can seemingly move ahead with plans to increase the participation of representative state organs in key national security decisions—including those on defense procurement and the use of Soviet troops abroad. At the Foreign Ministry conference this summer, Shevardnadze called for Supreme Soviet committees to review national security policy decisions. Soviet officials have sought information on the U.S. legislative review process, apparently hoping to apply similar procedures in the USSR. While Gorbachev is unlikely to allow the Supreme Soviet to block him from taking diplomatic or military actions that have the full backing of the Politburo, he could use a legislative review process to his advantage if he is having difficulty rallying support for his initiatives in the party leadership.

Gorbachev clearly hopes that a moderate line associated with his new leadership team will help overcome the damage done to Moscow's image by the aggressive national security policies of the Brezhnev era. The leaders on the new team are cognizant of the public relations value of diplomatic flexibility and military restraint, and they are not likely to feel bound to policies developed under Brezhnev and Gromyko. Thus, we believe that the United States will be faced with even greater activism in Soviet foreign and national security policy than in the past, and that Moscow is likely to generate new initiatives on a broad range of international arms control issues. [...]

[*Source: CIA declassification. On file at the National Security Archive.*]

Document No. 34: Diary of Anatoly Chernyaev on the Situation in the Baltics

December 10, 1988

This diary entry shows that Gorbachev, unlike the CIA analysts in the September "Housecleaning" analysis (see Document No. 33), began as early as December 1988 to sense the rising instability in the Soviet Union, and particularly the spill-over effect that the secessionist movements in the Baltics were having on the Russian "mainland." Nevertheless, Chernyaev registers the remarkable "self-delusion and naïveté" of his boss for believing it was in the self-interest of the Balts to stay in the USSR. A few months later, as political revival began in Poland, Hungary and the GDR, the Soviet leader would display the same lack of realism in expecting that these countries would voluntarily remain a part of the Warsaw Treaty Organization and not risk losing economic and trade relations with the USSR.

The Baltics are in a storm. In Armenia and Azerbaijan, ten people get killed in a week; there is all-out nation-against-nation banditry. Fifty-thousand refugees, children are in the cold, houses looted, terrorism in transportation, etc.

Both followers of M.S. [Gorbachev] and the Balts feel that Gorbachev is ready to go very far down the road towards federalization of the Union. It is no accident that he cares to preserve common bonds of a very general nature: The October [Revolution], socialism, adherence to Lenin's choice [...] Everything else seems to be negotiable. But he is concerned by the reaction of the Russian component of the Union. Several times, speaking to me one-on-one, he said that [Russian] great power "undercurrents" [*potentsii*] are "rumbling" menacingly. As for me, I believe that in Russian nationalism the prevailing trend is not towards a "single and indivisible" [Russian empire], but nationalism as such: [people think] "let them, all these Estonians and Armenians, go to hell!" [The Russian] public seems to not really care but the enemies of *perestroika* are making background noises: [screaming that Gorbachev is] breaking up the Soviet Union, our great achievement. [...]

Gorbachev asked me and, as I learned, asked Shakhnazarov and Yakovlev: is it really true that the Baltic people really want to secede? I told him: I believe they do [...] And he told me (does he mock me or seriously think so): they will perish when they cut themselves off from the rest of the Union. Self-delusion and *naïveté* [...]

[*Source: Anatoly Chernyaev's Diary, Manuscript. On file at the National Security Archive. Translated by Vladislav Zubok.*]

Document No. 35: Transcript of CC CPSU Politburo Session

December 27–28, 1988

This is one of a very few official records of Soviet Politburo proceedings that are available publicly. The December meeting it chronicles was the first following Gorbachev's return from the United States, having cut short his travels in order to deal with the disastrous earthquake in Armenia. Gorbachev devotes much time to summaries of the increasingly grave forecasts for his perestroika *program by foreign analysts, but then proceeds to dismiss their seriousness. Part of the context for his lengthy monologues and Shevardnadze's proposals for a "businesslike" withdrawal of Soviet troops from Eastern Europe is the growing bewilderment of certain military and KGB leaders who were not fully informed in advance about the scale and tempo of Gorbachev's announced unilateral arms cuts. Still, there is no trace of real opposition to the new course. The Soviet party leader has learned a lesson from the military's lack of a strong reaction to the previous discussions of "sufficiency," and he is now ramming change down their throats. Ever obedient, Defense Minister Yazov states, "everyone reacted with understanding," even after Shevardnadze's aggressive attacks against the military for retrograde thinking, directly contradicting the U.N. speech, and proposing only "admissible" openness rather than true glasnost. Ironically, when Shevardnadze and Ligachev suggest announcing the size of Soviet reductions "publicly," Gorbachev objects: if the Soviet people and party learn how huge Soviet defense expenditures really are, it will undermine the propaganda effect of his U.N. speech. In yet another call for strategy vis-a-vis Eastern Europe, a conservative Politburo member, Vitalii Vorotnikov, says, "I consider the situation in a number of socialist countries to be so complicated that we should clarify our thinking in one document or another." No such integrated strategy ever appeared.*

---

1. ON THE PRACTICAL IMPLEMENTATION OF AND PRACTICAL SUPPORT FOR
   THE RESULTS OF THE VISIT OF CDE. M.S. GORBACHEV TO THE U.N.

Gorbachev: [...] We can state that our initiatives pulled the rug out from under those who have been prattling—and not without success—that the new political thinking is just about words. The Soviet Union, they said, still needs to provide evidence. There was plenty of talk, many nice words, but not a single tank is withdrawn, not a single cannon. Therefore the unilateral reduction left a huge impression and, one should admit, created an entirely different background for perceptions of our policies and the Soviet Union as a whole. [...]

Such impressive positive shifts created among the conservative part of the U.S. political elite—and not only in the U.S.—concern, anxiety and even fear. Thatcher also shares some of it. This breeds considerations of another kind, the essence of which is to lower expectations, to sow doubts, even suspicions. Behind it is the plot to halt the process of erosion and disintegration of the foundation of the "Cold War." That is the crux of the matter. We are proposing and willing to build a new world, to destroy the old basis. Those who oppose it are in the minority, but these circles are very influential.

In the classified information that we receive, they speak directly: we cannot allow the Soviet Union to seize the initiative and lead the entire world. [...]

What kind of policy will the U.S. conduct with regard to us? There are several very interesting and serious possibilities. [...]

Here is one: changes in the policy of the USSR are caused by a profound crisis in communism and socialism, and what is happening in the socialist world and the Soviet Union is allegedly a departure from these ideas. In other words, we are dismantling socialism with our *perestroika* and renouncing communist goals. This version is being used to devalue our peace initiatives. These are just forced steps, so they say; they have no other way to go. Well, there is some grain of realism in this, but only to a degree. We had something different in mind when we formulated our policy. Of course, we considered internal needs as well.

On the basis of this version comes the conclusion that the United States should do nothing for its part to consolidate the positive shifts in international relations. The Soviet Union, so they say, as well as other socialist countries, have no way out. [The USSR] will give up its positions step by step. This is serious, comrades. The *Washington Times* is writing about it. And the Heritage Foundation prepared a recommendation for the future Bush administration along these lines.

And here is the viewpoint of the liberal circles: The USSR is not renouncing socialism but is rescuing it, as President Roosevelt once rescued American capitalism through the New Deal. They remind us that capitalism, to solve its problems, many times borrowed socialist ideas of planning, state regulation, and social programs based on the principle of more social fairness. So they do not want to allow the Right to play on their version and to devalue our peace initiatives. [...]

If this [conservative] version prevails, it will have a serious political effect. Incidentally, some elements from this concept are present in Bush's thinking, as if they are passing from Reagan to Bush. They are present in Western Europe: they say that under Reagan the United States built up its military potential, activated its support to freedom fighters in various regions, and thereby convinced the Soviet Union that an expansionist policy has no future. Some Europeans also want to see the source of change in Soviet policy as emanating from American power.

This seems to be the most influential current. In essence, it is close to the official viewpoint. Its harm is obvious since, if it takes root and is embedded in the policy foundation of the future administration, it will contribute to the arms race and to military interference by the U.S. in other countries. I am now following these things very closely. [...]

Now we should work out a longer-term plan of practical measures to implement the announced concept [at the U.N.] On this issue the Politburo has received considerations from departments of the CC, Foreign Ministry, Defense

Ministry, and the Committee of State Security [KGB]. They provide a program of action for the near and long term. Perhaps this is still a first draft. We should put our heads together and give it time. [...]

Among the things that were discussed during my stay in New York, the major issue was the future of *perestroika*. And this I would like to emphasize before the Politburo. Could there be a turn backwards? Incidentally, this is an object of most intense speculation among the Far Right. [...] And if you analyze the content of recorded foreign broadcasts in the languages of our country on all foreign stations, the emphasis is clearly on the difficulties of *perestroika*, on growing obstacles to the process in the economy, in relations among nationalities, in the process of democratization and *glasnost*, etc.

When I had to stay in isolation [during the trip], I tried during those twelve days, day by day, to analyze and systematize the materials in this regard and to give them my assessment. [Radio voices] are hammering away at the Soviet audience that *perestroika* is losing ground, grinding to a halt, that it has not given anything to the people, that chaos reigns in the leadership and the party, and that the country is sliding toward chaos. No matter what the leadership undertakes, it will sooner or later end up in a trap. And the future of the present leadership hangs by a thread. To be frank, they say that Gorbachev is living through his last days. According to most optimistic forecasts, he may have a year, or a year-and-a-half. True, Vladimir Aleksandrovich [Kryuchkov]?

Kryuchkov: People say many things.

Gorbachev: You do not want to speak up. It is so. I should not say we are very surprised by all this. I do not want to be excessively cheerful, but if they are upset, if they try to make these forecasts, it means that they are afraid of our *perestroika*. [...]

Of course, it is still premature to draw serious conclusions about the policy of the future administration, but something can be said on the basis of contacts and certain information. First, it is hard to expect that this administration will aggravate relations with the USSR or will get involved in a risky international venture that could undermine these relations. There seem to be solid grounds for saying this. On the other hand, comrades, I believe with full certainty that this administration is not ready for a new, serious turn in relations with the USSR, which would be adequate to the steps our side has undertaken. At least such is the picture today. So they say: we will remain prudent, we will not hurry.

Still, at the last moment, when I managed to tear myself away from Reagan, I spoke to Bush about this indecisiveness. He snapped back: you must understand my position. I cannot, according to American tradition, come to the fore until a formal transfer of power has taken place. This I understand, no question about it. We will have an understanding. And he assured me: there will be continuity. He believes we should build on what has been achieved and will make his own contribution.

All that we picked up from different channels says that from their side they will augment efforts to develop our relations.

We should take into account that Bush is a very cautious politician. They say that his idiosyncratic feature is "natural caution." It is inside him. We should see it. And what can make Bush act? Only [the threat] of a loss of prestige for the administration. So we need [the sorts of] circumstances that we have now created through our initiatives, to promote this process.

The mood of the present administration mostly reflects centrist sentiments in U.S. political circles. **And Bush himself says: I am in the Center.** Most of those who today turn out to be on Bush's team are people who are called traditionalists in America. These people were brought up in the years of the Cold War and still do not have any foreign policy alternative to the traditional post-war course of the United States with all its zigzags to the right and to the left, even with its risky adventures. We should understand that. And much will depend on how we act. I think that they are still concerned that they might be on the losing side, nothing more. Big breakthroughs can hardly be expected. We should produce smart policy.

[Georgy] Arbatov has just shared the following ideas. They [the Americans] have suddenly sent up a trial balloon: we are not ready; let's wait, we will see. In general, they will drag their feet, they want to break the wave that has been created by our initiatives. In response they heard that, of course, we could wait because we have much to do in other directions—European, Asian, Latin American. Then they say: well, you misunderstood us.

So we should have a thoughtful, dynamic, practical policy. We cannot allow the future administration to take an extended period of time and slow down the tempo of our political offensive. [...]

Shevardnadze: [...] There is a draft resolution [on point 1 of the Politburo agenda]. Of course, I do not consider it a final draft. We will have to work on it [...]

It is not true that the draft has not been cleared with the Ministry of Defense. The reasons are well known: comrades were not in place; only Comrade Lobov was present and all these issues, all these points we agreed upon with him. We went to him, obtained his signature, etc.[33] But this is not so important. I am worried about something else. What, for instance, does the Ministry of Defense propose in its report? To present data to the Supreme Soviet only after their consideration by the Defense Council and the Politburo, etc.? Should we do that, if we are getting ready for a new Supreme Soviet with a new status, new rights, new content and forms for its work? I believe that should not be done.

I have serious reservations about the proposal that the Supreme Soviet receive information only about the main lines of a military build-up and not the plans

---

[33] General Vladimir Lobov was chief of the Soviet General Staff. In an effort to keep the information on the actual number of reductions to a very limited circle, and to avoid wide discussion among the senior military, which would have opposed the reductions, the draft proposal was presented to the General Staff on the weekend, when conveniently only Lobov was in his office, and he signed without involving other top military officers.

for this build-up, as the draft suggests. This may result in the absence of any details in the Supreme Soviet's discussion of this issue and also in the same negative consequences we have already spoken about. Specific plans will continue to be adopted and implemented in secrecy without the Supreme Soviet. We should probably not let that happen. It is absolutely unclear how the Supreme Soviet, without information on specific plans, will be able to consider seriously and approve defense expenditures. This is a very serious issue. It is also hard to understand the reasons for the objection to these clauses of the [Foreign Ministry's Politburo draft resolution] where it speaks about the presentation of a plan and schedule for withdrawal of our troops from allied territories and about the discussion of this with our friends.

As far as I know, a specific schedule for withdrawal has not been discussed in the Committee of Ministers of Defense [of the WTO]. We should have plans, we should agree on them with the allies and announce them publicly so that everybody knows about our firm intention to carry out what was stated at the United Nations in a systematic, purposeful and orderly way. Otherwise, if everything is to be decided, as the comrades [from the Ministry of Defense] write, in the usual course of business, we will become a target for allegations that we are trying to sidetrack the issue of withdrawal and troop restructuring, and not do things as was announced from the podium at the General Assembly.

The following instance [in the Ministry of Defense proposals] is in direct contradiction to what was said from the Assembly's podium and to the clause of the [Foreign Ministry] draft resolution. I have in mind the Defense Ministry formula that [Soviet] forces that will remain on the territory of socialist countries after the [unilateral] cuts will adopt a more, I stress, more defensive posture. These are just words, but they have significance in principle. Cde. Gorbachev spoke about giving these forces a different, unequivocally defensive structure. This is an important and big difference. We will be caught at every turn, so to speak. And now they propose that we talk not about structure but about some kind of abstract direction. Behind this difference in terminology stand various methods of implementing the general secretary's address. In practice we should act in accordance with the speech at the U.N., so that deeds do not diverge from words.

I also cannot agree with how the Ministry of Defense draft treats the issues of *glasnost* and openness, which are today of principal importance, of the highest importance. When we carry out our unilateral steps, *glasnost* and openness will be maximized, in my opinion. Otherwise the desired effect will be lost, and, it seems to me, our policy will sustain a propaganda defeat. Our opponents will not hesitate to take us up on this and sow doubts [to the effect] that the announced steps are not being implemented in full.

[The military] proposes not a maximal level of openness, but a level that would be acceptable. What that means—acceptable openness—is not clear. Even more important is that even this acceptable *glasnost* and openness are suggested to be applied only to the withdrawal of our troops from allied territory. As to reduction measures on our territory, apparently no *glasnost* is admitted. This is probably wrong as well.

In general, my conclusion is that the amendments [to the Foreign Ministry draft proposed in the Ministry of Defense's] draft resolution, in particular to the military-political section, are designed not to allow genuine *glasnost* and openness. And I still believe that these issues are of great importance.

In conclusion, Mikhail Sergeyevich, several words. You spoke about certain information reports [...] They want us to be nervous. And look at them, they are serious people, serious politicians. [...]

Gorbachev: Yesterday in the morning [U.S. Ambassador Jack] Matlock asked for a meeting with Yakovlev and arrived. He listened to a broadcast from Leningrad, inspired by comrade [Yurii Filippovich] Soloviev [first secretary of the Leningrad Party Organization]. During this program the chairman of the Administration of the GDR also spoke and said that one should keep in mind the plots of the imperialist intelligence services and their subversive activities against *perestroika*. Well, Matlock then said: "I have a special request from my leadership, both the current and the future one, to declare that we support *perestroika*."

Shevardnadze: You know, sometimes we ourselves help to discredit certain foreign authorities. We found an analysis of this fellow, Kissinger. Look what remained of his theory after your speech.

Gorbachev: Nothing remained.

Shevardnadze: If one says something, then another, a second, a third, we should not take it as absolute wisdom. I think we should treat it more seriously.

Gorbachev: We get used to the fact that in our country if someone speaks up it is not necessarily an official viewpoint. And there they just prattle on, you see. [...]

Gorbachev: When we discussed [alternative military service] at the Defense Council and even considered it at the Politburo, we spoke about a reduction of troops by 500,000. Then, in order to resolve the issue with students, we said: add to these 500 another 100,000 to remove the issue of enlistment of students, but let's continue talking everywhere about 500,000. These 500 are army troops, and 100 are construction troops. Eduard Amvrosievich [Shevardnadze] would have liked to announce the figure 600,000, but I told him no, because when we start comparing numbers of troops, they will always poke their finger at the fact that these are construction troops, and we will insist that they are not. Therefore, officially we speak about 500,000. [...]

Yakovlev: Yesterday I met with Matlock. He told me that Bush is more professional, better informed, but at the same time is more cautious. He tried to convince me that he always took part in the preparation of specific decisions, was interested in details, and knew many—i.e. he cast the new president in the best possible light.

What else should we keep in mind in terms of putting pressure on the Americans? They are very afraid of our European and Pacific policies. They would not like to jump on a departing train, not to mention a runaway train. They are used to driving the engine. They are upset by our active foreign policy in other regions [...]

Most important, Mikhail Sergeyevich—you spoke many times about this—is the disappearance of the image of the enemy. If we continue to advance in this direction and we carry out this business, we will ultimately pull the carpet from under the feet of the military-industrial complex [of the United States]. Of course, the Americans will be forced radically to change their approaches. [...]

Yazov: In accordance with the decision of the Defense Council taken on November 9, the Ministry of Defense has already worked out the plans for withdrawing our troops from the GDR, ČSSR, HPR and PPR.

After your speech at the United Nations, I attended a party conference of the Group of Soviet Forces in Germany. There was not a single question or a provocative remark. Fourteen people spoke, and all accepted this with approval. On Saturday I was at a conference in the Kiev district of Moscow. There was this question: "Would the withdrawal affect preparedness for defense?" I answered. There were no more questions; everyone reacted with understanding. The entire armed forces of the country regard this with understanding. At the Committee of Defense Ministers' meeting in Sofia, all the ministers accepted it with understanding.

I believe that we are ready to report to the Defense Council on our plans for implementing the proposals that were announced at the United Nations.

The Ministry of Defense does not object to publicity of the issues of military build-up in the Commission of the Supreme Soviet. But while according to the Constitution the Defense Council exists I believe that all the issues should be considered at the Defense Council before they are moved to the Commission of the Supreme Soviet. I do not know why Cde. Shevardnadze disagrees with this. Before Mikhail Sergeyevich presented these proposals at the United Nations, this issue had been considered by the Defense Council and over here at the Politburo. How could it have been otherwise? The Americans do not let us know everything either. What we really want to learn from them we cannot buy for any amount of money in the world. And why should we pass everything right away through the Commission of the Supreme Soviet? Today the Commission of the Supreme Soviet will include a very broad circle. And not everybody should know everything.

Gorbachev: I think there is a misunderstanding [...] There are many things that Americans consider behind closed doors.

Yazov: Absolutely true.

Gorbachev: There are things that the Congress does not even consider. They can be carried out at the discretion of the president and the National Security Council.

Yazov: Now, on the formula about our defensive direction. In his speech Mikhail Sergeyevich has mentioned cuts by 10,000 tanks. In doing this, we have to touch on all troops that are located in the Group of Soviet Forces in Germany. We have to include our tank divisions. There are motorized regiments in tank divisions. We intend to preserve these motorized regiments, and to remove tank regiments from the tank divisions that will remain in Germany so that more tanks can be withdrawn. In this situation should we really reveal the entire structure only because we want more *glasnost*?

I believe that is the prerogative of those countries which provide their territory for our troops. In any case, we will reveal what can be revealed, but it is not necessary to go all the way.

As to the schedule for withdrawal, we are ready to make a report on it. We propose to withdraw three divisions from Eastern Europe this year and three divisions next year.

As to the part concerning the USSR and Mongolia, we are also prepared to report to the Defense Council regarding the schedule.

Ligachev: I would like to mention two or three circumstances [...] In a word, *perestroika* in international relations is very substantial. Meanwhile, it does not lose its class character, which was stressed by Mikhail Sergeyevich in his report at the XIX Party Conference. At the same time, we spoke, and justifiably so, about the priority of common human values, common human interests. I believe that if it were not for the common interests of the countries that belong to different socio-economic systems, there would be no unity of action. There is apparently a common interest in the following area: the huge burden of military budgets; this is felt by the socialist world as well as by the capitalist world. Issues related to the survival of humanity and ecological problems have become burning issues. All this, taken together, and above all our policy of initiatives, have led to some changes for the better. This is the first point I wanted to mention.

The second point: foreign policy is a very large complex of issues. The most important among them is disarmament. [...] We need disarmament most of all. We took such a burden upon ourselves with relation to the military budget that it will be difficult to dramatically solve anything in the economy; plus, sometimes we took on this burden without sufficient grounds for it. I've already mentioned this before.

But this does not mean that we should weaken the country's defense preparedness. We have enough ways, approaches and means to reduce excessively large military expenditures and to use rationally, pragmatically the means for strengthening the nation's defense readiness. We should tell the party and party activists about this. Today, when the world has already begun to disarm, slowly but surely, in the final analysis the power of the state will be determined not by military might but by a strong economy and by the political cohesion of society. [...]

Vorotnikov: [...] I would mention only one point. You, Mikhail Sergeyevich, in your speech have emphasized an ambiguous approach to *perestroika* and the reaction in capitalist circles, including the United States. But even in the socialist countries we run into serious problems.

Maybe in our draft resolution we should formulate the course for our policy towards the socialist commonwealth after all? Indeed, there is nothing in the draft besides telebridges [*telemostov*] that should be arranged with socialist journalists. I consider the situation in a number of socialist countries to be so complicated that we should clarify our thinking in one document or another. This flows from your speech.

Gorbachev: Comrades, let us call it a day. Our campaign, which we had prepared for so long and have implemented, has generated much publicity. It elevates us to a new level in our thinking and work. [...]

I think that our resolution encompasses in general all these areas [political, diplomatic, ideological follow-up]. But the comrades should read it once again. Perhaps they will add something useful to it or suggest some corrections.

I also have two points to add. Vitalii Ivanovich [Vorotnikov] said that people ask around the country and even at home: how did it come about that we are once again "stripping down" of our own accord? And Yegor Kuzmich [Ligachev] approached this theme from another angle: the party should know. We are still keeping it a secret, frankly. And we keep this secrecy for one reason: if we admit now that we cannot build a longer-term economic and social policy without [unilateral cuts], then we will be forced to explain why. Today we cannot tell even the party about it. First of all, we should bring in some order. If we say today how much we take for defense from the national revenue, this may reduce to nothing [the effect] of the speech at the United Nations since a situation of this sort does not exist in any other country—perhaps only in poor, destitute countries where half of their budget goes for military spending.

Shevardnadze: For instance, in Angola.

Gorbachev: Yes. But there the budget and everything is different. We are talking about another story. If we take this [*glasnost*] approach now, then people will tell us: your proposal is rubbish, you should cut your military expenditures by three-to-four times. How do we go about that, comrades? First, in our plans we build in military expenses that are twice as large as the growth of national income; then our national income turns out to be down the tubes; yet we stick to our military plans. So put two and two together about what is going on here. For this reason we should be patient a little bit longer. But you are all correct—we will have to speak about it. Meanwhile, only in the political sense. [...] By the time of 13th five-year plan, Yurii Dmitrievich [Masliukov], we will implement all these decisions and will have something to say. Then our expenses on this item will be somewhat closer to the American expenses. [...]

A lot of work should be done on our [military] grouping in Eastern Europe. We should do it in a systematic way. I know that all these proposals are in preparation for the Defense Council. We agreed to hold [a meeting] in early January and to discuss all these issues. [...]

Let's finish our exchange. It was necessary. This is really large-scale policymaking. I propose to instruct Comrades Shevardnadze, Zaikov, Yakovlev, Yazov, and V.M. Kamentsev to finalize the draft resolution of the CC on these issues, keeping in mind the discussion at the Politburo.

Members of Politburo: Agreed.

[*Source: RGANI. Published in "Istochnik" 5–6, 1993. Translated by Vladislav Zubok.*]

Document No. 36: Record of Conversation between Aleksandr Yakovlev and Henry Kissinger

January 16, 1989

The following series of documents from the Kremlin's talks with Henry Kissinger in Moscow provide the first primary-source evidence ever published on one of the most controversial subplots in the narrative of the end of the Cold War. The former U.S. secretary of state, largely excluded from official roles during the Reagan years, volunteers himself to the incoming Bush administration in December 1988 as an intermediary with Gorbachev, with the idea of proposing a cooperative superpower effort to maintain stability in Europe. The documents suggest there is interest in both Washington and Moscow, but to the outside world this would look like the Yalta division of Europe all over again—a great power condominium to decide everyone else's fate. By March 1989, Secretary of State James Baker would leak the Kissinger initiative and disavow it, shrewdly limiting the political damage for the president.

In this set of notes written by Yakovlev's aides, Kissinger begins by trying to convince Yakovlev of his closeness to Bush, then quickly moves to a warning about the potential for "unpredictability" in Europe "[i]f the balance of military forces on the continent shifts drastically." Kissinger continues, according to the Russian notes: "G. Bush, as president, would be willing to work on ensuring conditions in which a political evolution could be possible but a political explosion would not be allowed." Otherwise, Kissinger warns, German nationalism would rise, and U.S. troops would therefore need to stay in Europe because "[we] need a guarantee against the adventurism of Europeans themselves." Kissinger alerts Yakovlev not to expect rapid movement on Washington's part, because "the incoming President will need some time to grasp in detail all the discussions on military-political questions that are going on now in the United States." Yakovlev may well be asking himself at this point what Bush had been doing for eight years as vice president.

I received H. Kissinger upon his request.

At the start of the conversation, H. Kissinger made a statement about his closeness to the new president of the USA, George Bush, and to the people comprising his inner circle. At the present time, he said, in this circle Bush, Baker, Sununu, and Scowcroft are actively debating perspectives on Soviet–American relations. The general goal set by G. Bush comes down to the following: that in "four years we should be able to demonstrate a new quality in relations between the United States and the Soviet Union." For this purpose it is necessary to make a more decisive turn toward the most essential, substantive issues of relations between the two states, mainly the political ones.

I do not believe, said H. Kissinger, in the reliability of relations that are built only on personal contacts between the top leaders. Stable relations can only be built on the basis of the long-term interests of each side. In this connection, the coming U.S. administration is currently taking an inventory of U.S. interests for the future, and is developing a philosophy of its own foreign policy course, and so [the administration] is ready to accept relevant ideas from the Soviet side.

The long-term and principal interests of both the USA and the USSR require them to turn to the political side of their relationship. "The top leaders should not be preoccupied with counting warheads or confidence-building measures," said H. Kissinger. "This is the business of experts." The top leadership should mainly consider the political issues on which the content and the reliability of future relations will depend.

In H. Kissinger's opinion, those initiatives and proposals that have been presented up till now, even if they are 100 percent implemented, "will only touch the outer surface of Soviet-American relations, and will not engage them substantively." The key issue is precisely about how genuinely to engage the political essence of the relationship. H. Kissinger reiterated this idea numerous times in the course of the conversation.

In the United States, continued H. Kissinger, presently "a very serious discussion is taking place about political relations" between the USSR and the USA in perspective. "You are leaving Afghanistan," he said, "but other conflicts remain, for example in Angola and Nicaragua. Even in Afghanistan, the conflict will persist after your withdrawal."

But even the future of Europe carries within itself the potential for unpredictability. If the balance of military forces on the continent shifts drastically, "a very complicated situation might emerge." "G. Bush, as president, would be willing to work on ensuring conditions in which a political evolution could be possible but a political explosion would not be allowed."

Developing this theme, H. Kissinger said that if in the future something were to happen in Europe that would lead to "active Soviet military involvement" in some form—especially after conventional weapons have been reduced, nuclear weapons abolished, and the image of the USSR as an enemy removed—Germans in the FRG would feel as if they had been betrayed by the Americans. The growth of nationalism in both parts of Germany "will hurt us Americans in the next five years, but in 50 years it will hurt you." The countries of Eastern Europe are now entering a [stage] of "special evolution." As a result, after a period of time, Europe could become explosive once again, "and if that were to happen, 98 percent of Americans would say that the Soviet Union had envisioned all that from the very beginning."

It is impossible to stop history, as Kissinger summed up this part of his deliberations, but "it is possible to stop its explosions, to increase collective security before such explosions occur, and to discuss the emerging political problems." In Afghanistan, "we want you to withdraw, but we do not want to create problems for your security or any kind of difficulties for you. We accept the fact that your country has legitimate security interests there. But we have the same situation and same legitimate security interests in Nicaragua." We have to turn to a discussion of political problems—some of this could become part of official agreements as a result, and some can become a part of our mutual understanding.

We consider it our problem, continued H. Kissinger, that the United States has no tradition of foreign policy that would be genuinely based on a consciously understood national interest. Instead, we are thrashing about under the influence of emotions and ideological predilections. In the USSR, as I see it, you have a different problem: "you have never lived in balance with your neighbors. Either they invaded Russia, or Russia ensured its security by expanding its territory."

In our view, said H. Kissinger, the USA and the USSR will have to learn to live in balance with each other. "We should not be trying to reform you, and you [should] agree to live in conditions of relative and not absolute security. I do not believe that you have any plans for world revolution, and the Soviet Union does not have capabilities for that either."

Neither the USSR nor the USA needs a mutual confrontation. Any mutual conflict would weaken both sides and would not strengthen either one. It would only benefit third countries, "which are developing quickly even without it." "We discussed this in detail in G. Bush's inner circle," stated H. Kissinger, "and we believe that to create a serious balance we need a dialogue, some form of deliberation on essentially political relations. Then all the other issues, such as arms control or economic relations, will move much faster."

Developing the idea of the substance of such a political dialogue in response to a question, H. Kissinger spoke in a preliminary fashion about the possibility of separating issues of political evolution, which is impossible to stop, from those of security as such in the process of this kind of dialogue, in order to try to combine the continuation of political evolution with preservation of the status quo in the sphere of security. Without putting obstacles in the natural course of political evolution, but also without trying to energize it in an artificial way, without making efforts to suppress it, and while taking into account the legitimate interests of each side. The coming U.S. administration would be ready to discuss all these questions in a confidential manner. Scowcroft could serve as its representative.

H. Kissinger spoke very decisively against a complete withdrawal of U.S. troops from Europe: "We need a guarantee against the adventurism of Europeans themselves. In the case of a complete withdrawal of our armed forces from Europe, it would be politically more difficult for us to bring them back than it would be for the Soviet Union, if there were such a need."

Responding to the question in which areas he would envision the possibility of serious progress, H. Kissinger said that in his opinion one could expect an affirmation by the new administration of its adherence in principle to the idea of continuing the [present] course of relations with the USSR, as adopted by President Reagan. A statement to that effect, in a general form, will in all likelihood be included in G. Bush's inaugural address, as will a general point about the possibility of cooperation on the environment—about which the newly-elected president spoke earlier—and in the sphere of banning chemical weapons.

At the same time, noted H. Kissinger, the incoming president will need some time to grasp in detail all the discussions on military-political questions that are going on now in the United States. In part, these discussions are related to the necessity of responding to the budgetary situation. However, in part, [they are related] to the indefinite situation existing in the strategic sphere as such; for example, how should the USA react to SS-24 and SS-25 missiles?

We would also like, said H. Kissinger, to figure out the interconnections and interdependencies between strategic and conventional weapons. This analysis is especially challenging for the USA, "because earlier we did not study conventional weapons as closely and as comprehensively as we did in regard to strategic weapons. Besides, past experience shows that in contrast to strategic [weapons], in the conventional sphere the balance does not guarantee against war." There have been instances where wars have been started, and even won, by those with fewer weapons. In other words, in this sphere, one has to account for many more parameters than in the strategic one.

H. Kissinger showed detailed interest in the progress of *perestroika*, in its practical results and difficulties, in the reaction to it by various strata of the population, in the prospects for the price-formation reform, and in the resolution of problems that have accumulated in inter-ethnic relations.

January 17, 1989
[Signature] Aleksandr Yakovlev

[*Source: State Archive of the Russian Federation [GARF], Moscow. Yakovlev Collection. Fond 10063. Opis 1. Delo 258. On file at the National Security Archive. Translated by Svetlana Savranskaya.*]

Document No. 37: Record of Conversation between Mikhail Gorbachev and Henry Kissinger

January 17, 1989

This discussion between Gorbachev and Kissinger is not nearly the substantive back-and-forth that Kissinger experienced the previous day with Yakovlev (see Document No. 36). The meeting seems almost ceremonial rather than a negotiation, with the focus on the process of how to open a confidential channel rather than the pro's and con's of the superpower condominium idea. Kissinger remarks that former Ambassador to the U.S. Anatoly Dobrynin has the direct personal number of the new national security adviser, Brent Scowcroft, and, not surprisingly, Kissinger makes clear that he would like to be in the loop as well. The American also plays up to the Soviets regarding the Jackson–Vanik legislation from the 1970s, which limited economic cooperation with the Soviet Union and placed human rights and emigration conditions on any American aid or credits. Kissinger comments that the law was "directed against me in the first place, and only then against the Soviet Union. I agree with you. I always thought it was wrong. I believed that your emigration policy was your country's internal affair."

[...]

Kissinger: In practical terms, as I understand it, you implied to George Bush in your conversation on Governors Island that you would like to establish a channel for a confidential exchange of ideas. He understands that on your end Anatoly Dobrynin would serve as the contact.

Gorbachev: Yes, that's correct.

Kissinger: President Bush is very interested in this method of communication. We have not worked out a specific mechanism yet, but it is clear that Scowcroft will be an important figure on the president's side in such a dialogue.

We are ready to begin at any time convenient for you. At the end of February the President will visit Japan with a short stop in China. Maybe the beginning of March could be a convenient moment? It would be a good opportunity if Anatoly Dobrynin could be in the United States at the time, or maybe some other way.

This confidential channel could be used without any harm to our dialogue through all other existing channels. It will give us an opportunity to open up for you somewhat the course of our internal discussions of certain problems, so that when we introduce a proposal, you would know what ideas and goals are behind it.

George Bush would appreciate an opportunity to receive similar information from you. [...]

Gorbachev: Of course, the problem of coordinating our economies, the search for forms of cooperation, is a very real problem, and both sides should think about it. However, already today, the steps we have taken in our foreign economic policy—the creation of legal and economic bases, strengthening guarantees for our foreign partners—should be supported on your side by a repeal of the Jackson–Vanik Amendment. If you do not sweep it away with a broom, it would be difficult for us to enter your markets.

Kissinger: The Jackson–Vanik Amendment was directed against me in the first place, and only then against the Soviet Union.

I agree with you. I always thought it was wrong, I believed that your emigration policy was your country's internal affair. One cannot make external demands about that. One could, probably, discuss it with you confidentially, but without pressing any demands.

Gorbachev: Those problems are now substantially resolved.

Kissinger: Yes.

Gorbachev: We only fight against brain drain. As far as dissidents are concerned, let them all go to your country.

Kissinger: I always believed that dissidents are very difficult to deal with even for those countries that receive them. [...]

Gorbachev: We are waiting for a signal from the administration.

Kissinger: You will hear positive statements from the president from the very beginning of his term. The exchange of opinions we agreed to conduct could begin in the first days of March, if it is convenient for you. Our people are ready.

I already told Anatoly Dobrynin that I considered the first part of your U.N. speech exceptionally important. We should discuss how to implement those propositions in solving concrete problems. If we could do that, we would be able to harmonize our policy and to improve our bilateral cooperation.

As far as the mechanism of such communication, Anatoly Dobrynin already has Scowcroft's direct personal number and, on my part, I could help to establish the initial contact, so that it doesn't have to go through the apparatus.

Gorbachev: I would also like you to tell President Bush that I appreciate his letter, and the fact that he sent it at such an early stage, even before his inauguration. We attach special importance to contacts and to the confidential exchange of opinions.

Please give my regards to President Bush, and tell him that he can count not only on understanding but also on cooperation on my part. I think that in the context of this conversation, which I would also ask you to pass on to him, it will be clear to him what meaning I am putting in these words. [...]

[*Source: Archive of the Gorbachev Foundation, Fond 2. Opis 1. On file at the National Security Archive. Translated by Svetlana Savranskaya.*]

Document No. 38: Letter from George H.W. Bush to Mikhail Gorbachev

January 17, 1989

Henry Kissinger hand-delivered this personal letter from President-elect George H.W. Bush to Gorbachev just days before the inauguration. According to Chernyaev's notes (the letter remains classified at the George Bush Presidential Library), it is interesting for what it says and what it does not say. In Chernyaev's account, the letter reads: "my advisers responsible for national security and I will need some time to think through the entire range of issues." But there is no mention, much less an endorsement, of Kissinger's condominium efforts. Bush and his closest aides, particularly Brent Scowcroft, are looking for a "pause" in the US–Soviet rapprochement that had proceeded very rapidly in the last year of the Reagan presidency. They believe Reagan went too fast, and that Gorbachev's reforms are actually aimed at reinvigorating the Soviet Union in order to resume the strategic competition with the United States. The "pause" would produce no policy revelations as the months went by in the first half of 1989, but it would generate increasing frustration among the Soviet leadership (see Document No. 64, for example), U.S. allies and even some American foreign policy officials such as Ambassador to Moscow Jack Matlock, who in his account of the collapse of the Soviet Union titles the relevant chapter "Washington Fumbles." On the Soviet side, Chernyaev's memoirs use the chapter title "The Lost Year," referring to Gorbachev's belief that the change of U.S. administrations cost a precious year in moving toward their objective—the end of the Cold War.

Attachment

Handed by Henry Kissinger to Mikhail Gorbachev

Dear President Gorbachev,

I am using the opportunity of Henry Kissinger's visit to Moscow to send you a short personal letter.

First of all, I would like to tell you that I very much appreciate the attention given to my son and grandson during their recent trip to Armenia. They both are deeply shocked by this terrible tragedy, which they witnessed on the spot. They came back with a feeling of deep respect for the strength and devotion of the people who are repairing and rebuilding all that was destroyed in the catastrophe.

Also, I would like to reiterate what I said to you last year, when you came to the United Nations. As I explained then, my advisers responsible for national security and I will need some time to think through the entire range of issues, especially those concerning arms control, which occupy a central place in our bilateral relations, and to formulate our position in the interests of further developing these relations. Our goal is to formulate a solid and consistent American

347

approach. We are not talking about slowing down or reversing the positive process that has marked the last two years.

I am very serious about moving our relationship forward in the interests of our two countries and peace itself. I believe that we should elevate the dialogue, especially between you and me, above the details of arms control proposals, and discuss more general issues of more extensive political relations to which we should aspire.

I am ready to do everything possible in order to build and improve a reliable and solid relationship. I hope that we will continue our personal contacts in the process of solving the common problems our countries are faced with.

Respectfully,
George Bush

[*Source: Archive of the Gorbachev Foundation, Fond 1. opis 1. On file at the National Security Archive. Translated by Svetlana Savranskaya.*]

Document No. 39: Report from Mikhail Gorbachev to the CC CPSU Politburo regarding His Meeting with the Trilateral Commission

January 21, 1989

The Trilateral Commission was a powerhouse of statesmen and financiers from the United States, Western Europe and Japan. In his report to the Politburo about his recent meeting with the Commission, Gorbachev takes special note of a comment by former French Prime Minister Giscard d'Estaing, who postulated that "in 10–20 years we all will have to deal with a federation of states named Europe"—a sentiment exactly in sync with Gorbachev's own vision of the common European home. Referring to Kissinger's conversations with Yakovlev earlier in the month, Gorbachev also mentions that the former secretary of state "hinted at the idea of a USSR–USA condominium" so that the "Europeans do not misbehave."

Gorbachev's references to Kissinger use the word "Kisa"—a diminutive term for "cat," replete with connotations of slinking around, and also the name of the pretentious aristocrat in a classic 1960s Soviet movie based on a famous satirical novel by Ilf and Petrov published in the 1930s. On January 16, Kissinger had suggested to Yakovlev that the situation in Eastern Europe was comparable to that preceding World War I when the Great Powers set off a chain reaction which led to war. To avert catastrophe, Kissinger proposed high-level negotiations to reach a set of understandings, both formal and informal. Gorbachev's words to the Politburo suggest some attraction to the idea, but his assistants would later claim he was uninterested and even hurt by the Americans' apparent inability to take his "new thinking" seriously. In any case, for the first time, Gorbachev would initiate an actual process to analyze the developments in Eastern Europe seriously. In the following weeks, Yakovlev would receive a number of analytical documents from the CC International Department, the KGB, the Ministry of Foreign Affairs and the Institute of the Economy of the World Socialist System (see Document Nos. 41 & 42).

Communist Party of the Soviet Union
Central Committee

Gorbachev is speaking about the Trilateral Commission, with which he met (Kissinger, Giscard d'Estaing, Nakasone). It is interested in everything that is going on, especially in our country. It is working on all issues of European world policy. I would emphasize two issues.

The first is how you—meaning we, the Soviet Union—are going to integrate into the world economy. These issues are being considered within the Trilateral Commission. If you are going to integrate we should be ready for it, they said to me.

Giscard told me directly that for us (the USSR) this problem would be extremely difficult, but for them also.

Second issue. They are coming to the conclusion that the biggest battles for *perestroika* are still ahead of us. And in the international sphere the main problems for us will emerge in the Third World. They think that the West "let the Third World live," and the Third World, in turn, "let the West live." But how are we going to deal with the Third World? They believe that in 10–20 years we all will have to deal with a federation of states named Europe.

Kisa [Kissinger] just shrugged at this statement by Giscard, and asked me a direct question: How are you going to react if Eastern Europe wants to join the EC? It is not an accident that they asked me about this. They know that our friends are already knocking on the door. And we should also look at what processes are going on there now—economic and political—and where they are drifting.

What is going on in Hungary, for example? An opposition party led by [Miklós] Németh has emerged there. Hungary is on the eve of a serious choice. Of course, it will be different. And I think that every country should have, and has, its own face. And we will continue to be friends, because the socialist foundation will be preserved in all of them.

The paths of our development will be very diverse while we will preserve our commonality. We need a mechanism that will ensure our mutual understanding and interaction. There will be a lot of political, economic, and military-political questions. We should consider them in the Central Committee's Commission on Eastern Europe. We should undertake situational analysis with scholars. For example, how would we react if Hungary were to leave for the EC? Comrades, we are on the eve of very serious things, because we cannot give them more than we are giving them now. And they need new technologies. If we do not deal with that, there will be a split and they will run away.

And then there is the question of what we should present to the working groups of the leaders of the socialist countries. By the way, let the Commission give us a substantiated answer as to whether we need this meeting at all. Before that, we should work out what we can give to our friends, and compare it with what the West can give them.

The answer to this question, I am sure, lies with our *perestroika,* with its success. We should try to involve our friends, to get them interested in our economic reforms. Let Yakovlev, with scholars, look at it. We are facing a serious problem there.

The peoples of those countries will ask: what about the CPSU, what kind of leash will it use to hold our countries back? They simply do not know that if they pull this leash harder, it will break.

It is time to transfer our relations to the forms that we utilize in our relationship with China. But we can get to such forms only via the market, and, of course, via technological and scientific developments in our own country.

In that case, we would break the old rule that we keep them attached to us only by means of energy resources.

At the same time, we cannot just tell them that we will cut deliveries. That would be a betrayal.

Kisa hinted at the idea of a USSR–USA condominium over Europe. He was hinting that Japan, Germany, Spain and South Korea were on the rise, and so, let us make an agreement so that the "Europeans do not misbehave."

We should work on this range of issues also, but in such a way that it would not leak, because in Europe they are most afraid of what they understand the Reykjavik summit to mean. If you remember, in Reykjavik they saw an attempt at conspiracy between the USSR and the USA over Europe.

My impression from the meeting with the Trilateral Commission is the following: they understood in the West that the world needs a peaceful breathing spell—from the arms race, from nuclear psychosis—as much as we need it. However, we need to know it all in detail in order not to make mistakes. They want to channel the processes in such a way as to limit as much as possible our influence on the world situation. They are trying once more to seize the initiative; they are putting forward criteria for establishing confidence, as a test: if the Soviet Union, they say, does not want to agree to something, we will take steps in order to score points.

That is why we have to keep the initiative. This is our main advantage.

[*Source: Archive of the Gorbachev Foundation, Fond 2. Opis 2. On file at the National Security Archive. Translated by Svetlana Savranskaya.*]

Document No. 40: Notes of Telephone Conversation between Mikhail Gorbachev and George H.W. Bush

January 23, 1989

Chernyaev's notes of one of the first telephone calls between George Bush and Gorbachev capture the careful and noncommittal tone of the new American president with regard to the Kissinger condominium idea. "Even though Kissinger was on a personal, not on an official trip, we would like very much to hear his story. We do not always agree with him on everything ..."

[...]

Bush: Secondly, I would like to mention with appreciation that you were very generous to give so much time to your conversation with Henry Kissinger. In a couple of days my assistant [Brent] Scowcroft will invite him to the White House in order to be informed about that conversation in detail, although we already know some details. Even though Kissinger was on a personal, not an official, trip, we would like very much to hear his story. We do not always agree with him on everything, but he visited you as a friend, and we will listen to him carefully.

 Gorbachev: Thank you. I hope you will find his story interesting. [...]

Conversation recorded by V. Sukhodrev.

[*Source: Archive of the Gorbachev Foundation, Fond 1. Opis 1. On file at the National Security Archive. Translated by Svetlana Savranskaya.*]

Document No. 41: Memorandum from CC CPSU International Department, "On a Strategy for Relations with the European Socialist Countries"

February 1989

This fascinating analysis from the new combined International Department, headed by Valentin Falin, is one of the results of the Politburo's January 21 discussion (see Document No. 39)—in effect, the first serious attempt at a systematic analysis of possible Soviet strategy towards Eastern Europe. In practical terms, these analyses already are late in coming, since the Polish Roundtable begins to meet this month and would shortly agree on relatively open elections as soon as June. Still, this memo is indicative of the new thinking and the new candor of glasnost. For example, here is the Central Committee of the Soviet Communist Party admitting that the socialist model is in the midst of a prolonged crisis, and that the WTO, far from being a true alliance, "effectively represents a Soviet military headquarters with the purely formal presence of representatives of other countries."

The memo is cautiously critical of Gorbachev's non-interference policy since "it creates an impression in the eyes of our friends that we are abandoning them," while the role of Eastern Europe as a security belt for the USSR "remains unchanged to some extent." The authors agree "it is very unlikely that we would be able to employ the methods of 1956 and 1968, both as a matter of principle, and also because of unacceptable consequences." Yet, while this "[p]resupposes our affirmation of the principle of freedom of choice ... at the same time, it should retain a certain vagueness as far as our concrete actions are concerned under various possible turns of events, so that we do not stimulate anti-socialist forces to try to 'test' the fundamentals of socialism in a given country." Significantly, the memorandum recommends that Moscow move away from a policy of non-engagement, resume the mantle of leadership in Eastern Europe, and begin to "actively seek channels for establishing contact with all forces that stake a claim to participation in the realization of power in the socialist countries." Also noteworthy is the caution expressed with respect to East Germany, warning that the GDR could not survive its own perestroika.

Yet with all its candor, even this document provides only a minimum program for Moscow, essentially admitting that the USSR has little leverage, and that the Kremlin faces a choice between "preserving by all means the ruling communist parties at the wheel of power" and "preserving alliance relations with those countries." By declining to use force, Gorbachev essentially is choosing the latter.

ON A STRATEGY FOR RELATIONS WITH THE EUROPEAN SOCIALIST COUNTRIES

1. Our relations with the socialist countries, including our allies in the Warsaw Treaty Organization, have entered a difficult and critical stage. The transition to the principle of equality and mutual responsibility, which began in April 1985 and was affirmed during the working meeting in Moscow in 1986, gave us an

353

opportunity to remove many old layers, and to eliminate the perceptions of our conservatism. *Perestroika*, the development of democratization and openness, has confirmed the role of the Soviet Union as the leader in the process of socialist renewal. More and more, we are influencing our friends by our own example, by political means.

However, having broken with the former type of relations, we have not yet established a new mode.[34] And the problem is not only that the process of restructuring interactions between socialist countries on the basis of a "balance of interests," which we have proclaimed, is objectively difficult, and that subjectively it creates an impression in the eyes of our friends that we are abandoning them—abandoning the priority of relations with socialist countries. The problem is [also] that *the transition to a "balance of interests" is seriously aggravated by the prolonged crisis of the socialist model, whose main features were developed in the Soviet Union during Stalin's time* and then transferred to the countries that were liberated by us, or with our decisive participation. Their political system still suffers from a lack of legitimacy, and this stability-oriented socio-economic system is incapable of providing an adequate response to the challenge of the scientific and technological revolution.

The relaxation of tensions, the diminishing of the threat of war, to which the socialist countries have contributed in a decisive way, has caused deep changes in their national security priorities. *The economic factor, the ability of a country to join and to assimilate into the world economy, has moved to the top of their priorities*, because no single country can overcome the widening gap on its own individually, and because socialist economic integration is clearly in a stalemate so that if these countries remain with it they will risk being left out of world development. This constitutes the primary national interest of the majority of the socialist countries right now, and it should be taken into account above all in our relations with them.

The European socialist countries have found themselves in the powerful magnetic field of the West European states' economic growth and social well being. Against this background, on the one hand, their own achievements have dimmed, and on the other hand the real problems and difficulties that exist in the West are practically imperceptible. The constant comparing and contrasting of the two worlds, of their ways of life, production and cultures, have entered our life thanks to mass communications, and there is no way around it. We are speaking about countries in which they still remember times when they were close to, or on the same level of development with, the West European states. The influence of this magnetic field will probably grow even stronger with the introduction of the common European market [in 1992].

As a consequence, *in a number of socialist countries the process of rejecting existing political institutions and ideological values by these societies is already*

---

[34] Here and elsewhere in this document, emphasis is in the original.

354

underway. Nonconformity is spreading more and more widely among the youth, and it is moving from a passive, home-grown level toward a civic and political one.

2. The difficult and transitional character of this stage comes from a situation in which *the ruling parties cannot rule in the old way any more, and the new "rules of the game"—of managing the group interests that are pouring out, and of finding a social consensus—have not yet been worked out.* And to the extent that this process is being postponed and prolonged, the parties could find themselves in a more and more difficult situation.

In the context of general tendencies that are observable in all socialist countries, there are specific features in specific countries, which require a differentiated response from us.

In Poland and Hungary, events are developing in the direction of pluralism, toward the creation of coalition and parliamentary forms of governance. In these circumstances, the Hungarian Socialist Workers' Party (HSWP) and the Polish United Workers' Party (PUWP) can count on preserving their positions only within the framework of political alliances. A lot will depend on whether they are able to involve a part of the opposition in constructive cooperation. Taking into account the fact that a considerable part of the population of Poland is tired of crises, the probability of evolutionary development here is higher. In Hungary, at the same time, notwithstanding their seemingly better living standards, the situation might unfold in most unexpected ways.

Some of the party activists in both the HSWP and the PUWP have expressed their willingness to use force in case of a rapid deterioration of the situation. There is no unity of opinion on all of these issues in the leadership of the HSWP and the PUWP; therefore, we should expect a rise in factional fighting there.

In Czechoslovakia, tensions have risen considerably in recent times. Here the 1968 syndrome is still present, which interferes with the party's ability to define its position toward *perestroika,* especially in the sphere of democratization and openness.

A significant part of the leadership leans toward employing administrative measures in the struggle against opposition moods. In general, there is a tendency to begin to make changes in the economy and to postpone reform in the sphere of democratization and openness until a later stage.

The stabilizing factor is that so far they have managed to preserve a relatively high standard of living in the country, although they are achieving this with more and more effort now.

In Bulgaria, there is, in essence, a simulation of *perestroika,* which is to a large extent a consequence of T. Zhivkov's personal ambitions. The loud declarations about a comprehensive reconsideration of Marxist-Leninist theory and about the creation of a new model of socialism in principle lead in practice to endless reorganizations and shuffling of personnel, and to a further tightening of the screws. All this discredits the party and socialism, and casts a shadow on our *perestroika.* Nonetheless, T. Zhivkov still controls the situation rather well by employing methods of political manipulation and by relying on a well-developed administrative apparatus, even though discontent is growing in the party and in the country.

In the GDR, a particularly complex situation is developing against the background of apparent well-being. Even though the GDR can be distinguished from other socialist countries by the better state of its economy and standard of living, the country's economic situation is deteriorating. There is the pressure of debt and growing dependence on the FRG. The party leadership, to a large extent under the influence of personal ambitions, is striving to avoid problems of renewal. In making critical assessments of the conservatism of the GDR leadership, one has to keep in mind that it has some objective basis. The GDR was founded not on the national, but on the ideological—on a class basis; therefore, a rapid transition to democratization, openness, and free speech might be accompanied by special problems in this country.

In Romania, there is still the oppressive atmosphere of the personality cult and of Ceauşescu's authoritarian rule. Striving to isolate the country from our influence, he is now trying to dress in the robes of a "fighter for the purity of socialism" and is making indirect arguments against us. Some eruptions of discontent are possible in that country, but it is unlikely that they will become widespread now. The situation will, most likely, change only with Ceauşescu's departure, which could bring with it quite painful developments.

Yugoslavia has entered a phase of political crisis in the context of very deep economic problems; this could lead to a substantial weakening of the positions of the UJY [Union of Yugoslav Communists] and even to a split within the federation.

3. Several possible scenarios of the further development of the socialist countries are distinguishable now. One of them is a smooth movement toward democratization and a new form of socialism under the leadership of the ruling parties. Under this scenario, some concessions cannot be excluded regarding the issue of governance, a significant growth in self-governance, and a strengthening of the role of representative organs in political life bringing constructive opposition to the governing of society and possibly even its transformation into one of the forces contesting for power. This road toward a parliamentary or a presidential socialist republic in certain countries (PPR, HPR, ČSSR) would be preferable for us. If the initiative for democratic change originates with the ruling party, the chances of preserving internal political stability and alliance commitments are high.

Another possibility is a scenario of intermittent development, which would be a direct continuation of the preceding development, in which the ruling party makes concessions after a new mini-crisis. This scenario lets us avoid the worst—a political eruption—but it moves the party away, to the sidelines of political life, strengthens pessimism and skepticism about socialism, stimulates demands from the opposition, and gradually prepares society for abandoning the framework of socialism. The transition of a country to a traditional mixed economy and the free play of political forces would not, in all cases, lead it to abandon its obligations to its allies, but in such a case the foreign policy orientation of that country would become the subject of intense political struggle.

In the end, a third way is possible too—the preservation of the existing system of governance in society along with the suppression of the social and political activity of the masses. Under this scenario, it would be characteristic to take an openly conservative course, to limit reforms, mostly in the area of management of the economy, and to actively reject Soviet *perestroika*. In the future, such a course does not exclude a violent resolution of the crisis by way of a social explosion with unpredictable consequences for the country's domestic and foreign policy. The main catalyst of such a crisis could be an increase in dissatisfaction among the population as a result of economic deterioration and worsening living standards.

4. *In this critical transitional period, our relations with the socialist countries remain our priority.* But not in the sense that we implied before, when the Soviet Union and its allies were, in essence, in international isolation; and so our relations with each other considerably outweighed our ties with the rest of the world. Since then, the new political thinking and the energetic efforts by the USSR and its allies in recent years have rapidly changed the international situation. It is natural that the relative weight of our relations with the socialist countries in our foreign policy has changed. However, that does not alter the fundamental fact that *the degree of our interdependence with the socialist countries remains higher than with the rest of the world, or that the internal stability and influence of socialism in world affairs depends on that.*

From a geopolitical standpoint, the importance of the European socialist countries for the Soviet Union used to be determined by the fact that from the very beginning they *acted as a kind of security belt that created a strategic cover for the center of socialism.* Today, notwithstanding all the changes in the international situation, this role of Eastern Europe—especially of the GDR, Poland and Czechoslovakia—remains unchanged to some extent.

It is a complicated question—*what could and should be the forms of our influence on the socialist countries under the new conditions?*

Authoritarian methods and direct pressure have clearly outlived their usefulness. In the political sphere, even in the case of a sharp deterioration in one of the countries—and we cannot exclude that possibility today—it is very unlikely that we would be able to employ the methods of 1956 and 1968, both as a matter of principle and because of unacceptable consequences. The use of force would be admissible only in one case—if there were direct and clear armed interference by external forces in the internal developments of a socialist country. Therefore, essentially, our methods of leverage can only be our political and economic ties.

5. *The state of economic relations* is assuming growing political importance. Their role is evident for the majority of socialist countries. And for us they have great importance also. We should decisively discard the stereotype that those countries are our dependents. In contrast to routine perceptions, the economic effects of our trade with the European CMEA countries are rather favorable to us. This can be seen from the following examples.

The share of *goods imported from the CMEA* countries in the overall volume of goods consumed in the USSR:

Metal rolling machinery—40–50 percent; food technologies—40 percent; textile technology—50 percent; chemical industry technologies—35 percent; lumber and woodwork equipment—about 30 percent; polygraphic equipment—more than 40 percent; meat, meat products, vegetables and other produce—up to 10 percent; non-food consumer products—10–15 percent.

According to our calculations, we get up to 4 *rubles of profit for each ruble of oil sold in the CMEA countries* (the profitability of oil exports to these countries in 1987 was 493 percent [sic]). Apart from that, by buying food products and consumer goods in those countries, *we gain a substantial budgetary profit* when we sell them in the USSR at our retail prices. Thus in 1987, for each ruble of expenses on the import of meat and meat products, we had the following profit from domestic sales—96 kopecks; cotton textiles—1.76 rubles; coats and dresses—2.24 rubles; leather shoes—2 rubles; personal care items—2.92 rubles; china—2.81 rubles; furniture—89 kopecks; and so on.

Conditions for grain purchases, in particular, in the CMEA countries (Hungary, Bulgaria) are more favorable for us than on the world market. For example, we need to sell approximately 1.45–1.5 tons of oil to buy a ton of wheat on the world market for convertible currency; to buy it in the above-mentioned CMEA countries we would need to sell approximately one ton of oil.

At the same time, *the old forms of economic cooperation have been exhausted to a large extent.* The volume of commodity turnover is decreasing. The USSR is already unable to satisfy demand from the CMEA countries for increases in fuel and raw materials deliveries; and on a number of vitally important resources—oil, for example—we are actually planning to decrease deliveries in the coming five-year period. We are also unable to provide these countries with modern technology. As a result of a drop in prices for energy resources (mostly oil) by the end of the next five-year period, the Soviet Union could end up with a negative trade balance with the European CMEA countries of more than 7 billion rubles.

The issue of a transition to integration has already been raised. It is especially acute for our CMEA partners. Without actively joining the processes of international economic integration, they would simply be incapable of ensuring a radical renewal of their economies.

It appears that *the strategic policies established earlier for this sphere*—the course for creating a CMEA common market and appropriate instruments (currency convertibility, wholesale trade, and others)—*continue to be entirely relevant. However, their realization has been unsatisfactory.* Many joint decisions notwithstanding, industrial cooperation is clearly stagnant. The comprehensive program of scientific and technological cooperation among CMEA countries, which raised such hopes, has effectively been thwarted.

After the Working Summit in 1986, the joint work of CMEA countries picked up somewhat. *Direct ties between enterprises were developed, and joint enterprises were established.* However, the new forms of interaction have not had any significant impact on the volume and structure of exchange (direct ties represent less than 1 percent of the turnover volume).

The temptation to reorient the economies of the socialist countries toward the West is growing stronger. Exports of top-quality products to the West have become the norm. CMEA countries often compete with each other in capital markets.

Experience shows that it is impossible to solve the problem of economic integration with the help of general programs, even the best of them. It is necessary to accumulate relevant financial, organizational, legal, and other types of prerequisites in all countries. Success here will depend, first of all, on fundamental changes in the Soviet economy, in its structure, in the economic mechanism, and in the expansion of its export potential, which would take at least several years.

What can we do under current conditions? First of all, we should not allow our prestige as a reliable economic partner to decline. Each breach of contract—and such cases are becoming more frequent—puts the socialist countries in a difficult, sometimes even hopeless, situation. The accumulation of similar facts in the economic sphere leads to unfavorable political consequences for us. We should overcome this illness, to the point where we should reconsider our ministries' proposals on a complicated issue such as the volume of our oil deliveries during the next five-year period. This should be done in the spirit of our former agreements.

The coordination of efforts to convert the military economy could become one of the new channels of economic influence on the socialist countries, especially because the military-industrial complex in the socialist countries is integrated to a higher degree than their civilian economies. One more opportunity would be *to develop a common concept of alleviating foreign debt*, which is extremely large in a number of socialist countries.

Lastly, when we intensify our economic ties with the West, it is important to *try actively to bring our socialist partners into those contacts* in order to overcome the impression, which some of them have, that we are no longer paying attention to the fraternal countries. We should probably hold a specific discussion with them to talk about the possibility of their joining in projects that are carried out with the help of Western credits, and to elaborate finally *a coordinated strategy for integrating the socialist commonwealth into the [network of] global economic relations.*

6. *A number of new tasks has emerged in the sphere of political cooperation.* Just several years ago we would have considered many of the developments that are underway now in the socialist countries to be absolutely unacceptable for us. Today we need a deeper, more flexible, and differentiated approach to what is useful for us, what is admissible, and what is unacceptable. At the same time, it is important that we *realistically assess our opportunities,* find out exactly where we can realistically have an influence and where our interference could only aggravate the situation.

The measure of socialism in the transformations that are underway now in the socialist countries is a difficult question. Some of them are allowing not only extensive development of market relations but also forms of private property and the widespread influx of foreign capital. And still, it appears that *we should not exaggerate the danger of one of the countries simply switching to the capitalist way of development*. The roots developed by socialism are very deep. Such a transition would mean a rapid breakup of the entire economy [and] its structures, the development of crises, and a rapid deterioration of living standards for the majority of the population. And it is very unlikely that the West would be inclined to take on countries whose economies have been marked by crisis elements and heavy foreign debt.

It is characteristic that the ideas that are presented from time to time about the "marshallization" [i.e., a new "Marshall Plan"] of certain socialist countries (in particular Hungary and Poland, for example, converting their debt into foreign investment) have not enjoyed any noticeable support in the West so far. [This is] due to the volume of expenses and the unpredictability of the economic and political consequences. Although we should not completely discard this possibility in the [future], we should be more concerned about the possibility of an economic collapse or anarchic explosions in the context of social tensions and the lack of [future] prospects. This concerns countries where the regimes continue to stay in power by further tightening the screws (Romania, the KPDR [North Korea]).

We need to give special comprehensive consideration to *the processes of forming structures for political pluralism* of the coalition type and parliamentary type and to the processes of legalization of the opposition that are unfolding in a number of countries. Of course, this is an uncharted road that requires the parties to possess both strength of principle and tactical flexibility, as well as the ability to lead the process and not leave it up to the opposition forces.

The lessons of several crises have shown that the main danger posed by an opposition [force] is not the fact of its existence in itself, but that it could unite on a negative, destructive platform all kinds of forces and movements in the society that are dissatisfied with the existing situation. Therefore, pulling a portion of the opposition into the official structure and assigning it responsibility for constructive solutions to the problems that have accumulated could play a stabilizing role.

In the existing difficult circumstances, *the processes of our perestroika exercise a special influence on the internal processes of the socialist countries*. There also, in some sense, it has created a new situation. Whereas before, any mass expressions of dissatisfaction with the existing situation that flared up from time to time in the socialist countries assumed an anti-Soviet character almost automatically, now such a direct relationship has disappeared. A serious blow has been dealt to the idea that it is impossible to reform a one-dimensional form of socialism based on the experience and example of the Soviet Union.

Perestroika has brought us objectively closer to the countries that are trying to reform their economic and political system (China, Yugoslavia, Poland, Hungary); but at the same time it has created certain problems in relations with some of our traditionally close allies whose leadership continues to rely on administrative and command methods.

In this situation we have to face the question of *how to build our relations with the parties and the national leaderships that exhibit a reserved attitude toward our perestroika* (the GDR, Romania, Cuba, KPDR). Here, clearly, we need patience and tolerance, we need to understand the positions of such parties as the [SED] and the Communist Party of Cuba, which due to their specific and sometimes even front-like circumstances of development, experience particular problems in accepting and implementing the processes of economic restructuring and the democratization of society.

7. The general development of world politics and the increased differentiation of the national interests of the socialist countries require that we make corrections in our approach to *coordinating our joint steps in the international arena.*

Most importantly, *the process of reducing confrontation in the world, the decreasing weight of military-strategic factors and the increasing weight of the political factors of security are objectively increasing the role of our friends.* And it is not only because conventional weapons reductions in Europe have moved to the forefront of the all-European process in all its dimensions, taking into account the new quality that was conferred on it by the Vienna meeting. Without the active and positive participation of our allies, progress on those issues is simply impossible. Therefore, we can talk about not just mutual information, about providing information sometimes at the last minute, but about the preliminary coordination of our actions.

However, the problem is much bigger. Essentially, the period when a reduction in the military threat was achieved primarily within the framework of Soviet–American relations is not that far from its logical conclusion. The *internationalization* of major international issues is growing. And if that is so, then our friends' advice [and] consultations with them should involve not only the specific topics under consideration but *the entire complex* of issues involving the world economy and politics. Only in this case can they experience a real, not just an affected, feeling of belonging to the development and implementation of a common socialist foreign policy. At the same time, our initiatives would become more respectable, and in some ways, considering the experience of our friends, more substantive.

However, there is also another side of this. *The pluralism of interests of different socialist countries* is more and more noticeable. The reduction of military budgets in some of those countries is moving at a rate that is ahead of our own; in other countries it creates anxiety over the future of their own rather developed military industry [that is] integrated with ours. In a similar fashion, the humanization of international relations and the introduction of human rights in international relations are perceived by some of the governments as a threat to socialism; for others it serves as an additional impulse to set off on the road to "openness" in their own countries.

Differences of opinion sometimes lead to flashes of nationalist feelings that aggravate relations between countries (Romania–Hungary). It could be anticipated that internal socio-economic and political difficulties would strengthen the desire to play on the sensitive strings of nationalism within the leaderships of certain countries.

Taking into account all these different interests, *it is not at all necessary to try to achieve consensus as a goal in itself at any price* during our discussions and consultations with our friends. We should not allow a situation in which one of the countries would tie our hands as a matter of their national ambitions. Each country should have a right to preserve its freedom of action, of course, along with explaining its position to the allies and substantiating it. Also, it is not in our interest to transfer any kind of aggravated nationalist tensions between our friends onto a multilateral level, especially if such an "argument" involves us directly. Of course, it is a different matter if we are faced with opposition to our actions on the part of many or even the majority of the socialist countries; in that case it would be a signal for us to have another look at whether that step was the right one.

8. In spite of the fact that we have repeatedly stressed that we have discarded our administrative-command approach toward the socialist countries, the syndrome of such an approach persists in the thinking of our friends. At the same time, the conservative factions of the leadership would like, in essence, for the Soviet Union to continue its role as a kind of "protector" of the socialist countries. However, a significant part of the public is expressing its anxiety over the existing situation in which they see vestiges of that kind of paternalism. This finds its expression in different attitudes toward the presence of our troop contingents in the socialist countries, and it is linked with the influence on internal processes, not with external threats to their security. There is continuing anxiety about how the Soviet Union would react in a political crisis in one of the countries in which the ruling party's control of the situation was threatened. There is dissatisfaction with the ongoing inequality in the military apparatus of the Warsaw Treaty, the leadership of which effectively represents a Soviet military headquarters with the purely formal presence of representatives of other countries.

Herein lies a significant reservoir of possible steps for removing the above-mentioned "irritants," including ensuring *real* participation by our friends in the military procedures of the Warsaw Treaty, and eliminating the negative domestic political aspect of the presence of our troops, possibly through "internationalization." It would be advisable to direct our efforts toward achieving a situation where in some countries, where necessary, they would deploy joint formations of troops from those Warsaw Treaty countries which agree to do it, rather than Soviet troops.

It is most important to work out a balanced approach to the problem of the possibility of our interfering in one of the countries in the event of a political crisis. This presupposes our affirmation of the principle of freedom of choice as a universal basis for world order. But at the same time, it should retain a certain vagueness as far as our concrete actions are concerned under various possible turns of events, so that we do not stimulate anti-socialist forces to try to "test" the fundamentals of socialism in a given country.

Finally, it is necessary to take into account the growing attention of our friends to the still remaining "white spots" in our relations; this interest will most likely become even more pronounced this year in connection with the 50th anniversary of the onset of World War II and the signing of the Soviet–German pact. It would be expedient to work on our interpretation of the nature and the origins of World War II *employing newly defined approaches* to the assessment of our policy in the 1930–40s, and to discuss it with our friends ahead of time.

9. In the present circumstance we could formulate the following *"minimum program" for our relations with the socialist countries in the transitional period*:

First of all, we should have a balanced and unbiased analysis of the development of the socialist countries and of their relations, and we should prepare scenarios for our reaction to possible complications or sharp turns in their policies ahead of time, while simultaneously decisively rejecting the old stereotypes and avoiding willful improvisations that caused us a lot of harm in the past. We should step up our *joint* study of and efforts to find ways out of the existing crisis, as well as our studies of the new vision of socialism and of modern capitalism, and of the possibilities and limits of their interaction, mutual influence, and mutual assimilation.

Second, we should keep in mind that our contacts with the party and state leaderships of the socialist countries remain just as important as, if not more important than, before, particularly in light of the possibility that our friends may develop an "abandonment complex," and the suspicion that our claim that relations with our friends are a priority is not filled with real meaning. Inter-party contacts, if they are accompanied by an open analysis of problems, discussions, and an exchange of information about intentions, would allow us directly to feel the pulse of the fraternal parties, and to give them moral support.

Third, in explaining the essence of *perestroika* policy, we should carefully try to avoid any artificial projection of our experience onto other countries, which they could perceive as a reversion to administrative-command methods and a restriction of their independence, and could eventually lead to undesirable circumstances.

Fourth, by strictly adhering to our obligations we should preserve the existing ties that link the socialist countries to the USSR and try to ensure that the inevitable process of integrating the socialist economies with the West, which is to a certain extent beneficial to the common interest, develops in a balanced and coordinated way; that it is not accompanied by unacceptable economic and political costs; and that it would strengthen the processes of integration among the socialist countries.

Fifth, taking into account the key role of the armed forces in case of a deteriorating situation, it is important to keep up a genuine partnership among the armies of the socialist countries both on a bilateral basis and in the framework of the Warsaw Treaty by eliminating all elements of inequality.

Sixth. We should continue our policy of lowering our military presence in the socialist countries, including the possibility in the future of a complete withdrawal of our troops from Hungary and Czechoslovakia. We should consider a scenario of "internationalizing" the remaining troops, and creating joint formations.

Seventh. It is certainly in our interest that the changes that are ready to occur in the socialist countries, with all their possible variations, develop as much as possible without extra shocks and crises in the framework of socialist solutions. But we have to account for the possibility of a different course of events. *In that situation, it would be important that ideological differences* over the renewal of socialism and over finding ways out of the crises that have manifested themselves in the socialist world *do not assume the character of a conflict and do not have a negative influence on relations between our states, nor lead to antagonism toward the Soviet Union.*

This presupposes making a distinction between the interests of preserving by all means the ruling communist parties at the wheel of power and the interests of preserving alliance relations with those countries.

Eighth. By making use of the favorable opportunities created by *perestroika*, which have overturned the stereotypes of "Moscow conservatism," we should actively seek channels for establishing contact with all forces that stake a claim to participation in the realization of power in the socialist countries. Contacts [with] churches are becoming more important because church influence is on the rise in the socialist countries.

* * *

In general, at this stage, it is particularly important to reject the old stereotypes in our approaches that have outlived their usefulness. If a country disagrees with us, sometimes even seriously, this does not necessarily mean it is turning to the West; if the role of the party in one of the countries is questioned, this does not yet determine that it would definitely distance itself from us. The dialectics of the real processes, as our experience has shown, are much more complex. Yugoslavia and China "distanced" themselves from us some time ago, but they have not turned into capitalist states. In Poland, the party could realistically become just one [component], and perhaps not even the main one, in the structures of power; however, the geopolitical situation of the country is such that even the opposition understands the necessity of preserving some form of alliance with our country.

All this presupposes studying and trying to predict concrete scenarios for the development of the situation in every country, including the most extreme ones; making decisions as to what those scenarios could mean for our relations; and implementing them in a practical form on that basis.

[*Source: Archive of the Gorbachev Foundation. On file at the National Security Archive, donated by Professor Jacques Levesque. Translated by Svetlana Savranskaya.*]

Document No. 42: Memorandum from the Bogomolov Institute, "Changes in Eastern Europe and their Impact on the USSR"

February 1989

Like the International Department memo above, this assessment is sent to Yakovlev (and read by Gorbachev, according to his aides) as part of the analytical process commissioned by the January 21 Politburo discussion. But the think-tank reformers here go much further than the Central Committee staff, both in terms of frank description and support for change. The head of the institute (officially, the Institute of the Economy of the World Socialist System) is Oleg Bogomolov, one of the "people of the Sixties" who was disillusioned by the 1968 Soviet invasion of Czechoslovakia. (He publicly opposed the 1979 invasion of Afghanistan.) This memo does not just refer to the crisis of the socialist system, but concludes that "[t]he model of economic and political development imposed on these countries after 1948 has clearly exhausted itself." Compare the word "imposed" to the word "transferred" employed as recently as October 1988 by Shakhnazarov (see Document No. 29). The document explicitly warns that "[t]he direct use of force by the USSR, its intervention in the course of events on behalf of conservative forces that are alienated from the people, will most evidently signify the end of perestroika and the crumbling of trust on the part of the world community in [our reforms]. But it will not prevent a disintegration of the social-economic and social-political systems in these countries."

At the same time, the Bogomolov memo provides reassurance about the outcomes of reform and even about more fundamental processes that might occur—what historian Timothy Garton Ash would later call "refolution." The memo says: "By itself the fact of a transfer of power to alternative forces does not mean an external and military threat to our country." Likewise, even though an Eastern Europe that successfully instituted perestroika would inevitably gravitate to the West economically, they would be "pioneers" not traitors; and the process would benefit the USSR.

Missing from even this radical vision, however, is any sense of how much of their legitimacy the region's communist parties have already lost; any inkling of the possible dissolution of the WTO; and any foresight that East Germany might end up folding into West Germany rather than becoming a neutral confederate state. The memo tracks remarkably with the actual attitudes that Gorbachev would display through 1989, indicating that it may have been an important influence on, or reflection of, his thinking. As such, its limitations would explain in part why Gorbachev would be so ill-prepared for the eventual discussions on German unification.

CHANGES IN EASTERN EUROPE AND THEIR IMPACT ON THE USSR

Societies in the Eastern European countries are beginning to change their character. Attempts to build socialism with Stalinist and neo-Stalinist methods, not without active involvement by the Soviet side, have ended in a deadlock. This situation carries with it an aggravation of contradictions and crisis developments.

The degree and scale of conflicts vary from more or less hidden social-political tensions pregnant with sudden explosions to a chronic crisis without any visible ways out—a crisis that signals the beginning of the disintegration of the social-political system and also does not exclude cataclysms. Such processes are irreversible; they result from the long-term evolution of the regime, and in a majority of countries they favor the transition to a new model of socialism but can also possibly lead to the collapse of the socialist idea. In the last year or year-and-a-half there has been a rapid acceleration of developments in Eastern Europe, and there are more elements of unpredictability there.

A GENERAL CHARACTERIZATION OF SOCIAL-POLITICAL PROCESSES IN THE COUNTRIES OF EASTERN EUROPE

Crisis symptoms are visible in all spheres of public life inside those countries as well as in relations among them.

In the national economy, the intensity of these symptoms varies from a slow-down of economic growth, a widening social and technological gap with the West, a gradual proliferation of the deficit in domestic markets and the growth of external debts (GDR, Czechoslovakia, Bulgaria), all the way to the real threat of economic collapse (Yugoslavia, Poland). Particularly dangerous is the open and hidden inflation that has become a common phenomenon and only varies by degree: creeping and galloping inflation are predominant, but one cannot exclude its escalation into hyperinflation (Poland, Yugoslavia). A "black market economy" and corruption are gaining in strength everywhere and periodically burst forth in scandals and "affairs" that carry political connotations.

In the political sphere, the crisis manifests itself first of all in the dramatic decline of the position of the ruling communist parties, in some cases so dramatic that one can speak about a crisis of confidence in them. Some of these parties are undergoing an internal crisis: their membership is decreasing since rank-and-file members do not want to share responsibility for decisions that had nothing to do with them. The old social base is eroding. Infighting in the leadership is pregnant with split-ups (most likely in Yugoslavia; there are also obvious symptoms in Hungary and low-key signals in Poland and Czechoslovakia). Under pressure from multiplying and growing alternative political structures (embryos of new parties, clubs, and movements) the HSWP and PUWP have become so weak that they have to share power and accept coalition forms of government, as well as agree to a transition to a genuine multi-party system and the legalization of dissenting opposition forces. This is occurring in somewhat different forms in the UJC [Union of Yugoslav Communists]. Alternative forces are developing an international character. Conservatives are acquiring international contacts (for instance, GDR—ČSSR—SRR).

A very much crisis-ridden field is that of *ideology*. Its old forms block the renewal of the socialist order and provide the rationale for counter-reformism (GDR, Romania, Czechoslovakia). Dogmatic social sciences are incapable of working out a convincing ideological rationale for long-needed reforms. In public opinion, particularly among the youth, there is the spread of apathy, a sense of doom, nostalgia for pre-Revolutionary times (i.e. pre-World War II or even earlier), and a lack of faith in the potential of socialism. Extreme manifestations of these sentiments can be seen in the increase in emigration (Poland, Yugoslavia, Hungary, GDR, Czechoslovakia, Romania). The positions of some social groups are becoming dangerously radical; there is a growing trend towards anarchy and violence (Poland, Hungary, GDR, Czechoslovakia, the Yugoslav Confederation). The spread of video equipment, satellite broadcasting, and personal computers with printers is producing an explosion of independent culture (Poland, Hungary, Czechoslovakia).

The degradation of *common ties* is taking place in various forms. Interest in present-day forms of integration is visibly lower, as are the hopes for substantially increasing its effectiveness through direct ties and cooperation in technology. Due to profound structural problems and flaws in the mechanism of trade cooperation, bilateral trade exchanges with the USSR are dropping, which is producing very negative consequences for the national economies of our partners and is creating additional obstacles in the way of economic reforms (underutilized capacities in most countries, inflation of mutual in-kind [*klivingovoie*] indebtedness). In some cases inter-ethnic relations have grown worse: the Hungarian–Romanian conflict has become explicit; and mutual antipathy between Germans and Poles, Poles and Czechs, Czechs, Slovaks and Hungarians has increased.

Two groups of countries stand out by the degree of their crisis tendencies.

In *Poland, Hungary, and Yugoslavia*, crisis processes are developing intensely and openly: having broken to the surface once, they have acquired a certain inertia. The acuteness of the social-political situation in these countries stems first of all from the mass scale of workers' protests. "A new working movement" is being born. Its scope is such that it is no longer possible to treat the strikes as sporadic excesses or, as was the case in Poland, to attribute them to the influence of anti-socialist forces domestically and from abroad. The strikes obviously are escalating into the ongoing social conflict between the working strata and the party and government techno-bureaucracy. Rank-and-file communists often actively take the side of the strikers. Trade union movements are being rapidly politicized (some symptoms of this can also be observed in Bulgaria and Czechoslovakia). Official trade unions are beginning to play the role of the legal opposition; independent trade unions are proliferating; trade union pluralism is taking root.

In all three countries, the living standards of very substantial parts of the population are sinking; their revenues are shrinking to the social minimum and lower. Simultaneously, differentiation in income is becoming more pronounced, and a speculative stratum is emerging.

Public opinion is becoming aware of the processes heretofore hidden from it, such as the fact of the continuing exploitation of employed labor. Some leaders of the UJC have publicly admitted the existence of a struggle for redistribution of added value produced by workers, and the fact of their exploitation (for instance,

367

through inflation). Discussion about specific forms of exploitation has begun in Poland.

The public consciousness of the working class and other working people is increasingly being formed outside of the ruling communist parties. Pressure from "below" plays an ambiguous role: by pushing the leadership to enact reforms, it simultaneously curbs and even sometimes blocks attempts to revitalize the economy, and to modernize structures of public production at the expense of income growth and living standards. When an ongoing crisis erupts from time to time ("crisis within a crisis") without getting a peaceful and constructive resolution, problematic and even deadlock-type situations emerge as a result. The probability of social explosions is getting higher.

The social-class nature of ruling parties that are undertaking the turn toward radical reforms is in question now since there will be problems relying on the entire working class, particularly on its largest groups employed in the coal industry, metallurgy, ship-building industry, and other traditional industries which are in decline all over the world. Besides, it is well known that Marxist-Leninist parties traditionally saw their historic mission first of all as expressing the interests of workers as the most progressive class, and whose interests objectively coincide with the interests of the working people. Under present conditions this understanding has been increasingly complicating practical steps towards the revitalization and modernization of the economy since the short-term material interests of the working class (at least its substantial part—those employed in physical labor) clash with longer-term interests of society at large. [...] The governments of Poland and Hungary are seeking to accelerate changes in the structures of public production by carrying out the policy of "socialist Thatcherism." Since such a policy hurts substantial segments of the working class and lacks ideological justification, the workers, among them rank-and-file party members, rise in protest while referring to old ideological formulas.

The ruling parties fail chronically and badly in their reaction to the course of social-political developments. None of them has so far proved to be capable of seizing the initiative. Apparently this is due to the lack of clear prospects for renewal, the lack of a contemporary socialist vision. So far this problem has been alleviated because of the absence of alternative constructive platforms. But today the opposition has most obviously been attracting intellectual potential (Poland, Hungary) and has been developing its own ideology and political program.

The developing situations in Yugoslavia, Hungary, and Poland touch on the geopolitical and geo-strategic interests of the Soviet Union to varying degrees. Whatever the outcome of the Yugoslav crisis, it would only marginally affect our society without any serious, direct ideological effect. On the contrary, the course of events in Hungary and especially in Poland will affect us directly and very painfully by buttressing the position of [our] conservative forces and breeding doubts about the chances of survival for *perestroika*.

In *Czechoslovakia, GDR, Bulgaria and Romania* (all the differences in economic position notwithstanding) analogous internal social-political conflicts are still implicit and hidden, even though they are clearly detectable. They tend, however, to exacerbate [matters], and there are telling symptoms that demonstrate (to political scientists) real harbingers of tension:

- Under-fulfillment of excessively optimistic plans and programs (particularly regarding consumption); unexpected growth of inflation; declining indicators of living standards; proliferation of uncontrollable, spontaneous processes in economic life.
- Growing dissatisfaction with the existing situation in the distribution of material goods and equality of opportunities; aggravation of the problem of social justice.
- Intensifying discussions at party congresses; more frequent resignations of politicians, reshuffling of the staff.
- Ferment within the intelligentsia, particularly in its creative components.
- Exacerbation of the generational conflict.
- Crisis of morale; proliferation of social pathologies (crime, drug-addiction, etc.).
- Accumulating feelings of social frustration (deprivation) in large social groups spilling over into "witch hunts," sometimes into aggressive ethnic conflicts, and anti-worker and anti-intellectual sentiments.

These symptoms are manifesting themselves in various combinations and at different volumes. Social-political conflicts remain hidden largely due to harsh controls exercised by repressive structures over public life and to strict limitations on mass media. But in some cases these factors are no longer sufficient to prevent acts of protest (in Czechoslovakia, GDR, and even Romania). A further tightening of controls and more persecutions can either trigger an uncontrollable chain reaction—all the way to an explosion (quite possible in Czechoslovakia)—or encounter a negative reaction in world public opinion and the introduction of very painful economic and political sanctions. For instance, the repressive totalitarian regime in Romania is increasingly finding itself in international isolation, and amicable contacts with N. Ceaușescu, while promising no preferential treatment on the part of the SRR today, even less in the longer term, may only compromise politicians [who engage in such contacts] in the eyes of world public opinion.

POLITICAL FORECAST

In the *countries of the first group*, the crisis has acquired visible forms and the sides in the conflict are lined up, but the prospect of further developments is not clear; there are several alternatives. None among them would presuppose the preservation of traditional forms of governance by the ruling parties and their full control over society. Despite all assurances and words, real chances to keep developments within the framework of socialist renewal are shrinking. The existing model of socialism can be transformed only with enormous difficulty into a more

369

effective and modern social setup. There are serious obstacles to a less-than-costly resolution of the crisis. Furthermore, scenarios of deadlock and catastrophe are coming to the fore.

Poland

1. *Most favorable scenario*: The conclusion of a so-called anti-crisis pact at the "Roundtable" talks, which could mean an unstable compromise between the PUWP (and its allied parties), Solidarity (and the forces of the opposition intelligentsia) and the GCITU [the General Council of Industrial Trade Unions]. The gradual transition to a mixed economy, and de-centralization and privatization of "the giants of post-war industrialization" through shareholding. Transition to one or another variant of a market economy. Advancement towards genuine party-political pluralism (free elections, redistribution of seats in the Parliament, co-optation of representatives of the present opposition into the government, access of the opposition to mass media) could increase support on the part of the population of the country and the West. The latter could ameliorate the situation with payments on external debt, and by opening channels for new credits, which could somewhat reduce internal economic tensions. However, even in this case popular protests would hardly be neutralized, and political instability would continue for a long time, producing micro-crises periodically. This would complicate a decisive and energetic program of reforms. The weakening of the PUWP would inevitably continue as a result of the ideological crisis and internal struggle, but it would take a more gradual course in a form that could allow an explosion to occur. Relations with the USSR would remain ideologized while Poland would remain a member of the WTO.

Terms of realization: preservation and consolidation of the authority of the present-day party-political leadership (W. Jaruzelski); containment of pressure from "below" in a framework that would preclude the radicalization of both trade union confederations.

2. *Pessimistic scenario*: Failure of the anti-crisis pact resulting from a clash between the conservative forces in the PUWP, a radicalized GCTU and the extremist wing of Solidarity, while minimal political contacts between the party-government leadership and the opposition survive. A protracted "deadlock" situation. Slow and ineffective changes in the economy, a de facto pluralism in society without effective mechanisms for taking and implementing decisions. Growing elements of anarchy. Transformation of Poland into the chronically "sick man of Europe."

3. *Deadlock scenario*: Failure of the anti-crisis pact followed by an aggravation of relations with the opposition. Rapid escalation of the conflict until an explosion (the most probable timing in this case—spring 1989). Renewal of martial law or a situation approximating a civil war—"Afghanistan in the middle of Europe."

4. Recently, the first weak symptoms of yet another scenario have emerged. It is close to the first but is related to the formation of the Christian Democratic

Party of Labor which, hypothetically, may grow into a big political force if supported by Solidarity (in the role of a Catholic trade union) and the oppositionist Catholic intelligentsia. The PUWP may well welcome such a scenario since it could promise cooperation with the Church, which seeks to avoid an explosion. Yet existing information provides no clues as to the change in the Church's position, which has so far preferred to remain in the role of mediator.

This last month produced good chances for developments according to the first scenario. There is no absolute guarantee that this will be realized, since there are no assurances that the traditionalist forces would not defy the course of the 10th Plenum of the CC PUWP at the forthcoming party conference, and that Solidarity would and could contain the rising mass protest and observe the two-year armistice. Specific conditions in Poland may lead the first and especially the second scenarios to a dead end. The chance for an explosion in the PPR is far greater than in other countries of Eastern Europe.

In a longer-term perspective even the most favorable scenario does not ensure preservation of the socialist choice. Evolution towards a classic bourgeois society of the type of Italy or Greece is highly likely.

Hungary

1. *Most Probable Scenario*: Radical reforms in the state sector of the economy, partial re-privatization of industries and agriculture, transformation of the economy into a mixed one, functioning on the basis of market relations. Further strengthening of organizational ties with the European Union and perhaps with EFTA [European Free Trade Association] growing cooperation with Austria. Step-by-step rebuilding of the parliamentary system on the foundations of party pluralism. Along with the inevitable decline of cooperation with the CMEA and formal continuation of membership in the WTO, there will come a tendency towards neutralism and possibly a movement towards some kind of Danube federation if this idea takes shape and gains support among Hungary's neighbors.

Terms of realization: as a result of a considerable strengthening of the positions of the reformist wing in HSWP's leadership and in the party as a whole, the reformist wing is seizing the initiative in transforming social-economic and political structures; the gradual formation of a coalition with the Social Democratic movement (not excluding the transition of a considerable number of party members to the Social Democrats or the peaceful split into two parties). Even if the influence of other parties increases in the short run, the course of events will probably become a modification of the first scenario since none of the movements can compete in strength and influence with the reformist circles of the HSWP and the forces of Social Democratic orientation.

2. *Pessimistic scenario*: Concessions to the conservative wing of the party, which retains strong positions in the medium and lower ranks. Attempts to minimize deviations from the traditionalist schema. Inconsistency and compromises in carrying out reforms. The growth of economic and political tension. Further

decline of living standards, the growth of a strike movement, politicization of trade unions. Possible declaration of bankruptcy on the external debt, aggravated relations with creditors, including international monetary-financial institutions. Building obstacles on the way to the legal construction of some oppositionist parties and movements. Postponement of parliamentary elections. Further drop in the authority of the reformist wing in the present-day leadership of the HSWP and of the supporting forces in the party and state apparatus. Weakening electoral chances of the HSWP (including an electoral defeat). Transfer of initiative to alternative political forces. As a result, there is a return to the necessity of radical reforms but under new, economically and politically less propitious circumstances. [...]

The first scenario's implementation is not yet out of the question, but the most probable seems to be some kind of middle way between the first and the second scenarios. The inevitable aggravation of the internal situation in this case may propel events towards the first scenario or raise the chances of complete slideback towards the second scenario. [...]

In the longer term, the present-day situation in the countries of the second group appears to be more dangerous for the future of socialism and crisis phenomena there will inevitably take an open form. Czechoslovakia is the first candidate. In Bulgaria and Romania (possibly, also in the GDR) changes will come with a change of leader, which will occur from natural causes. The character and tempo of subsequent events will depend on the degree to which the new generation of leadership, willing to defuse the accumulated tensions and raise personal prestige, comes to decrease the grip of the repressive apparatus over society. The available data provides no evidence for a substantial forecast of alternatives, but it seems obvious that the more the tension is driven inside, the higher the chances for an explosion in one of these countries, with all the consequences that flow from this.

Czechoslovakia

With a high degree of probability one can expect rapid escalation as soon as this coming spring or in the fall. Causes: a combination of strong public discontent with the unjustifiably harsh crackdown on the last demonstration[35] with the first unpopular results of the economic reforms (the absence of bonuses in many unprofitable plants, etc.). Preventing such a course of events is possible by undertaking, at M. Jakeš' initiative, a resolute change in a considerable part of the current party-state leadership, removal of publicly compromised people, joint efforts together with L. Adamec and the initiation of practical steps towards socialist renewal and broad democratization. However, first, since the General Secretary

---

[35] On the anniversary of the February events and of the death of T. Masaryk this crack-down will probably take place again. [Footnote in the original.]

of the CC CCP has already twice failed to live up to public expectations and to declare himself an advocate of a new course, and, second, since there is too little time left for preparation of such a step, the chances for such a favorable outcome are minimal. Extrapolation of the current situation points to a crisis, where order would be restored by force and all problems would again be driven inside.

In the course of events, one may expect the appearance of a new political force in the country's political arena—the Club of socialist *perestroika*, headed by well-known leaders of the Prague Spring, C. Císař and Černík, who adhere to socialist positions. This group has a solid constructive platform and can expect an influx of a large number of supporters—possibly up to 500–750,000. In a struggle with this political adversary, the leadership of the CCP has minimal chances of victory. However, the struggle against the politicians and ideas of 1968 will be acute and will lead to a quick and rapid escalation of the crisis.

Romania.

1. *Favorable scenario*: Changes take place in the leadership of the country. As a result, N. Ceaușescu is replaced by reasonable politicians capable of carrying out radical reforms and ideas for the renewal of socialism. There are good preconditions in Romania for the use of market-type relations, for a relatively dynamic restructuring and modernization of the people's economy with a real unfettering of economic initiative and the creation of a multi-sector competitive economy.

2. *Middle-dead end scenario*: The present leadership of the country stays and so too the policy. If the resources that are freed as the external debt is paid off are used for reducing social tensions, then it is possible to maintain general political stability for quite a while, while conserving political problems in the country and ensuring a slowdown in technological-scientific progress. If, however, the leadership chooses to ignore the task of improving living standards for the population and diverts the obtained resources for the realization of new ambitious projects, then one cannot exclude a social explosion. In a case where renewal processes in other socialist countries by that time have not proven the feasibility of reform, there could be a danger of a decisive turn by the country—[i.e. Romania], whose population gets disenchanted with socialist values and is traditionally raised in the spirit of common destiny with the Latin [*romanskii*] world—in the direction of the West (including its exit from the WTO). Financial and material support from the West, highly probable under conditions of real change, may prove to be very effective for a country possessing a good deal of natural and economic resources.

Since the regime still has not exhausted its resources and has recently been accumulating the experience of combined repressive measures and social maneuvering to maintain social stability, the second scenario seems to be more likely. In its favor there is also a relatively low level of national self-consciousness and an absence of organized opposition in Romania. At the same time, the obvious irrationality of the policy of the current leadership produces growing dissatisfaction not only on the grass-roots level but even among the ruling elite [*verkhushki*]. Therefore, the possibility of some kind of changes "from the top" cannot be excluded.

German Democratic Republic.

The conservative nature of the party leadership, the sectarian and dogmatic character of its positions on ideological questions, authoritarianism and harsh control of the repressive apparatus over society are weakening the prestige of the party and heightening tensions in the country, as well as negativist sentiments among the population. Nevertheless the current line may survive the change of leadership for some time.

There is no formal center of opposition in the GDR, although non-conformist movements with more or less formalized platforms do exist. So far they do not represent any force capable of applying palpable pressure from below and of destabilizing the situation. With a degree of probability one can surmise that there are forces in the current ruling apparatus who not only can evaluate the situation soberly and analyze critically, but who can work out a constructive program of changes. Reformist sentiments do not come to the surface, most likely because potential advocates of a new course do not have sufficient assurances that the process of renewal in the USSR is inevitable. Besides, they understand that far-reaching reforms in the GDR will hardly remain an internal affair and may trigger a change in the status quo in the center of Europe.

With this in mind, *perestroika* in the GDR, if it occurs, will require from the USSR and other socialist countries the reevaluation of a number of established assumptions and perhaps a reappraisal of its interests in the center of Europe. Under conditions of democratization and *glasnost*, this question will probably become the central one, and the mode of its resolution will depend on the determination of the [GDR] leadership in carrying out reforms. In the long run, one can foresee the declaration of such goals as the creation of a unified neutral German state on the basis of a confederation. A mid-term slogan, "one state—two systems," may be also advanced.

Bulgaria

Underground ferment and differentiation of social-political forces have become fact. So far they manifest themselves in local, impulsive flashpoints of resistance to the official ideology and the concept of social development, without growing into any significant movements. Further dynamics and the direction of social-political shifts will be determined primarily by economic trends.

The country's leadership has worked out a concept for economic reform, but practical measures for its realization have not yet been sufficiently prepared, so in the near future real results can hardly be expected. A deterioration in the economic situation is more likely, particularly because of the growing debt to the West and the threat of bankruptcy, which will inevitably bring about unwanted social, and then political, consequences. Against this background hotbeds of tension might proliferate—including strikes, particularly among non-qualified and less-qualified workers.

The party's ideological influence on society is declining. There are opposition sentiments among intellectuals who resent the use of force against ecologists and the persecution of a number of scientists for critical speeches. There are seeds of alternative movements, and extremist elements are coming to the fore. Alternative political forces are still weak and not organized, but they could broaden their social base.

The withdrawal of the present number one in the party from the political scene may provide an impetus for intra-party differentiation between the supporters of the old leadership and those who seek a genuine renewal. Forces capable of carrying out more balanced and reasonable policies do exist in the party; they enjoy enough authority, but they will face a difficult legacy.

The overall trend of social-economic and political development in the country tends to repeat the Hungarian scenario—with certain deviations, time gap and national peculiarities, and the eclectic emulation of experiences of other countries. The fate of the Hungarian experiment may exercise a serious influence on future developments in the PRB.

Possible consequences for the USSR

The prospect of the weakening of the ruling parties' positions—including their removal from power, its transfer into the hands of other political forces, the decline of Soviet influence in the countries of Eastern Europe, and its attachment to the orbit of Western economic and political interests—require the formulation of a more rational and deliberate reaction by the Soviet Union. We face a dilemma: to thwart the evolution described above or take it in stride and develop the policy accepting the probability and even inevitability of this process.

Attempts to thwart emerging trends would be tantamount to fighting time itself, the objective course of history. In the long term, these kinds of steps would be doomed and in the short run would mean wasting means and resources for an obviously hopeless cause. Attempts to preserve in Poland, Hungary and Yugoslavia the status quo that has lost its objective foundations, as well as the support of conservative forces in the GDR, ČSSR, Romania and Bulgaria will weigh as an excessive burden on our economy, for the price of maintaining existing relations will increase in time. The use of forceful pressure from our side will inevitably reinforce the conservative wing in the upper echelons of power, rupturing reforms where they have begun, and worsening the crisis. Social-political tensions in societies will increase, anti-Soviet sentiments will grow stronger, which might spill over into a delicate balance on the brink of a most acute social-political conflict, with an unfathomable outcome. The direct use of force by the USSR, its intervention in the course of events on behalf of conservative forces that are alienated from the people, will most evidently signify the end of *perestroika* and the crumbling of trust on the part of the world community in [our reforms]. But it will not prevent a disintegration of the social-economic and social-political systems in these countries, nor will it exclude mass outbreaks of protest, including armed clashes. Besides, not only nationally isolated events, but mutually interacting, chain-reaction "fuse-type" explosions can be expected.

In the framework of possibilities created by new thinking and cooperation between the USSR and the United States, East and West, the "architects" of American foreign policy can be seen as changing their priorities. They prefer the support of *perestroika* in the USSR and the creation of an external environment favorable to its success. Serious Western politicians warn against playing on the problems of the socialist community, and on its disintegration, which in their opinion may bring about unexpected consequences for the Western world. Western circles of authority are coming to the conclusion that, by cooperating with reformist forces, they can achieve more than by attempting to pull the socialist countries from the USSR's sphere of influence one by one.

Working through the options for a future Western strategy towards Eastern Europe, bourgeois political scientists and some think tanks are considering a "Finlandization" scenario for a number of countries of the region.[36]

What could be the possible consequences of such a scenario for the USSR? The following aspects should be considered: military, international politics, internal politics, economic and ideological.

1. Poland will certainly not leave the WTO, since this is against its national, state, and geopolitical interests. Hungary will also hardly raise this issue in the foreseeable future. The forthcoming withdrawal of a portion of Soviet troops stationed on the territories of both countries will significantly reduce the political acuteness of this problem. The GDR will also not raise the question of leaving the WTO since its party and state cadres consider this organization as one of its props. Only in the long-term, if détente and the construction of a "common European home" progress sufficiently, will the issue of a unified German confederate state possibly be put on the agenda. From the international angle, this will most

---

[36] In the political dictionary this term mostly signifies the return of our neighboring states to the mode of capitalist development while preserving special, friendly relations with the Soviet Union that guarantee the security of its borders. Such an understanding of the notion of "Finlandization" overlooks two significant moments in relations between the USSR and Finland. First, they are built on the neutrality of our northern neighbor which does not join any military bloc; second, the Finnish communist party by definition cannot come to power and carry out a revolutionary coup which guarantees the stability of the [Finnish] social-political regime. Since the countries of Eastern Europe will hardly raise the issue of leaving the WTO in the near future and the ruling parties, even provided their rapid weakening, will retain for a while some social base, "Finlandization" can be used here only with very significant qualifications. [Footnote in the original.]

likely end up in the neutralization of both parts of Germany and the establishment of special relations between the GDR and NATO, and the GDR and the WTO. The positions of Bulgaria and Czechoslovakia depend on many uncertain factors, but they will hardly leave the WTO in the foreseeable future. If relations with us worsen, the Romanian leadership may take up this issue, but with skillful ideological orchestration of this step we will not lose anything since its geopolitical location will force the self-isolated Romania to consider our interests. In the case of Yugoslavia, as is well known, the question of the WTO does not figure at all.

So we can expect that the WTO—at least in the foreseeable future—will not necessarily sustain significant losses; and we can expect that all of the Eastern European countries, which are currently undergoing serious transformations, will stay in alliance with us.

2. As long as new foreign policy trends emerge in the countries of Eastern Europe, which became the object of special aspirations for the U.S. and the West as they conducted their policy of differentiation, the USSR may consciously take over the initiative from the West as well as from the oppositionist, social-reformist forces inside those countries (Poland, Hungary) by consciously adopting a certain degree of "Finlandization" of these countries. Such a policy will demonstrate the seriousness of our global aims to get involved in world economic, political and cultural ties. Renunciation of the diktat with regard to the socialist countries of Eastern Europe will nurture a more benevolent image of the USSR in the public opinion of these countries and around the world, and it will make the U.S. seriously correct its foreign policy towards Eastern Europe.

The very chance that European socialist countries may take a mid-way position on the continent will intensify the interest of Western Europe in maintaining the economic and political stability of Eastern Europe as well as in stimulating the process of disarmament and détente on the continent and around the world. Inevitable consequences of this will be the growth in significance of the European factor in world politics and economics, which will favor Soviet efforts aimed at containing an anti-Soviet consolidation of the Western world and at developing a "common European home." The economic burden of the USSR will be alleviated. Anti-Soviet and nationalist influences will operate on shrunken ground, and the prestige of the Soviet Union and its ideological-political influence on broad strata of the population will grow—of course, the political shift will be viewed as a result of our conscious decision and not a result of the pressure of hostile forces. This will be a "revolution from above" in foreign policy, which will prevent a "revolution from below."

3. It cannot be excluded that in some countries of Eastern Europe the crisis will have gone so far and reforms will have come so late that the ruling parties will not be able to retain power or will have to share it in a coalition with other political forces. By itself the fact of a transfer of power to alternative forces does not mean an external and military threat to our country. On the contrary, history provides examples of when the Soviet Union developed relations with non-communist leaders of Eastern European countries that were not too bad. Normal

political activity by communist parties (along with other political parties) should not instill the fear in non-communist governments that, under the guise of international aid, there will be a violation of popular sovereignty with a possible violation of its will expressed through free elections. Guarantees of non-interference in the internal affairs of neighboring countries and respect for their political stability should, under present circumstances, be seen differently than in the 1950s–1970s, for we ourselves have recognized the need for a different understanding of socialism in principle, and have stopped trying to expand over the entire world the model that was in existence in our country. We have begun to realize the need in the socialist model for accounting for some basic characteristics of the Western mode of development (markets, competition, civil society, civil liberties, etc.)

There is no question, of course, of renouncing the support of communist and workers' parties, but an obligatory precondition for such support should be voluntary recognition of their leadership by their people, their legitimacy. For the loss of trust, they should pay as any other party in normal democratic society. Similar logic dictates to us the need for support of business, civilized contacts not only with those political parties in the countries of Eastern Europe which are currently at the tiller, but also with the internal opposition, the constructive opposition in society—equal to our practice toward non-socialist states. An unwillingness to accept contacts with alternative forces in these countries could be interpreted as a form of interference in internal affairs, i.e. something which we have rejected as a matter of principle.

4. The objective outcome of the natural development of the trends towards "Finlandization" could be a new, middle-of-the road position on the part of the East European countries since they, according to their internal order, the nature of their economic ties and their real international position, would pass from the sphere of monopolistic influence of the USSR into the sphere of mutual and joint influence by the Soviet Union and the European "Common Market." It cannot be excluded that in the near future the European Economic Union will convey associate member status to some countries of Eastern Europe. They could, in this case, become the pioneers in the process of integration between East and West. This process not only poses no threat to the interests of the USSR but, on the contrary, will allow the benefits we receive today from our cooperation with Finland and Austria—by linking to Western markets—to multiply. [These include] the achievements of Western science, know-how and technology, When a common market starts functioning in Western Europe in 1992, East European countries involved in the orbit of the EU may facilitate our access to this sphere.

5. In a new situation, we will have to liberate ourselves from certain persistent ideological stereotypes, for instance the assumption that only a communist party in power can provide guarantees for the security of Soviet borders. We will have to rethink the notion of a "world socialist system." But the utility of these [notions] was purely fictional; it existed only in a realm alienated from life, in a didactic ideology which we have been striving to overcome. Consequently, the rejection of such categories and dogmas may only promote a new system of

ideological coordinates that are emerging in the process of *perestroika* and the formation of new political thinking.

An optimal reaction by the USSR to the evolutionary processes taking place in Eastern Europe would be, as it turns out, active involvement which would place them [the processes] under control and make them predictable. Even if some decline of Soviet influence in Eastern European affairs takes place, this would not cause us fatal damage but, perhaps on the contrary, resulting from self-limitation, it would place our means in rational harmony with our capabilities. For we speak about a voluntary abandonment of only those levers of influence that are not in accordance with the principles of international relations proclaimed by the Soviet Union in the spirit of "new thinking."

Of course, such a turn may produce collisions and conflicts, for example if openly anti-Soviet, nationalistic groupings are legalized in this or that country. But their persecution, their underground existence will only help them gain in popularity, and their legalization against the backdrop of our reserved policy, and with thoughtful criticism of them on the part of friends of the USSR, will lay bare the lack of perspective and short-sightedness of anti-Soviet assumptions.

Favorable international conditions for the progress of reforms in the socialist countries of Eastern Europe will lend a powerful side-effect to the process of internal *perestroika* in the USSR. Structural modernization of their economies, and the development of market relations will help to overcome the elements of parasitism in their economic relations with the USSR and to transfer them to the healthy ground of mutual profitability.

Possible practical steps of the USSR

In light of the aforementioned, the following measures seem to be justified:

Work on a strategic program to develop our relations with the East European socialist countries within the framework of the new model of socialism and a calibrated reflection of this program in official documents and speeches.

Advancement of our proposals to reform the Warsaw Treaty Organization, presupposing a bigger role for the fraternal countries in the management of the WTO, and the creation of regional commands (taking the example of NATO) under the leadership of representatives of hosting countries. This would help to "tie" them into the WTO, which in practice is still regarded as a predominantly Soviet construct.

A further gradual reduction of our military presence in Eastern Europe taken at our own initiative and upon agreement with the hosting countries, working on a schedule for withdrawal of troops, the creation of the most propitious conditions for demilitarization in Central Europe (with its possible neutralization), and a reduction of American presence on the European continent.

Working through bilateral consultations on mutually beneficial measures to alleviate the consequences of restructuring in the countries of Eastern Europe, particularly where strong tensions might end up in an explosion.

In case certain proposals are made, we should agree to some form of continuous and periodic consultations with West European countries and the U.S. on the issue of preventing explosions in this or that country of Central and Eastern Europe.

Developing a practice of genuine consultations on issues of foreign policy with our allies instead of informing them about decisions already taken.

Carrying out a serious analysis of the activities of Soviet embassies in the East European socialist countries, in some cases leading to replacement of ambassadors and leading officials of the Embassies who act against the interests of our foreign policy in its new phase. Special attention should be paid to our cadres in the countries where a potential escalation of tensions and even explosion are possible. During the change of cadres we should send to these countries those officials whose appointment will be a sign of the attention and high priority the USSR assigns to relations with socialist countries.

While arranging summits in socialist countries, one should borrow the methods utilized in leading capitalist countries (the organization of appearances by leading Soviet scientists, cultural figures, etc.)

It is necessary to work out without delay an integral line of behavior on the issues of "blank pages"[37] in relations with each East European country. (We should not ignore the accumulating negative fallout that resulted from our postponement of the resolution of these problems with regard to the PPR and HPR.)

It is highly important to radically change our informational policy with regard to events in the socialist countries of Eastern Europe, to cover in an objective light and to explain and justify the processes that are taking place there, since it is equal to the explanation and justification of the measures that lie ahead for us in carrying out our economic and political reforms.

While covering events in the fraternal countries and responding to the speeches of their leaders, we should express a manifest support for those pronouncements which signal their acceptance of reformist ideas (particularly with regard to the leaders of the GDR, Czechoslovakia, Bulgaria and Romania), thereby showing on what side of the forces and trends the sympathies of the Soviet Union lie.

Popularization of Soviet publications merits all kinds of support. Proposals of our embassies in some countries to eschew such support are clearly in contradiction with our interests.

SOME CONCLUSIONS

Overcoming the crisis in the countries of Eastern Europe presupposes outright de-Stalinization. This should encompass their domestic life as well as their

---

[37] The terms "blank pages" or "blank spots" referred to events in the history of Soviet relations with the East European countries that were controversial or censored in Soviet history books, such as the massacre of Polish officers at Katyń in 1939.

relations with the Soviet Union. The model of economic and political development imposed on these countries after 1948 has clearly exhausted itself. The search for more fruitful ways and means of development is leading to a rethinking of the socialist ideal, including the revival of assumptions that formed in the communist and workers' parties of the East European countries in 1945–1948 (mixed economy, parliamentary democracy, etc.). This means a return to a natural, historical form of social progress—instead of one deformed by external pressure—that stems from the national peculiarities of each country. To a certain degree, one may speak about overcoming the Yalta legacy of splitting the world into two enemy camps, and about the gradual formation of a more varied and simultaneously more united Europe.

From the world socialist perspective, any attempt to stop this evolution by force could have the gravest consequences: the inevitable slide of the East European countries back to the ranks of the poorly developed (the so-called "fourth world"), the undercutting of the socialist idea in all its versions, and the provision of a new hand of cards to neo-conservatives in the West to use in their offensive against the social achievements of the working masses. Besides, Eastern Europe will inevitably acquire "hot points" [*goriachie tochki*]" and quasi-dictatorial regimes which would continuously deplete the material resources of the Soviet Union and effectively exclude the prospects for renewal of socialist society in our country. However, the peaceful evolution of East European states (without serious explosions) would to a great extent improve the world situation and enhance international relations. In that way, the chances of accelerated development in Eastern Europe would grow, as would the prospects of certain socialist elements that can be found in the practice of highly developed capitalist countries. Overall, the prospects for forming humanistic and democratic post-capitalist societies in accordance with socialist ideals would be preserved.

[*Source: Donation of Professor Jacques Levesque. Document on file at the National Security Archive and at the Gorbachev Foundation. Translated by Vladislav Zubok.*]

Document No. 43: Cable from Jack Matlock to State Department, "The Soviet Union over the Next Four Years"

February 3, 1989

Career foreign service officer and Soviet specialist Jack Matlock became U.S. ambassador to Moscow in April 1987 after almost four years as a key National Security Council staff member during President Reagan's growing rapprochement with Gorbachev. Now, less than a month into the new Bush administration's "pause," Matlock tries to influence U.S. policy towards greater engagement by sending three cables (see also Document Nos. 45 & 47) that cumulatively remind the reader of the famous "Long Telegram" from George Kennan in 1946. Matlock begins his first cable with an extraordinary finding that the Soviet Union has "declared the bankruptcy of its system" and, like a corporation in "Chapter 11," there is "no turning back." At the same time, Matlock's crystal ball is off: he tells Washington that "Mikhail Gorbachev is likely to remain the top Soviet leader for at least five (probably ten) more years ..."

No doubt the seasoned ambassador already knows the proclivities of the new White House team and constructs his prose to push only so far. Even so, compared to the policy choices already made by Gorbachev, and to the forecasts in the Bogomolov and even the International Department memos (see previous two documents), Matlock's analysis seems distinctly behind the pace of events. He would follow up these cables with a Washington visit on March 3, urging an early summit, only to find Bush noncommittal.

---

1. Secret—Entire Text

2. Begin Summary. In my personal assessment, we can plan our foreign policy with a high degree of confidence that the Soviet leadership's preoccupation with internal reform will continue throughout the first Bush administration. It is almost as certain that *perestroika* will not rpt [repeat] not bring marked improvements to the Soviet economy in this period and that internal resistance to major aspects of the reform programs will force those at the Soviet helm to tack against the wind much of the time. The potential for severe outbreaks of public disorder will grow. This will contribute to a sense of anxiety in the supreme councils of the party and state, though I believe that they in the end will maintain order.

3. Mikhail Gorbachev is likely to remain the top Soviet leader for at least five (probably ten) more years, but my confidence in this prospect is lower than that in the continuation of a Soviet preoccupation with internal reform. That preoccupation, combined with the multitudinous difficulties of forcing the Soviet mastodon to adapt to the modern technological world, will bring an inexorable pressure to curtail the amount of resources devoted to the military sector.

4. In sum, the Soviet Union has, in effect, declared the bankruptcy of its system, and just as with a corporation which has sought the protection of Chapter XI, there is no turning back. End summary.

5. Crystal balls are never as clear as one would like, and they tend to cloud over during times of rapid and fundamental change. Nevertheless, it seems to me that we can make some assumptions about the Soviet domestic scene over the next four years with a high level of confidence. This message will attempt to encapsulate my personal assessment of the most salient trends. Subsequent messages will look at prospects for Soviet foreign policy and U.S.–Soviet relations.

FOCUS ON INTERNAL AFFAIRS

6. I believe we can state with near certainty that the current Soviet preoccupation with internal reform will continue at least for another four years—and probably much longer. This preoccupation will not preclude an activist foreign policy (as will be discussed in a separate message) but will mean that foreign policy decisions will be heavily—and often decisively—influenced by domestic needs and imperatives.

7. While this is not the first time Soviet leaders have attempted some change in Soviet political and economic practice, today's *perestroika* is potentially the most profound—and therefore most destabilizing—effort to push the economy, political system, and social structure into a new mold. Although many individual aspects of this effort can be stalled or even reversed, enough of the old structure, the old habits and the old ideology have been discredited to make return to the status quo ante quite impossible. It is as if a delicate (but still ill-functioning) machine has been partially dismantled before a new design has been developed, let alone tested and new parts fabricated. Many of the old parts have broken so the machine cannot be quickly restored even to its earlier inefficient condition, such is the dilemma the Soviet leaders face, and it will claim their priority attention for years.

THE IDEOLOGICAL FOUNDATION

8. *Perestroika*, as it has developed, differs from past efforts to reform this or that Soviet practice (Khrushchev's attack on Stalin's terror) or this or that aspect of the system (the abortive "Liberman" reforms of the 60's) by its increasing attention to fundamentals. Earlier attempts at "reform" tried to keep the ideology intact and simply change the way it was implemented. This sufficed to eliminate the grosser aspects of Stalinist terror, but not to improve the managerial efficiency of the economy.

9. When Gorbachev first came to power it appeared that he, too, was going for superficial "fixes" in economic management. Nevertheless, as his program developed, it began more and more to confront the ideological foundation of the old practices—and to change the old assumptions.

10. This process followed several paths. One was an all-out attack on Stalinism, which implicitly—and sometimes explicitly—denied that that Stalinist system of state monopoly was even a legitimate form of socialism. Concomitantly, a gradual rehabilitation of non-Stalinist Marxist thinkers such as Bukharin has occurred with the obvious intent of providing variant and more congenial interpretations of Marxist principles.

11. Lenin has remained sacrosanct, but his utterances on topics of the day were so varied that the diligent researcher can find a quote to bolster virtually any proposition. "Leninism" in effect becomes what the current leaders want it to be—even if this requires an unacknowledged transformation of Marxism itself.

12. Among the major ideological points which the reformers are trying to establish are the fundamental role of the market in determining economic value (we don't see much on Marx's labor theory of value anymore!); the importance of fostering individual initiative and tapping individual creativity; the necessity for more powerful economic incentives; the need to shift from "administrative" to "economic" (read market) controls of economic life; and—not least—a downgrading of the "class struggle" to a position subordinate to the "common interests of mankind."

13. None of these propositions has figured prominently in past Marxist thinking—to put it mildly—and an intense struggle is still underway here over them. Many (including Ligachev) are openly skeptical about basing so much on market forces, and the practical effects of moving in that direction (rising prices) are fiercely resented by an overwhelming majority. Still, it seems clear that if *perestroika* ever is made to work, ultimate adoption of these very un-Marxist principles will be essential.

"DIVIDENDS" SLOW TO MATERIALIZE

14. Given the depth of the Soviet Union's problems, and the difficulty of breaking through institutional and attitudinal barriers, it should not be surprising that concrete economic dividends in the form of goods in the shops have been slow in coming, but while it should not be surprising, the Gorbachev leadership seems to have been surprised. They clearly have been required to stretch out their plans and adjust their interim targets downward, even as they were devising even more ambitious final goals.

15. An objective look at the major economic initiatives launched under the banner of *perestroika* shows a recurrent flaw. Top Soviet leadership is having to revisit each initiative in order to sustain or rebuild momentum which is otherwise lost when the leadership itself is not focused on it. The political thrusts of each major economic initiative (e.g., land-leasing, consumer goods, free trade zones, financial autonomy, industrial policy, consumer good production) have far outdistanced economic substance, and provision of the specifics necessary for implementation and overcoming resistance to reform at all levels. Moreover, the failure to engage adequately on key reform issues like monetary and price

reform, creation of wholesale markets, external competitiveness and convertibility, combines with the momentum problem to ensure that there is effectively no integrated, mutually reinforcing, sequentially sensitive economic reform program.

16. As the intractability of the economic problems became ever more evident, leadership attention focused increasingly on political and social reform. Most Soviet observers I talk to attribute this to a recognition that political reform is a precondition for effective economic reform. (Since one of the root problems in the economy is the stranglehold exercised by the rigid party bureaucracy, one must limit the powers of party officials, pare down the bureaucracy, and make what is left more responsive to public opinion if the economic reforms are to be feasible.) In addition, one suspects that another motivation for some of the political reforms was a desire to provide popular benefits to the public at a time when economic results were disappointing. If bread was short, at least there could be circuses: local meetings to "nominate" candidates to a brand-new "parliament," for example. But political reform is proceeding neither smoothly nor automatically. Its achievements are partial and qualified ones, and the initial enthusiasm of many is turning into frustration and even despair as they sense the magnitude of the task ahead.

STRUCTURAL AND ATTITUDINAL BARRIERS

17. Fundamentally, Soviet reformers have to contend with much more than the familiar and daunting problems of over centralization, red-tape, bureaucratic resistance, party arrogance, unrealistic plans, corruption, and all the other ills which have received so much attention of late. The (for them) sad fact is that the Soviet political and economic system was designed to work only from the top down, on a command basis, and to resist change and spontaneity, much as the body's immune system resists infections. Moving to a system with the opposite orientation—clearly implied by *perestroika*—may not be possible on the basis of incremental change. To put it another way, each change tends either to be smothered by the system itself or—if it is pressed relentlessly—to threaten collapse of the entire system.

18. If the bulk of the population had a better understanding of what is required to get out of the mess all acknowledge they are in, the structural barriers noted might seem somehow erodible. Alas, most people here have not the foggiest notion of what constitutes market economics. Nurtured for decades on the myth that there is a "free lunch" (socialist "benefits" of "free" education, "free" medical care, cheap food and housing) and that it is immoral to live better than one's neighbor, there is fierce resistance to market prices, if they higher prices—as they inevitably do in an economy of scarcity and printing-press money. Thus, we now witness the phenomenon of the public demanding price and other controls on the fledgling cooperative (i.e., private) sector, which would at best force upon them the same inefficiencies as the state sector and more likely kill them off altogether.

19. Difficult as the current problems are, they are likely to get worse. The exasperation of the Soviet consumer is almost palpable. The combination of shortages and inflation, the latter rapidly becoming a major problem, are moving the Soviet Union toward a barter economy. Soviets, from taxi drivers to intellectuals, are not interested in having rubles: they want goods. Large-scale strikes and riots are conceivable if the situation deteriorates further and the legendary patience of the Soviet people is exhausted. Most likely, such outbursts can be controlled—but at enormous cost to the forward momentum of reform.

20. More serious is the potential for major eruptions of nationalist feeling, as the Baltics and the Caucasus have shown over the past year. Indeed, despite all of the changes in Soviet society over the past several years, the *glasnost* and the *perestroika*, only nationalism has been capable of igniting popular passions. And we must remember that the Ukraine and Central Asia—areas where, because of population size, resources and religion, nationalism could represent a major danger to the Soviet empire—have remained thus far almost eerily quiet, a calm that neither we nor the Soviet leadership should expect to continue.

21. A backlash of Russian nationalism has already begun. We can expect it to intensify over the next several years as the minority nationalities become more assertive, either in the press or in the streets. No matter what the danger to his reform program, there are limits beyond which no Soviet leader will be able to go, and still remain in his job, in tolerating nationalist outbursts. For that very reason, Gorbachev and the Soviet leadership will invest great energy and resources in the effort to head off or manage nationalist explosions.

GORBACHEV'S POSITION

22. The gloomy outlook for tangible improvements in Soviet economic performance has led many to question Gorbachev's staying power. Mindful especially of Khrushchev's fate and also, perhaps, influenced by the logic of Western political processes, some observers feel that without an upturn in the availability of food and consumer goods fairly soon, Gorbachev could be successfully challenged by rivals.

23. This is possible, but I do not consider it likely. My guess is that Gorbachev will remain the Soviet leader for a considerable time to come, whether or not his domestic policies are successful. In the first place, the Soviet Union is by no means a parliamentary democracy. Gorbachev will not be voted out by a public impatient for tangible rewards. If he is removed, the only plausible scenario for his removal by political means would involve a conspiracy against him in the Central Committee. Any successful conspiracy would have to involve a fairly wide circle, so that the organizers could be confident of overwhelming support once the issue were joined. Khrushchev fell victim to such a conspiracy, so we know it can happen. So does Gorbachev, of course, and that is probably why he

386

has placed the KGB and (less importantly) the army in loyal hands. So long as the KGB chairman, the commander of the Kremlin guard and the Minister of Defense are loyal to him, it is difficult to see how a conspiracy could be mounted successfully, since he would be warned in time to take "prophylactic" steps—and would have the means to do so. Even the first two of the trio named would probably provide adequate insurance.

24. In addition, the constitutional changes now planned will create an added institutional barrier to a sudden, conspiratorial removal of the Soviet leader. Once Gorbachev occupies the revamped office of president, those who would plan his removal by other than constitutional means would face a possible hurdle which does not exist today. Since strict adherence to constitutional procedure has never been a noticeable Soviet or Russian trait, one cannot say that he could not be removed by a conspiratorial clique with the support of the Central Committee, but it would be a more complicated task than that facing Brezhnev and his associates when they moved against Khrushchev. This is probably the most important of Gorbachev's motivations in pressing so hard for the creation of a stronger presidency with a fixed term, to be held simultaneously with the office of party general secretary.

THE MILITARY BURDEN

25. As *perestroika* founders and pressures on Gorbachev to deliver increase, one fact looms larger and larger: the policy of allocating disproportionately large resources to the military sector has impoverished the civilian sector and is one of the roots of today's economic disarray. Furthermore, given its size and technical sophistication, the military sector provides a tempting "reserve" which can be tapped to alleviate today's shortages. Thus, the recent decision to proceed with the unilateral arms reductions—and even more substantial cutbacks in the industrial capacity devoted to military production—are a reaction to what the Gorbachev leadership must view as an urgent necessity.

26. The military—and the military industrial complex as a whole—can hardly be enthusiastic over such moves, and we can assume that those elements of society will put up a stiff fight, especially if attempts are made to continue retrenchments beyond those already announced. This would not be trivial resistance, but it might not automatically carry the day.

27. The Soviet concentration on building up their military machine has led many to conclude that the Soviet military is an invincibly powerful political force within the country. However, the Soviet military build-up may have been caused more by the militarized thinking of the previous party leadership than by the disproportionate influence of the Soviet marshals. The political leaders most likely ordered up the military hardware because it served their perceived political needs and not because the general staff forced them to procure more than they wanted.

28. If this is the case, then Gorbachev in fact may have a freer hand to squeeze the military-industrial complex than many have supposed.

29. I, of course, may be guessing wrong in predicting Gorbachev's political longevity—and it would be just my luck if I wake up the day after this cable is dispatched to learn that the CC has elected a new general secretary in an unannounced session and Mikhail Sergeyevich has assumed the duties of *kolkhoz* chairman at some location to the East.

30. Though I doubt that this will happen, let us assume that this does—if not tomorrow, then next year or the year after. What then? Would that be the end of *perestroika*?

31. Essentially, any successor over the next four years would face precisely the same problems Gorbachev does—possibly in more acute form. Presumably, an initial attempt would be made to apply the throttle to those aspects of the reform process which are considered particularly painful or destabilizing. More severe limits might be placed on the expression of opinion and on unofficial groups, nationalist tendencies might be opposed more forcefully, implementation of a market price mechanism postponed further, and private entrepreneurship actively discouraged. Such slowdowns or reversals of policy could occur. As a matter of fact, they can occur even if Gorbachev stays in power. But such shifts would only cause the economy to sink deeper into the quagmire of inefficiency, technological backwardness and unrequited human needs. The Soviet leadership's preoccupation with domestic problems would continue and eventually another radical reformer would likely emerge. There is a lot of truth in Gorbachev's frequent assertion that *perestroika* is conditioned by objective necessity and is not dependent on any individual. Over the long run, this is probably right.

32. One thing a successor regime could not do is put things back like they were, vintage late 70's or early 80's. The Soviet Union has, in effect, declared the bankruptcy of its system, but is sticking stubbornly to most of its primary social goals, and like a corporation under Chapter XI, is now seeking to reorganize its mode of operation in order to achieve those objectives. There is no turning back, however, and in time, even ideologically-based guarantees of social equity may have to give ground to market-based efficiencies, with all the implications that carries for a reorientation of government and society.

33. Leningrad minimize considered. Matlock

Secret

[*Source: U.S. Department of State, obtained through FOIA. On file at the National Security Archive.*]

Document No. 44: Memorandum from Anatoly Chernyaev to Vadim Zagladin

February 4, 1989

After the success of the United Nations speech in December 1988, Gorbachev decides his next major audience should be Europe, and the July meeting of the European Parliament in Strasbourg becomes the chosen venue. With this memo, Chernyaev commissions Vadim Zagladin to work on a draft text, a highest-priority assignment direct from the general secretary to be handled in total secrecy. Zagladin at this time is a deputy head of the CC International Department with highly relevant experience with communist and "progressive" parties in Western Europe dating back to the 1960s. Chernyaev tells Zagladin the speech needs to "keep Europe in the movement" towards a common European home and that "it is important that they do not try to destabilize Eastern Europe." Chernyaev's shorthand reference to "Mitterrand's approach" encompasses the notion Gorbachev seized on at the Trilateral Commission session (see Document No. 39) about a borderless Europe in 10–20 years, and a Euro-focus rather than, for example, Thatcher's (and the Americans') more Atlanticist concepts.

Vadim!

The General [Secretary] sends his regards and asks me to give you a general assignment: think about a speech for the European Parliament [to be delivered by Gorbachev]. Do not contact anyone or seek anyone's advice; do not disclose what you are working on. We need to meet about the arguments [we want to make], as well as about the reasons we are in favor of a new Europe and what we mean by "a common European home." [...]

In addition to general structural positions, we need something specific—so specific that it would implicitly support Mitterrand's approach. It is very important for us now to keep Europe in the movement that began as a result of our philosophical approaches and negotiating processes. It is important that they do not try to destabilize Eastern Europe. We should try to balance their approaches (based on a European consciousness) with the American approaches to Eastern Europe.

In short, we should try to accomplish a difficult task: not to repeat ourselves very much, but to produce something similar to the U.N. speech, only with a specifically European angle.

Mikhail Sergeyevich suggests that you set aside all routine business and concentrate on this issue, work through it thoroughly, and prepare it at a good scholarly level. He plans to talk with you about it after you have done some work on the above-mentioned tasks.

Yours, Chernyaev

[*Source: Archive of the Gorbachev Foundation. Fond 2. Opis 1. On file at the National Security Archive. Translated by Svetlana Savranskaya.*]

Document No. 45: Cable from Jack Matlock to State Department, "The Soviet Union over the Next Four Years"

February 13, 1989

Matlock's second cable in a series (see Document Nos. 43 & 47) echoes the hard-line position in Washington held most prominently by Scowcroft and Gates: "New Thinking in Soviet foreign policy probably started as a tactical shift to buttress a limited reform ... The intent most likely was to provide a temporary breathing space during which the Soviet Union could consolidate its strength and resume its expansionist policies with enhanced prospects for success." He goes on to give a traditional analysis of Soviet foreign policy that includes the comment: "Histori-cally, Russia and the Soviet Union have been most threatening to their neighbors and the rest of the world when the political leaders felt strong and confident." This view would be significantly contradicted by internal Kremlin documentation describ-ing the insecurity and paranoia underlying landmark decisions by Soviet leaders ranging from Stalin in Germany to Brezhnev in Afghanistan.

Closer to the mark, Matlock's second cable tells Washington exactly what Bogo-molov has just told Yakovlev—that military intervention in Eastern Europe "would of course mean the end of reform in the Soviet Union." But unlike Bogomolov, Matlock warns that the U.S. "should not dismiss the possibility" of outside inter-ference even though the "threshold of pain" that would trigger such an interven-tion is currently much higher than in the 1960s and 1970s. The U.S. ambassador, like almost everybody else, does not foresee any rapid transformations in the region and predicts erroneously that Soviet tolerance for changes in the GDR, Poland and Czechoslovakia would not be as high as in Bulgaria, Romania and Hungary. Even as the Polish Roundtable begins meeting, Matlock uses the conditional "if" on the possibility that Solidarity might be legalized; yet within six months Solidarity would sweep national elections and assume the leadership of a non-communist government in Poland. Matlock still does not see Gorbachev's intention to end the Cold War, and describes Soviet policy in terms that perhaps Moscow's hard-liners would have endorsed, though not Gorbachev and his inner circle: "If they are lucky, they will induce the West to disarm as fast or faster than they do ... If they are doubly lucky, they will cajole the West into picking up the tab ... But even if the West is sufficiently prudent to deny them these advantages, their tactics create problems for our alli-ances and drive wedges."

---

1. Secret—Entire Text.

BEGIN SUMMARY:

2. While Soviet foreign policy may show a considerable degree of unpredict-ability in its details, its broader thrusts must, willy nilly, conform to domestic

demands and domestic capabilities. These require a reduction of international tension, so that a greater measure of resources and leadership attention can be devoted to solving domestic problems. This situation suggests that we are likely to see:

A—Continued effort to pare down (but not eliminate) military commitment abroad.

B—Increasing use of political and economic means of exerting influence—but no flagging in the determination to be a global power.

C—Ideological revisionism to provide a conceptual framework for a shift to a less confrontational stance vis-à-vis the capitalist world.

D—Growing willingness to engage in joint bilateral or international efforts to deal with specific global problems: e.g., chemical weapons proliferation, environmental protection, terrorism, traffic in illicit drugs.

E—A major drive to break into the world economic system, particularly the financial councils of the developed world.

F—A continued concentration on the Soviet–U.S. relationship, combined with attempts to improve relations with Western Europe, China, and Japan and to drive wedges whenever possible.

G—No letup in espionage and no end to "direct action" when attractive; possibly some decrease in outright disinformation.

3. In sum, Soviet policy will not only seem to the outside world less aggressive, it will in fact be less threatening militarily—at least in the short to medium term. Yet, even with projected cuts in the Soviet military establishment, the potential long-term Soviet capacity to use force for political ends will not disappear. Furthermore, despite Soviet economic weakness and political confusion at home, Soviet influence in some areas of international life may actually grow as the rest of the world responds to perceived non-threatening, "cooperative" behavior.

End Summary.

4. This message, the second in a series, contains my personal assessment of likely trends in Soviet foreign policy over the next four years. In my view, these years will be marked by political and diplomatic activism to cover a retrenchment in Soviet armed forces and in Soviet military involvement abroad.

5. The extent and pace, as well as the concrete manifestations of increased reliance on political instruments of influence will be determined by many factors, some unpredictable at this point: domestic developments in the Soviet Union, the policy of other countries—most importantly the United States—and the occurrence or absence of major events such as widespread public disorders in Eastern Europe or the Soviet Union. Nevertheless, we can predict with confidence that the tendency to shift from intimidation to persuasion in dealing with the outside world will continue. Soviet conditions at this time, and over the coming few years, permit no other course.

6. Some well-informed observers have expressed the fear that a "failed" *perestroika* could result in a Soviet Union even more threatening to our interests than the USSR of the 1970's. The "sick bear" could go on a rampage, lashing out in all directions in a desperate effort to distract attention from his illness through aggressive behavior.

7. I do not believe that such a scenario is plausible. The failure of *perestroika* might be a tragedy for the Soviet people, and for those of Eastern Europe, but it would not in itself threaten the West's vital interests. The most important reason for this is that a Soviet leadership, weakened by an abortive reform process, is most unlikely to have either the means or incentive to make serious trouble abroad. Even a change of leadership to one which discarded many of today's policies is unlikely to bring more threatening external activity.

8. Historically, Russia and the Soviet Union have been most threatening to their neighbors and the rest of the world when the political leaders felt strong and confident. When they felt weak and troubled at home, they turned inward. Therefore, while another ruling group might well be more truculent, more secretive, more given to propaganda and bluster, and less interested in negotiation and cooperation, its external policy is likely to resemble a sulk in the corner more than a rampage through the neighborhood.

"NEW THINKING": HOW NEW?

9. For decades the Soviets have resorted so consistently to misleading propaganda that one is entitled to approach slogans like "new thinking" with great circumspection, if not outright cynicism. There is no reason at all for us to take the Soviets at their word until their actions provide concrete proof; in fact, there is every reason for us to refuse to accept words at face value in the absence of corroborative evidence.

10. Nevertheless, we would be negligent if we failed to recognize that much of the "new thinking" is in fact genuinely new in a Soviet context. To the extent that this "new thinking" becomes established as the accepted norm, and implemented in concrete policies and actions (a process which is far from complete), it could signal a lasting and fundamental change in the Soviet approach to the rest of the world. If it is truly accepted that mankind has interests which transcend and supersede Marxist class interests, and that security and prosperity can be achieved only by cooperation with other countries in a[n] interdependent world, then this would represent a fundamental break with the traditional Soviet view of international relations as a zero/sum struggle of irreconcilable classes, one of which is destined to defeat and supplant the other.

11. "New Thinking" in Soviet foreign policy probably started as a tactical shift to buttress a limited reform of the Soviet economic management system. The intent most likely was to provide a temporary breathing space during which the Soviet Union could consolidate its strength and resume its expansionist policies with enhanced prospects for success. But, even if this was the original intent, some unexpected things happen on the road to the quick fix: the quick fix itself dissolved like a mirage on the horizon, and the efforts to produce some limited controlled changes began to have ramifications far beyond their planned effect. *Perestroika* has already produced effects in the body politic which will impede efforts to revert past policies.

12. One of the most important of these effects is a fundamental attitudinal change in regard to the rest of the world. For decades after World War II the world's most pervasive propaganda machine drummed into the Soviet population the theme of the external threat, particularly from the U.S. Though it was never accepted a hundred percent by the Soviet Public, this hostile propaganda had an undeniable effect on attitudes. It, combined with the absence of information regarding the magnitude of the Soviet military effort, permitted the diversion of enormous resources to the military without any effective complaints from the citizenry. After all, even those who were hostile to the Soviet rulers and much of their policy were usually willing to sacrifice to defend their motherland.

13. Now, after little more than three years of U.S.–Soviet summitry, these old propaganda themes have been shattered—and very likely shattered beyond repair. It turns out that the rest of the world is not hostile: Would the U.S. agree to eliminate INF missiles if it were? Would the world have rushed to aid earthquake victims if it were? Would Ronald Reagan be seen kissing babies in Red Square if it were?

14. But that is not all. It also turns out that it was not Western hostility which created difficulties for the Soviet citizenry, but the Soviet system itself. It was not the West that caused the Chernobyl disaster or flimsy construction in seismic zones, but their own system which ignored safety considerations. It was not western economic boycotts which deprived the[m] of consumer goods, but rather their own leaders' propensity to give all the goodies to the military. The decision to reduce Soviet military forces unilaterally suggests unmistakably to the average Soviet citizen that the Soviet military was built up beyond any objective need, just as the withdrawal from Afghanistan makes clear that the rest of the world had good reason to fear the Soviet Union.

15. These "revelations" are still reverberating through the Soviet public consciousness, and they will make it very difficult for a future Soviet leadership to obtain automatic public acquiescence to a renewed military buildup or to aggressive military actions abroad. Once facts and attitudes are out in the public domain, they cannot easily be rounded up and forced back into the old stockade—particularly if the stockade fence itself has tumbled down in many places.

16. Ultimately, however, what will give the "new thinking" its staying power is its fundamental accuracy: we do in fact live in an interdependent world; there are in fact common interests of mankind, and though there is no constitutional barrier to any Soviet political leadership reverting to fallacious Marxist slogans as a basis of policy, those slogans will never reflect objective reality. They are simply wrong, and no policy based on them is likely to work—particularly the second time around, when they are more likely to produce a farce than a tragedy.

CONVERGING AND CONFLICTING INTERESTS

17. The Soviet leaders are now beginning to see areas where their and Western interests converge rather than conflict, and these go beyond such obvious and traditional ones as avoidance of nuclear war, nuclear non-proliferation, and environmental protection. There is clearly growing interest (though not always identical approaches) in areas such as chemical weapons control, non-proliferation of ballistic missile technology, and combating terrorism and illicit drug trafficking. Also, as the Soviets move to reduce their own conventional military forces, their interest in finding political solutions to regional conflicts is growing.

18. Though they talk about it much less in public, the Soviet leaders are doubtless aware that Soviet and Western aims remain incompatible in many key areas. In particular, the announced cuts in Soviet military forces will not eliminate the potential threat to the West from that quarter. There is a manifest Soviet interest in stimulating the disarmament of the West more rapidly than their own, the erosion of our alliances and system of overseas bases, and the hobbling of the U.S. Navy. They continue to back clients who are hostile to Western interests, and to provide military support to them. Their extensive efforts to conduct espionage continues unabated, and there is no reason to suppose that they will be less willing in the future to pursue covert action to further their goals. Even in some areas where the Soviets have acknowledged a need to cooperate with the West, the old competitive habits still dominate their practice. The Soviets, thus, still have far to go before their deeds will fully match the words of their "new thinking."

THE EAST EUROPEAN "WILD CARD"

19. A future Soviet decision to intervene militarily to put down disorders in Eastern Europe would of course mean the end of reform in the Soviet Union for a long period thereafter. One certainly should not dismiss the possibility of such a retrograde event, given the history of the area and the pressures for change which are mounting there.

20. Nevertheless, my guess is that the Soviet leaders will manage to avoid such a traumatic event—at least over the next four to five years. The fact is that the "threshold of pain" which would trigger Soviet intervention is much higher today than it was in the sixties and seventies. This gives governments in the area considerable leeway to liberalize, if they are so inclined. It is clear, for example,

that the Soviets will not try to block a legalization of Solidarity in Poland, if that should emerge from the current Roundtable. If a Dubček II were to create a Prague Spring this year or next, Moscow would almost certainly tolerate it and might even cheer it on.

21. This means that if major disorders occur in Eastern Europe, they most likely will result from the rigidity of the East European regimes, and not from a Soviet effort to block all internal change. Even if confronted with widespread disorders, the Soviet leaders might well refrain from military intervention so long as Soviet installations were not attacked and there was no serious effort to leave the Warsaw Pact. (The degree of Soviet tolerance, of course, varies with the country in question: it is doubtless greater in respect to Bulgaria, Romania, and Hungary than it would be with the GDR, Poland, and perhaps Czechoslovakia.)

THE POWER OF POSITIVE THINKING

22. If, as is likely, the Soviet Union will avoid a repeat of 1948, 1956, and 1968, its diplomacy is likely to feature the smile, and its speech the language of compromise and conciliation. The smiling face did not come naturally to this regime, but the Soviet leaders have learned to enjoy wearing it. Being popular in the world is such a novel experience for a Russian that it tends to go to the head. Furthermore, the current leaders are beginning to learn something their cyni[c]al predecessors would have jeered: as Willy Loman said, You can go a long way on a smile and a shoeshine.

23. Of course, the Soviet leaders are not into smiling just for the kicks. They expect the smile to translate into political benefits. Their constant talk of their defensive doctrine, their announcements of unilateral military cuts, the periodic proclamation of various "peace" initiatives, are elements of an overall strategy designed to maintain Moscow's great power status and influence during a period of military and economic retrenchment. If they are lucky, they will induce the West to disarm as fast as or faster than they do, and thus remain at a military disadvantage. If they are doubly lucky, they will cajole the West into picking up the tab for some of their economic reconstruction. But even if the West is sufficiently prudent to deny them these advantages, their tactics create problems for our alliances and drive wedges. And even when the West holds firm and the Soviets are forced to meet Western terms, their tactics ensure that much of the Western public will credit them for initiatives they did not in fact make.

24. Does this make all the defensive talk and "new thinking" a fake? I think not. In my view, the Soviet leaders are making a virtue of necessity. They are covering their retrenchment with a hyperactive diplomacy in an attempt to preserve their great power position (or at least as much of it as possible) on a diminished base of military power.

25. Vorontsov's frenzied diplomacy in the last months of Soviet military withdrawal from Afghanistan exemplifies this overall technique. The fact that he did not obtain his ostensible goals (a general ceasefire and an acknowledged future

political role for the PDPA) does not mean that his efforts will be [j]udged unsuccessful in Soviet eyes. The ostensible goals were maximum ones and nobody would have been more surprised than the Soviet leaders if they had been reached. Real Soviet goals were probably more modest: to prevent the humiliation of Soviet forces during their withdrawal (the fall of major cities as they left); to stimulate disputes among the Afghan opposition forces; to drive wedges between the Mujaheddin forces and other countries, especially Pakistan and the U.S.; and— not least—to demonstrate solidarity with their friends in Kabul, so that the latter would have to assume full responsibility for their own future collapse.

26. Such, in my estimation, will be the Soviet approach to many other issues, mutatis mutandis (and of course the specifics vary widely). The bottom line for the Soviet leadership will be whether they can cloak—and thus make politically acceptable at home—a diminished use of military force in their foreign policy. If they manage to pick up a few extra dividends along the way in the form of gratuitous western concessions, they will of course accept them with pleasure (though without gratitude). The challenge for the West is to deny unbalanced concessions and thereby maintain the pressure for a further evolution of Soviet policy along the path the Soviet leaders have ostensibly taken. Matlock

[Source: U.S. Department of State, obtained through FOIA. On file at the National Security Archive.]

Document No. 46: Report on Vadim Medvedev's Visit to Romania

February 16, 1989

In this document, Politburo member and head of the ideology department Vadim Medvedev reports to the Politburo on his just-completed visit to Romania, where, as he describes it, Ceauşescu has changed his stance 180 degrees. From insisting on independence for each of the allies, to becoming the enforcer of the communist faith, he is now proposing ideological excommunication for apostates such as Hungary. But, Medvedev says, "it is not in our best interest to react to these maneuvers;" Moscow should simply alert the other bloc allies as to what to expect at upcoming meetings. Here we see the Soviets' non-interference policy at work. Kremlin leaders are hoping that more progressive leaders in the bloc will commit to perestroika, be dismissive of the old Brezhnevites (even Stalinists), but still try to stay out of direct personnel discussions, not to mention the string-pulling that would be necessary actually to change the leaderships. Noteworthy is Gorbachev's colorful comment about the Romanians: "they are afraid to catch the 'AIDS' of perestroika from us."

[...]

Gorbachev: To all appearances, over there they are afraid to catch the "AIDS" of *perestroika* from us. [...]

Medvedev: During the visit we signed a plan for ideological collaboration between the CPSU and the CPR [Communist Party of Romania] for the years 1989–90. It consolidates and deepens the opportunities for strengthening our influence on Romania in the sphere of ideological collaboration, opportunities that we developed at the top level meetings. A bilateral committee on social sciences could play an important role in this matter. At the same time, we should not entertain any illusions in this respect. The Romanian leadership's attitude toward new, more promising forms of interaction remains evasive and essentially negative. The Romanians have once again avoided answering our proposal to open bilateral cultural-informational centers, or at least libraries, similar to the ones the U.S., FRG, Italy and France have in Bucharest.

As the meetings in Romania have shown, particularly the meetings with professors from the Party Academy, there is great interest in our country's *perestroika* processes. Regrettably, a two-hour-long talk with Ceauşescu confirmed the Romanian leadership's cautious and critical attitude toward *perestroika* and the reforms [taking place] in the Soviet Union and other socialist countries. Ceauşescu stated that he is concerned about the return of forms of capitalist property to some of the socialist countries. He insists on conducting a special meeting of fraternal party leaders; he refuses to conduct an exchange of opinions when the fraternal parties' leaders will be in Bucharest at the PCC session.

Ceauşescu has undergone yet another metamorphosis. It is as if he has changed his position diametrically. He used to give absolute value to independence; he spoke about the sovereignty of every party in developing policies. Now he talks about general principles, claiming the role of a judge trying to pronounce peremptory judgments about what in other countries' policies does or does not correspond to the principles of socialism. Ceauşescu does not specify whom exactly he has in mind when he speaks of apostasy, however it is absolutely clear that he is talking primarily about Hungary. He also throws comments at our camp. At the same time, the Romanian leadership would not be against pulling us into the anti-Hungarian campaign as its ally.

In our propaganda to Romania, in the contacts with Romanian representatives we should pay special attention to clarifying those elements of the concept of *perestroika* that are misunderstood and distorted in Bucharest. These are: the leasing, the contracts, *glasnost* policy, the condemnation of mistakes and the warping of the past, and elements of our electoral system.

It can be expected that the Romanian leadership's views will be reflected in the behavior of the Romanian representatives at the approaching fraternal CC party meetings on ideological and economic problems, and at other multilateral forums. Most likely, Ceauşescu will raise [these views] at the general secretaries' working meeting. It is possible that he has made them known to leaders of a number of parties. It seems that it is not in our best interest to react to these maneuvers by the Romanians. We should give the leaders of other parties some orientation regarding Ceauşescu's intentions.

[*Source: Archive of the Gorbachev Foundation. Fond 2. Opis 2. On file at the National Security Archive. Translated by Anna Melyakova.*]

Document No. 47: Cable from Jack Matlock to State Department, "U.S.–Soviet Relations: Policy Opportunities"

February 22, 1989

U.S. Ambassador Matlock's third cable (see Document Nos. 43 & 45) drives home the point that U.S. influence has never been greater, and "[t]hat leverage should be used not to 'help' Gorbachev or the Soviet Union, but to promote U.S. interests. The most central of such interests is the long-term transformation of the Soviet Union into a society with effective organic constraints on the use of military force outside its borders." Even the expert Matlock does not recognize that Gorbachev has already decided against the application of force. The ambassador is more worried about the stresses on NATO stemming from Gorbachev's popularity, and asserts that the main challenge will be alliance management because "the smiling face will have a more divisive effect than the belligerent growl." Even Matlock's specific recommendations are underwhelming (including encouragement for joint ventures and producing more printed materials in Russian), and there is no real attention to what was about to become revolutionary change in Eastern Europe.

---

1. Secret – Entire text.

BEGIN SUMMARY:

2. We have an historic opportunity to test the degree the Soviet Union is willing to move into a new relationship with the rest of the world, and to strengthen those tendencies in the Soviet Union to "civilianize" the economy and "pluralize" the society. U.S. leverage, while certainly not unlimited, has never been greater. That leverage should be used not to "help" Gorbachev or the Soviet Union, but to promote U.S. interests. The most central of such interests is the long-term transformation of the Soviet Union into a society with effective organic constraints on the use of military force outside its borders.

3. Our traditional four-part agenda remains relevant, but we should review current policy to determine what specific adjustments may be required by rapidly changing circumstances. We should continue negotiations for verifiable arms reductions but refuse to make these the centerpiece of the relationship. We should increase political pressure on Moscow to end, once and for all, its military involvement in Central America and to scale back substantially its military presence in Cuba.

4. If momentum can be sustained in all of the areas of our traditional agenda, we should gradually put more substance in two additional areas, perhaps eventually giving them the status of points five and six: multilateral cooperation and

economic relations. Neither should involve aid, but be based strictly on mutual profitability and reciprocal obligations.

5. As Soviet policy changes and Soviet diplomacy becomes more active, effective management of our alliance relationships will become more complex and difficult. The challenge in this area may in *fact*[38] be greater than the challenge of managing U.S.–Soviet relations, but a forward-looking policy toward the Soviet Union with well defined goals, should be helpful *regarding*[39] alliance management.

6. The current disarray on the Soviet domestic scene has given the United States an unprecedented potential for influence on Soviet foreign and domestic policy. Our leverage is by no means unlimited—we cannot force them to hand over the store—but it is sufficient to tilt the balance of decision on many key issues, provided we are wise enoqh [sic] to use our latent influence skillfully, consistently, and persistently. This message will suggest a general framework for a policy to maximize our influence over developments in the Soviet Union. More detailed descriptions of some of the policy proposals mentioned illustratively in this presentation will follow in subsequent messages.

THE WRONG QUESTION

7. Unfortunately, many observers, giddy from the surprise of seeing rapid change in a society which was closed and seemingly static for so long, are asking the wrong question—and drawing the wrong conclusions. "*Perestroika*," they say, is in the U.S. interest; Gorbachev is essential to "*perestroika;*" ergo the U.S. should devise a strategy to "help" *Gorbachev:*

8. Even though the first of these propositions is true (if only because *perestroika* tends to demobilize the Soviet Union while it is underway), the others are not. Indeed, they contain several highly questionable assumptions: that we know enough about the ins and outs of Soviet politics to "help" individuals effectively; that we should ever identify U.S. national interests with those of individual Soviet political leaders; that concessionary policies would in fact be of assistance in stimulating radical reform. Even more fundamentally, these observers are posing the wrong question. The question should not be how we can help "*perestroika*" or Gorbachev, but rather how we can promote the interests of the United States. If the pursuit of our goals has the collateral effect of strengthening the position of political leaders who have espoused policies consistent with our own, well and good. But we should be clear in our own minds that our objective is to serve our interests, not theirs.

---

[38] This word is a handwritten correction on the cable.
[39] Handwritten correction on the cable.

400

9. We of course have many specific interests which we must pursue, but no long-term goals are more important than the transformation of the Soviet political system into one with effective structural constraints on the use of military force outside Soviet borders, along with the evolution of the Soviet military machine into one suitable primarily for defensive purposes. For long, many have doubted that the Soviet Union would or could move in this direction except as the result of a total collapse of the system. The doubters may eventually prove to be right. Nevertheless, for the first time in at least sixty years, these goals are consistent with avowed Soviet aspirations. We would be remiss if we did not reinforce incentives for Soviet movement in this direction.

10. Reinforcing incentives, however, does not mean "aid" in the traditional sense. The deployment of Pershing II's and cruise missiles in Europe beginning in 1983 provided powerful incentives to conclude an INF agreement on western terms. In contrast, all the financial aid given Poland in the 1970's actually reduced incentives to carry out reforms necessary for the viability of the economy. These examples argue for a policy which sets high but fair standards for agreements and cooperation and requires full reciprocity of obligation and benefit.

OUR AGENDA:

11. The four-part agenda which we have successfully pursued over the past six years addresses both the external manifestations of the Soviet threat (Soviet military involvement in regional conflicts; arms reduction) and also its internal causes (human rights; puncturing the Iron Curtain). It has been successful in the sense that it has finally produced significant Soviet positive movement in all these areas. It has not yet exhausted its full potential, however, since much remains to be done in all four areas.

ARMS REDUCTION AND REGIONAL CONFLICTS:

While the Soviets have now formally accepted our four-part agenda as the framework for discussion and negotiation, it is obvious that they still give arms control, and particularly the conclusion of an agreement on START, coupled with some "reinforcement" of the ABM treaty, pride of place. There is no reason for us to copy them in this respect, though of course we should continue to negotiate in good faith on START and DST when our review of the issues has been completed.

13. The point is not that a good START agreement would be more in the Soviet interest that ours—if it is a good agreement, it will serve U.S. objectives equally as well as Soviet ones. The point rather is that it is important for us to avoid an unbalanced concentration of attention on arms control issues to the detriment of those parts of our agenda which have a more direct impact on the evolution of

Soviet society in a pluralistic direction and on the conversion of Soviet industry to a greater concentration on civilian production.

14. Furthermore, while it may be difficult in practice to establish formal diplomatic linkages between the arms reduction issues and problems in other areas of the relationship, we should be alert to the possibility of adjusting the pace of arms control negotiations to match progress on other issues important to our national security.

15. One example which comes to mind is the Soviet supply of military equipment to Nicaragua. We should press them hard for an immediate end to this practice (including provision of what Gorbachev has called "police-type" weapons), and it will not hurt to leave the impression that our review of START issues may be more rapid if there is a resolution of this important problem. Our push for an absolute cessation of Soviet military supplies to the Central American isthmus should be particularly forceful if we decide not to press Congress for a near-term resumption of arms supplies to the Nicaraguan opposition. If that is to be our policy in any case, then we should certainly invite the Soviets to use it as a "justification" for their abstention.

16. Concomitantly, we should develop a strategy for diminishing gradually the Soviet military presence on Cuba. A gradual approach which provides the Soviets with some pretexts for retrenchment is likely to be more effective over the long run than public threats which encourage Moscow to prove that it is not abandoning friends or bowing to U.S. pressure.

HUMAN RIGHTS:

17. Human rights must of course remain a key element in U.S. policy. Although much remains to be done, prospects for further progress are better than they have been in living memory. In pursuing our policy in this area, we have at our disposal both negative and positive incentives, and in addition a very extensive mechanism for consultation which did not exist even two years ago. The CSCE process provides both leverage on and opportunity for the Soviets; they must defend their practice at the upcoming Paris and Copenhagen meetings, plus continue their progress at home if they are to have U.S. and British participation at the 1991 meeting in Moscow.

18. We should use our bilateral consultation machinery to continue to push vigorously on the remaining issues. In regard to emigration practices, the Jackson–Vanik amendment gives us a tool which can be used more actively—as I will discuss subsequently. In dealing with the Soviets on human rights issues we have one new asset: the Soviet avowed policy to improve protection of the rights of its citizens. This allows us to approach many of the human rights issues under the rubric of "cooperation" rather than confrontation.

19. Progress in eroding the Iron Curtain has been rapid of late, what with the cessation of jamming, growing U.S. access to Soviet media, the rapid growth of private travel and the beginnings of youth exchanges on a substantial scale. We should be prepared to move rapidly to take advantage of these new opportunities as fully as possible. While nobody should expect wider personal contacts and a better flow of information to translate immediately into a non-aggressive policy or democracy inside the Soviet Union, there is no question that that handful of the Soviet elite which has had recent and extensive exposure to the West are among the driving forces for pluralism and individual rights. We should not underestimate the force of our example on Soviet minds and it will serve our interest to increase opportunities for the Soviet political elite to see life in the United States.

20. With this in mind, we should lose no time in devising innovative programs to influence Soviet thinking in the right direction. They might include some of the following:

– A systematic plan to invite to the United States, under one rubric or another, the remaining Politburo and Secretariat members who have not been there, plus many party and government leaders in major republics and *oblasts*.

– Expansion of printed materials in Russian, including an extensive book program, in the fields of philosophy, political science, economics, and international relations.

– Expanded programs to provide U.S. speakers, T.V. panelists and T.V. documentaries for broadcast in the Soviet Union.

– Rapid movement to establish a major U.S. cultural center in Moscow, now that the Soviets have agreed to one in principle, following decades of refusal.

– Expansion of the U.S. presence into major non-Russian republics, where the population has been exposed only sporadically to U.S. influence. To minimize budgetary costs, technical delays and counter-intelligence problems in the U.S., we should study the possibility of small unclassified posts (6–8 employees with personal diplomatic immunity, but without immunity of premises).

EXPANDING THE AGENDA: INTERNATIONAL COOPERATION:

21. The most obvious candidate for an expanded agenda is in joint participation in multinational cooperation to solve common problems. Previously, when the Soviet leadership was still in the grip of a "zero-sum" psychology, opportunities for U.S.–Soviet cooperation in most international efforts were severely limited. The Soviets had a propensity to politicize even the most purely humanitarian issues and to misuse the international organizations established to deal with them. They considered this a perfectly acceptable form of political warfare against the West in general and the United States in particular. The results were quite apparent in organizations such as the ILO and UNESCO.

22. Now that the Soviets are trumpeting their conversion to a more cooperative doctrine, we should put them to the test by challenging them to play a more constructive role in international cooperative efforts. However, we should refuse to bend the ground rules of existing organizations to accommodate the Soviets, and we should insist that the Soviet Union pull its full weight. In addition, we should make clear to the Soviet leadership that using international organizations as a cover for intelligence operations is unacceptable, and—if this practice is continued—will militate against the acceptance of the Soviet Union as a formal partner in future international cooperative arrangements.

23. Areas of international cooperation which might be more actively explored with the Soviets (with the caveats set forth above) include the following:
  – environmental protection on a global scale;
  – combating terrorism;
  – chemical weapons non-proliferation—and ultimately a verifiable global ban;
  – non-proliferation of ballistic missiles;
  – planning and eventually building a prototype power plant based on nuclear fusion;
  – famine and other disaster relief;
  – nuclear power plant safety and nuclear non-proliferation.

24. We should, however, proceed very slowly in one area in which the Soviets will show great interest, that of international trade and finance institutions (e.g., GATT, IMF, World Bank). Our policy in respect to these organizations should be considered in the framework of our overall economic policy toward the USSR. The economic area has sufficient potential for influencing Soviet behavior to make it a strong candidate for a sixth point on our overall agenda.

EXPANDING THE AGENDA: ECONOMICS

25. Up to now economic relations with the Soviet Union have formed a barely-mentioned subunit of the bilateral agenda category. We have hardly used it as a tool in the relationship, despite its intrinsic importance, for a number of reasons, most quite sound. With the exception of trade in agricultural products, which we promoted quite vigorously and even subsidized, we have been ambivalent about exports of industrial products, particularly of those capital goods which interested the Soviets most. This attitude was shaped by legitimate concern over the danger of new technology seeping into the Soviet military industrial complex. The tension between the desire to prohibit damaging technology transfer and the desire to promote U.S. export markets often led in practice to a total bureaucratic impasse: aside from prohibiting certain types of exports and delaying permissible exports for months or years, the federal government remained largely passive, occasional rhetoric to the contrary notwithstanding.

26. The time has now come for us to develop and implement a more vigorous and forward-looking policy in regard to East–West economic relations, and to use the economic lever to promote the sort of changes in the Soviet Union which are congenial to our interests. Our policy should stop short of aid or subsidy and should provide for strict enforcement of agreed COCOM controls, but within those bounds it should offer significant incentives for the Soviet leaders to develop a decentralized, pluralistic, civilian-oriented economy.

27. The key element in our economic policy would be an effort to define for Soviet policy makers those conditions which would induce the U.S. government to facilitate unsubsidized trade and investment in areas not prohibited by CO-COM. This could have some effect in encouraging developments within the Soviet economy which we favor. Simultaneously, we should provide more effective support for American firms doing legitimate business with the USSR. Specific examples of such possibilities are:

A. – Joint Ventures: We should offer to provide encouragement to U.S. firms to consider investment in large-scale joint ventures, provided the Soviet authorities create conditions which increase the possibility that these will be profit-making enterprises. The conditions should be defined on the basis of a careful study, but might include such elements as management rights for the non-Soviet partner, currency convertibility, or at least protection against arbitrary exchange rate shifts. Reasonable tax and tariff treatment, reduction of bureaucratic controls to the minimum necessary form, reasonable health, safety and other generally recognized standards, and the right of Soviet employees to travel abroad for training and other business purposes. Criteria such as these tend to converge with those defining a more open, decentralized and civilianized economy such as we would like to see in the Soviet Union.

– Development of such criteria would not only provide some incentive to the Soviets to move in the direction indicated, they could also provide a valuable service to American businessmen who are now exploring the possibility of joint ventures without clearly understood criteria to judge the viability of proposals being made.

B. – Jackson–Vanik: Although the Soviet authorities have improved their emigration practices substantially over the past year, they still fall short of qualifying for a waiver of Jackson–Vanik sanctions. They are, however, within hailing distance of qualification, and we should use this fact to hasten the resolution of the remaining refusal cases and the institutionalization of more liberal procedures overall.

– Therefore, we recommend that the administration consult with the Congress and interested private organizations with a view toward defining whathre [sic] must be done to qualify for a waiver and thus eligibility for MFN. When we have determined what conditions will be acceptable politically to justify a waiver, we should describe these conditions to the Soviets privately. (Needless to say, if they then meet the conditions, a waiver on Jackson–Vanik should be granted, and

MFN granted—one year at a time. Government-financed credits and guarantees should however not be resumed.)

C. – Training: We should encourage cooperative projects to train Soviet economists, managers, entrepreneurs (for the "coop" sector), and specialists in areas such as marketing which are little known here yet crucial for a decentralized economy with a significant private sector.

D. – International economic and financial organizations: We have quite properly opposed Soviet association with organizations such as GATT. The Soviets, however, are certain to continue their campaign to enter the international economic and financial community. It would probably be useful for us to replace our current flat "No" with an "If": if they meet certain rigorous but fair standards, we would be willing to support their membership. For example, the criteria for GATT might involve a real decentralization of decision-making in the Soviet economy, including creation of a substantial private/cooperative sector. It should be made clear that, in addition to meeting certain criteria of suitability, the Soviet Union would be required to assume the same obligations as other members with developed economies.

– Establishing such criteria would serve a two-fold purpose: it would indicate to the Soviets what we must do to qualify for membership, and it would also provide a credible rationale to resist any future attempts by other member countries to bend the rules to accommodate the USSR.

E. – Support for U.S. business: We should continue to review our export regulations and licensing procedures to ensure that they are effective in implementing COCOM controls, but that they do not exceed COCOM restrictions (which only shifts trade to other countries). Furthermore, we should ensure that restrictions on exports are clear, easily understood, and applied consistently in the licensing process. A mechanism should be established to ensure that interagency disputes are settled promptly and not allowed to drag on for months without resolution.

PROBLEMS: ALLIANCE MANAGEMENT:

28. As the Soviet Union retrenches in response to the requirements of *perestroika*—or in consequence of *perestroika*'s failure—U.S.–Soviet relations will become more "manageable" than they were in the 1970's and early 1980's. We may well find, however, that our alliances will become more difficult to manage. In the past, alliance problems have often been solved when the Soviets committed some outrageous act that rallied the allies to our side. We can no longer count on such Soviet "assistance" in the future: the smiling face will have a more divisive effect than the belligerent growl.

29. General advice on alliance management is of course beyond the scope of this message. However, inasmuch as U.S. policy toward the USSR has a major and often decisive effect on our relations with our allies, we believe that the sort of policy stance suggested in this message would assist in maintaining alliance cohesion in the face of Soviet blandishments. A largely static policy buttressed

mainly by periodic warnings of the potential threat the Soviets still present is likely over time to exacerbate strains in the alliance system, no matter how valid the warnings are in fact. We are much more likely to hold the allies to a reasonable course if we take the lead in defining the future—and in pressing the Soviet Union to live up to its currently avowed aspirations. Matlock

[Source: U.S. Department of State, obtained through FOIA. On file at the National Security Archive.]

Document No. 48: Record of Conversation between Mikhail Gorbachev and Achille Occhetto

February 28, 1989

Gorbachev's interlocutor at this meeting is the Italian communist leader Achille Occhetto, who in 1994 would declare the communist experiment over and dissolve the Italian party into a social democratic institution. The notes of this conversation, which focus in part on the significance of the Prague Spring of 1968, were probably prepared by Valentin Falin of the International Department. The Italian communists had been early critics of the Soviet invasion of Czechoslovakia, and Occhetto goes out of his way to praise the Czechoslovak leader at that time, Alexander Dubček. But Gorbachev responds with remarkable ambiguity, still unready to admit that the intervention was a mistake. He says that by July–August of 1968 the Czechoslovak reforms had amounted to "not just extremism" "but also anti-socialism and anti-Sovietism." His reluctance to reinterpret those events, which Moscow insists were Czechoslovakia's own internal affair, stems from a concern that if he did so the entire CPCz leadership would have to go. "In the present situation, we are trying to be especially delicate."

Occhetto: I would like to touch upon the Labor Movement question. We view the processes taking place in Eastern Europe positively: the introduction of a multi-party system in Hungary, the beginning of talks with "Solidarity" in Poland. But at the same time we are worried by the state of affairs in the socialist countries where the developing situation contradicts the commitments that were assumed with the Helsinki agreements.

I would like to tell you about a moving meeting I had with Dubček. I must say, I formed an impression of Dubček as not only a convinced communist, but also a sincere supporter of socialism. He follows the process of *perestroika* with great enthusiasm and faith, and in many respects evaluates the situation in Czechoslovakia reasonably. He says that we cannot speak of *perestroika* in Czechoslovakia without determining the historical place of the "Prague Spring" of 1968. And the point is not even the historical evaluation, but the fact that it could revive and restore the desire to fight for socialism on the part of thousands and thousands of people who took part in the "Prague Spring." If the connection between that historical moment and today is not strengthened, the right will take the lead. Dubček said that some dissidents in Czechoslovakia want to fight outside the framework of the party. He thinks that they should remain in the party.

During his stay in Italy, Dubček disappointed the reactionary powers, which had been expecting him to make statements against socialism. His speech at the University of Bologna turned into the praise for humane socialism. Dubček publicly gave a positive evaluation of the *perestroika* policies of the Soviet Union. We understand that to restore Dubček's good name and to return him to his former position are different matters. But it is necessary to give the "Prague Spring" its due.

The Hungarian comrades said that elements of a people's uprising played a part in the events of 1956, although later reactionary powers took root there. Perhaps this is even more true for Czechoslovakia as well, especially since the processes there developed differently. A reform process in Czechoslovakia would have enormous significance for us all.

Gorbachev: The entire socialist world, all the socialist countries, one way or another, are in the process of change. Not *perestroika*, but change. This is as characteristic for Cuba as for Mongolia and Vietnam. I want to emphasize that all the countries are being overtaken by a process of rethinking of history and changes under the influence of what is going on here, as well as under the influence of their own internal imperatives. To a significant extent this is tied to the economy. But it is no less tied to the realization of what socialism is today. With all the differences in these processes, they are characterized by the development of democracy. Perhaps Romania does not fit in here, even though Comrade Ceaușescu always brings up claims that his country is developing democratically. One's attention is of course drawn by the specific regime in place there. The main direction of developments in the socialist world is toward democratization. And this is very interesting. The spheres of economics, politics, and culture are affected by this. Our friends in Eastern Europe are returning to history. In a word, normal development is taking place.

You spoke about Dubček and about Czechoslovakia. It is probable that the lessons of 1968 left an imprint on the situation in this country. That is why our colleagues are being careful, so as not to spur destructive tendencies. But they intend to keep moving forward. The resolution of many issues there is tied to personnel changes. We are taking this position: it is their internal affair. This approach fits well with the type of relations that we have now assumed and maintain. We believe that the events of 1968 should be analyzed in their development. There was a promising beginning in December 1967 and January 1968, and we welcomed that.

Falin: Novotný asked for help then. We said no.

Gorbachev: Yes, there was a request for help. But we thought that everything had matured on its own there. The latter stage of that process, in July–August, was a different matter. That was not just extremism—it would probably be impossible to do without that—but also anti-socialism and anti-Sovietism. That came from over the border. All of it escalated the situation significantly. This is our perception of those events. But there will be changes in Czechoslovakia. We are sure of this. The problem is already coming up of how to deal with communists expelled from the party. We are trying to assume a careful attitude toward these processes, especially since the Czechoslovak comrades are trying to understand them themselves. This must take its natural course.

As for Hungary, the economic and social tensions in this country led to the necessity of seeking a resolution. It is difficult there. Recently I spoke with Grósz over the phone about Pozsgay's speech. We will meet with Grósz on March 18 or 20. The new premier, Németh, will soon be coming. There everything depends on the economy. But all of this is an incentive to look for a new model for socialism.

Every country—China, Poland, Hungary—enriches us with its experience. Bulgaria has its own. I think that each party's task is to understand the necessity for change and to lead these processes, these changes—not vice versa. And those who lose time will see how these losses will tell on the nature of the changes taking place in the country.

In the present situation, we are trying to be especially delicate. Let them observe our experiences, and we will observe theirs.

There are some who would like to throw explosives into these processes. In these circumstances not only democratic decisions come through, but the completely opposite kind as well.

We must be open to these changes. Otherwise socialism will not be able to unfurl. There can be only losses. We are firm supporters of these processes; we value highly each party's search. And they are all different. In the past everything was simple: the "one size fits all" approach. Now that is impossible.

[*Source: Archive of the Gorbachev Foundation, Fond 1. Opis 1. On file at the National Security Archive. Translated by Anna Melyakova.*]

Document No. 49: Notes of CC CPSU Politburo Session

March 3, 1989

Yet another Politburo member returns from a trip to Eastern Europe and sounds the alarm. In these notes, Ryzhkov describes his talks with the prime minister of Czecho-slovakia, Ladislav Adamec, and reports that the country is in total crisis: "half of Czechoslovakia does not support the government, because all of them—and their children and grandchildren, too—are connected to 'the year 1968.'" If Gorbach-ev had changed his interpretation of those events during his 1987 trip—as many Czechoslovaks had hoped he would—or simply encouraged the CPCz to do so, the communists might have gotten out ahead of the issue.

Concerning talks with Adamec (Prime Minister of Czechoslovakia)

Ryzhkov: Five hundred thousand have been expelled from the CPCz. Already half of Czechoslovakia does not support the government, because all of them—and their children and grandchildren, too—are connected to "1968." [...]

The CMEA. We need to finally stop apportioning who gets what for every brick; we need to start just trading with one another.

Gorbachev: This Adamec is a reliable man. He told me: we will get nowhere with this kind of personnel!

[*Source: Archive of the Gorbachev Foundation. Fond 2. Opis 1. On file at the National Security Archive. Translated by Anna Melyakova.*]

Document No. 50: Record of Conversation between Mikhail Gorbachev and Miklós Németh

March 3, 1989

At this juncture, Miklós Németh represents the new, reform-minded crop of Hungarian communists. His visit with Gorbachev comes just as turmoil is spilling out into the streets of the Baltic capitals, in Tbilisi, Georgia, and even in Moscow. Just two days after this conversation, thousands of people would demonstrate to support the candidacy of Boris Yeltsin for the Congress of People's Deputies. Gorbachev and his top advisers are being increasingly engulfed by the political struggle at home, and are not paying close attention to Eastern Europe. This together with his long-standing non-interference policy may explain his casual attitude when Németh probes his reaction to the Hungarian decision to remove the "Iron Curtain" (the barbed wire fence) on their border. Németh clearly realizes that the issue touches on the stability of the entire bloc, especially the GDR. Yet, Gorbachev gives a non-response: "We have a strict regime on our borders, but we are also becoming more open."

Thus we are already seeing interesting differences in the Big Brother relationship. Whereas a few months earlier Károly Grósz had gingerly solicited Moscow's understanding on the question of recognizing Israel (see Document No. 32), here Németh merely informs the Soviets of what Hungary is doing—and Gorbachev's advice is simply "not to sell my trump cards too cheap." In the second excerpt below, Gorbachev supports Németh's attempt to occupy the Hungarian political center, which he is willing to concede "does not exclude the existence of some opinions on the right and on the left." Németh comments in this connection that the events of 1956 "turned into a counterrevolution and bloodshed," even though it started with "genuine dissatisfaction among the people."

Németh: One more question. We made a decision—to completely remove the electronic and technological defenses from the Western and Southern borders of Hungary. They have outlived their usefulness and now serve only to catch citizens from Romania and the GDR who are trying to escape illegally to the West through Hungary. Hungarians no longer violate the border, they have an opportunity to leave the country legally. Of course, we will have to talk to the comrades from the GDR.

Gorbachev: We have a strict regime on our borders, but we are also becoming more open.

Németh: About relations with Israel. At the end of April–beginning of May, if nothing bad happens in the Middle East, we plan to establish diplomatic relations with Israel. [...]

Gorbachev: You know that Eduard Shevardnadze just returned from the Middle East. He met with the Israeli foreign minister. The Israelis put a lot of pressure on us, but we are not in a hurry because establishing diplomatic relations is currently our strongest argument. Therefore we tell them: go to the Arabs, agree to an international conference, and we are ready for normalization. The Soviet Union will recognize the state of Israel and its security on an equal basis with the security of other states of the region; we are even ready to give our guarantees. We have a lot of contacts, as you do. However, now we, together with the West Europeans—for example the British and the French—want to pressure Israel to take a more constructive position. Something of that kind is going to happen, and I would not want to sell my trump cards too cheap, so to speak. Maybe it would be helpful for your foreign minister to meet with our foreign minister and discuss this issue. [...]

Gorbachev: It is important to be honest everywhere—in the Central Committee and in the Parliament, in conversations with people, and with oneself, with one's own conscience. Otherwise, a disintegration and collapse of personality is unavoidable.

Németh: We believe that now it is most important to create a majority in the Central Committee, which would unite around a single program.

Gorbachev: This, of course, does not exclude the existence of some opinions on the right and on the left.

Németh: Yes, it is important that the center stays strong. [...]

Németh: I think that in this sense there are some extreme moments among [Imre] Pozsgay's statements. At the beginning of the events of 1956, there was genuine dissatisfaction among the people. However, later, the events turned into a counterrevolution and bloodshed. You cannot discount that.

[*Source: Archive of the Gorbachev Foundation, Fond 2. Opis 1. On file at the National Security Archive. Translated by Svetlana Savranskaya.*]

Document No. 51: Notes of Mikhail Gorbachev's Meeting with Soviet Ambassadors to Socialist Countries

March 3, 1989

These notes reproduce a remarkable oration by Gorbachev to an audience that traditionally consisted of party functionaries picked for their ideological correctness rather than their diplomatic skills. But by now the Soviet leader and his foreign minister are in the midst of a process of installing more reform-oriented emissaries to the socialist community. Gorbachev's consistent message leaps from this text—and one can imagine how vividly this must have come across in person. He insists over and over on a policy of non-intervention and the rejection of force—"we are excluding the possibility of bloody methods"—and connects this policy to the new Soviet sense of the allies as burdens, rather than as unquestioned assets for the USSR. He further shows his resentment of the allies who "reproach us" for "giving up [our] leadership role." But if we "go back to this practice ... we will once again assume full responsibility for their actions." However, the allies are also taking advantage of the Soviet Union: even though the GDR enjoys much higher meat supplies per capita than Soviet citizens, the East Germans still "demand raw materials for special prices!" Chernyaev's notes convey the written equivalent of Gorbachev banging the podium: "They resell the specially priced resources they get from us to the West for hard currency. Such is their reciprocity! This is where I turn into a nationalist!" Small wonder the Soviet leader and his circle show so little reluctance to see Eastern Europe go.

Gorbachev: Nothing is going to be easy. Everything depends on the staff and the people. We need to change the approach to our work—all of it, entirely. This is the most important thing.

Even our first reaction, as we were rotating the flywheel of *perestroika* and feeling that it was not working as planned, was to reach for the stick and to punish someone because of ideological or economic issues. Either do what we tell you or leave, so to speak.

This concerns Politburo members as well. We ourselves are gaining experience and wisdom, and in society everything is still very tentative. Routine work is holding us up more than anything. We still have to finish thinking through and making a prognosis at least of what the contours of future society might be as conceptions become transformed into policy.

There is movement forward. But so far we have not acquired much through *perestroika*. *Perestroika* is moving deeper into society, and we must offer society forms of life that everyone is able to understand. The philosophy of our movement is another matter. But we must not be naïve. We must reach each person through reform. The individual is our main focus.

414

Sometimes we hear from different sides: *perestroika* will not give you anything, you will not succeed, the country will fall apart and you will return to Brezhnev, if not to Stalin.

Yes, there are many mistakes, but that is inevitable. We have no other choice but to add more to *perestroika* and to move forward. The people are growing stronger. The people believe. A CPSU candidate to the Congress of People's Deputies[40] traveled around the entire Urals region and then came to me. Everything is in motion, he told me, but it bumps up against old thinking and habits. Novelty is frightening. I told him: what kind of a revolution would it be if there was nothing new in it. We are not just applying new wallpaper, as [Kurt] Hager said.

We have started such a project! And we started it after serious analysis. The fate of the country is [tied up] in it; this is the country's chance for a future. If we go back now, the fate of socialism in general will be up in the air.

Even the Social Democrats want very much for *perestroika* to be successful. They say they have their model and we have our model. But the socialist idea is shared in common between them.

The ambassador of Cuba said to me: the reactionaries in the West have come to the conclusion that *perestroika* is not beneficial to them. Yes, a real struggle is going on. *Perestroika* has hit the military industrial complex hard, and it is clear that it is not profitable for weapons manufacturers. Baker traveled around Europe and he is in a panic: Europe is breaking away from their control. Their society is reacting powerfully to our work.

The *perestroika* concept is being tested by real life right now. It has affected everybody—the party, the peasants, the workers, the intelligentsia. We have a general program, but it has not been developed in some aspects. We do not have a tax policy, we still hope for leftovers from the administrative system. We do not know how to deal in this sense with the cooperatives, with customs, with insurance. And for now the government must control every detail. We do not have a mechanism that would function without being pushed.

The work being done is already enormous. But it will be some time before everything starts working. [...] [And] what to do with our monopolies? These are not capitalist corporate monopolies. These are absolute monopolies.

There are many people profiteering from our problems: both conservatives and leftists. They are coming together in attacking us. Yeltsin for example—he is insulted and ambitious. The Yeltsin phenomenon is characteristic of a pivotal moment, when society has come up against real difficulties.

We proposed a triad after the XIX Party Conference: housing, goods for the people, and services. But we need time to become accustomed to it. And life is

---

[40] The first free elections, allowing for several names on the ballot, were scheduled for March 26, 1989 (see discussion of results in Document No. 53). By agreement, 100 seats in the new parliament were reserved for representatives of "public organizations," which included the communist party. The Central Committee organized a very active electoral campaign for communists throughout the Soviet Union.

moving on and tensions are growing. And the people are listening to the demagogues. The leadership does not help by securing scarce goods for itself. This is
how the "defenders of the people" arise. They profit from hardship.

It is a pity that Yeltsin took this road. I tried to stop him. Among other things,
his ignorance prevented him from. [...]

How can we respond? There is one answer—intensify *perestroika*. Raise the
quality of all work. Work, work and persist! Difficult years are ahead of us. Some
people are proposing a solution: buy provisions from abroad, saturate the market.
[...] But Hungary's and Poland's experiences are before us. Should we ignore
that? Of course, if we were frightened we could do that. We will smooth some
things out temporarily. But it would be a mistake from a strategic point of view.

We are searching. Nevertheless a vacuum is left in places and somebody immediately fills it. [...]

Working in your countries you will have to explain the goals and tasks of *perestroika* every day. Our friends have a major interest in it. Our "best friends," the
Chinese (animation [in the room]), are studying our experience very seriously.

They have "open zones," appendices to the international market. That did not
work out [for us], and even the leadership was overtaken by corruption. The village grows. But now it has run up against the need to use technology. [...]

But we will not dissolve the collective farms, rather we will change them
from within by leasing them.

Lomakin: (ambassador to Czechoslovakia). The issue is not with the collective farms. Yegor Kuzmich [Ligachev] came to Prague to assure Jakeš that we
will keep the collective farms.

Aristov: (ambassador to Poland). Poland produces less than the GDR. We will
advocate leasing in industry. But there have been cases when factories were ru-
ined through leasing. [...] The individual at the point of production is the most
important factor in Poland. Here, it is the director!

Gorbachev: The reforms are influencing the personnel. When leasing, the
number of specialists needed is 3–4–5 times smaller. Why should they want to
lease? They get their 600–700–1500 rubles and are happy with it. Why should
they change?

We are losing 20 billion [rubles] from unprofitable industries. The Cubans did
not believe me when I told them.

We have not succeeded in turning society toward the new yet, but some work
has already been done. The most important question right now concerns the cadres of *perestroika*. [...]

How is all this reflected in the minds of our friends and foes? [...] Your position
should be as follows: we, the Soviet Union, need *perestroika*. We must find a new
quality of society with it. We can no longer tolerate the situation our people find
themselves in now. *Perestroika* is vitally important to us. It is also important for our
friends to understand that the fate of socialism in general is at stake here as well.

Our friends are worried about socialism's fate. But we will reveal the potential of socialism through democracy, through the individual.

416

And as far as they are concerned: let them take what suits them from our *perestroika*. Do not impose anything on anybody! Every country is very specific. Considering this specificity, we are not playing with them. We reject force in everything, in all our policies.

Take Cuba. [...] They are worried. They are afraid to lose what they have been getting from the other socialist countries. As a matter of fact, the GDR has long ago stopped giving anything to Cuba. The Czechs don't know what to do with meat, but to us they sell it at world market prices. There is 100 kilograms of meat per capita in the GDR. And they continue to demand raw materials for special prices. This is their solidarity! They could not care less about our problems and difficulties.

They think over there that since we swore to [follow] internationalism, we should go ahead! They reproach us: how is it that you are giving up your leadership role?! You will not teach us anymore and tell us what to do?!

We will not go back to this practice! If we do, we will once again assume full responsibility for their actions.

We will think of our own people.

We are not abandoning Cuba, but we will bring our assistance to within reasonable limits.

We gave Zhivkov 400 million dollars for no particular reason [*prosto tak*]. That is 30 percent of Belgium's national income! What is going on?

Soviet GNP growth in the last five years[41] has been 20 percent [sic] and military spending grew by 40 percent, including for the Warsaw Treaty.

We will hold people strictly responsible!

We are in favor of industrial cooperation with our friends. But they do not want it, they want us to provide them with the achievements of our basic science for the modernization of their industry. [...] They resell the specially priced resources they get from us to the West for hard currency. Such is their reciprocity!

This is where I turn into a nationalist!

We are not changing the course of the socialist community, but we will add some adjustments.

What is all this for? We need *perestroika*. The people deserve it. We will persevere and make it through the hindrances and resistance of the bureaucracy.

We will not follow the path of jumps and races; we will not be erratic. We will conduct a realistic policy.

So you know what to defend in your assigned countries, what to tell them. The people are pressuring the party, demanding more energetic action. There is impatience. And the oppositionists and demagogues are playing off of this.

For now we are not equipped with the necessary defensive mechanisms. We are excluding the possibility of bloody methods.

[*Source: Archive of the Gorbachev Foundation, Fond 2. Opis 1. On file at the National Security Archive. Translated by Anna Melyakova.*]

---

[41] The phrase "in the last five years" is handwritten as an insert.

Document No. 52: Record of Conversations between Mikhail Gorbachev and Károly Grósz

March 23–24, 1989

These Hungarian notes on the meetings between party leader Grósz and Gorbachev reveal plainly the ambiguities that still permeate the Soviet leader's deliberations with the East Europeans—or perhaps his naïveté about the party's ability to constrain change. Gorbachev responds to an extended discussion of the events of 1956 and 1968 by insisting again that "we have to preclude the possibility of repeated foreign intervention in the internal affairs of socialist countries" and that reassessing 1956 "is entirely up to you." Yet the Hungarians take special note that Gorbachev "emphasized that we clearly have to draw boundaries ... The limit, however, is the safekeeping of socialism and assurance of stability." Of course, any such boundaries would soon crumble along with the Berlin Wall, and the warning signs are here in Grósz's presentation, not simply in his remark that "we have to face our past, hard and painful as it is," but in the observation that a "lack of self-confidence is palpable enough in the party." Grósz claims somewhat lamely that the direction of change is "according to our intentions," while the "pace is somewhat disconcerting." The pace would soon quicken.

Comrade Grósz informed the negotiators about the Hungarian situation. He said that events in Hungary have lately accelerated. Their direction is according to our intentions, while their pace is somewhat disconcerting. Comrade Grósz emphasized that we wish to retain political power and find a solution to our problems by political means, avoiding armed conflict.

We have a good opportunity to reach our goals. People are afraid of a possible armed conflict. Workers, peasants and professionals want to work and live in peace and security, safeguarding their property. [...]

Another major concern is the history of the last 30 years. We have to face our past, hard and painful as it is, since the participants are still alive. On the other hand, by drawing the necessary conclusions, we might dishearten certain strata among the active supporters of our policy within the party. A lack of self-confidence is palpable enough in the party anyway. [...]

Comrade Gorbachev agreed that the Western world does not want instability in Eastern Europe, including Hungary, because in the present situation it would be adverse to their interests. Nonetheless, it is quite apparent that they intend to facilitate the realization and strengthening of developments which suit their own political ideas.

Comrade Gorbachev emphasized: "The assessment of the events of 1956 is entirely up to you." You have to stand on firm ground; you have to examine what really happened then and there. The Soviet leadership has recently analyzed the events of 1968 in Czechoslovakia, and they continue to maintain that what happened there was a counterrevolution, with all the idiosyncratic traits of such an event. There were different periods within the Czechoslovak events, but the Dubček regime was unable to prevent counterrevolutionary forces from gaining ground through them. [...]

Comrade Gorbachev emphasized that we clearly have to draw boundaries, thinking about others and ourselves at the same time. Democracy is much needed, and interests have to be harmonized. The limit, however, is the safekeeping of socialism and assurance of stability.

Comrade Grósz emphasized that when referring to 1956 we adhere to the original evaluation that the party endorsed in December 1956. The process is described in three consecutive words [sic]: student protest, uprising, and counterrevolution.

Comrade Gorbachev agreed with the above. He emphasized that today we have to preclude the possibility of repeated foreign interventions in the internal affairs of socialist countries. [...]

[*Source: MOL M-KS-288-11/4458 o.e. Document obtained by Magdolna Baráth. From* Political Transition in Hungary, 1989–1990; *International Conference, June 12, 1999, Hungarian Academy of Sciences, Budapest; A Compendium of Declassified Documents and Chronology of Events. Translated by Csaba Farkas.*]

Document No. 53: Transcript of CC CPSU Politburo Session, "Outcome of the USSR People's Deputies Elections"

March 28, 1989

This weekly Politburo meeting follows the March 26 vote for the USSR's first popu-larly-elected national Congress of People's Deputies. The discussion features both Gorbachev's positive spin and a thinly veiled sense of shock on the leadership's part. The new super legislature of 2,250 members—elected by 170 million voters—would meet from May 25 through June 9, elect a standing legislature—the new 542-mem-ber Supreme Soviet—and become the focus of national and world attention thanks partly to live telecasts spotlighting noted dissidents such as Andrei Sakharov in their extraordinary new roles as elected deputies. At this session, Gorbachev lays claim to achieving the Politburo's goals of advancing democratization and successfully holding free elections. Yet there is a serious discordant note: some 20 per cent of party candidates lost—even with no opposition—including the top party leaders in Moscow and Leningrad. The Leningrad party chief drew only 110,000 votes while 130,000 of his constituents crossed out his name—a practice that would become epidemic in the June Polish elections. And Boris Yeltsin, the reformer bounced by Gorbachev from the Politburo in 1987, won overwhelmingly as Moscow's at-large candidate. As in Poland, the CPSU went into the elections without a sense of how dramatically it had squandered its legitimacy. In the short term, this new reformist Congress would strengthen Gorbachev's agenda; but subsequently it would become a platform for the radical democrats.

OUTCOME OF THE USSR PEOPLE'S DEPUTIES ELECTIONS

Gorbachev: These elections were exceptional in all our history. This is a major step in realizing the political reforms and the subsequent democratization of our society. With good reason we can speak of the further progress of *perestroika*. The progress of *perestroika* was at the heart of the electoral campaign. Despite all the different thoughts and opinions, the policy of *perestroika* was never put in question.

Today, I think, we will have a preliminary discussion. There is no simple an-swer as to whose victory or loss this is. The results are what we have. The out-comes realistically reflect the progress of *perestroika*.

The outcome of the campaign shows us that at all stages—in the nominations and in voting—the elections went most successfully, with fewer losses and ex-penses, where people saw the real fruit of *perestroika*. This is the north Caucasus, and the central Chernozem *oblast*, Ukraine, and the Altay region.

It is characteristic that not everything came down to financial inter-ests. Non-formal movements—the ones that joined in the general process of change—were able to integrate smoothly into this current. But there were also some surprises.

After all, this is the first alternative campaign! These are the first democratic elections! And I must say that it will be like this from now on in all elections. The people have to understand that we need to act differently now. The working class missed its deputies, and we missed them too, we did not help [the working class] to get them. In Moscow from the six nominated candidates only one worker is left, and even he is a *raikom* [regional committee] secretary, i.e. a worker only by social origin.

The elections are progressing within the framework of a normal process. And we must analyze everything maturely and calmly. We cannot cover the entire gamut of impressions right now. It is not a simple picture. In any case, right now we must not follow the line of thinking that if someone did not receive support he is not trustworthy or should be dismissed.

We must pay particularly close attention to the outcomes of elections in Moscow and Leningrad.[42] The special characteristics [of the cities], the crisis in the cultural sphere, the problems with prices all took their toll. The lineup of candidates was worthy, although there were some who acted for personal gain. This was more evident in the capitals than anywhere else. Some candidates used all the methods of cheek, impudence, demagoguery, and irresponsible promises. And they won in that way. This also requires analysis.

It would be difficult to assume that we would have everything the way we wanted on the first try. But our tactical blunders are not the only reason for that. That would be an oversimplified and superficial approach. The realistic policies we are conducting do not permit such approaches.

In Moscow and in Leningrad we faced broad dissatisfaction from the workers with the progress of *perestroika*. Real problems did not receive appropriate solutions here. People might say that the market is in this state not only in Moscow but in the entire country. This is correct. And yet, we have to consider the fact that we give a great deal of our attention to Moscow and Leningrad, sometimes more than to other places. And the market situation here is not worse than in other places, even though there are many problems. This means that the matter lies not only in this, but in the fact that the *perestroika* processes in general are moving slower than they could be. This is a very serious signal for the government and for the CC, not to mention the *gorkoms* [city committee] and *raikoms*. The state of dissatisfaction is what caused the criticism and carping, which was heated up by the press and the avant-garde artists. The seeds they sowed fell on soil that was capable of receiving them. The voters did not give their preference to people we had counted on, which is evidence of the fact that the people wanted

---

42 In Leningrad all party and soviet leaders, as well as the commander of the military region, failed to be elected. In Moscow almost all party workers lost. Yeltsin, on the other hand, received 90 percent of the votes. [Footnote in the original, see source below.]

421

to convey their dissatisfaction to the CC and the government. So the matter is not the candidates personally. This is where we need to look. This is a major lesson for the entire party.

We could also say that this is the price of democracy and the result of the mass media's willfulness. Here too, the lack of a general political culture is telling, as is unsubstantiated fault-finding. In some magazines and newspapers it came down to speculation and running people down left and right. But the essence is still in something else. We came across this while traveling around the country. I, for example, saw a different people in Krasnoyarsk. The democratization process has produced its major results. People are beginning to take a stand and do not want to reconcile themselves to the things they come across in everyday life. This process grew and revealed itself in the electoral and reporting campaign, and even earlier—at the XIX conference we saw it during meetings with workers and in other circumstances.

The majority of the people understand the state the country is in right now and because of that they support the *perestroika* policies. But they believe that in four years more could have been achieved. They see how ineptly issues are resolved sometimes, how good initiatives come to naught. They understand that *perestroika's* major goals require more time. Yet they know that there are issues that can be resolved right now. But they often come across the old atmosphere, when [the leaders] listen to them for a while but do nothing, and sometimes even reprimand them. Now people do not want to accept this anymore. Our people are prepared to forgive and understand a great deal if they are treated with respect.

Our mistakes were: amelioration [of farm lands] and the anti-alcohol campaign; miscalculations at the level of central organs as well as in the provinces. We did not recognize the depth of the difficult state the country is in.

One could argue whether we acted correctly at the beginning of *perestroika*, whether we had an option to act some other way. We may and should argue about this, and bear responsibility for it. Arguments can be presented in favor of any of these points of view.

For example, people say that Cuba does not give us hard currency for oil and we lose billions of dollars. We could have bought 20 billion rubles worth of goods with that money. We are sustaining enormous losses in Chernobyl, in Armenia, in Afghanistan.

The situation in the market has become aggravated. We will not be able to solve the food problem or any other problem until we stabilize the monetary situation. And everyone present here today has contributed to the acuteness of this problem. We have our errors at the level of the center, and in the provinces. The main error is that we did not realize the difficulty of the financial and economic situation in due time.

Right now we are in a more critical situation than we were in 1985. For a long time we have felt that it is worsening, but we did not react appropriately. We allowed, for example, an increase in capital investment over and above the plan. We did this because it was urgent. Work that has started but not been completed is strangling us because salaries are being paid, but there is no product from these units. And these salaries were also thrown into the market. Our decisions do not have a sufficient economic basis. Gosplan must have a firmer rationale for its activities.

We are most disturbed by the reduction in the rate of economic growth. Have we lost our way here? All of this had an effect on the general situation, on people's state of mind. It is not just the intrigues of *Ogonyok, Moskovskie Novosti*,[43] and Yeltsin. It would be very easy to explain everything that way. We did not resolve the matter ourselves, and everyone here must admit to that. We must take the responsibility. After all, decentralization is only gathering momentum. We could have done more with the unprofitable and low-profit enterprises. They take 20 billion [rubles] a year.

So the criticism we have heard was fair. It provided an argument to those who have been depicting themselves as protectors of the people's interests.

I repeat: a great deal could be remedied by paying attention to the population in the provinces. The mechanism of relating to the people has been twisted over the decades, and I see that it is difficult to break it. And this is despite the fact that during this time we have replaced two-thirds of the regional committee leaders, chairmen of *kolkhozy* [collective farms], *sovkhozy* [state farms], and *obkoms* [*oblast'* committees]. But the situation is changing slowly.

What should we concentrate on?

The government has to consider the new goals quickly, and intensify the development of the economic-organizational function of Soviet governmental agencies in the provinces. The Politburo will not carry out this function anymore. The party should only provide help. More efficiency, overcome the parasitic attitude and nods toward the center. Decentralization means rights and responsibilities.

Bureaucratism—it is our and the workers' drama.

Control over trade, we need to establish order, give workers rights. We need to pass resolutions on labor control more quickly, we need to write more about this.

We need to intensify the fight against crime, which is getting out of hand. So far everything that has been done about this is only on paper. Crime is raging in Moscow, people have stopped going on evening strolls. Mobilize the workers' patrol. Present the issue sharply, publicly, so the people know what is going on. They will support us.

I conclude my speech with two assessments.

First: I have come to the conclusion that all problems must be resolved through *perestroika*—not instead of it, not by digressing from it, and not by twisting the line of *perestroika*—and in all of its directions. Once again we are lagging behind. The people are once again ahead of us. And again the only excuse available to the party is that it was the initiator of everything and as a result

---

[43] *Ogonyok* is an illustrated weekly magazine, *Moskovskie Novosti* a weekly newspaper.

deserves a high evaluation. We must eliminate the stumbling about, the frightening of the people and of ourselves. We are living through the most difficult period—when *perestroika* touches us all.

Second: [...] Perhaps some officials see that they are in an uncomfortable situation, they find themselves face-to-face with the people, they are experiencing a state of uncertainty. And democratization is taking place, comrades, as is the growth of people's political and social activity, even while there are negative outcomes from this process. And here we must keep our heads and not get lost.

Ryzhkov: March 26 was a turning point. We got a realistic picture of what is going on in society. It is one thing when we make speeches, and another when people cast secret ballots. What puts me on guard is that the unresolved questions are falling to the party. We should not panic, but we should also not underestimate this. We have a strong party, a strong state, but we also should take concrete measures.

Moscow and Leningrad did not vote the way they did solely because of the food shortage. We were put too much at ease when everything went normally in 1986 and 1987. Then 1988 knocked us off our feet. We need to explain to people that they can receive only the money they earn. I draw your attention to the responsibility of the mass media. We should call them to order. We have watched as even CC bodies came out against the CC.

Vorotnikov: We are all concerned about our colleagues who did not make it. We must not allow people from the staff who were not elected to feel that the attitude toward them has changed. The law about elections before local elections needs to be corrected. People in the provinces are upset. People there are also disturbed by the behavior of the mass media, which fosters negative attitudes toward party personnel. In 14 military districts [the party candidates] were not elected. We should think about a special Plenum, we should not go solely with the election results. The negative attitude toward army candidates for deputy positions is very disconcerting.

Shcherbitsky: An election campaign in general is an important stage. We should conduct the Plenum shortly before the Congress. We should examine the issue of the responsibility of CC CPSU party members who spoke from antisoviet positions.

Shevardnadze: We should welcome and work with all the officials who succeeded in the elections. The people must be convinced that the party takes its responsibilities seriously and sees its mistakes. We have to dissociate from the past. We cannot save the authority of the party without that. We should use the election results to strengthen the party.

The elections took place during a transitional period. The people have not yet received the material fruit of *perestroika*. We were punished for the deficiencies and mistakes, for the sugar and the laundry detergent. We were not prepared for the logic and dynamics of the election campaign. The demagogues came to the forefront without our help. The best forces came through the party and civic organizations, but had not mastered the tactics of the election campaign

424

(*consultants, training, etc.*). Many independent people led the campaign competently.

The elections have provided us with an argument: *democratic elections are possible within a one-party system.*

The elections showed that we were not able to use what we have won in the process of *perestroika*. The entire world acknowledges the party's merits in instilling new thinking in the international arena. What breakthroughs we have had: disarmament, leaving Afghanistan, etc! We used this capital inadequately.

Still, we passed through this stage with fewer losses. The elections in the provinces are troubling.

Ligachev: The elections reflect the *perestroika* process. But we sustained serious political losses. Many objective factors influenced the elections: deficits, reductions in the armed forces, etc. In many places people voted against party officials.

The main cause is the position the mass media took in relation to party history and party work. Negative opinions had accumulated in people's minds, and that is very dangerous. We must remember that in Czechoslovakia and in Hungary (in 1956 and 1968) everything began with the mass media. We need to subordinate certain press agencies to the CC. If we do not move from words to deeds it will become worse. We do not need repression. But we must keep order. And where necessary we should use power. I am speaking of certain newspapers that are well known to everyone. Anywhere I go people speak loudly about this.

Of course, there were major weaknesses in party work. We withdrew support from worthy people who gave all their knowledge, all their power to *perestroika*. The party will be able to maintain its position only through deeds. We gave way to demagogues who feed like parasites on our difficulties. But we have no other way than the way of *perestroika*. Stratification is taking place, the poverty layer is growing and at the same time there are excesses. In the mass media we should develop criticism and struggle against excessive enrichment, and we must not allow party workers to be defamed. We need information on the selfless work and moral character of party workers. Take for example Polozkov:[44] he does not eat or sleep, he gives his all to the party and the people.

Medvedev: The elections took place in an entirely new setting, when the old political system had already broken, but the new one had not yet been thought through and worked out. Therefore this could not have happened without surprises. What before would have shaken our very foundations now has to be accepted as a normal phenomenon. An electoral system of this kind has never been used anywhere. The regional candidates are nominated not by parties but by individual citizens. After all, it is a paradox when representatives of one party have to compete with each other, promote their programs, etc. It is impermissible for

---

[44] Ivan Polozkov, chairman of the Communist Party of the Russian Soviet Federative Republic.

425

a member of the party to speak in the name of the party and not defend it but criticize it. And we have often had *obkom* and *raikom* secretaries fighting each other for a deputy position. In conditions of a one-party system we have allowed a procedure that weakens party control. And we had to close our eyes to all of this because any interference might have trampled the first shoots of democracy. We have allowed many things to take their own course.

A question: how should a communist behave if he is nominated as a candidate? In the West everything is controlled by party lists.

Gorbachev: There is one party, and if we set off down this road we will clamp down even tighter.

Medvedev: The *obkom* and *gorkom* secretaries ended up on the same list. They are competing. We have to either absolutely exclude a party approach, or keep it.

The election campaigns have not been analyzed. What kind of elections are these if they are not evaluated by society and by the press? But it is true that by attacking some programs it would be possible to trample the first shoots of democracy.

A critical attitude prevails, not about *perestroika* itself but about the way it is taking place. The gap is growing between *perestroika* in the spiritual and ideological spheres on the one side, and in the material sphere on the other. We have criticized our past but have not overcome elements of the command-administrative system; we have not overcome egalitarian mindsets.

The press' critical attitude toward us stems from this. We cannot blame it for everything. After all, the press not only forms society's views, and it has plenty of shortcomings there, it also reflects them. It is impossible for the press to think one thing and for the people to think another. Journalists, leading figures of the press, they are all people who live and work together with us. They are not from some other world. If the newspaper pages, radio and television programs express certain attitudes it means that those attitudes exist in society, even though the press might not adequately portray society's views as a whole. Of course we have to work on this, and we are working on it. It is important for the press to act according to the main directions of *perestroika* and aid these processes.

I agree that the most vivid expression of dissatisfaction with *perestroika's* progress came in the election of regional leaders. The people who, in the public's opinion, spoke either directly or indirectly against *perestroika* suffered defeat.

My practical proposal is that at the CC Plenum we need to subject the election results to open and relentless analysis, and that we need to publish them. We need to show that we understand everything and are drawing the necessary conclusions.

Soloviev: Our opponents are directing active work against us. Our press does not oppose it; on the contrary: *Pravda* maintains that *obkoms* are the forces of evil.

In Leningrad all seven heads of the party, administrative, and military regions lost the elections. We have an opposition, we do. We underestimated them.

And I must say that the election campaign showed that there is a struggle for power going on. Our opposition worked with the youth and the elderly in residential areas in their regions—i.e. with the majority—while we worked in labor collectives.

Our leadership has been widely renewed, and we were not able to prepare it in time. Meanwhile, our opposition recruited psychologists and people who know how to work a crowd.

The press not only reflects, but also forms society's attitudes. *Pravda* and *Izvestiya* are criticizing the *obkoms*. The result is that the majority of attacks is not aimed at specific candidates, but at the party: "No to the CPSU! Out with the one-party system of functionaries, vote for Yeltsin!" In Leningrad, 9 out of 21 people were elected; three of them are communists. The authority of the party organization is declining. Today people do not ask [the party organization] but go [instead] to the labor collective council. In addition to that, we have started electing directors through the labor collective. But they [must be] managers.

Our opposition used to be an informal entity; now it is a clear structure with its own center. There are the democratic unions in Moscow. The prosecutor's office is stalling on the criminal action that is being brought against them. For the first time in 70 years the mass media has so sullied the party that nothing remains. The "heroes" [now] are [Mikhail] Shatrov, Yeltsin, [Vitalii] Korotich.[45]

We have to work energetically not to fail in the regional elections. They want to take all the mandates and seize power.

Chebrikov: The colleagues who lost must be retained and supported. In Armenia and the Baltic states they are rocking the boat from two sides. In Armenia there were picket lines against party workers by the voting stations. They made blacklists. The Balts went around the entire country, campaigning against party candidates. They made it as far as Irkutsk! Who gave them the right? Meetings between Politburo members and voters were given four minutes on television, no more. Television should provide more time to Politburo members' appearances.

Gorbachev: Why do we have such spineless people in the Politburo?

The work after the earthquake[46] had positive results. The workers did not give in. And the "structures" already worked at the elections.

Chebrikov: The Balts went around the cities of Byelorussia and Ukraine. In Leningrad they posted flyers aimed at local leaders. Politburo members have seven minutes to appear on television, while Yeltsin speaks for the entire evening.

---

[45] Shatrov was a playwright who had supported dissident causes. Korotich was editor of *Ogonyok*.

[46] The Spitak earthquake, in which more than 50,000 died, occurred on December 7, 1988, while Gorbachev was at the U.N. General Assembly in New York. The tragedy exposed abuses of power and corruption in the region, and resulted in the removal of a number of party officials in Armenia.

We need to think about the Congress, about the Supreme Soviet's composition. There will be many people incapable of carrying out parliamentary functions.

Zaikov: The press is attacking the headquarters and is not taking a stand regarding discrimination against the [party] apparatus. For example: Onikov's article on democracy and centralism.

The MGK [Moscow city committee] and the *raikoms* were out of favor. All the candidates for deputy positions took to criticizing party organizations and Soviet society, going as far as to criticize the system itself. If somebody spoke in favor of the party platform, he lost immediately. That means that in essence the attitude was against Soviet power. The *raikoms* cannot work. The standard scenario is "Are you from a *raikom*? Take a walk!"

I said that we will deal with it after the campaign. They conducted the campaign so as to undermine the two remaining [candidates] in the three electoral districts and to nominate Korotich once again. In a settlement where only generals live, 89 percent voted for Yeltsin. The same occurred at the Military and Political Academy.

Gorbachev: The dissatisfaction of the officers and the officer corps with the generals and with protectionism had an obvious effect.

Zaikov: Seventy-four percent of Supreme Soviet and Council of Ministers officials voted in their place of residence for Yeltsin and 90 percent of the diplomats are for him. The mass media has formed the opinion that the foundation of the bureaucracy is the party-state apparatus. They, so to speak, do not know how to work.

We need to change the tone of the propaganda, we need to show the party's role in *perestroika*, and stop discrimination against the [party] apparatus, especially since it is the new apparatus. Offenses occurred against the flag and the Soviet anthem. Tricolor flags appeared.[47] There were demands to convene a CPSU Congress ahead of schedule in order to elect a new CC. This is also in L. Onikov's *Pravda* article.

In enterprises non-conformists are being pulled into the leadership of labor collectives while party organizations are ignored.

Crime is on the increase in Moscow.

Pugo: There were many attacks on the party. And there is a danger that the election outcomes will begin to be portrayed as a defeat of the party. We must not allow such an assessment to spread. Party organizations are not growing. The party is being drained; the number of those leaving the party is growing. Young people are not joining the party. The party is losing authority. Its unity is being blurred by the election campaigns of party-member candidates for deputy positions. In the Baltics the popular fronts have achieved everything they wanted. A nationalistic August is approaching[48] (*the 50th anniversary of the incorporation*

---

[47] The traditional Russian colors—white, blue, red.

[48] The 50th anniversary of the Molotov-Ribbentrop Pact. [Footnote in the original.]

of the Baltic States [into the USSR]). We need to find political answers to stop dangerous processes, especially those related to republic-level elections.

Yakovlev: There must be no word of any defeat. Eighty-four percent of voters came to vote and 85 percent of communists have been elected. This is a referendum on *perestroika*. The results of this referendum are clearly not favorable to the CPSU (*he cites Die Welt*).

We were a little scared. In reality the Soviet people voted for *perestroika*, against stagnation and the command-administrative system, against negligence and slovenliness. Socialist democracy has advanced to a new level.

We are at a difficult stage; there are problems in the economy, etc., but even in these circumstances society has shown great maturity.

I agree with Shevardnadze that it has been demonstrated that democracy can develop within a one-party system. Let us not rush to conclusions. Elections provide good insight into the current moods of society. We should accent the fact that democracy also has to be defended legally.

I am more concerned by something else: when a newspaper writes 10 times about the same thing there is no reaction from the party organs or any other organs. Letters have not been answered. We should check the press for the promises made by "bawlers'" [*krikunov*] and ask them to deliver.

Razumovsky: We have spent too much time with documents. We shouted "Ivanov, Sidorov!"[49] in congress halls and registered people arbitrarily. The Department (*of organizational party work*) and I overlooked a great deal. Thirty *obkom* and *gorkom* secretaries were not elected. There will be new elections in 200-plus regions.

We should not dramatize the outcomes. And we should not accent the fact that some of the leaders were not elected. In a number of cases (*Chelyabinsk*) there were no surprises. Some were too involved in their campaigns and missed the region's politics as a whole. We need to develop [new] procedures and remind people of CPSU regulations, of party discipline and responsibility. If a communist takes the floor, he must remember that he represents the party.

Slyunkov: This is a normal process. There are losses. That is natural. There is anxiety about the party. We allowed the situation to be portrayed as if everything was the fault of the party. History comes into play here, as do the goods that are missing from the store shelves. Attacks on the party and the government are really picking up. We need to strengthen the ideological support for *perestroika*, and opposition to attacks on the party.

We should hold the Plenum before the Congress.

Shalaev: People's deputies from civic organizations always were and will continue to be our tower of strength. And they themselves have stirred, but regrettably they participated very little in the regional elections because they were busy with their own election campaigns. In the work environment the atmosphere

---

[49] Typical Russian names, the equivalent of "Smith, Jones!"

is demanding, but good. There is one wish: follow through with your promises. The mass media revealed very little of what was done over [the past] four years.

We did not give anything to the population before the elections (*in terms of food and goods*). In some places people were not even paid their salaries.

Mironenko: A politician cannot take offense at his people. Many party committees were simply not ready to work on a broad front. The habit of sending commands through organizational departments was telling. In the provinces this habit is very strong. To the youth, the elections are a symbol of *perestroika's* success. We need a clearer line to strengthen the Komsomol's organizational independence. Members of the Politburo should give interviews to the youth press.

Lukyanov: One-fifth of the party organizations' secretaries did not go through. The reasons for this are economic, especially the falling standard of living for pensioners and the poor. Now it is being said that the CC set the party organizations adrift, that it left the party committee secretaries to be devoured by demagogues. We must take measures against "*Memorial*" and "*Pamyat'*."[50] They are close to becoming anti-soviet organizations.

In nine months there have been over 1,200 mass demonstrations encompassing 13 million people. The mass media's colossal attack on the party cadres set off a discussion of the possibility of an alternative party. Party workers feel that the CC is not protecting them. It is significant that the majority of the military voted against the party secretaries. Even in the KGB graduate school 80 percent voted for Yeltsin.

Masliukov: We are missing something. Why are the people filling up with dissatisfaction? We see the results of our disorganization. We must prepare people for the fact that inflation is inevitable, that rising prices are inevitable, that difficulties with foodstuffs and the freezing of salaries are inevitable. In order to normalize the financial system we need draconian measures and at least 50 billion [rubles] worth of goods. Machine building and defense would increase the production of goods for the people by 40 percent.

Gorbachev (concluding): We achieved a major political victory in extraordinarily difficult circumstances. Defeat is out of the question. We are in the most acute stage of *perestroika* right now. We touched everyone—workers and peasants, scholars, and military men. The countryside is experiencing a drought, and on top of that there is Chernobyl, Armenia, Afghanistan, oil prices and pressure from the West. And despite everything we received active support in this situation. This is how we have to look at it from the political perspective, otherwise we could get lost, especially if we consider how Western propaganda works: saying that the empire is crumbling, the Politburo is being torn by opposition, etc. And [even] in this situation people came and voted.

[50] *Memorial*, a non-governmental human rights organization, was established in 1987 to uncover information on, and build a memorial to, the victims of Stalinist repression. *Pamyat'*, founded in the same year, was a Russian nationalist group especially active among college students.

On the CPSU. This is a major subject. To say that the people voted against the party would not be right. Let's not compare apples and oranges.[51] What kind of unity do we need in the party? [A unity] based on *perestroika* and new approaches, under conditions of democracy and *glasnost*, i.e. not on the basis of force, or fear that you will be dismissed and punished. Unity only on the basis of the *perestroika* platform. This does not exclude, of course, the need to provide a reminder of the communist's traditional duties. And we are shy about talking about it. Communists must feel like they are masters [of their own party]. The committees are there for them, not the other way around. There can be no socialism without a party that has a socialist program.

The party built up its authority through the policy of *perestroika*, not through threats and fear but by going to the people openly and calling for criticism of itself.

But this is authority at the first stage. Now we need to win authority at the stage when we solve practical matters. And we cannot make anybody shut up; authority is not won in that way. It must be won by activity and closeness to people.

Perestroika must mainly be defended by continuing *perestroika*; by real actions, first and foremost in the economy; by working with people, through the staff.

A great deal right now comes down to the staff. The elections reflected that very clearly. We need to consolidate the best party and non-party powers, including information organizations that support *perestroika* and are not just after a pay check. Our party worker receives a salary and asks the CC to protect him, while he should himself plug into the process and begin to act.

It is a very critical time for us in the Center. Much depends on us. Politics are developing in the direction of the people. We should not lose time in worry and self-analysis. Let us act calmly and with confidence.

We have to go to the CC Plenum with a profound analysis of the political outcomes of the elections. Do not hand over the initiative in interpreting them.

The Congress begins on May 25. Yeltsin says that he is already looking at which deputies he can include in his group. Additional elections are on May 14.

[*Source: Archive of the Gorbachev Foundation, Fond 4, Opis 1. On file at the National Security Archive. Also* V Politburo TsK KPSS... Po zapisyam Anatolya Chernyaeva, Vadima Medvedeva, Georgiya Shakhnazarova (1985–1991) *[In the CC CPSU Politburo... From the Notes of Anatoly Chernyaev, Vadim Medvedev, Georgy Shakhnazarov (1985–1991)], Eds. A Chernyaev, A. Weber, V. Medvedev. (Moscow: Alpina Business Books), pp. 460–466. Translated by Anna Melyakova.*]

---

[51] The Russian expression here is *"Ne putat' Bozhii dar s yaichnitsei."* Literally, "Don't confuse a gift from God with fried eggs."

Document No. 54: CIA Intelligence Assessment,
"Rising Political Instability under Gorbachev: Understanding the Problem and Prospects for Resolution"

April 1989

Only four months after concluding that Gorbachev's process of change "could take decades," the CIA now concludes that "[e]ven Gorbachev realizes ... that it is far from certain that he will be able to control the process he has set in motion." In this assessment, the Agency's analysts, primarily in the Office of Soviet Analysis (SOVA), which is markedly more pessimistic than the rest of the intelligence community at this time, go beyond Ambassador Matlock's prediction of impending bankruptcy to a new finding—that the Soviet Union is less stable today "than at any time since Stalin's great purges in the 1930s." Read with hindsight, this conclusion is quite prescient in that the second and third possible outcomes described here actually would come about: the hard-line reaction in the form of the attempted coup in August 1991, followed by the maximalist-reformer takeover and ouster of Gorbachev by December 1991. The specific policy recommendations made here fit perfectly with President Bush's characteristic prudence and caution, urging that the West not be seen to "exploit the USSR's internal weakness during this vulnerable period" because that "would undercut Gorbachev's arguments that Soviet security can be maintained by diplomatic, rather than military, means and could threaten his reform process."

KEY JUDGMENTS[52]

The Soviet Union is less stable today than at any time since Stalin's great purges in the 1930s. General Secretary Gorbachev clearly hopes that, by shaking up the Soviet system, he can rouse the population out of its lethargy and channel the forces he is releasing in a constructive direction. Even Gorbachev realizes, however, that it is far from certain that he will be able to control the process he has set in motion. That process could create so much turmoil and unrest that it will be very difficult for him to achieve his goals. In the extreme, his policies and political power could be undermined, and the political stability of the Soviet system could be fundamentally threatened.

Gorbachev's reforms—while yet to remedy existing problems—have caused new challenges to surface. Having seen their quality of life stagnate under Gorbachev, Soviet citizens are becoming increasingly skeptical of reform, seeing it more and more as a threat to the secure existence they recall they enjoyed under

---

[52] Information Available as of March 31, 1989 [as indicated in original document].

432

Brezhnev. Moreover, the aspects of reform that are potentially most destabilizing are only in their early stages. The political reforms being introduced could further erode central authority and could give disaffected groups new platforms to challenge the regime. Radical economic reform appears further away because the kinds of market-oriented measures required to meet economic objectives would heighten social tensions by raising prices, creating unemployment, and increasing income inequality. Moreover, such a transition could create a period of economic chaos and a sharp drop in production before the reforms began to yield positive results.

Over the past two years, incidents of political unrest in the USSR, ranging from benign small gatherings to major acts of political violence, have sharply escalated. Under the banner of *glasnost*, Soviet citizens are organizing groups that could form the basis of a political opposition and are advancing a wide range of demands that challenge central authority. The most dangerous of these are the nationalist movements that have blossomed in many republics, unleashing centrifugal forces that, if unchecked, could threaten to tear the system apart. This increasing assertiveness by national minorities is provoking a backlash among the Russians, emboldening Russian nationalist groups and setting the stage for violent clashes in the republics where the Russians are in danger of becoming second-rate citizens.

The next several years promise to be some of the most turbulent in Soviet history. Indeed, while the kind of turmoil now being created in the USSR has been effectively managed in many countries, in other countries it has contributed to the destabilization of the political system. There are too many unknowns to determine whether Gorbachev will be able to control the process he has started, or if it will increasingly come to control him, making a wide range of outcomes possible over the next five years:

- If Gorbachev's reforms begin to produce tangible results and if he is lucky, he should remain in power and prevent any of the potential problems he faces from getting out of control, while continuing to move his reforms ahead.
- A growing perception within the leadership that reforms are threatening the stability of the regime could lead to a conservative reaction. This would probably, but not necessarily, involve a transfer of power—with a majority of the Politburo voting Gorbachev out, as happened with Khrushchev in 1964—and a repudiation of many aspects of reform.
- Those pressing for a maximalist agenda could gain control of the political system as a result of democratization and *glasnost*—as happened in Czechoslovakia in 1968—and force Gorbachev out.
- Should a sharp polarization of the leadership prevent it from acting resolutely to deal with a growing crisis, the prospects would increase for a conservative coup involving a minority of Politburo members supported by ele-

ments of the military and KGB. The prospects of a unilateral military coup are much more remote.

- If ethnic problems mount, consumer and worker discontent grow, and divisions in the leadership prevent it from acting decisively, organized political opposition could threaten the regime. Under these conditions, opposition groups could come to share power, as Solidarity did in Poland in the early 1980s, or individual republics might win de facto independence.

To get through this difficult period, the Soviet leadership can be expected to continue to place a high premium on creating a stable and predictable environment—minimizing the possibility of threats to Soviet interests from abroad. East–West relations, especially with the United States, will be particularly important. To help ease the strain on the economy and improve the prospects for delivering on promises to the consumer, the Soviet leadership will continue to vigorously pursue arms control and seek ways to reduce military spending.

Gorbachev can be expected to seek more foreign policy successes to enhance his legitimacy, build his personal prestige, and distract attention from domestic problems. For this and other reasons, he can therefore be expected to maintain a very high profile in the international arena, continuing to advance major foreign policy initiatives. At times, however, domestic crises—some of which may not be visible on the surface—will probably distract the Soviet leadership from foreign policy. This could result in temporary reversals on specific issues, or unexplained periods of indecision—such as occurred during the U.S. Secretary of State's October 1987 visit to Moscow in the midst of the Yeltsin crisis—when the Soviet leadership failed to set a date for a summit.

IMPLICATIONS FOR THE UNITED STATES

The next several years promise to be turbulent ones in Soviet domestic affairs, regardless of the path followed. There will almost certainly be continued turmoil within both Soviet society and the leadership. Such ferment is not only a natural byproduct of the reform process, but it would also result from any effort to turn that process back. Consequently, continued or even increased turmoil in itself cannot be taken as an indication that Gorbachev or the political stability of the Soviet Union is in jeopardy. Indeed, it could be an indication that the reform process is moving ahead and tackling the difficult issues that need to be addressed to build a more effective system. [...]

In the near term, Gorbachev can be expected to continue a foreign policy line that will create the most favorable international climate for the changes he is trying to bring about in the Soviet Union. Consequently, he will continue to place a high premium on creating a stable and predictable international environment, minimizing the possibility of threats from abroad to Soviet interests. To this end, the leadership is likely to continue to take a more flexible approach in most areas of foreign policy, and the prospects for the USSR becoming engaged in regional conflicts will remain relatively small.

East–West relations, especially with the United States, will be particularly important. To help ease the strain on the economy and improve the prospects for delivering on promises to the consumer, the Soviet leadership will continue to vigorously pursue arms control and seek ways to reduce military spending. More important, the Soviet leadership will need to feel confident that other nations will not try to exploit the USSR's internal weakness during this vulnerable period. A perception that the West was actively trying to do this—particularly in the field of military competition—would undercut Gorbachev's arguments that Soviet security can be maintained by diplomatic, rather than military, means and could threaten his reform process.

Gorbachev can also be expected to seek more foreign policy successes to enhance his legitimacy, build up his personal prestige, and distract attention from domestic problems. As long as his reforms continue to produce results, he can be expected to continue to seek these successes by the conciliatory route. Gorbachev can therefore be expected to maintain a very high profile in the international arena, continuing to advance major foreign policy initiatives. At times, however, domestic crises—some of which may not be visible on the surface—will probably distract the Soviet leadership from foreign policy. This could result in temporary reversals on specific issues or unexplained periods of indecision—such as occurred during the U.S. Secretary of State's visit to Moscow in October 1987 in the midst of the Yeltsin crisis, when the Soviet leadership failed to set a date for a summit.

[Source: CIA declassification. On file at the National Security Archive.]

Document No. 55: Report from Vadim Zagladin on Conversation with Jan Pudlák

April 1, 1989

Even while working on his secret task of drafting Gorbachev's Strasbourg speech (see Document No. 44), the International Department's Vadim Zagladin continues his official role as liaison with "progressive" East and West Europeans. Here, Zagladin's report on conversations with a leading Czechoslovak official, Jan Pudlák, provides yet another of the many "early warnings" that reach Gorbachev's desk long before the events in Czechoslovakia take a dramatic turn. Zagladin describes a "deep moral and political crisis" in Czechoslovakia comparable to "the one that preceded 1968." He tells Chernyaev that "in the working class, among intellectuals and the youth, there is a time bomb of discontent." Also noteworthy is the way this leading Moscow expert judges the political role of Václav Havel, a "mediocre writer" who "could have been dealt with through softer, political means." Obviously, the old habits of looking at dissidents as Western agents of influence are still strong in Moscow. Zagladin also gives a candid reason for not reassessing the events of 1968: because "one part of the leadership was thoroughly involved in those events, and another fears a repetition of 1968 through inertia."

[Pudlák] is now also director of the Institute of International Policy at the Foreign Ministry of the ČSSR. He participates in the work of the Commission of the CC CPCz on international affairs. I have known him for a long time.

[According to him, Czechoslovakia] is in a "deep moral and political crisis." This crisis can be compared with the one that preceded 1968. One difference today is that the living standards of the masses are considerably higher than in 1967. This means a lot for the Czechs. [...] However, these positive factors are about to disappear. [...] On the mass level, among all groups of society but above all in the working class, among intellectuals and the youth, there is a time bomb of discontent.

Gradually a broad opposition is being formed. But it is a diverse phenomenon. It would not be all that bad if there were only hostile groups like "Charter-77" or "Renewal."[53] But along with them there is a considerable group of former party members (up to half a million) who, without joining the opposition [...] voice their active dissatisfaction both with their own situation and that in the country. Simultaneously, the mood of discontent has spread among a great

---

[53] Charter 77 was a groundbreaking Czechoslovak dissident group founded in January 1977. The human rights activists who signed the initial Charter included future President Václav Havel and prominent members of the Czech and Slovak intelligentsia. Their goal was to uphold principles of the Helsinki Final Act in the daily lives of Czechoslovak citizens

number of party members and members of the Communist Youth. And non-p⸱ members are not calm either. [...] The youth is comparing the activities of thᴜ authorities to the actions of "fascists."

[Václav] Havel's arrest [and] imprisonment have converted this mediocre writer into a martyr, and for the discontented he has become a national hero. This is a priceless gift for the West. In all truth, he could have been dealt with through softer, political means. [...] The leadership failed to demonstrate the skill "to think several moves ahead." Today it is most important to operate by political means, to "cage" discontent into discussions. [...]

[It is necessary to reassess 1968 and the role of Alexander Dubček.] However, it has been difficult to do that so far; one part of the leadership was thoroughly involved in those events, and another fears a repetition of 1968 through inertia (although if the party became a true political leader of *perestroika*, this would not happen). We must approach it cautiously, gradually. [...]

[*Source: Archive of the Gorbachev Foundation. Fond 3. Opis 1. On file at the National Security Archive. Translated by Vladislav Zubok.*]

by using non-violent legal means in accordance with the Czechoslovak Constitution. "Renewal" is a reference to *Obroda—Klub Za Socialistickou Přestavbu,* the Club for Socialist Restructuring, an organization formed in early 1989 by reform communists who had been pushed out of the party after the Prague Spring. It became a part of Civic Forum in November 1989.

Document No. 56: Record of Conversation between
Mikhail Gorbachev and Margaret Thatcher

April 6, 1989

The candor and depth of the conversations that took place between Gorbachev and the British prime minister testify to their close relationship, which contributed to Thatcher's instrumental role as the first Western leader to take notice of the Soviet party boss ("a man you can do business with," as she said in 1984). Her voice persuaded President Reagan to engage the new Kremlin leader, and her personal reassurances helped dramatically to reduce Gorbachev's own sense of threat from the West. After Gorbachev's U.N. speech in December 1988, Thatcher would proclaim the Cold War over and spearhead the effort to bring Gorbachev into the club of world leaders.

Several striking impressions emerge from the talks in London: the quality of the discussion recorded in these notes, Gorbachev's willingness to listen to Thatcher, her treatment of him in turn as a peer, the learning process occurring between them, and the prime minister's sense that "political pluralism" in Poland and Hungary is well ahead of Gorbachev's own conception. (Their discussions take place just after the conclusion of the Polish Roundtable agreement on reforms, which include relatively free elections scheduled for June.)

[...]

Gorbachev: On the one hand, there is a point of view emerging in the White House that the success of our *perestroika*, the development of the new image of the Soviet Union, is not beneficial for the West. Secretary of State James Baker returned from his trip to Western Europe on the verge of panic. Europe, according to him, is ready to respond to our invitation to build new relations in Europe and in the entire world. The West Germans, in this sense, have simply lost their minds. And so they are beginning to think about how to stem the influence of our policy and of our initiatives in the minds of the West.

Of course, these processes are going through a struggle in the United States. There are a lot of people there who sympathize with our policy, who think that the continuation of *perestroika* is good for American interests because it would allow us to ensure security, development of the economy, and cultural and other kinds of exchanges. These forces are sufficiently large and influential. However, there is also another wing, which thinks in the tradition of the well-known statements by Kissinger, Brzezinski, and other right-wing individuals who have now gotten closer to the new American administration and are trying their best. We receive letters from George Bush and we see entire passages there that are copied from known public statements by Kissinger. In short, there is a clear concern

438

there that the West is losing public opinion, and so they are trying to dilute the mood of cooperation with us.

On the other hand, as we see from the negotiations that George Bush and James Baker had in Western Europe, the process of working out a response to our proposals is slowing down in the West. And from this fact comes the desire to undermine interest in *perestroika*, in our initiatives, and to present it all under the cover of general considerations—let's see where *perestroika* will lead, how will it end, whether it is associated with the person of Gorbachev only, and if so, whether we should make the future of the West dependent upon it. I tell you frankly, we are concerned about it.

Even you, Mrs. Thatcher, as we can see, are exhibiting more reservations recently. We are informed that you are being advised, especially by banking circles, not to rush, to be careful. And this shows through, both in your statements and in your practical policy.

Thatcher: If anybody made such a recommendation, it has not reached me. How did it reach you?

Gorbachev: That's how it happens. What an interesting world, isn't it? [...]

Thatcher: That is why we are concerned about the immensity of your tasks. It is one thing to tell people what to do and where to work, and quite a different thing to make it so that they work properly under conditions of major production and complex technology. People start feeling less confident in themselves and their future. I saw this during my trip to the Soviet Union in 1987. The old order is being broken, and the people do not know what will take its place. And what is it like to rely on one's own labor and entrepreneurship—will it bring a better life? This is what we are concerned about in your *perestroika*.

Gorbachev: Why are you so scared of our *perestroika*?

Thatcher: Precisely because I was the first to start an analogous *perestroika* in my country. And also because I was the first to say that your success is in our interest. It is in our interest that the Soviet Union becomes more peaceful, more affluent, more open to change so that this would go together with personal freedoms, with more openness and exchanges. Continue your course and we will support your line. The prize will be enormous. But you have to see the economic difficulties. Not too long ago I discussed these issues in detail with a Soviet academician. He said that Gorbachev would need our common support for ten years. I do not know the exact length of time, but in principle that is right.

We are glad to see the political changes in the Soviet Union. Your recent elections [for the Congress of People's Deputies on March 26, 1989] were a real watershed. They showed that the people are not afraid of using political power. But in addition to this, you need finances, you need a strong economy, educated and capable managers. I know that you have enough talent, but it is not yet as clear as in the political sphere.

And in the international sphere—I am thinking about your allies in Eastern Europe—promising changes are taking place. I visited Hungary, and I saw that that country is experiencing a stage of new freedom in politics and in the economy. But they have already been moving two or three steps ahead of you in terms of introducing new economic forms and freedom of enterprise for some time. Most interesting developments are under way in Poland. I met with Wojciech Jaruzelski. He is a prominent and honest politician who is doing everything he can for his country at a very difficult stage in its development. Let's take the latest events—the recognition of Solidarity. In my view, this is the beginning of political pluralism, because Solidarity is a political movement, not just a labor union. Young people and retirees take part in it, not just workers. I met with Solidarity's leadership, and I repeatedly advised them to seek a dialogue with the government, not to limit themselves to confrontation. I said to them that you can never leave the negotiating chair empty, it would not lead to anything, and I can see that they have listened to my advice.

More complicated developments are under way in Czechoslovakia. In our analysis, everything is unclear there. And there is some evil irony in this, because Czechoslovakia was one of the most affluent and democratic states in Europe.

In the more general international context I can see the first fruits of our joint effort and the new approaches. The agreement on Namibian independence has been signed. We are working together in the United Nations, in the Security Council, in a spirit of cooperation that was unimaginable only recently. It has led to the cease-fires between Iran and Iraq and to positive changes in the Middle East peace process. There are fewer positive signs in Central America. The United States is very concerned about the situation in that region. Everything there arises from the fact that when the Sandinistas overthrew Somoza, they did not deliver on their promise to restore democracy in Nicaragua. The rebels in El Salvador receive weapons above and beyond any reasonable limit. All in all, there are reasons to be concerned there, as well as in the Horn of Africa.

The world represents a calico picture. In some regions, there are more positive signs than in others. But we all want international success that would make the world safer, and put an end to bloodshed in the hot spots.

You touched upon the policy of the new American administration. I know George Bush and James Baker very well. I do not see how they could make policy that would contradict President Reagan's course. Of course, Bush is a very different person from Reagan. Reagan was an idealist who firmly defended his convictions. But at the same time, it was very pleasant to deal with him, to have a dialogue, and to negotiate. Bush is a more balanced person, he gives more attention to detail than Reagan did. But as a whole, he will continue the Reagan line, including on Soviet–American relations. He will strive to achieve agreements that would be in our common interest.

Gorbachev: That is the question—in our common interests or in your Western interests?

Thatcher: I am convinced in the common interest.

Gorbachev: Here you need to be super-convinced. [...]

For example, we now have a financial system and budget deficit that are out of balance. There is a large volume of free money in the country that is not

440

supported by consumer products. People's incomes are growing faster than the production of consumer goods. This is where the deficit is coming from. I remember that only 15 years ago the shelves of these stores were overstocked with butter, milk, meat, and then we consumed 1/3 or even 1/2 the quantity of those products that we do now. Demand was limited because incomes were unlimited [sic]. Now we have a new problem—not only to produce more goods of better quality but also to balance incomes with the volume of production. We think that this is a task of primary importance; if this is not done, it will be hard to hope for economic improvement in general. That is why we are trying to regulate incomes through economic mechanisms and at the same time to stimulate entrepreneurship and initiative, as well as self-financing. We cannot change the entire economic mechanism at once; that would simply blow up the economy. We could, of course, undertake some temporary measures to alleviate the situation for the people; for example, we could get foreign loans and saturate the market with goods purchased with that money. Some people here advocate that.

Thatcher: But that is not a solution to your problem. That is not a policy.

Gorbachev: Exactly. And as far as our budget deficit, it would simply be a violation of our obligations to our country. That is why we are developing a policy for building an economic, industrial base for the production of consumer goods so that later we will be able to eliminate the deficit with our own goods. […]

[*Source: Archive of the Gorbachev Foundation, Fond 1. Opis 1. On file at the National Security Archive. Translated by Svetlana Savranskaya.*]

Document No. 57: National Intelligence Estimate 11-4-89,
"Soviet Policy toward the West: The Gorbachev Challenge"

April 1989

This remarkable estimate from the U.S. intelligence community provides one of the clearest expressions anywhere in the American documentary record of the split between hardline skeptics of Gorbachev—a group that in 1989 included President Bush as well as his top advisers Brent Scowcroft, James Baker, and Robert Gates—versus those who saw fundamental change happening in the Soviet Union, a less influential group that included former President Reagan as well as most of the senior career analysts at CIA such as Douglas MacEachin. The extraordinary "Disagreements" section of this estimate summarizes the views of both sides, without mentioning that the first group was actually in charge of the U.S. government at that moment. The opening bullet points of the "Key Judgments" are especially striking for their obtuseness, warning that the first two effects of changes in "the nature of the Soviet challenge" would be to "threaten the security consensus developed in the West to combat Soviet expansionism" and "undercutting support abroad for defense programs"! The evidence now available from the Soviet side, including the documents published in this book, which intelligence analysts at the time could only dream of gaining access to, demonstrates that the "fundamental re-thinking" view was precisely on target; yet this view did not have nearly as much influence on U.S. policy after the 1986 Reykjavik summit, (or especially in the first year of the Bush administration), as did the opinions of the hard-liners who were so wrong in these judgments because of their presumptions about the Soviet Union.

KEY JUDGMENTS[54]

Dramatic changes in approach to the West under Soviet leader Gorbachev are driven by economic and social decay at home, a widening technological gap with the West, and a growing realism about trends in the outside world. For the foreseeable future, the USSR will remain the West's principal adversary. But the process Gorbachev has set in motion is likely to change the nature of the Soviet challenge over the next five years or so:

- New Soviet policies will threaten the security consensus developed in the West to combat Soviet expansionism.

---

[54] Information available as of April 17, 1989 [as indicated in original document].

442

- The Soviets are likely to succeed to a degree in undercutting support abroad for defense programs and in reducing political barriers to Western participation in their economic development.
- At the same time new policies will make Moscow more flexible on regional issues and human rights and pave the way for a potentially significant reduction of the military threat.
- Alliance cohesion will decline faster in the Warsaw Pact than in NATO, giving the East Europeans much greater scope for change.

We believe Moscow wants to shift competition with the West to a largely political and economic plane. In order to prepare the ground for such a shift, Soviet leaders are making major policy changes and promoting a broad reassessment of the West. These new policies serve domestic as well as foreign policy needs:

- They aim to create an international environment more conducive to domestic reform and to undermine the rationale for high defense budgets and repressive political controls.
- They are seen as more effective than past policies in advancing Soviet foreign interests.

There are limits on how far the new Soviet leadership wants to go in the direction of a less confrontational East–West relationship:

- Vigorous efforts to protect and advance Soviet geopolitical interests and selective support for Communist regimes and revolutionary movements will continue.
- Moscow will continue to employ active measures and covert efforts to advance its objectives. Foreign intelligence activity is likely to increase.

Given the turmoil unleashed by the reform process, we cannot predict policy trends during the period of the Estimate with high confidence. Nevertheless, we believe that Gorbachev is likely to stay in power and that the reform effort is more likely than not to continue. If so, we believe the following developments are probable:

- *Military power*. While increasing so far under Gorbachev, Soviet defense spending will decline significantly in real terms. Moscow will maintain vigorous force modernization programs and a strong R&D effort in key areas, but production and procurement of many major weapons will decline. Gorbachev is likely to make further concessions to achieve a START agreement, show flexibility on chemical weapons, and take further steps to trim and redeploy Soviet conventional forces—moving unilaterally if necessary.
- *The Western Alliance*. Moscow will attempt to translate its more benign image into expanded credits, trade, and technology sales and reduced support

for defense spending and force modernization in Western Europe. While trying to reduce US influence and military presence, Moscow does not see an abrupt unraveling of current Alliance arrangements as serving Soviet interests.

- *Third World competition.* The Soviets will seek to expand their influence and continue support to leftist causes deemed to have some future. But they will be more careful to consider how such moves affect broader Soviet interests, including relations with the West. They will encourage their clients to make economic and political reforms and seek Western aid. It is highly unlikely that Moscow will become directly involved in military support to another leftist seizure of power in the Third World as it did in the 1970s.

ALTERNATIVE SCENARIOS

We see a number of developments that—while unlikely—could disrupt current trends and push Gorbachev onto a different course:

- A widespread crackdown on unrest at home or in Eastern Europe would probably trigger a re-escalation of East–West tensions, causing Gorbachev to tack in a conservative direction. A shift of this sort would limit Gorbachev's freedom of maneuver in negotiations and his ability to transfer resources away from defense.
- Were nationality unrest to threaten central control or the territorial integrity of the country, we see a risk that the leadership would revert to more hostile rhetoric and policies toward the West in an attempt to reunify the country.

Gorbachev's removal—unlikely but not to be ruled out—would have a significant impact:

- A more orthodox regime would slow the pace of change, be more supportive of military interests and leftist allies abroad, and eschew unilateral arms control concessions.
- We see little chance that a successor leadership would completely roll back Gorbachev's policies or revert to a major military buildup and aggressive policies in the Third World.

DISAGREEMENTS

There is general agreement in the Intelligence Community over the outlook for the next five to seven years, but differing views over the *longer term* prospects for fundamental and enduring change toward less competitive Soviet behavior:

- Some analysts see current policy changes as largely tactical, driven by the need for breathing space from the competition. They believe the ideological imperatives of Marxism-Leninism and its hostility toward capitalist countries are enduring. They point to the previous failures of reform and the transient nature of past "detentes." They judge that there is a serious risk of Moscow returning to traditionally combative behavior when the hoped for gains in economic performance are achieved.

• Other analysts believe Gorbachev's policies reflect a fundamental rethinking of national interests and ideology as well as more tactical considerations. They argue that ideological tenets of Marxism-Leninism such as class conflict and capitalist-socialist enmity are being revised. They consider the withdrawal from Afghanistan and the shift toward tolerance of power sharing in Eastern Europe to be historic shifts in the Soviet definition of national interest. They judge that Gorbachev's changes are likely to have sufficient momentum to produce lasting shifts in Soviet behavior.

INDICATORS

As evidence of Moscow's progress over the next two to three years toward fulfilling the promise of more responsible behavior, we will be watching for:

• Soviet acceptance of real liberalization in Eastern Europe.
• Full implementation of announced force reductions.
• A substantial conversion in the defense industry to production for the civilian economy.

[*Source: Central Intelligence Agency:* At Cold War's End: US Intelligence on the Soviet Union and Eastern Europe, 1989–1991. *Ed: Benjamin B. Fischer, 1999.*]

Document No. 58: Session of the CC CPSU Politburo

April 20, 1989

Gorbachev was out of the country on April 9 when Soviet forces cracked down on pro-independence demonstrators in Tbilisi, Georgia, killing at least 20 and drawing widespread condemnation. Eleven days later, this Politburo meeting is the first sustained high-level discussion of the still-murky affair. Gorbachev denounces the Georgian communist leadership who called in the troops for having "sat in a bunker and relied only on force." He turns directly to the head of the KGB, Vladimir Kryuchkov, to criticize the slanted intelligence given to the leadership, while Prime Minister Ryzhkov chimes in that "we, the people in the government, the Politburo members, knew nothing" and had to read about the deaths in Pravda.

The Tbilisi events become the center of debates when the new Congress of People's Deputies convenes in May; the Congress would appoint an investigating commission, and the acting head of the Politburo at the time of the massacre, Yegor Ligachev, would be pilloried on national television by the radical democrats and independence advocates. For his part, Ligachev would maintain he had been set up, and that Gorbachev had been aware of the order to use force, even though in the post-event debates Gorbachev would unequivocally side with the opponents of violence.

On a broader level, Tbilisi later becomes a watershed event that undermines the prestige of the Soviet military, delegitimizes the use of force against political movements in the USSR, reinforces Gorbachev's own commitment to nonviolent change, and leads to the erosion of state power based on fear of violence and repression. Yet, in April, the leadership's views appear to be considerably more guarded. Left with the final word in this version of the Politburo meeting, Defense Minister Dimitry Yazov (later a coup plotter in August 1991) advises grimly: "Still, the troops should not be moved far from Tbilisi."

Shevardnadze: In 1921 there was no revolutionary situation in Georgia. The 11th army just entered [the country]. From here stems the traditional attitude toward Kirov and Ordzhonikidze.[55]

Our version of the April 9 events was absolutely groundless. The crisis is in the manifestation of contradictions between the new situation and the old leadership methods. We should have prevented the use of the army. In general, the army should not be drawn into resolving internal political conflicts.

---

[55] Sergey Kirov (1886–1934) and Sergo Ordzhonikidze (1886–1937) were Bolshevik revolutionaries who played integral roles in establishing Soviet control over the Transcaucasus region, including Georgia, in 1921–1922.

Gorbachev: The crisis in Georgia was not a bolt out of the blue. The whole country suspected that something was brewing there. Eduard Amvrosievich [Shevardnadze] drew our attention to this many times. The Georgians and Ossetians have a fiery temper, they are not like the Armenians. [Georgian First Party Secretary Jumber] Patiashvili, as far as we know him, is not deaf to national interests but he shares with other comrades elements of panic-mongering, suspicion and, even more, reliance on force. He lacks the guts to conduct political work.

The Georgian leadership did not establish ties with the intelligentsia. And this is the Georgian (!) intelligentsia. It is historically deeply tied to the people. It is the carrier of Georgian national symbolism. Everything there—theater, film, music—everything carries a very strong national element, an underlying connection between the intelligentsia and the people. Had the intelligentsia been involved in due time in the process of change it would have responded sincerely and actively. But this was not done. Patiashvili has a taste for "decisive action."

I have long been saying—let us learn how to work under conditions of democracy. And now events confirm that. Our cadres regard political methods as a manifestation of weakness. Force—that is the real thing! In Georgia they could not transform themselves in the democratic way, to lead genuine advocates of *perestroika*, to listen to opponents, even to people with extreme views. Patiashvili is the man with whom I was most closely tied in the Georgian leadership, so it is difficult for me to give a full political and accurate analysis of what happened. And right now this is important for our work with the entire country.

The crisis in work methods is showing through in more than just relations with the intelligentsia. It is necessary to understand everything correctly in order to work not only with the intelligentsia, but with the entire country. Herein lies the source of what happened. It is very important to understand this for the sake of political analysis. Otherwise we will not find ways to consolidate the people in this time of change.

Regarding this, I would touch upon another theme: the information necessary for decision-making. When I receive ciphered telegrams, for instance, I immediately see the handwriting of the GRU or the KGB or any other ministry. When they analyze the situation in the Baltics, I can see right away what is true and what is packaged as truth. (He turns to [KGB head] Kryuchkov) Vladimir Aleksandrovich, I am looking at you! It is important to what extent one should attribute [nationalist] disturbances to trouble-making teenagers, and to what extent it is about the profound undercurrents in the nation.

From the point of view of information, let us look at the events in Tbilisi. I land in Moscow. At Vnukovo I am told that troops were brought into Tbilisi. What is this? Was it necessary? At that time in the airport I did not go to the heart of the matter, I did not question this decision. But right away I understood that something was about to happen. I was told that this was necessary to protect objectives, nothing more. Why was the curfew necessary? It was not necessary. The Georgian CC members should have walked out to the people. But as it turned out, they sat in a bunker and relied only on force. Only later did we begin to receive truthful information from Tbilisi. Perhaps someone from the KGB should have gone there to obtain information. In a word, if we don't have truthful and timely information, or objective data; we cannot make correct decisions. And in these matters one should think seven times, one hundred times, and only then make a decision and act.

Ryzhkov: We were in Moscow in those days, and what did we know? I am chairman of the government and what did I know? I read about the deaths of people in Tbilisi in *Pravda*. The CC secretaries knew [what happened]. And we, the people in the government, Politburo members, knew nothing. And why Shevardnadze's trip [to Georgia] was canceled I also do not know.

True, we in the Politburo should not panic. But we must have timely and truthful information. How could this have happened? The army was used against the people. The military district commander was acting there, and we in Moscow knew nothing about it. And if he comes and arrests the entire Georgian Politburo? Will we also learn about it in the newspapers? And, it turned out, Mikhail Sergeyevich [Gorbachev] also did not know. So what is actually going on here? Armed forces were used, and the general secretary learns about it only the next morning. How then do we appear before Soviet society, before the whole world? In general, wherever you turn, things go on without the Politburo knowing about them. This is even worse than if the Politburo had made bad decisions.

Gorbachev turns to *Yazov*: Dmitri Timofeyevich, from now on the army cannot take part in such actions without Politburo decisions.

Ryzhkov: Why is our government removed from such matters? Why are other members of the Politburo removed from them? By the way, the same [trend] came up during the elections in Moscow and Leningrad [...] they blame the general secretary; they say that he has split the country. They insist on a "firm hand." These are all serious matters. [...]

[*Source: Archive of the Gorbachev Foundation, Fond 2. Opis 2. On file at the National Security Archive. And:* The Union Could Have Been Preserved *(Moscow: April Publishers, 1995) Translated by Vladislav Zubok and Anna Melyakova.*]

Document No. 59: Diary of Anatoly Chernyaev regarding Gorbachev's State of Mind

May 2, 1989

After Tbilisi and the mixed results from the election for the Congress of People's Deputies, this diary entry reflects the feeling among Gorbachev's reform-minded assistants that perestroika *has lost its bearings and Gorbachev himself is beginning to feel deprived of political levers to control and steer the processes he himself unleashed. The reference to "velvet gloves" points to Gorbachev's rejection of the use of force in his policies. Chernyaev, along with Yakovlev and many others, believes that Gorbachev must break with the communist party altogether and build a new "democratic" authority and, along with it, political legitimacy for himself. Gorbachev's refusal to do so, in their opinion, leaves him caught in the middle and in danger of being outmaneuvered by the radical democrats who are rallying around Boris Yeltsin.*

Depression and alarm are growing within me, a sense of crisis for the Gorbachevian Idea. He is prepared to go far. But what does it mean? His favorite catchword is "unpredictability."

Most likely we will come to a collapse of the state and something like chaos. He feels that he is losing the levers of power irreversibly, and this realization prevents him from "going far." For that reason he is holding to conventional methods but acting with "velvet gloves." He has no concept of where we are going. His declarations about socialist values and the ideals of October, as he begins to tick them off, sound ironic to the cognoscenti. Beyond them is emptiness.

Now it is "socialist security." What is going on, when 22 million people have a salary of less than 60 rubles?! Etc. He is fighting off the demagogues who are breaking down "values" not aware (or maybe they are aware) that it will bring us to what we moved away from in 1917, i.e. to capitalism. But, really, we did not step away at all, or rather we stepped "into nowhere"; we ourselves do not know what kind of society we are living in.

[*Source: Anatoly Chernyaev's Diary, Manuscript. On file at the National Security Archive. Translated by Vladislav Zubok and Anna Melyakova.*]

Document No. 60: Session of the CC CPSU Politburo

May 11, 1989

The March elections in the Baltics are evidently yet another shock to members of Gorbachev's circle, such as Vadim Medvedev, who reports on their significance to the Politburo, below. Most of the elected deputies, he notes, "share a separatist and nationalist mood" and contrast the "interests of their individual nations to the interests of the Union as a whole." Yet in response Gorbachev argues, "[t]he Popular Fronts are supported by 90 percent of the population of the Republics, we cannot identify them with extremists. And we should learn how to talk with them..." This discussion demonstrates that by May 1989 the Soviet leadership is conscious of the real prospect of the disintegration of the Soviet Union. In comparison, developments in Eastern Europe—the dismantling of the barbed wire fences on the Austria–Hungary border, preparations for the Polish elections—occupy relatively little of Moscow's attention. Most important for the imminent events in Eastern Europe is Gorbachev's declaration that the use of military force "against people" in the Baltics or in foreign policy is "out of the question." This is a strong statement, particularly given the serious political problems Gorbachev is facing, and it is clearly connected to the disaster that has just unfolded in Tbilisi.

[...]

Medvedev: Formal data on the outcome of elections for USSR people's deputies in the Baltic republics (participation in elections, percentage of communists among deputies, etc.) should not create illusions. Most of the elected deputies are members and active participants of Popular Fronts, they share a separatist and nationalist mood, and the Popular Fronts themselves ran as a force opposing the CPSU, opposing the interests of their individual nations to the interests of the Union as a whole. [...] The tactic of so-called flexible tacking [*lavirovaniie*] by the leadership of the Republics has so far been leading to continuous concessions, and negatively affecting the unity and combat-readiness of the party. [...] In the emerging situation, the party and state leaderships of the Republics need political will and determination to fulfill the course of the CPSU towards the renewal and consolidation of socialism. At the same time the Republican leadership badly needs our assistance and moral-political support. [...]

Gorbachev: We should look into the roots of the situation. Without [understanding] them we will not figure it out. Within the framework of *perestroika* there is a stormy process of growing national self-consciousness in those Republics. And a very serious issue arises about a more modern and complete interpretation of the notion of "sovereignty." This is a real issue. When a population has an intelligentsia, it digs into history and bares its roots. By itself this is a rich process. But it has negative repercussions. [...]

The roots of the situation are in the specifics of history, in particular the history of the 1930–1940s. And this requires a precise ideological characterization. But we are lagging behind. Meanwhile more and more armfuls of wood are being thrown onto the fire. And we are not providing answers to the people.

Perestroika has demonstrated how many distortions had accumulated in everything—in culture, in language, in our productive forces. Earlier we could somehow muddle through, but now we will not. And force does not help in this business. We have accepted that even in foreign policy force accomplishes nothing. But internally especially—we cannot and will not resort to force. [...]

The leaders of the communist parties of Latvia, Lithuania, Estonia who were present at the Politburo meeting, left at this point.

We trust all three of them, there is no question about that. [...] Well, our comrades are at the end of their patience! Omissions were made during the stage when their predecessors ruled. Let us consider that not everything is lost. And we should be careful in our assessments so as not to push them into despair [or] into an open break.

Voices from the Politburo members: Maybe we should really agree to hold referendums in these Republics? None of them will secede. [...]

Gorbachev concludes: The Popular Fronts are supported by 90 percent of the population of the Republics, we cannot identify them with extremists. And we should learn how to talk with them. [...] Trust in the people's common sense. [...] Do not be afraid of experiments with full economic self-accounting in the Republics. [...] Do not be afraid of differentiating among the Republics according to the level of sovereignty that is practiced. [...] And in general: think, think how in practice to transform our federation. Otherwise everything will really collapse. [...] The use of force is out of the question. We have excluded it from our foreign policy, but especially against our people it is out of the question. [...]"

[*Source: Archive of the Gorbachev Foundation, Fond 4. Opis 1. On file at the National Security Archive. Translated by Vladislav Zubok.*]

Document No. 61: Transcript of CC PUWP Secretariat Meeting

June 5, 1989

On the day after Solidarity's sweep of Poland's first open elections since communist rule, ultimately netting the union 99 of 100 Senate seats, the Polish party leaders vent their shock and dismay in this transcript from the Polish archives, opened in the 1990s. The Secretariat's members rant that this has been "a bitter lesson," "the aktiv and the party are not connected with the masses," "[w]e trusted the Church, and they have turned out to be Jesuits," and "50 percent of our party now consists of all sorts of managers and retirees" who were unable to show any "self-protective instinct in the elections." Aleksander Kwaśniewski (who would later be elected president of Poland in the 1990s as the country joined NATO) remarks that even "party members were crossing out our candidates" on the ballots. (In fact, only two of 35 party candidates survived the epidemic of X's).

Like Gorbachev, the Polish communists have no idea of the degree to which the "System" has already lost its legitimacy. Also like Gorbachev, they believe they can still enact reforms and frame a modified arrangement with the opposition in which the party would retain the leading role. But the whole edifice is coming down around them, and even in their current state of shock these Polish officials understand there is no choice but to negotiate a coalition government, and they specifically "[w]arn against attempts at destabilization, pointing at the situation in China." By contrast, on the same day as the Polish elections, the Chinese Communist Party ordered the army to crush the popular demonstrations that took place on Tiananmen Square in Beijing—in effect, choosing the methods of 1956 and 1968. For Gorbachev and the Poles in 1989, that brutal approach was the road not taken.

The Agenda:

An exchange of views on the first round of elections to the Sejm and Senate.

Cde. W. Jaruzelski stated at the beginning that the election results are very bad for the coalition. What should be done right away in the next few days?

- In today's TV newscast, a statement preceding the official election results—decide who will speak;
- Today, a meeting with the allies;
- June 6, hold a Politburo meeting and a conference with first secretaries of the Voivodeship committees;
- Consider different dates for a CC meeting (in an extraordinary procedure before June 18, after June 18), adopt a decision at the Politburo, set dates for consultations with CC members;
- Get in touch and hold talks with the Church hierarchy, consider a meeting with Primate J. Glemp. The Church is the major culprit in the situation that has arisen;

- Hold informational meetings with ambassadors accredited to Warsaw;
- Consider the advisability of going ahead or postponing the planned visits of the chairman of the Council of State to London and Brussels and President Mitterrand's visit to Poland.

Cde. Czarzasty said an analysis of the election shows that they had the character of a plebiscite, a referendum, which we had not been assuming. So far full results of voting for the national list are not available.

The Voivodeship committees are signaling that the clergy, particularly on election day, were issuing calls to vote for "S". Youth participation in the election was very low.

Cde. J. Czyrek assessed that electoral assumptions could not be met. The personal formula turned out to be ineffective. The result has been decided in the first round. The opposition is not interested in the second round. Forecasts of election turnouts also were not on target. The coalition side, the party itself, has proven ineffective in its campaigning and propaganda effort. The majority of voters decided beforehand whom to vote for.

Now the most important thing is to master moods in the party and in the entire coalition. The allies are uneasy, "Solidarity" has already shown support for some of their candidates and it can still do it in the second round.

Urgently establish contacts with the Church, but also with the leadership of the opposition (decide on the forms and levels). Urgently hold a meeting of the Commission on Understanding.

Undertake visits to London and Belgium, but postpone Mitterrand's visit to our country.

Cde. S. Ciosek: Today someone from the leadership or Cde. Urban should appear on television. He is signaling a mood of depression among the engaged journalists.

Cde. Cz. Kiszczak: The adversary has been fighting intensively from beginning to end, using different means. We have been acting with "white gloves," without taking advantage of even obvious opportunities. Election results have exceeded the opposition's expectations. They are shocked and don't know how to behave. Elections to the Senate are a total disaster for us. The general had warned, we were saying that 65 percent of the mandates in the Sejm would not provide sufficient protection for the coalition since it is known that "S" stands behind some of our candidates (e.g. [Tadeusz] Fiszbach in Gdansk). This is true not only of party members, but also of the SD [Democratic Party] and ZSL [United People's Party]. This needs to be taken into consideration. [...]

Cde. Kiszczak acknowledged that the visits planned earlier should be undertaken.

Cde. F. Siwicki explained that in all closed military districts the military (not the staff) voted on average 52–62 percent for the national list. Cde. Kiszczak added that similar indicators, or even higher, up to 70–72 percent, held for the Vistula units, WOP and ZOMO.[56]

Cde. J. Urban was of the opinion that there should be a statement on the television news in the nature of a commentary and not a communiqué from the Secretariat meeting, which can be given separately. The statement should emphasize that independent of the results we are for accepting a broad reform coalition, and that all extreme measures would be dangerous.

Geremek stated at a press conference that they are not interested in a coalition with the present system of government.

Cde. J. Czyrek: A statement on TV should be agreed on with the allies and made on behalf of the coalition. Cde. Reykowski shared this point of view. He thought that in that statement it should be pointed out that the elections were democratic in preparation and implementation. Our electorate amounts to about 30 percent, which proves that we are not altogether in isolation. Warn the opposition against the possibility of destabilization under the influence of success.

Cde. W. Baka proposed emphasizing in the statement that we had taken into account the unfavorable result. We are consistent, we have no other alternative. Warn against attempts at destabilization, pointing to the situation in China.

Hold the XIII CC plenary meeting at the turn of June and July and present the party's strategy there.

Cde. W. Jaruzelski: Urgently prepare who is going to appear on TV today. Perhaps spokesmen from the PUWP, ZSL and SD. Perhaps Cde. Urban or Cde. Reykowski.

Cde. A. Kwaśniewski emphasized that an extremely important matter after announcing the election results is to prevent spontaneous demonstrations, which neither side might be able to control. The opposition is also afraid of this. Get in touch with "S", so that any appearances will be peaceful and without triumphalism.

Cde. J. Urban proposed that Cde. Kiszczak should appear on TV as a host of the "Roundtable."

Cde. Kiszczak suggested that Cde. Urban might appear and that on this matter it is appropriate to consult with Onyszkiewicz.

Cde. M.F. Rakowski: Cde. Kwaśniewski might also appear as chairman of the Socio-Political Committee of the Council of Ministers, or Cde. J. Bisztyga as a press spokesman of the CC PUWP.

Cde. A. Gdula: It is enough if Cde. Bisztyga appears. He informed that Kuroń in a telephone conversation had expressed concern about the central list. He mentioned that it would be advisable to convene the Commission on Understanding. He stressed the need to secure peace.

---

[56] WOP (*Wojska Ochrony Pogranicza*) was the Border Defense Guard. ZOMO (*Zmotoryzowane Odwody Milicji Obywatelskiej*), the Mechanized Detachments of Citizens' Police, was the security force relied upon to impose martial law in December 1981.

Cde. W. Jaruzelski: We don't know how the Solidarity base will behave. Consider a simultaneous speech by spokesmen for the PUWP, ZSL and SD.

Cde. K. Barcikowski thinks that from the "S" side there will be high-level spokesmen, so he proposes Cdes. Kwaśniewski or Urban from our side.

Cde. J. Bisztyga: We can propose to Onyszkiewicz that he appear with me, or with the participation of spokesmen for the ZSL and SD.

Cde. Cz. Kiszczak: Present them with three variants: Cde. Kwaśniewski, Cde. Urban or Cde. Bisztyga with colleagues from the coalition.

Cde. Kwaśniewski thought that if Onyszkiewicz's name comes up from the "S" side, then J. Bisztyga should appear from our side. The most important matter are talks with "S" on joint efforts to prevent loose public feelings that neither side will be able to control. Let's not disregard the mood in small centers and in very modern plants.

He thought it advisable to hold an urgent meeting of the prime minister with the head of Solidarity.

Cde. Z. Sobotka: He favors a TV appearance by Cde. Kwaśniewski.

Cde. J. Bisztyga: Some youth groups may behave as after a victorious match. No appearance is going to silence euphoria. It would be good if Cde. Kwaśniewski would appear.

Cde. S. Ciosek: It would be best if Bisztyga and Onyszkiewicz would appear simultaneously. Inform our allies of this and obtain their authorization.

Cde. M.F. Rakowski recognized that a plenary meeting should be called urgently, this week. Election results and in particular the results of voting for the national list will hit the party hard. Consider how we are going to react to the loss of the party and state leadership. What might be the consequences of this defeat?

Talks with the opposition are necessary. My meeting with Wałęsa should be considered. Geremek is talking about a change in the system of exercising power.

Cde. J. Reykowski: Absolutely hold talks between the party leadership and the OPZZ. Geremek mentioned in a conversation that they would be willing to enter into the Presidential Council with people from the national list (he said so before the elections). If it is possible from the legal point of view, negotiate with the opposition to turn to the Supreme Court to introduce an amendment to the electoral law, which would enable candidates from the national list to run in the second round.

Cde. J. Kubasiewicz: Hold talks with the opposition on the national list. Take into consideration that in the second round the opposition may support some candidates from our mandates.

Cde. J. Czyrek: A discussion was held with Kuroń about how to resolve the situation if candidates from the national list do not get elected. Then, based on a legal act, those 35 candidates would run again within that 65 percent pool.

Cde. K. Barcikowski: The main argument is a political agreement on the distribution of mandates. There is no possibility of repeating the national list in the second round because if they fail again it is going to result in total discredit.

Cde. A. Kwaśniewski: Repetition of the national list in the second round is unacceptable. It was crossed out by our people as well. There is no guarantee it would pass [a second time]. We need to agree with the opposition that within the 65 percent pool we will transfer one mandate to each electoral district. This is the only chance. The national list was a mistake and it should not be repeated. An important matter is to analyze who did not participate in the elections and by what motives they were guided. Is this a passive resistance? It is well known that party members were also crossing out our candidates.

The plenary meeting should be called quickly. Consider convening a party congress.

Cde. Cz. Kiszczak: An important and urgent matter is to ensure participation in the second round. Hold the plenary meeting later.

Cde. J. Kubasiewicz: In the first place hold consultations with CC members, then the plenum.

Cde. A. Gdula: Hold consultations with CC members very soon and the plenary meeting towards the end of the month. Present a penetrating assessment of the domestic situation and motions for party work.

There is little we can do about the national list. We cannot annul the elections. It is possible for the new Sejm to adopt an amendment to the electoral law and hold new elections, or issue a statement that the Sejm has 425 deputies. Also examine whether it might be possible to make a new distribution of mandates on the basis of an understanding between the parties.

Cde. L. Miller expressed anxiety over the condition of the party. A segment of it did not support its own candidates. In the second round participation may be weak. Also our trade unions and social organizations did not support us. We have to keep in mind that as triumphalism within the opposition rises, frustration in the party will be rising too. Any effort which we put into the campaign will be disproportional to the results.

Cde. J. Urban: Do not renew the national list since we would ridicule ourselves before our own base. Negotiate with the opposition over supplemental elections and the composition of the Sejm defined in the Constitution. The opposition should accept this proposal. Start these talks right away. An example of a part of the apparatus (party, state) voting for "S" can be found in the results in Ulaanbaatar, Pyongyang and Tirana. He recognized that meetings of the party leadership with the military circles, security apparatus and the mass media are urgently needed to calm moods and present further perspectives.

The CC plenum should be held soon despite some risk. Postponing it would be evidence of paralysis in the party structures, of a crisis. The election results prove that the party in its present form has outlived itself. It needs an innovative political, ideological and organizational concept, otherwise there will be disintegration.

Cde. Cz. Kiszczak: We are faced with the campaign to elect a president. Examine whether the plenum could help or hurt us in this. It is worth pondering this, it is very important.

456

Cde. Z. Michałek: The election result represents a crisis of confidence in us. Initiate talks with the opposition to save the names on the national list. Hold consultations with CC members soon. Postpone the plenum. Define the tasks for party members in the second round of elections. Conduct an efficiency assessment of the regional apparatus on the basis of the election campaign.

Cde. M. Stepień: Postpone discussion on the reasons for the present situation till another time. Today the most important question is to master the moods in the party through direct contact by the leadership. He proposed that the Politburo turn to all party members with a letter announcing a plenum and a congress.

Cde. E. Szymański: Negotiate with the opposition a legal procedure which would enable candidates from the national list to run in the second round of elections.

Cde. I. Sekuła: The election results prove that society wants changes. The party has initiated the process of changing, but is conducting it very slowly, not radically. We have not fulfilled expectations; that is why "S" has won.

Cde. Z. Czarzasty: We need to strive for a renewed vote for the national list, with different names, through a decree by the Council of State.

At the plenary meeting talk about a congress (towards year's end or March 1990), initiate discussion on a program, a statute, the name of the party, a vision for changes.

Cde. A. Kwaśniewski: A plenum within a short period is necessary. Losing the national list is putting the party leadership in a dramatic position. Urgently resume negotiations with the opposition relating to the national list, the president, and the government. Hold talks on these matters with the Church. Set the date for the plenum and for talks about a congress only after negotiating and working out a position on these major questions.

Cde. B. Kołodziejczak: We cannot convene the plenum without having a position on the president and the government, and an assessment of the situation. If the plenum is going to be prepared as the election campaign was, its result can be predicted. We have to draw conclusions based on the mistakes we made. Present a comprehensive analysis to CC members of the reasons for the situation that has arisen. Talks with the opposition regarding a president must be conducted reliably.

Cde. F. Siwicki: Convene a plenum once we have a thorough analysis of the reasons [for the defeat] and a concept of the functioning of the state within a new configuration of political forces. Urgently resume consultations with the opposition on the selection of a national list by a simple majority of votes. Start an evaluation of the situation within basic party cells. Come to terms with the youth organizations regarding their participation in the election campaign, with conclusions. The most urgent questions are consultations with the opposition regarding the national list, the government, and the president.

Cde. J. Reykowski: The party turned out to be weak. What has happened is the result of a joint mistake in assessing the situation. Now the most important thing is the security of the state and the president.

Cde. Z. Sobotka: Turn very urgently to party members. The triumphing [sic] of "S" has already started. Soon pressure will mount to remove the party from the workplaces. Let's not count too much on an understanding with the opposition. They have already got what they wanted and are not interested in the second round. Let's not create a plenum without preparing for it. Lately we have not been seeking their advice on important decisions. Urgently hold consultations with CC members, then hold the plenum at a later date.

Cde. S. Ciosek: I don't understand the reasons for the defeat. The party has to pay for it, it didn't follow us. It is a bitter lesson. Those responsible will have to bear the consequences. Now the most important question is the election of the president, for which we need 35 mandates—which were lost. On this we need to talk with the opposition, as the president is the protection for the entire system; it is not only our internal matter, it is a matter for the whole socialist commonwealth, even for Europe. On this matter seek urgent talks with the opposition (Commission on Understanding) and with the Church. The guilt belongs to us. We trusted the Church, and they have turned out to be Jesuits. We overestimated our possibilities and have turned out to be deprived of the base. We have to keep in mind that very soon various claims and pressures will be rising like an avalanche—e.g. against the mass media. Radical changes must take place in the party.

Cde. Z. Michałek: What does that mean—radical changes in the party?

Cde. M.F. Rakowski: We had a false assessment of the situation. The first secretaries of the Voivodeship committees estimated our chances better. And the conclusion is that the perception of moods, of what people think, is weak, that the *aktiv* and the party are not connected with the masses. We cannot use the thesis that the party has not backed us up. That is false. The fact is that the party has not proved to be a mobile force. There was a lack of awareness that crossing out their own people would cause self-destruction.

There is a fear that there may be strikes, wage pressures, and demonstrations which will complicate the economic situation even more.

One may agree with the notion that the plenum should not be held right now. But one needs to be aware that the party in its present structure is not in a position to stand up to current challenges. At the X plenum of the CC we proposed another model for the party, but this has not been noticed. And we need to go even further.

Talks with the opposition are necessary. It has proven to be trustworthy. It has called all along for crossing out the national list. What has happened in Poland is going to have a tremendous impact abroad (USSR, Hungary, other countries). This may lead to upheavals in the whole camp; we have to make our society aware of this. We need to draw all conclusions from the fact that a considerable part of society said "no".

Cde. K. Barcikowski: In the analyses point out the reasons for the relatively low election turnout. Who are those who did not vote, how were they motivated? In part they were also party members. One of the reasons was the personal formula of the elections.

458

Do we now have the right to take offense at the party? We have been managing it for the past 10 years. To whom should we then direct our claims? The same relates to the youth and social organizations. Examine this matter quietly, draw conclusions, ponder what to do to regain trust and how to do it. What should we expect from the opposition now? They will make an assault on the national councils and on territorial self-government. Urgently seek talks on the question of the 35 mandates, the president and the government. They are also afraid of power disintegrating.

Cde. W. Jaruzelski suggested adopting the following findings:

- On June 6 hold a Politburo meeting, and in the afternoon a conference with the first secretaries of the Voivodeship committees and division heads of the CC, jointly with the Politburo
- Urgently seek talks with the opposition leadership, including a meeting of the prime minister with Wałęsa
- Urgently hold a meeting of the Commission on Understanding of the "Roundtable"
- Hold talks with the Church (*modo privato*), possibly a meeting with Primate Glemp
- Set the date for the XIII plenum in consultation with the first secretaries of the Voivodeship committees
- Submit for decision by the Politburo and consultations with the first secretaries of the Voivodeship committees the matters of visits to Belgium and England and a visit by President Mitterrand to Poland
- Send a Politburo letter to all party members (submit the draft to the first secretaries of the Voivodeship committees).

Fifty percent of our party now consists of all sorts of managers and retirees. Therefore it must be disquieting that just such a party (clerical) has not shown a self-protective instinct in the elections. This problem needs to be worked out in particular, and conclusions drawn. A considerable portion of the party consists of state administration and employees of the justice system. How can we reach them? (Quickly staff vacant positions on the Supreme Court—Cde. Gdula). Think about what to do to lift the spirits of the people engaged on our side and working in the mass media to convince them that they are not lost. Hold meetings with those groups at the central level (W. Jaruzelski, M. Rakowski) and in the regions.

Cdes. Reykowski, Stepień, Czarzasty, Tabkowski will prepare a draft letter tomorrow from the Politburo to party members (encl. No. 1). [Omitted]

[*Source: PUWP Secretariat files, copies obtained by the Institute for Political Studies, Polish Academy of Sciences; published in* Tajne dokumenty: Biura Politycznego i Sekretariatu KC, Ostatni rok wladzy 1988–1989 *(London: Aneks Publishers, 1994) pp. 390–398] Translated by Dr. Jan Chowaniec.*]

Document No. 62: Record of Conversation between Erich Honecker and Eduard Shevardnadze

June 9, 1989

This is one of many documents that became available in the party archives of the former German Democratic Republic after the fall of the Berlin Wall. The hardline leader of the GDR, Erich Honecker, at this time is surpassed only by Ceauşescu of Romania in his resistance to perestroika *and to the new thinking in Moscow represented in this meeting by Shevardnadze. Honecker has even banned a number of Soviet publications from distribution in the GDR. The conversation below reveals Honecker's ideological concerns, but also his understanding of the geostrategic realities in Central Europe. He reminds Shevardnadze that "socialism cannot be lost in Poland" because that country controls communications between the USSR and the Soviet troops stationed in the GDR that are facing NATO's divisions. This is the same consideration that led Honecker and his predecessor, Walter Ulbricht, to urge Soviet military intervention as a means to suppress previous Eastern European uprisings such as in Poland in 1980–81. But Honecker here is most dismayed by Gorbachev's upcoming trip to West Germany, which threatens Honecker's "balancing" act, which in turn depends on poor relations between the USSR and the FRG. Shevardnadze has an impossible mission: to assuage the East German's concerns about developments in Poland, Hungary and inside the Soviet Union. His words—"our friends in the GDR need not worry"—sound more than ironic today. He not only does not believe his own statement, he does not believe in the entire concept of East German "socialism."*

Shevardnadze: Our friends in the GDR need not worry. The party will remain the leading force in society. It exercises control over all-important processes despite great difficulties. The most important decisions, which the Politburo or the Central Committee has put before the Congress, are meeting with the consent of the Congress. Developments at the Congress are being followed very attentively. In the opening days, ambitious and demagogic speeches received support. As the Congress has proceeded, the ability of the deputies to differentiate between the truth, lies and demagoguery has grown.

A similar learning process is taking place among the people as well. In the beginning there were threats of strikes in case certain representatives were not elected to the Supreme Soviet. The publishing of everything from the Congress has proven to be correct. The CPSU must in the future adapt itself in its style of work to the new conditions.

Altogether one may be content with the results of the People's Congress. The Party has passed a difficult test. Henceforth the task is to solve urgent sociopolitical matters.

Here the Soviet Union can learn much from the GDR. A compelling example of this was the most recent exhibition in Moscow on "Berlin Days," in which the mastery of social problems was vividly shown. Millions of Soviet citizens live in poverty. Twenty million pensioners receive less than 70 rubles a month. In spite of great financial difficulties the Congress decided to raise the minimum pension to 80 rubles, for which the State must spend a total of 4 to 5 billion rubles per year. This is happening [despite] awareness of the fact that buying power has already considerably exceeded the supply of goods as it is. A further task of greater political importance is to increase the production of consumer goods. In addition it is necessary to solve the housing issue. The GDR has focused on this correctly and in a timely manner. A third difficulty is the extremely complicated national question. An assessment which found earlier that the national question had been solved forever was a big mistake. These problems existed long ago and have built up over the years. During the course of democratization, they have been revealed. Special problems exist in the Caucasus, in the Baltic republics, and recently in Uzbekistan as well.

One cannot be sure whether tomorrow will witness new conflicts erupting in other regions. The party requires a new nationalities policy. In this respect, the CPSU is preparing itself for a corresponding plenary session. The writing of a new constitution is also a pressing matter.

It is known that our friends in the GDR are well informed on the developments in the GDR, and are compassionate. Your valuable support would be highly appreciated in the Soviet Union.

Comrade Eduard Shevardnadze stated that Comrade Yakovlev will be received on Saturday by Comrade Czyrek, at the request of Comrade Jaruzelski, to receive information on domestic developments in Poland. At the moment it is still difficult to guess how the situation in Poland will continue to unfold. The most recent events are having serious consequences.[57] A profound analysis is necessary. It should be taken into account that Solidarity represents a genuine force. The PUWP must accept a real defeat and finds itself in a very difficult position. In Hungary as well, an unsettling development is taking place.

Comrade Erich Honecker emphasized that he shares fully the evaluation made of Poland. At a meeting with Comrade Jaruzelski, [Jaruzelski] still gave an optimistic evaluation of the expected election results, although defeat was already becoming apparent.[58]

It is well known that Poland lies between the GDR and the USSR. Socialism cannot be lost in Poland.

In Hungary the processes are most probably unstoppable. Many Hungarian comrades fear that in connection with the planned reburial of the prime minister

---

[57] A reference to the June 4 national elections in Poland.
[58] The discussion between Honecker and Jaruzelski took place on May 22, 1989, in Berlin.

from 1956, [Imre] Nagy, counterrevolution will break out again.[59] What Pozsgay proclaimed has nothing at all to do with socialism.[60] The question is whether it is possible to prevent a split within the Hungarian working class. If not, Hungary will slip further into the bourgeois camp. Comrade Erich Honecker remarked that he remembers quite well the events of 1956 and the role Imre Nagy played.

[*Source: Stiftung Archiv der Parteien und Massenorganisationen der DDR-Bundesarchiv, SED, ZK, JIV2/2A/3225. Translated by Christiaan Hetzner.*]

---

[59] Nagy, who had been executed in 1958, was ceremonially reburied on June 16, 1989.
[60] Pozsgay, in one instance, had appeared on West German television in early June and described the Prague Spring as a reform attempt whose outcome had yet to be determined.

Document No. 63: Record of Conversation between Mikhail Gorbachev and Helmut Kohl

June 12, 1989

In June 1989, Gorbachev travels to West Germany in pursuit of his foreign policy strategy of building the "common European home," and to satisfy concerns over the "pause" in U.S.–Soviet relations. The ensuing "Gorbymania" among West Germans marks the peak of Gorbachev's popularity in the West and evokes serious apprehensions in the Bush administration. However, as this document reveals, Gorbachev badly wants to resume the dialogue with the U.S. president, whom he really does not understand—"where is Bush genuine, and where is Bush rhetorical?" Gorbachev has already been talking with the key European leaders—Thatcher, Mitterrand, Kohl—but it would not be until December at Malta that he would come face-to-face with Bush.

In particular, during this visit Gorbachev is seeking an understanding with the Western countries that no-one should take advantage of Solidarity's victory in Poland. His clear rejection of the "Brezhnev doctrine" in his talks with Kohl follows the two leaders' tacit understanding that both sides would steer clear of developments in Poland, Hungary and other Eastern European countries. ("[Y]ou should not poke a stick into an anthill. The consequences of such an act could be absolutely unpredictable.") Only a few weeks later, speaking to the Council of Europe in Strasbourg on July 6 (see Document No. 73), Gorbachev would make the rejection of force even more public.

We can also see in these notes precisely the kind of development Honecker was so concerned about, as Gorbachev and Kohl agree to establish a backchannel involving Kohl's assistant Horst Teltschik and Anatoly Chernyaev. By this time, for Gorbachev, relations with West Germany have taken priority over relations with the East.

Kohl: [...] I have known George Bush for a long time, we have a very good, friendly relationship. In evaluating him as president, after just several months on the job, we have to take into account his previous career.

George Bush was vice president under President Reagan for eight years. He was always a loyal person. In this respect we probably have a common point of view; we perceive such qualities as positive. However, for George Bush personally, such an assessment had a negative aspect, hurt him, because everybody was constantly asking whether he would be able to emerge from Reagan's shadow and acquire his own political face, or whether he would always remain in a position of loyalty.

In terms of public relations, Bush has a long way to go to compete with Reagan: he has neither the actor's charisma, nor the art to communicate with people via TV, nor any other similar qualities. He is an intellectual. In America they distinguish between people from the West coast and from the East coast. People from California are very different from people from the Western [sic: Eastern] United States.

In this sense Bush, as a politician, is very important for Europe—he has a more European vision of things than Reagan had. By the way, Reagan, as a politician, grew literally before my eyes; I have known him since 1979 when he still was the leader of the opposition. One time he came to Bonn, I received him, and we talked for three hours. Helmut Schmidt, who was chancellor then, did not receive him, stating that he did not have time. I had a depressing impression from that conversation with Reagan. It became clear that he did not understand anything in European affairs. My assistant, [Horst] Teltschik, was present at that conversation, and he can tell you even now how discouraged we were then. But later Reagan became president, and you, Mr. Gorbachev, were able to find a common language with him.

Bush is a completely different person. Do not forget that he inherited a difficult domestic political situation, above all in terms of the economy. Now the ghost of the united European market, which will be created in 1992, is knocking at the U.S. door. Japanese entrepreneurs are working in the United States, and they are capturing new positions all the time. The living standards of the U.S. population, above all those of the disadvantaged strata, continue to stagnate.

Recently I had a chance to see it with my own eyes. Last week I flew to America on a personal, unofficial trip, to visit my son, who took exams at Harvard University. I spoke with students and with professors—and I did not hear any positive assessments from anybody of how the American people now live. Bush has an overwhelming load of things to do in the social sphere, which could become his Achilles' heel. At the same time, in Congress his situation is more favorable than Reagan's was. I would say that dramatic changes have happened there. The current leader of Congress, [Rep.] Tom Foley [D-Wash.], represents a politician of a quiet, non-aggressive type. He is oriented toward cooperation, not confrontation. He wants to build positive political capital for himself, so that in the future he might become a presidential candidate for the Democrats. In short, it is important to follow American domestic developments, and to account for them in formulating your own political line. [...]

Gorbachev: I had many meetings with Bush, including personal meetings. Last time we talked in [New York City in] December of last year, when he had already been elected president. We agreed confidentially that we would develop Soviet–American relations on the basis of the following formula: continuity, plus what we should supplement it with. There are a lot of sensitive issues in our relations, which is why it is important to improve trust between Moscow and Washington. So far, I have not noticed any significant deviations from the agreement on Bush's part. However, as I have already mentioned, his last speeches gave us grounds for concern.

Kohl: Are you talking about his statements on arms control? What speeches do you have in mind?

464

Gorbachev: The speech at the University of Texas on May 12, and the speech at the Coast Guard Academy [May 24]. Also, he made quite unpleasant statements concerning Eastern Europe and the Soviet Union at the [March 6] "Veterans of Foreign Wars" conference before Americans of Polish origin, and so on. This is what comes to mind. However, there were other statements of this kind in recent months, too. I don't see either realism or a constructive line in those statements. Frankly speaking, those remarks reminded us of Reagan's statements about the "crusade" against socialism. He appealed to the forces of freedom, called for an end to the "status quo," and for "pushing socialism back." And all this at a time when we are calling for de-ideologization of relations. Reluctantly, the questions come to mind—where is Bush genuine, and where is Bush rhetorical? Where does he just play up the rhetoric, and where does he lay down the state line?

Kohl: We will wait and see. I am convinced that everything will take its course, and with good speed. There will be progress in disarmament also. Here everything depends on the two great powers.

If we can achieve decisive progress in Vienna in the next 12–15 months, it will change the situation on all arms control issues in a crucial way. Now there are no taboos or irresolvable problems any more.

[...] We are watching developments in Hungary with great interest. The United States, and of course you, Mr. General Secretary, are following them too. I told Bush that as far as Hungary is concerned, we are acting on the basis of an old German proverb: let the church remain in the village. It means that the Hungarians should decide themselves what they want, but nobody should interfere in their affairs.

Gorbachev: We have a similar proverb: do not go to another monastery with your own charter.

Kohl: Beautiful folk wisdom. Both sides share it. And if so, there can be no talk of "crusades."

Gorbachev: I am telling you honestly—there are serious shifts underway in the socialist countries. Their direction originates from concrete situations in each country. The West should not be concerned about it. Everything is moving in the direction of a strengthening of democratic foundations. Every country is deciding on its own how to do it. It is their internal affair. I think you would agree with me that you should not poke a stick into an anthill. The consequences of such an act could be absolutely unpredictable.

Kohl: There is an opinion on one side, there is an opinion on another side, but there is also a third opinion—a common opinion. This is the common opinion of the Soviet Union, of the United States, of the FRG, and of other countries. In short, we should not interfere with anybody's development.

Gorbachev: The situation is very tense in a number of countries. If someone were to try to destabilize that situation, it would disrupt the process of building trust between West and East, and destroy everything that has been achieved so far. We want a rapprochement, not a return to the attitudes of confrontation. [...]

Kohl: However, it is no secret to anybody that Erich Honecker is not inclined to undertake any changes or reforms, and thus he himself destabilizes the situation.

I have problems because of that in the FRG. I say all the time that I am not interested in destabilizing the situation in the GDR. However, the people ask me all the time, why does the GDR remain frozen in its positions? I am told that we should do something in order to let the people there experience the same freedom that now characterizes Hungary, Poland, and, of course, the Soviet Union,

You cannot imagine what was going on here when the GDR banned distribution of the Soviet magazine *Sputnik*. Everybody laughed. But I did not, because they demanded that I, as chancellor, take new steps to improve relations with the GDR, and I could not do anything about it.

Gorbachev: As far as our friends are concerned, we have a firm principle: everyone is responsible for his own country. We are not going to teach anyone, but we are not asking anyone to teach us either. I think that what I have just said makes it clear whether there is a "Brezhnev Doctrine." We are in favor of positive changes in all spheres, in favor of political normalization, and strengthening the economy. But at the same time we are also in favor of preserving the special features and traditions of the socialist states. [...]

Kohl: I support your ideas. To tell you honestly, we understand Moscow much better, and we feel much closer to it than to [East] Berlin now. Ninety percent of the population in the GDR watches our television. They are informed about everything but are afraid to speak publicly. I just feel sorry for the people. But let me reiterate that I am not doing anything to destabilize the situation. This applies to Hungary and Poland as well. To interfere with anyone's internal political development now would mean taking a destructive line which would throw Europe back to the times of caution and mistrust.

Gorbachev: That is a very important statement. It fits the spirit of the times.

Kohl: [...] As far as conventional weapons are concerned, the key to that issue is in your hands. We have a real opportunity to reach an agreement—and in a fundamental sense—on conventional weapons in the next 12, or if not, then in the next 14–15 months: An agreement on conventional weapons would put the entire arms control agenda on a qualitatively new level. I will be one of those who makes a clear and sound statement about that.

I would like to propose to you, Mr. General Secretary, that in the next several months we should stay in direct contact—not via departments—on the issues of negotiations in Vienna. And in general, I believe that we should intensify our contacts, call each other more often, even if there is no concrete business to discuss. If we talk regularly, hear each other's voices, all problems will be easier to solve.

As far as special representatives are concerned, as I have already told you, I will send my closest assistant, Teltschik, who is present here. And you can send Chernyaev to me.

Gorbachev: I agree.

466

Kohl: We are not exaggerating our role, but we are not underestimating it either. Others will listen to our opinion more and more. I can already feel it.

Gorbachev: We need to cooperate more closely, because our cooperation can produce very effective impulses and lead to positive changes on still-unresolved issues.

[*Source: Archive of the Gorbachev Foundation, Fond 1. Opis 1. On file at the National Security Archive. Translated by Svetlana Savranskaya.*]

Document No. 64: Record of Conversation between Mikhail Gorbachev and Richard von Weizsäcker

June 12, 1989

This conversation between Gorbachev and West German head of state Richard von Weizsäcker demonstrates the FRG's role as intermediary, bridge, and messenger between the superpowers. The country's leaders were eager to see the two sides engaged and talking. Weizsäcker comments that the atmosphere in the United States is much less conservative than it was even three months earlier. Gorbachev expresses his frustration with the Bush administration's "pause", which he sees as yet another "characteristic" of the U.S. approach—to wait for the USSR's "difficulties" to force movement "toward more concessionary positions" rather than engage directly with Moscow. However, we now know from American memoirs and documents that the pause actually represented something of a policy split in Washington as well as a reflection of Bush's own go-slow mentality, not a strategic angling for concessions.

Weizsäcker: [...] Kissinger told me about your conversation, and he emphasized the importance of keeping up confidential contacts. Such conversations should be held not just between Gorbachev and Bush. They could be conducted by specially authorized representatives as well.

In any case, I can say that the atmosphere in the United States now is much less conservative than three months ago. And the numerous conversations that the chancellor, the minister of foreign affairs, and other representatives of the FRG had with the American leadership made a significant contribution to the change in atmosphere.

Gorbachev: Since we touched upon President Bush's line, I would like to emphasize that we enjoyed a confidential, positive atmosphere during our personal conversations. In order to preserve that atmosphere, even though the administration took such a long time to clarify its line regarding the further development of Soviet–American relations, we contained our impatience and did not criticize Bush and his government. We did not get pulled into polemics even when criticism over such a long pause began to grow exponentially among the public in the United States and Western Europe. Now we can see that we made the right decision.

Speaking of American foreign policy, I should point out that it has a number of inherent, permanent weaknesses. First of all, when President Bush speaks one-on-one, he exhibits both pragmatism and the desire not to get stuck on ideological principles. However, when he makes public appearances, he makes statements that often sound like what we used to call "Reagan's crusade against communism." We believe that such returns to the past do not help to establish the atmosphere for a long period of peaceful interaction and cooperation [of the kind] we are proposing to the Bush administration. Those are things the American president needs to think about.

And secondly, the position of waiting and taking their time in their approach to developing relations with the USSR is characteristic of the Bush administration as well as of its predecessors. Again and again they make efforts to see if the Soviet Union, because of various difficulties it is experiencing now, will move toward more concessionary positions, which would give an advantage to the United States. We have told them repeatedly about the illusory nature of such an approach, and about the fact that one cannot build policy on the basis of misconceptions. But they continue to cling to such an approach.

[*Source: Archive of the Gorbachev Foundation, Fond 1. opis 1. On file at the National Security Archive. Translated by Svetlana Savranskaya.*]

Document No. 65: Transcript of Opening Full Session of Hungarian National Roundtable Negotiations

June 13, 1989

This remarkable document, transcribed from previously unpublished video recordings of the Hungarian Roundtable process, points to the unwritten "rules" of mutual civility that arose in the nonviolent dissident movements of Eastern Europe and found an echo among the communist reformers during the negotiated revolutions of 1989. For example, here Dr. István Kukorelli from the Patriotic People's Front (part of the "informal" opposition, but formerly allied with the communists) proposes to "refrain from questioning each other's legitimacy ... since the legitimacy of each of us is debatable. Who will be given credit by history and who will be forgotten is a question which belongs to the future." Communist party secretary Károly Grósz begins the negotiation process on his side by announcing the party's intention to "separate ourselves from the remnants of the Stalinist model;" in fact, the party "has begun to transform from a bureaucratic state-party into a left-wing socialist reform party." (Formal dissolution of the Hungarian party would take place in the fall.) We have obligations towards our allies, Grósz says, but we are striving to create a Europe without blocs. The formal opposition, in the person of Imre Kónya, declares that "the goal of the negotiations is to assure a peaceful transition from the existing dictatorial ruling system to a representative democracy that genuinely asserts the will of the people." The communists would succeed in delaying free elections until 1990, but would nonetheless lose badly. Ironically, their reform candidates would have had a better chance if they had opted for elections right away in the fall of 1989.

Károly Grósz: Ladies and Gentlemen, my Honorable Compatriots, there are few positive events unfolding in our hectic world nowadays. A lot of people are facing the future with anxiety and uncertainty. Against this background, let me greet with confidence and optimism the participants of this meeting and those who are going to follow the beginning of real political negotiations in front of their TV screens in Hungary and abroad.

[...] Just a few months ago, at the February meeting of the Central Committee of the Hungarian Socialist Workers' Party, we arrived at the conclusion that we must find a peaceful transition to representative democracy based on party pluralism and presupposing competition between the parties. Our resolution met with the political goals of all those, whose representatives are seated at this table together. We are responsible for the success of this undertaking not only to the Hungarian people, but also to the community of nations. The public is looking forward to, and is concerned about, the outcome of this attempt at the same time. [...]

Let me stress that we do not intend to exaggerate or appropriate the results of building a democratic constitutional state which have been attained so far. In our opinion, apart from the political realism of the Hungarian Socialist Workers' Party, these results were due to the social organizations and movements present and the constructive efforts of the evolving parties. It is our solid determination to separate ourselves from the remnants of the Stalinist model. The Hungarian Socialist Workers' Party, together with other political forces, strives to build a democratic and socialist constitutional state which asserts the intention of the people. We expect economic and political reforms based on public consensus to help us overcome the economic crisis and to enable us to approach the most developed regions of the world instead of being irreversibly pushed to the periphery. Apart from the universal values of peace and humanism, we are trying to find socialist solutions that are particularly Hungarian. We observe our obligations towards our allies; at the same time, we are striving to create a Europe without blocs. [...]

The stakes are high. The negotiations entering a new phase should provide programs based on a consensus on as many issues as possible. This is the precondition for forming a viable coalition and for avoiding the paralyzing of party pluralism in Hungary through petty party disputes. For this reason we must concentrate on the common points instead of the differences between us. I am convinced that these negotiations can foster the development of a viable coalition and of future political alliances. It would be too early to predict the content of these. Reviewing interests and programs properly, however, can guarantee lucrative political cooperation.

The Hungarian Socialist Workers' Party has begun to transform from a bureaucratic state-party into a left-wing socialist reform party. It urges, for example, differentiation based on performance; at the same time it aims to reduce social differences that cannot be accounted for by performance. It strives for economic efficiency without disregarding social solidarity. Its goal is to ensure that private property stimulates economic performance while it insists on the determining role of efficiently operating public property. [...]

Imre Kónya: Mr. Chairman, Ladies and Gentlemen, Hungary has belonged to the Hungarian people *de jure* for a thousand years. This is so notwithstanding the fact that during its history the people could hardly dispose of their property as owners or free citizens, in spite of trying to take possession of it from time to time.

Assuming our historical responsibility and in accordance with our agreement with the Hungarian Socialist Workers' Party, we, the delegates of the Opposition Roundtable organizations, have appeared today at the Parliament in order to begin negotiations with the representatives of the ruling Hungarian Socialist Workers' Party and the delegates of other organizations it has invited. We wish to put it on record that the goal of the negotiations is to assure a peaceful transition from the existing dictatorial ruling system to a representative democracy that genuinely asserts the will of the people. In the course of the negotiations we do not wish to divide power between ourselves and those who are holding it now. We do not wish to exercise power above the people's heads, without being entitled to it by the people. Our aim is to enable Hungarian citizens to decide whom, which political forces, they commission to exercise power during the periods extending from election to election. [...]

After thirty years of numbness, our society has finally arisen. The formation of independent organizations and of large-scale demonstrations is an indication that it wants to control its own fate. It is not only our moral obligation to facilitate that, but also our common interest; moreover, many of us believe that it has already become a precondition for our nation's survival. A reliable and already tested form of the continuous assertion of the will of the people is representative democracy. The peaceful method of its creation is free elections.

We are convinced that free elections will not only lead to the significant revival of public life and policy-making, they can also affect the fate and history of our nation. We must be aware that free elections can only be held in a society which has been freed from its fears and suspicions. And fears and suspicions take time to fade. Burying the martyrs of the Revolution and commencing these talks can mark the beginning of a national reconciliation. Real reconciliation, however, can only be achieved by burying the existing dictatorial power system. That can only be done by depoliticizing repressive organizations and through free elections.

Therefore, we wish to enter into negotiations with the power-holders based on the following principles. The basis of power is the sovereignty of the people. None of the political forces can appropriate sovereignty and declare itself the only representative of the will of the people. The will of the people must be expressed in free elections with an open outcome, not allowing for the exclusion of any party or political organization which accepts the principles of democracy and rejects the use of repressive instruments. Until the political will of society is expressed by the election of members of parliament, no other nation-wide elections, for example the election of the president of the republic or the election of local authorities, should take place. The power-holders should also accept the results of free elections and should not try to change them by any means afterwards. A strong opposition in parliament is a basic institution of democracy, counterbalancing the operation of the government. No political party or organization can have its own armed forces. Parties and political organizations cannot exert influence on the operation of the armed forces through their members. The armed forces cannot be used for solving political conflicts under any circumstances. It is constitutionally legitimate to react to violence only to the extent that is necessary for abating violence. It is not enough to renounce using instruments of oppression, the possibility of using them must be excluded. Workers' militias should be disbanded, the operation of political police should be contained within well-defined limits, public security police should be subordinated to local governments and the use of guns should be controlled publicly.

This is the only way people can stop being afraid, this is the only way for—not the silent but the silenced—majority to participate in politics. We, the organizations constituting the Opposition Roundtable, see the goal of the negotiations as regulating the way political forces are going to act and be compared publicly.

At the same time, we are ready to do anything within our own range of competence, anything that is necessary to solve the conflicts brought about by the crisis. However, we cannot take responsibility for resolving [our] economic bankruptcy until the elections, since opposition organizations—being in opposition—can and would only monitor those who have governed this country for 40 years and who have caused this situation. We are aware that the economy is about to collapse and is burying under itself the lives of several thousand people every day. There, that is to say, our situation will not be improved by any political demagogy. The precondition for halting the economic decline is to change the political system.

Finally, we would like to emphasize that the organizations of the Opposition Roundtable did not sit down at the negotiating table in order to acquire their share of power, but in order to give rise to a situation where the people themselves can acquire power without using violence, with the help of peaceful means. Hungary is the property of the people, therefore it is not necessary for the people to take by force what is their own property. The people only have to lift up their heads, organize themselves and take possession of the country, of their own homeland with due self-consciousness. [...]

István Kukorelli: Mr. Chairman, our Honored Political Partners, we have initiated today's Roundtable talks and we are ready to take responsibility for them, though the table, let's face it, has turned out to be rather square. It is still very significant for peaceful social development.

The agreement we also signed is the result of mutual and realistic compromises. These compromises, the arrangement of the seats, will not give rise to illusions, will not deceive the public. These three sides express a lot of things and conceal a lot of other things as well. Placing the power-holders and the opposition opposite each other cannot be disputed. Democracy can hardly be imagined without an opposition protected by minority rights in the future. There is no doubt that the opposition and certain other civil organizations still lack an economic infrastructure, the creation of which is a task for our negotiations and for the government.

We also have to admit, however, that the way we are seated cannot represent all the major divisions in society. To mention just a few of them: the country has started to break into two along lines separating public figures who organize themselves into parties and become the so-called elite and people who reject the formation of parties; separating the capital from the countryside; separating the haves and the have-nots. Other dividing lines also appear in the structure of society. All those tensions shall be tackled by us here—we are able to do it since around the table we represent a horizontal cross-section of society as well.

Organizations that make up the third side do not pretend to appear as a unified force. They are present as independent political organizations representing the interests of their memberships, and their policies are formed independently on the basis of the agenda along the way. I am well aware of the fact that few people are able to find a common characteristic in this heterogeneous group intending to

473

participate in the negotiations as an independent force. We do not make a secret of the fact that we are not a homogeneous delegation, but we possess, we will possess, a great amount of tolerance within our group.

We wish the same to the unified delegations as well. We are drawn together through having a common interest in tackling the social and economic crisis. [...]

In the case of most organizations of the third side the role of being a formal partner of the old power structure is a common burden. That is why a lot of people wanted our delegation to take seats on the side of the HSWP. But they do not take into account the recent developments of our accelerating times, that is, the significant modifications that have occurred in the structure of the sphere of power. [...]

To refrain from questioning each other's legitimacy could determine the success of our Roundtable, since the legitimacy of each of us is debatable. Who will be given credit by history and who will be forgotten is a question which belongs to the future. For our part, we do not intend to apply such arguments during the negotiations and we accept that all of us are negotiating partners with full rights representing smaller or larger segments of society. [...]

We are in the year of the creation of the constitutional state; reliable professional workshops are offering various significant draft bills for us to "buy," and the government is working hard, it does what it must. We should also pick up speed, because the sociopolitical foundations of the law, that is, the political consensus, is still missing. We have stated in our agreement that legislative work cannot precede political agreements. We agree with this and also suggest that the Parliament should only include in its agenda draft bills that have been made public already, such as the party law, after the agreements are completed. Instead of being governed by decree, Hungary needs consensus law; the rule of law is the most important feature of the constitutional state. [...]

The third side agrees that two main topics should be included in our agendas, namely, the definition of principles and roles that support the execution of the democratic political transition, and of the strategic tasks in tackling the economic and social crisis. It would be a misunderstanding of our role to pull a government-level economic and political strategy out of a hat. It cannot be the goal of the opening plenary session; its goal is that we declare to the public our intention to cooperate and to negotiate. [...]

[*Source:* A rendszerváltás forgatókönyve. Kerekasztal-tárgyalások 1989-ben *[Scenario of the Transition. Roundtable Talks in 1989] Editor-in-chief: András Bozóki, editors: Márta Elbert, Melinda Kalmár, Béla Révész, Erzsébet Ripp, Zoltán Ripp, Magvető Kiadó, Bp. 1999, Vols. I–IV (From:* Political Transition in Hungary, 1989–1990; *International Conference, June 12, 1999, Hungarian Academy of Sciences, Budapest; A Compendium of Declassified Documents and Chronology of Events). Translation provided by the Cold War History Research Center, Budapest.*]

Document No. 66: Record of Second Conversation between Mikhail Gorbachev and Helmut Kohl

June 13, 1989

In these notes of the continuation of Gorbachev and Kohl's talks in Bonn, we see the beginnings of the "beautiful friendship" that led to German unification in 1990. Earlier in 1989, Gorbachev wanted to make Bush his main foreign partner, but the "pause" in Washington meant the two leaders would not meet until December. So by June the Soviet leader has settled for Kohl, remarking on "the trust that is growing between us with every meeting." It is hard to imagine any other Soviet communist and any other West German politician appealing to each other through their personal experiences of World War II.

[…]

Kohl: I am in favor of progress in all negotiations, in all spheres of arms control. I took 1992 as a benchmark. And the "Lances" are not the only ones that matter. The point is that in 1992 there will be a year left until the elections in the U.S. We should take that into account in all respects. We have to work in all directions.

Gorbachev: We have a common destiny. Why should we be anybody's hostages?

Kohl: We have not only a common destiny, but also a common history. Now, as we are talking, our wives are visiting the memorial in Stuckenbrück—the place where Soviet citizens killed in the war were buried. There is not a single family in either the USSR or the FRG whom the war did not touch. My two sons are officers in the Bundeswehr, and my brother was killed in the war.

Gorbachev: Policy without morality cannot be considered serious policy; immoral politicians cannot be trusted.

Kohl: At a recent NATO meeting at the highest level I told my colleagues directly that I was the only one among them whose two sons served in the army integrated into NATO. I also stressed that I was not a coward, of course, but that I was a German, and knew history and geography very well.

Gorbachev: I very much appreciate your honest and sincere judgments. And I value the trust that is growing between us with every meeting.

Kohl: Let us communicate more often, let's call each other on the phone. I think that we could accomplish many things ourselves without delegating to the bureaucracies, which can drag their deliberations on and on.

[*Source: Archive of the Gorbachev Foundation, Fond 1. Opis 1. On file at the National Security Archive. Translated by Svetlana Savranskaya.*]

Document No. 67: Record of Third Conversation between Mikhail Gorbachev and Helmut Kohl

June 14, 1989

Friendship blooms as Kohl says to Gorbachev, "I am telling you once again that I like your policy, and I like you as a person." In turn, Gorbachev reveals to Kohl his worries about America: he has intelligence that a "special group" is now "charged with discrediting perestroika *and me personally." According to various sources, including former CIA Director William Webster (in a 1999 speech at Texas A&M University), the White House did form a highly secret contingency group to look at the possibility of a collapse of the Soviet Union, or of Gorbachev's own ouster (secret because disclosing it publicly might help make it so). But most U.S. accounts describe the group as having started much later, in September 1989, and been coordinated by the NSC's Condoleezza Rice. Kohl's response here, like the later American versions, also suggests the group's role was to monitor rather than to undermine.*

Most striking here is how candid the Kohl and Gorbachev assessments are of events in other countries, compared to Soviet Politburo discussions and certainly to the stilted presentations of the "fraternal" parties. Moreover, Kohl and Gorbachev actually agree on what they think about Jaruzelski, Ceaușescu, and the Hungarians, for example. Kohl continues to assure Gorbachev that the FRG will do nothing to destabilize the situation in Eastern Europe. At the same time, taking advantage of their new close relationship, he complains for the first time about Honecker's policies in the GDR, and Gorbachev seems receptive to his views. Of course, the Soviet leader is weighing his reactions based in part on the financial power of West Germany which gives it immense influence regarding Eastern Europe.

As an interesting aside to the fate of Yugoslavia, Kohl suggests to Gorbachev that "we need to think about how to prevent the Balkans from becoming a source of destabilization." The talks end with a joint declaration by the two leaders that, according to Chernyaev, "de facto began the process of reunification of Germany." [61]

[...] *Kohl:* We would like to see your visit, Mr. Gorbachev, as the end of hostilities between Russians and Germans, as the beginning of a period of genuinely friendly, good neighborly relations. You understand that these are words supported by the will of all the people, by the will of the people who greet you in the streets and the squares. As chancellor, I join this expression of the people's will with pleasure, and I tell you once again that I like your policy, and I like you as a person.

---

[61] Chernyaev, *Shest' Let s Gorbachevym*, 291.

Gorbachev: Thank you for such warm words. They are very touching. I will respond equally, and I will try not to disappoint you.

I would like to tell you the following with all sincerity. According to our information, there is a special group that was created in the National Security Council of the United States charged with discrediting *perestroika* and me personally. When Baker was in Moscow, we openly asked him about that. He and his colleagues were somewhat confused and did not give us a clear answer; they only tried to convince us that it was not so. However, I have some evidence that such a group does, in fact, exist. I think you understand me well, Mr. Federal Chancellor; you understand how I feel about it.

Kohl: Thank you for your openness. I have heard nothing about such a group. Even if it does exist, I do not think it was created at George Bush's initiative, or that it was charged with the tasks you have just formulated. Maybe if it exists it has some kind of monitoring functions, but not subversive ones. [...]

Kohl: Now a couple of words about our mutual friends. I will tell you directly that Erich Honecker concerns me a great deal. His wife has just made a statement in which she called on the GDR youth to take up arms and, if necessary, defend the achievements of socialism from external enemies. It is clear that she implied that the socialist countries which implement reforms, stimulate democratic processes, and follow their own original road are the enemies. Primarily, she had Poland and Hungary in mind. This is certainly a strange statement.

Gorbachev: What are your relations with Poland like?

Kohl: The country is in a difficult situation right now. But we want to help it to get out of the crisis. As is the case with the GDR, we do not want any destabilization.

Tomorrow François Mitterrand will travel to Poland. We agreed that France will be the first to extend aid to Poland, to give them financial assistance in the form of credits. Then George Bush will visit Poland. As for me, I consciously decided to be the third to visit Poland—after the French and the Americans. The Germans and the Poles are connected by something else. This year will mark the 50th anniversary of the beginning of World War II. I will probably visit Poland on those dates. Anyway, I would like my visit to contribute to the improvement of relations between Germans and Poles, even though I realize that it will be very, very difficult.

Gorbachev: We need to support the Poles; they do not have anybody who has more authority and respect than Wojciech Jaruzelski now.

Kohl: We also plan to give Poland financial support. I understand your words, Mr. Gorbachev.

We have rather good relations with the Hungarians. However, we also do not want destabilization there. That is why when I meet with the Hungarians, I tell them: we consider the reforms that are underway in your country your internal affair, we are sympathetic. However, if you would like to hear our advice, we recommend that you do not accelerate too much, because you might lose control over your mechanism, and it will start to work to destroy itself.

Of all the socialist countries, we have the most hopeless relations with Romania. There is no movement at all; just complete darkness and stagnation. I do not understand Ceaușescu. How does he not see what a ridiculous cult he has created in his own country? I cannot believe that he can seriously think he has made the Romanians the happiest people on Earth.

Gorbachev: It is certainly strange that this kind of family clan would be established in the center of civilized Europe, in a state with rich historical traditions. I could imagine something like that to emerge somewhere else, like it has in Korea; but here, right next to us—it is such a primitive phenomenon.

Kohl: I like the Bulgarians. If you compare Bulgaria in the first post-war years and now, the progress is impressive—like night and day. Bulgarian representatives—leaders as well as simple professionals—often visit my country. They think and operate with very modern concepts, and they avidly absorb our economic experience. They also, as we can observe, implement it in their economic life quite effectively. I really like Todor Zhivkov. He has been in power for a very long time—I think since 1956, when I was still taking final exams in high school. He is a very flexible politician. I met with him several times, and every time we met he criticized those leaders of various branches of the Bulgarian economy who could not manage their responsibilities. It is curious that he speaks about that as if those individuals were not members of his own circle and as if he gave them no directives, just observed them from a distance.

I am mostly concerned by the situation in Yugoslavia. The economy there is choking, and nobody knows how to help it. We need to think about how to prevent the Balkans from becoming a source of destabilization.

I have already said that in our policy toward the socialist countries, toward the Soviet Union, we remain on a clear course of non-interference in their internal affairs. However, a policy of non-interference could be of two sorts. It is one thing to sit in a theater seat, to watch what is unfolding on-stage and, when the play is almost over, to rise and say that we foresaw everything that happened, and that it could not have been otherwise. How smart we are. [...]

[*Source: Archive of the Gorbachev Foundation, Fond 1. Opis 1. On file at the National Security Archive. Translated by Svetlana Savranskaya.*]

Document No. 68: Memorandum of Telephone Conversation between George H.W. Bush and Helmut Kohl

June 15, 1989

Here we see Kohl in his role as superpower matchmaker, as he debriefs the American president about his discussions with Gorbachev. All the substance in this conversation comes from Kohl while Bush listens and says almost nothing. The chancellor is very positive about Gorbachev, and suggests strongly to Bush that he needs to have direct contact with the Soviet leader and to "signal the President's confidence, which is a key word for Gorbachev, who places a high premium on 'personal chemistry.'" Kohl directly challenges the Scowcroft-Gates view of the USSR, repeating Gorbachev's emphatic assertion that "wedge-driving was not his intention" and that he does not want "destabilization in Europe." The German leader reassures Bush about negotiations over conventional forces in Europe (CFE), which have dragged on since the 1970s: Gorbachev does not see a 12-month deadline as a problem, he says; on the contrary, he is ready for "rapid progress."

Chancellor Kohl initiated the call, as he said he would do in his June 7 telephone conversation with the President. After opening greetings, Chancellor Kohl gave a lengthy debrief of Chairman Gorbachev's just-concluded visit to the Federal Republic. He found Gorbachev in very good shape, much more optimistic than when the Chancellor had visited Moscow in October. The Chancellor said Gorbachev is in a stronger position following his election to the presidency and the structural reorganization of the Supreme Soviet. These general impressions were echoed by Aleksandr Yakovlev, who accompanied Gorbachev on the visit.

Chancellor Kohl then turned to a discussion of Eastern Europe, which he thought the President would find useful in light of his forthcoming trip to Poland and Hungary. The Chancellor emphasized Gorbachev's very close personal relationship with General Jaruzelski and their common approach toward developments in Poland. No such personal relationship exists with any one Hungarian leader, the Chancellor added, but Gorbachev also supports Hungary's reform efforts. By contrast, there is an enormous distance between Moscow and Bucharest, and also East Berlin.

Chancellor Kohl said that Gorbachev was dismayed about developments in China but offered no elaboration. On the Middle East, the Chancellor found it interesting that Gorbachev is very eager to find a settlement—partly because he thinks he will have a problem with Islamic fundamentalism in the Soviet Union.

Chancellor Kohl noted that he and Gorbachev had talked for quite some time about the President. It was clearly apparent, Kohl said, that Gorbachev has greater hope for establishing good contact with the President than he had with President Reagan. At an intellectual level, Gorbachev sees eye to eye with the

President and wants to deepen contacts with the U.S. and the President personally. The Chancellor said he had told Gorbachev that there will be no opportunities for driving wedges between the U.S. and the Federal Republic or between the President and the Chancellor. Gorbachev, the Chancellor reported, said emphatically that wedge-driving was not his intention, and that the Soviet Union does not want destabilization in Europe, because this would mean disruption in the USSR as well.

Chancellor Kohl said again that it was his impression that Gorbachev is seeking ways of establishing personal contact with the President, adding that Gorbachev also has a favorable impression of Secretary Baker. Kohl thought that if the President moves forward with talks, there will be a good basis for progress. While noting that there is lingering Soviet mistrust toward the U.S., Kohl felt nonetheless that Gorbachev was serious in his desire for establishing better relations and moving forward on the issues.

Chancellor Kohl said that he was somewhat surprised that Gorbachev does not seem to think that a twelve-month timetable (for a CFE agreement) is a problem. Gorbachev thought there could be rapid progress. The Chancellor said he had agreed with this view, citing the INF Treaty as an example of how fast progress can come when there is real political determination.

Chancellor Kohl then made a suggestion and a request. Once negotiations are underway in Vienna and work has begun through official negotiating channels, the Chancellor said, it would be a good idea for the President to send direct messages to Gorbachev from time to time. This would signal the President's confidence, which is a key word for Gorbachev, who places a high premium on "personal chemistry."

Chancellor Kohl found it interesting that Gorbachev spoke openly about Soviet domestic problems and about the crimes of the Stalin era. Gorbachev said he was resolved to make all the facts available to the (Soviet) public and to bring the truth out, as the Hungarians were doing (with regard to the 1956 revolution). Gorbachev had been frank in admitting Soviet economic problems and anticipated a few tough years ahead.

Chancellor Kohl said that Gorbachev's most important message to the Germans had been that the war is over and a new generation has come to the fore. The Soviet Union and the Federal Republic have their differences but want reasonable cooperation. Gorbachev acknowledged that the two countries have different views on central issues like Berlin, but Kohl found him much more restrained than he had been in October.

Chancellor Kohl, summing up, said he was very satisfied with the visit. Gorbachev knows which side the FRG is on, Kohl said, and knows he must respect that. But Gorbachev is trying to make improvements and has created a reasonable basis for future work.

The President thanked the Chancellor for his debrief and said he had listened very carefully, adding that if the Chancellor had further thoughts the President would like to hear them.

480

Chancellor Kohl said he would call again in a couple of weeks to discuss preparations for the Economic Summit.

The President welcomed the idea and proposed that he call the Chancellor at the end of the following week. It would be his nickel, the President said.

[Source: George Bush Presidential Library. Obtained through FOIA. On file at the National Security Archive.]

Document No. 69: Memorandum of Telephone Conversation between George H.W. Bush and Helmut Kohl

June 23, 1989

This telephone transcript of another in a succession of conversations between Bush and Kohl seems most remarkable in retrospect for the absence on the American side of any sense of the pace of change in Eastern Europe. President Bush appears simply to be conveying a series of talking points given to him by the bureaucracy about the Vienna CFE talks and the economic summit, with no sense of the big picture at all. The telling phrase comes from Bush regarding the possibility of debt forgiveness for Poland. The notes paraphrase Bush as saying: "emotions run high regarding Poland. While the President shared those emotions, he also felt it important to act carefully and to avoid pouring money down a rat-hole." The U.S. ambassador to Warsaw, John R. Davis, would hear virtually this exact phrase from White House Chief of Staff John Sununu while sitting on a park bench in Warsaw during the Bush trip in July. The U.S. administration's refusal to put its money where its mouth is undercuts the claim that the White House has a "grand strategy" for Eastern Europe during these crucial months of revolution that changed the world. Ironically, this may have been a good thing, since it probably helped reduce Soviet paranoia about American intentions, and thus created a vacuum into which the Eastern European "refolutionaries" would rush.

The President said he was calling back, as he promised he would do during the previous week's telephone conversation. The President mentioned that he had a very pleasant visit with Foreign Minister Genscher (on June 21).

Chancellor Kohl said he would be talking with Genscher in two days. They would be going to Madrid for a European Community meeting and had a lot of work ahead of them. The Chancellor also noted that this was the last week before the parliament took its summer break. In this context, the Chancellor wanted to reassure the President about the results of the June 18 elections to the European Parliament. These are unusual elections, he said. There is no European government, no European opposition, and none of the normal give and take of politics. The Christian Democratic Union and Christian Social Union once again emerged in the strongest position. The Chancellor also assured the President that the *Republikaner* were not Nazis. Their top leaders were nationalists, but not National Socialists, and those who voted for them were expressing anger rather than real support for the *Republikaner.* The Chancellor was confident that these voters could be won back. This would not be easy, but it could be done.

The President noted that experts here concluded that the Chancellor's party came out better than had been predicted a couple of months ago, before the NATO Summit. The President said he was pleased with that.

The President said he wanted to raise two other subjects: follow-up to the NATO Summit and preparations for the Paris Economic Summit. As he had told Foreign Minister Genscher, the President said it would be a big mistake to divide the Vienna talks into phases. This would undermine the Alliance's CFE initiative. The Alliance's first priority must be an agreement at Vienna on conventional reductions. For that reason, the U.S. does not want to see discussions within NATO on SNF negotiations. The Alliance has a good formula, the President said, and should stick with it.

Chancellor Kohl agreed, saying he was very much against taking up the SNF issue again. The Alliance should continue with what was agreed to at Brussels.

The President then turned to the Economic Summit, saying that U.S. priorities would be to discuss the international debt situation and macro-economic policy coordination. The Summit Seven need to get back to the level of policy coordination they had in the past. This pattern produced good results and should be followed once again. On the Polish situation, the President noted that he would be going to Poland soon and would welcome any suggestions the Chancellor might have. The President observed that President Mitterrand had called for the Paris Club to be more "imaginative" and "flexible" on the Polish debt. This will be discussed at the Economic Summit, but the President also welcomed Chancellor Kohl's personal views on what the West should do to help on the economic side and also on facilitating the transition the [sic] democracy in Eastern Europe, especially in Poland and Hungary. The President added that he would be arriving in Poland on July 9 and would go to Budapest the following Tuesday.

Chancellor Kohl said he would send a letter to the President laying out his views on Poland and Hungary. He would prepare the letter by the middle of the next week, following his return from Madrid.

The President said he would look forward to receiving the letter, which he would treat with strict confidence. He noted that emotions run high regarding Poland. While the President shared those emotions, he also felt it important to act carefully and to avoid pouring money down a rat-hole.

The President said he wanted to raise two additional points regarding the Economic Summit. He felt it important to work hard to complete the Uruguay Round by the end of next year. This is essential to stave off protectionist pressures everywhere. The President also wanted to have intensive discussions on the environment, urging that the Summit participants be realistic in their approaches.

Chancellor Kohl said that raising those issues was his intention as well. He saw no problems between the U.S. and the Federal Republic at the Uruguay Round, but felt that other countries would be more difficult. The Chancellor agreed that the environment and rain forests were among the most important issues that needed to be discussed at the Summit.

The President, before concluding the conversation, said that he might have specifics to propose to Poland bilaterally and would keep the Chancellor informed.

[*Source: George Bush Presidential Library. Obtained through FOIA. On file at the National Security Archive.*]

Document No. 70: Letter from Helmut Kohl to George H.W. Bush

June 28, 1989

---

*In their telephone conversation on June 23 (see previous document), Bush men-
tioned his upcoming trip to Poland and Hungary, and asked Kohl for his suggestions
and personal views on what the West should be doing to help the transition to democracy. Kohl responded that he would send a letter laying out his views, and Bush
assured him it would be treated in strict confidence. That communication, which appears here, includes a briefing that compares the "painful" history of German–Polish relations to the "exemplary" relations between Germany and Hungary, and details the backstage negotiations between Germans and Poles over a "package" that
is being put together to resolve ongoing controversies before Kohl travels to Poland
for his own "breakthrough" trip. Ironically, Kohl's visit would put him in Warsaw on
the day the Berlin Wall fell in November 1989, and his attention to Poland would be
supplanted by the demands of dealing with East Germany and ultimately unification
(see Document No. 100). Here, Kohl highlights for Bush the "paramount Polish interest" in "economic-financial cooperation," while reinforcing Bush's own cautious
and parsimonious approach by warning that the grim Polish economic situation is
the result of earlier "careless policies on national debt" and "failed attempts by the
West to provide aid." Kohl explicitly rejects the analogy of the Marshall Plan (a version of which Poles like Lech Wałęsa would continue to ask for) in favor of treating
the Poles the way Western financial institutions handle developing countries, with
a donor conference making all decisions about aid.*

Dear George,

As we agreed during our telephone conversation at the end of last week, I would
like to inform you about the main points of my policy and my concrete plans regarding Poland and Hungary.

The German–Polish relationship is stamped with a long, painful history,
which has left a heavy political toll on the relationship between the states and
deep emotional wounds in the consciousness of the people that have not yet
healed. This history painfully returns to our consciousness in connection with
the 50th anniversary of the start of World War II, which began with the attack on
Poland and the creation of the Hitler–Stalin pact that shortly beforehand divided
Poland for the fourth time.

Precisely because of this I would like to make a political and psychological
breakthrough this year in our relations with Poland and open new ways for understanding between the states and for reconciliation between our peoples.

Poland and Hungary make up the leading group of the Warsaw Pact countries that have undertaken radical reforms in the political, economic, and social
spheres and thereby paved the way toward more political pluralism, increased

attention to human rights, more private initiative, and the step-by-step introduction of market economics. The West should use its best powers to support these processes—and I know we are of the same opinion on this—not least because successful reforms in Poland and Hungary promise to have a positive effect on the Soviet Union as well as on the GDR, and herein lies our particular German interest. I would like to reinforce both the new beginning in our bilateral relations and our support for the Polish reform process through an official visit to the People's Republic of Poland this year. Of course, before then a multitude of open questions must be resolved and a "comprehensive package" has to be proposed, as I discussed with Prime Minister Rakowski earlier this year. We have appointed delegates to negotiate this package (from our side it is Horst Teltschik). The delegates have met seven times since late January and have already to a large extent brought their positions closer together, but their talks have to continue. We have agreed from the beginning that until we have a conclusive "comprehensive package," the date for my visit will not be set. The comprehensive package consists of a number of difficult questions. To some extent, the federal government under my leadership and that of my predecessors has been striving to find solutions to these problems for decades. Among other things, this concerns the following issues:

– A number of agreements, such as a youth exchange, the formation of cultural institutions, collaboration in scientific-technological work, collaboration in environmental work, protection and promotion of investments;

– humanitarian and historical issues: care for the graves of war casualties, remembrance of the German opposition to Hitler and of German historical figures;

– one of the focal points of our interests is the rights of Germans and people of German descent living in Poland: support for their religion, language, culture, and traditions, according to the Vienna Final Act on Security and Cooperation in Europe and other international deeds;

– the paramount Polish interest is economic-financial cooperation: Horst Teltschik has outlined our offer in a telex to Brent Scowcroft from June 27.

From the Polish side there is also a desire to integrate this comprehensive package into a "joint statement."

The negotiations over economic-financial collaboration have proven to be particularly difficult for the following two reasons:

– First of all, the current devastating economic situation is primarily the result of the system, of the careless policies on national debt of the 1970s as well as the failed attempts by the West to provide aid during the same era (to which the earlier FRG government contributed); Western countries alone cannot resolve the Polish economic problems.

– New Western support measures have to be very closely coordinated so that they benefit concrete and workable projects in Poland, particularly in the private sector. Poland should not play off the Western countries against each other, as is regrettably the case today with the national creditors of the Paris Club and the private banks of the London Club.

Therefore, I would like to propose to you that at the economic summit in Paris we discuss with our partners a coordination mechanism for Western countries that would allow us to organize the support measures of potential donors and provide political guidelines for the upcoming deliberations of the International Monetary Fund, the World Bank, and the Paris Club, which naturally must also include larger foreign policy considerations. Additionally, we could think about the possibility that under the authority of this mechanism we could establish an office in Poland for a coordination committee of experts from mainly Western countries including the Scandinavian countries and Switzerland. This group would select and inspect cooperation projects locally, and assign them to particular donor countries (this would be comparable to the so-called donor conference in developing countries, rather than the mechanism of Marshall plan aid, except that we would not introduce this terminology).

My preliminary queries lead me to believe that it would be possible to reach agreement with the Polish government on this issue. We have already bilaterally conducted some conceptual preliminary work: during talks with the delegates, the Poles announced their agreement that in conjunction with the reopening of export credit guarantees [*Hermes-Bürgschaften*] a new mechanism for joint project inspections would be introduced, which one could now make multilateral. I would greatly appreciate it if before the Paris economic summit you could communicate your assessment of this proposal, which I have not yet taken up with the other partners.

With Hungary the issues are politically much easier for us. For over a 1,000 years—which is arguably a singular European record—there have been no armed conflicts between Germany and Hungary. After World War II, exemplary good-neighborly relations developed between the Federal Republic of Germany and the People's Republic of Hungary.

Hungary carries on commendable policies toward its national minorities. In 1987 we reached a bilateral agreement regarding the Hungarian Germans, which allows us to provide cultural support to the German minority population. This is an exceedingly valuable precedent for our dialogue with the Soviet Union, with Romania and, last but not least, with Poland.

In terms of foreign policy in relation to us, Hungary has consistently shown itself to be open and understanding; in particular, it did not take part in the Soviet Union's confrontational policy in the first half of the 1980s. Even then it sought to bridge the differences between East and West and at the same time introduced political, economic and social reforms in the domestic sphere.

These factors persuaded me to support Hungary more than the other countries of the region. Thus, during the official visit of former General Secretary Grósz in 1987, Hungary received an untied term loan for 1 billion DM from a German commercial bank, which the FRG government vouched for in consideration of larger political reasons. Now there is a plan to increase this credit by an additional 250 million DM, and the FRG government will renew its guarantee on the loan. Additionally, it is expected that two federal states will grant a credit facility to the amount of 750 million DM; so in an interval of less than two years, Hungary is receiving 2 billion DM of "fresh money." We hope that this new financial aid will already enable Hungary in this critical phase to continue steadily with its political reforms and economic openness to the West.

I intend to come to Hungary on an official visit this year. There is no set date yet; in any case it will be after the forthcoming October 7 Congress of the Hungarian Socialist Workers Party.

At the forthcoming economic summit we should come to an agreement on our policies towards Hungary. Despite the difficult economic situation and the still high per-capita indebtedness in comparison with Poland, active help from the West could be particularly beneficial because of the relatively small size of the country. In Paris we should further consider whether to propose for Hungary the kind of cooperation mechanism I described for Poland, as well as a local project inspection committee.

Dear George, since you are going to be in Warsaw in a few days and will be visiting Budapest, you will have the most current information from both countries for the Paris economic conference. Therefore I am looking forward to our talk even more. I wish you every possible success for this visit and send you and Barbara, also in Hannelore's name, the warmest greetings and best wishes.

Kind regards,
Helmut Kohl

[*Source:* Deutsche Einheit: Sonderedition aus den Akten des Bundeskanzleramtes 1989/90. *Eds. Hanns Jürgen Küsters and Daniel Hofmann. R. Oldenbourg Verlag, Munich, 1998. Translated by Anna Melyakova.*]

Document No. 71: Record of Conversation between Mikhail Gorbachev, François Mitterrand and Their Spouses

July 4, 1989

During a sequence of discussions in Paris, the French leader effectively joins Margaret Thatcher and Helmut Kohl as an informal member of Gorbachev's primary international peer group, the support of which becomes a crucial source of his self-esteem and sense of security. In the conversations reproduced in this volume (see also Document Nos. 72 & 74), Gorbachev discusses his ostensible Warsaw Treaty Organization partners with a Western leader in terms far more frank than those usually employed in the Kremlin, or certainly with those "allies" directly. Both leaders' commentary about President Bush is perhaps even more candid. Interestingly, Chernyaev's notes show Raisa Gorbachev as an active participant in the conversations.

Gorbachev: Thank you for your kind words. We also count on the success of our meeting. I recall my visit in 1985. So many things have transpired since then! You probably noticed how our statements have changed compared with 1985. In general, I feel as though I have lived four lives since 1985.

[Raisa] Gorbachev: I think a person should always be who he is.

Mitterrand: I cannot resist recalling the words of the poet [Walt] Whitman: "Become who you are!"

Gorbachev: Let me ask you: what about *perestroika,* and an individual in *perestroika,* where people are trying to become better, more pure?

Mitterrand: I am convinced that a person becomes better if he manages to remain himself. [...]

Mitterrand: The most difficult issue for you is inter-ethnic relations.

Gorbachev: You are right, it is a difficult problem; but we will have the necessary approaches.

Mitterrand: If I were in your place, I would probably still be unable to find the right solution.

Gorbachev: You would be able to, because you simply would have to seek a solution for this problem. As far as we are concerned, we are on the verge of taking the right steps. That is why we do not have any grounds for pessimism.

[Raisa] Gorbachev: In our country everybody understands the inevitability of change. But there are some who are scared, who are confused. And there are also those who push in the wrong direction.

Gorbachev: But that is normal, as in any revolution.

***

The conversation continued during the walk in the park of the Élysée Palace.

Gorbachev: It would be inadmissible if, during the period of important formative shifts that are now underway in our country and in the other countries of Eastern Europe, someone tried to interfere crudely with this process under the pretext of all these emotions.

Mitterrand: France understands this issue very well from the ideological and the political point of view. I count myself among those who sincerely wish success to *perestroika* in the USSR.

[Source: Archive of the Gorbachev Foundation, Fond 1. Opis 1. On file at the National Security Archive. Translated by Svetlana Savranskaya.]

Document No. 72: Record of Conversation between Mikhail Gorbachev and François Mitterrand

July 5, 1989

In this congenial and candid conversation, Mitterrand and the Gorbachevs discuss the internal conditions and leaderships of Romania, Bulgaria and Poland. Each participant is highly critical of Ceauşescu, whom Gorbachev is due to visit after leaving Paris. They are more sympathetic to Zhivkov although there is a tacit agreement that he is in frail health and will have to go. By contrast, Gorbachev is very positive about Jaruzelski. Among other topics, the Soviet leader shows an interest in better understanding the American political system, while Mitterrand offers the startling assessment that "Bush, as a president, has a very big drawback—he lacks original thinking altogether."

[…]

Mitterrand: So, you are going to Romania tomorrow. I appreciated the answer about Romania you gave during your interview with the TV show "Antenne-2" and the radio station "Europe-1." (The interview took place after the press conference at the Élysée Palace on July 5). But at the same time, we all understand that Romania is a real dictatorship. The only unclear point is whose dictatorship is it—Ceauşescu's himself or his wife's?

Gorbachev: Still, we should make a realistic assessment of the situation. Romania used to be a backward agrarian country, and now it is an industrialized, developed state. The challenge is to complete the economic and social base that has been created with a suitable political establishment. For example, Romania has completely solved the housing problem. This is a big victory.

But Ceauşescu is scared of democracy. By the way, he told me that the measures that we are now undertaking in the USSR in the framework of *perestroika* he already implemented in Romania 10 years ago.

Mitterrand: He told you that? Romania, of course, could use *perestroika*. I visited Romania several years ago. After that I never went back.

Gorbachev: Ceauşescu probably "wrote out" a whole plan of actions for you.

Mitterrand: Precisely. Since what year has he been the general secretary of the Romanian Communist Party?

Gorbachev: Since 1965.

Mitterrand: Every power is seeking a way to find its place in history. Besides, and I already quoted these words by Tacitus yesterday, "every man always reaches the limit of his own power." That is why democracy must have a mechanism for political balances.

490

Contrary to Ceauşescu, who is cracking down, Todor Zhivkov is acting in a smarter, I would even say more cunning, way. For how many years has he been in power?

Gorbachev: He has led the Bulgarian Communist Party for 35 years now. I recall being at his meeting with students of the University of Sofia. They criticized him quite harshly, and he kept responding, "They are right about everything."

Mitterrand: 35 years!

[Raisa] Gorbachev: And you thought that two presidential terms in France—14 years—is too long for you.

Mitterrand: (Laughing.) It is also long. Zhivkov is about 80 years old now.

Gorbachev: He is not in complete control of his legs and facial muscles. When I see him, I remember Brezhnev. […]

Mitterrand: In the past, U.S. presidents used to be the masters of the game. Roosevelt and Truman made their own independent foreign policies. By impeaching Nixon, the Congress took its revenge. However, George Bush would make very moderate policy even without the congressional constraint because he is a conservative. Not all conservatives are alike. Bush, as a president, has a very big drawback—he lacks original thinking altogether.

Gorbachev: The American internal political process also interests me in terms of building relations between parliament and the president. In Italy, for example, the complicated relations between various democratic institutions sometimes lead to inconclusiveness, to a disruption of the political process. In our country we have to concentrate on the implementation of radical reforms. Therefore it is undesirable that the center's initiative be compromised by disorderly relations with the regions and with other democratic institutions. We need to find a golden median here. […]

Mitterrand: For a revolution you need a new class that can take power in its hands. The Decembrists were able to use a powerful popular burst of discontent, but they were not ready to take power and nothing came out of it.

[Raisa] Gorbachev: There was a lot of violence during the French revolution. Names of such heroes as Robespierre, Danton, and Marat are associated with revolutionary terror.

I think the situation in the world now is such that when people want to change their regime, their government, it is not by way of revolution anymore.

Gorbachev: In Poland, for example, people want to avoid repeating the events of 1980 more than anything else. By the way, this is the reason why Jaruzelski's path toward a dialogue with Solidarity, Lech Wałęsa, and all of Poland's political forces is gaining wide support among the Poles.

Mitterrand: By employing cruel methods, the leaders of the French revolution were able to unite the population against the foreign threat. They were very effective in this. Just as Stalin was in his time.

[Source: Archive of the Gorbachev Foundation, Fond 1. Opis 1. On file at the National Security Archive. Translated by Svetlana Savranskaya.]

Document No. 73: Address by Mikhail Gorbachev to the Council of Europe in Strasbourg

July 6, 1989

This document may be seen as Gorbachev's cri de coeur *for Soviet integration into Europe and the strongest expression of his vision of the new Europe. When he charged Zagladin with preparing a draft in early February 1989 (see Document No. 44), he intended this speech to be the equivalent of his December 1988 United Nations address, but aimed at European audiences. In it he lays out the meaning and the intended structure of the "common European home," repeatedly emphasizing that the Soviet Union belongs with the Western democratic community.*

Significantly, Gorbachev begins by quoting the French poet and novelist Victor Hugo, who in the 19th century predicted that "all the nations of the continent ... will merge inseparably into a high-level society and form a European brotherhood." The Soviet leader maintains this theme, using phrases such as "European unification" and "co-creation of all nations," which go beyond the simple idea of integration. The speech further links the idea of an integrated Europe with the inadmissibility of the use of force and attempts to limit the sovereignty of states, a vision with wider meaning for the world as Europe should be "seeking to transform international relations in the spirit of humanism, equality and justice by setting an example for democracy and social achievements." Importantly, the transformation of Europe is to be achieved on the basis of European common values and is intended to "make it possible to replace the traditional balance of forces with a balance of interests."

The common European home would be built on four main cornerstones: collective security—ruling out the very possibility of the use or threat of force; economic integration—"the emergence of a vast economic space from the Atlantic to the Urals;" protection of the environment; and humanitarianism—respect for human rights and a community based on laws.

Gorbachev also calls for a summit of signatories of the 1975 Helsinki Accords and hopes to use that model to build a European Community of the 21st century. This summit was eventually held in Paris in November 1990 and produced the Charter of Paris for a New Europe. Gorbachev's passionate dream of Europe was eventually overtaken by events in the heart of the continent—Poland had already had elections which brought about the defeat of the communists, and Hungary had begun its Roundtable negotiations leading to a multi-party system. But Germany had not yet moved toward unification, and thus the vision of a Europe without military blocs and borders still sounded quite realistic to its supporters.

Esteemed President, Ladies and Gentlemen, I thank you for the invitation to take the floor here, one of the epicenters of European politics and European thought. We may assess this meeting as proof that the all-European process is a reality and that it is advancing.

Now that the twentieth century is drawing to a close and the postwar period and the Cold War are becoming things of the past, the Europeans are beginning to face the unique opportunity of playing their role in building a new world, a role that is worthy of their history and their economic and intellectual potential. [...]

Victor Hugo said: "A day will come when you, France; you, Russia; you, Italy; you, Britain; and you, Germany—all of you, all nations of the continent will merge tightly, without losing your identities and your remarkable originality, into some higher society and form a European fraternity. [...]—A day will come when markets, open to trade, and minds, open to ideas, will become the sole battlefields."

It is not enough now merely to state the interdependence and joint destinies of the European states. The idea of European unity should be collectively rethought in the process of the concerted endeavor by all nations—large, medium, and small. [...]

Social and political orders in one or another country have changed in the past and may change in the future. But this change is the exclusive affair of the people of that country and is their choice. Any interference in domestic affairs and any attempts to restrict the sovereignty of states—friends, allies, or any others—are inadmissible.

Differences among states are not removable. They are, as I have already said on several occasions, even favorable—provided, of course, that the competition between the different types of society is directed toward creating better material and spiritual living conditions for all people. [...]

In the course of centuries Europe has made an indispensable contribution to world politics, economy, and culture, and to the development of the entire civilization. Its world historical role is universally recognized and praised.

Let us not forget, however, that the curse of colonial slavery spread worldwide from Europe. Fascism was born here. The most devastating wars began here. Europe may take legitimate pride in its accomplishments, but it has far from paid all its debts to humankind. This is yet to be done. This is to be done by pressing for changes in international relations in the spirit of humanism, equality, and justice and by setting an example of democracy and social achievements in their own countries.

The Helsinki process initiated this immense effort of world significance. Vienna and Stockholm have led it to fundamentally new frontiers. The documents adopted there are the most complete expression to date of the political culture and moral tradition of the European peoples.

We all, participants in the European process, are yet to use as fully as possible the prerequisites created by our common effort. This aim is served by our idea of the common European home.

Our idea of the common European home was born of the comprehension of new realities and the understanding of the fact that the linear continuation of the movement along which intra-European relations developed up to the last quarter of the twentieth century no longer matches these realities.

The idea is connected with our domestic economic and political restructuring, which was in need of new relationships primarily in that part of the world to which we, the Soviet Union, belong and with which we had been connected most of all for centuries.

We also took into account that the tremendous burden of armaments and the atmosphere of confrontation not only hindered the normal development of Europe, but at the same time prevented our country from joining in the European process economically, politically, and psychologically, and deformed our development.

These were the motives from which we decided to revitalize our European policy, which in itself, incidentally, had always been of importance to us.

Matters concerning both the architecture of a "common home" and methods for building it and even "furnishings" were touched upon during meetings with European leaders recently. Conversations with President François Mitterrand on this subject in Moscow and in Paris were also fruitful and rather wide-ranging.

I do not claim today that I have a ready-made blueprint for such a "home." Instead I shall speak of what, in my view, is the main point—namely, the need for a restructuring of the international order in Europe to bring to the fore all European values and make it possible to replace the traditional balance of forces with a balance of interests.

But what does this involve? Let us first take security issues. [...]

The philosophy of the "common European home" concept rules out the probability of an armed clash and the very possibility of the use of force or the threat of force—alliance against alliance, inside the alliances, wherever. This philosophy suggests that a doctrine of restraint should take the place of the doctrine of deterrence. This is not just a play on words, but the logic of European development prompted by life itself. [...]

If security is the foundation of the common European home, multifarious cooperation is its superstructure.

An intensive interstate dialogue—bilateral and multilateral—has become a sign of the new situation in Europe and the world in recent years. The range of agreements, treaties, and other accords has been considerably extended. Official consultations on diverse issues have become a feature of life.

The first contacts have been formed between NATO and the Warsaw Treaty organization, the EC and the CMEA, not to mention many political and public organizations in both parts of Europe. [...]

The need for a second conference of the Helsinki type is becoming increasingly topical. It is time for the present generation of leaders of the European countries, the United States, and Canada, to discuss, apart from most pressing issues, how they visualize the subsequent stages in the movement toward the European community of the twenty-first century.

As concerns the economic content of the European home, we consider the prospect for forming a vast economic space from the Atlantic to the Urals with

494

a high degree of interdependence between its Eastern and Western parts as real, although not immediate.

The Soviet Union's transition to a more open economy is of fundamental importance in this sense. And not only for ourselves—for enhancing the efficiency of the national economy and meeting consumer requirements. This will enhance the interdependence of the economies of East and West and, consequently, have a salutary effect on the entire complex of European relations. [...]

We have no doubt that integrational processes in Western Europe are acquiring a new quality. We do not underestimate the likelihood of the emergence of a single European market in the coming years.

The CMEA has also taken a course toward the formation of a joint market, although we lag far behind in this respect. The rate of internal transformations within the CMEA will in many respects determine what will undergo a more rapid development in the coming years—relationships between the CMEA and the EC as groupings or between individual socialist countries and the EC.

It is quite possible that from time to time this or that form will come to the fore. It is important that they both should fit into the logic of the formation of an all-European economic zone.

The next step in this process is perhaps a trade and economic agreement between our country and the EC. We also attach substantial importance to it from the viewpoint of all-European interests.

Naturally, we by no means counterpose our contacts with the BC to contacts with other associations or states. EFTA countries are our good and long-standing partners.

It would also be sensible perhaps to speak of the development of relations through CMEA and EFTA channels and to utilize this channel of multilateral cooperation in the building of a new Europe.

A common European home will need to be kept ecologically clean. Life has taught us bitter lessons. Ecological hazards in Europe have long transcended national boundaries.

To form a regional ecological security system is a matter of urgency. It is quite likely that the CSCE process will evolve most quickly in this really high-priority field.

The first step could be to elaborate a long-term continental ecological program. [...]

The humanitarian content of the CSCE process is decisive.

A world in which military arsenals would be cut but in which human rights would be violated cannot feel secure. We, for our part, have arrived at this conclusion finally and irrevocably.

The decisions made at the Vienna meeting signify a genuine breakthrough in this sense. A whole program for joint action by European countries has been mapped out with provision for the most diverse measures. Mutual understanding was reached on many issues which until recently were a stumbling block in East–West relations.

We are convinced that a reliable legal foundation should be furnished for the CSCE process. We visualize a common European home as a legal community, and we, for our part, have begun moving in that direction. [...]

Ladies and Gentlemen. Europeans can meet the challenges of the next century only by pooling their efforts.

We are convinced that they need one Europe—peaceful and democratic—a Europe that preserves all of its diversity and abides by common humane ideals, a prospering Europe that extends a hand to the rest of the world. A Europe that confidently marches into the future. We see our own future in this Europe.

Perestroika, which has as its goal the fundamental renewal of Soviet society, also predetermines our policy aimed at the development of Europe exactly in this direction. [...]

[*Source:* Vital Speeches of the Day; *9/15/1989, Vol. 55, Issue 23, pp. 706–711.*]

Document No. 74: Record of Concluding Conversation between Mikhail Gorbachev and François Mitterrand

July 6, 1989

In this conversation, Gorbachev shares with Mitterrand his concern about Bush's statements during his recent visit to Warsaw calling for the withdrawal of Soviet troops from Poland. He warns against a situation where "someone would try to behave like an elephant in a china shop" at such a sensitive time in Europe. Mitterrand promises to raise these issues with Bush at their forthcoming meeting. Gorbachev also informs the French leader that his negotiations with the Americans on the 50 percent strategic weapons reductions will not affect French and British nuclear weapons.

Gorbachev: It is good that you and I are discussing this topic now, in the context of the current deep changes. It is very important now, when responsibility and large-scale thinking are necessary.

I am not inclined to overdramatize the situation. I can tell you that we are going to continue taking the initiative in conducting our relations with the United States. I merely thought it was necessary to share with you our latest observations and thoughts about how the United States looks at the world, and moreover, how they act. To go to Poland and to talk about restoration of the 1939 borders in Europe, and to call for the withdrawal of Soviet troops—all this looks very strange to me.

Mitterrand: (Asks his assistant, J. Musitelli, when Bush made those statements.)

Frankly, I am also surprised by those statements, which do not take into account the experience of 45 years of post-war development. I do not think that we can open a new era in Europe if we begin with this type of proposals. I can only hope that that was a conclusion, not a preamble.

Gorbachev: It is important, Mr. President, to avoid a situation where in these times, which are marked with signs of big changes and common hopes, someone would try to behave like an elephant in a china shop.

Mitterrand: I am going to have a meeting with Bush in the near future and, of course, I will raise the issues that we discussed here. I promise that it will be a substantive conversation.

Gorbachev: I would like to touch upon the issue of French and British nuclear forces. We understand and take into account the specific nature of these weapons. I would like to ask you, Mr. President, to see that this situation does not affect French actions in the context of the processes unfolding now in Europe, in Geneva. I have in mind, for instance, the Soviet–American negotiations about a 50 percent reduction in strategic offensive weapons. This is all I would like to ask you about. However, it is not a small request.

[*Source: Archive of the Gorbachev Foundation, Fond 1. Opis 1. On file at the National Security Archive. Translated by Svetlana Savranskaya.*]

Document No. 75: Notes of Meeting of Warsaw Treaty Member-States

July 8, 1989

These notes of Gorbachev's meeting with the "fraternal" party leaders in Warsaw present an extraordinary contrast—in their shallowness, superficiality, and lack of specifics—with the candor seen earlier in his talks with Kohl and Mitterrand. Gorbachev cannot seem to stop talking, and his remarks are filled with generalities about perestroika *in the USSR with almost no attention paid to the crises in Eastern Europe. There is only a single paragraph in which the Soviet leader comments that "[a] number of countries are experiencing crises" and "[o]nly an objective, precise analysis of the causes will allow us to map out a way to overcome them. We have come to the conclusion that deep reforms are necessary." But what reforms? This is what Grósz described to Yakovlev as the "dialogue of the deaf." Here, Gorbachev appears to be just as hard of hearing as his colleagues, perhaps having been "deafened" by the quadruple shock of the Soviet elections, Tbilisi violence, Baltic vote, and the ongoing Polish transition.*

(Record of main content of conversation)

[...]

Gorbachev remarked in his speech that the conversation about topical problems of socialist construction had already begun at the PCC conference. Gorbachev joked: N. Ceauşescu spoke especially prolifically about this—he may have even exhausted his time limit for today.

It is evident that the need to exchange information and opinions on internal development issues in the socialist countries is great for everybody. However, right now we cannot explore this subject in depth because of time restrictions.

A detailed conversation can take place at the general secretaries' and fraternal parties' working meeting, which was prearranged to be held in Czechoslovakia. That meeting is being prepared; M. Jakeš will be the team leader. Although questions of economic collaboration were to be at the center of attention, everything is concentrated in this realm of cooperation. In a word, the most important conversation is still ahead of us.

Today I will only touch upon what concerns us all the most. The interest in questions of domestic policy development in our countries is natural. No one is indifferent to each other's state of affairs, because this is our fate. And considering socialism's international role, the fate of the entire world is concerned.

We are hearing about our friends' concerns in relation to the processes of socialist renewal in the Soviet Union.

The changes taking place are neither of a tactical nor opportunistic nature. It is not some kind of short-term election campaign that aims only at temporarily relieving the acuteness of the situation. It is a process of deep, fundamental changes.

Our friends' wish to comprehend what is going on in the Soviet Union is understandable. Regrettably, in some of the concerns that arise in this connection a note can be heard that is not in proportion to the problem. Sometimes not only anxiety crops up, but fear, even with a trace of panic. It is in consideration of these kinds of attitudes that I would like to speak about our affairs right now.

Every day life presents problems that acutely concern the broadest social spheres. It is as if we are under their press. Because of routine it is not always possible to evaluate the stage and context in which events develop. But without understanding this, one can only get tangled in details.

That is why when evaluating what is happening in the Soviet Union it is necessary to get up from our familiar seats and look at events from higher historical and philosophical positions.

It is very important to approach reality from this point of view—then the theory and policies of the changes can be understood.

For a long time we have been thinking carefully about the processes going on in the world. And we came to the conclusion that it is time to shift from the international order that has taken shape over the decades to a new one. And the nature of this new order largely depends on the process of development in the socialist countries.

The context of our internal development is also essential. We feel acutely that the goal of advancing to new boundaries requires an elevation of the productivity of social labor by the strictest standards. That is why we believe that in all areas of our collaboration—in the Council for Mutual Economic Assistance, in the Warsaw Treaty Organization, and at the general secretaries' meetings—it is necessary to assist the adaptation of socialism to the demands of the time and the current stage of the STR. Without this we will not accomplish the historic task of uncovering the potential of the socialist system.

Of course, we must sensibly evaluate socialism's services to humanity. Capitalism and the entire world would be different without socialism. And the future of the world depends on the future of socialism.

But a realistic approach does not allow us to close our eyes to the problems and shortcomings present in all socialist countries. Of course each country has its own, some more and some less. A number of countries are experiencing crises. Only an objective, precise analysis of the causes will allow us to map out a way to overcome them. We have come to the conclusion that deep reforms are necessary.

New impulses and stimuli, new dynamics of development will not appear without changing the relationships of production. We came to a new reading of the content of socialist property, to the diversity of its forms.

After all, the main goal of October 1917 was to overcome the alienation between working people and property. Here is the source for another motivation for

500

labor and human behavior. Regrettably, this did not happen. Decades of a command-administrative system separated the person from property and from developing his inner creative potential.

According to Lenin, socialism presupposes the closest ties with democracy. The development of democracy prepares socialism, and socialism develops democracy. This goal was not achieved. From here stems the second goal that stands before us—overcoming the alienation of the people from power. From there we moved on to the necessity of policy reform and democratization.

Finally, a very relevant problem is to overcome the alienation of the person from culture. We will have to include him in all cultural processes, and wake up the individual in each one.

In short, such is the philosophy of *perestroika*; it is based on a critical analysis of experience. In the four years since we took the course for *perestroika*, there has been no alternative and there is none [today].

The discussions are mainly only about the pace of reforms. Mostly, two extremes emerge.

Some are afraid that *perestroika* will infringe upon their interests and therefore avoid the changes and hinder the *perestroika* processes.

Others would like to solve all problems in one big sweep, to jump over the abyss in two leaps, so to speak. These radicals speculate on the natural expectations of the masses.

We have to implement *perestroika* within the framework of these complicated processes. You must consider this when you evaluate the flow of information you receive about the progress of *perestroika* in the Soviet Union. In a word, we understand: this is not maintenance, not some kind of whitewashing, but a deep transformation. And it is taking place in a multinational country, which leaves a special imprint on all processes.

That is why it is important to have an idea about how difficult and complicated our path is. But we cannot conceive it without socialism. [...]

Of course, in a specific interpretation of the goals of *perestroika* not everything is sufficiently clear yet. There have already been blunders during the *perestroika* processes, especially in the sphere of economics. The old forms are taken down decisively, while the new ones have not been developed yet. The market is out of balance, which causes natural discontent. We are forced to try quickly to remedy the situation.

It seems that at the forthcoming meeting of general secretaries, which could last perhaps for 2–3 days, we will try to present more detailed material on our affairs. But now we can already say that we have the main guarantee of *perestroika*'s success—the people have joined it. The Congress of People's Deputies has shown this conclusively. There were, of course, elements of naïveté, illusions, and even demagoguery. But on the whole, these are different people now who are ready for active participation in the affairs of government and society. Thirteen days of the Congress' work had a deep impact on all of society. *Perestroika* is acquiring an irreversible character. But if we are asked where we are right now, there will be one reply: in the most difficult period, accompanied by confused minds and conflicting interests.

The party's lagging behind the processes of change is also part of our current reality. We seek answers to demands of these new times.

As has happened in some other fraternal parties, we are thinking about moving forward the date of the next Party Conference; perhaps it will be convened in fall 1990. We will have to consolidate the present stage of *perestroika* and build a way toward its next stage. New changes in the party and in the economy are needed. A further rotation of the staff is also forthcoming. Even V.I. Lenin said that new policies need new people. And this does not depend only on subjective wishes anymore. The very process of democratization demands it. [...]

[Source: Archive of the Gorbachev Foundation, Fond 2. Opis 1. On file at the National Security Archive. Translated by Anna Melyakova.]

Document No. 76: Information Note regarding George H.W. Bush's Visit to Poland (July 9–11)

July 18, 1989

In this summary of Bush's conversation with Jaruzelski, prepared by the Polish For-eign Ministry, one sees Bush's caution and sensitivity about undermining Gorbach-ev's policy or destabilizing Eastern Europe in any way. He mentions several times his respect for Gorbachev and his resolve not to interfere in the processes in Poland. Jaruzelski makes it very clear to Bush that Western economic assistance is needed if the Polish reform is to succeed and that its success or failure would have wide implications throughout Eastern Europe. When discussing the idea of the common European home, Jaruzelski expresses a preference for a little more privacy—"that it should be a house with free corridors between respective rooms." Bush, however, seems to agree with Gorbachev's more radical vision—"a united Europe, without foreign troops (including American troops)." He sees this as "a vision of the future, but he is not waiting for a unilateral withdrawal of Soviet troops from Poland." Bush also asks Jaruzelski to make it clear to Gorbachev that his recent remarks were not a call for a Soviet pullout, which was a concern for the Soviet leader.

[…]

Pres. Bush expressed great satisfaction with the fresh possibility of visiting Po-land. He is impressed by the changes, which the world is watching with bated breath and admiration. He underscored that he did not come to Poland to com-plicate the very difficult work Gen. Jaruzelski has to perform. He does not want to engage in "super rhetoric" that could be received well in the West but would hinder actions by the Polish authorities.

It is not his goal to make Gorbachev's life more difficult and to trigger in-ternal tensions in the socialist camp. He came to pay tribute to the reforms and changes and to encourage their intensification and expansion, to speak about how the United States could contribute to Poland's economic renewal, but not to in-terfere in any way in our internal affairs. That is the general goal of President Bush's visit to Poland, and [he was] pleased to hear the comments by his host, who is in a position to realize that goal.

Also, he does not intend for the present visit to create a peculiar contest about who is more popular: Gorbachev in the West, in the FRG and France, or Bush in the East, in Poland and Hungary.

He is prepared to discuss every aspect of Polish–American relations. He also wants to emphasize that because of the course Gen. Jaruzelski has declared and taken, his personal standing and popularity have never been as high in the United States as they are at present.

Thanking [Bush] for expressing such relevant intentions for his visit, Gen. W. Jaruzelski stressed that we are all aware of the superpower leaders' tremendous responsibilities with regard to global problems, but also in reference to our country. He added that during his visit to France and the FRG M. Gorbachev did not do and did not say anything that could damage U.S. interests. It is invigorating that people of such high prestige approach politics in such a responsible manner, in a spirit of mutual trust and respect for a partner's interests. Only in this way is it possible to move forward. [...]

Reporting specifically on the results of the meeting of the Political Consultative Committee of the Warsaw Pact nations in Bucharest, Gen. W. Jaruzelski underlined that it was another step on the path toward progress in arms reductions and international cooperation, and toward achieving stability and security in Europe. The main emphasis in Bucharest was on political cooperation, and not military confrontation. The internal problems of the allies were also discussed, on which there is greater pluralism than in NATO. The PRL, Hungary and the USSR find themselves at the forefront of change and reform. But another viewpoint also exists. Some allies are concerned that the situation will slip out of control, that it will explode. Thus, the Polish situation might represent an incentive [for reform], or discourage [others] from reform if there are only empty shelves in Poland. Therefore if the West is interested in success for our reforms, they should see them not only in the Polish context but also in terms of spreading conditions. In Bucharest we spoke in favor of arms control, détente, the development of East–West relations, and a common European home. At the same time, if you are dealing with Poland we support the American concept, that it should be a house with free corridors between the respective rooms.

Pres. Bush asked if in Bucharest all of the allies were interested in the development of Poland's situation or [if] they expressed anxieties that [the Poles] were moving too rapidly toward reform. In response, Gen. W. Jaruzelski stated that one must understand their anxieties. Some see the achievements of the Korean People's Republic or Romania. It turns out that [those] results were generated by a dictatorship or a strong hand or money. We do not have either the first or the second. Bush added that Poland has the respect of the entire world and has never been in the same league [as the others], whereas who knows or talks about the achievements of the PDRK or Romania. [...]

In the conversation, Pres. Bush repeatedly returned to the topic of the Soviets. Several times he underscored that he did not regard his visit as a test for meddling in Poland or internal bloc matters. Similarly, one should not think that it is his intention to break up the socialist bloc and to hinder M. Gorbachev's life.

He stressed, nevertheless, that in the preceding administration he was the vice president and that after winning the election he insisted on completing a thorough inter-departmental review of American policy regarding the USSR and the socialist bloc. Its outcomes were apparent in Bush's speeches in Hamtramck and in Texas.

As a result of this review it was decided to unambiguously support Gorbachev and his *perestroika* policy.

Bush personally values the candid dialogue with Gen. Jaruzelski and would be pleased if a similar one existed with Gorbachev.

After Gen. Jaruzelski encouraged frequent contacts between leaders of both powers, Bush responded that they are thinking about that in Washington. Secretary of State Baker already maintains contacts with Min. Shevardnadze. The Soviets related that J. Baker is not only a talented secretary of state, but Bush's best long-term friend. Contacts with him are nearly tantamount to contacts with the president of the United States. [Bush] worries, he added, that [his] meeting with Gorbachev could create too great an expectation, particularly regarding arms reduction agreements which are still not ready. They noted many signs of good relations. The Soviets did not reject the American arms reduction proposals, a Soviet ship helped clean up the oil in the sea near Alaska, and Americans sent burn experts to treat victims of a train collision in Siberia, with serious cases being treated in San Antonio. The head of the U.S. Joint Chiefs of Staff returned not long ago from unusually successful meetings in the Soviet Union. There were no antagonisms or hidden motives that could avert or keep the U.S. far away from the USSR.

Bush expressed satisfaction with the USSR's positive reaction regarding the quick attainment of success in conventional arms reductions, so that the deadlines set for reductions could be met.

Finally Bush requested that Gen. Jaruzelski clarify to Gorbachev that he did not comment on withdrawing the Soviet army from Poland. He added that his comment was poorly interpreted. A united Europe, without foreign troops (including American troops) is a vision of the future, but he is not waiting for a unilateral withdrawal of Soviet troops from Poland. It would be good if Gen. Jaruzelski would be willing to inform Mr. Gorbachev of that and to clear the atmosphere in relations for both leaders.

[*Source: Archive of the Polish Ministry of Foreign Affairs, 2/94, W-8, Dep III (1989), AP 220-15-89. Located and translated by Gregory F. Domber.*]

Document No. 77: Record of Conversation between Aleksandr Yakovlev and Jack Matlock

July 20, 1989

This memorandum from the Yakovlev files in the Russian State Archive highlights several significant points relating to U.S.–Soviet ties during the important early period of the Bush presidency. For one, it provides an indication of how extensive the "pause" in the relationship was in 1989 (despite the crush of events in Eastern Europe), when veteran U.S. Ambassador Jack Matlock comments to Russia's leading "new thinker"—"We have not met for several months." One of the consequences of this lack of direct contact is the likelihood of misunderstandings. When Yakovlev complains about President Bush's remarks in Poland, which raised the issue of withdrawing Soviet troops, Matlock assures him the statement was not "planned," and that Bush had made a "mistake" which "he did not repeat." (Compare this with Bush's account of the incident to Jaruzelski in Document No. 76.) Matlock calls for "a constant dialogue between our countries in order to understand better the acceptable limits of statements"—a dialogue that would not resume, however, until the Malta talks in December.

Another interesting revelation is the serious underestimation on Yakovlev's part of the forces of nationalism within the USSR—"nobody is seriously planning to secede from the Soviet Union," he insists.

But the most astonishing exchange is the repudiation of the shared vision that Gorbachev and Reagan reached at Reykjavik in 1986, when the two leaders came close to agreement on the abolition of nuclear weapons. Yakovlev twice raises the subject, but Matlock does not pick up on it until the second mention. When Yakovlev says the most important subject is "how better to liquidate nuclear weapons," Matlock corrects him, saying: "Reagan believed in the possibility of liquidating nuclear weapons. Bush thinks that we need to reduce them to a minimum, but we should not liquidate them." Matlock goes on to say that even "an agreement in principle about the liquidation of nuclear weapons" would be "premature" at this moment, to which Yakovlev responds, "in five years it will be too late."

For Matlock, the key issue is Yakovlev's comment on lifting travel restrictions to the U.S.: the only limit on visits is "the absence of the necessary financial means. There are no political limitations."

Matlock: Thank you for receiving me. We have not met for several months. During this time President [George] Bush has visited Eastern Europe and M.S. Gorbachev visited Western Europe. In our opinion, those visits were constructive. What is your assessment? I would also like to know your opinion about the overall state of Soviet–American relations.

Yakovlev: From our point of view, the trips to Europe produced results that were not bad. One may say that there has been a change from a confrontational approach to cooperation. Both leaders in their statements avoided anything that could inspire hostile feelings with regard to the other side. One exception was Bush's response to the question about withdrawal of Soviet troops from Poland. M.S. Gorbachev emphasized the need for U.S. participation in the resolution of European problems.

Gorbachev's appeal to the "Seven" is an appeal for a transparency in policy. We need more trust in the relations among all countries. The absence of information sometimes leads to an aggravation of relations, when in reality there might have been no problem at all.

I cannot avoid saying that the resolution NATO adopted in Brussels surprised us. The language in which it is written is at least ten years out of date.

There is only one danger—nuclear weapons. As long as they exist, there exists a threat to peace. If we liquidate them, there will be no threat. Some people cite the fact that before the era of nuclear weapons, bloody wars took place as well. However, times are very different now, and it is impossible to compare the situation today with the prewar situation.

Matlock: As far as foreign policy is concerned, there are no substantial disagreements between the political parties of the United States. There are some disagreements on secondary issues. For example, the Congress, which is dominated by the Democrats, wants the president to endorse more serious sanctions against China, and Bush stands by a more moderate policy. He also introduced changes in U.S. policy toward Latin America. But in general, in contrast to the first half of the 1980s, the administration and the Congress are working well together.

The same can be said about U.S. policy toward the Soviet Union. Here, too, Congress and the president are in agreement.

Expressing my personal opinion, I would like to say that the statement regarding the withdrawal of Soviet troops from Poland was not planned by President Bush. It was asked at the press conference, and Bush expressed his opinion. Later he understood that he made a certain mistake, and he did not repeat it again.

Of course there are issues of contention and different approaches. The United States is in favor of democratization, freedom, but we do not want a destabilization of the situation in the USSR or in other countries of Eastern Europe. The processes unfolding in Eastern Europe may not always be correctly understood in Washington. That is why it is important for us to maintain a constant dialogue between our countries in order to understand better the acceptable limits of statements, and to highlight those sensitive moments on which it would be better to abstain.

We understand well that the issue of inter-ethnic relations is one of the most acute in the Soviet Union. It has not found a solution yet. It is also known that the United States does not recognize the inclusion of the Baltic states in the Soviet Union. However, we do not want this issue to be resolved forcibly. We believe sincerely in the goals of *perestroika*. We realize that if the *perestroika* process succeeds in the Soviet Union, it would be to our benefit as well. That is why we do not want to interfere with this process. But we would like to know more precisely what in our actions or statements could potentially, even unintentionally, harm this process, because sometimes we simply do not possess the necessary information.

Yakovlev: Since our conversation is unofficial and quite sincere, I would like to say that I believe that the United States is not trying to destabilize the situation in the Soviet Union, because, simply speaking, it would not be profitable for you. But we all need to be more careful in any statements that touch upon the other side. Recently there appeared a resolution regarding the so-called captive nations. It resulted in demonstrations, rallies, and hunger strikes in support of this statement in the Baltics. However, if we look at the present situation in the Baltic republics, who is captive there? This word is not appropriate to the real situation. At the same time, the statement by the U.S. President made a certain impression on the extremist circles, which put forward an appeal to secede from the USSR. But speaking seriously, where would they go?

Matlock: That statement was adopted in accordance with the resolution of the Congress, and it is adopted annually.

Yakovlev: I am aware of that, but the situation is changing radically. And now the price of words has gone up significantly. We know it from our own experience.

The USSR is really going through some difficult times now. *Perestroika* is passing through a critical stage, and the nationalities issue is one of the most acute. At the same time, the calls of the extremists notwithstanding, nobody is seriously planning to secede from the Soviet Union. For decades we accumulated problems, about which we could not speak publicly. Now we can do that, and we start from the assumption that we need to give these emotions an opportunity to surface. The people will figure out the situation on their own, and everything will stay within a reasonable framework.

I think that for some time passions will rage in our country. However, I am an optimist. Beginning in 1990 we are introducing republic-level economic self-sufficiency, for some republics at first. Let them experience firsthand economic and political problems that need to be solved.

The period of transition is a very complex one. In the economy, the reform has not been completed yet, wholesale trade has not been introduced, and our economists, citing different American experts, give contradictory advice.

Matlock: We tell the following story as a joke: when Truman became U.S. president, he listened to the opinions of various economists, who always said, "on the one hand," and "on the other hand." Then he asked his aide to find him a one-armed economist, who would have only one hand.

Yakovlev: Returning to the problems of foreign policy, I would like to say that we need to conduct negotiations on reducing both conventional and nuclear weapons more actively. Anti-nuclear feelings, which have always been strong, are becoming more acute now. If we continue perfecting nuclear weapons, then we will not be able to stop this process. We should find "one-armed" scientists, who could give us advice on how better to liquidate nuclear weapons.

Matlock: One has to take into account that positions and approaches change slowly. Reagan believed in the possibility of liquidating nuclear weapons. Bush thinks that we need to reduce them to a minimum, but we should not liquidate them. He believes that without nuclear weapons the risk of war being unleashed would increase. For the time being the question of liquidating nuclear weapons has rather a philosophical, but not a practical, character. That we need to reduce the number of nuclear weapons substantially is clear to everybody. If conventional weapons are reduced, that would make the approach to the issue of liquidating nuclear weapons easier, although these problems are not directly linked. Nuclear weapons were developed in the United States as a counterbalance to the conventional weapons of the Soviet Union, in order to achieve a balance of forces and carry out the policy of deterrence. Reducing conventional weapons to a minimum would create a psychological climate, which would help to move on to the solution of the problem of nuclear weapons. I think that the proposals introduced in Vienna and Geneva are constructive and open the way toward an agreement. We are on the right track.

I personally believe that it would be premature now even to achieve an agreement in principle about the liquidation of nuclear weapons in the future.

Yakovlev: I, naturally, do not agree with this point of view. Our mistrust toward each other was the basis for the accumulation of nuclear weapons. Today, it seems to me, we have abandoned the previous stereotypes, and we don't think that we want to destroy each other. And today we are talking not just about Soviet and American nuclear weapons, but in five years a number of other countries will possess nuclear weapons. A danger emerges that in the course of regional conflicts one of those countries will not be able to resist the temptation to use nuclear weapons. The USSR and the USA can achieve an agreement about liquidating nuclear weapons, but I am not absolutely sure that it would be possible to do that with all other countries. Today we can put nuclear weapons and their liquidation under strict international control. We could introduce a rule, according to which inspection visits could be arranged on the basis of any suspicion. In five years it will be too late.

Matlock: What is your assessment of the work of the USSR Supreme Soviet, and what kind of relationship exists between the CC CPSU Commission on International Relations and the International Commission of the USSR Supreme Soviet?

Yakovlev: So far we have not experienced any problems in discussing foreign policy issues. We have not thought yet about coordination of the actions of the Commissions of the CC CPSU and the Supreme Soviet. We believe that in contrast to economic activities, where one needs a separation of functions, as far as foreign policy is concerned they require a partnership.

Matlock: Will the principle of party discipline work during voting on any Supreme Soviet resolutions on foreign policy issues?

Yakovlev: This question remains open so far, but I think that it will not. It is natural that unity is needed on questions of principle and in approaches to the main course of foreign policy.

Matlock: Do you need to change the CPSU Charter for that?

Yakovlev: No, we don't, because at least in theory we never rejected the pluralism of opinions. And besides, it is impossible to address all questions in charters or resolutions of any kind. Life itself will advise us.

Matlock: I sent to Washington my ideas about the necessity to find some method for inviting Soviet leaders, especially those at the republic and *oblast* levels, to the United States. Of course, this proposal has to be thought through still, but I think that it will be done in two or three months. I think invitations will be sent on behalf of congressmen and governors of individual states of the United States. We need to expand channels of contacts between our countries.

Yakovlev: Our reservations in developing extensive personal contacts with the United States can mainly be explained by the absence of the necessary financial means. There are no political limitations.

Matlock: We in our Embassy have issued 30,000 tourist visas for visits to the United States in the last six months. We expect the number to reach 70,000 by the end of the year.

Let me thank you for the time you have given me. I would like to repeat once again that in my opinion we are on the right track, we are trying to understand better the processes that are unfolding in the Soviet Union. I would like to have an opportunity to meet with you in the future from time to time.

As far as the congressional resolution "On Captive Nations" is concerned, it would be hard to change it. I expect that a large number of members of Congress and U.S. Senators will come to Moscow. I will be talking to them about this problem.

Yakovlev: The new times call for new terminology. We should be looking for non-standard ways of improving relations between our countries.

Candidate Member of the CC CPSU, First Deputy Head of the International Department of the CC CPSU K. N. Brutents was present during the conversation.

The conversation was recorded by senior staff member of the International Department of the CC CPSU E. S. Lagutin.

[*Source: State Archive of the Russian Federation [GARF], Moscow. Yakovlev Collection. Fond 10063. Opis 1. Delo 264. On file at the National Security Archive. Translated by Svetlana Savranskaya.*]

Document No. 78: Report from Rezső Nyers and Károly Grósz on Negotiations with Mikhail Gorbachev

July 24–25, 1989

During this visit to Moscow, the Hungarian communists are no longer quite the suppliants of the previous year, but they are still probing Moscow's reactions, still working to ascertain the limits of Gorbachev's tolerance, still uncertain themselves of how far to go—and receiving very little direction from their Big Brothers in the Kremlin. This document from the Hungarian archives provides the delegation's report back to the comrades in Budapest about their surreal experience in the Soviet capital. At one level, the talks provided yet another warning to the Kremlin of how far the situation had disintegrated among the "fraternal allies." The new leadership of the Hungarian party, prominent among them the reform economist Rezső Nyers, told Gorbachev that the Hungarian party was in tatters, its legitimacy gone, the cadres paralyzed, and disintegration imminent. Among the political factors that "can defeat the party," Nyers lists first of all "the past, if we let ourselves [be] smeared with it." Indeed, the Soviet repression of 1956 was, as Timothy Garton Ash put it later, like Banquo's ghost, destroying the legitimacy of the Hungarian party, just as the crushing of the Prague Spring in 1968, martial law in Poland in 1981, and all the other communist "blank spots" of history did to communist ideology in 1989. For their part, of course, Soviet party reformers (including Gorbachev) did not quite know how to respond as events accelerated in 1989—except not to repeat 1956. They did not know what to do, only what not to do.

REPORT
to the Political Executive Committee

Invited by the Central Committee of the Soviet Communist Party, comrades Rezső Nyers and Károly Grósz visited the Soviet Union on 24 and 25 July 1989. They took part in a two-hour negotiation with Comrade Mikhail Gorbachev, general secretary of the Central Committee of the Soviet Communist Party. The Central Committee of the Soviet Communist Party invited the delegates for dinner, with the participation of several Soviet leaders. Comrades Nyers and Grósz negotiated with leaders of the Soviet–Hungarian Friendship Society. Comrade Nyers met Soviet social scientists; Comrade Grósz met leading officials of the Central Committee of the Soviet Communist Party.

Comrade Nyers described the situation of Hungary and the Hungarian Socialist Workers Party. He said that the party is preparing for a working congress.[62] A decision has not been made on every issue yet but it is quite definite that internal issues of the party will be on the agenda. A task set for the congress is to render the unity of the party. Comrade Nyers pointed out that the party is already becoming active, and new platforms are being formed. The basic concept of the congress is democratic socialism, self-government, parliamentary democracy, and economic democracy. Comrade Nyers emphasized that property reform is considered the primary element of the reforms. We wish to democratize public property, indeed making it available for the public. We are considering a new system that utilizes available capital more efficiently. We are planning to increase the ratio of private capital in the economy and the investment of foreign capital.

Comrade Nyers mentioned the experiences of parliamentary by-elections.[63] He emphasized that one should not jump to immediate conclusions from the results. We consider the elections neither a success nor a complete failure. The present state of paralysis within the party, however, has become apparent. He referred to the fact that in one constituency the opposition united their forces in the campaign against the MSZMP, but this is not expected to be a broad tendency when it comes to the general elections. Comrade Nyers stressed that there are three factors that can defeat the party. First: the past, if we let ourselves get smeared with it. Second: the disintegration of the party. The third factor that can defeat us is the paralysis of party membership.

Speaking about Hungary, Comrade Gorbachev said that Hungarian events are followed with much interest in the Soviet Union. The leadership of the Soviet Communist Party refers to our policy with understanding. In the course of negotiations they understood our intention to find our way on the path of democratic socialism. At the same time, Comrade Gorbachev posed several questions relating to Hungary's situation and the policy of the MSZMP. Among other things, he inquired about our orientation in foreign policy, the role of private property and foreign capital, the experiences of by-elections, the goals of the party congress, and about the unity of the party. Comrade Gorbachev put special emphasis on the fact that Soviet leaders interpret the mass sympathy towards the MSZMP demon-

---

[62] The 14th Congress of the MSZMP was held on October 6–10, 1989. During the congress the party dissolved itself and on October 7 formed a new entity, the Hungarian Socialist Party.

[63] On July 22, 1989, parliamentary by-elections were held in four constituencies but the first round brought a final result in only one of them, where the opposition parties formed a coalition and won. The second round of elections was held on August 5 when candidates of the Hungarian Democratic Forum acquired two of the seats while in one constituency the election was void. [Footnote in the original.]

strated at the funeral of János Kádár[64] as an important political resource to rely upon. [...]

IV.

In the course of the visit, several issues of the bilateral relationship were discussed. Negotiators mutually agreed that we should widen the scope of relations between the MSZMP and the CPSU, and increase the exchange of experiences. In this way the recently aggravated laxity that has been hindering the cooperation of Soviet and Hungarian party organizations can be effectively eradicated. Hungarian negotiators suggested that the CPSU and other Soviet social organizations begin collaborating with Hungarian democratic organizations and newly forming parties as well.[65]

The negotiations proved that it is our mutual intention to maintain the friendship of the Hungarian and Soviet nations, and create a new basis for reinforcing the friendship movement, winning over the best professionals and the youth for the friendship of the two nations.

In the course of negotiations, Hungarian and Soviet leaders examined the most urgent issues regarding the stationing of Soviet troops in Hungary. Comrade Nyers reminded the negotiators that at the meeting between Comrades Grósz and Gorbachev in Moscow in March, they agreed in principle that troops would continue to be withdrawn. At that time, Soviet negotiators asked that this agreement not be publicized. This time, Comrade Nyers suggested that the March agreement be reinforced, and the question of withdrawing Soviet troops further considered and publicized in one way or another. Speaking for the Soviet leadership, Comrade Gorbachev agreed with the idea. His suggestion was that when dealing with the issue, one should start from what the Soviet press release says about the subject: "In the course of negotiations, the issue of Soviet troops stationed in Hungary was brought up, and the parties decided that steps will be made to further reduce the number of Soviet troops in accordance with the European disarmament process and with the continuation of the Vienna talks." Comrades Nyers and Grósz agreed with the suggestion.

In the course of the negotiations, we reaffirmed our mutual political intent to seek the possibility of establishing a new basis for Hungarian–Soviet economic

---

[64] The aging János Kádár, holding the honorary title of party president since the party conference in May 1988, died on July 6, 1989; his funeral on July 14 was attended by tens of thousands of people.

[65] On July 27, just a few days after the return of the two MSZMP leaders from Moscow, József Antall, Hungarian Democratic Forum representative, made a proposal to the Opposition Roundtable to invite the Soviet ambassador in Budapest and inform him of the opposition's ideas. This move strengthened the probability that a secret communications link existed between the MSZMP and certain opposition representatives, as was commonly believed (but never proved) at the time.

cooperation. Comrade Nyers indicated that the Hungarian government is presently working on a new fiscal system, and that the proposals might be submitted this autumn.

The president of the MSZMP emphasized that the situation of Hungarian minorities in the Sub-Carpathian region is improving, which is of great importance for us in terms of domestic and foreign affairs alike. Comrade Gorbachev indicated that they are determined to head in this direction.

Another subject was raised: many Hungarian soldiers died in action on the Soviet front or in POW camps in World War II. Hungarian public opinion is exerting pressure to preserve the memory of these victims in an appropriate fashion. Comrade Gorbachev emphasized that the Soviet Union is ready to cooperate in this field as well. They said that mass graves on battlefields are virtually impossible to find now. However, they are ready to specify cemeteries where Hungarian prisoners of war were buried. They would preserve the tombs, memorial monuments could be installed, and Hungarian citizens could visit these sites. The same practice is working well with the Federal Republic of Germany. [...]

[*Source:* A Magyar Szocialista Munkáspárt Központi Bizottágának 1989. évi jegyzokönyvei. *[Minutes of the 1989 meetings of the Hungarian Socialist Workers' Party Central Committee] Editors: Anna S. Kosztricz, János Lakos, Karola Vágyi, Mrs. Németh, László Soós, György T. Varga.* Magyar Országos Levéltár *[Hungarian National Archives], Bp. 1993, Vols. I–II. Translation provided by the Cold War History Research Center, Budapest.*]

Document No. 79: Transcript of SED Politburo Sessions

September 5, 1989[66]

At this stage, the East German communist leadership is just catching up to the fact that the Hungarian communists have already decided—with some support from Moscow—to open their borders to the West (see Document No. 50). The scenes of East Germans hiking en masse to the Austrian border and flocking to embassies in Prague and Budapest while awaiting train tickets to the West, would dramatically degrade what little GDR prestige remained from its higher-than-average living standards in the bloc. In this record, we see the unvarnished discussions of the GDR leadership, featuring repeated attacks on the Hungarians for doing the bidding of the FRG, and "betraying socialism." This discussion takes place two months after Gorbachev's candid conversations with Kohl whom he treated as a peer and partner to an extent that would have appalled the members of the SED, although some may have feared as much in light of evidence such as that cited below—that the Soviet Foreign Ministry is trying to prevent the GDR from calling a foreign ministers' meeting to rein in the Hungarians.

[Oskar] Fischer: The letter from Comrade Shevardnadze was forwarded by Comrade Gorinovich. He emphasized the Soviet Union's concern over the further escalation of the campaign against the GDR. Kvitsinsky will speak with Genscher's representative to cool or temper feelings in the FRG. Fischer told Gorinovich that the article in *Pravda* was indeed good, but the Soviet side has far more possibilities.[67] O. Fischer's proposal to convene the Committee of Foreign Ministers of the Warsaw Treaty states met with misgivings from Gorinovich. That did not materialize too quickly. One must take into consideration the deviating viewpoints in Poland and Hungary as well. Fischer stuck to the proposal, but Shevardnadze's representative, Aboimov, had reservations too. It seems clear that Hungary will be yielding to the pressure from the FRG. Németh, Pozsgay, and Horn are not playing their cards openly. Minister of the Interior Horváth views the situation better. A change in the Hungarian position, beginning with the emigration of GDR citizens from September 11, should not be expected.

[Willi] Stoph: The West wants to continually raise the stakes. Hungary supports this in reality, particularly with the open borders. That goes against all treaties. The FRG's campaign also goes against the agreements between Erich

---

[66] Standing in again for Egon Krenz at the session was Wolfgang Herger, who took down the minutes. [Footnote in the original.]

[67] Under the headline "Hour of the Hypocrites," *Pravda* ran an article by M. Podklyuchnikov. The West German media was made responsible above all for the situation in Hungary. See *Neues Deutschland*, September 1, 1989.

Honecker and Kohl. We must present our situation more aggressively to our allies and other countries. [...]

[Kurt] Hager: Hungary is playing a double game. Their meeting in Bonn is further kept in secret.[68] The Hungarian gate remains open. It is therefore necessary for the Warsaw Treaty states to present our point of view to Hungary. In the long run such a negative position by Hungary does not bode well for friendly discussions between the two of us. What they are doing is a breach of hitherto normal relations. We are faced with the question of how we should continue to conduct ourselves with Hungary. For me, that is still an open question. But the Hungarian position worsens with respect to us—in favor of Bonn. They will obey orders from Bonn. [...]

[Werner] Krolikowski: I am in agreement with the letter by Erich Honecker,[69] the newscast declaration, and the other materials. We must continue unwaveringly:

To strengthen the GDR

To strengthen the alliance system, particularly with the Soviet Union

To expose the FRG campaign

One must fundamentally assess the enemy's entire campaign and present it to the Politburo. We should use Shevardnadze's letter as an opportunity to make the first proposals. We must also continue to work with Hungary, so that what is planned does not occur. [...]

[Erich] Mielke: Hungary is betraying socialism. The proposal by Fischer for a foreign ministers' meeting is very important. It concerns the power relationships in socialism in general. If Hungary continues to proceed with this, we risk having Hungary become a transit country. We must, however, support our comrades in Hungary, too. We provide our comrades with theoretical articles, which are being read and studied. What matters though is to clarify the practical questions in the spirit of these good, theoretical articles. [...]

[*Source: Stiftung Archiv der Parteien und Massenorganisationen der DDR-Bundesarchiv. Translated by Christiaan Hetzner.*]

---

[68] During a surprise visit to Bonn, Hungarian Prime Minister Németh and Foreign Minister Horn reached agreement with Chancellor Kohl and Foreign Minister Genscher to open the Hungarian border to the West to those GDR citizens who wanted to emigrate. See Horn, *Freiheit, die ich meine.*

[69] On September 5, *Neues Deutschland* first published an article by Erich Honecker entitled "40 Years of the German Democratic Republic," which was originally written for the theoretical journal of the Central Committee of the SED, "Unity." See *Einheit,* 1989 Volume 9/10, p. 788. [Footnote in the original.]

Document No. 80: Memorandum of Conversation between Oskar Fischer and Vyacheslav Kochemassov

September 7, 1989

In this discussion, East German Foreign Minister Oskar Fischer seeks reassurance from the Soviet ambassador to East Berlin in the midst of the refugee crisis precipitated by Hungary's decision to open its border with Austria. Ambassador Kochemassov tells Fischer that his colleagues are in fact actively rebuking both the West Germans and the Hungarians. In particular, Moscow's envoy to Bonn, Yuli Kvitsinsky, is a hard-line holdover who has been blasting the FRG for encouraging the East German émigrés, and "condemn[ing]" repeated statements by politicians to the effect that the GDR's days are numbered. The latter remark comes in the wake of highly-publicized comments by the U.S. ambassador to the FRG, Vernon Walters, in the International Herald Tribune predicting the speedy reunification of Germany.[70]

Comrade Kochemassov provided information first of all about the activities of the Soviet ambassador to Hungary aimed at influencing the appropriate Hungarian comrades and afterwards preparing a detailed report on the course and results of the discussions conducted between the Soviet ambassador in Bonn, Comrade Kvitsinsky, and the chancellor's Office minister, Seiters. Therefore, Comrade Kvitsinsky expressed on behalf of the Soviet Foreign Ministry their serious apprehensiveness concerning the line being pursued by the West German authorities and mass media in regard to GDR citizens' attempts to illegally emigrate to the FRG. He stated that continuation of the situation could lead to a limitation of contacts between citizens of both German states, especially since the GDR controls these possibilities. [...]

Referring to the repeated statements by Bonn politicians that the days of the GDR are numbered and the reunification of Germany is on the agenda, Comrade Kvitsinsky condemned such a course and called for realism in view of the understanding that the GDR has a place in Europe. If the FRG is endeavoring to limit the influx of refugees and not to bury the GDR, it must recognize GDR state citizenship and put an end to immigration from the GDR through economic aid. It makes martyrs out of these so-called "cross-settlers," however, warriors fighting against socialism. [...]

It was agreed that Comrade Oskar Fischer and Comrade Kochemassov should remain in continual contact, and, as needed, keep one another promptly informed.

[*Source: Stiftung Archiv der Parteien und Massenorganisationen der DDR-Bundesarchiv. Translated by Christiaan Hetzner.*]

---

[70] Hutchings, *American Diplomacy,* 80, 380, footnote 90.

Document No. 81: Letter from Gerd Vehres to Oskar Fischer

September 10, 1989[71]

This personal letter from the GDR's man in Budapest to the foreign minister reports on his recent talks with Rezső Nyers. Responding to East Berlin's condemnation of Hungary's émigré policy, Nyers claims that the border openings are "only a temporary measure." But Ambassador Gerd Vehres dismisses this and other comments from the Hungarians as "an attempt at stalling and deliberately misleading the GDR." Rather than understand the flight of so many East Germans as a popular judgment on the regime, the SED is only able to conceive it as "a coordinated and successful attempt by the imperialist states ..."

Dear Comrade Minister:

In addition to my CT 385 from September 10, I would like to inform you of some further aspects of my conversation with Comrade Nyers.

After I had given our initial position on the decision by the Hungarian government and the following recognition by the Party Presidium, Comrade Nyers replied:

Comrade Nyers does not wish the events mentioned to be viewed in the GDR as an anti-GDR campaign.

Comrade Nyers believes that a great part of the original problem was caused by the sudden opening of the border with Austria. This fact strengthened existing intentions among a number of GDR tourists to leave the country illegally. The quickly increasing numbers willing to leave under existing circumstances make it impossible to convince such a huge number of people by words or declarations. Had Hungarian organs been placed deep in the affair, that is, in the situation themselves, many substantial conflicts would have been started that would have been undesired by both Hungary and the GDR.

The only political victor in this case is the FRG. Comrade Nyers expressed his conviction that in the future the Hungarian side must deal with us on a more mutual level. He believes that the present wave of emigration is unique and that later this will start to abate, and consequently the problem will become manageable. Related to this, he emphasized once again that the Hungarian decision is only a temporary measure, valid for just a short time. Afterwards the Hungarians will again apply our existing bilateral agreement.

---

[71] Oskar Fischer further relayed the letter to Günter Mittag and then to all members and candidate members of the SED–Politburo as well on September 11, 1989. [Footnote in the original.]

Comrade Nyers stated that until last month the Hungarian leadership had examined whether the Berlin Formula would make a solution possible. "We wanted very much to proceed, but unfortunately had to find out that with such a number of people willing to leave the country under these particular conditions in Hungary, success was unfortunately not a possibility." [...]

In judging Hungarian actions one must observe that "Hungary is in a dilemma, we have fallen into a political trap." Hungary could not choose between good and bad, but rather between only bad and worse. (I refrained from remarking that in that statement the GDR is the lesser evil.) Comrade Nyers lastly referred to the exceptional nature of the present situation, namely that it was now being pushed into a defensive position politically, and he can only hope that it will once again be able to go back on the offensive. [...]

Thus far, the course of today's discussion in the Central Committee of the HSWP permits me to draw attention to still other points in connection with the entire event. [...]

2. In spite of the verbally declared willingness on behalf of the Hungarians to solve the problem facing the GDR, the discussions with the GDR (foreign minister, head of the Consular Affairs Department, MfS, DRK[72]) represent an attempt at stalling and deliberately misleading the GDR. The Hungarian organs undertook no serious attempts of their own to persuade those GDR citizens wishing to emigrate to return to the GDR. The efforts by our embassy's consular section to contact the GDR citizens in these [refugee] camps and explain the GDR's point of view were both delayed and impeded.

Simultaneously the Hungarian media provoked and supported a campaign directed against the GDR, which, upon being observed, encouraged the GDR citizens staying in the camps. Battle groups which were temporarily placed at the border as reinforcements were defamed by opposition groups, anti-socialist forces, and the majority of the press.

3. This campaign is judged at the same time to be a coordinated and successful attempt by the imperialist states, in particular the FRG, to take advantage of Hungary's political and economic position to exert pressure on the Hungarian leadership to solve the problem of those GDR citizens wishing to leave with the aim of looking out for all Germans. Here the imperialist policy of discrimination was consciously directed to foil, via the purposeful introduction of extensive economic means into Hungary, the solutions already initiated in accordance with the Berlin formula for the FRG's representation in Berlin and Prague with regard to the HPR. With the massive scale of the migration [*Ausschleusang*] of thousands of GDR citizens, a socialist country will establish in effect a public precedent supporting the FRG position, which is not in the spirit of international law. That follows the process already initiated of expelling Hungary from the socialist state community.

---

[72] The Ministry for State Security, or Stasi, and the [East] German Red Cross, respectively.

Characteristic of the preparation and implementation of the migration was the fact that the FRG always more openly and directly conducted the maintenance and care of the camp [...] and the deliberate preparation of the migration campaign. The Hungarian organs tolerated and covered up these acts by the FRG.

[Source: Stiftung Archiv der Parteien und Massenorganisationen der DDR-Bundesarchiv. Translated by Christiaan Hetzner.]

Document No. 82: Record of Conversation between Evgeny Primakov and Margaret Thatcher

September 18, 1989

These notes capture the congruence between the British prime minister's attitude towards Eastern Europe and that of Gorbachev's top aides, including the future Russian foreign minister, Evgeny Primakov. When the Soviet official expresses appreciation for Thatcher's position "in favor of stability in Europe," the prime minister confirms the need for "a stable 'background'" and goes on to extend high praise to the Polish leadership for its skill in managing the current situation—an exact parallel to Gorbachev's own assessment of Poland's former dictator, and now elected president, Wojciech Jaruzelski.

[…]

Thatcher: We are also watching the developments in the other Eastern European countries with great interest. What is happening there now should have happened inevitably sooner or later.

Primakov: Indeed, many of the developments happening now in the world draw increasing attention. It is clear that stability on the continent will depend on how they play out. Our Parliament highly appreciates your position in favor of stability in Europe.

Thatcher: Under conditions when big changes are underway, we need to ensure a stable "background." We are very impressed by the skill the Polish leadership has shown in their management of the processes in the country. Western countries are willing to provide assistance, and such assistance is already being provided. […]

[*Source: Archive of the Gorbachev Foundation, Fond 2. Opis 1. On file at the National Security Archive. Translated by Svetlana Savranskaya.*]

Document No. 83: CIA Intelligence Assessment, "Gorbachev's Domestic Gambles and Instability in the USSR"

September 1989

This controversial assessment from the CIA's Office of Soviet Analysis separates SOVA from the consensus of the rest of the U.S. intelligence community regarding Gorbachev and his chances for success, or even survival.[73] The document carries a scope note calling it a "speculative paper" because it goes against the general view that would soon be expressed in a Fall 1989 National Intelligence Estimate. That NIE would predict that Gorbachev would survive the coming economic crisis of 1990–91 without resorting to widespread repression (only targeted acts of suppression, as in Tbilisi)—a relatively optimistic conclusion that would play a major role in the Bush administration's embrace of Gorbachev at Malta in December.

In the assessment below, authored by senior analyst Grey Hodnett, SOVA takes a much bleaker view, essentially concluding that Gorbachev's reforms will fail, precipitating a coup, a crackdown, and perhaps even the piecemeal breakup of the empire. The United States "for the foreseeable future will confront a Soviet leadership that faces endemic popular unrest and that, on a regional basis at least, will have to employ emergency measures and increased use of force to retain domestic control." The paper further predicts that "Moscow's focus on internal order in the USSR is likely to accelerate the decay of Communist systems and growth of regional instability in Eastern Europe, pointing to the need for post-Yalta arrangements of some kind." What exactly "post-Yalta" means is unclear, but may simply be a reference to the new non-communist government in Poland (installed in August), that explicitly chose to remain a part of the Warsaw Treaty Organization. Under any circumstances, orchestrating such an arrangement would be a major challenge for the United States.

Key Judgments:[74]

Gorbachev and other Soviet leaders are concerned about serious future breakdowns of public order in the USSR. This concern is well justified. The unrest that has punctuated Gorbachev's rule is not a transient phenomenon. Conditions are likely to lead in the foreseeable future to continuing crises and instability on an even larger scale—in the form of mass demonstrations, strikes, violence, and perhaps even in the localized emergence of parallel centers of power. This instability is most likely to occur on a regional basis, not nation-wide—although overlapping crises and a linking together of centers of unrest could occur.

---

[73] The background for this document comes from Lundberg, "CIA and the Fall of the Soviet Empire."

[74] Information Available as of September 21, 1989 [as indicated in original document].

Instability in the USSR is not exclusively a product of *glasnost*, and some of it is indeed a sign—as Gorbachev asserts—that reforms are taking hold. But Gorbachev's claim that instability otherwise merely reflects the surfacing of problems that were latent or repressed under Brezhnev is only partly true. The current budget deficit and consumption crisis is largely due to policies Gorbachev himself has pursued since 1985. And the prospects for further crises and expanded turmoil in the future are enhanced by key policy gambles he is taking now:

- In the *nationality* arena, Gorbachev is gambling on defusing ethnic grievances and achieving a more consensual federative nation through unrestrained dialogue, some concessions to local demands aimed at eliminating past "mistakes," a constitutionalization of union/republic and ethnic group rights, and management of ethnic conflict to a substantial degree through the newly democratized soviets.
- In the *economic* arena, Gorbachev is gambling that, by putting marketization on hold through the postponement of price reform, and by pursuing a short-term "stabilization" program, he can avoid confrontation with the public *and* reengage in serious economic reform without steep costs at a later date.
- In the *political* arena, Gorbachev is gambling that, by transforming the Communist Party from an instrument of universal political, social, and economic management into a brain trust and authoritative steering organ, while empowering popularly elected soviets, he can create a more effective mechanism for integrating Soviet society and handling social tensions.

[...]

Gorbachev's gambles and the centrifugal trends they have set in motion are already viewed with extreme alarm and anger by many members of the Soviet political elite. But Gorbachev's major gains in the Politburo at the September 1989 plenum of the Central Committee demonstrated once again how difficult it is to translate conservative sentiment in the ranks into effective opposition to Gorbachev's rule at the top. For the time being, his power looks secure. If, somehow, a successful challenge were mounted against him over the next year or so, the most likely outcome would be a traditionalist restoration that would attempt to "draw the line" in various areas—especially with respect to democratization of the party and soviets, *glasnost* in the media, the conduct of informal groups, and expression of "nationalist" views—but would accept the need for significant change, including reduction in military spending and decentralization of management. Unless such a regime chose to move ahead vigorously with marketization (not impossible, but highly unlikely) it would obtain possible stability in the near term but suffer high medium- to long-term instability, leading toward Ottomanization or upheaval from below. If Gorbachev were not overthrown in the near term, an attempt to turn the clock back would become more difficult—given the reaction of increasingly well-entrenched pluralistic forces—and could thus also be nastier, possibly involving the armed forces and taking on a xenophobic Russian nationalist coloration.

Whether or not Gorbachev retains office, the United States for the foreseeable future will confront a Soviet leadership that faces endemic popular unrest and that, on a regional basis at least, will have to employ emergency measures and increased use of force to retain domestic control. This instability is likely to preoccupy Moscow for some time to come and—regardless of other factors—prevent a return to the arsenal state economy that generated the fundamental military threat to the West in the period since World War II. Moscow's focus on internal order in the USSR is likely to accelerate the decay of Communist systems and growth of regional instability in Eastern Europe, pointing to the need for post-Yalta arrangements of some kind and confronting the United States with severe foreign policy and strategic challenges. Instability in the USSR will increase uncertainty in the West about proper policies to pursue toward Moscow, reflecting nervousness about Soviet developments but nonchalance about defense, and will strain domestic and Alliance decision-making.

Domestic policy successes or failures will be the paramount factor ultimately determining Gorbachev's retention of office, but foreign policy achievements that allow him to justify further cuts in military spending on the basis of a reduction in the external "threat" would give him more room for maneuver. Western actions that could be presented by his opponents as attempts to "take advantage" of Soviet internal instability could hurt Gorbachev. [...]

The chances that Gorbachev will successfully overcome the dilemmas (many of his own making) that confront him are—over the long term—doubtful at best. But the process of pluralistic forces taking root in Soviet society strengthens the rule of law, builds constraints on the exercise of power, and fosters resistance to any turnaround in military spending and to reinvigoration of an expansionist foreign policy—which, as argued above, will be strongly inhibited in any event by the insistent demands of consumption and the civilian sector. This process, and the deterrence of a military reactionary restoration that might attempt to bring about a basic shift in the Soviet Union's foreign posture, benefits greatly from each year's prolongation of Gorbachev's rule. [...]

[*Source: CIA declassification. On file at the National Security Archive.*]

Document No. 84: National Security Directive (NSD) 23, "United States Relations with the Soviet Union"

September 22, 1989

This National Security Directive, representing the formal expression of U.S. foreign policy at the highest levels, was apparently drafted as early as April 1989, and its conclusions duly reflect how divorced U.S. policy in this period is from the radical transformations occurring in Eastern Europe. Among the document's hesitant predictions: "[t]he character of the changes taking place in the Soviet Union leads to the possibility that a new era may be now upon us. We may be able to move beyond containment to a U.S. policy that actively promotes the integration of the Soviet Union into the existing international system." First, however, "Moscow must authoritatively renounce the 'Brezhnev Doctrine' and reaffirm the pledge of signatories to the U.N. Charter to refrain from the threat or use of force against the territorial integrity or political independence of any state." It is almost as if the authors never read Gorbachev's United Nations speech in December 1988, much less his Strasbourg address in July 1989. Perhaps the most sterile prescription in the document is the president's directive to the secretary of state to eliminate "threatening Soviet positions of influence around the world." Precisely what positions were these in the latter half of 1989? Again reflecting a sense of caution that willfully ignores the events on the ground in Eastern Europe, the authors declare hopefully: "[w]e may find that the nature of the threat itself has changed, though any such transformation could take decades." These policy recommendations would perhaps be appropriate for 1986, but they are completely outdated in 1989.

For forty years the United States has committed its power and will to containing the military and ideological threat of Soviet communism. Containment was never an end in itself; it was a strategy born of the conditions of the postwar world. The United States recognized that, while Soviet military power was not the only threat to international stability, it was the most immediate and grave one. The U.S. challenge was to prevent the spread of Soviet communism while rebuilding the economic, political, and social strength of the world's long-standing and new democracies. Those who crafted the strategy of containment also believed that the Soviet Union, denied the course of external expansion, would ultimately have to face and react to the internal contradictions of its own inefficient repressive and inhumane system.

This strategy provided an enduring pillar for the growth of Western democracy and free enterprise. While the most important goal of containment has been met—the development of free and prosperous societies in Western Europe and in other parts of the world—the Soviet military threat has not diminished. Rather, in the last two decades, the Soviet Union has increased its military power across the spectrum of capabilities, drawing on that power to exacerbate local conflicts and to conduct a global foreign policy opposed to Western interests. The Soviet Union has stood apart from the internal order and often worked to undermine it.

The character of the changes taking place in the Soviet Union leads to the possibility that a new era may be now upon us. We may be able to move beyond containment to a U.S. policy that actively promotes the integration of the Soviet Union into the existing international system. The U.S.S.R. has indicated an interest in rapprochement with the international order and criticized major tenets of its own postwar political-military policy.

These are words that we can only applaud. But a new relationship with the international system cannot simply be declared by Moscow. Nor can it be granted by others. It must be earned through the demilitarization of Soviet foreign policy and reinforced by behavior consistent with the principles of world order to which the Soviet Union subscribed in 1945 but has repeatedly violated since. The Soviet Union cannot enjoy the fruits of membership in the community of states while holding ideological principles and engaging in conduct that promote the overthrow of that community.

The transformation of the Soviet Union from a source of instability to a productive force within the family of nations is a long-term goal that can only be pursued from a position of American strength and with patience and creativity. Our policy is not designed to help a particular leader or set of leaders in the Soviet Union. We seek, instead, fundamental alterations in Soviet military force structure, institutions, and practices which can only be reversed at great cost, economically and politically, to the Soviet Union. If we succeed, the ground for cooperation will widen, while that for conflict narrows. The U.S.–Soviet relationship may still be fundamentally competitive, but it will be less militarized and safer.

We are in a period of transition and uncertainty. We will not react to reforms and changes in the Soviet Union that have not yet taken place, nor will we respond to every Soviet initiative. We will be vigilant, recognizing that the Soviet Union is still governed by authoritarian methods and that its powerful armed forces remain a threat to our security and that of our allies. But the United States will challenge the Soviet Union step by step, issue by issue and institution by institution to behave in accordance with the higher standards that the Soviet leadership itself has enunciated. Moscow will find the United States a willing partner in building a better relationship. The foundation of that relationship will grow firmer if the Soviet reforms lead to conditions that will support a new cooperative relationship between Moscow and the West. Those conditions include:

- Deployment of a Soviet force posture that is smaller and much less threatening. The United States believes that the Soviet Union has legitimate security interests but Soviet military power is far greater than that needed to defend those interests.

- Renunciation of the principle that class conflict is a source of international tension and establishment of a record of conduct consistent with that pledge.
- Adherence to the obligation that it undertook at the end of World War II to permit self-determination for the countries of East-Central Europe. Moscow must authoritatively renounce the "Brezhnev Doctrine" and reaffirm the pledge of signatories to the U.N. Charter to refrain from the threat or use of force against the territorial integrity or political independence of any state.
- Demilitarization of Soviet foreign policy in other regions of the world and serious participation in efforts to ameliorate conflict, including bringing pressure to bear on Soviet clients who do not recognize the legitimate security interests of their neighbors.
- Participation in cooperative efforts to stop the proliferation of ballistic missile technology as well as nuclear, chemical and biological weapons.
- Willingness to cooperate with the United States to address pressing global problems, including the international trade in drugs and narcotics, terrorism, and dangers to the environment.
- Institutionalization of democratic internal laws and human rights practices, political pluralism, and a more market-oriented economic structure, which will establish a firm Soviet domestic base for a more productive and cooperative relationship with the free nations of the world. [...]

POLITICAL-DIPLOMATIC OBJECTIVES

Regional Issues

U.S. policy will encourage fundamental political and economic reform, including freely contested elections, in East-Central Europe, so that states in that region may once again be productive members of a prosperous, peaceful, and democratic Europe, whole and free from fear of Soviet intervention. Our policy of differentiating among East European states based on their internal political and economic processes, and our support for the CSCE process, will help in the achievement of this goal.

We will engage the Soviet Union on a variety of regional issues not only to seek their resolution, but also in order to test the reality of new Soviet thinking and whether Soviet behavior matches rhetoric in key areas around the world. We also shall seek to limit the expansion of Soviet power through arms transfers, force projection, and proxy forces by continued U.S. political, economic and military support for friends, and allies and for freedom fighters.

I direct the Secretary of State to:
Consider the most appropriate ways to engage the Soviets in discussions on resolving regional conflicts and eliminating threatening Soviet positions of influence around the world.

The United States and the Soviet Union share an interest in reversing the spread of drugs and narcotics. The United States must challenge the Soviet Union to refrain from directly or indirectly supporting or training terrorists and insist that its allies do the same.

I direct the Secretary of State to:
> Lead an interagency effort to develop a detailed plan for cooperating with the Soviet Union on these matters, including the boundaries of such cooperation given security and intelligence constraints.

I also direct the Secretary of State to:
> Examine ways in which the Soviet Union and the United States might cooperate on environmental issues.

The Vice President should:
> Explore through the National Space Council ways that the United States and the Soviet Union might jointly use space to advance our mutual interests. A particularly promising area might be research on the environment in support of multilateral efforts to protect our planet. [...]

DEMOCRATIZATION

The United States is encouraged by emerging trends in the internal political processes in the Soviet Union. Our concern about the character of the Soviet system, which denies its people basic political and economic liberties and pursues a policy of expansion abroad, is at the heart of our differences with Moscow. Let no one doubt the sincerity of the American people and their government in our desire to see reform succeed inside the Soviet Union. We welcome the positive changes that have taken place and we will continue to encourage greater recognition of human rights, market incentives, and free elections. To the extent that Soviet practices are modified and institutions are built based on popular will, we may find that the nature of the threat itself has changed, though any such transformation could take decades.

Where possible, the United States should promote Western values and ideas within the Soviet Union, not in the spirit of provocation or destabilization, but as a means to lay a firm foundation for a cooperative relationship. I direct the United States Information Agency, within budgetary limitations, to find new ways to promote the flow of information about American institutions and ideals to the Soviet Union. A special effort should be made to encourage private sector initiatives in support of this objective.

The Secretary of State is directed to:
- Review carefully Soviet compliance with the commitments that led to our conditional agreement to attend the 1991 Moscow human rights conference.
- Develop new initiatives in the area of U.S.–Soviet exchanges designed to promote Soviet understanding of the rule of law, free-market economic principles, U.S. business management concepts, and other principles of free Western societies.

PUBLIC DIPLOMACY

The United States should make every effort clearly and responsibly to communicate our message about U.S.–Soviet relations at home and abroad. Our goal is a consistent, responsible and sustainable policy toward Moscow. We must stress the comprehensiveness of our agenda as well as the fact that the relationship is moving forward on the basis of long-supported Western objectives to which the Soviet Union is now adapting.

CONCLUSION

The goal of restructuring the relationship of the Soviet Union to the international system is an ambitious task. The responsibility for creating the conditions to move beyond containment to integrate the Soviet Union into the family of nations lies first and foremost with Moscow. But the United States will do its part, together with our allies, to challenge and test Soviet intentions and, while maintaining our strength, to work to place Soviet relations with the West on a firmer, more cooperative course than has heretofore been possible.

[Source: FOIA request, published in Presidential Directives on National Security, Part II: From Harry Truman to George W. Bush (National Security Archive/ Chadwyck-Healey, 2003), Document No. 01738]

Document No. 85: Record of Conversation between Mikhail Gorbachev and Margaret Thatcher

September 23, 1989

These notes of Margaret Thatcher's conversation with Gorbachev contain the British leader's most sensitive views on Germany—so confidential that she requests no written record be made of them during the meeting. Chernyaev complies but immediately afterwards rushes outside and writes down her comments from memory. The talks open with a candid exchange in which Gorbachev explains the recent (September 19–20) Party Plenum's decisions on ethnic conflict, and why he does not believe in the Chinese model: "how can you reform both the economy and politics without democratizing society, without glasnost, which incorporates individuals into an active socio-political life?" Thatcher replies, "I understand your position [on Eastern Europe] in the following way: you are in favor of each country choosing its own road of development so long as the Warsaw Treaty is intact. I understand this position perfectly."

At this point, the prime minister asks that note-taking be discontinued. Her words are indeed forceful, and imply a certain tradeoff—I understand your position on Eastern Europe, please accept mine on Germany: "Britain and Western Europe are not interested in the unification of Germany. The words written in the NATO communiqué may sound different, but disregard them. We do not want the unification of Germany." Of course, "[w]e are not interested in the destabilization of Eastern Europe or the dissolution of the Warsaw treaty either ... I can tell you that this is also the position of the U.S. president." No doubt the Russians took note that the U.S. reassurance only applied to Eastern Europe and not to German unification; but the vehemence of Thatcher's opposition to the idea of unification provides a certain comfort to Gorbachev that he would rely on until it was too late for him actually to prevent the merger.

Thatcher: [...] I know that it is not easy to carry out political reform. You began to implement the reform from above, and it would be impossible otherwise. Here, as I understand it, you are in full control of the situation. But to carry out economic reform is even more difficult; I know this from my own experience. [...]

You have now reached the stage where every new step is more difficult than the previous one. It is important for people to see results, even though it is a politically ungratifying task. For instance, I had to wait for two years before the first results. All that time I was criticized, and when the success came it was received as something natural, and nobody thanked me. [...]

Thatcher: But you need to teach the people to live day by day, not on future credits.

Gorbachev: We are teaching—teaching with life.

If you add to what we have just said the fact that these processes are unfolding in a country with 120 nationalities and ethnicities, you can imagine what a tight knot all the problems together present. As you know, the CC CPSU Plenum which has just ended analyzed the issues of inter-ethnic relations in depth. The Plenum's resolutions are very important. Their essence is to balance the nationalities policy, to rejuvenate the Soviet federation and to fill it with real meaning. I will tell you honestly, until now our state has been considered a federal one only formally, but in reality everything worked like in a typical unitary state—from the top down. The decisions of this Plenum are supposed to change that, to create mechanisms which in practice would help to remove tensions from inter-ethnic relations without interfering with the basic interests of individuals, nationalities, and society in the economic, cultural, and other spheres. Otherwise, inter-ethnic tensions could bury *perestroika*. This is how the issue stands now.

I would also like to state openly the following thought. Sometimes I hear, even here in the West: Why do we have to open up so many fronts simultaneously? But how can you reform the economy without reforming the political system? It will not work. And we already have the sad experiences of Khrushchev, and Kosygin with Brezhnev. How can you reform both the economy and politics without democratizing society, without *glasnost*, which incorporates individuals into an active socio-political life? That will not work either. How can you make prognoses and form healthy inter-ethnic relations separately from the economic, political, and democratic reforms in society as a whole? How can you carry out *perestroika* itself without rejuvenating the party?

All these issues are inseparably linked, and that is why we are saying that *perestroika* is not just a reform, it is a genuine revolution, our second socialist revolution. And we are making great efforts to carry it out. [...]

Thatcher: I would like to raise the issue of the situation in the countries of Eastern Europe. I was very impressed by the courage and patriotism of General Jaruzelski in Poland. For you, of course, the future of Poland and its alliance with you has great significance. I noted that you calmly accepted the results of the elections in Poland and, in general, the processes in that country and in other East European countries. I understand your position in the following way: you are in favor of each country choosing its own road of development so long as the Warsaw Treaty is intact. I understand this position perfectly.

Now I would like to say something in a very confidential manner, and I would ask you not to record this part of the conversation.

Gorbachev: As you like.

(The following part of the conversation is recorded from recollections.)

Thatcher: We are very concerned with the processes that are underway in East Germany. It is on the verge of big changes, which are being caused by the situation in that society and to some extent by Erich Honecker's illness. The thousands of people who are escaping from the GDR to the FRG are the primary example. All that is the external side of things, and it is important for us; but another issue is even more important.

531

Britain and Western Europe are not interested in the unification of Germany. The words written in the NATO communiqué may sound different, but disregard them. We do not want the unification of Germany. It would lead to changes in the post-war borders, and we cannot allow that because such a development would undermine the stability of the entire international situation and could lead to threats to our security.

We are not interested in the destabilization of Eastern Europe or the dissolution of the Warsaw Treaty either. Of course, the internal changes are apt in all the countries of Eastern Europe, but in some countries they are more pronounced, in some countries not yet. However, we are in favor of those processes remaining strictly internal; we will not interfere in them and spur the decommunization of Eastern Europe. I can tell you that this is also the position of the U.S. president. He sent a telegram to me in Tokyo in which he asked me to tell you that the United States would not undertake anything that could threaten the security interests of the Soviet Union, or that could be perceived by Soviet society as a threat. I am fulfilling his request.

Gorbachev: Thank you for the information. In general, you formulated our position correctly. We think that the socialist countries should make their own decisions about their internal affairs; they should be able to choose which road to take, and at which tempo, in implementing their socialist choice. We do not want to, and we will not, interfere in these processes; but we were, of course, helping, and we shall be helping our friends and allies.

As far as Erich Honecker's health is concerned, he is planning to participate in all the events commemorating the 40th anniversary of the GDR. I can inform you that I am planning to visit the GDR on October 6 and 7 for the celebration of the anniversary.

Thatcher: Thank you.

The confidential part of my talk is over; you may now resume recording. [...]

[*Source: Archive of the Gorbachev Foundation, Fond 2. Opis 1. On file at the National Security Archive. Translated by Svetlana Savranskaya.*]

Document No. 86: Protocol No. 166 of CC CPSU Politburo Session

September 28, 1989

This document reflects the first in-depth Soviet Politburo discussion of Poland after the June elections and the Mazowiecki government's accession to power in August. The report to the Politburo prepared by Shevardnadze, Yakovlev, Yazov, and Kryuchkov opens with a blunt statement that the Polish "situation is unprecedented for a socialist country—the ruling communist party was not able to convincingly carry the parliamentary vote and had to yield to the opposition the right to form a government." Yet the analysis is strikingly non-ideological and gives a sober assessment of the new realities of Soviet–Polish relations, already signaled by Moscow's acquiescence to the Solidarity-led government as well as Mazowiecki's pledge in his inaugural speech that Poland would remain in the Warsaw Pact. Overall, the authors of this report find that positive collaboration between the two states is possible and should be pursued on the basis of mutual interest. It notes that the new regime "will not be able to function" without Soviet energy supplies and raw materials, which will continue to tie the two countries together economically.

Interestingly, even though stressing the need for further support for the Polish communists, the Politburo decides to invite the head of the party, Mieczysław Rakowski, only if he repeats his request for an invitation to come to the USSR, while the Politburo resolution specifically mentions inviting Prime Minister Mazowiecki, President Jaruzelski and Foreign Minister Skubiszewski. The report devotes surprisingly little space, about two paragraphs, to relations with the fraternal party, and there is some sense of distancing the CPSU from the Polish communists for the time being while expanding ties with forces across the political spectrum. The general tone of the report is not alarmist, although the authors do show concern over the spillover effect of a non-communist scenario in the region, and the possible impact on perestroika there.

ON THE SITUATION IN POLAND, POSSIBILITIES FOR ITS DEVELOPMENT, AND THE OUTLOOK FOR SOVIET–POLISH RELATIONS.

1. Agree with the thoughts stated in the note by Cdes. E.A. Shevardnadze, A.N. Yakovlev, D.T. Yazov, V.A. Kryuchkov from September 20, 1989 (see attached).

2. Soviet–Polish relations should develop with consideration for the necessity to collaborate with all constructive political powers in the PPR that are in favor of developing Soviet–Polish relations and following Poland's allied responsibilities within the framework of the Warsaw Treaty.

Soviet ministries and departments, social organizations and creative unions should strictly adhere to all agreements and treaties signed with our Polish partners, not allowing a decrease in the level of collaboration with Poland.

3. Continue to consider connections between the CPSU and the PUWP as an important element of Soviet–Polish relations, specifically concentrating on helping our friends in the organizational and ideological strengthening of the party, and on restoring its political thrust and authority.

4. In accordance with existing plans, have Cdes. N.N. Slunkov's and A.N. Yakovlev's visit to the PPR come before the end of 1989. Allow for meetings with leaders of "Solidarity" and other political organizations during the visit.

5. In accordance with the existing agreement, receive First Secretary of the PUWP CC M. Rakowski on a working visit to the Soviet Union (if he repeats his request).

The CC CPSU's International Department should prepare material for the talks between M.S. Gorbachev and M. Rakowski.

Send an invitation to PPR President W. Jaruzelski to come to the Soviet Union on an official visit in 1990.

6. Invite Chairman of the PPR Council of Ministers T. Mazowiecki to the Soviet Union on an official visit.

7. Receive in Moscow PPR Minister of Foreign Affairs K. Skubiszewski.

8. In accordance with the CC CPSU resolution of August 2, 1989 (P164/18), assign the Soviet ambassador in the PPR to meet with L. Wałęsa and discuss the possibility of his visiting the Soviet Union. Discuss the dates for the visit with the PUWP leadership beforehand.

9. Consider it expedient to establish connections between the Supreme Soviet of the USSR and both chambers of the PPR National Assembly, and to send invitations to marshals of the Sejm and Senate to come to the Soviet Union on official visits.

Cdes. E.M. Primakov and R.N. Nishanov should develop a collaborative program for the USSR Supreme Soviet and the PPR National Assembly.

It is important to establish contacts with committees and deputies' clubs of all the political forces represented in the PPR National Assembly.

Increase interactions among the national groups in the Interparliamentary Union.

10. Consider it expedient to carry out a number of working visits to Poland by representatives of the chairman of the USSR Council of Ministers and heads of ministries and departments to discuss topical questions of Soviet–Polish economic collaboration; among the visits for 1989, plan Masliukov and Katushev's trips to the PPR.

11. USSR Gosplan, MFER [Ministry of Foreign Economic Relations], and Ministry of Finance are to *register* their *concrete* views before the end of the current year on the following: the possibility of a transition to current world market prices in trade with Poland; the use of freely convertible currency in mutual payments; the establishment of real exchange rates for national currencies; the expansion of wholesale trade; and the improvement of banking services. They are to create a joint group made up of representatives of planning organs, the USSR MFER, and the ministries of finance from both sides in order to work out a system of payments and prices.

Develop a position on possible requests by Poland's new government to defer the deadlines for Polish debt servicing to the Soviet Union, taking into consideration the interests of our country.

12. Based on an analysis of developments in the domestic economic situation and foreign economic relations with Poland, USSR Gosplan, the Social-Economic and International departments of the CC CPSU, the MFA, the MFER, and the Academy of Sciences are to prepare by March 1, 1990, general directions for the necessary structural *perestroika* of our economic relations with Poland for the future, including such questions as possible changes in our present approach to coordinating economic plans, the creation of joint stock companies on Polish territory, and other forms of Soviet–Polish financial-economic collaboration under the new conditions.

13. The CC CPSU International Department is to prepare thoughts and concepts on relations between the CPSU and the United Peasants' Party and the Democratic Party, holding consultations with them before the end of 1989.

14. Recommend that S.A. Shalaev (ACCTU [All-Union Central Council of Trade Unions]) take measures to broaden collaboration with the All-Polish trade union agreement [organization]. If needed, help in training and re-training embassy trade-union-worker personnel, and in publishing.

With the goal of networking with all categories of Polish ACCTU workers, determine the "Solidarity" leadership's readiness to make contact with Soviet trade unions.

15. To strengthen the material base and increase the effectiveness of the Polish–Soviet Friendship Society's work, Cde. V.V. Tereshkova (USFS [Union of Soviet Friendship Societies]) together with Cdes. L.E. Davletova (State Committee for Light Industries under USSR Gosplan), K.Z. Terekh (USSR Ministry of Trade), the USSR Ministry of Culture, S.A. Shalaev (ACCTU), and the USSR State Committee for International Tourism have one month to consider proposals to carry out joint events on a commercial basis.

16. The CC CPSU International Department, together with Cde. U.N. Khristoranov (Council on Religious Matters under the USSR Council of Ministers) are to submit proposals for broadening contacts with the episcopate of the Polish Catholic Church. Liven up our policy to develop Soviet–Vatican contacts with the aim of helping our Polish friends, primarily in their work with practicing Catholics and with the leadership of the Polish Catholic Church.

17. Cdes. D.T. Yazov (USSR Ministry of Defense) and V.A. Kryuchkov (USSR KGB) are to be provided with a three-month period to develop ideas on maintaining collaboration with their PPR partners under the new circumstances.

18. The USSR MFA, Ministry of Defense, and CC International Department should conduct negotiations with the PUWP leadership and the PPR Ministry of National Defense, as well as hold bilateral consultations with allied nations on questions of the future political and military operation of the Warsaw Treaty, considering the developing situation in the PPR and our long-term line in European and world affairs.

Provide additional views regarding improving the mechanism of political and military collaboration within the framework of the Warsaw Treaty.

Develop our position on the Polish government's possible request for a further reduction or withdrawal of the Soviet troop contingent from PPR territory.

19. The USSR permanent mission to CMEA together with the USSR MFA and other concerned departments should prepare views concerning possible changes in the PPR's approach toward economic collaboration organizations within the framework of the Council for Mutual Economic Assistance and its work.

20. The CC CPSU Ideology and International Departments are to conduct a briefing with the heads of major newspapers, magazines, radio, and television with respect to elucidating the developing situation in Poland in the Soviet mass media. We should recommend that they regularly publish materials and articles by prominent political writers, statesmen, and diplomats that would express our view of the processes unfolding in the PPR.

Cde. M.F. Nenashev (State Television and Radio of the USSR) should go over Solidarity's proposal to create a "Warsaw–Moscow" tele-bridge that would represent from the Polish side all the political forces that took part in creating the Roundtable agreements. In the course of the discussion we would aim to exchange opinions on "methods of de-Stalinization in Soviet–Polish relations, and their consolidation."

21. The USSR MFA, Ministry of Defense, MFER, Ministry of Culture, Ministry of Education, and other concerned Soviet departments and organizations are to take stock of the major active Soviet–Polish treaties and agreements from the point of view of their accordance with today's demands and Poland's possible requests to review them.

Secretary of the CC

ON THE SITUATION IN POLAND, POSSIBILITIES FOR ITS DEVELOPMENT, AND THE OUTLOOK FOR SOVIET–POLISH RELATIONS (SUPPLEMENT)

The drawn-out crisis in Poland has entered a new stage. The PUWP gambled on reaching a national consensus by collaborating with the opposition but was not able to keep the developing events under control. The ensuing situation is unprecedented for a socialist country—the ruling communist party was not able to convincingly carry the parliamentary vote and had to yield to the opposition the right to form a government.

The information we are receiving leads us to believe that right now Solidarity's efforts will be directed primarily at consolidating the authority of the government of national accountability and at the same time at undermining the PUWP's positions. Solidarity leaders have followed tactical considerations, particularly taking into account international factors, with the election of W. Jaruzelski as president of Poland and the inclusion of PUWP representatives in the government. However, with a favorable set of circumstances in the future, it is likely that they will try to take back both these concessions.

Solidarity's most immediate political goal is to hold elections for local offices ahead of schedule. It aims to carry a significant victory while riding the wave of its popularity, which would allow it to establish control over the entire structure of the state. The goal is to considerably transform the state and economic administrative apparatus and get rid of loyal PUWP personnel, which would affect around 15,000 people just in the initial stages.

Solidarity is working to liquidate PUWP organizations in ministries and departments, industry and institutions, in education and the military; it is limiting PUPW's financial resources and reducing subsidies for social organizations tied to the PUWP.

By 1991, the 200th anniversary of the first Polish Constitution, we can expect a new PPR law to be adopted that would consolidate the changes in Poland's political life and become the foundation for further transformations.

It seems we should proceed from the fact that Poland is entering a lengthy period with serious far-reaching social and political consequences, which is characterized by the struggle for the ability to choose the path for the country's further development.

Within Solidarity there is a broad spectrum of political views—from social democrats to the bourgeois-conservative, and at present it is difficult to say who will prevail. But under the current circumstances, representatives of a number of social groups, including some PUWP members, are united by the hope of leading the country out of its crisis through a concept developed in Solidarity. This concept of the evolutionary reorganization of Poland is based on Swedish social-democratic ideas and the standpoints of Catholic social doctrine. It would seem that this kind of evolution would also imply changes in the foundation, including the denationalization of state property and every kind of encouragement for private enterprise.

The PUWP is in an exceptionally difficult position right now. The trust of the masses has been considerably undermined. Members of the party are demoralized, many are condemning the policies that led to "a voluntary surrender of power, an increase in withdrawals from party ranks, and the danger of a split in the party."

Headed by M. Rakowski, the party leadership views the situation realistically and is preparing for a serious political struggle. But enormous amounts of energy and time would be necessary to reconstitute the PUWP and restore its lost positions. A great deal will depend on the resolutions of the forthcoming XI Party Congress.

Also important will be the fact that on the political level, right now, the PUWP leadership places national interests as its first priority, expressing a readiness to cooperate in order to promote the success of T. Mazowiecki's government.

537

The "grand coalition" government faces a major challenge—how to pull the country out of a deep social and economic crisis and get workers' support for unavoidably severe economic stabilization measures while the economic situation worsens and workers grow more and more discontented. They will have to overcome the tendency to reduce industrial production and normalize a troubled financial system; deal with frightful inflation; and arrest the disintegration of the domestic market. If they cannot achieve tangible results in this respect, then a new social explosion will be unavoidable. As the protests have shown, Solidarity cannot expect to possess a special capability to maintain social peace at the enterprises.

Aspects of foreign policy in general are favorable to T. Mazowiecki's government. Even though there is as yet no major financial support materializing from the West, leading West European countries and the U.S., which view the "Polish experiment" first and foremost through the prism of their political interests in Eastern Europe, are working on options for offering Poland food assistance.

At the same time, T. Mazowiecki's government is interested in maintaining economic relations with the USSR, because it will not be able to function without Soviet energy-fuel and raw material resources in the foreseeable future. Therefore, both poles of attraction—the East and the West—will influence the foreign policy course of the new Polish government. The Solidarity leaders' strategic plan, which is aimed at reorienting Poland's economic ties towards the world capitalist market and its political ties towards achieving neutrality, will present a major problem that will affect not only the interests of Poland and its society's political forces, but also those of the PPR's allies and neighboring countries.

Naturally, the conditions under which we conduct our policies towards the PPR are becoming more complex. But in the new situation we have the opportunity to maintain friendly, good-neighborly relations with Poland. A number of factors provide for this: Poland's geopolitical situation in Europe, the traditional ties between two Slavic peoples, the Poles' German syndrome and the dependence of Poland's economy on our energy sources. The progress of socialist transformation in our country, first and foremost the realization of plans for *perestroika* in economic and foreign economic relations, will have an undeniable impact on the development of the situation in Poland and on the formation of Soviet–Polish relations.

Right now the head of the new Polish government and the political leaders of Solidarity are emphasizing their interest in stable Polish–Soviet relations. Time will tell how sincere these statements are. Even though T. Mazowiecki's government needs to have good relations with us, at the same time it is clear that within Solidarity's leadership and the government there will be a struggle over foreign policy and foreign economic orientation. [...]

Under these circumstances it is important to keep in mind that a resolution of the protracted crisis and a normalization of Poland's political situation is in our interest. In this sense we should support corresponding efforts by the new Polish coalition government. On these grounds we could reach a business understanding with the new government, which would not contradict our support for the PUWP. Intergovernmental efforts in our bilateral relations with Poland have to work together with improvements in inter-party relations between the CPSU and PUWP and with reaching out to other political forces in the country.

On a number of foreign policy issues at the intergovernmental level considerable differences in positions and evaluations could occur. It seems that the new government will raise questions more sharply than the PUWP leadership has done—questions related to our troop presence on Poland's territory; the "blind spots," especially Katyń; and other difficult problems in Soviet–Polish relations.

Right now in our approach to Soviet–Polish relations in the political sphere we have to proceed from the realities in the PPR. We have to be prepared to cooperate with the new Polish government, the political parties, and the forces represented in the parliament.

Taking into account the changes in the PPR MFA leadership, we have to diversify the contacts of our Ministry of Foreign Affairs with them, using them not only to influence the formulation of the course of foreign policy, but also to discuss high-priority issues in Soviet–Polish relations, which will most likely be raised by the Polish side more and more frequently.

It seems expedient to invite the new PPR minister of foreign affairs for a visit to Moscow before the end of the year. In accordance with existing practice we should also plan a meeting with him and other foreign ministers from Warsaw Treaty Organization member-states during the U.N. General Assembly session in New York.

Individual work with prominent members of the Sejm and Senate, leaders of the United Peasants' Party and the Democratic Party, leaders of Catholic lay organizations [text interrupted], influential social figures and representatives of the intelligentsia acquires special significance. It is important to expand collaboration with the All-Polish administration of labor unions and other Polish social organizations (youth, the society for Polish–Soviet friendship, and others).

Considering the important role of the Catholic Church in Poland's social life, it seems expedient to maintain a political dialogue with the Episcopate leadership, not limiting contact to the Council on Religious Matters under the USSR Council of Ministers. The subject of Poland will undoubtedly take up a significant part of the meeting with the Pope during Cde. Gorbachev's trip to Italy.

In this context, the further intensification of Soviet–Vatican contacts, especially the establishment of diplomatic relations, could create fundamentally new opportunities. This position would unquestionably create a much more favorable situation for the PUWP's work with practicing Catholics and with the leadership of the Polish Catholic Church.

In trade-economic collaboration it is becoming necessary to transfer our bilateral relations onto a mutually beneficial basis, to make payments in freely convertible currency and at current world prices. It would be useful to prepare our position in advance in case the Polish government asks us to defer the deadlines for its debt servicing, or to have a partial remission of the PPR's debt to the Soviet Union.

The course of events in Poland is having a negative impact on European socialist countries, is increasing concerns about the fate of socialism, and sometimes leads to false conclusions about the flaws of *perestroika's* processes. It will be important to consider this detail when we state our positions at the meeting of CC secretaries of communist and labor parties on international issues in Varna.

The position of the PPR's new government on issues of multilateral collaboration among the socialist countries so far has not been finally determined.

At the same time it is already clear that Solidarity's assumption of power will create problems for the operation of the Warsaw Treaty. Even though its leaders still speak of honoring the alliance, it is possible that they will change their approaches in the future.

The new Polish situation could necessitate amendments to the multilateral political and military interactions that have been established. At the same time we should look for approaches in our contacts with representatives of the current Polish leadership that would not cause them to suspect a lack of trust on our side and thereby lead to a decrease in the level of collaboration by the allied states. This is especially important when conducting meetings within the framework of the Political Consultative Committee and the Committee of Foreign Ministers, sessions of the Committee of Ministers [text interrupted] and the Military Council, at WTO headquarters, and in the special commission on questions of disarmament where issues vital to the allied states are considered and mutual positions are coordinated.

In particular, it is important to adhere strictly to equal partnership relations when forming collective negotiating positions among the allied states on the subject of disarmament, especially for conventional weapons. We should reject the practice of "informing:" imposing our point of view on our allies as we develop and coordinate a common line on this or that issue; we should carefully consider our partners' opinions.

Overall we can expect that the alliance's work will proceed strictly along intergovernmental lines. Taking into account the Solidarity leaders' demands to sharply reduce military spending we cannot exclude the possibility that Poland will begin to disregard the total fulfillment of its allied responsibilities. It is possible that participation in the Warsaw Treaty will become a formality.

More difficult questions could arise should the Polish leadership eventually raise the question of withdrawing from the military organization or from the alliance as a whole. However we can scarcely expect that such a step could be taken in the near future.

It seems that it would be expedient first to discuss the developing situation with the PUWP leadership and on a bilateral basis with our allies, especially since many of them have already expressed this wish at the working level.

The need also arises to review some of the proposals that are being worked on within the framework of the alliance right now. These are proposals for improving the mechanism of political and military collaboration (P143/10 from December 2, 1988 and P160/9 from May 26 1989). We should initiate work in this direction. It appears that the issue of creating a permanent political working body is especially relevant under the present circumstances.

Considering Solidarity's announced radical transformations in the Polish economy it would be important to prepare for possible changes in Poland's approach toward questions of bilateral and multilateral economic collaboration. We can expect that the new government will embark on a review of collaborative strategies within the framework of CMEA and the PPR's relations with this organization. Most likely it will try to achieve a more radical development of the mechanism of multilateral economic interaction on a market basis and a relaxation of the processes of integration. It is likely that the PPR will refuse to collaborate on a preferential basis with less developed members of CMEA such as the SRV [Socialist Republic of Vietnam], the Republic of Cuba, and the MPR [Mongolian People's Republic]. It is also possible that the question of reducing the PPR's financial share in CMEA will be raised, as well as the assigned personnel of the Polish segment of its Secretariat. The radicalization of the PPR's position in CMEA will further complicate relations among participating countries and the search for a compromise in resolving key issues of economic collaboration. This could lead to an increase in confrontational episodes in the course of fulfilling the *perestroika* program in CMEA's work and the politicization of the work of the session, the executive committee, and the committees.

Serious difficulties could arise in the work of such CMEA organs as the standing commission on issues of military collaboration of European member-states of CMEA, the Committee on Foreign Economic Relations and certain others.

All of this requires that we work out new approaches in principle toward developing relations with Poland on many issues. In this respect it seems necessary to undertake a number of practical measures in the near future.

E. Shevardnadze, A. Yakovlev, D. Yazov, V. Kryuchkov,
September 20, 1989.

[*Source: State Archive of the Russian Federation [GARF], Moscow. Yakovlev Collection. Fond 10063. Opis 1. On file at the National Security Archive. Translated by Anna Melyakova.*]

Document No. 87: Diary of Anatoly Chernyaev regarding Mikhail Gorbachev's Visit to the GDR

October 5, 1989

This diary entry, written on the eve of Gorbachev's visit to an East Germany in crisis, describes the Soviet leader as anxious and ambivalent about the radical changes underway in Eastern Europe, yet determined not to say anything that will prop up the hard-line Honecker. Chernyaev knows what the drafters of American national security policy at this time do not, that "the total dismantling of socialism as a factor of world development is underway"—and it is a spectacle Chernyaev applauds. Here is striking proof of the profound radicalization of political thinking that is unfolding inside the reform-minded echelons of the Soviet political elite. Chernyaev has by now resolved his personal doubts in favor of supporting the anti-communist "revolutions" in Eastern Europe. However, while he clearly sees the future of the Soviet Union on the path of total rejection of the Leninist-Stalinist legacy, Gorbachev's own thinking in this period is more complex and, unlike Chernyaev, is not completely free from the "syndrome of Leninism." In particular, Gorbachev still seems to nurture an ideological belief in "democratic socialism" as a road for Eastern Europe, and the GDR in particular.

Tomorrow M.S. is flying to the GDR for its 40th anniversary. He really does not want to. He called me twice, said that he polished his speech to the letter, knowing that they will be examining it under a microscope... there is not a word in support of Honecker [...] but he will support the [GDR] Republic and revolution.

Today in Dresden 20,000 people came out to demonstrate. Yesterday in Leipzig there were even more. We are receiving information that during Gorbachev's visit they will storm the Wall. There were terrible scenes surrounding a special GDR refugee train passing through Dresden on the way from Prague. The West-German TV recorded this and is showing it in the GDR. The Western press is brimming with articles on the "reunification" of Germany.

Tomorrow a Congress of the Hungarian Socialist Workers Party [HSWP] in Budapest will declare the self-liquidation of the "Socialist Hungarian People's Republic." Needless to mention Poland: the Polish United Workers Party not only lost power, but it is doubtful whether it will survive till its next Congress in February.

In a word, a total dismantling of socialism as a factor of world development is underway. Maybe this is inevitable and good. For this is a matter of humanity uniting on the basis of common sense. And this process was started by a regular guy from Stavropol.

Perhaps Thatcher is right when she admires him precisely because she thinks that "in his heart" he envisioned the self-liquidation of a society that is alien to human nature and the natural order of things.

It is another matter [...] whether Russia needed the year 1917 [...] and once again (!) our great sacrifices so that humanity would come to this conclusion.

[Source: Anatoly Chernyaev's Diary, Manuscript. On file at the National Security Archive. Translated by Anna Melyakova.]

Document No. 88: Record of Conversation between Mikhail Gorbachev and Members of the CC SED Politburo

October 7, 1989

When Gorbachev visits Berlin in early October, thousands of East Germans are already pressing to leave the GDR and demonstrations against the regime are taking place in Leipzig and elsewhere. Chernyaev's notes of the discussions with the SED Politburo show the Soviet leader actually pushing for leadership changes—contrary to his own repeated insistence about staying out of bloc "personnel" matters. While not even mentioning the refugees, Gorbachev reminds the East Germans about the crises of the 1970s when the leadership felt the need to accelerate reforms. "Life itself will punish us if we are late," he says. He goes on to tell a story about the miners of Donetsk, where "some leaders cannot pull the cart any more, but we don't dare replace them, we are afraid to offend them." There could hardly be a clearer reference to Honecker and, sure enough, within 10 days the SED Politburo replaces him with another of those present at this meeting, Egon Krenz.

Gorbachev: In this connection, I would like to return to the 1970s. Then everybody in the world acutely felt the challenges of the scientific and technological revolution. We all remember how energetic the West's actions were in adjusting to it. By the way, they did so without taking the interests of the working class into account. At that time we had a pointed discussion of those urgent issues in the CPSU. It was then that the thesis appeared that if we did not latch on to scientific and technological developments socialism would lose. The processes causing us to lag behind became so apparent that L. I. Brezhnev agreed that it was necessary to hold a special Plenum of the CC CPSU devoted to the problems of accelerating scientific and technological progress in the USSR. We are not going to talk about the specific reasons why that Plenum was never held. It was a miscalculation. It was a strategic miscalculation, and we are still feeling the consequences of it. You approached those problems differently in the GDR. I could see that myself when I studied your experiences with economic reform in 1966 here.

In the 1970s you understood the challenge of the times, and actively responded to it. And that was correct, it allowed you to do many things. These are two examples of different reactions to the needs of social development which require a transformation in the party's practical policy.

This has direct relevance to our *perestroika*. Where the party is lagging behind the times in theoretical and practical terms, there we have to harvest bitter fruit. You all know how inter-ethnic conflicts and passions have flared up in our country recently. Inter-ethnic problems are very complex. There are many issues interwoven there: economics, demographics, problems of sovereignty, history, the traditions of separate peoples. We had to present society with thoroughly developed approaches to these problems. But while we were working intensively on those problems, which of course took some time, other forces were planting poisonous seeds in the soil of inter-ethnic relations. And only when we passed the platform of inter-ethnic policy at the September [19–20] Plenum of the CC CPSU did society calm down in a certain way. The people got clear signals that allowed them to consolidate the social forces.

[…] You know, it was important for me to hear everything here because our *perestroika* is also a response to the challenge of the times. In the end we, communists, think about what we are leaving behind and what we are preparing for the generations to come.

I did say to Erich [Honecker], however, that it seems that it would be much easier for you than for us. You do not experience such tensions in the socio-economic sphere. But to make a decision to undertake political reforms is also not an easy thing to do. In the future you will have to make courageous decisions. I am speaking from our own experience. Remember, Lenin used to say that in turbulent revolutionary years people get more experience in weeks and months than sometimes in decades of normalcy. Our *perestroika* led us to the conclusion that the revolutionary course would not receive working class support if living standards did not improve. But it turned out that the problem of sausage and bread is not the only one. The people demand a new social atmosphere, more oxygen in the society, especially because we are talking about a socialist regime. I am saying this to remind you of the problems we face at home. Figuratively speaking, people want not only bread but entertainment, too. If you take it in a general sense, we are talking about the necessity of building not only a material but a socio-spiritual atmosphere for the development of society. I think this is a lesson for us. It is important not to miss our chance here. The party should have its own position on these issues, its own clear policy in this respect also. Life itself will punish us if we are late. By the way, in this connection, we have moved up the dates of the XXVIII Congress of the CPSU [to July 2, 1990].

There is an understanding in society—the state of affairs in the society will determine [the timing]. […]

From our own experience, from the experience of Poland and Hungary, we saw that if the party pretends that nothing special is going on, if it does not react to the demands of reality, it is doomed. We are concerned about the fate of the healthy forces in Hungary and Poland, but it is not easy to help them. They have given up their positions. The positions were given up because they could not provide a timely response to the demands of reality, and the processes took a painful turn. The Polish comrades did not use the opportunities that opened up for them in the beginning of the 1980s. And in Hungary, at the very end of his life Kádár deeply regretted that he did not do what he could and should have done in time. So, we have only one choice—to move decisively ahead, otherwise we will be defeated.

It is even more true, if you keep in mind as we have already mentioned, Erich, that they are already rubbing their hands waiting for social revenge on a global scale, for a constricting of the socialist sphere. It makes it even more important not to slow down—that would mean defeat.

The CPSU and the Socialist Unity Party of Germany, as the most powerful of the fraternal parties, have an opportunity not only to strengthen their authority but to widen it on the basis of the original principles from which they were created, and in the name of our ideals, the ideals of October. Now is a good moment for you to act. And what could be more important for communists than the future of our movement! We, for our part, are ready to be with you in the future, to cooperate closely and constructively. In this we are open to you without any reservations. [...]

Gorbachev: The miners taught a good lesson to the secretary of the Donetsk Regional Party Committee. At the enterprises workers were saying right in the shop: why is it that the leaders of the country and of the party care about the workers, are interested in their feelings—the new minister paid a visit recently, for example—but they had no water in the workers' town for two weeks, and they could not get the chairman of the local Executive Committee to come? It is no surprise that the workers actively supported certain communists, but demanded that others be immediately replaced. And we often see that some leaders cannot pull the cart any more, but we don't dare replace them, we are afraid to offend them. Meanwhile, the problems grow and become very painful. In short, there are many "warning bells" for the party.

[*Source: Archive of the Gorbachev Foundation, Fond 2. Opis 1. On file at the National Security Archive. Translated by Svetlana Savranskaya.*]

Document No. 89: Diary of Anatoly Chernyaev regarding German Reunification

October 9, 1989

This diary entry reflects the overestimation, by Gorbachev and his top aides, of the strength of West European opposition to German reunification. Chernyaev notes with approval the chorus of French official voices that have spoken quietly against "one Germany," as well as the earlier Gorbachev conversations with Margaret Thatcher (see Document No. 85). But a note of realism emerges as Chernyaev concludes that the West Europeans want Moscow to do their dirty work: "they want to prevent this [reunification] with our hands."

All of Europe is raving about M.S. [Gorbachev] in Berlin. And many people are "whispering in our ear:" it is very well that the USSR has spoken up now, although in a delicate way, against the "reunification of Germany."

[Vadim] Zagladin has just returned from a tour across France. He met with many people—from Mitterrand to city mayors. He sent a shower of cables to Moscow about his conversations. And everyone says in a single voice—nobody needs one Germany. And [Secretary of the French President] Attali talked with us about a revival of a solid Franco-Soviet alliance, "including military integration—camouflaged as the use of armies in the struggle against natural disasters."

Thatcher […] in her conversation with M.S. […] suddenly asked us "not to take notes." She is decidedly against "the reunification of Germany." But, she says, I cannot speak about it back home, or in NATO.

In brief, they want to prevent this [reunification] with our hands.

[Source: Anatoly Chernyaev's Diary, Manuscript. On file at the National Security Archive. Translated by Vladislav Zubok.]

Document No. 90: Diary of Anatoly Chernyaev regarding Erich Honecker

October 11, 1989

Events are moving quickly in the GDR, marked by the beginning of maneuverings in the SED Politburo against Honecker. Here Chernyaev records a conversation with Gorbachev and Shakhnazarov in which the Soviet leader refers to Honecker with an obscenity for not stepping down gracefully and thus preserving "his place in history." Chernyaev and Shakhnazarov doubt a graceful exit is possible for the East German party boss, who "has already been cursed by his people."

Today M.S. met with Rakowski (the Polish Premier). I was not present, but read the record of his meeting with Jaruzelski and Rakowski in Berlin. One on one, M.S. said to them and Honecker some things that he probably should not have said. He was playing along, or maybe paying tribute to whatever orthodoxy is left in him when he said that the PUWP and the HSWP have lost, let things get away, receded from the positions of socialism.

He did not say this to the Hungarians. As for the Poles, he agrees with them when they say it themselves.

Record of conversation with Honecker [...] when speaking with me and Shakhnazarov, M.S. called him scumbag [*mudak*]. M.S. said, "He could have said to his people that he has had four operations, he is 78, he does not have the strength to fill his position, so could they please 'let him go,' he has done his duty. Then, maybe, he would have remained an esteemed figure in history." Shakhnazarov and I were doubtful that he would get a place in history if he did this right now. Two or three years ago, maybe. Right now he is already in Kádár's situation. He has been cursed by his people.

The PB in Berlin is meeting for the second day. Krenz asked our ambassador to convey to M.S. that he will raise the question about change. Honecker warned Krenz that should he do this, they will be enemies. But it looks like he did it anyway. What will come of it?

The day before yesterday, Kohl wanted to speak with M.S over the phone. Yesterday I reminded M.S. about this, but he brushed it aside—he did not want to. Today he called me and said: "go ahead, put the call through. [...]" As soon as I reached for the phone, he called again: "Should I? The results of the Berlin PB are not clear yet. And in general. [...]"

I told him that he should, otherwise it would be awkward. Plus, I am sure that Kohl is calling to disassociate himself from his statements regarding reunification (in connection to the flight of GDR citizens to the FRG).

The conversation lasted 17 minutes. Kohl promised to help in Hungary and Poland, planned a visit to Warsaw, and most importantly, assured M.S. that he will not destabilize the GDR. M.S. replied: "This is a very important statement. I will take it into consideration." They talked about bilateral economic ties in follow up to M.S.' visit to Bonn.

[*Source: Anatoly Chernyaev's Diary, Manuscript. On file at the National Security Archive. Translated by Anna Melyakova.*]

Document No. 91: Session of the CC CPSU Politburo, Discussion of Mikhail Gorbachev's Talk with Mieczysław Rakowski

October 12, 1989

In a telephone call with Gorbachev, former Polish prime minister and current party leader Mieczysław Rakowski bemoans how "helpless" the Polish party is. To this Gorbachev replies: "It is just like ours," and adds that Poland's resort to "military-administrative methods have yielded the opposite results" from what was intended. The most intriguing part of Chernyaev's notes, however, is the hint of an alternative Soviet response to problems in Poland: "I told him that if affairs in Poland develop 'not as they should,' we will react." Is this a veiled threat? Is Gorbachev merely protecting himself in the Politburo against the potential charge of losing Poland? Did Gorbachev say this directly to Rakowski or just to the Politburo? In his notes, Chernyaev places several question marks next to this phrase, as if to ask what it means.

Gorbachev: He told me that military-administrative methods have yielded the opposite results. Jailing and releasing people is not a method for leading the government. [...] The PUWP was "under the KGB umbrella," and turned out not to be ready for political struggles.

What a huge thing this party of ours is (the PUWP), he says, and how helpless! It is just like ours—an exact copy.

He complained about nostalgia for the simple and clear decisions. Is it any different with us?

He said that we still will have to prove that socialism can be achieved without dictatorial methods. But democracy cannot live long without bread. [...] The reforms could provoke a counterrevolution, and a dictator of the Piłsudski[75] type could arise.

I told him that if affairs in Poland are to develop "not as they should," we will react. [...] (?? A.Ch.)

(*Gorbachev said that he spoke with Kohl on the telephone. –A.Ch.*)

[*Source: Archive of the Gorbachev Foundation, Fond 2. opis 2. On file at the National Security Archive. Translated by Anna Melyakova.*]

---

[75] Field Marshal Józef Piłsudski (1867–1935), a Polish socialist and revolutionary, later became a military strongman and celebrated political leader of Poland. He viewed Russia, under the tsar and the Bolsheviks alike, as Poland's chief military threat.

Document No. 92: Record of Conversation between Vadim Medvedev and Kurt Hager

October 13, 1989[76]

Just a week after Gorbachev's visit to Berlin, senior GDR party leader Kurt Hager and the Soviet Politburo member in charge of ideology, Vadim Medvedev, meet for several hours in Moscow. This memorandum provides an ample dose of the kind of party jargon that was the staple of such "fraternal" conversations in the Soviet bloc. Rote invocations of eternal Soviet–East German friendship are followed by rhetorical commitments to continuing the building of socialism. But the real problems of the day continually force their way into the discussion. Hager admits that an "inconsistency" between "everyday experiences" and "official reporting" has led to the spread of "a justifiable discontent" across society. Yet, the two party loyalists conclude, all this is really the result of "a massive campaign by the enemy" of "psychological warfare against the GDR, the SED, and socialism." For them, the campaign has been a "complete failure," notwithstanding the thousands of recent East German émigrés, the church dignitaries joining the political opposition, the street demonstrations, and all the other visible evidence of the GDR's imminent collapse.

At the beginning Comrade Medvedev expressed his delight to be able to greet Comrade Hager in the CC of the CPSU as an old, trusted friend. He considered the GDR Cultural Days in the USSR to have been a great, memorable event in the realm of cooperation between both countries.[77] This cooperation is meaningful particularly in the present circumstances where the situation in both countries is marked by important events. For the CPSU, support for the GDR is very important, as is an understanding of the process of reorganization and its problems. This aspect [of Soviet–GDR understanding] is also important during the Cultural Days.

Important processes are also taking place in the GDR, most of them positive, including the 40th anniversary of the GDR, for it means the 40-year existence of a socialist state on German soil.

The CPSU is equally aware that the SED is confronted with problems today. The Soviet comrades hope very much that they will be overcome.

---

[76] Before this discussion, CPSU Member of the Politburo and CC Secretary Vadim Medvedev and Kurt Hager signed a "Long Term Conception for the Development of Cooperation between the GDR and the USSR in the sphere of Culture until the year 2000."

[77] The "Days of GDR Culture" in the USSR opened on October 12, 1989, in Moscow in the presence of Hager and CC CPSU Secretary Lev Zaikov.

Comrade Hager on his behalf expressed thanks for a friendly reception. He conveyed greetings to Comrade Mikhail Gorbachev and the Politburo of the CC CPSU from Comrade Erich Honecker and of the Politburo of the CC SED.

The visit by Comrade Gorbachev to Berlin, his encounters with citizens and the youth, particularly at the FDJ's[78] torch-light procession, revealed a great deal of support towards Comrade Gorbachev.

Especially important was the meeting with Comrade Erich Honecker and the entire Politburo. In these discussions the problems of both countries were referred to openly and candidly, and a deepening of cooperation was stressed as absolutely necessary, both in the economy and technology, and in the realm of social sciences and culture.

The "Long Term Conception" just signed is an important document and offers a good foundation for both countries, for cultural and artistic figures, and for the ministries, to raise cooperation to a qualitatively higher level and develop new forms. The Cultural Days have begun successfully and have proved once again that culture makes a contribution as only it can—namely an emotional one, which has an effect on the feelings. In this spirit the party has resolved unanimously to fulfill this Conception. Comrade Hager proposed that the departments of both Central Committees act in coordination toward that aim, and make the corresponding proposals for conversion of the Conception.

Proceeding to the issue of the present situation in the GDR, Comrade Hager reported on a two-day Politburo session, in which all the issues and faults in the work of the party and State had been discussed openly. Altogether it was a very critical discussion. Problems of the role of worker-and-farmer-power, the party, and also cooperation between the fraternal parties were discussed. To that effect, there was unanimous agreement to throw out everything which was unproven, to give up what is routine, and to carry out changes both in party work as well as in the state organs, people's representatives, and in the media and information policies. As a result of the discussions, the Politburo adopted a declaration which will be published. Excerpts can also be found in *Pravda*.

Comrade Medvedev made the point that the possibility of a verbatim publication is being looked into.

Comrade Hager informed further that artists and cultural figures have spoken out increasingly critically, [on subjects] having nothing to do with cultural or social problems, but rather mostly about the emerging general situation. Statements by the Academy of Arts and by the Cultural League have been published.[79] On the general situation and its origins Comrade Hager said the following:

[78] *Freie Deutsche Jugend*, the Free German Youth, was the official youth movement of the German Democratic Republic.
[79] The declaration of the Presidency of the Academy of the Arts in the GDR and the Communiqué of the Presidential Session of the GDR Cultural League were already published in *Neues Deutschland* on October 4, 1989, and October 13, 1989, respectively. [Footnote in the original.]

552

1. The emigration of tens of thousands of citizens to the FRG is creating great anxiety and raises a question as to the causes.

2. The GDR is at the mercy of a massive campaign by the enemy—psychological warfare against the GDR, the SED, and socialism—which has been a complete failure.

3. An array of opposition groups has emerged; they are trying to organize themselves, the Social Democratic Party among others, of which 7 of 14 founders are clergymen.[80] A group of church dignitaries is playing a negative role and stirring up the atmosphere. Others opposed to this are searching for a way to reach agreement with the state organs.

4. Artists and cultural figures, scientists, and other members of the intelligentsia, workers, and farmers feel that there is an inconsistency between words and deeds, their everyday experiences do not correspond to official reporting.

Consequently a justifiable discontent is forming.

On this basis the Politburo adopted the above-mentioned declaration, which contains all these aspects and opens up new paths for the development of the party and for life in the GDR.

Presently consultations are taking place with district and municipality leaderships as well as with friendly parties. A plenary session of the CC SED is being prepared, which will comment on the situation and present a platform of tasks for the further development of socialism in the GDR for discussion in preparation for the IX Party Congress. All these steps and plans mean the initiation of a great dialogue with all circles of the population, the majority of which supports the strengthening of socialism.

There are also forces, however, which support anti-socialist positions and choose other forms of discussion, namely demonstrations, and attacks on armed [state] organs. In this respect heightened vigilance is required to prevent counter-revolutionary actions. An adjustment in media policy is also important to moving forward.

In all, a great change is occurring in life in the GDR, in the spirit of the motto of continuity and change, where stress is being placed on change. In this stormy time it is necessary to hold course, to allow for no pessimism, and to defend the values of socialism—all of these being tasks for ideological work, in which the role of culture is not unimportant.

Comrade Medvedev was thankful for the detailed statement and for his part reported on the recent Politburo session of the CC CPSU. In these deliberations the outcome of Comrade Gorbachev's visit to the GDR was discussed. Comrade Gorbachev gave a detailed report on the jubilation, the festivities, his talks with people on the sidelines, and on the meetings with the party leadership and with

---

[80] The Social Democratic Party in the GDR (SDP) was founded on October 7, 1989, in Schwante (Municipality Oranienbarg). The founding appeal "For an ecological social democracy" was first published in *Die Welt* on October 9, 1989. [Footnote in the original.]

Comrade Honecker. There was complete agreement on the view that the CPSU will always support the GDR. In the past they always granted aid and support and that will also be so in the future:

- towards the workers' and farmers' state on German soil;
- towards the party leadership;
- and always aid as well [against] attacks from outside.

At the same time the Politburo expressed hope and confidence that the SED party leadership will solve these problems on the basis of a far-reaching analysis and find ways to continue to build socialism. Above all, steadfastness regarding the tenets of socialism is the most important by far for both states and equally for all other socialist states.

Comrade Medvedev expressed a determination to deepen the cooperation between both states, parties, and peoples. This is necessary in the fields of science and the economy—just as his talk with Professor Scheler[81] stressed—and similarly in the cultural realm. In this respect, the "Long Term Conception" has great importance; it will also have repercussions on ideological and theoretical work. Therefore, coordination must take into account the present conditions of socialism and in the world at large. In the party spheres both parties should see that this cooperation gains in speed and strength, so that concrete goals may be achieved. In conclusion, Comrade Medvedev reported that Comrade Gorbachev was informed of this meeting and conveyed his warmest greetings. He likewise gives his regards to Comrade Honecker and the entire Politburo leadership, [and states] that there is much sympathy for their current problems and that he will follow attentively what is happening in the GDR. One hopes that the party leadership can cope with the situation and that the position of socialism will be strengthened.

Comrade Hager expressed his thanks for the discussion and said that the positions of socialism will never be surrendered. However, what was achieved could not be undone, and that remains so. The GDR is always closely bound to the Soviet Union, and knows what it obtained in friendship and solidarity, without which it would not have been able to survive. This points to the responsibility that the GDR bears at this point in Europe and in view of the sentiments heard already from the FRG.

[*Source: Stiftung Archiv der Parteien und Massenorganisationen der DDR -Bundesarchiv, SED, ZK, IV2/2039/283. Translated by Christiaan Hetzner.*]

---

[81] Medvedev met beforehand with President of the GDR Academy of Sciences Prof. Dr. Werner Scheler.

Document No. 93: Memorandum from Georgy Shakhnazarov to Mikhail Gorbachev regarding Military Détente in Europe

October 14, 1989

This policy memorandum marks a kind of apogee for "new thinking" which combines a vision of a post-Cold War Europe with a concrete proposal for the unilateral withdrawal of Soviet troops from Poland, Hungary and Czechoslovakia. The author, Georgy Shakhnazarov, is enough of a realist to argue that the Soviet Union needs to take the initiative before either its domestic political opponents—or, more likely, the new governments in Eastern Europe—demand such withdrawals, leaving Moscow on the defensive. Shakhnazarov indulges in some wishful thinking about the dissolution of both NATO and the Warsaw Treaty Organization by the end of the 20ᵗʰ century, but also gives very pragmatic reasons for the pull-out—among them, that their "function of scaring the opposition" "has now disappeared," and that domestic Soviet reaction would be enthusiastic because of the "substantial savings" to be gained. But events in Eastern Europe would continue to take the initiative away from Moscow, and all Gorbachev can do (in his November 30 speech at Rome city hall just before the Malta summit) is call for a re-convened Conference on Security and Cooperation in Europe (CSCE) as a replacement for the two opposing blocs.

Mikhail Sergeyevich!

I present for your consideration a proposal for our new move on military détente in Europe. I have in mind a proposal to give the process of weakening the confrontation between the military blocs a more plan-based quality, presupposing the liquidation of the WTO and NATO by the end of the XX century. Within the framework of this process, it would be expedient to outline several intermediate stages, the most important of which should be the abolition of the military organizations of the two blocs by 1995.

Similar ideas literally fill the air. One can have no doubt that this proposal will find a positive response, and will define clear timelines in the future development of the European process. It is important that in this case the initiative will be ours.

However, this proposal will sound much stronger if it is supplemented by our concrete actions to limit the military activities of the blocs. What I have in mind is a unilateral withdrawal of Soviet troops from Poland, Hungary and Czechoslovakia.

The following arguments support this decision:

First of all, the military significance of the units stationed in those countries under current conditions is not great. In essence, they used to serve the function of scaring the opposition, [a function] which has now disappeared.

Moreover, the continuing presence of our military units is becoming an "irritant" in the development of normal interstate relations with the new regimes that already exist in Poland and Hungary, and obviously will emerge in Czechoslovakia in the very near future.

We should not have any doubts that sooner or later, the new governments of Hungary and Poland will present us with demands to withdraw our troops. Therefore, it would be better to do it on our own initiative, and not withdraw under pressure, accompanied by our enemies' whoops and howls.

Secondly, if the troop withdrawal is carried out under pressure, it would look like a capitulation by the Warsaw Treaty Organization, one more indication of the failure of communism, and—especially dangerous—a dismantling of the system that came together in Europe after World War II (or, as we say, postwar European realities).

However, if we start withdrawing troops on our own initiative, then it will look like a sign of peace-making and one more indication of the effectiveness of our new political thinking.

Thirdly, it is very important that our allies, having received the satisfaction of the withdrawal of Soviet troops, at the same time will be "tied down" by the plan to liquidate the military blocs by the year 2000, which would be codified by an agreement among all states. It would be simply unseemly [*neprilichno*] to violate such an all-European consensus. This, in essence, will eliminate the question of [their] leaving the WTO now, which is an obsession of the extremist wing of the Polish and Hungarian opposition.

Fourthly, one more winning element related to such an initiative on our part will be a colossal increase in trust toward Soviet policy with all the favorable circumstances resulting from that.

Fifth, we should state openly that under current conditions it is not yet possible to withdraw Soviet troops from the GDR, but:

a) we are willing to reduce them in accordance with the agreement that will be reached at the negotiations in Vienna;

b) we will be ready to withdraw them immediately, the moment the USA agrees to withdraw their troops from the FRG.

Sixth, this initiative will find even wider support if it includes a proposal, along with the dissolution of the military blocs, to liquidate all foreign military bases on the territory of the European states before the end of this century.

And lastly, in addition to the foreign policy effect, this action, without doubt, will be met with enthusiasm in our own country, primarily because it will mean a substantial savings of the resources that we now need so much.

By the way, it is quite possible that if this initiative is not proposed from above, it could be proposed in the very near future by all kinds of party opponents or simply by reasonable people's deputies. In that case, we would have to take the step anyway, but the political victory would belong to others.

And the last [thought]. It seems to me that it would be expedient to unveil this large-scale proposal in Rome, because it is precisely in that country [sic] that it would be received with greater enthusiasm than anywhere else. The time factor is important as well.

The month-and-a-half left before the trip to Italy will not delay our proposal of this significant measure by too much, and at the same time it will allow us to conduct the necessary work on this idea inside the country and in coordination with our allies.

Shakhnazarov

[Source: Published in G.Kh. Shakhnazarov's Tsena svobody *[The Price of Freedom] (Moscow: Rossika-Zeus, 1993), pp.423–425. On file at the National Security Archive. Translated by Svetlana Savranskaya.]*

Document No. 94: Record of Telephone Conversation between George H.W. Bush and Helmut Kohl

October 23, 1989

Not only does Helmut Kohl initiate this telephone call, he also leads the entire conversation, giving the American president a detailed briefing, country-by-country, about the changes in Eastern Europe. Kohl says he is supporting the Hungarian reform communists "quite vigorously," and that "our Western friends and partners should be doing more" to aid Poland. He foresees more than 150,000 refugees from the GDR by Christmas, and reaffirms his commitment to NATO. Bush's response shows his concern from media stories "about German reunification resulting in a neutralist Germany and a threat to Western security"—"we do not believe that," he insists—and he almost plaintively seeks credit for the $200 million that the U.S. will contribute to a Poland stabilization fund (hardly the new Marshall Plan that would be called for by, among others, Lech Wałęsa in his November 15 address to a joint session of the U.S. Congress). But Bush, characteristically, is determined not to move "so fast as to be reckless."

CHANCELLOR KOHL INITIATED THE CALL.

The President: How are you?

Chancellor Kohl: Fine. I am glad to hear your voice. I saw pictures of your visit to San Francisco and hope you will be able to give as much support as possible for that tragedy.

The President: It is terrible, but the authorities there are doing well. We will help at this end in any way we can.

Chancellor Kohl: I wanted to tell you briefly how I see events in Hungary, Poland, and the GDR. In Hungary, things are going the best. The people are incredibly courageous, and very determined. The present government is taking an enormous risk: the changes have their origin with the reform movement in the Communist Party, but it is not at all certain that the reformers will be able to get credit in the course of the election. It is quite possible that the Party will come in only second, and there might be a coalition. We have supported the Hungarians quite vigorously. In December I will go over for two days to give further support, also optically.

The President: Where will you go?

Chancellor Kohl: I will go to Budapest and perhaps also to a second city, but that is not certain. The economic situation is relatively good there. They can make it, though the next two years will be decisive. On November 9 I will go to Poland for four days. Our negotiations have been essentially concluded. I will do all I can to support the new government, especially in the economic area.

With the EC, I intend to give assistance in human resources. This seems to be the problem, if I may put it bluntly: there is a lot of good will and many good ideas, but the Poles do not know how to put them into practice. They have to introduce currency reforms, a new banking system, and other steps to open up a new market-oriented economy. I will be doing what I can, and I will also take into account and work on what you have suggested, so that Western activities can be homogeneous. My feeling is that our Western friends and partners should be doing more. There is a difference between words and deeds. I also want to enter into a new phase with the Poles, 50 years after the outbreak of war.

In the GDR, changes are quite dramatic. None of us can give a prognosis. It is not clear whether the new man will have the determination and the strength to carry out reform. Gorbachev told me that he had encouraged reform during his visit, but I am not sure how courageous he [new Party and State leader Egon Krenz] [sic] is. There is an enormous unrest among the population. Things will become incalculable if there are no reforms. My interest is not to see so many flee the GDR, because the consequences there would be catastrophic. Our estimates are that by Christmas we will have reached a total of 150,000 refugees, with an average age of under 30.

My last point concerns the climate among the media in New York, the coast, London, the Hague, Rome, and Paris that, crudely speaking, holds that the Germans are now committed to Ostpolitik and discussions about reunification and that they are less interested in the EC and the West. This is absolute nonsense! I will again and again explain and declare my position. At the beginning of January, I will go to Paris to deliver a speech at a major conference. I will say publicly—also to the left wing in the FRG—that without a strong NATO, without the necessary development of the EC, none of these developments in the Warsaw Treaty would have occurred. I am firmly convinced of that, and that will be my message. It would also be good for you, as soon as you can, to deliver a public message that progress in disarmament and changes in the east are possible only if we stand together.

The President: I couldn't agree more. I have seen some of those stories, but I know your position and think I know the heartbeat of Germany. The strength of NATO has made possible these changes in Eastern Europe. We are seeing a spate of stories about German reunification resulting in a neutralist Germany and a threat to Western security. We do not believe that. We are trying to react very cautiously and carefully to change in the GDR. We have great respect for the way the FRG under your leadership has been handling this situation. You have done a great job.

I understand that Horst [Teltschik, the Chancellor's security advisor] [sic] is coming soon. We are very anxious to talk with him on this subject and also about Poland and Hungary. We are getting criticism in the Congress from liberal Democrats that we ought to be doing more to foster change, but I am not going to go so fast as to be reckless. On Poland, the Congress is pushing us to put forward more money, but we are moving forward. I asked our Congress to approve a $200 million grant, which would be our contribution to the $1 billion stabilization fund the Polish government has requested. I consider it vitally important that we help Poland as it implements its economic reform program in the context of an IMF agreement. I am also sending a high level team from the public and private sectors to consult with the Poles and help them as they decide how to implement these reforms.

Chancellor Kohl: I consider that a very important step, especially to have people from the public and private sectors. Let me ask you to have one of your collaborators call Horst Teltschik to talk this over. We have a similar approach, which we discussed with Mr. Delors. We want the EC to do the same. After my trip to Poland, I will send Horst to discuss these matters.

The President: Is Horst here now?

Chancellor Kohl: He was in New York a couple of days ago. The next time I will have him come down.

The President: I thought he was coming to Washington.

Chancellor Kohl: No. He is back now.

The President: I will ask General Scowcroft to call him.

Chancellor Kohl: Any time.

The President: We ought to get together for an informal session, perhaps a few hours at Camp David.

Chancellor Kohl: I will think it over and find out when I can make it. It would have to fit into one day.

The President: We can do that. It is important to talk things over about Eastern Europe. I will see Thatcher around the time of our Thanksgiving. It is important to signal the importance I attach to U.S. relations with the FRG, especially when we see some of these mischievous stories around.

Chancellor Kohl: I understand and think it is a very good idea.

The President: Let's stay in touch. General Scowcroft will call Horst and tell you more about our approach toward Poland and our support for the stabilization fund. Let me also say that I appreciate this call very much.

Chancellor Kohl: Thank you. I will call again before I go to Poland, around the 6th or 7th of November.

[*Source: George Bush Presidential Library. Obtained through FOIA. On file at the National Security Archive.*]

Document No. 95: Record of Conversation between Mikhail Gorbachev and Mauno Koivisto

October 25, 1989

The first Social Democrat to be elected president of Finland (1982), Mauno Koivisto maintained Helsinki's traditional deference to Moscow throughout the revolutions of 1989 and the collapse of the Soviet Union in 1991, even declining to recognize neighboring Estonia until after major European powers had done so. But he also led Finland's move to join the European Union before ending his tenure in 1994, even though in this 1989 conversation in the Finnish capital, he is pleased with Gorbachev's idea for a new Helsinki conference, perhaps in 1992, leading to a convocation of all 35 European countries. Here, just at the time that Eastern Europe is moving toward the West, Koivisto repeats U.S. and West European assurances that they do not want to take advantage of developments such as the Baltic independence movements or otherwise provoke the Soviet Union. Gorbachev is moved to reiterate his commitment to non-interference, referring to "friends" (no doubt Ceauşescu and others) who are urging him "not to allow" the Polish developments: "But what does 'not to allow' mean? To interfere in their internal affairs, to take all the responsibility for the future of Poland, and also for all its debts." Here, yet again, the "fraternal allies" are a drain, not a benefit, for Moscow. The real news from Gorbachev's trip to Finland came from his public comments that the Soviet Union (as well as the West) has "no right, moral or political," to interfere in Eastern Europe—at which point Soviet spokesman Gennadii Gerasimov joked that the Brezhnev Doctrine had given way to the "Sinatra Doctrine," referring to the 1969 hit song, "My Way."

Koivisto: [...] As far as the Baltics are concerned, we are, indeed as well as Sweden, interested in what is happening there. The Swedes pay more attention to Latvia and to Estonia. It appears that the situation in Latvia is deteriorating. The Estonians have approved programs, according to which they are switching to economic self-sufficiency beginning next year. Last summer the Supreme Soviet approved the economic self-sufficiency of the republics in general. But the law has not been worked out yet. Plus, the elections are coming, and everything will deteriorate again.

What could we do in this situation? We have tried to send you signals repeatedly: we need clarity—in case of problems we need one political line, and in case of the complete success of your policy another [line].

I am glad that [Estonian party leader] Vaino Valjas is here now. I hope that I can talk to him. If those in the Baltics believe they will find general sympathy if they push their demands far enough, they are mistaken. Even Baker said that they did not base their calculations on the disorders in the USSR. He put it in even stronger words. The governments of the West European countries are thinking along the same lines. They do not want to take part in an activity that would be provocative toward the USSR. That is why it is important to know now how the situation will develop in the future.

Besides, from the point of view of the environment and resources, we have an interest in Karelia and the Kola Peninsula. The Kola Peninsula has resources that we do not have, and we would like to take part in industrial cooperation there.

Gorbachev: I share your ideas and accept your opinion. [...]

The society is very tense as it is. And if there are outside attempts to profit from these tensions, there could be the most negative consequences. We firmly stand for non-interference in the internal affairs of socialist countries. As far as the situation in Poland is concerned, we have received some letters from our friends in other countries with appeals "not to allow it!" But what does "not to allow" mean? To interfere in their internal affairs, to take all the responsibility for the future of Poland, and also for all its debts. We have a firm position here—non-interference. But the West should not interfere either, it should not provoke them. [...]

All in all, Mr. President, it seems to me it would be important to think about how to lift the entire European security process to a new level. Recently, I noted the fact that of all the people who signed the Helsinki Final Act, only Zhivkov, Ceauşescu and [Agostino] Cardinal Casaroli [Vatican secretary of state] are still in power. Almost 15 years have passed since that moment. It would probably be interesting for the new generation of leaders of the 35 states to get together and see what horizons of the European security and cooperation process are opening up now, and what the possibilities for building the common European home are. From my point of view, it would be natural to meet again in Helsinki in 1992.

Koivisto: (with irony, but evidently pleased). I would like to think hard about that. [...] You mean to meet in 1992 in the framework of the forthcoming all-European forum?

Gorbachev: Yes, exactly. It would be natural to meet again in the location where the original act was signed. If you do not have any problems with that, I will make the proposal tomorrow in my speech.

Koivisto: (Laughing) Let's say that it took you a great deal of effort to convince me to agree. [...]

[*Source: Archive of the Gorbachev Foundation, Fond 1. Opis 1. On file at the National Security Archive. Translated by Svetlana Savranskaya.*]

Document No. 96: Record of Conversation between Aleksandr Yakovlev and Zbigniew Brzezinski

October 31, 1989

The leading Soviet reformer on the Politburo finds surprising agreement on the German question in this meeting with the Polish-American observer, Zbigniew Brzezinski, whom the Soviets had vilified as an enemy of détente when he served as President Carter's national security adviser in the late 1970s. (Cementing his reputation for iconoclasm, Brzezinski would subsequently endorse Ronald Reagan for re-election in 1984.) In a tribute to glasnost, Brzezinski thanks Yakovlev for permitting a ceremonial visit to Katyń, the site of the World War II massacre of Polish officers by Stalin's NKVD, which Soviet propaganda had long blamed on the Nazis.

This frank discussion of the future of Europe features Yakovlev's repeated notion of the mutual dissolution of NATO and the Warsaw Pact versus Brzezinski's argument that the blocs should remain stable, and even the new governments of Poland and Hungary should remain part of the Warsaw Treaty Organization. Like Gorbachev's quotation of Giscard d'Estaing (see Document No. 39), Yakovlev foresees a Europe with "a common parliament, common affairs and trade relations," along with open borders. He warns against any intervention by the U.S. or Western Europe in the processes underway in the East; and he declares that the lesson of Afghanistan is that "not one Soviet soldier should be in a foreign country with the purpose of conducting warfare." Yakovlev wants the "same understanding" from the American side.

For his part, Brzezinski makes a number of prescient observations, contrasting the state of reform in the USSR (a "rift" between political and economic reform, with the former much further along) to that of China (economic but not political change), predicting that Czechoslovakia would soon follow the path of Poland and Hungary (this would happen only seven weeks later), and warning that any crumbling of the East German regime would soon lead to German unification—a development that "does not correspond to either your or our interests." Here we see the Polish nationalist worried about "the Prussians" and preferring to keep Europe divided into two blocs rather than deal with "one Germany, united and strong." The next day (see following document), Gorbachev would compliment Brzezinski for possessing "global brains."

Brzezinski: I have a very good impression from this visit to your country. As you probably know, I had an opportunity to present a lecture at the Diplomatic Academy. I also thank you very much for organizing a trip to Katyń for me. For me personally this is very important both politically and symbolically. As you probably know, I gave an interview to Soviet, Polish, and American television. In this interview I wanted to say three things. Firstly, I am glad that my trip to Katyń took place. Secondly, I am glad that right now the truth about Stalin and his crimes is being spoken frankly. Thirdly, and most importantly, I said that the truth should serve to bring the people of the Soviet Union and Poland closer, rather than pushing them apart.

I would like to use this meeting to ask you a number of questions. First of all, I would like to ask you how you see the changes taking place in the countries of Eastern Europe, and what you expect in the future. After all, the countries of Eastern Europe are undergoing a period of dynamic development, new relations between socialist countries are forming; what formed between 1945 and 1950 is rapidly changing. Also, if you have time, I would like you to answer the question of how you see the further development of the Soviet Union. It seems to me that the rift between political reform and the real economic situation has never been so great. In this, your country can be compared to China, with the difference that in China everything was exactly the opposite—the economic reforms there were far ahead of the political system's reform.

Yakovlev: I have known of your work for a while. In particular I see in you the embodiment of the union between theoretician and pragmatic politician.

About Eastern Europe.

I would like first of all to point out that we are strictly following what we said at the very beginning of *perestroika*, for example the statement about respecting freedom of speech. Since 1985, when we said this, we have continued to strictly follow this.

Brzezinski: Did you expect that it could go so far?

Yakovlev: Why not? We are troubled by something else. If the processes taking place in Eastern Europe right now continue to proceed strictly on the basis of those countries' internal development, then there is nothing to worry about. It would be a mistake for Western Europe or the USA to intervene in these processes in any way. We must not forget that we have a common border with these countries and without question we have our own interests in connection with this. But right now we see no direct threat. We have not changed our relations with Poland one bit, and the new Polish leadership assures us that it is interested in upholding normal friendly relations with our country, and does not intend to change existing agreements.

Brzezinski: Over a year ago, during my meeting with Wałęsa, I recommended that he visit Moscow before his visit to Washington.

Yakovlev: Why not? Let him visit. I do not see any obstacles.

Brzezinski: At the same time I would like to know how you define intervention and what exactly you mean by this.

Yakovlev: Frankly speaking, it would be quite unpleasant if the Poles were egged on against Russia. Some people are doing this in the mass media in other ways. In present-day Poland, sometimes people allow themselves to do this. For example, one of the representatives of the present Polish government started saying that we have to pay some kind of compensation. But 700,000 of our soldiers died there. Sometimes Soviet soldiers' graves are defiled. I believe that soldiers' graves should not be touched.

Let everything develop gradually in Poland. They are in a very difficult economic situation right now. You know the situation in Poland better than I do. But I do not take it upon myself to predict when they will be able to overcome the current crisis. One should help. But at the same time, the Poles are now already beginning to understand that they need to work better themselves. The day before yesterday Wałęsa spoke about this. In general, no one will solve their problems for them.

And no one will solve our problems for us. Our point of view is the same for Poland and Hungary. Right now in Hungary they have formed a Socialist Party. But I see that people are not too eager to be part of this Socialist Party. Now they have created an organizing committee to reconstitute the HSWP [Hungarian Socialist Workers Party]. What will come of this? I do not know and I do not take it upon myself to say anything; let them analyze it themselves.

Brzezinski: Nikolay Shishlin, your politician, says that he thinks that nothing bad would happen if both Poland and Hungary withdrew from the Warsaw Treaty Organization. Is this the official position or only his point of view? Personally I think that the Warsaw Treaty Organization must be a political union, not an ideological one. But at the same time a coordination of the member countries' actions must be maintained.

Yakovlev: In this case I agree with you absolutely that there must not be any individual withdrawals from military-political alliances. This would disturb stability. It would be a different matter if we come to an agreement and disband both military-political unions.

Brzezinski: Here I do not agree. I do not think that the time has come to disband these alliances. Gradually, new opportunities for a transition to a new system will arise. Only then can the alliances be disbanded. On the basis that exists right now, East and West can conduct discussions about all issues. However, if some continue to provoke the population of Eastern Europe with all kinds of statements—which can be interpreted by certain elements in their own way, considering the sensitivity of the German question—it could cause a most acute political crisis.

Yakovlev: Yes, in this you are right. During this transitional period both our sides must be very mindful and careful. A moment could come when all past offenses, pretensions, etc., overtake people's common sense, and then everything could simply explode. We must pass this stage very calmly. Both sides must exhibit maximum vigilance.

With all its negative aspects, Afghanistan had one positive moment for us. From Afghanistan's example we came to the conclusion that not one Soviet soldier should be in a foreign country with the purpose of conducting warfare. In the end, we should come to an agreement so that we have the same understanding from your side.

Brzezinski: To resolve the Afghan problem it is necessary for [President Mohammad] Najibullah to leave. He was and remains for the country's entire population a successor to Babrak Karmal and a symbol of the former regime. If he leaves, the Jirga and other organs will be able to negotiate a national agreement faster.

Yakovlev: This is a decision for that country's people. Let them decide.

Brzezinski: But you have enormous influence there. You could resolve this issue. After all, many Afghans do not want a compromise. If Najibullah had to urgently leave the country due to health concerns and go to the Soviet Union or some other place for treatment, it would answer the interests of all sides.

Yakovlev: I have already told you that the people themselves must decide this.

Matlock: It seems to us that for the Afghans themselves resolution of the issue with the participation of Najibullah is unacceptable.

Yakovlev: So let them express this.

Brzezinski: Right now insurgents control around 90 percent of Afghanistan's territory. Najibullah controls only the major cities, and the roads between them have already been cut off.

Yakovlev: You will, however, agree with me that in the end Afghanistan shares a border with the Soviet Union and not the United States.

Brzezinski: Of course I agree that in this case the interests of your state's security are involved. However, we would like [Afghanistan] to be a neutral country, maintaining good-neighborly relations with you, as it was under Daud until the Afghan tragedy occurred.

What changes do you expect to take place in Eastern Europe, considering the fact that there as well you have an interest in securing stability and security? By my calculations, events similar to the ones in Poland and Hungary must soon take place in Czechoslovakia, and we will most likely react calmly to this. But if the process of democratization begins in East Germany then that artificial state, created on an ideological basis, will soon crumble. And if ideology as an element of its existence falls away, then the current regime will quickly tumble and the question of reuniting the two Germanys will immediately arise. This is dangerous. How should the German question be solved? What will it be: a confederation, the ratification of a new agreement between former allies in World War II? All of this needs to be thought through thoroughly.

Yakovlev: I think the fact that right now [Egon] Krenz, after being chosen to the position of leader of the GDR and SED, has verbally stated that he needs to establish working contacts with the FRG leadership signifies that a very good step was taken. Who knows what it will lead to in the future? I think that right now no one will take it upon himself to predict it. One thing is clear—democratic and peaceful states must exist in the heart of Europe, on the German territories, not states that are increasing their armaments. We had enough with the destructive war of the past. For us this is a matter of principle. We do not want another war. As a veteran of World War II, I know that while I live I will be unambiguous about it, and my generation will always be mindful. One careless movement can change the balance of power and the situation in Europe. [Alfred] Dregger from the FRG and his ilk must clearly perceive the problem in its entirety. By the way, I met with him recently. During the war we were of about the same rank; one could say we fought against each other. He, of course, is a nationalist and is only for himself; he speaks against you and against us. You cannot call him a fascist, but nationalism does not lead to democracy either. In my opinion, he should be more careful. Also troubling were his statements along the lines of saying that the processes in Eastern Europe are a sign of our weakness. The most important thing is to understand that any changes are [to be] made by the people. We have said this and we will hold this course.

Brzezinski: The conception of European stability provides for a combination of different social-political and social-economic interests, including the introduction of such forms as multi-party systems, free markets, etc. It seems as though this coincides with the USSR's national interests, which cannot be unconcerned about maintaining stability in Europe.

Yakovlev: In this respect we have a mutual concern: not to have hostile nations at our borders.

Brzezinski: That is why I openly said that I am in favor of Poland and Hungary remaining within the Warsaw Treaty Organization. Both blocs should not be disbanded right now. I do not know what will happen if the GDR ceases to exist. There will be one Germany, united and strong. This does not correspond to either your or our interests.

Yakovlev: How would you keep the GDR? By force?

Brzezinski: I think that is also not necessary. Political possibilities always exist.

Yakovlev: But right now many demonstrations are going on there.

Brzezinski: These are the Prussians. By their nature, they are very disciplined people. And if 300,000 people came out to demonstrate, it is evidence of a very serious crisis.

Yakovlev: I was informed that the situation there is stabilizing. A dialogue has begun between members of the government and participants in the demonstrations.

Brzezinski: In terms of approaching the collaboration of Warsaw Treaty members with European Common Market countries or United Europe, do you on the whole allow that in the future such countries as Poland, Hungary, and Czechoslovakia will, on the one hand, effectively collaborate with West European countries in the economic sphere and, on the other hand, remain loyal members of the Warsaw Treaty Organization?

Yakovlev: There are many questions about Europe's future. What will happen? The European countries will have a common parliament, common affairs and trade relations; the borders will be open. And what will happen with long-established bilateral relations between Western Europe and the socialist countries? How, for example, will economic relations between the USSR and Belgium develop further? How will military issues be resolved considering the fact that United Europe will include some neutral states?

At the same time, this has to be considered a component of the policies directed at building a Common European Home. If this project succeeds in creating an effectively functioning economic association, if it succeeds in following the social interests of the workers, then it deserves our interest, and we are prepared to cooperate with Europe.

Brzezinski: Of course, right now you have many cares, including concerns about ideological issues. If in the near future there is no catastrophe in Poland and Hungary, they will become stable, multi-party democratic systems with market economies. And your people will also begin to say: do what they did.

I am in your country for the sixth time. This time I was most struck by the gap between the Soviet Union and the West in its present form. Right now one can say that you are not going through merely an economic crisis. Even against the background of what was here a short while ago one perceives a decline. And considering the depth of the gap one can draw the conclusion that it is very likely that a political crisis could strike your country as well. I am digesting all of this right now, but I am afraid to predict concrete outcomes.

[*Source: State Archive of the Russian Federation [GARF], Moscow. Yakovlev Collection. Fond 10063. Opis 1. Delo 266. On file at the National Security Archive. Translated by Anna Melyakova.*]

Document No. 97: Record of Conversation between Mikhail Gorbachev and Egon Krenz

November 1, 1989

Here the Soviet leader receives the new East German replacement for Honecker, Egon Krenz. As interior minister, Krenz had declined to use force to suppress the Leipzig and other demonstrations, yet he would later serve time in unified German jails (unlike Honecker, who would be excused for health reasons) as punishment for the GDR's policy of shooting Berlin Wall jumpers. Krenz tells Gorbachev, in effect, that his country's policy has changed, citing "orders to our border troops not to use weapons at the border," as part of an attempt to address the pressing refugee crisis.

Apparently meeting with Gorbachev's approval, Krenz mentions in passing a new draft "law on foreign travel" that would loosen restrictions. This proposed law would figure directly in the most dramatic moment of the entire period. On November 9, a party spokesman's unplanned announcement of the new law's immediate effect (rather than the gradual change intended by the SED) at a Berlin press conference would lead to huge crowds pressing through checkpoints at the border with West Berlin culminating later that night in the actual tearing down of the Wall itself. Perhaps at this point Gorbachev is already resigned to the refugee exodus and this presages Moscow's relative calm when the Wall would fall.

With such developments as yet unimagined, the two leaders commiserate about the failures of Krenz's predecessor. Gorbachev even claims that Honecker might have survived had he reformed earlier, but Krenz says Honecker was too threatened by Gorbachev's own popularity. They frankly discuss their mutual economic problems, including Soviet resentment over providing the raw materials for the GDR's factories, and Moscow's sense of Eastern Europe as a burden. The Soviet general secretary also tells a remarkable story about the Politburo's own ignorance of economic matters, describing an episode in the early 1980s when Gorbachev and Ryzhkov tried to obtain some budget information only to be warned away by then-leader Yurii Andropov.

On the German question, both the Soviet and the East German take comfort that "the majority of Western leaders do not want to see the dissolution" of the blocs nor the unification of Germany. But within a month the East German parliament would revoke the leading role of the communist party, and Krenz himself would resign on December 6.

Gorbachev: The Soviet people are very interested in everything that is going on now in the GDR. We hope to get the most recent information from you, although, of course, we know a lot. The situation in the GDR, judging by everything we see, is moving at an increasing speed. Is there a danger of being left behind the reforms? Remember, we said in Berlin that to be behind is always to lose. We know that from our own experience. [...]

I cannot tell you that we have already "broken the horse of *perestroika*," [a horse] that has turned out to be quite restless. In any case, we have not completely tamed it yet. Sometimes it even tries to throw off its rider. But we have gained very valuable experience.

Krenz: [...] At the Politburo we came to the conclusion that a crisis has not emerged in the last several months. Many problems have accumulated over the years.

But the main mistake was probably that we did not draw serious conclusions from the new processes of social development, which began in the Soviet Union and other socialist countries, and which were ripe in the GDR itself. Because if you have a primary ally, you have to understand and share its problems and hardships. One cannot declare friendship in words and at the same time stay on the sidelines when your ally is trying to deal with its difficult problems. People who are used to this felt that we suddenly lost our unity with the Soviet Union and that we ourselves erected this barrier.

Gorbachev: From the political point of view the situation is clear, but from a simply human standpoint it is dramatic. I was also concerned about this. In general, I had good relations with Honecker, but it seemed recently as if he had gone blind. If he had been willing to make the necessary changes in policy on his own initiative two or three years ago, everything would have been different now. But apparently he underwent some kind of shift; he ceased to see the real processes [occurring] in the world and in his own country. It was a personal drama, but because Honecker occupied a very high position it grew into a political drama.

Krenz: Yes, you are right; it is a drama, and for me too because Honecker brought me up, he was my political mentor.

Gorbachev: Some people now speculate on that, but I think you should not react to it.

Krenz: For Honecker the turn probably occurred exactly in 1985 when you were elected general secretary of the CC CPSU. He saw in you a threat to his authority, because he considered himself the most dynamic political leader. He lost all touch with reality and did not rely on the Politburo collective. [Secretary of the Economy Guenther] Mittag and [Secretary of Agitation and Propaganda Joachim] Herrmann did him a very bad service in this respect. The first as a strategist, the second as an executive. [...]

Gorbachev: This is a familiar picture. Some time ago, when I was already a Politburo member, I basically did not know our budget. Once we were working with Nikolay Ryzhkov on some request of Andropov's that had to do with budgetary issues, and we naturally decided that we should learn about them. But Yurii V. Andropov said: Do not go there, it is not your business. Now we know why he said so. It was not a budget, but the devil knows what. [...]

Gorbachev: We knew about your situation, about your economic and financial ties with the FRG, and we understood how it all could turn out. For our part, we were carrying out our obligations to the GDR, including those on oil deliveries, even though some of it had to be reduced at a certain time. Erich Honecker was not very honest with us about those things. We knew about that, but led by the highest political considerations we exercised reserve and patience.

570

Krenz: It is very important to define the division of labor between the GDR and the Soviet Union better. It is one of our main reserves. The situation here is far from ideal. We need to remove existing barriers. There should be only one criterion—effectiveness and mutual benefit.

Gorbachev: The issue of the division of labor stands as a major problem in our country as well. The republics that produce raw materials demand a redistribution of money, because they think that those that produce finished products get too much. They are presenting very harsh conditions, up to the point of limiting and halting deliveries.

By the way, yesterday in the Supreme Soviet one of the deputies—Nikolay Shmelev—raised the question of getting real information about all our foreign economic relations, including relations with the socialist countries, to the Supreme Soviet.

Krenz: We are prepared to discuss those issues seriously once again with our Soviet comrades.

Gorbachev: I suggested the topic of cooperation to Honecker many times. He was in favor of direct connections, but spoke about cooperation without any enthusiasm, and especially about joint ventures. But it was precisely cooperation that had the greatest potential for mutual benefit. You cannot coast on deliveries of our raw materials all the time. There are some strict limits here. [...]

Gorbachev: Yesterday Aleksandr N. Yakovlev received Zbigniew Brzezinski [see Document No. 96] and, as you know, he has a head with "global brains." He said: if today events transpire in such a way that the unification of Germany becomes a reality, it will mean the collapse of many things. I think that so far we have held to the correct line: we stood firmly in favor of the coexistence of two German states, and as a result achieved broad international recognition of the GDR, realized the Moscow Treaty, and gave a boost to the Helsinki process. Therefore, we should confidently follow this same course.

You must know: all the serious political figures—Thatcher, Mitterrand, Andreotti, Jaruzelski, and even the Americans, though their position has recently exhibited some nuances—are not looking forward to German unification. Moreover, in today's situation this would probably be explosive. The majority of Western leaders do not want to see the dissolution of NATO or the Warsaw Treaty Organization. Serious politicians understand that they are factors that make up a necessary equilibrium. However, Mitterrand feels he has to indicate his sympathy for the idea of German unification. The Americans also speak about sympathies for the Germans' pull toward unification. But I think they are doing it as a favor to Bonn, and also because to some extent they are anxious about too close a rapprochement between the FRG and the USSR. Therefore, I repeat, now the best course of action is to continue the same approach in German affairs that we have successfully developed so far. By the way, Willy Brandt shares this opinion also. He believes that the GDR is a great victory for socialism, even though he has his own understanding of socialism. The liquidation of the republic, in his opinion, would have been a bust for the Social Democrats. Therefore, I think, we all should start from the following formula: history itself decided that there should be two German states. But of course you cannot get away from the FRG. The need for human contacts presupposes normal relations with the FRG. You should not disrupt your ties with the FRG, although certainly they should be kept under control.

I am convinced that we should coordinate our relations with the FRG better, although Honecker tried to evade this necessity. We know about your relations with the FRG, and you know about our relations with it. Why should we try to hide anything from each other! It would make sense to talk about the possibilities of trilateral cooperation between the USSR, the GDR and the FRG, especially in the economic sphere. [...]

The situation in Hungary and in Poland today is such that they have nowhere else to go, as they say, because they have drowned in their financial dependence on the West. Today some people are criticizing us. They say, what is the Soviet Union doing allowing Poland and Hungary to "sail" to the West? But we cannot take on the support of Poland. Gierek accumulated $48 billion dollars of debt. Poland has already paid off $49 billion, and it still owes almost $50 billion. As far as Hungary is concerned, the International Monetary Fund had already dictated its harsh ultimatum under Kádár.

Krenz: This is not our way.

Gorbachev: You need to take this into account in your relationship with the FRG. [...]

Gorbachev: We need to think through all this, and find formulas that would allow people to realize their human needs. Otherwise we will be forced to accept all kinds of ultimatums. Maybe we can direct our International Departments and Foreign Ministries to think about possible initiatives together. Clearly, your constructive steps should be accompanied by demands for certain obligations from the other side. Chancellor Kohl keeps in touch with me and with you. We need to influence him. Once, under the pressure of the opposition, he found himself riding the horse of nationalism. The right wing is starting to present their demands for the unification of Germany to the Soviet Union and appeals to the U.S. The logic is simple—all [other] peoples are united; why do we Germans not have this right?

Krenz: We have already taken a number of steps. First of all, we gave orders to our border troops not to use weapons at the border, except in case of a direct attack against our soldiers. Secondly, we adopted a draft of the Law on Foreign Travel at the Politburo. We will present it for public discussion, and we plan to pass it in the People's Council even before Christmas. [...]

Gorbachev: Kohl was visibly worried when I mentioned the perverse interpretations of some of our agreements with the FRG in my speech in Berlin. He immediately called me on the telephone regarding that.

Krenz: Yes, he is worried; I noticed it in my conversation with him. He was even forgetting to finish phrases.

Gorbachev: Kohl, it seems, is not a big intellectual, but he enjoys a certain popularity in his country, especially among the petit bourgeois public. [...]

Gorbachev: I was told that he (Honecker) did not adequately understand even our discussions in the Politburo. But we do not have any ill feelings towards him. Had he made the right conclusions two or three years ago, it would have had great importance for the GDR and for him personally. In any case, one cannot deny the things your party and people have achieved in the past. We have a complete mutual understanding about that.

Krenz: cordially thanks Gorbachev for the support, openness and good advice.

[*Source: Archive of the Gorbachev Foundation, Fond 1. Opis 1. On file at the National Security Archive. Translated by Svetlana Savranskaya.*]

Document No. 98: Cable from U.S. Embassy in Sofia to State Department, "The Nov 10 CC Party Plenum: Little Prospect for Major Changes"

November 9, 1989

On the day the Berlin Wall would fall, few could imagine that dramatic events were about to take place across the bloc. Typical of the cautious diplomatic discourse only hours before the ultimate Cold War symbol cracked is this cable from the U.S. Embassy in Bulgaria predicting calm and continuity, no "major personnel changes" and no "major change towards a more reform-minded system" as a result of the Communist Party plenum about to meet in Sofia. The Embassy's information comes from limited sources—two Party officials and a published plenum discussion paper. In fact, at this moment, the 78-year-old Bulgarian party boss Todor Zhivkov is trying to fire his more moderate foreign minister, Petar Mladenov, who within a day would take Zhivkov's job, promise a "modern, democratic, and law-governed state" and receive effusive public congratulations from Gorbachev.

---

1. Conf[idential]: Entire Text

2. Summary. The Bulgarian Community [sic] Party Central Committee will hold a plenum on Nov 10 to discuss restructuring efforts and to pave the way for the next party congress. Since Todor Zhivkov has used similar gatherings in the past to announce major personnel changes, rumors abound in Sofia as to who might me demoted, promoted, or reassigned. Given the backdrop of events in other Eastern European countries, rumors of more open dissatisfaction with the pace of reform here, and the frank admissions of the failure of recent reform efforts contained in a published report prepared by Zhivkov for the plenum, there has also been speculation about major reform measures in the political and economic fields or even the possibility of considerable voiced criticism by CC members of the GOB's policies.

3. Zhivkov is probably the only one who really knows the answers to the above questions, however, and he plays his cards close to his chest. Chudomir Aleksandrov, former Zhivkov heir apparent, doubts that there will be major personnel changes and we tend to agree with him. Even if there are, the result would not be a major change towards a more reform-minded system. It will only be a continuing of Zhivkov's routine reshuffling of his personnel. While criticism of the Bulgarian system does appear to be growing more open and widespread, Zhivkov and company will almost certainly continue the policy of plenty of rhetoric about reform, but little concrete action.

4. On November 10, the Bulgarian Communist Party will hold a Central Committee plenum with the announced purpose of discussing progress towards restructuring in Bulgaria and also to prepare for the next party congress. A lengthy report (REFTEL) prepared by Todor Zhivkov was published last week to form the basis for discussion at the plenum. It contained frank admissions that the reform efforts thus far have not been successful and contained a variety of proposals for reforms in the political, economic, and social fields. As has been the case with previous reform efforts, the proposals were long on rhetoric and short on specificity.

5. Similar meetings in the past have been used to announce major personnel changes and rumors therefore abound in Sofia about senior party and governmental officials who may be demoted, promoted, or reassigned in this instance. Prominent rumors include the outright dismissal of Foreign Minister Mladenov or his reassignment as Chairman of the National Assembly; the retirement of Atanasov as Prime Minister and his replacement by Deputy Prime Minister Danchev; the breaking up of the Ministry of Economics and Planning and reestablishment of a Ministry of Finance; and even the replacement of Minister of the Interior Tanev (for failing to foresee the May demonstrations of ethnic Turks.)

6. Given events in East Germany and other Eastern European countries, there has also been speculation as to whether the Central Committee would maintain its traditional role as rubber stamp for Zhivkov's wishes or begin to voice dissatisfaction with current policies. The [Excision] Ambassador, for example, said he was hesitant to predict how the plenum might turn out. While CC members have always "kept silent and done what they were told," the Ambassador said that there is now an undercurrent of dissatisfaction among CC members and a new willingness to voice criticism openly. There is some chance, he speculated, that that willingness to speak out might be a factor in the plenum itself.

7. During a Nov 9 meeting related to his early December visit to the U.S., Chudomir Aleksandrov, currently chairman of the Committee for Geology, and until mid-1988 the heir apparent to Zhivkov, made the following comments to the Ambassador about the Nov 10 Central Committee plenum. If the plenum really discusses the issues raised in Zhivkov's report (REFTEL), the meeting should last two days and pave the way for preparations for the next party congress. However, things could change as a result of the Politburo meeting which is normally held on the eve of the CC plenum. Zhivkov usually plays his cards close to his chest and may reveal his intentions only at the Politburo meetings. While there were no domestic reasons calling for any major personnel/policy changes, it was hard to know how the "external" factors (i.e., the developments in the GDR) might influence the CC's deliberations.

8. Aleksandrov did not expect any major policy changes from the plenum, a policy which he described as a gradual, controlled opening up of Bulgarian society. There is, as was evident from a reading of Zhivkov's report, a tremendous

emphasis on "unity," since everyone was aware of the developments in Poland, Hungary and, most recently, in the GDR. In Aleksandrov's view, foreign observers would be "disappointed" if they expected major personnel changes from the plenum. At the same time, he did not preclude—but did not expect—the disappearance from the Politburo of some of its older members to make way for some new blood. This would not, however, mean Zhivkov's replacement now.

9. This same sense of uncertainty about personnel changes was conveyed by a Bulgarian CC staffer during the Soviet Embassy's November 7 reception. This source claimed that no one knows what Zhivkov has in mind about the possible Politburo personnel changes. That people wanted changes (unspecified) was clear; what was equally clear was that no one is prepared to mount any direct challenge to Zhivkov.

10. Comment. On balance, we tend to agree with Aleksandrov that there probably will not be major personnel changes. Even if there are, the basic Zhivkov policy of tight control over a reform process long on rhetoric and very short on concrete action will certainly continue. At the same time, the candid admissions of the failure of reform efforts thus far and the fact that Zhivkov thought it necessary to issue a report on restructuring efforts before this plenum (and to discuss restructuring at the plenum) demonstrate that the question of reform is becoming even more pressing in Bulgaria today.

End comment.

[Source: U.S. Department of State, obtained through FOIA. On file at the National Security Archive.]

Document No. 99: Session of the CC CPSU Politburo

November 9, 1989

On this historic day featuring the breaching of the Berlin Wall, the Soviet Politburo pays no attention at all to Eastern Europe. The leadership's regular weekly meeting mentions not a word about the changes in East Germany, but the reason becomes understandable when one realizes that the subject is the even more chilling prospect of the dissolution of the USSR itself. There is a sense of fatalism in the air about the inevitability of the Baltic countries seceding, and even Gorbachev can propose only a media strategy to try to convince the Balts that separating from the USSR will "doom their people to a miserable existence." As he often does, Prime Minister Ryzhkov plays the role of the panicked Cassandra: "What we should fear is not the Baltics, but Russia and Ukraine. I smell an overall collapse. And then there will be another government, another leadership of the country, already a different country." This time, his prediction would come true.

Gorbachev: I met before the holidays [of November 7, commemorating the Bolshevik revolution] with representatives of Estonia and Latvia. They have a feeling that there is no way other than to leave the USSR. No attempts to adopt republic-wide economic autonomy [*khozraschet*] will give them independence. So they think. They are convinced that because the Center is not ready to grant real independence there will be no real economic autonomy either. This is being used as an excuse to leave the USSR.

On the one hand, this is blackmail. But we must retain the initiative. And experience shows that the most blatant nationalists can go far. Tomorrow we will revoke the laws the republics have passed about their independence. However, we must keep in mind that aside from separatist attempts there are real problems and we should decide on them. And fill [the concept of] republican economic autonomy with real substance so that later we will not have to agree to yet another "wretched Brest-Litovsk peace."[82] We have no other option but to stick to our concept, and to implement it instead of beating around the bush and wasting time.

Sitaryan: There is and will be no compromise with the Baltics.

Pavlov also believes that compromise would be impossible to achieve.

Gorbachev: And you expect to keep them [in the Union] through fuel prices, via the energy sector?

---

[82] The Treaty of Brest-Litovsk was signed on March 3, 1918, between Soviet Russia and the Central Powers. As the price for extracting itself from World War I, Russia incurred heavy territorial and resource losses, and was subject to widespread criticism as a result, although the effects were short-lived due to the Allies' victory in the war.

Vorotnikov: If we confront them with unacceptable economic terms, then it would be a signal for them to leave the USSR.

Gorbachev: But we should show them: those who choose separation doom their people to a miserable existence [*proziabanie*]. And they should come to feel it. We must take a progressive stand in general, instead of bargaining here and there.

Vorotnikov: If we publicly reveal everything about how we are conducting negotiations with the Balts, Russia will blow up.

Gorbachev: We must sort out the main issues: 1) The Federation; 2) Property; 3) Prices. If a Federation exists, prices should be common for everyone, otherwise there will be borders, customs. 4) social differentiation from republic to republic. All the experience we have in the different republics should be summarized in a single new concept.

Abalkin: We need a law on the order of secession from the USSR.

Gorbachev: As the economic situation worsens in the country, the Balts come up with a new tune: "We do not want to perish in this common chaos."

Ryzhkov: Among them everything is aimed at preparations for secession. All these discussions with us are just for show, for buying time. As soon as they win elections, they will adopt a decision to leave. What should be done? Introduce a common free market among isolated republics? But that would mean chaos. What we should fear is not the Baltics, but Russia and Ukraine. I smell an overall collapse. And then there will be another government, another leadership of the country, already a different country. There is an evolution visible among the Russian collectives in the Baltic Republics—from confrontation to unity with the local population.

Medvedev: The only way is to act through economics. I do not believe that everybody will necessarily and single-mindedly vote for secession.

Gorbachev: Task number one, also for the mass media, is to propagandize our platform. All that is there we will fight for. And we are lagging behind in this. Even the term "our common home" has disappeared from television screens. We must have a program of action for the mass media. I ask you, Ivan Timofeyevich [Frolov],[83] do whatever it takes but get this program done. Our decisions are gradually getting pulled apart [*rastaskivaiut*]. They have gotten used to us making decisions and just moving on. And the next day these decisions are already forgotten.

In the republics we are already being attacked on the issues of language and citizenship. And where are we? We need to form a pan-Union consciousness, common agreements, we need to argue and argue that separation is fraught with very serious consequences. Our platform must be defended and propagandized on television daily. We must convince [people] that we are prepared to take

---

[83] Ivan Frolov, editor-in-chief of *Pravda*, had just been promoted to his position in October 1989. He later became a full member of the Central Committee.

a step, and that this would be a substantial step in the direction of solving national issues.

Vadim Andreyevich [Medvedev] is right, progress can be achieved through economics. But even here we need to thoroughly and concretely show the constructiveness of our approach and through that bare the intentions of their endless "new propositions." Perhaps we should work out a draft for republican economic autonomy. An exemplary one. And publish it with commentary, discuss it at the USSR Supreme Soviet. We must act to forestall them.

Many alarmist words have been said here. Are we exaggerating a bit? Is the situation really so menacing that we should cry wolf? No? No. Then we must act. Summarize what has been said at this Politburo session and work out a line. So far the Balts have been imposing their logic on us, not we on them. And the problem of secession is not the problem of a single republic; this problem will be resolved by the whole country.

A commission is created including: Slyunkov, Vorotnikov, Lukyanov, Karimov, Girenko, Sitaryan, Pavlov, Nikitov.

[Source: Archive of the Gorbachev Foundation, Fond 2. Opis 2. On file at the National Security Archive. Translated by Vladislav Zubok.]

Document No. 100: Record of Conversation between Helmut Kohl and Lech Wałęsa

November 9, 1989

When the Berlin Wall is breached, West German Chancellor Helmut Kohl is out of the country—visiting the new democratic leaders of Poland for the second time this fall. The Poles, represented by Solidarity hero and Nobel Prize winner Lech Wałęsa, are not at all eager for more change in East Germany. Wałęsa is virtually the only major political figure who foresees the Wall coming down soon—"he wonders whether the Wall will still be standing in one or two weeks"—and is anxious that "events in the GDR are developing too quickly." He even suggests to Kohl that "one must try to slow them down" because "what would happen if the GDR completely opened its border and tore down the Wall—must the Federal Republic of Germany rebuild it [East Germany] again?" The problem for Poland, Wałęsa explains, is that West Germany "would be compelled to direct its gaze toward the GDR as a top priority" and no longer help Poland with its reforms. Kohl demurs and reassures Wałęsa that no matter what, Poland's reforms would remain a priority. Besides, he adds, "[t]here is no military alternative [in the GDR]—either involving their own or Russian soldiers." So events in the GDR, he declares, would remain under control. Within hours, however, the news of the Wall would arrive and Kohl would scramble back to Berlin—and ultimately fulfill Wałęsa's prophecy.

The Chancellor greeted Lech Wałęsa and reminded him of the last meeting at the beginning of September. Since then a lot has happened in Europe!

He hopes that a new chapter in the German–Polish relationship can now truly begin. The strength of his delegation—among them 80 persons from business—demonstrates strong interest. If Poland [could] only create the necessary political infrastructure, one could do much jointly: promote agricultural cooperatives, industrial concerns, middle class enterprises—there is already the potential for cooperation.

The joint document negotiated by [our] personal representatives is rational and forward-looking.

Indeed, one must know that the left in both states does not want this visit to be successful. The discussion over the Annaberg[84] has shown this, as does the way one psychologically punishes an entire segment of the population, such as exiles—who are completely obliging—until they react.

---

[84] The Annaberg, in Upper Silesia, is considered by many Poles to be a holy mountain. It was also the site of a 1921 Polish uprising against German control of the region. Kohl was criticized for accepting an invitation to attend a German–Polish Catholic Mass there.

A success in German–Polish relations in view of the dramatic developments in the GDR would be especially compelling. No one can say how it will continue—not even Krenz. Every day between 10,000 and 15,000 people simply flee the GDR. Krenz told him—the chancellor—over the telephone that he wants to continue with reforms, but following the Moscow model, not Warsaw's or Budapest's. He wants to keep the present party control in practice. But this will not work; if Krenz does not permit parties and guarantee free elections there will be no peace. Had Honecker implemented this two years earlier, this would perhaps have worked, but now in the face of demonstrations by 500,000 people in Leipzig, 600,000–700,000 people in Berlin, it is too late. One can no longer align with the police and tanks against such a crowd of people. Gorbachev also realizes this.

This is why a success with reforms here in Poland is so important. This success would be a first-class European event. Therefore, he—the chancellor—wants to do everything to contribute to this success. Clever politics is necessary on both sides.

Wałęsa thanked [the chancellor] for the opportunity to have these talks and responded to the Annaberg theme—that in this case one does not wish to emphasize it too much. One should not forget that there was an iron curtain between the two states, that the Polish people would have been poorly informed on the chancellor's plans and efforts. The present opening is still too new to overcome these molds, these moods. In a month one could not imagine this. In half a year such a problem will no longer exist.

Today, however, the widespread fear of German aggression, German tanks, continues to have an effect. The communists have psychologically maintained this image—*the chancellor* interjected: And exploited it.

Wałęsa advises waiting calmly for things to develop.

He sees the developments in the GDR as very dangerous. One must try to slow them down. He had said earlier that it would be good if the GDR remained in fifth or sixth place (among the reform states). He would have preferred it if developments had maintained a certain order—with Poland and Hungary on top. But now one stands unprepared before a new situation. One requires brave solutions—for instance a complete opening: everyone could go where it suits him. But no one is prepared for such solutions.

In the GDR everything works in the short-term and is thought of belatedly. A stream of people moves to the West and no one is left to turn off the light. He asks himself if the Federal Republic of Germany could stop this influx. For Poland, the developments are coming at the wrong time: the Federal Republic of Germany would be compelled to direct its gaze toward the GDR as a top priority—in which case the Polish reforms would inevitably be in the background.

The Chancellor interjected that this is not his policy—without the developments in Warsaw, these developments would not be occurring in the GDR—and if the Warsaw reforms were to fail, nothing further would happen in the GDR.

Wałęsa replied that admittedly this is logically correct; on the other hand the situation in the GDR is developing with swift leaps and bounds. He asks himself

581

what would happen if the GDR completely opened its border and tore down the Wall—must the Federal Republic of Germany rebuild it [East Germany] again?

The Chancellor continued: if the number of refugee-seekers grew dramatically again, the GDR would collapse.

Wałęsa continued anew: the development of reforms in the GDR is late—and if the GDR cannot and will not go further, it will seek to shift the debt to the Federal Republic of Germany.

The Chancellor views such a course as unlikely: yesterday in the German Bundestag he said that there were three points that were crucial: admission of free parties, free elections, and credible guarantees. Then the Federal Republic of Germany could also help.

Wałęsa views such developments as coming too late. If it were up to him to decide in the GDR, he would announce that the complete opening (of the border) has been prepared, proclaim a political program along these lines, and introduce a clever solution that would not result in confusion. But this is not possible now. One already knows this in Poland from personal experience. He would have preferred a clean solution—"with gloves." But now one must improvise. In spite of everything, the attempt must also be made in the GDR to implement a well-thought-out solution, otherwise there will be chaos.

The Chancellor repeated: truly free parties and free elections are what the people in the GDR are now waiting for.

Wałęsa asked if there is anyone with whom one can talk rationally.

The Chancellor repeated his view of the GDR leadership: It is not about one person, rather it is about many who feared losing their advantages and now are feeling genuine anxiety. Within the leadership there are three groups:

- Those who still believed ten days ago that things could be brought back to order through the removal of Honecker; now they have detached themselves. "The old cement-heads" [*die alte Betonköpfe*] are gone.
- Krenz and his followers, who would like to implement reforms, such as a leading role for the party, following the model of the Soviet Union, meaning with a leadership role for the party. He, the chancellor, does not believe this will happen.
- Finally, the third group is difficult to characterize—however, it clearly wants actual changes. He has received inquiries regarding conditions, but of course answered that the Federal Republic of Germany has no conditions to impose; rather, all decisions must come from the GDR itself.

Above all, he emphasized that he could provide comprehensive help if there were actual reforms: the founding of free labor unions, free parties, free elections, guarantees. [...] [I]f the GDR does not go down this path, they will be swept away.

Wałęsa emphasized anew his fear and concern over uncontrollable developments: the situation in the GDR calls for a brave solution. [...] He sees no (long-term) planning. The SED is not in a position to carry out reforms, no one would believe them. Perhaps one should think about including the U.N. But there is no person, no institution in particular—such as the Church in Poland—with which one can discuss [matters] rationally and control the situation. There is no earnest organization, although certain people from the *nomenklatura* could play with military power.

The Chancellor repeated: Military power will help no one now. However, the example of Hungary could help. There some people have realized that reforms were important.

Wałęsa does not see a second Hungary in the GDR as possible. He wonders whether the Wall will still be standing in one or two weeks.

The Chancellor emphasized that the peaceful course of the demonstrations has very clearly proven that the people are not radical.

Wałęsa reported from his own experience that he also first emphasized results after the "Roundtable" talks, but was overtaken by the outcome. Particularly because of that, he has concerns that events in the GDR are developing too quickly.

The Chancellor pointed out that the GDR, in contrast to Poland and Hungary, is not a country, rather it is a part of Germany. If there were a firm arrangement on the admission of parties and a guarantee of free elections, then the people would no longer leave. Since there are still remnants of earlier parties—though this does not count for the East CDU—there could be a new infrastructure in three months.

Prof. Geremek interjected that the same question presents itself in the GDR as in Poland: Society wants freedom, not parties. If one were to put this to the test, then why does the Wall still stand?

The Chancellor replied: with these developments the Wall will without a doubt be cleared away. On the other hand, if someone were to open fire, everything would be over.

Wałęsa sees difficulties with the re-establishment of parties because many of the most active leadership personalities are already gone. Perhaps the party problem is even on the back burner. For the people the cry "we want parties" is, as in Poland, about freedom.

Wałęsa asked about the economic and benefits situation in the GDR.

The Chancellor sees this as a small problem. Besides, yesterday in the German Bundestag he emphasized our preparedness to help if free labor unions and parties are allowed and free elections are guaranteed. One could activate the GDR economy quite quickly. Naturally the level of help must be significant—he harbors no illusions about this. Especially in the current situation, the Chancellor continued, he wants to clear things up with Poland. He wants to achieve results through bilateral relations, but also as a result of developments in the GDR. It would be utterly wrong to allow the GDR current priority and to claim that Poland is no longer a theme because the developments are not a German, but rather a European, problem. He evaluates everything he does as a German in this situation from the perspective of how it will work in Europe.

In Paris, London, Rome, Warsaw there are many people who did not wish for these developments. That is exactly why one must try to reach a consensus. He spoke with President Mitterrand about this eight days ago and then stated with him at a press conference: now more than ever the Federal Republic of Germany needs a partnership with France—it is existential, for we are a piece of Europe. The Germans are not the measure of all things.

He can only repeat: if things in Poland develop for the worse, then the same will happen in the GDR. That is exactly why he would give important impetus here.

Wałęsa asked if the Federal Republic of Germany could accept a million people from the GDR.

The Chancellor saw such an influx of refugees as unlikely. From his own conversations, he knows that these are normal people who actually didn't want to leave; rather, through their flight they wanted to force better living conditions in their homeland.

Wałęsa clarified anew his concerns about uncontrolled developments and "revolutionary chaos." There is a joint interest that things develop peacefully.

The Chancellor emphatically agreed. However he—the chancellor—cannot make the decision together with Wałęsa. People in the GDR leadership need yet another lesson, specifically that the party cannot continue with the same leadership. There is no military alternative—either involving their own or Russian soldiers. But just because a few people wanted to save the leadership, they would not carry out a scorched earth policy.

Wałęsa nevertheless does not rule out a development in which martial law or a state of emergency [are declared].

The Chancellor repeated anew: the people want change, not revolution.

Wałęsa and Geremek doubt that this also holds for the youth.

The Chancellor repeated: naturally they want changes and a better standard of living, but they also see the costs and risks.

Next week there will be a new government in East Berlin. He does not know the designated minister president, perhaps a few people of his background. It would not surprise him—the chancellor—if he attempted after a while to push Krenz to the side and take over his role.

Besides, the people in the GDR are well informed on relations with us. They knew what they expected in the Federal Republic of Germany. Fourteen million travelers over the past year also conveyed personal impressions.

For this reason, too, he believes there will be no radicalization. In demonstrations of 500,000 people, no broken windows—this was indeed notable. (Digression: GDR refugees in the embassies in Warsaw and Prague.)

In closing, *the Chancellor* gave his convincing impression that one can place things under control in the GDR with determined steps in the direction of admitting free trade unions, free parties and, in a realistic perspective, free elections. The Catholic and Evangelical churches have played a stabilizing role throughout.

After the arrival of [Franz] Cardinal Hengsbach, *the Chancellor* clarified anew that developments in the GDR would not change his policy. He wants success for the reforms in Poland and Hungary. They are significant for all of

584

Europe—if they are not successful, there will be no rational developments in the GDR.

He expressed his readiness to remain in contact with Wałęsa in case of a dramatic worsening [of the situation].

Wałęsa: thanked [the chancellor] for the talk.

[*Source: Published in* Deutsche Einheit: Sonderedition aus den Akten des Bundeskanzleramtes 1989/90, *Hans Jürgen Kusters and Daniel Hofmann, eds. (Munich: Oldenbourg Verlag, 1998), document number 76, pp. 492–496. Translated by Catherine Nielsen.*]

Document No. 101: Diary of Anatoly Chernyaev regarding the Fall of the Berlin Wall

November 10, 1989

This extraordinary diary entry from inside the Kremlin on the day after the Wall's collapse captures the "snapshot" reaction of one of the closest and most loyal of Gorbachev's assistants. Chernyaev practically cheers "the end of Yalta" and the "Stalinist legacy" in Europe, and sees "the shift in the world balance of forces" towards ideas like the common European home and the Soviet Union's integration with Europe. All of this he attributes to Gorbachev leading, not standing in the way.

The Berlin Wall has collapsed. This entire era in the history of the socialist system is over. After the PUWP and the HSWP went Honecker. Today we received messages about the "retirement" of Deng Xiaopeng and Todor Zhivkov. Only our "best friends" Castro, Ceauşescu, and Kim Il Sung are still around—people who hate our guts.

But the main thing is the GDR, the Berlin Wall. For it has to do not only with "socialism," but with the shift in the world balance of forces. This is the end of Yalta [...] the Stalinist legacy and "the defeat of Hitlerite Germany."

That is what Gorbachev has done. And he has indeed turned out to be a great leader. He has sensed the pace of history and helped history to find a natural channel.

A meeting with Bush is approaching. Will we witness a historic conversation? There are two main ideas in the instructions M.S. gave me to prepare materials: the role of two superpowers in leading the world to a civilized state and the balance of interests. But Bush might disregard our arguments. [...] We do not really have anything to show except for the fear that we could return to totalitarianism.

[Source: Anatoly Chernyaev's Diary, Manuscript. On file at the National Security Archive. Translated by Vladislav Zubok and Anna Melyakova.]

Document No. 102: Record of Telephone Conversation between George H.W. Bush and Helmut Kohl

November 10, 1989

This memorandum of conversation reads as if the agenda had been set before the Berlin Wall fell. The West German chancellor leads off with a report on his trip to Poland, where the new leaders are "fine people" but with "too little professionalism" because they "spent the last couple of years in prison, not a place where one can learn how to govern." Only after the president says he has no questions about Poland does Kohl launch into a description of the extraordinary scene in Berlin, "a dramatic thing; an historic hour," "like witnessing an enormous fair" with "the atmosphere of a festival" where "they are literally taking down the wall" and "thousands of people are crossing both ways." Kohl hopes that the opening will not lead to more brain drain since 230,000 East Germans have already moved to the West this past year alone. Bush especially appreciates the political gesture Kohl mentions of publicly thanking "the Americans for their role in all of this;" and the president emphasizes his wish to be thoroughly briefed by Kohl before the upcoming Malta summit with Gorbachev. Bush repeats his recurring refrain about wanting "to see our people continue to avoid especially hot rhetoric that might by mistake cause a problem." (In other words, no dancing on the Wall).

Chancellor Kohl: The reforms in Poland are moving ahead. They have a new government with fine people. They are too idealistic with too little professionalism. Many of their professionals have spent the last couple of years in prison, not a place where one can learn how to govern. They are committed to democracy and market economics; we must help them. My request is as follows. I just told Margaret Thatcher and will tell Mitterrand tomorrow that we should give instructions to our representatives at the IMF that the negotiations with Poland should be completed speedily. These negotiations are not nice for the Poles but they are aware of the need and they seek clarity and clear cut conditions. We should help to get an agreement completed by the end of November. So I ask you, help us. Go and do this in the interest of the people. With respect to the rest of my trip to Poland, I will tell you next week after I return. Do you have any questions on Poland.

The President: I have no questions. I'll be interested to hear from you next week. I'm very interested in the GDR.

Kohl: I've just arrived from Berlin. It is like witnessing an enormous fair. It has the atmosphere of a festival. The frontiers are absolutely open. At certain points they are literally taking down the wall and building new checkpoints. At Checkpoint Charlie, thousands of people are crossing both ways. There are many young people who are coming over for a visit and enjoying our open way of life. I expect they will go home tonight. I would cautiously tell you that it appears that the opening has not led to a dramatic increase in the movement of refugees. It may be with the frontier open, people will simply go back and forth, looking, visiting and going home. This will work only if the GDR really reforms and I have my doubts. Krenz will carry out reforms but I think there are limits. One of those limits seems to be one party rule, and this simply will not work. Certainly, in particular, it will not work without pluralism, free trade unions and so forth. I could imagine that this will continue for a few weeks—that for a few weeks people will wait to see if the reforms come and if there is no light at the end of the tunnel they will run away from the GDR in great numbers. This would be a catastrophe for economic development; good people are leaving. The figures this year—230,000 have come. Their average age has been between 25 and 30. This is a catastrophe for the GDR. They are doctors, lawyers, specialists who cannot be replaced. They can earn more here. This is a dramatic thing; an historic hour. Let me repeat. There were two major manifestations (political gatherings) in Berlin. One was in front of the Berlin Town Hall where there were a lot of left wing rowdies, these are the pictures that will be shown on TV around the world. The second was at the Kurfurstendamm organized by our political friends. It was at about 6:30PM and the estimates are that there were 120,000–200,000 people. The overall spirit was optimistic and friendly. When I thanked the Americans for their role in all of this, there was much applause. Without the U.S. this day would not have been possible. Tell your people that. The GDR people in the protests and demonstrations have been sincere, not aggressive. This makes it very impressive. There have been no conflicts, even though in East Berlin, Leipzig and Dresden hundreds of thousands have been in the streets. I hope they will continue to be calm and peaceful. This is my short report.

The President: First, let me say how great is our respect for the way the FRG has handled all of this. Second, my meeting with Gorbachev in early December has become even more important. I want to be sure you and I spend enough time on the telephone so I have the full benefit of your thinking before I meet with him.

Kohl: We should do that. It's important.

The President: I will call Brady today or tomorrow to tell him of your suggestion for a rapid completion of the IMF agreement on Poland. Fourth, I want to see our people continue to avoid especially hot rhetoric that might by mistake cause a problem.

Kohl: That's very good of you.

The President: Fifth, I want to tell the U.S. press of our talk, that you gave me a thorough briefing, that you did publicly acknowledge the role of the U.S., and that you and I agreed to talk later next week.

Kohl: Excellent.

The President: Take care, good luck. I'm proud of the way you're handling an extraordinarily difficult problem.

Kohl: Thank you. Give my best to Barbara.

The President: I'm in Dallas. Same to Hanalore.

Kohl: Thank you and kind regards. Tell her to save her money that I intend to send sausages for Christmas.

[*Source: George Bush Presidential Library. Obtained through FOIA. On file at the National Security Archive.*]

Document No. 103: Record of Telephone Conversation between Mikhail Gorbachev and Helmut Kohl

November 11, 1989

With the tearing down of the Wall, the West German chancellor takes the initiative in Europe, reaching out to both Moscow and Washington with assurances of stability in the two Germanys—the epicenter of the Cold War—while simultaneously pursuing his ultimately successful campaign for German unification. Here Kohl calls Gorbachev to express some of the same points made in the previous day's telephone conversation with Bush: the need for more dynamic reforms in the GDR, the crossing back and forth of hundreds of thousands through the open Wall, and the potential impact of high numbers of East Germans migrating to the FRG. But Kohl's core message is that he opposes destabilization in the GDR, and he indicates that he will check in with Gorbachev on all relevant topics immediately after his upcoming trip to Poland.

This appears to reassure the Soviet leader, who mentions their previous "philosophical" discussions about "relations between our two peoples" and how "mutual understanding is improving" as "we are getting closer to each other." Gorbachev also applauds what he calls "a historic turn toward new relations, toward a new world;" but his worries show through when he urges Kohl to "use your authority, your political weight and influence to keep others within limits that are adequate for the time being..." On a day when banners calling for German unification are billowing on both sides of the former Wall, Gorbachev resorts to euphemisms about this touchy subject, and hears what he wants to hear in Kohl's commitment to stability.

The conversation took place at Helmut Kohl's request.

Kohl: I am glad to hear you, Mr. General Secretary, I would like to express my appreciation with regard to your address yesterday. It is a very good step. [...]

We want the people of the GDR to stay home, and we do not strive to have the entire GDR population move to the FRG. And not at all because, as some are claiming, we would not be able to resolve the problems that would result from that. For example, 230,000 people have moved from the GDR to the FRG this year, and all of them were accommodated. But a mass migration to the FRG would be an absurd development; we want the Germans to be able to build their future at home.

I would also like to inform you, even though the information is still preliminary, that today by 12 noon hundreds of thousands of people have crossed the GDR border. However, there is an impression that the majority are just visitors, and have no intention of staying in the FRG. The number of people who actually want to move to the FRG for permanent residency is much lower than the level we would be concerned about.

I recently told you that we did not want a destabilization of the situation in the GDR. I am still of the same view. I do not know on what scale Egon Krenz really plans to carry out reforms. However, in a situation such as they have now, the GDR leadership should act in a more dynamic way.

I would like to repeat that I appreciate your contacting me in connection with these events. Next week, immediately after I return from Poland, I would like to give you a call again if you do not have any objections, to discuss the new developments with you.

Gorbachev: That would be good. I recall how we discussed relations between our two peoples, and general developments in Europe in the philosophical sense. As you can see, Mr. Chancellor, those discussions were not simple exercises in rhetoric. Deep changes are underway in the world. This also concerns the East European countries. One more example of that is the beginning of the reform process in Bulgaria. And changes are happening even faster than we could have imagined recently.

Of course, the changes could take different forms in different countries, and reach a deeper level. However, to preserve stability it is important for all sides to act in a responsible way.

All in all, I think that the basis for mutual understanding is improving. We are getting closer to each other. And this is very important.

[...] In particular, I recommended to Egon Krenz that the leadership of the republic should prepare reforms while carefully taking into account the mood of society, and on the basis of an open dialogue with public forces, public movements in the country.

I understand that all Europeans, and not only Europeans, are closely following developments in the GDR. This is a very important point in world politics. But it is also a fact that you and I—the FRG and the Soviet Union—have even more interest in these developments both because of the history and because of the character of our relations today.

In general, I can say that there is a certain kind of triangle forming now, in which everything has to be thought-out and balanced. I think that our relations today allow us to do everything the way it should be done.

Of course, any kind of change means a certain instability. That is why, when I speak about preserving stability, what I mean is that we, on all sides, should take steps that are carefully thought out in relation to each other.

I think, Mr. Chancellor, we are experiencing a historic turn toward new relations, toward a new world. And we should not allow ourselves to impair this turn by our awkward actions, or, moreover, to push developments toward an unpredictable course, toward chaos, by forcing events. That would be undesirable in all respects.

That is why I take the words you have spoken in our conversation today very seriously. And I hope that you will use your authority, your political weight and influence to keep others within limits that are adequate for the time being and for the requirements of our time.

591

Kohl: I think that it is fortunate that relations between the USSR and the FRG have reached the high level of development that they have now. And I especially appreciate the good personal contacts that have developed between us. In my opinion, our relations are beyond simply official contacts, they have a personal character. I believe that they could continue to develop like this in the future. I am ready for that. I understand that a personal relationship does not change the essence of the problems, but it can make their resolutions easier.

Coming back to the assessment of the situation in the GDR, I would like to mention that the problem now lies in the realm of psychology. Honecker's course, which rejected any reforms up until the end, put the new leadership of the GDR in a very difficult situation. Krenz's "team" now has to operate under horrible time pressures, and this is where I see the main problem. You are right, they need time to draft and implement the reforms. But how would you explain this to the population of the GDR? [...]

[Source: Archive of the Gorbachev Foundation, Fond 1. Opis 1. On file at the National Security Archive. Translated by Svetlana Savranskaya.]

Document No. 104: Record of Telephone Conversation between Mikhail Gorbachev and François Mitterrand

November 14, 1989

Alarmed by "all the excitement that has been raised in the FRG around the issue of German unification," Gorbachev reaches out to the French president to confirm that "we have a mutual understanding" on this issue. Mitterrand's tone is reassuring: "There is a certain equilibrium that exists in Europe, and we should not disturb it." But his words are more equivocal than Gorbachev would have wanted. The French position is to "avoid any kind of disruption," but Mitterrand does not think "that the issue of changing borders can realistically be raised now—at least until a certain time." When that time would be, however, he does not say. Gorbachev believes he has assurances from Kohl that he will "abide strictly by the existing agreements" and that "the Germans should live where they are living now;" but such categorical commitments are not in evidence in the actual texts of Kohl's conversations.

[…]

Gorbachev: I thank you, Mr. President, for this information. I am also glad to talk to you.

In general, the events in the GDR were not unexpected for us. I can only note that if such events—the change of leadership in the GDR—had taken place earlier, everything would have been much calmer. We would support the direction in which the situation is moving now, with the exception of one aspect. I have in mind all the excitement that has been raised in the FRG around the issue of German unification.

Mitterrand: I understand what you are saying.

Gorbachev: We have already discussed this problem with you. Therefore, I am not going to develop my position in detail here, especially because of the specific nature of a telephone conversation. I would like to stress, though, that as far as I understand it we have a mutual understanding on this really cardinal issue.

Mitterrand: […] I knew your point of view regarding the German issue. But I thought it was necessary to contact you again to hear a confirmation directly from you.

The French position is as follows: we would like to avoid any kind of disruption. We realize that it is necessary to take into account the real feelings that exist among people both in West and East Germany. At the same time, I do not think that the issue of changing borders can realistically be raised now—at least until a certain time.

Our two countries are friends of East Germany. I plan to visit the GDR in the near future. I am convinced that they should not undertake any hasty actions which could destabilize the situation. There is a certain equilibrium that exists in Europe, and we should not disturb it. We will also talk about this with the leaders of 12 members of the European Community in Paris.

I hope that we will have an opportunity to continue this conversation, but not over the telephone. [...]

I would like to reiterate: taking into account the recent acceleration of events, I think it would be necessary to organize some direct contact between us. This is, by the way, the reason for my call. I would like to find out your assessment of the evolution of the situation in Europe, and to tell you that for my part, I plan to keep my cool.

Our two countries are old countries. They have been in contact for a very long time, and it is important that they should understand each other in the future [...]

Gorbachev: But at the same time we should not allow any artificial stimulation and forcing of the events.

Mitterrand: As you know, I have warm, very cordial relations with Chancellor Helmut Kohl. I will discuss all these issues with him in a couple of days.

Gorbachev: I also spoke with him not so long ago. He assured me in particular that he was going to abide strictly by the existing agreements.

Mitterrand: Yes, he is a sober thinker.

Gorbachev: He promised to act in such a way that the situation would remain normal. I carefully noted his words that the Germans should live where they are living now. And if there is a possibility to improve relations between them, it would be a very positive process, of course.

Mitterrand: I understand such an approach.

Gorbachev: I like your idea about the possibility of meeting.

Mitterrand: I would think such a meeting would be good for Europe. I will try to inform [Foreign Minister] Roland Dumas about more specific thoughts regarding such a meeting. Thank you for your willingness to talk to me on the phone.

[*Source: Archive of the Gorbachev Foundation, Fond 1. Opis 1. On file at the National Security Archive. Translated by Svetlana Savranskaya.*]

Document No. 105: Record of Telephone Conversation between George H.W. Bush and Helmut Kohl

November 17, 1989

Again, the West German leader initiates this telephone conversation with the president. Here, Kohl reports on his talks with Gorbachev and with East German leader Egon Krenz, and promises "we will do nothing that will destabilize the situation in the GDR." Bush responds: "The euphoric excitement in the U.S. runs the risk of forcing unforeseen action in the USSR or the GDR that would be very bad." But he assures Kohl that "[w]e will not exacerbate the problem by having the President of the United States posturing on the Berlin Wall." Kohl's initiative also shows in his offer to match a U.S. contribution of up to $250 million for a proposed Polish stabilization fund; (earlier in 1989, Bush had offered only $125 million for Poland over three years). Bush tells Kohl "I am absolutely determined to get advice and suggestions from you personally before I meet with Gorbachev... so that I can understand every nuance of the German Question... [and] nuances of difference in the Alliance." But Kohl remarks that "[w]ith the developing situation, I would like to stay here" – perhaps thinking ahead to his surprise announcement of the 10 Points unification plan to the Bundestag on November 28. Kohl would give his advice on Gorbachev in the same November 28 letter to Bush that tells the American president about the 10 Points. Ultimately Bush and Kohl would meet face to face only after Malta (see Document No. 111).

Chancellor Kohl initiated the call.

Chancellor Kohl: In my talks with [new East German leader] [sic] Krenz, I raised the issues of free elections, free trade unions, and freedom of the press. I suggested that we in the FRG will give comprehensive assistance under the condition that these reforms, which the people are expecting, will be carried out. If they do not carry them out, the government will fall. There will be more movement on Saturday and Sunday. I expect more than a million people will visit the FRG. I hope that the opening of the border has had the consequence that travellers do not have to stay but can return to an improving home.

In view of world political developments, we will do nothing that will destabilize the situation in the GDR. I had a long conversation with Gorbachev. Of course, the Soviets are concerned. I told Gorbachev that if Krenz does not carry out reforms as in Poland and Hungary, the system will fail.

The President: Thank you for your support in your public comments. It is important that Germans see that they have the support and sympathy of their allies.

Chancellor Kohl: Tomorrow night at the EC meeting, I will report on Poland, Hungary, and the GDR. I will put in an urgent plea to support the American initiative for Poland. I will pledge that if the U.S. is willing to put up $250 million for stabilization, we will put up the same amount. All in all, that amounts to $500 million as a stabilizing measure. I do hope that others will be able to put in the remainder.

The President: Let me say that we appreciate the FRG's stand and your stand personally. In spite of Congressional posturing, the U.S. will stay calm and support reforms in just the way you talk about. The euphoric excitement in the U.S. runs the risk of forcing unforeseen action in the USSR or the GDR that would be very bad. We will not be making exhortations about unification or setting any timetables. We will not exacerbate the problem by having the President of the United States posturing on the Berlin Wall.

The Wałęsa visit went well. He was reasonable, and relatively pleased about the Congressional aid package. I have followed up on giving the IMF a push in its negotiations with Poland. It will be difficult to reach a conclusion by the end of November—which is your timetable—but may be possible in December.

Chancellor Kohl: If negotiations are completed by mid-December, that would be acceptable, but it cannot be later than that.

The President: We will push and encourage others to do the same. You might tell the EC that we have talked and push others to help.

Chancellor Kohl: I had hoped we might get together as you prepare for Malta, but unfortunately I cannot come before your meetings. What about our meeting in Spain, even for two hours?

The President: We are in a tight time frame. I would value your judgment and would like to get together. I gather you cannot come to Camp David.

Chancellor Kohl: I have an enormous problem with freeing myself for two days. With the developing situation, I would like to stay here. There is also a budget debate in our parliament. You have a Naval base [in Spain] [sic]. Perhaps you could make a stopover.

The President: Here is my point: I am absolutely determined to get advice and suggestions from you personally before I meet with Gorbachev. That is very important, because of the German Question. I understand your logistical problems. I want to suggest that after Genscher is here, you and I set aside an hour or more next weekend to talk by phone. Maybe we can have secure communications, so that I can understand every nuance of the German Question. I will be available for as much time as possible. Input from the FRG, from Chancellor Kohl, to Gorbachev is more important than at any other time or for any other meeting.

Chancellor Kohl: We should try to arrange that. Perhaps Monday we should have a long conversation.

The President: That would be good if we cannot figure out another way. I think there are nuances of difference in the Alliance. I want to understand them.

Chancellor Kohl: That is true.

The President: I will have proper consultations. More important than large consultations, I need to understand Germany. Woerner has invited us to come to Brussels. I will do that. You and I could have a separate breakfast—or supper if we get in early.

596

Chancellor Kohl: When will you arrive?

The President: Sunday night, maybe in time for dinner. Maybe you would buy me dinner.

Chancellor Kohl: I would be able to do that. We can arrange that, either on December 3 or December 4.

The President: Or before the meeting, for two hours over breakfast.

Chancellor Kohl: That is possible. Let us envisage having breakfast on the 4th.

The President: Let's do it.

Chancellor Kohl: We can talk about it.

The President: It is important, so that I do not miss the nuance of Germany's or Kohl's positions. After Genscher is here to see Jim Baker, we can talk. Brent can also talk to Teltschik. If there is any disconnect, I may request that our top people get together.

Chancellor Kohl: Let me make a suggestion. Genscher will be in Washington on Tuesday. The second part of the week I will send a personal memorandum of my position. I will call you on November 27 for an extensive discussion, and we will meet before the conference in Brussels.

The President: We will get back to you on which time is better.

Chancellor Kohl: All right. Let's envisage a meeting on the 3rd. Next week you will receive a paper from me.

The President: Let me make one personal comment. When you told me that you thanked the American people for their steadfastness, I passed that along and it was received warmly. I want to thank you for that comment.

Chancellor Kohl: It was only natural.

The President: If anything comes up that is unforeseen, call me or I will call you.

Chancellor Kohl: I will do so.

[*Source: George Bush Presidential Library. Obtained through FOIA. On file at the National Security Archive.*]

Document No. 106: Record of Conversation between Mikhail Gorbachev and Brian Mulroney

November 21, 1989

Canadian Prime Minister Brian Mulroney hears an earful from Gorbachev about the Americans, but the Soviet leader's annoyance is focused less on Bush and Secretary of State James Baker ("after a difficult period of doubts they came to very realistic positions") than on the U.S. Congress, which he accuses of interfering in Soviet affairs with actions such as a proposed Senate resolution on the Armenian-populated Nagorno-Karabakh enclave in Azerbaijan, scene of nationalist protests and a future civil war. "The habits of the global policeman are still very strong," Gorbachev remarks. "Americans have an itch: to give everybody advice how to live. For Americans this is like an illness..." Mulroney agrees that Bush and Baker "have a reasonable and balanced approach to Eastern Europe," and describes as "mature" the president's refusal to "go to Berlin" for "a big speech" "in front of the wall," despite pressure from leading Democratic politicians. Then the Canadian poses a series of tough questions about the limits, if any, for developments in Eastern Europe, including German unification and the future of the Warsaw Pact. The Soviet leader does not respond directly, but falls back on his vision of "the Helsinki process"—perhaps there should be another Helsinki summit involving Europeans, part of a process of mutual contacts, slow integration, and gradual change in the character of the blocs. As for Germany, Gorbachev appears to be in full denial: "let history itself solve it. This is not an issue to be solved today."

[...]

Gorbachev: [...] Now all the world's intelligence services and the press are debating the question of how much time is left for Gorbachev. Well, they have their work to do, they have a subject to talk about. But this is not the decisive factor. The country will not go back, it has to change. Maybe some other team would be able to affect the speed of the changes, but the country will change anyway. And in this sense, one can say that Gorbachev has already accomplished his mission. Of course, I am not going to abandon the course that I began.

Mulroney: I have more confidence in your political longevity than in my own. And I, by the way, plan to work for several more years. [...] Better let somebody else make sacrifices. There can be no changes without problems.

Gorbachev: Our people are prepared to persevere. But they want to know, they want to be confident in the results, in the success of *perestroika*. Our people are patient, but their patience is not endless. You cannot test the limits of the people's patience. They can rise like no other people. [...]

Mulroney: This brings us to the question of specific features of different peoples, for example the Americans and the Canadians. The Americans see the world in a very simple way: free enterprise, capitalism, the American flag, McDonald's—everything is OK.

Gorbachev: If it were only that. [...] No, they have other specific traits too.

Mulroney: In any case, they have achieved a lot implementing the principle of free enterprise. [...]

Gorbachev: I would like to emphasize one more issue. We are faced with attempts to interfere in the affairs of our federation on the part of the USA—by the administration, and especially by the Congress. It is not easy for the Americans to comprehend the essence of the new world, of the new values. The habits of the global policeman are still very strong, as are the desire to impose their opinion and the efforts to dictate to others.

I will have to tell the president in Malta: if you want to help somebody, try to help Quebec. It is closer to you, and we will sort out our problems on our own. It seems like the American senators have lost sleep over Nagorno-Karabakh. Why is their sleep not disturbed by what has been happening in Northern Ireland for 15 years now? And that is in a country where almost 30 percent of the population is of Irish origin.

Interference is impermissible. You know that every federation has its own problems. Take, for example, Yugoslavia. We need sensitivity here, attentive and careful consideration. And the Americans have an itch: to give everybody advice on how to live. For Americans this is like an illness—AIDS. So far there is no treatment for it. [...]

I have to say that as far as Eastern Europe is concerned it is hard for the United States to give up the habit of teaching others. It is not an accident that they call the American Ambassador in Hungary *"Gauleiter."*[85] People notice his behavior. However, as far as President Bush and Secretary of State Baker are concerned, it seems to me that after a difficult period of doubts they came to very realistic positions, not only on Eastern Europe but the entire spectrum of international problems. That is why I think we will have a good conversation in Malta.

Mulroney: I agree with your assessment of President Bush's position.

Gorbachev: By the way, recently you visited him for four days. What did you talk about?

Mulroney: About you (laughter).

Gorbachev: Well I take it as a statement.

Mulroney: Indeed, Bush and Baker have a reasonable and balanced approach to Eastern Europe. Meanwhile, there were demands that the president should immediately go to Berlin, stand in front of the wall, and deliver a big speech.

Gorbachev: Was it a request of the Democrats?

---

[85] From the German *"Gauleiter,"* meaning the leader of a local branch of the Nazi party who often wielded a great deal of power.

Mulroney: Yes, it was a request of the Democratic leader, [George] Mitchell, who is generally speaking quite a reasonable person.

In these circumstances, Bush showed himself to be a mature politician. The majority of European leaders are behaving in the same way.

I would like to ask you one more question about Eastern Europe. You implied that these countries are free to search for their own road in terms of economic development. Do you place any limits on that? What if the GDR begins to experience the same processes that are underway in Hungary and Poland—the emergence of new political parties and demands for free elections? Is a situation possible where a certain country would want to reconsider its relations with the Warsaw Treaty Organization? Do you think that the status quo should be preserved—two Germanys, and existing political institutions under conditions of more freedom?

Posing these questions, I would like to assure you that you cannot find two more reasonable people than Bush and Baker in the entire West. And I would like to ask you again to look five years ahead. What do you think? What changes might happen in the next five years in international political structures, in relations between the Soviet Union and the Warsaw Treaty Organization as a whole, and Europe, the European Communities, the West as a whole? Do you anticipate any fundamental changes?

Gorbachev: First of all, I tell all my guests: let us develop the Helsinki process, let us not destroy what we have built. I think that now we are entering a new stage in this process, a stage where it is necessary to have a new understanding of the changes that are happening. That is why, when I was in Finland [in late October 1989], I suggested convening a Helsinki-2 summit.

We proceed from the fact that we support the changes that are underway in Europe, not only in the East but also in the West. We say that they should continue in conditions of stability; I would say strategic stability. We can help this process by giving new substance to the activity of the existing military and political organizations. This has already begun. We can see that representatives of the Warsaw Treaty Organization are meeting NATO representatives, getting to know each other, inspecting the military technology, discussing military doctrines. The character of these organizations should change.

Contacts between the CMEA and the European Community are being established, and we need to stimulate this process. It is important that the new relations between them take into account the requirements of our time. New ecological and cultural organizations and new foundations are emerging. That creates new opportunities for contacts between people, youth exchanges. We need to support and stimulate all this.

As far as the German issue is concerned, as I said many times before, that issue emerged under certain historical circumstances. And let history itself solve it. This is not an issue to be solved today. To force progress on this issue would be to feed people an unripe fruit, to poison us.

600

Today the reality is that there are two states that are members of the United Nations and of existing military-political structures. I am not a prophet but at some stage, in the framework of the new Europe toward which we are moving now, there could be some changes that would involve the two German states. But this is an issue for the future. Today we must act on the basis of existing realities without forcing the processes. We need to walk all the way through, without leaping over stages. Otherwise we may make a lot of mistakes; we will make a mess, not policy.

[...]

Mulroney: You know Reagan spoke from his [index] cards even when we spoke on the phone. Bush is a completely different person.

Gorbachev: But you cannot deny Reagan's impressive political intuition.

Mulroney: That is completely true. By the way, I saw him recently—for the first time after his operation. I have to say that he has changed a lot, he looks older.

[Source: Archive of the Gorbachev Foundation, Fond 1. Opis 1. On file at the National Security Archive. Translated by Svetlana Savranskaya.]

Document No. 107: Record of Conversation between Mikhail Gorbachev and Tadeusz Mazowiecki

November 24, 1989

This historic meeting is Gorbachev's first with a non-communist East European leader. The exchange is quite respectful, even at points approaching the peer-to-peer candor found in Gorbachev's talks with Thatcher or Mitterrand. In this case, Polish Prime Minister Tadeusz Mazowiecki is well aware that he was able to take office as head of the Solidarity-led government in August 1989 in significant part because Gorbachev declined to interfere. (As part of the same arrangement, the communist martial law ruler, General Wojciech Jaruzelski, has become the Polish president).

Mazowiecki is also in Moscow seeking help, "a few percent more" supply of oil, gas, and cotton to ease Poland's economic crisis. Gorbachev replies: "we are in a complicated situation" but "we will do what we can." The two leaders go into detail on the politics and the means surrounding economic reforms, and Gorbachev candidly admits the huge Western lead in technology—"we are even in different technological eras, it seems."

On the historically sensitive matter of Poland's membership in the WTO, the Polish leader takes the opportunity to confirm existing alliance commitments, while Gorbachev gives reassurances about maintaining "good-neighborly relations," "keeping the peace," and guaranteeing "the inviolability of borders."

The most difficult part of the conversation is about history, with Mazowiecki pressing for glasnost on the Nazi–Stalin protocols of 1939 and the 1940 massacre in the Katyń Forest, on the grounds that continued silence on these matters only feeds anti-Soviet sentiment in Poland. But Gorbachev drags his feet, claiming that the original documents cannot be found. His real problem is with domestic critics, who are already accusing him of losing Eastern Europe, and who would strongly oppose any revelations that would put the Soviets in a negative light. (Gorbachev's successor, Boris Yeltsin, would ultimately release these and other incriminating documents about past Soviet activities.)

Gorbachev must have appreciated Mazowiecki's endorsement when the latter commented, "In connection with your idea of a Common European Home, I would like to note that in this home our apartments share the same landing," implying that Poland and the Soviet Union would remain closest neighbors.

Gorbachev: Greets his guest, wishes success to the new government of friendly Poland.

Mazowiecki: Expresses thanks for the greeting. Speaks of his interest in Soviet *perestroika*. Conveys greetings from Jaruzelski.

Gorbachev: Jaruzelski is our great friend. I have a high regard for his civic and personal qualities, his propensity for constructive dialogue. If someone else occupied his post, it would be difficult to say how the situation would take shape in this difficult time for Poland.

Major capital has been built up in Soviet–Polish relations. It encompasses all spheres: the economy, politics, culture, human contacts. We intend to continue developing our relations with Poland in the future, especially since we do not plan to resettle anywhere. Much good has been done in our relations in recent years. Together we set off down a fine road of collaboration. That is why I hope that we will develop collaborative capital; otherwise what kind of politicians are we?

Mazowiecki: I think so too. I would like to thank you, the Soviet leadership, for showing openness, goodwill, and a positive attitude from the start—this is very important. We also do not plan to resettle anywhere. That is why we would like to demonstrate that despite the new leadership's change of party, other political powers in Poland also understand what the alliance with the USSR means to us. We can be a dependable ally. It is important that you and the entire leadership are certain of that. We understand that ideological connections exist between the CPSU and PUWP. But from my point of view, the intergovernmental alliance is particularly important. It could be guaranteed by different powers representing broad circles of Polish society. You would not be against this kind of competition between them for the development of relations with the Soviet Union?

Gorbachev: Of course not. We recognize every nation's right to decide its fate on its own. And of course it is the Polish people's decision what government to have. Since we have good relations with the Polish people, naturally we are prepared to cooperate with the government they have chosen. I think the good-neighborly relations between our countries also satisfy Poland's strategic interests. This pertains to your relationship with the West as well, because good-neighborly relations with us give you additional security, especially since the West knows how to set traps, too. We have a shared interest in keeping the peace on our borders and in Europe. We are both interested in respecting post-war realities, the inviolability of borders, and not permitting attempts to undermine them. In general, in all directions our strategic interests are in harmony. This is the position of the entire Soviet leadership.

Mazowiecki: I would like once again to confirm what I already have said in parliament: now and in the future, Poland intends to keep to its alliance commitments, including the Warsaw Treaty and CMEA.

But I believe that there is something greater in the relations between our two countries than mere mutual treaty commitments. In my understanding, it is historically important that the alliance between our two countries rested on a most expansive social base. Right now such an opportunity exists.

Gorbachev: I agree with you.

Mazowiecki: Mikhail Sergeyevich, I know that you personally and W. Jaruzelski, who was previously in a different camp than mine, did a great deal for the development of Soviet–Polish relations.

Gorbachev: I would like to note that W. Jaruzelski always thought about all of Poland. I do not see any obstacles to our relations resting on a most expansive social base. This pertains to the PUWP, to those powers-that-be in "Solidarity," and to other parties and organizations that understand the necessity and mutual benefit of good-neighborly relations and collaboration. The more so, I repeat, since the people support your government. We are prepared to lead a constructive dialogue with everyone; you can proceed reliably from this basis.

I think it is very important for you to maintain a consensus, a broad coalition, in the country. While all of society supports Mazowiecki's government, it can feel more confident, especially in the difficult circumstances Poland is facing right now. Our circumstances right now are not simple either.

Mazowiecki: Nevertheless, I think our conditions are more difficult than yours right now. But the most important thing is that we need each other.

I see two dangers in our situation. The first is in pushing the PUWP into the opposition [camp]. This would be a mistake and a trap. That is why I am for a broad coalition.

Gorbachev: I agree with you. Let all the political powers divide the responsibilities and work constructively. I have known the PUWP for a long time. I think it has serious socio-political potential for collaboration.

Mazowiecki: All the socio-political associations including "Solidarity," the Peasant Party, the Democratic Party, and others must once again review their roles in order to understand that right now the new situation places new demands on them. This is a painful, difficult, and lengthy process, for "Solidarity" as well.

Gorbachev: It is possible that your government will be criticized [by "Solidarity"]. Your government will have to make some unpopular decisions.

Mazowiecki: Overcoming inflation is our first priority.

Gorbachev: This problem is also interesting for us. What do you intend to do?

Mazowiecki: Freeze salaries, allow free price movement on the market, remove subsidies and achieve market regulation for prices. In terms of this we have already attained the first positive results. After the rise in fuel prices the peasants sharply raised the prices for agricultural goods. But after a while they began to decrease because demand fell sharply. Now butter is available in stores and is being sold for lower prices. That is the way we intend to lower the inflationary processes by the end of the year. Of course we do not rely on everything taking its course. A certain amount of regulation will also take place. [...]

Gorbachev: [T]he workers are looking after this carefully. A draft of a Property Act is being discussed; it should provide new incentives for interest. Of course, your situation is different. Private property, including land ownership, has already been developed to quite a considerable extent.

Mazowiecki: We have quite neglected this sphere.

Gorbachev: Right now we are developing antitrust legislation. We have such giants that could take everything under and even bring the country to its knees. If extremely large enterprises remain, the government will dictate prices for them. But the main approach is to break them up into smaller units and create competing enterprises. In the past, we thought that the creation of industrial giants was the peak of success. But it turned out that therein lay one of the sources of interference with the rapid development of scientific-technological progress. This work will take many years: you cannot fix things all at once in one big stroke; stages are necessary here.

But it is also dangerous to lapse into over-decentralization. It seems you leaned toward that in the first stage of your reform.

Deng Xiaoping's daughter came to visit us recently. We invited her when we were in Beijing. She says that right now China is trying somehow to correct over-decentralization in the economy. Some people managed to snatch up control of the provinces, while the State, the center, was left almost empty. This is also experience, and it probably should not be ignored.

Mazowiecki: The second danger we face is the people's impatience, especially now when we are firmly struggling against inflation. This is a major problem.

Today in a talk with Council of Ministers Chairman Ryzhkov we discussed a number of serious economic problems. We asked to leave supplies of fuel and energy raw materials at the previous levels. But to speak frankly, we need at least a few percent more than we have right now. This particularly concerns oil, gas, and cotton.

Gorbachev: Yes, these are all very "simple" questions. But we will not see the change of government in Poland as grounds for abandoning our commitments, although I must say that we are in a complicated situation. N.I. Ryzhkov just told me that the Council of Ministers will examine the questions you have raised. As they say, we will do what we can.

But both you and we need to work on resource conservation. The West did much in this sphere in the 1970s. They have applied a new level of technology. We are almost a level behind. We are even in different technological eras, it seems. To produce one unit we use up to two times more energy, resources and materials than in the West. It is true, however, that the West achieved this not only through scientific and technological breakthroughs, but also by leaving tens of millions of people without jobs.

We are intensively working on economic problems right now. And this is absolutely necessary. But we also need powerful stimulation for the scientific-technological process. We have not gotten to that yet. If we had a more modern level of resource conservation it would of course be easier for us to respond to your requests. But then you probably would not be making those requests. We need to work earnestly together on this problem. Both you and we have the scientific force to do that. […]

Mazowiecki: We do not have any suspicions [regarding the Soviet investigation into the Katyń tragedy]. It is possible that it is not yet the right time for you. But we can work together in this direction and see to it that there is no anti-Soviet reaction. Standing idle in this matter actually provides grounds for anti-Sovietism, although anti-Soviet displays are indirect.

I spoke with our historians. They say that they have studied and said everything possible on this problem, and there is nothing more to say. It is all clear to them. We need to make a policy decision; the silence in the political sphere has lasted too long.

Gorbachev: We are now ready to acknowledge facts. But there is a similar situation with Katyń as with the secret [Soviet–Nazi] protocols for the 1939 agreements. We have approached a certain threshold where logic dictates a certain conclusion. But no one has seen any documents, so I cannot sign such a decision. Kohl did not provide me with the secret supplements—he promised to do it at first, but then could not find them. That is why an official statement on this issue is difficult. A similar situation is forming with Katyń. After Jaruzelski's request I gave instructions to find the documents on Katyń, but we have not discovered anything so far, although they are finding many other documents. And there are no people left in the appropriate organs who might know. Some say that many of our people are also buried in Katyń. Accordingly, it is our responsibility to see the matter through. In any case, I understand your request. We will continue the work. We need to think about what we can still do without putting this matter off.
[...]

Mazowiecki: It is understandable that everyone is being careful. No one foresaw such rapid developments.

Gorbachev: The way the situation has developed could have been foreseen. The GDR had serious problems, and we had warned that it was impossible to ignore them. They should have seized the initiative ahead of time. Regrettably, it was not done at that time.

I recall the progress of events in Poland in the early 1980s. It is good that we did not send in our troops then, it would have created a permanent rift between our peoples. It is good that a leader like Jaruzelski appeared in the political arena, with his devotion to the idea of national accord.

Mazowiecki: I would like to touch upon the question of your upcoming meeting with Bush.

Gorbachev: The road to Malta was not easy. We corresponded for two months before we agreed on Malta. Bush invited me to the U.S., but I did not deem it expedient to go there right now. Moreover, it is our joint opinion that it is important not to allow a deterioration of the international political climate, and much here depends on relations between the USSR and the U.S.

What questions would it be useful to examine with Bush, in your opinion?

Mazowiecki: The main topic is disarmament. I think it has great significance for the USSR as well as for Poland, economic considerations not being the least part of it.

Before the meeting with Bush you will have a meeting with a distinguished Pole in Rome, namely at the Vatican. [...]

Gorbachev: Our policy is to provide a solution to complex international problems. As difficult as the problems of Eastern Europe are, we must maintain a pan-European process. For this to happen, all its members must exhibit a very mature approach.

We are not the only ones who must change; you must too. Regrettably, not everyone realizes this, and not all the time. For example: my old partner in questions on Western Europe—Mrs. Thatcher—has recently again judged the processes in Eastern Europe to be the "failure of socialism." I will be blunt—this is no breakthrough concept. Socialism is renewing itself. We will still see a renewed socialism. We cannot enter the XXI century on an old horse, with the old notions and distrust for each other. We all know what a dead-end confrontation that has brought us to.

That is why I emphasize once again—not only do we have to change, but you do as well.

Mutual changes that would lead us away from confrontation are necessary. We need a historic turn toward mutual tolerance and respect.

We have many similar problems, especially since every social system has many possibilities for development. We must not try to fit all countries into one model. Let every people seek its own place, its own forms and ways of development while preserving its uniqueness and originality on a foundation of respect for values common to all mankind.

If we are true to the recognition of freedom of choice and the primacy of values common to all mankind, we will be able to build a new world.

Mazowiecki: In connection with your idea of a Common European Home, I would like to note that in this home our apartments share the same landing.

Gorbachev: We proceed from that. And let me tell you in a neighborly way— we do not have to cede our floor space to anyone, just as we do not ask others for anything for ourselves. And our good relations with Poland are by no means a political tactic. In a certain way Poland is our destiny. And we would like the achievements in our relations of recent years to be consolidated and to continue to multiply.

Mazowiecki: I would not be a person from "Solidarity" if I did not ask you for your views of Lech Wałęsa's visit to the USSR. He would not forgive me if I did not ask you this question.

Gorbachev: I view this question in the broad context of reality. Poland for us is a close partner, a neighbor, an ally. We respect the choice of the Polish people. Within the framework of a natural exchange, this visit is as practical as a visit by any political and social figure. There should not be any sensationalism surrounding this visit. It is a normal process. As pertains to specific dates, we could work that out together a little later. You can convey this to Mr. Wałęsa.

Mazowiecki: I thank you for the conversation. It is extremely significant to me. I attach great importance to our personal contacts. I am glad to have found you to be as I had imagined you.

Gorbachev: I also imagined you as you are. Please convey my best wishes to Mr. Jaruzelski. I hope for constructive collaboration.

[*Source: Archive of the Gorbachev Foundation, Fond 1, Opis 1. Donated by Georgy Shakhnazarov. On file at the National Security Archive. Translated by Anna Melyakova.*]

Document No. 108: Speech by Ladislav Adamec at CC CPCz Extraordinary Session

November 24, 1989

The "Velvet Revolution" in Czechoslovakia is in full swing when the CPCz's Central Committee meets in special session to debate whether or not to repress the mass demonstrations with force. A week earlier, the forcible suppression of a student march sparked a general strike and continuing protests that filled Wenceslaus Square in the center of Prague; and dissidents from the 12-year-old Charter 77 movement already are in the process of establishing the Civic Forum as the organized opposition to the regime. This transcript of the speech by Prime Minister Ladislav Adamec to the Party's "extraordinary session" provides perhaps the clearest expression in any Soviet bloc document of the complicated mix of reasons why most of the political elites running the regimes imposed by Stalin's force ultimately would not use violence in 1989 to save their own power. Such a solution would only temporarily "return calm," it would radicalize the youth, "the international support of the socialist countries [could] no longer be counted on," and "the capitalist states" might react with a "political and economic boycott." The view is that political methods are the only option, and the current communist leaders are hoping to utilize them to mobilize the party. But within the month, the dissident playwright Václav Havel would be on his way to the Castle at Hradčany as the next president of Czechoslovakia.

[...]

Making decisions is not simple. Events are developing rapidly and are not the same everywhere. I therefore regard it as my duty to express my opinion of the situation and its resolution. I am aware that we do not have much choice. The pressure of circumstances is rising day by day and possibly hour by hour. We have to deal with it. I am considering the alternatives along with everybody else. There are basically two ways to go—both have their advantages and drawbacks, merits and risks. None of them are guaranteed to fully succeed. With these thoughts, following up what Comrade Jakeš has said, I would like to contribute to finding the optimal political variant internationally and domestically. To explain the first alternative, let us assume that mass demonstrations and spreading strike movements constitute a direct attack on the socialist establishment, and that therefore there is no other way but to immediately halt all protest actions. On the basis of this evaluation, we may decide that a general strike must be prevented even at the cost of extensive use of extraordinary means, including force. This operation could be complemented by a large number of protest letters from party collectives in industrial and agricultural factories, and other workplaces.

One cannot passively watch the law being violated. To allow anarchy would be the direct opposite of democracy, whereas taking extraordinary measures could, if only temporarily, return calm to the streets. But experience with administrative measures has shown a significant risk. After a certain period the situation could explode again, bringing on another crisis with still more unpredictable results.

For all these reasons, I would clearly prefer the second alternative: a political solution. We must count on making certain acceptable concessions. I believe that we have not nearly exhausted these possibilities. I also rely on the fact that most of our people, including young people, have no reason to be against socialism. They are unsatisfied with many things, even stirred up by all kinds of disinformation, but are able and willing to repay trust with trust. To drive the young generation into the arms of the enemies of socialism would be an unforgivable mistake. This must be prevented under any circumstances.

I also advocate political methods because the recent intervention by the forces of order has led to the radicalization of the youth, allowed various groups to unite behind its condemnation, and has not contributed to the authority of either the party or the state. Next time we must avoid things like this. It would also be a mistake to underestimate the international risks of a broad application of force. We must not labor under the illusion that various democratization, environmental, and other movements end at our borders. Also, signed international treaties dealing with human rights cannot be taken lightly. When selecting methods for managing internal political problems, the international support of the socialist countries can no longer be counted on. From the capitalist states, one must take into account the results of a political and economic boycott. This warning should not be understood as a call for concessions at any price, without regard to the loss of socialist values.

To look truth in the eye means to realize that the loss of political trust as a result of mistakes in leadership must be paid for. There have been many in the last twenty years, and not small ones. I am convinced, however, that we need not pay too high a price if we can manage to mobilize the party. No one else has such a numerous membership, such an experienced cadre of functionaries, and close connections with each collective. [...] Today it has come down to the very status of the party in society. If our meeting helps to energize all its members, it will fulfill its historic mission. If not, we shall pay dearly, and only very slowly repair the damage. I consider it especially important and sensitive to take a position on the basic demands, especially those that are most often voiced. They are extremely varied, correct and incorrect, feasible either now or only later. This must be clear. Those that we are unable to answer immediately, at least let us say when we will address them. Under no circumstances should there arise the impression that we are avoiding something, using delaying tactics, and somehow maneuvering.

Let us choose our course so as not to give impetus to further waves of still-more-radical demands. I consider it crucial to announce the convening of another meeting of the Central Committee within a fortnight to evaluate political

questions, especially the program of accelerated restructuring and expanded dialogue. We would gain time, mobilize the party, and improve its level of information on the preferred strategy. The party needs a short-term action program,
a plan for the unification of the greatest possible number of communists toward
a concrete goal in the coming weeks. It would then even be possible to organize a broad public discussion centered on the positions and proposals of the CC
CPCz. We could also, for example, quickly submit proposals on the constitution
for public discussion and publicize proposed laws on association and assembly
for citizen comment. This would provide a certain framework and solid content
to an exchange of views that thus far has been less than constructive. We could
take the wind out of the sails of the daily proclamations, various calls and peti-
tions. I am convinced that only an active approach can give our side the initiative, and with that we shall also turn the majority of our citizens in favor of party
policy. This is the best reply to the demands of party organizations for more assistance from the CPCz Central Committee. [...]

*[Source: Stenographic minutes of the Extraordinary Session of the CC CPCz,
November 24, 1989, pp. 21–3, State Central Archive, Prague, CC CPCz record
group, W-0154/89. Translated from the Czech by Todd Hammond]*

Document No. 109: Letter from Helmut Kohl to George H.W. Bush

November 28, 1989

This remarkable letter arrives at the White House at the very moment that Chancellor Kohl is surprising both the allies and the Soviets with his "10 Points" speech at the Bundestag in Bonn, pointing toward reunification. The letter is couched as a response to Bush's repeated entreaties to Kohl (for example in phone calls on November 10 and 17) for his input before the Malta meeting with Gorbachev; in fact, Bush had practically implored Kohl to come and meet in person, but the chancellor demurred in order to tend to his domestic political situation.

The letter has a much more formal tone than the telephone transcripts convey, likely due to the participation of Kohl's aides in drafting and editing it. Here, the German leader encourages Bush to engage with Gorbachev across the board, but uses the president's own mantra of "stability" to emphasize that "the most important decisions over stability or destabilization will be made by the countries in Central and Eastern Europe. The duty of the West on the other hand must be to support the ongoing reform process from the outside." Kohl emphasizes that "Western help is coming far too slowly" to Poland and Hungary in particular—a rebuke to Bush's caution. Kohl also pays quite a compliment to Gorbachev, telling Bush that for the reform changes in Eastern Europe, "we have General Secretary Gorbachev's policies to thank."

But all the Malta advice is really secondary to the letter's final section laying out the "10 Points," along with a personal appeal in which he attempts to cover his bases with Bush. Kohl's aide, Horst Teltschik, had drafted the "10 Points" based largely on secret messages from Moscow—a gambit by Soviet expert Valentin Falin to spark a Kohl-Gorbachev dialogue on confederation. But Kohl rushed to go public, thinking Gorbachev was already on board (see pages 35–36, above). Kohl had informed neither the Americans nor the NATO allies (nor his own foreign minister) in advance of his speech. Bush later wrote that Kohl was "[a]fraid of leaks, or perhaps of being talked out of it" and that "I was surprised, but not too worried," because Kohl "couldn't pursue reunification on his own." Scowcroft was more concerned: "If he was prepared to go off on his own whenever he worried that we might object, we had very little influence." Scowcroft commented that in his telephone conversation the next day, November 29, Kohl repeatedly "pledged that there would be no going it alone—only one day after he had, in fact, 'gone it alone.'"[86] These phrases, such as "little influence" and "support ... from the outside," provide further testimony of how American policy lagged, instead of led, the miracles of 1989.

Dear George,

Thank you for your telephone request for information on the German situation for your upcoming meeting with General Secretary Gorbachev in Malta.

---

[86] Bush and Scowcroft, *A World Transformed*, 194–196. See also Savranskaya essay, 35–36.

I welcome this. This is a great sign of German–American friendship and partnership. At the same time, I would like to thank you for your friendly words in your Thanksgiving television address.

In order to take full advantage of your offer, I ask that you understand that your meeting with General Secretary Gorbachev will likely deal with themes that touch on the interests of the Federal Republic of Germany and all Germans.

1. MALTA PHILOSOPHY

I am much obliged to you, George, for the clarity with which you have rejected every parallel between Yalta and Malta. I mention this point not from a German or European status perspective. My point is more that the historical reform process we are currently experiencing in East and Central Europe is not only proceeding in the direction of our Western values—free self-determination, democracy, private enterprise—but is also being carried out by the people themselves. Lech Wałęsa impressively underscored this recently in talks with you and before the Congress of the United States.

That is why attempts to steer these reform developments from above or to channel or limit the movement of the people fail to meet the demands of this historic epoch. This is of course a consideration that applies to us and to our European neighbors.

In this sense, the talks in Malta should avoid any appearance of a status quo summit.

2. STABILITY OF THE REFORM PROCESS

The issue that General Secretary Gorbachev will in all likelihood address—warding off of all destabilization, increasing stability through reform—should be handled from this perspective.

Towards these goals, I would like to recommend full and complete agreement—in my name as well. The same goes for your assurance that America greets these reforms—and not as an opponent looking for an advantage, but rather as a people that offers support.

That is why it is important to establish with General Secretary Gorbachev the definition of both concepts:

– Contrary to what some Eastern propaganda still claims, destabilization does not come from Western influence or an invasion from the West. Its source is more from an awakening after many decades of violent, oppressive conflicts (for example ethnic conflict), or from the rejection of reforms and the subsequent reaction—or flight—of the people. The GDR and the ČSSR are the latest examples of this, and the fate of Romania is an occasion for much concern.

– Stability means stable development of reforms that guarantee the self-determination of the people—in the words of Gorbachev, "freedom of choice"—that allow citizens a democratic share in the political developments in their country and open to the people a tangible future outlook in their homeland. In short: as in 1776, it is about life, liberty and the pursuit of happiness!

– Last but not least, stability means a positive foreign policy environment, especially dynamic progress in disarmament and arms control.

If these definitions are correct, then the result will be that the most important decisions over stability or destabilization will be made by the countries in Central and Eastern Europe. The duty of the West, on the other hand, must be to support the ongoing reform process from the outside. The concrete forms and conditions of this support could be a major topic of discussion in your meetings with Secretary Gorbachev.

3. SITUATION IN THE SOVIET UNION

Based on our analysis, you will face a General Secretary Gorbachev who wants to continue his policies resolutely, consistently and dynamically, but is meeting internal resistance and is dependent on external support.

The economic situation in the Soviet Union is, based on the judgment of our analysts, worse than when Gorbachev took office. The already difficult supply situation could worsen this winter due to an energy crisis.

Our analysts say that General Secretary Gorbachev's position currently is safe, and his acceptance as number one, even from government colleagues who are critical of the direction and tempo of *perestroika*, is unchanged. There is also no indication that his popularity among the people has decreased due to the absence of concrete results.

4. DISARMAMENT AND ARMS CONTROL

On top of that, together—with General Secretary Gorbachev—we can work on advances in foreign policy. The agenda that Secretary of State Baker and Foreign Minister Shevardnadze worked with in Wyoming[87] has far-reaching meaning for American–Soviet relations.

I hope that your meeting with General Secretary Gorbachev will give strong stimulus to the arms control negotiations, even if no concrete agreement is concluded.

I would welcome it if the goals established in Wyoming for the START negotiations were further solidified. This could strengthen the hope that in the next year an agreement could be reached, or be very close to it, in this important area that also has significant meaning for us Europeans.

---

[87] The two foreign ministers met in Jackson Hole, Wyoming, on September 22–23, 1989. The day before the start of their meeting, Shevardnadze delivered a letter from Gorbachev to President Bush on arms control. This, along with discussion of a possible summit, Soviet domestic developments, regional conflicts, and human rights constituted their agenda in Wyoming.

An outstanding interest of the Federal Republic is speedy, substantial results in the Vienna conference on conventional weapons in Europe. Here I am also in agreement with our NATO partners, especially with you. This deals with a key issue of European security.

Given the strength of Soviet armed forces in the countries of Central and Eastern Europe, dynamic events in the Warsaw Pact states have given these negotiations extra meaning. I think it especially important that progress in the Vienna negotiations keep up with the general political changes in this region of Europe.

I would therefore welcome it if you could explain to GS Gorbachev the Western determination to come to a preliminary result in Vienna within the timeframe laid out by you at the NATO summit in May. I believe that the Soviet Union is striving toward this goal as well. It should be reinforced in this interest, which after all was expressed in GS Gorbachev's proposal for a meeting of heads of state and government in the second half of 1990 for the purpose of signing an agreement on conventional weapons.

We welcome the agreements on chemical weapons reached by the USA and the Soviet Union because they give hope for the possibility of soon reaching a global, comprehensive and effectively verifiable ban on chemical weapons in Geneva.

I would welcome it if you could again commit General Secretary Gorbachev to this goal and could thereby move him, too, to campaign actively for comprehensive participation.

For the overall plan for arms control and disarmament, at the NATO summit we adopted a clear position with respect to the question of nuclear deterrence and land-based short-range nuclear systems. We wrote down a precisely defined negotiating perspective for this area. General Secretary Gorbachev should be constantly reminded that his unilateral dismantling of the large military superiority in the East should make later negotiations easier.

Let me be clear on this point: I heard with joy and satisfaction your renewed assurances in your Thanksgiving television address that you will leave American forces in Europe as long as they are wanted and needed by your European friends. I assure you: as before, we view the presence of your forces as vital to European security.

5. DEVELOPMENTS IN OTHER WARSAW PACT STATES

Regarding the reform process in Poland, Hungary, Bulgaria, the ČSSR, and not least the GDR, we have General Secretary Gorbachev's policies to thank. His *perestroika* has let loose, made easier, or accelerated these reforms. He pushed governments unwilling to make reforms toward openness and toward acceptance of the people's wishes; and he accepted developments that in some instances far surpassed the Soviet Union's own standards.

General Secretary Gorbachev has more or less declared the Brezhnev Doctrine dead and instead has sanctioned the right of every state and people to "freedom of choice" in their political and social systems (in, among other things, the joint declaration he signed with me in June, as well as the last communiqué of the foreign ministers of the Warsaw Pact).

Here it will depend on General Secretary Gorbachev committing to his own promises and in particular stressing that the ban on interference goes for everyone—for the Soviet Union in particular where it has its own troops stationed.

With respect to the situation in Poland and Hungary, my visit to Warsaw and a last-minute talk with Németh have firmly convinced me that with winter coming both countries are facing considerable problems in providing for their people due to a reduction of Soviet energy supplies and the liquidity crisis. In both countries, "social eruptions" are not excluded, particularly as orthodox party circles could be interested in that.

In the face of this critical situation, I must emphasize that Western help is coming much too slowly. In particular, neither the International Monetary Fund nor, in the case of the Poland, the Paris Club discussions have been completed, nor is the Stability Fund in the amount of 1 billion dollars, which you suggested in the beginning of the October, secured. With the exception of the United States of America and the Federal Republic of Germany, no other Western country has promised contributions.

I am going to use our alliance meeting on December 4 to push for quick passage of a resolution by the international financial institutions and to plead for further contributions to the stabilization fund.

6. SITUATION IN THE GDR

What I said about the importance of respecting "freedom of choice" is especially relevant for the GDR.

Based on our information and, in particular after talks with the head of the Federal Chancellery in East Berlin, Minister Seiters, we have come to the assessment that the leadership situation is no longer stable, and the people are restless.

In spite of the opening of the border and the Wall, in spite of changes in the leadership and the prospect of proposed reforms, mass demonstrations continue and Germans are fleeing from the GDR to the Federal Republic of Germany in significant numbers.

The upcoming party Congress in the middle of December will answer key questions:

– Is the communist party prepared to renounce its monopoly on power and to change the corresponding constitution?

– Is the communist party prepared to allow for free elections in the near future, to allow new and non-socialist parties and unions, and to initiate urgent economic reforms?

Positive answers to these questions depend on whether the Federal Republic of Germany can fulfill its offer to help the GDR in new financial dimensions.

Should General Secretary Gorbachev criticize this view of the Federal Republic as interference, I would be indebted to you if you could clarify that for both us and the West it cannot be about stabilizing a discredited leadership and an intolerable situation; it must be about a process of far-reaching political, economic and social change supported from the outside—[while being] mindful of the wishes of the population.

7. GERMAN REUNIFICATION

Let me thank you in the name of all Germans for your clear statement that the USA welcomes German reunification and that it is an issue for the Germans, or rather both states, to decide.

General Secretary Gorbachev may address this question in the sense that we must continue to respect post-War realities, and that for that reason the reforms in the GDR could at any rate not go as far as altering the existing borders between East and West and reestablishing the unity of Germany in whatever form.

I ask you emphatically—in particular in the vein of my statement at the outset—not to agree to any commitments that could be interpreted as limitations (containment)[88] on a policy "of working towards a state of peace in Europe, in which the German people could regain their unity through free self determination."

This goal was renewed by the NATO heads of state in their declaration of May 30, 1989, and we already demonstrated this to the Soviet Union in the conclusion of the 1970 Moscow Treaty.

The crux of the matter is and remains the free self-determination of Germans in the GDR. The events of the past summer have proven that they do not feel or think as members of a separate nation. Since the opening of the Wall and the border, more than half of the citizens of the GDR—as of today, more than 9 million people!—have visited the Federal Republic of Germany and were welcomed with warmth and solidarity. With the mass demonstrations in the GDR, calls for freedom, free elections and free unions were increasingly joined by the call for unity. This will continue to grow if the promised reforms fall apart.

Naturally, it is in the common interest of the West and East, and all Germans, that a "chaotic situation" does not arise, such as General Secretary Gorbachev feared in his message to you on the 10th of this month.

The Germans in the GDR really have shown considerable attention, reason, and level-headedness when face-to-face with the repression that was still being carried out at the beginning of October.

The German government has in no way used the current situation in the GDR to single-handedly achieve its own goals. On the contrary, we have strengthened our unbreakable loyalty to the Alliance and our active cooperation with European

---

[88] "Containment" appears in English in the German text.

integration. This has been acknowledged by you and by our European friends and allies, for which I at this point again thank you.

Even General Secretary Gorbachev in a telephone conversation with me spoke in favor of the German government's practice of clever restraint. I hope very much that he does not tell you anything different. I assured him that the German government stood firmly by the Moscow Treaty and the CSCE obligations, whereby self-determination must apply to everyone.

It is in accordance with the legitimate security interests of all Europeans and the entitled interests of the German people, in particular the people of the GDR, to harmonize a long-term perspective.

Before the German Parliament, I summarized in 10 points what the German government intends to do to move toward this goal:

First:

Immediate concrete help for the people of the GDR in the humanitarian and medical spheres and through financing their newly won freedom of travel.

Second:

Strengthened cooperation with the GDR in all areas that would be of immediate benefit to the people: economy, science and technology, culture, environment, communications.

Third:

An expansion of our help and cooperation in new areas if there are fundamental changes to the political and economic system.

Fourth:

Picking up the concept of President Modrow regarding a contractual association: the development of joint institutions, such as for business, traffic, environmental protection, technology, health, culture. The full incorporation of Berlin.

Fifth:

As soon as the other side is available as a democratic and legitimate partner, the development of confederate structures between the two states.

Sixth:

The embedding of the future structure of Germany within the pan-European process, for which the West has paved the way with its concept of a lasting and just

European order of peace. Just as we described to the Soviet Union, the building blocks of this structure [are]: unrestricted observance of the integrity and security of every state, the right of every state to freely choose its own political and economic system, observance of the principles and norms of international law, in particular the right of self-determination of the people, and—not least—the realization of human rights.

Seventh:

Openness and flexibility on the part of the European Community with respect to all reformed countries in Central, Eastern and Southeastern Europe, naturally including the GDR: speedy conclusion of trade and cooperation agreements; in the long-term, the development of associations to assist with dismantling the economic and social differences of the continent.

Eighth:

Energetic progress in the CSCE process using the imminent forms.

Ninth:

Far-reaching and speedy steps in disarmament and arms control (compare with part 4 above).

Tenth:

Organic development toward a situation in which the German people through free self-determination regain their unity, whereby the interests of all involved are taken into account and peaceful coexistence in Europe is guaranteed.

Dear George,

I would be especially obliged to you if, when you meet with General Secretary Gorbachev, you could support the policies in these 10 Points and make clear to him that the best interests of his country do not lie in clinging to obsolete taboos, but rather in this forward-looking course. For this I thank you in advance.

With friendly greetings,
Yours,
Helmut Kohl

[*Source:* Deutsche Einheit: Sonderedition aus den Akten des Bundeskanzleramtes 1989/90. *Eds. Hanns Jürgen Küsters and Daniel Hofmann. R. Oldenbourg Verlag, Munich, 1998. Translated by Catherine Nielsen.*]

Document No. 110: Soviet Transcript of the Malta Summit

December 2–3, 1989

Originally intended as an "interim" meeting to prepare for a full-scale summit in 1990, the Bush–Gorbachev meeting at Malta would take on a life of its own, symbolically closing the Cold War. Bush came up with the idea for the meeting after his July trip to Hungary and Poland, when Jaruzelski, among others, urged American support for Gorbachev and encouraged Bush to meet with the Soviet leader. Gorbachev's own frustration with the Bush "pause" and review of policy made the Soviet leader more than eager for such a meeting; but between the July idea and the December reality, the entire Soviet empire in Eastern Europe fell. Stormy weather and raging seas in Malta would play havoc with the meeting planners' idea of alternating U.S. and Soviet ships as picturesque sites for the meetings—thus providing something of a metaphor for the rush of events in Eastern Europe that ran out of the control of both superpowers. While the U.S. transcript of Malta is not yet declassified, the Gorbachev Foundation has published excerpts of the Russian version, although several sections relating to Central America are not included in the published Russian volume.

Gorbachev's remarks at Malta include intriguing hints that date back to the Yakovlev–Kissinger conversations at the very beginning of 1989 (see Document No. 36). The Soviet leader seems to probe the idea of a superpower condominium (though he refers to "speculations" and claims not to be suggesting a condominium) that he did not seize upon in January. Now, however, it is much too late to slow the pace of change in Eastern Europe. Gorbachev keeps insisting that the U.S. should stay in Europe, that the U.S. and USSR "are equally integrated into European problems" and that they need to work together to keep those problems from exploding. The American president responds with classic expressions of reserve and prudence, insisting that he does not intend to posture over East Germany even though he is under severe domestic political pressure to "climb the Berlin Wall and to make broad declarations." Bush affirms his support for perestroika, *and reassures Gorbachev that they both remember the Helsinki Final Act's pronouncements on the inviolability of borders. In general, the American wants to talk about practical details, such as specific congressional amendments on the U.S. side or arms deliveries in Central America from the Soviet bloc, while Gorbachev is more interested in broad philosophical discussion: "The world is experiencing a major regrouping of forces."*

But both men are uneasy about the dramatic transformations taking place. Bush frankly pronounces himself "shocked by the swiftness" while Gorbachev says "look at how nervous we are." After warning Bush not to provoke or accelerate the changes, the Soviet leader in particular seems to ask what kind of collective action they should take. He stresses the Helsinki process as the new European process and also mentions the Giscard d'Estaing comment in January 1989 (see Document No. 39) about a federal state of Western Europe: "Therefore, all of Europe is on the move, and it is moving in the direction of something new. We also consider ourselves Europeans, and we associate this movement with the idea of a common European home." Gorbachev hopes for the dissolution of the blocs—"what to do with institutions cre-

ated in another age?"—and suggests that the WTO and NATO become, to an even greater degree, political organizations rather than military ones.

On the German question, neither leader expects events to move as fast as they would the following year. Just days earlier, on November 28, Helmut Kohl announced his "10 Points" towards confederation in a Bundestag speech that the Soviet Foreign Ministry denounced as pushing change in "a nationalist direction;" and here, Gorbachev attributes the speech to politics and says Kohl "does not act seriously and responsibly." But then Gorbachev asks whether a united Germany would be neutral or a member of NATO, suggesting that at least theoretically he imagines the latter, although he may simply be acknowledging the U.S. position. His clear preference is for the continuation of two states in Germany and only very slow progress towards any unification: "let history decide." The president is not eager for rapid progress either; he says "I hope that you understand that you cannot expect us not to approve of German reunification. At the same time ... [w]e are trying to act with a certain reserve."

Malta's most significant outcome would simply be the reassurance it provided to the two leaders through a face-to-face meeting, and the building of a personal relationship on which both would rely in the difficult next two years. Gorbachev, for example, tells Bush: "First and foremost, the new U.S. president must know that the Soviet Union will not under any circumstances initiate a war. This is so important that I wanted to repeat the announcement to you personally. Moreover, the USSR is prepared to cease considering the U.S. as an enemy and announce this openly." Gorbachev also makes an impact on Bush in the discussion of values. He bristles at Bush's repeated reference to "Western values" and argues that the U.S. approach of "exporting 'Western values'" would cause "ideological confrontations [to] flare up again" in "propaganda battles" with "no point." Bush subsequently adopts Gorbachev's phrasing, saying in his Brussels remarks immediately after the summit that the need to end the division of Europe is in accord with "values that are becoming universal ideals."

Gorbachev: Welcome, Mr. President, and members of the American delegation, aboard the Soviet cruise ship *Maxim Gorky*. It was you who took the initiative for organizing this meeting between us. I would first like to say that we regard the president's initiative highly.

Bush: Thank you very much.

Gorbachev: I have been thinking: what has happened in world developments that has prompted the USSR and the U.S. to meet like this? Not only what has happened, but that so much is happening. That is the important thing. For that reason we need to find a new, deep dialogue, one that will be integrally linked with those changes and new events that need to be faced in the international arena. We must conduct our affairs in some other way; we must address the changes. Therefore, we can no longer limit the active work being conducted to the level of foreign ministers. Life demands that we organize more frequent working meetings and increase contacts between our nations' leaders.

This meeting is undoubtedly a prelude to an official meeting with you. In any case, it will have a meaning of its own. I am generally impressed by unofficial meetings which are not accompanied by particular formalities. You and I carry on a substantial correspondence. But it is important to sit down at the table and talk. This has a symbolic significance not only for the USSR and the U.S., but for the whole world.

In the Soviet Union and the United States, and throughout the world, people are hoping that the negotiations in Malta will not simply be a nice symbol of our relations, but that they will bring results.

Let our experts work together with the leaders. Opportunities will be created for them to do this.

Once again, I sincerely welcome you, Mr. President.

Bush: Thank you for your kind words. It was I who came forward with the suggestion for this meeting. But I proceeded along the assumption that such negotiations would be acceptable to the Soviet side as well. Therefore, I feel that we prepared this meeting together. When I was on my way from Paris to Washington this past summer and was on the plane editing the draft of my letter to you concerning this meeting, I realized that I would be changing my former position 180 degrees. This change in our approach was understood by the American people.

Since the idea of this summit was proposed, many important events have taken place in the international arena. I expect that during the forthcoming exchange we will be able to share our views of these changes, not only in Eastern Europe but in other regions as well, in order to come to a better and deeper understanding of our respective positions. I am in favor of an exchange not only in the presence of our delegations, but also one-on-one. I think that we should meet more often.

Gorbachev: I agree. I have a feeling that we have already talked and that this meeting is a continuation of our useful discussions.

Bush: Yes, that's right. We have already had productive discussions. I would like, if you will permit me, to outline some of the thoughts of the American side.

I fully agree with what you have stated regarding the importance of our meeting on Malta. I was prepared to make similar points. Therefore, I will not repeat them.

Concerning our attitude toward *perestroika*. I would like to say in no uncertain terms that I agree completely with what you said in New York: the world will be better if *perestroika* ends as a success. Not long ago there were many people in the U.S. who doubted this. At that time you said in New York that there were elements that did not wish for the success of *perestroika*. I cannot say that there are no such elements in the U.S., but I can say with full certainty that serious-thinking people in the United States do not share these opinions.

These shifts in the public mood in the United States are affected by the changes in Eastern Europe, by the whole process of *perestroika*. Of course, among analysts and experts there are differing points of view, but you can be certain that you are dealing with an administration in the U.S. and with a Congress that wish for the crowning success of your reforms.

I would now like to offer a number of positive steps, which, in our opinion, might provide a general direction for our joint task of preparing an official summit in the United States.

A few comments concerning economic issues. I want to inform you that my administration intends to take measures toward suspending the Jackson–Vanik Amendment, which prevents the granting of Most Favored Nation status to the Soviet Union. [...]

I also want to inform you that the administration has adopted a policy of repealing the Stevenson and Baird amendments, which restrict the possibility of extending credit to the Soviet side. [...]

These measures, which the administration is now proposing in the realm of Soviet–American relations, are guided by a certain spirit; they are not at all directed toward a demonstration of American superiority. And in this sense, as we understand it, they are in line with your approach. As it stands to reason, we in the U.S. are deeply convinced of the advantages of our type of economy. But that is not the issue right now. We have attempted to construct our proposals in a way that does not give the impression that America is "saving" the Soviet Union. We are not talking about a plan of assistance but about a plan for cooperation.

After the Jackson–Vanik Amendment is repealed, conditions will be favorable for eliminating restrictions on granting credit. The American administration considers this a question not of granting assistance, but of creating the conditions for the development of effective cooperation on economic issues. We plan to convey our considerations on this issue to the Soviet side in the form of a document. It involves a number of serious plans in the areas of finance, statistics, market function, etc. [...]

I would like to say a few words to clarify our position with respect to the wishes of the Soviet side to gain observer status in the GATT. There used to be a division of opinion among us on this issue—the U.S. was against admitting the USSR into this organization. Now the position has been reexamined. We are for granting the Soviet side observer status in the GATT. This is based on the view that participation of the USSR in the GATT will be conducive to its becoming familiar with the conditions, operation, and development of the world market. [...]

There is one other area in which new approaches can be used to develop economic cooperation. I have in mind the establishment of contacts with the Organization for Economic Cooperation and Development. This would provide a good framework for cooperation on economic issues between East and West. The administration is in favor of active progress in this direction. [...]

[Bush moved on to discuss regional issues, and stated the U.S. position with regard to the situation in Central America. Then he proposed that the two sides discuss the issue of disarmament.]

Gorbachev: I agree.

Bush: You know that my administration is in favor of eliminating chemical weapons from mankind. Today I want to state our new proposal, which contains a certain new element. If the Soviet side will give its agreement in principle to our proposal on the issue of chemical weapons, which was set forth in my speech to the United Nations General Assembly in September, then within the framework of this approach the U.S. could agree to abandon our program of modernization, that is, the [program of] further production of binary weapons after comprehensive convention on the prohibition of chemical weapons would enter into force.

In practical terms this would mean that in the near future the two sides could come to agreement on a significant reduction in supplies of chemical weapons, bringing to 20 percent the current figure on chemical agents in the U.S. arsenal, and, eight years after entering into the arms convention, [bringing it down] to 2 percent. We propose to carry out the plan so that by the time of the summit meeting in the U.S. in the middle of next year the draft of a bilateral agreement would be ready, and it could be signed at that time.

On conventional weapons. Although this matter requires serious work connected, among other things, with the necessity of overcoming certain barriers not only in our countries but in other countries, for example in France, we could expect to reach an agreement sometime next year. I think that in this connection, we could set the following goal: to aim toward signing an agreement in 1990 on radical reductions in conventional forces in Europe, having obtained signatures on such an agreement during the summit meeting of representatives of the countries participating in the Vienna negotiations.

On the issue of a future treaty for the reduction of strategic offensive weapons. The American side seeks to provide the proper initiative for negotiations on that matter. We are in favor of jointly resolving all outstanding key issues for the forthcoming summit meeting in the U.S. We are also not excluding the possibility that by then the draft treaty on reducing strategic offensive weapons and its attachments will be agreed upon in full. In this case, the treaty could be signed in the course of the summit meeting.

We are hopeful that at the forthcoming Soviet–American talks between our foreign ministers a solution might be found in the near future to issues such as a procedure for accounting for long-range air-launched cruise missiles, telemetry encryption, restrictions on non-deployed missiles, etc. On the eve of the meeting between our foreign ministers, which could take place at the end of January, the American side is planning to formulate its position on these questions and to offer it at these negotiations.

We are also planning to provide instructions to our delegation at the Geneva negotiations to withdraw the previous American proposal on banning mobile intercontinental ballistic missiles.

I would like to ask the Soviet side to turn once again to the issue of restrictions on SS-18 intercontinental ballistic missiles. We would like to prohibit the modernization of these missiles and would like the Soviet side to explore the possibility of deeper unilateral reductions.

Regarding preparatory protocols to the treaties of 1974–1976 on underground nuclear testing, there is, in our opinion, every possibility for completing this work soon and signing the stated protocols at our meeting in the U.S.

It is becoming increasingly important at the present time to find a solution to the problem of preventing the proliferation of missiles and missile technology. In this regard the United States would welcome the Soviet Union's joining the arms limitation convention to which seven Western nations already belong.

Gorbachev: This issue is already under discussion.

Bush: We would like to raise the question of whether it would be possible for the Soviet Union to publish roughly the same amount of data on the Soviet military budget as we do in the United States. I think that our publications give quite a comprehensive idea of the kind of military activity undertaken in our country. I am sure that your intelligence services can confirm this authoritatively.

Gorbachev: They report to me, on the contrary, that you do not publish everything.

Bush: I am certain that the publication of more detailed data on military budgets, on a mutual basis, would encourage trust in this sphere.

I would like to touch on a few questions which are important for the future. [...]

Particularly critical at the present time are problems of environmental protection. We are now forced to take into account even the economic consequences of global climate changes. Some Western countries are going so far as to drastically curtail even essential economic activity for the sake of averting these changes.

We are trying to approach these issues rationally, to avoid extremes. At the present time, the USSR and the U.S. are working actively on a committee preparing an international conference on the climate under the aegis of the U.N. This is bringing satisfactory results. Looking ahead, we are planning two more important steps in this direction. First, after the committee work is finished by autumn of next year we intend to host a conference to draw up a limited treaty on climate change.

Environmental protection demands the attention of leading scientists. I have asked the White House Assistant for Science [and Technology], Director [B]romley, to organize a conference for next spring on the environment, to bring together the finest scientific minds as well as leaders of appropriate departments from many countries. I hope that Soviet representatives will also attend this forum.

The development of cooperation between our countries depends largely on the participation of young people in this process. Here student exchanges are intended to play a great role. We suggest making arrangements so that in the 1990–91 school year, this type of exchange could be increased to approximately 1,000 persons from each side. The expanded program would involve young people up to 25 years of age. In addition, special attention should be paid to student exchanges in the humanities and sociology. The practical experience would be very productive with respect to agricultural studies programs.

Gorbachev: Thank you for sharing these interesting ideas. This is possibly the best proof of the fact that President Bush's administration has set its political focus along Soviet–American lines. I intend to touch on some specific issues a little later.

Now I would like to make some observations of a general philosophical nature. It seems very important to me that we talk about the conclusions we can reach from our past experience, from the "Cold War"—what took place, what will linger in history. Such, if you wish, is the advantage of the historical process. But trying to analyze the course of past events is our primary obligation. Why is this necessary? We can probably assert that we have all lived through a historic turning point. Entirely new problems, of which people in the past could not even conceive, have arisen before mankind. And so—are we going to resolve them using old approaches? Absolutely nothing would come of that.

By no means is everything that has happened to be considered in a negative light. For 45 years we succeeded in preventing a major war. This fact alone shows that in the past all was not bad. But all the same, the conclusion is obvious—the emphasis on force, on military superiority, and along with it the arms race, has not justified itself. Both our countries apparently understand this better than any of the others.

The emphasis on ideological confrontation did not justify itself either and resulted only in our continual criticism of each other. We reached a dangerous line. And it is good that we knew enough to stop. It is good that a mutual understanding has arisen between our countries.

And the emphasis on the uneven exchange between developed and underdeveloped nations is also being weakened. In what way? The colonial powers gained a lot from that relationship. But so many problems arose in the developing world, problems that are literally taking us by the throat. Indeed everything is interrelated.

On the strategic level, Cold War methods and confrontations have suffered defeat. We recognize that. And perhaps it is even better recognized by the general public. I am not going to start preaching. It is just that people are rushing into politics. Problems have arisen with respect to the environment and the preservation of natural resources that are linked to the ill effects of technological progress. And this is entirely understandable—after all, this is essentially about the problem of survival. Public opinion of this kind has a strong effect on us politicians as well.

Therefore we—in the USSR and in the U.S.—can do a lot together at this stage to alter radically our old approaches. We were aware of this in our dealings with the Reagan administration. The process is continuing now. And look at how we have opened up to each other.

On the political level, we lag behind the public mood. And this is understandable—after all, there are many forces acting on political leaders. It is good that Marshal [Sergey] Akhromeyev and your adviser, [Brent] Scowcroft, understand the problems arising in the military sphere. But in both countries there are people—and a considerable number—who simply frighten us. In the area of defense there are many people who are accustomed to their profession and who do not find it easy to change their way of thinking. But this process has begun all the same.

Why have I started off with this topic? In American political circles a certain premise is persistently put forward: the Soviet Union, they say, began its *perestroika* and is changing direction under the influence of Cold War politicians. It is said that in Eastern Europe everything is collapsing and, they say, that also supports the self-righteousness of those who relied on Cold War methods. And since this is so, then no political changes need to be made. What needs to be done is to increase the force of oppression and prepare more baskets for reaping the fruits [of this approach]. Mr. President, this is a very dangerous misconception.

I realize that you see all this. I know that you have to listen to representatives of various circles. However, your public announcements and the concrete proposals you put forth today, which are aimed at developing cooperation between the USSR and the U.S., signify that President Bush has formulated a conception of the world that meets today's challenges.

It goes without saying that each person makes his own choices. But it is also clear that as far as relations between the USSR and the U.S. are concerned, mistakes and errors in politics are unacceptable. We must not let our politics be built on misconceptions either in relations with each other or in relations with other countries.

At first I even considered delivering some sort of reproach—saying that the U.S. president time and again has expressed his support of *perestroika* and wished it well and has commented that the Soviet Union should carry out its reforms on its own; but that we expected from the president of the United States not only a statement but also concrete action to back up the statement.

Now there is both a statement and an action. I come to this conclusion having listened to what you just said. Even if this means only plans for action, it is very important.

My second consideration. The world is experiencing a major regrouping of forces. It is clear that we are moving from a bipolar to a multipolar world. Whether we want to or not, we will have to deal with a united, economically integrated Europe. We could discuss the issue of Eastern Europe separately. Whether we like it or not, Japan is another center of world politics. We once discussed China. This is another most serious reality, which neither of us should exploit against the other. And we must think about how not to make China feel excluded from the processes that are taking place in the world.

All these, I repeat, are major factors in the regrouping of forces in the world. I am watching political developments in India—these politics are dynamic. I have spoken at length with Rajiv Gandhi. India has a balanced approach aimed at establishing good relations both with us and with you.

What role do we play in this regrouping? Very serious things follow from this. I began discussing this question with [George] Shultz. After one of the discussions he showed us some diagrams reflecting changes that will occur at the end of the century in economic relations between the leading countries of the world. Now it is simply essential to understand the role of the USSR and the U.S. in these major changes. The changes cannot always be accompanied by a peaceful flow of events.

626

Take Eastern Europe. Its specific share in the world economy is not very large. And look at how nervous we are. What form of action should we take? Collective action?

And what lies ahead in terms of economics, the environment, and other problems? We must think about this together, too.

For a long time the Soviet leadership has pondered this. And we are coming to the conclusion that the U.S. and the USSR are simply "doomed" to dialogue, joint action, and cooperation. It cannot be otherwise.

But for this to happen we must stop viewing each other as enemies. There is a lot of this in our heads. We must take care not to look at our relations solely from a military standpoint.

This does not mean that we are suggesting a Soviet–American condominium. This is about realities. And this in no way puts into question allied relations or cooperation that have built up with other countries. We need to understand all this. I do not think that this was there before. We have just now entered the process of mutual understanding.

We have asked the question: what kind of Soviet Union is in the U.S. interest—the dynamic, stable, solid one or the one struggling with all kinds of problems? I am informed about the advice you have been receiving.

As far as we are concerned, we are interested in a U.S. that feels confident in the decisions it makes on national security and progress. This thought is present in all discussions with my Western partners. And there have been hundreds of such meetings. I believe that any other approach is dangerous. Ignoring domestic political processes, an unwillingness to take into account the practical interests of the U.S. in the world—that is a dangerous policy.

And the U.S. must take into account the interests of other countries. Meanwhile, there is still a desire to teach, oppress, and step on throats. It is still there. We all know this. Therefore, I would like to hear your opinion on this. For the question is how to build a bridge between our countries—across the river or down its course.

Since there is much time remaining in the president's leadership of the U.S., this point must be made clear. I think that we will not achieve this in just one meeting. But the main issues must be sorted out. I repeat: we need clarity. All the rest is concrete detail, specifics that in the final analysis are integrally linked to mutual understanding on these basic problems. [...]

Bush: I hope you noticed that while the changes in Eastern Europe have been going on, the United States has not engaged in condescending statements aimed at damaging the Soviet Union. At the same time, there are people in the United States who accuse me of being too cautious. It is true, I am a cautious man, but I am not a coward; and my administration will seek to avoid doing anything that would damage your position in the world. But I was persistently advised to do something of that sort—to climb the Berlin Wall and to make broad declarations. My administration, however, is avoiding these steps; we are in favor of reserved behavior.

627

Gorbachev: [...] I want to reply to the views you expressed at the beginning of the discussion. I welcome your words. I regard them as a manifestation of political will. This is important to me.

From my own experience, and the experience of working with President Reagan, I know how we found ourselves more than once in a situation concerning disarmament where everything came to a halt and was stuck in the mud. The delegations sat in Geneva sipping coffee, and there was nothing to do.

At that time I received a message from President Reagan. I read the text carefully and concluded that nothing would come of it. Of course, I could have written a formal reply but I do not like wasting words. I had to make a decisive move. And that is how the idea arose for a meeting in Reykjavik. Some people were frightened by the results of the Reykjavik talks. But in reality Reykjavik became a genuine breakthrough on questions of arms limitation. After this, the mechanism for negotiations began to work actively and effectively.

Or take another area—economic ties. Here there are limited possibilities for advancement. In order to overcome these limitations, political will is needed. A signal is needed from the president. American businessmen are disciplined people, and as soon as they see a new way of thinking in the economic sphere, they respond very quickly.

At the Geneva talks, the delegations squeezed literally everything they could from the directives given to them. It is essential to give impetus to all work. I noted your views in this connection. They appear to me to be worthy of attention.

I thank you for placing top priority on the question of bilateral cooperation. We are prepared to discuss all issues related to this.

The following situation often arises: when discussing relations between our countries, we are told: "Come to an agreement with the Americans, we will support you." But as soon as we start to negotiate, they scream: "A new Yalta." That is somewhat natural. Much depends on our work with our allies, and with the non-aligned countries.

We will move to adapt our economy to the world economy. Therefore we consider it important to be part of the GATT system and other international economic organizations. We believe that this will be useful to our *perestroika*, and will allow us to understand better how the world economic mechanism functions.

In the past, the U.S. took a negative stand on the question of the USSR's participation in international economic organizations. It was said that participation in the GATT would politicize this organization's activity. I think that this is a vestige of old approaches. There really was a time when we placed ideological issues in the forefront. By the way, you did, too. Now times have changed, there are other criteria, other processes, and there will be no return to the old ways. [...]

We are allowing for the possibility in our country of various forms of private property. We will aim toward making the ruble convertible. *Perestroika* is also happening within the framework of the Council for Mutual Economic Assistance in order to bring this organization's operational principles closer to generally accepted world economic standards.

Now, on Central America. We see how you perceive the situation in Latin America. But it is not quite clear to us what you want from Nicaragua. There is political pluralism in that country, there are more parties there than in the United States. And the Sandinistas—what kind of Marxists are they?! This is laughable. Where are the roots of the problem? At the core are economic and social issues. Why does the U.S. fail to see them? You say that the main problem in Nicaragua is the question of power. Well, there will be elections there. Let the United Nations monitor them. Frankly speaking, it is not our business. Let this process go where it will.

On Cuba. Cuba came into being without our assistance. Rather, it was the United States that played some role in that. When the new Cuba was born, we learned about it from the newspapers. But let us not touch on history. The issue now is how to improve the current situation. There is a simple and well-proven method: one has to speak directly to Castro. You must learn: nobody can lord it over Castro. He has his own ideas about our *perestroika*, too.

I want to emphasize again: we are not pursuing any goals in Central America. We do not want to acquire bases or strongholds there. You should be assured about this.

Let us return to the problem of disarmament. We are familiar with the U.S. approach to solving the problem of chemical weapons. However, in the past this approach has been missing an important element—a U.S. readiness to curtail production of binary weapons after the convention banning chemical weapons went into effect. Now this element has appeared, and that is very substantial. There has been progress here.

Therefore we, you and we, believe that a global ban is essential. We hold to this goal. But there are two-sided measures and definite stages to be negotiated. Our foreign ministers can discuss this.

Bush: The issue of nonproliferation of chemical weapons is also highly critical. I hope that our experts will touch on this subject.

Gorbachev: I agree.

Now on the Vienna negotiations and the reduction of conventional arms in Europe. You came out in favor of concluding an agreement on this most important issue in 1990 and on its signing at the highest level. Our approaches here coincided. We are ready for active and constructive cooperation to attain this goal. There are difficulties, of course. But I will not elaborate on the details.

On negotiations for limiting strategic weapons. Here political will is needed to give impetus to the work being done. I listened to you attentively, and you emphasized some of the elements. But, unfortunately, I did not hear you mention the problem of sea-launched cruise missiles.

Now the climate is favorable for preparing a draft treaty on the reduction of strategic offensive weapons for signature by the time of our meeting next year. And if by this time a solution to the problem of sea-launched cruise missiles has not been found, then a serious difficulty will arise. Here you are at a great advantage. The American side must consider this question again in the context I mentioned.

Bush: That is a problem.

Gorbachev: We are not trying to achieve mirror symmetry. Each side has a choice; there is the situation of the country to consider, the different structures of the armed forces.

But in working toward a reduction of strategic offensive weapons, it is impossible to ignore sea-launched cruise missiles. The U.S. has a serious advantage in this area. Put yourselves in our position. Our Supreme Soviet will not agree to the ratification of a treaty if it avoids the problem of sea-launched cruise missiles.

I very much welcome your proposals on the environment. You can expect our experts to take an active part in the conference on environmental issues planned by the White House.

I am glad that you touched on the question of increasing student exchanges. We began this good work during Reagan's presidency. For young people it is easier to find a common language. And I am sure that they will make a contribution toward the positive development of Soviet–American relations.

In summary, I would like once again to emphasize that I am happy with the steps that you outlined here. The Soviet–American dialogue is gaining a certain momentum. And to give it a new breath, new efforts and new steps will be necessary. [...]

RECORD OF CONVERSATION BETWEEN GENERAL SECRETARY MIKHAIL
GORBACHEV AND PRESIDENT GEORGE BUSH (ONE-ON-ONE) DECEMBER 2, 1989

Gorbachev: In our confidential conversation, I would like to raise three issues:

First, the issue of Central America, primarily Cuba. Mr. President, perhaps you remember that after my visit to Cuba I wrote a letter to you. My talks there were not simple. I must admit that Castro expressed a certain concern regarding our course. We clarified a number of issues for him, and in general everything ended well. Among other things, we said to him: What we are doing in our country is dictated by our needs. What you are doing in your country is your business; we are not interfering with it.

In a one-on-one conversation, Castro essentially asked for our assistance with the normalization of relations with the U.S. Recently the chief of staff of the Cuban Air Force visited the Soviet Union. He talked with [officials] at the Defense Ministry of the USSR, as well as with Marshal Akhromeyev. And he confidentially repeated this request. I am confiding it to you in a one-on-one conversation and hope that this will remain between us. Otherwise Castro's reaction may be rather strong.

Bush: Certainly. I am not going to put you in an embarrassing situation. There cannot be leaks from my side. I understand how delicate this matter is for you.

Gorbachev: Perhaps we should think about some kind of mechanism to begin contacts on this issue. We are ready to participate, but perhaps it will be unnecessary. It is up to you to decide. We are ready to assist you in starting the dialogue, but it is certainly your business, and I could only ask you to think about it.

It seems to me that Castro understands how much the world has been changing. I felt it in my conversation with him. But he has a remarkably strong sense of self-esteem and independence.

Bush: Could you please repeat verbatim what he told you.

Gorbachev: His words were the following: During your contacts with the president, we request that you find the ways and means to convey Cuba's interest in normalizing relations with the United States. That is what I have done just now.

Bush: I would like, so to speak, to show you all my cards on Central America and on Cuba. If we take our NATO allies, including Thatcher, Kohl, Mitterrand, in general they do not care about Central America. Of course, they say good words about democratization and free elections, but they have no vital interests in what is going on there. The same concerns the "left flank" of the American body politic. However, young fledgling democracies to the south of the Rio Grande, as well as the overwhelming majority of American people, take this issue very close to heart.

We see also that, compared to your movement forward, Castro looks like an anchor which makes this movement more difficult. This man is clearly out of step with the changes and processes that have enveloped the Soviet Union, Eastern Europe and our hemisphere. Democratic changes are alien to him.

The leaders of Latin American countries, of course, avoid criticizing other Latin Americans in the United Nations. Therefore I was surprised when Costa Rican President Oscar Arias pointed out that Castro was now in complete isolation. Castro poses yet another grave problem. I am talking about many Cubans who have been expelled from Cuba and whose relatives in Cuba are being persecuted. Many such Cubans tend to live in southern Florida, and there passions run high against this man who is considered to be the worst dictator.

Castro sounded us out before; however, he never followed through with any signs of readiness to change his behavior.

Now, about Nicaragua. You said that the Sandinistas are not real Marxists. Earlier I had a different opinion, but today I would tend to agree. Nevertheless, they still export revolution. I am deeply convinced that the "Cessna" episode was not just an accident. Whatever they say to you, they methodically transfer arms—here it does not matter from what sources—for the FMLN. I am concerned that now a new shipment of helicopters from the Soviet Union to Nicaragua is being delivered, although I do not doubt Mr. Shevardnadze's declaration regarding the missiles. Indeed they could get them from other sources.

Gorbachev: Your weapons are also in the region.

Bush: This is possible. We should look for a way to remove this source of tension in our relations. We see holding free elections under appropriate monitoring as such a way.

Gorbachev: I agree.

Bush: Today both of us should hope and pray that free elections will really take place and that [Daniel] Ortega, if he is not elected, will not try to cling to power somehow with the help of the army. If there are really free elections certified by a group of foreign observers, then the United States will accept their results and will in no way attempt to influence or sabotage their outcome.

There is another malignant issue in Latin America; I would say an open wound. I am speaking of Panama. I must tell you that nobody in the United States believes that the Soviet Union might have a stake in Noriega's success. For us he poses a terrible problem. By the way, I inquired of our attorney general how sound the incriminating evidence against Noriega is.

To tell you frankly, I would be ready to look for a way to give him a chance to leave without losing face, to alleviate the problem somehow. I am telling you this, of course, in confidence. However, I received a response that the evidence against him is very convincing and, considering how acute the issue of drugs in the United States is, we cannot simply dispose of an official indictment of Noriega.

Gorbachev: I would like you, Mr. President, to know how the Soviet Union perceives some of your administration's steps with regard to such countries as, for instance, Panama, Colombia and, most recently, the Philippines. In the Soviet Union people ask: The fact that these are sovereign countries—is this not a barrier for the United States? Why does the U.S. arrange a trial, reach a verdict and carry it out by itself?

Bush: What do you have in mind when you include Colombia?

Gorbachev: I have in mind the use of force against the drug business.

Bush: Now, we do not carry out any military operations. But you must have no doubt that when we are asked to help a democratically elected government in its struggle against the drug-mafia, we will do it. But President [Virgilio] Barco is a very courageous man and he will not ask us for it.

As for the Philippines, your reaction surprised me. President [Corazon] Aquino was elected democratically, and now she is being challenged by a group from the military led by Colonel [Gregorio] Honasan. She asked for aerial cover for her palace, which was under threat of bombardment. It seems to me this should not have caused problems for the Soviet Union. And the scale of assistance was not that large. If this creates problems for the Soviet Union, then at least it is good that you mentioned it. Otherwise, it would never have occurred to me. In any case, it is not my wish that such minimal assistance cause difficulties in our relations with the Soviet Union.

Gorbachev: Some are beginning to speak about the "Bush Doctrine" that is replacing the "Brezhnev Doctrine."

Bush: Do they really say so with regard to the Philippines? I simply cannot understand this. We are talking about the legitimate elected leader. She is asking for help against an insolent colonel.

Gorbachev: I agree. However, I think one can explain such a reaction in the context of the current situation. Just take a look; Europe is changing;

governments are falling—governments that were also elected on a legitimate basis. One wonders if during this power struggle someone were to ask the Soviet Union to intervene, what should we do? Should we follow the example of President Bush?

Bush: I see.

Gorbachev: Sometimes I hear that in the current situation we are not fulfilling our mission with regard to our friends. I always respond in such cases: first, nobody asked us to help; second, the changes are proceeding according to the Constitution.

Bush: I would say more—that it is thanks to you that they are proceeding peacefully. But there is a big difference between this and a colonel who intends to overthrow Aquino.

The whole thing is that changes should come about peacefully. President Aquino is the very symbol of peaceful change in the Philippines. But I can see how some people in the Soviet Union might have a different reaction.

Gorbachev: I understand you. We stand for peaceful change; we do not want to interfere, and we are not interfering in the processes that are taking place. Let the people themselves decide their future, without external interference. But, you see, such colonels, such people can pop up in any country.

Bush: I do not want to sound like an old, bad record, but let me repeat: public opinion in the U.S. supports you, firmly supports *perestroika* as well as your role in the pluralist processes in Eastern Europe: a role that cannot be reduced merely to restraint, but also is the catalyst for change. But in the eyes of our people, your continuing assistance to Fidel Castro causes you serious damage. I should be frank: it is simply incomprehensible. He is opposed to your course.

It would be nice if you could also find a way to terminate this extremely expensive outpouring of assistance that gives nothing back to you. These billions of dollars you could spend with great benefit for yourself, while removing this serious element of friction in Soviet–American relations.

Yet, even at the risk of contradicting myself, I would say: all this testifies to the fact that Castro is out of step with you and, therefore, he is not your puppet. People understand this. Well, in any case, it would be very good to find a way to halt assistance to Cuba and to certain forces in Central America so that we do not stand divided on such issues as Panama, Nicaragua, and Cuba.

Positive changes are taking place now in Chile, in other countries of Latin America. And this is good not only for the United States, but also for democracy and freedom of choice. Against this background Cuba and Nicaragua stand out like alien bodies, and, besides, they stand in the way of Soviet–American mutual understanding.

Gorbachev: The Soviet Union has no plans with regard to spheres of influence in Latin America. This was and will continue to be the case. This continent is now in motion. You know it better than I do. I agree with you: the general trend is positive, democratic; dictatorships give way to democratic forms, although these are young, newly formed democracies with the heavy burden of the past, and their road will be a difficult one. We sympathize with these processes. We do not intend to interfere with what is happening.

As to Cuba, we have certain established relations with it; they go back to a certain period of history characterized by economic blockades, etc. Now we would like gradually to transfer our economic relations to a normal track. One should not forget that Cuba is a sovereign country with its own government, its own ambitions and perceptions. It is not up to us to teach Cuba. Let them do what they want. [...]

Gorbachev: I would like to say a few words about reactions and behavior in connection with the events in Eastern Europe. First of all, I would like to say that the vector of these changes in Eastern Europe and the Soviet Union is bringing us closer to each other, and this is the main thing. But there is an important point. I cannot accept it when some American politicians say that the process of overcoming the split in Europe should be based on Western values. It seems that earlier we were blamed for the "export of revolution," and now they speak about the export of American values. I believe this goes against the spirit of today's changes; it may complicate the processes that are taking place. I wanted to share that with you, although I know that your position is different.

With regard to the "German Question." We have the impression that Mr. Kohl fusses and bustles around too much. He does not act seriously and responsibly. We are afraid that the topic of reunification may be exploited for electoral gain, that it will not be strategic factors but the mood of the moment that will take the upper hand. By the way, opinions in the FRG vary on this issue, both inside the governing coalition and between the coalition and the Social Democrats. It is important for both of us to convey to everyone that certain actions may cause damage to constructive processes. Moreover, they may put in question very important and serious issues, including trust in the government of the FRG.

So what would happen? Would a unified Germany be neutral, not a member of any military-political alliances, or would it be a member of NATO? I believe we should let everyone understand that it is still too early to discuss either of these options. Let the process take its course without artificial acceleration.

None of us is responsible for the division of Germany. History occurred this way. Let history continue to decide on this issue in the future. It seems to me we have developed an understanding in this regard.

Bush: I believe that in his actions Helmut Kohl was greatly influenced by an emotional reaction to events. The same concerns Genscher. True, the 10-point program does have a flavor of electoral political considerations. But we should not overlook the wave of emotions there. Kohl knows that some Western allies who pay lip service to reunification when the people of Germany support it are [actually] quite upset by the prospect.

Gorbachev: Yes, I know about that. And Kohl was informed about this viewpoint. But unlike you and your allies, I am speaking openly. There are two German states; this is the way history happened. Let history decide how the process will develop and what it will lead to in the context of a new Europe and a new

634

world. Kohl declared repeatedly that he understands his responsibility and that he will abide by the understandings we reached in Bonn. In general, this is an issue where we should act with maximum consideration to avoid hurting the chances that have opened up.

Bush: I agree. We will not take any rash steps; we will not try to accelerate the outcome of the debate on reunification. When you speak to Kohl, you will find that he is in agreement with my approach. And if his public declarations often contradict this, one should take into account the specifics of the political equation and the emotional aspects, especially the latter. They speak about this topic with tears in their eyes.

Gorbachev: I would like to stress that we view positively the change that created these possibilities for normal contacts, broader cooperation and trade between the two German states.

Bush: As strange as it may seem, on this issue you are in the same boat with our NATO allies. Most of the conservative ones among them welcome your approach. At the same time they have to think beyond the time when notions of the FRG and the GDR are history. I would tread cautiously on this issue. If our Democrats criticize my timidity, let them do it. I do not intend to jump up onto the Wall because too much is at stake on this issue.

Gorbachev: Well, jumping on the Wall is not a good activity for a president (Laughter).

Bush: If Bush and Gorbachev can express satisfaction about the changes, it will be great. But I will not be tempted to take actions that, while they might look attractive, could lead to dangerous consequences.

Gorbachev: Correct. The times we live in are not only promising, but also demanding.

Bush: I hope we will have another chance, today or tomorrow, to speak in confidence on one or two other issues.

Gorbachev: I have one such issue. It is Afghanistan. Today you skillfully dodged it. At another time I said to your predecessor that Afghanistan is a testing ground that will show whether our two countries can resolve even the most difficult issues. I believe we should discuss it.

Bush: I would say that today this issue is more important for you, not for us. I must admit that some time ago I was wrong in my forecast of what would happen after the pullout of your troops. I am ready to discuss this issue.

From my side I would suggest discussing one issue concerning the domestic affairs of the USSR. It could be discussed at the plenary meeting or in a one-on-one conversation. And, if you object, we may not discuss it at all. But I would like to have the clearest understanding of your approach to the Baltics. No mistakes should be made there. I believe it would be preferable to talk about this issue confidentially, since I would very much like to understand the essence of your thinking on this extremely complicated issue.

Gorbachev: We shall discuss this issue.

THIRD MEETING BETWEEN GORBACHEV AND BUSH (PLENARY SESSION),
DECEMBER 3, 1989.

Gorbachev: [...] I will start off by saying that we are pleased with the work that was done yesterday, but I believe there is a possibility for advancing even further. If you do not object, I would like to start first. Nevertheless, today I am your guest. [...]

Bush: I like "my ship" very much.

Seriously, we would like to express deep gratitude for the excellent opportunity extended to our delegation to work on the Soviet liner. Although the press is putting pressure on me right now, bombarding me with questions about our shortening the talks yesterday, I believe the changes in the program affected the content of our discussion substantially. For my part, I consider our discussion to have been very good and productive. Actually, we essentially continued the talks at breakfast.

Gorbachev: Yes, we have made a calculation and it turns out that the discussions lasted over five hours.

Before we begin discussing fundamental issues, I want to make one suggestion to you of an organizational nature. Why don't we hold a joint press conference? I think that there would be great positive symbolism in this.

Bush: That is a good idea. In principle I agree. Only I am afraid that our American journalists might think that I am avoiding their questions, since I did not agree to a separate press conference.

Maybe we can arrange a press conference in several parts. First we will speak to the journalists together, and then I will answer questions on my own.

Gorbachev: I also planned to meet with Soviet television after our joint press conference. So that is fine with me.

Bush: Excellent. So it is decided.

Gorbachev: Mr. President, yesterday I responded very briefly to the views you expressed on the military-political questions. Today it is our turn. I assume that our positions in this area are of great interest to you as well. I am revising my statement to take into account yesterday's exchange of opinions.

Even though this is only an informal meeting, we are meeting like this for the first time, and I would like to begin with a few statements on matters of principle.

First and foremost, the new U.S. president must know that the Soviet Union will not under any circumstances initiate a war. This is so important that I wanted to repeat the announcement to you personally. Moreover, the USSR is prepared to cease considering the U.S. as an enemy and announce this openly. We are open to cooperation with America, including cooperation in the military sphere. That is the first thing.

Secondly. We support joint efforts for providing mutual security. The Soviet leadership is dedicated to continuing the disarmament process in all aspects. We consider it essential and urgent to overcome the limitations of the arms race and prevent the creation of new exotic types of weapons.

636

In passing, I will note that we welcome the process of cooperation that has begun between our military leaders. In particular, we are grateful for the opportunity provided to the Soviet minister of defense to become familiar with the U.S. armed forces.

One more thought on a matter of principle. We have adopted a defensive [military] doctrine. We made great efforts to explain to you exactly what this was. Our armed forces are already involved in serious reforms. The structure of the military grouping in Eastern Europe is becoming defensive: the divisions now have fewer tanks, and they are removing ferrying equipment. And air force deployments are changing; aviation attack forces are reverting to the second echelon, and fighter aircraft, that is, defensive aviation forces, are moving to the front line.

We are not making a secret of our plans for a *perestroika* in the armed forces. The Soviet military is prepared at any time to meet with its American colleagues, to provide essential information, and to discuss questions that arise.

But [new] questions also arise in return. While the Soviet Union has approved and implemented a purely defensive doctrine, the U.S continues to be guided by a rapid reaction strategy that was adopted over 20 years ago. That could formerly have been justified somehow. But now, when on the military-political level it is recognized that the threats formerly emanating from the Warsaw Treaty no longer exist, we naturally pose the question: why is the U.S. being so slow in enacting *perestroika* within its own armed forces? I have familiarized myself with the voluminous—around 60-page—Brussels statement. And, unfortunately, I found that there is no progress yet to be found on the part of NATO in altering its policy at the doctrinal level in this most important area.

The next question of principle. To some degree we touched on this already when we looked at the dynamic of the negotiating process. However, I want to return to this problem and single out one very important point.

You and I have admitted that as a result of the arms race truly unimaginable military power arose on both sides. We have come to the same conclusion that such a situation is fraught with catastrophe. An extremely important negotiating process was initiated, at the forefront of which were questions about nuclear arms reductions.

Bush: Excuse me for interrupting you, but I would like in this context to thank you for the deeply symbolic gift which you sent to me through Ambassador Dobrynin—a memento made out of disassembled missiles.

Gorbachev: Yes. The treaty on shorter-range and intermediate-range missiles became a historic watershed.

Generally speaking, the prospects that are opening up are not bad, and your comments yesterday convinced me that a promising basis for further progress has been established.

But what worries us? Until now, the negotiations have left out one of the three fundamental components of military power—naval forces. Both the previous and the current administration have reacted very emotionally whenever this question has been raised.

Meanwhile, there has been no infringement on American security. I want to announce with full responsibility that we are taking into account the interests of the U.S. Your country is a sea power with vitally important lines of communication conveyed via seas and oceans. Building up naval forces is for you both a historical tradition and an entire system in science and industry that is deeply integrated with economic interests. For that reason changing the approach here is not so easy. We understand this well, since we ourselves are experiencing similar difficulties in other areas of military build-up.

But what is to come of this? As early as the beginning of the 1950s we were literally encircled by a network of military bases. They consisted of more than 500,000 people, hundreds of fighter planes, and powerful naval forces. The U.S. has 15 aircraft carriers, approximately 1,500 fighter planes. And what immense forces are already deployed along our shores, or could be deployed at any moment? I am not even speaking about strategic submarines—at least those fall under the nuclear [strategic] offensive weapons negotiations. As a result of the Vienna talks, the level of military confrontation on land will be substantially lowered.

As I have already said, there are good prospects for concluding a treaty on the reduction of strategic offensive weapons [START]. Under these circumstances we have a right to expect that the threat to the Soviet Union from the sea will also be diminished.

Our ministers have already talked about this. I am taking the initiative upon myself and am officially raising the issue of starting negotiations on the problem of naval forces. As for how to begin them—here we are prepared to be flexible. In the beginning let it be through measures of trust, then a general reduction in the scale of naval activity. Then, when the situation becomes clear at the same time in Geneva and in Vienna, the time will come to deal in earnest with the question of reducing naval forces.

I will say in advance that we will adopt a realistic position. In particular, we are aware that the U.S. has other problems aside from Soviet military forces. But I would still like to stress once again with total certainty: just as European security is important to the U.S. and its allies, we are interested in the security of the seas and oceans.

Now, after delineating some of our fundamental approaches, I would like to comment on specific negotiating points. Since we agreed in advance not to get carried away in the details, I will, as you did yesterday, limit myself to the main issues.

I would like to make things clear between us, at least concerning three very important negotiating positions. First, our ministers and military leaders have clarified the interconnection between the future treaty on strategic offensive weapons and the ABM Treaty. Second, we consider it of utmost importance— and the initiative of E.A. Shevardnadze in Wyoming is evidence of this—to come to an agreement on the rules of accounting for heavy bombers and strategic air-launched cruise missiles. If we take the current American formula, then the U.S.

can claim as a result not 6,000 but around 8,500 warheads. We are not trying to bargain here; as a starting point we must simply accept the facts of the matter.

The third problem, which I already touched upon, are the strategic sea-launched cruise missiles.

There are, of course, other questions, but I am not going to speak about them now. If I understood the president correctly, we are setting for ourselves a common frame of reference, at least to resolve all remaining major questions by the time of the summit meeting in Washington, and to sign the START treaty itself by the end of next year.

One more important point. I understand that this point was "pushed" by Akhromeyev and Scowcroft. The USSR and U.S. navies have nuclear weapons, both strategic (submarine-launched ballistic missiles and sea-launched cruise missiles) and tactical (short-range sea-launched cruise missiles, nuclear torpedoes, and mines). The subject of the Geneva negotiations is the strategic nuclear component of the navy. We are left with tactical nuclear weapons. We propose that they be destroyed. For the moment this is an unofficial conversation, but I am making a proposal to begin official discussions. The Soviet Union is prepared to completely destroy the navy's tactical nuclear weapons on a mutual basis. Such a radical decision would immediately simplify the procedures for monitoring its implementation as well.

Now a few words about Vienna. On the whole I agree with the president's evaluation of the negotiations. However, even here three important problems remain. The first is the question of reducing not only arms but also military personnel. We proposed a reduction to 1,300,000 on each side, that is, by one million on each side. NATO representatives do not agree with this, but for some reason they do not name their own figures. I think that people will simply not understand us if we limit ourselves only to a reduction in weapons [when] groupings that are enormous in strength face each other in Europe.

The second issue relates to troop reductions on foreign territory. We propose limiting them to a ceiling of 300,000, but we are being drawn in another direction—to the reduction of only Soviet and American troops. But there are also English, French, Belgian, Dutch, and Canadian troops. In short, we are being offered an unfair solution.

Now on the problem of air forces. We have proposed for each alliance a level of 4,700 tactical theater aviation aircraft and a separate level for interceptor aircraft. But so far things here have also been progressing slowly. We suggest that special attention be paid to this issue at the next ministers' meeting.

Briefly, about the president's proposal on "open skies." We support it. We will participate in the Ottawa conference. We are ready for productive joint work with the U.S. As it seems to us, there are substantial reserves in this proposal. Let us have our ministers and military specialists discuss expanding the open status of the oceans and seas, space and land. [...]

To summarize what I have said, I wish to stress once again most strongly that we are disposed toward peaceful relations with the U.S. And based on that premise, we propose to transform the current military confrontation. That is what is most important. [...]

Gorbachev: Perhaps we should now end the discussion of military issues and talk about Europe, and reflect on how to react to the efforts regarding developing cooperation there?

Bush: That is an excellent idea. But allow me to add a few words. I am very pleased with the cooperation between our diplomatic departments, in military as well as in other areas. I believe that the channels for discussing military-political problems are now integrally supplementing the contacts initiated by Akhromeyev and [Chairman of the Joint Chiefs of Staff Adm. William] Crowe. Meetings between military specialists help matters greatly, and I hope that we will continue to develop this practice.

Gorbachev: That is exactly what we intend to do.

Bush: I will say frankly that our military has immense influence in NATO. I have just asked them to do an analysis of military expenditures in the U.S. and the West combined, and to present their recommendations. I think that in this crucial period, contacts between our military leaders are particularly significant.

Gorbachev: So we will have them meet more often. Would you like to go first in discussing European issues?

Bush: You are closer to Europe, but I would like to preface our conversation with a few comments.

First of all, I admit that we were shocked by the swiftness of the changes that unfolded. We regard highly your personal reaction and the reaction of the Soviet Union as a whole to these dynamic, and at the same time fundamental, changes.

Although we did not go into details, during yesterday's conversation we discussed eye-to-eye the problem of the reunification of Germany. I hope that you understand that you cannot expect us not to approve of German reunification. At the same time, we realize the extent to which this is a delicate, sensitive issue. We are trying to act with a certain reserve. I will phrase this thought a little differently: there is no desire on my part, nor among the representatives of my administration, to be in a position that would appear provocative. I emphasize that point.

Another example of our policy with respect to Eastern Europe: we sent a high-level delegation to Poland. It included my senior economic advisers, other representatives of the administration, businesspeople, union leaders, etc. They went there not to create difficulties but to explain to the Poles what mechanisms, in our opinion, are effective in the economic sphere.

I will not elaborate on each Eastern European country but will stress the thought that we understand very well the meaning of the section of the Helsinki Act governing national boundaries in Europe.

It stands to reason that I am ready to answer any of your questions. Personally, I am most interested in how you view the possibility of moving beyond the limits of the status quo.

Gorbachev: I do not agree that we are "closer to Europe." The USSR and the U.S. are equally integrated into European problems. We understand very well

640

your involvement in Europe. To look at the role of the U.S. in the Old World any differently is unrealistic, erroneous, and ultimately unconstructive. You must know this; it is our basic position.

Bush: That is not exactly what I meant. I just meant that historically we were not as close to Eastern Europe. Of course we are close—and will be close—to Europe; we are vitally interested and involved in NATO. The U.S. is, properly speaking, the leader of NATO.

I want to emphasize apart from this that you are catalyzing changes in Europe in a constructive way.

Gorbachev: I reaffirmed our fundamental position on the U.S.' role in Europe for a reason. There is too much speculation on this issue. It is aimed both at you and us. We should be absolutely clear on such important matters.

Now, on the changes in Europe. They are truly fundamental in nature. And not only in Eastern Europe—in Western Europe, too. I received representatives from the Trilateral Commission. After one of the conversations, Giscard d'Estaing, who was the speaker, addressed me and said in a very meaningful way: "Be ready to deal with a united federal state of Western Europe." By saying that, I think, he meant that when European integration reaches a qualitatively new level in 1992 it will be accompanied by a deep reorganization of political structures that will reach the federal level as well.

Therefore, all of Europe is on the move, and it is moving in the direction of something new. We also consider ourselves Europeans, and we associate this movement with the idea of a common European home. I would like to ask E.A. Shevardnadze and Secretary of State Baker to discuss this idea in more depth, because I think it is in the interests of both the USSR and the U.S.

We should act—and interact—in a particularly responsible and balanced way during this period when all of Europe is undergoing such dynamic changes.

Bush: I agree with you.

Gorbachev: After all, as the saying goes, every five years a gun goes off by itself. The fewer weapons, the less chance for an accidental catastrophe.

In the process, the security of the U.S. and its allies should not be less by even one millimeter than our own security.

Shevardnadze: Yesterday the president introduced an interesting proposal on chemical weapons. The secretary of state and I discussed this issue in great detail and very constructively. As is apparent, it deserves the strictest attention.

Gorbachev: I have already stated my first reaction. As I understand it, there are two areas in which we agree. As a common goal we have before us a global prohibition on chemical weapons, but we are moving in stages and in so doing are rejecting the modernization of binary weapons. This is a good basis for negotiations.

Bush: If you will allow me, I would like in this connection to raise the very critical question of the proliferation of chemical weapons outside our two countries. In particular we are concerned about Libya. I, of course, understand that you are not in a position to control the Libyan leader. However, we, as before, are convinced that the factory in Rabta is designated to produce chemical weapons.

We would like to work with you not only on this specific problem, but on the whole issue of preventing the spread of chemical weapons, which are still sometimes called the "poor man's atom bomb." The whole world has already seen the horrible consequences of the spread of chemical weapons during the Iran–Iraq conflict. Therefore, we propose reaching an agreement in this area, too. Personally, this issue worries me greatly.

Gorbachev: I want to assure you that our positions on this issue coincide. The Soviet Union is decisively against the spread of chemical weapons. I suggest that our ministers continue their discussion of this problem on the basis of directives set by us.

Bush: We must make immediate progress in this area. For now, you and I are morally vulnerable. Others do not want to move, or they are moving in the opposite direction, alleging that Soviet and American chemical arsenals will remain untouched.

Gorbachev: I am convinced that even here we can work together successfully. If the USSR and the U.S. begin to reduce their chemical arsenals gradually, we will have the moral right to argue even more strongly for nonproliferation of chemical weapons. [...]

Bush: I fully agree with these views.

Gorbachev: When I meet with political leaders from Eastern as well as Western Europe, I tell them all that this is an objective process that brings together countries across the continent. They are now looking for optimal variants for combining economics, technology, and various standards. [...]

What is the essence of this essentially consensus-based approach? We are convinced that we must work toward continuing and developing the Helsinki process, and by no means toward destroying what was created on the basis of it. After this, Helsinki II will be needed so that we can interpret the new situation and work out joint criteria and frameworks. It is understood that all the countries that signed the Helsinki Act, including of course the U.S. and Canada, must take part in this meeting.

Another important question: What to do with institutions created in another age? This also demands a balanced and responsible approach. Otherwise the current positive direction of the process of change might turn into its opposite, and lead to the undermining of stability. Existing instruments for supporting the balance must not be shattered but modified in accordance with the demands of the age. They must be utilized to strengthen security and stability and improve relations between states. Let NATO and the Warsaw Treaty Organization become to an even greater degree political, not just military, organizations; and let there be a change in their confrontational nature. It is good that our generals have already begun to grasp the spirit of the times, to visit each other, and to discuss the most complex questions.

I am certain that there are good prospects for cooperation in the CMEA. In the CMEA we are planning complex measures to ease entry into the structure of the world economy.

642

Our members of parliament are already cooperating—and are not doing a bad job: a "people's diplomacy" is developing. Such a comprehensive, positive atmosphere will protect all of us from unexpected and unpleasant surprises in the future.

I am under the impression that U.S. leaders are now quite actively advancing the idea of conquering the division of Europe on the basis of "Western values." If this premise is not solely for propaganda purposes, and they are intending to make it a basis for practical policy, then I will say bluntly that they are committing many follies. At one time in the West there was anxiety that the Soviet Union was planning to export revolution. But the aim of exporting "Western values" sounds similar.

I would put it this way: The times are now very complex and therefore particularly crucial. The fact that Eastern Europe is changing in the direction of greater openness, democracy, and rapprochement toward general human values, and creating mechanisms for compatibility and world economic progress, all this opens unprecedented possibilities for stepping up to a new level of relations; a step utilizing peaceful, calm means. Here it is very dangerous to force artificially or to push the processes taking place, all the more so for the purpose of satisfying certain unilateral interests.

The possibilities for European integration in the cultural and political spheres can be most varied, including those never before experienced. This will not take place painlessly. In some locations the situation will even become critical. And this is natural, for there are immense and varied social forces being drawn into the events.

I can make this judgment at least about the Soviet Union. Our country is a genuine conglomerate of peoples. They have various traditions and historical features of development. We are now fiercely discussing the future of the Soviet economy, or, for example, the question of what kinds of political institutions are needed under conditions of serious democratization. The task of transforming our federation has once again become critical. Recently I exchanged views on this issue with the Canadian prime minister. He is worried about Quebec, which for many years has been pursuing separatist goals. By the way, even at that time the thought occurred to me: why is the American Congress involved in the Baltic region and not in helping the Canadians resolve the Quebec problem?

Our own experience allows us to predict that the processes in Europe will not always go smoothly. In general, this has already been confirmed. But on the whole we are looking at things optimistically. When you think on the level of a simple reaction to events, it can make you shiver; some people might even begin to panic. But if you rise to the political, philosophical level, then everything falls into place. After all, if the nature of the process is a deep one, if it broaches fundamental matters involving millions of people, whole nationalities, then how can it flow smoothly and easily?

It is essential to proceed from an understanding of the immense importance of current changes. We must avoid any possible mistake and utilize the historical possibilities opening up for a rapprochement between East and West. Of course, differences will remain. We discussed that yesterday. Even in the Soviet Union—in one state—differences between republics and different regions are visible to the naked eye. I am certain that such differences exist in the U.S. as well. Even more so, they must be present on the vast European continent.

We are in favor of having a common understanding with the U.S. of the events taking place in our country. I have ascertained that today such a common understanding exists. But the process will continue to develop. And I want this understanding not to weaken but, on the contrary, to become even stronger.

I want us to cooperate continually on the basis of this understanding throughout this complex transitional period. Otherwise the process might fall apart, and we will all end up in a chaotic state, which will create a multitude of problems, will bring a halt to the changes, and will throw us back to an age of suspicion and mistrust.

I emphasize: great responsibility lies with the Soviet Union and the U.S. at this historic moment.

Bush: I want to clarify one point. You expressed concern about Western values. This would be understandable if our adherence to certain ideals caused difficulties in the USSR or in Eastern Europe, if it disturbed the progressive processes developing there. But we have never pursued such goals. Any discussion of Western values in NATO or in other Western organizations is completely natural and does not have a destructive purpose. After all, what are Western values? They are, if you will, free speech, openness, lively debates. In the economic realm—stimulus for progress, a free market. These values are not something new or of the moment; we have shared them for a long time with the Western Europeans; they unite the West. We welcome changes in the Soviet Union or in Poland, but by no means set them against Western values. So I want as best as possible to understand your point of view in order to avoid any misunderstanding.

Gorbachev: The main principle which we have adopted and which we are following in the framework of the new way of thinking is the right of each country to a free election, including the right to reexamine or change its original choice. This is very painful, but it is a fundamental right: the right to elect from within without interference. The U.S. adheres to a certain social and economic system, which the American people chose. So let other people decide for themselves which God, figuratively speaking, to worship.

For me it is important that the tendency toward renewal that has taken shape in Eastern and Western Europe is moving in the direction of rapprochement. The result will not be a copy of the Swedish, English or Soviet model. No. Something will turn out that will meet the demands of the current stage of development in human and European civilization.

I have just discovered that people have no fear of choosing between one system and another. They are searching for their own unique possibility, one that will provide them with the best standard of living. When this search flows freely, then there is only one thing left to say: good luck.

Bush: I do not think that we differ on this. We approve of self-determination and the debates that go along with it. I want you to interpret our approach in a positive light: Western values by no means signify the intrusion of our system on Romania, Czechoslovakia, or even the GDR.

Gorbachev: That is very important for us. Fundamental changes are happening, people are coming together. That is the most important thing. I see that on East European soil, ways of resolving problems that involve a different system—in the fields of economics, technology, etc.—are becoming established. That is natural.

If we share a common understanding, then all our practical actions undertaken under changing conditions will be appropriate and will come to acquire a positive character.

Baker: I would like to clarify our approach to self-determination. We agree that each country must have the right to free elections. But all this makes sense only when the people in the country are really in a position to choose freely. This also falls under the concept of "Western values," and by no means is it a right to thrust one's ways upon others.

Gorbachev: If someone is making a claim to the ultimate truth, they can expect disaster.

Bush: Absolutely right.

Baker: That is not exactly what I meant. Take, for example, the question of reunification of Germany, which is making both you and us nervous, as well as many Europeans. What are we advocating there? For reunification to happen based on the principles of openness, pluralism, and a free market. By no means do we want the reunification of Germany to reproduce the model of 1937–1945, which, evidently, is something that worries you. Germany of that time had nothing in common with Western values.

Gorbachev: A.N. Yakovlev is asking: Why are democracy, openness, [free] market "Western values?"

Bush: It was not always that way. You personally created a start for these changes directed toward democracy and openness. Today it is really much clearer than it was, say, 20 years ago that we share these values with you.

Gorbachev: There is no point in entering into propaganda battles.

Yakovlev: When you insist on "Western values," then "Eastern values" unavoidably appear, and "Southern values" …

Gorbachev: Exactly, and when that happens, ideological confrontations flare up again.

Bush: I understand and I agree. Let us try to avoid careless words and talk more about the content of these values. From the bottom of our hearts we welcome the changes that are taking place.

Gorbachev: That is very important. You see, as I said, the most important thing is that the changes lead to greater openness even in our relations with each other. We are beginning to become organically integrated, freeing ourselves from everything that divided us. What will this be called in the final analysis? I think it is a new level of relations. For that reason, for my part, I support your proposal; let us not conduct the discussion at the level of the Church. In history this has always led to religious wars.

Baker: Maybe, by way of compromise, we will say that this positive process is happening on the basis of "democratic values"? [...]

[*Source: Archive of the Gorbachev Foundation, Fond 1. Opis 1. Excerpts published in: M.S. Gorbachev,* Gody Trudnykh Reshenii, 1985–1992 *[Years of Difficult Decisions], (Moscow: Alfa-print, 1993), pp. 173–185. Translated by Vladislav Zubok.*]

Document No. 111: Memorandum of Conversation of George H.W. Bush, John Sununu, Brent Scowcroft, and Helmut Kohl

December 3, 1989

This conversation immediately after the Malta summit marks a turning point in the process of German unification, where President Bush effectively joins Chancellor Kohl's program—yet neither man expects unification to happen even in two years, much less by October 1990 when West and East would actually join . Bush gives Kohl a rundown on the conversation at Malta, describing Gorbachev as "tense" during talks about Germany and convinced that Kohl is moving too quickly: "I don't want to say he went 'ballistic' about it—he was just uneasy." Both men agree to reassure Gorbachev and "not do anything reckless." The key moment here comes when Kohl tells Bush the opposite, in effect, of what Bush told Gorbachev about inviolability of borders under the Helsinki Final Act. Kohl reminds the American that Helsinki actually allows borders to be "changed by peaceful means;" and this seems to be the first time Bush internalizes this possibility. At the same time, Kohl outlines three deliberate steps: first, a free government in the former GDR, second, "confederative structures, but with two independent states," and finally a "federation; that is a matter for the future and could be stretched out. But I cannot say that will never happen." Kohl scoffs at predictions that this will take only two years: "It is not possible; the economic imbalance is too great." He is using similar language to Gorbachev's—"the integration of Europe is a precondition for change in Eastern Europe to be effective"—but says that European resistance to unification really comes from envy over Germany's economic growth ("[f]rankly, 62 million prosperous Germans are difficult to tolerate—add 17 million more and they have big problems"). Bush asks about GDR opinions on unification, and neither he nor Kohl foresees the rush to reunification that would dominate the March 1990 elections there. As for European opinions, Kohl gives a candid summary, calling Mitterrand "wise" for disliking unification but not opposing it, while "Great Britain is rather reticent." Bush exclaims, "That is the understatement of the year"—referring to Thatcher's total opposition. Kohl says, "She thinks history is not just. Germany is so rich and Great Britain is struggling. They won a war but lost an empire and their economy." The German version of this conversation contains more detail than the American version below, including an interesting discussion of Gorbachev and values (12 lines in the German, but only a parenthetical comment below) where Bush says "the entire discussion about economic issues had an unreal aspect to it more because of ignorance on the Russian side rather than narrow-mindedness. For example, Gorbachev took offense to the expression 'Western values.'"

The President: We had no particular agenda for our meeting in Malta, and President Gorbachev was very accommodating on that point. Gorbachev displayed little emotion, unlike my first meeting with him. The most contentious issues were discussed without rancor—the issue of Soviet bloc arms supplies to the

647

Sandinistas, for example. This could have been a shouting match, but it was very calm.

We spent much time on the German question. Gorbachev said you are in too much of a hurry.

Chancellor Kohl: Can I tell you about what happened today in the GDR? Everyone has resigned. There is a crisis supposedly in just running the government. The people want to know about special privileges being given to the leaders. That is only the beginning. In Rostock people broke into a factory and found arms there. They will now want to find where the arms were going. (He then described Krenz' situation.)

I told Gorbachev it was not in my interest to invite things to get out of control. I think Modrow will be the new General Secretary. I will be in Hungary on December 18 to speak to the parliament, and then will go to meet the new leaders of the GDR.

We cannot pay the 100 marks for each visitor anymore. It already amounts to $1.8 billion. (He then discussed how East Germans were taking advantage of this program.) It will be phased out at the end of the year. We will help the GDR in several areas; such as the country's big shortage of doctors, environmental protection matters, and building-up the telephone system.

Gorbachev said to me that he would not stand in the way of free, open elections. He has abandoned the old leadership. The Hungarians will be OK in two or three years; but this is not so in Poland.

Let me say a word about my ten-point program. First, I want to thank you for your calm reception of the ideas.

I will not do anything reckless. I have not set up a timetable. We are part of Europe and will continue as part of the EC. I have always planned carefully with President Mitterrand.

The ten points are *not* an alternative to what we are doing in the West. Those actions are a precondition to the ten points. The integration of Europe is a precondition for change in Eastern Europe to be effective.

Yesterday some of my colleagues said the ten points were OK. Andreotti was most difficult. Everyone in Europe is afraid of two things: (1) that Germany would drift to the East—this is nonsense; (2) the *real* reason is that Germany is developing economically faster than my colleagues. Frankly, 62 million prosperous Germans are difficult to tolerate—add 17 million more and they have big problems.

Once the GDR has a *really* free government, we could set up confederative structures, but with two independent states. Phase III is federation; that is a matter for the future and could be stretched out. But I *cannot* say that will never happen.

The President: Gorbachev's chief problem is uncertainty. I don't want to say he went 'ballistic' about it—he was just uneasy. We need a formulation which doesn't scare him, but moves forward.

Chancellor Kohl: That is one reason I will do nothing to disturb the smooth running course. The CSCE [Helsinki Final Act] says the borders can be changed by peaceful means. I don't want Gorbachev to feel cornered. I need to meet with him. I don't want to create difficulties. Newspapers write such nonsense. Even Henry Kissinger mentions two years. It is not possible; the economic imbalance is too great.

The President: What is the attitude of the people in the GDR toward reunification? Are there difficulties between the parties in West Germany?

Chancellor Kohl: In the GDR they are badly informed about the issues. The East Germans need time to figure out what they really want. I need a period of quiet development. One year ago talk like this would have been crazy.

In the FRG most people and parties are supportive. The Greens see an opportunity. They want the army abolished and neutrality. They are against reunification. The SPD agreed last Tuesday. Now there is a feeling that this is Kohl's victory. The liberals are in favor of the program but are angry because it is *my* success. The economy is good: never have my people earned so much as now, but now they want entitlements rather than work.

The President: I think the answer is self-determination, and then let things work. Then avoid things which would make the situation impossible for Gorbachev.

Chancellor Kohl: Did he talk about internal developments?

The President: Oh yes. But that was very discouraging. (They then discussed how little Gorbachev knows about Western values.)

Chancellor Kohl: We are helping Hungary and Poland. We are carrying the whole burden in Europe. Where is everyone else but you and me? It's going to be a tough winter in Poland.

The President: And in the Soviet Union. Are any of the EC leaders opposed to your ten points?

Chancellor Kohl: Gonzalez was very positive. With respect to France, Mitterrand is wise. He knows it would be bad to oppose this. But he wants it to proceed moderately. On the future of the EC, Mitterrand also knows it will be difficult to maintain the current structure of the European Parliament. But he can remember, from the Fourth Republic, when the parliament was too strong. Now it is too weak. The attitude of the Benelux countries is fine. Great Britain is rather reticent.

The President: That is the understatement of the year.

Chancellor Kohl: Switzerland and Austria are OK.

The President: Don't the Dutch still harbor resentments from the Hitler period?

Chancellor Kohl: Yes, very much so. The Nazis were very tough on the Netherlands. They were the worst Nazis from Vienna.

Thatcher says the European Parliament can have no power because Whitehall cannot yield a bit of sovereignty. Her ideas are simply pre-Churchill. She thinks the postwar era has not come to an end. She thinks history is not just. Germany is so rich and Great Britain is struggling. They won a war but lost an empire and their economy. She does the wrong thing. She should try to bind the Germans into the EC. (There was then a discussion of Thatcher and the EC, and of French pride.)

Did Gorbachev talk about arms control?

The President: Yes. (He described the discussions.)

Chancellor Kohl: Was there a discussion of the follow on to *Lance*?

The President: No. Did Cheney's comments here cause a stir?

Chancellor Kohl: No. Reagan had the reputation as a hardliner. Toward the end he changed—too quickly. Then you were elected, the Vice President to Ronald Reagan, and the groups under you just continued. Your visit last spring changed all that. Barbara helped that a lot.

These days now will be very important. Your leadership is essential and you will have every respect from me.

The President: (He elaborated further on the arms control discussions at Malta, mentioning agreement to a CFE Summit in 1990, START signed hopefully in 1990, and an agreement on chemical weapons—which Kohl especially hoped could be concluded in 1990 for electoral reasons.)

Chancellor Kohl: The schedule you outline would be fantastic. Let's work these things closely. If we can do something in CFE, chemicals, and START this would have a big impact on the Soviets and Eastern Europe. Nobody now believes that the East European troops would fight, so the numbers have changed dramatically.

The President: That is true. But I will still feel better when the Soviet divisions pull back.

The Chancellor: But that creates problems for Gorbachev.

[*Source: George Bush Presidential Library. Obtained through FOIA. On file at the National Security Archive.*]

650

Document No. 112: Record of Conversation between Mikhail Gorbachev and Petar Mladenov

December 5, 1989

This record of conversation covers the first meeting between Gorbachev and the new party secretary in Bulgaria, Petar Mladenov, who replaced the longest-serving East European communist leader, Todor Zhivkov, the day after the Berlin Wall fell (termed "the November 10 changes"). Gorbachev applauds Mladenov's "brave protest" in a "resignation letter" that provided a "Mladenov spark"—a reference to the latter's conflict with Zhivkov in October, when the Bulgarian boss refused the resignation and insisted that the then-foreign minister continue his travel to China, transiting Moscow twice on the way. Outside observers assumed Moscow's hand in the changes, but Gorbachev here repeats his non-interference line, although he does say the Kremlin refused Zhivkov's appeal for a visit in the middle of the crisis. Mladenov provides an insider's description of how decrepit the Bulgarian party process had become under Zhivkov, and Gorbachev (without a trace of irony) decries Politburo sessions that turn into monologues.

Gorbachev: Welcome. I am, of course, interested in your opinion on the prospects for developments in Bulgaria.

Mladenov: Overall, we are in control of events in the country. The people received the November 10 changes in the country's leadership with enthusiastic support. Once again we are convinced that even though we have been in politics practically our entire lives, we still do not always know the people's true attitudes.

Except for a small segment of the population, everyone is keenly in favor of *perestroika* in Bulgaria. Right now in our country there is an extremely high level of interest in Soviet *perestroika*.

It has now become absolutely clear to everyone that Bulgaria is ripe for real changes. After all, for a number of years the socio-political climate in the country has been deteriorating. The party was losing its authority; it became more and more noticeable that the words and actions of the leadership did not agree. The Central Committee was turned into a talk shop: the leader was praised during sessions, people said how wise he was, they supported his every speech and voted in unison. But the real, truly topical problems were never discussed at the CC Plenums, and the Politburo was not a collective organ. I was a part of it for 15 years and we never discussed or resolved the most important questions.

The moral climate of the country was seriously deteriorating. Everybody saw that the leader was unfairly promoting his relatives. Some other unbecoming acts—to put it nicely—were also committed. That is why the people saw the No-

651

vember changes as an aspiration to put an end to all the negative experiences that we have accumulated over the years.

Gorbachev: I heard that your Politburo met irregularly, and the rare sessions that you did hold all turned into a monologue.

Mladenov: Usually at the Politburo new theses and concepts would be presented, but there was almost no discussion of practical matters. Now we will have to say goodbye to a number of people who contributed to maintaining that style of work.

Gorbachev: We appreciate your courage and understand what it took for you to write a resignation letter, which many perceived to be a brave protest. Somebody had to start, and you took that responsibility upon yourself. It is very important that you developed a positive line. It's a sign of the fact that in the party and in society there is a potential for political wisdom and civil well-being. We rejected Zhivkov's request to come to Moscow with the excuse of seeking advice.

Our principal position was that the Bulgarians have to take care of their issues themselves. And that in no way means that we do not care about Bulgarian affairs. Nothing of the sort! Bulgaria is, of course, very close to us. We know our friends well, but we cannot interfere in their internal affairs and tamper with the ripening of the situation. And the "Mladenov spark," so to speak, which started the movement toward change, only showed that the situation had objectively become ripe, and even over-ripened. [...]

[*Source:* Mikhail Gorbachev: Zhizn' i reformy *[Mikhail Gorbachev: Life and Reforms], Novosti: 1995, pp. 371–373. Translated by Anna Melyakova.*]

652

Document No. 113: Record of Conversation between Mikhail Gorbachev and Hans Dietrich Genscher

December 5, 1989

A week has passed since Helmut Kohl announced his "10 Points" in a Bundestag speech, and Gorbachev, unlike his demeanor regarding Germany at Malta, does go "ballistic" in this conversation. This is perhaps because he is receiving the German foreign minister, Hans Dietrich Genscher, who heads a separate political party from Kohl but participates in the coalition government, but more likely because Bush has apparently weighed in on Kohl's side, despite the cautious talk at Malta. Gorbachev angrily remarks, "Yesterday, Chancellor Kohl, without much thought, stated that President Bush supported the idea of a confederation. What is next? ... What will happen to existing agreements between us? ... I cannot call him [Kohl] a responsible and predictable politician." Gorbachev says he thought Kohl would at least consult with Moscow, but "[h]e probably already thinks that his music is playing—a march—and that he is already marching with it." From the Soviet view, the "10 Points" are "ultimatums" and "crude interference in the internal affairs of a sovereign state." Gorbachev is personally offended because "[j]udging from all this, you have prepared a funeral for the European process"—his own vision of the common European home. Genscher tries to defend the "10 Points" as requiring "no conditions" and representing "just suggestions," and that "the GDR should decide whether they are suitable or not." Gorbachev rebukes Genscher for becoming Kohl's "defense attorney" and raises the rhetorical attack to the point of making a reference to the Nazi era: "You have to remember what mindless politics has led to in the past." Genscher responds, "We are aware of our historical mistakes, and we are not going to repeat them. The processes that are going on now in the GDR and in the FRG do not deserve such harsh judgment." (Shevardnadze is even more blunt with his comparisons, mentioning Hitler by name.) As a final debating point, Gorbachev notes that Genscher himself only heard about the 10 Points for the first time in the Bundestag speech. The German confirms it—"Yes, that is true"—but then deftly slips in a rejoinder to the new champion of non-interference that "this is our internal affair." Gorbachev replies, "You can see that your internal affair is making everybody concerned."

Gorbachev: I have to tell you directly—I cannot understand Federal Chancellor Kohl who spoke about his famous 10 points concerning the FRG's intentions regarding the GDR. It must be stated directly that those are ultimatums that are being imposed on an independent and sovereign German state. By the way, even though he only mentioned the GDR, what the chancellor said concerns us all.

First of all, these 10 points appeared after we had a constructive and positive exchange of opinions, after we had reached agreement on several fundamental issues. You would think that he should be presenting that kind of document only after relevant consultations with partners. Or does the federal chancellor think that he does not need them anymore? He probably already thinks that his music is playing—a march—and that he is already marching with it. I do not think such steps will contribute to the strengthening of trust and mutual understanding, or contribute to fulfilling our agreements with life. What kind of "Europe building" can one talk about if they act that way?

You know that I spoke with Chancellor Kohl on the telephone. I told him that the GDR was a factor in not only European but world politics, and that both East and West would carefully follow everything that is happening there. Kohl agreed with that; he assured me that the FRG did not want destabilization in the GDR, and that they would act in a balanced way. However, his practical steps deviate from his assurances.

I told Kohl that the GDR is an important partner and ally of the Soviet Union. We are also interested in developing our relations with the FRG. This is a triangle that plays a special role in European and global developments. Everything has to be carefully balanced in this triangle. And now he is issuing an ultimatum. He is giving directions for what road the GDR should take, what structures they should create. The FRG leadership is simply bursting with a desire to command, and let me assure you—everybody can feel it.

Maybe it is Bush who is heating the situation up? Still, you have to think through your moves two or three or five steps ahead, to foresee their consequences.

[...] Yesterday, Chancellor Kohl, without much thought, stated that President Bush supported the idea of confederation. What is next? What does a confederation mean? Confederation presupposes a common defense, and a common foreign policy. Where will the FRG find itself then, in NATO or in the Warsaw Treaty? Or maybe it will become neutral? And what would NATO mean without the FRG? In the end, what will come next? Did you think about everything? What will happen to existing agreements between us? Do you call this politics?

Shevardnadze: Today you apply this style to the GDR, tomorrow you might apply it to Poland, Czechoslovakia, and then to Austria.

Gorbachev: With all responsibility I can tell you that you have not demonstrated the best style of politics; you are not differentiating your position from Kohl's. In any case, I cannot call him a responsible and predictable politician.

Genscher: [...] On the eve of my trip to Moscow I spoke with Chancellor Kohl in Brussels. His statement of the 10 points does not represent a schedule of urgent measures, it defines the long-term perspective. The GDR will decide on its own whether to respond to his proposal.

We are interested in the internal stability of the GDR. We believe that by his statement the federal chancellor contributed to the strengthening of that stability. There were no directives or ultimatums in that statement. We know that neither Poland nor Hungary has that impression. These 10 points, and our policy, are supported by all parties represented in the Bundestag, including the SPD.

At the same time, we dissociate ourselves from the internal problems of the GDR, for which the FRG bears no responsibility.

654

Gorbachev: I could not even anticipate that you would assume the role of Federal Chancellor Kohl's defense attorney. Let us take the third point of his statement. He spoke for the "comprehensive expansion of our assistance, and our cooperation, if the GDR makes the necessary basic changes in its political and economic system," and if the state leadership of the GDR reaches agreements with "opposition groups," and if the GDR follows this course irreversibly. What do you call that except crude interference in the internal affairs of a sovereign state?

Shevardnadze: Even Hitler did not allow himself anything like that.

Gorbachev: More than that, Chancellor Kohl demands that the Socialist Unity Party of Germany give up its monopoly on power. He speaks about the need to abolish the "bureaucratic planned economy." Economic improvement, according to him, can only be achieved when the GDR opens its doors to Western investment, creates conditions for a market economy, and ensures opportunities for private enterprise.

I think that the GDR has to undertake fundamental reforms. However, this is their internal affair. Chancellor Kohl, meanwhile, is treating the citizens of the GDR, in essence, like his own subjects. This is simply blatant revanchism, which leaves nothing of his positive assurances, and puts all the agreements we have achieved in question. [...]

Genscher: I would like to draw your attention to point 2, where it is said that the federal government of the FRG would like to expand cooperation with the GDR on the basis of equality in all spheres.

Gorbachev: Stop defending it, Mr. Genscher. Point 2 is completely devalued by point 3. In tsarist Russia, when a political prisoner was released he was told that he could live wherever he chooses except in 18 counties—and there were only 18 counties in Russia. Where do you think he could live? It is the same with this statement.

Genscher: That is not so. [...]

Gorbachev: The Chancellor's statement is a political blunder. We cannot just let it go unnoticed. We are not inclined to play diplomacy with you. If you want to cooperate with us, we are ready. If not, we are going to draw political conclusions. I am asking you to take what I have just said seriously.

Genscher: I am speaking seriously. There are no conditions in the 10 points. These are just suggestions, and the GDR should decide whether they are suitable or not.

Gorbachev: Then it is even more of an ultimatum. Judging from all this, you have prepared a funeral for the European process, especially in this form.

Genscher: That is not so. I am in favor of speaking openly. You should not interpret point 2 and point 3 in that way. I would not want to be accused of a lack of good will. The FRG does not want to interfere in anybody's internal affairs. [...]

Gorbachev: We think that the changes in the GDR are good, but you should not interfere with all kinds of instructions and advice.

655

Genscher: We respect these changes.

Gorbachev: I am speaking about the FRG now. There is some confusion in [people's] minds there, a bustle. One can feel that some people there are already bursting from what is going on. Some people are beginning to lose their minds, and they do not see anything around themselves. Politics without brains is not politics. This way you may spoil everything that we have created together. The Germans are emotional people, but you are also philosophers. You have to remember what mindless politics has led to in the past.

Genscher: We are aware of our historical mistakes, and we are not going to repeat them. The processes that are going on now in the GDR and in the FRG do not deserve such harsh judgment. [...]

Gorbachev: In short, you want to say that you are acting correctly and responsibly. That is my conclusion. I would like to emphasize once more that we assign special importance to what is going on, and that we will monitor everything very carefully.

Genscher: Yes, the policy of the federal government is responsible and predictable; otherwise, I would have nothing to say.

Gorbachev: I am not speaking now about your overall policy, only about the 10 points. You are forgetting the past. Everybody can see that Chancellor Kohl is rushing, that he is artificially stimulating events, and by doing that he is undermining the European process that is being developed with such difficulty. How can he think that we are unable to render a dispassionate judgment about his behavior?

Genscher: I have already said that you should not dramatize the events. [...]

Gorbachev: [...] By the way, it seems to me, Mr. Genscher, that you only learned about his 10 points from the speech in the Bundestag.

Genscher: Yes, that is true, but this is our internal affair. We will deal with it ourselves.

Gorbachev: You can see that your internal affair is making everybody concerned. But the main thing is that we understand each other.

It seems to me that you are satisfied with what we are going to tell the press. Today we are still speaking like this. However, keep in mind that if some in your country do not come to their senses, then tomorrow we will make another statement.

Genscher: Let me assure you that we will take the most responsible approach. Please do not think that I do not mean what I am saying.

Gorbachev: Do not take everything I said personally, Mr. Genscher. You know that we feel differently about you than we do about others. We hope that you understood everything correctly. Thank you for the conversation.

[*Source: Archive of the Gorbachev Foundation, Fond 1. Opis 1. On file at the National Security Archive. Translated by Svetlana Savranskaya.*]

Document No. 114: Record of Conversation between Mikhail Gorbachev and François Mitterrand

December 6, 1989

Gorbachev finds the French president seemingly in complete agreement about Kohl, but not much help in doing anything specific to slow down the rush toward German unification. On the common European home idea, Mitterrand's language is music to Gorbachev's ears: "We should not change the order of the processes. First and foremost among them should be European integration, the evolution of Eastern Europe, and the all-European process." But, he adds, "Kohl's speech, his 10 points, has turned everything upside down." Yet, Mitterrand falls back on his treaty commitments with the FRG that make it "more difficult for me than maybe for others to deny the Germans the right to make mistakes." Gorbachev reports in detail on his conversation with Genscher (see previous document), but all the Frenchman can offer is moral support to Gorbachev for his "courage" in "reject[ing] established ideas inherited from the past. But you radiate calm, and you are even in a good mood." There is a hint, however, of the factor that would ultimately tip the balance toward unification, when Mitterrand asks about the response to the idea in East Germany. Gorbachev deludes himself that "more than half of the population of the GDR would like to preserve the existing character of their country, with changes in its political structure, of course ..." The March 1990 elections in the GDR would prove otherwise.

Gorbachev: I will tell you honestly—I am not satisfied with the results of this part of my conversation with Bush. Here is my conclusion. The Europeans should do the pioneer work in terms of making sense of the new world—of course with U.S. participation. But nonetheless, nothing will work without Europe. [...]

Gorbachev: I have a feeling that the U.S. is not completely open about their position, that they are not presenting it fully.

Mitterrand: That is true [...] The Americans are not telling the complete truth, including on the German issue. Nevertheless, I do not think that they are ready to take the position of changing European borders. [...]

I am speaking with you absolutely freely. We have special relations with the FRG. In 1963 De Gaulle and Adenauer signed an alliance treaty, and I am abiding by that treaty. That is why it is more difficult for me than maybe for others to deny the Germans the right to make mistakes. But I am being true to my duty—to preserve the balance in Europe.

We should not change the order of the processes. First and foremost among them should be European integration, the evolution of Eastern Europe, and the all-European process, the creation of a peaceful order in Europe. If the

United States participates in these processes, it would give all of us additional guarantees.

Kohl's speech, his 10 points, has turned everything upside down. He mixed all the factors together, he is rushing. I told Genscher about it, and he did not oppose my conclusions very much.

Gorbachev: That is interesting! But I will speak about that later. […]

Mitterrand: What exactly are you going to do next?

Gorbachev: First of all, we are going to continue the line of peaceful change. Let every country determine its direction on its own. We are convinced that there should be no external interference; the will of the people should not be misrepresented.

[…] You are right in saying that we should not only observe, but act. We need to trust every country, and to expand cooperation. […]

Gorbachev: […] We had a major conversation with Genscher. And it could not have been otherwise—for us, the German issue is a painful one. Our society reacted sharply to the chancellor's actions. And I told him directly—if you want to blow up, to destroy everything that we have achieved, then continue to act as you are. But then all the responsibility lies with you. Do not forget that even mid-level politicians should calculate their actions two or three steps ahead.

The chancellor spoke about a confederation of the GDR and the FRG. By the way, he said in Brussels that Bush supported the idea. I asked Genscher what a confederation means. Doesn't it mean a single foreign and defense policy? That is what is written in all the textbooks. But how can two German states work out this single policy? I asked what this new confederation would be a part of—NATO or the Warsaw Treaty? Or will it be neutral?

Then what will be left of NATO, I asked. Did you think about everything? Then I asked Genscher whether he knew about Kohl's 10 points before they were made public. Genscher admitted that he heard them for the first time in the Bundestag. Then I asked him whether he was going to behave that way in the future?

Mitterrand: You know, we, like Genscher, were not informed about Kohl's proposals beforehand.

Gorbachev: I asked: could you talk to him? What are all our agreements on consultations worth? Do you know what your behavior is called? Provincial politics. You are acting so crudely on such a universally sensitive issue.

Genscher was very confused. He assured me of his loyalty to the all-European process, reminded me of everything that he had personally done for its success. I told him that we knew him and valued him. But two questions still remain: why he assumed the role of Kohl's attorney, and whether he, Genscher, was prepared to reject everything that has been achieved in recent years with his help.

I said: it is your business to decide how you will act. It is within your authority. And it is within our authority to draw conclusions. I asked him to pass all this on to the chancellor.

Genscher tried to persuade me for a long time that we misunderstood Kohl's 10 points. And then he asked: how are we going to present our conversation to the press? I told him, let us say that we had an open and serious conversation. So far, we do not want to cast doubt over everything that we have done these past years. And I stressed "so far." But we will monitor future developments very carefully, because the FRG's behavior resembles that of an elephant in a china shop. [...]

Mitterrand: Is there any serious response to the idea of unification among the people of the GDR?

Gorbachev: Yes, there is a response. But you know, more than half of the population of the GDR would like to preserve the existing character of their country, with changes in its political structure, of course, with democratization, etc. They see relations between the GDR and the FRG as relations between two sovereign states. [GDR leader Hans] Modrow is speaking about a new agreement-based community.

Mitterrand: I will visit the GDR regardless of the developments. But I will stress that it would be a state visit.

Gorbachev: I think that would emphasize the natural character of the processes unfolding in the GDR. [...]

Mitterrand: You are working under a lot of stress. You are loyal to your heritage, and at the same time, you continue to deepen your revolution.

Gorbachev: We are trying to do what is necessary for our country, for the entire world, and for the socialist idea, to which we both are devoted. In this respect, our contribution should also be decisive.

Mitterrand: I appreciate your courage in the struggle for the goals that you have set. One has to be brave to reject established ideas inherited from the past. But you radiate calm, and you are even in a good mood. This gives us hope.

Gorbachev: I have made my choice.

[*Source: Archive of the Gorbachev Foundation, Fond 1. Opis 1. On file at the National Security Archive. Translated by Svetlana Savranskaya.*]

Document No. 115: Cable from James Baker to U.S. Embassy Sofia

December 19, 1989

This document represents one of the few pieces of evidence available on an actual behind-the-scenes intervention by Soviet officials in the reform and revolution processes in Eastern Europe. Gorbachev himself would proclaim non-interference over and over, and would only go so far in encouraging the ouster of the old guard—as when he told a parable to the SED Politburo in Berlin (see Document No. 88) about miners in Donetsk whose old leaders could not pull the cart any more. But here the State Department tells the U.S. Embassy in Sofia about a conversation between a senior Soviet official and the assistant secretary of state for human rights, Richard Schifter, in which the Soviet credits Foreign Minister Shevardnadze for actively working to help Petar Mladenov oust Todor Zhivkov in Bulgaria (on November 10).

SUBJECT: SHEVARDNADZE'S ROLE IN ZHIVKOV'S OUSTER

1. Secret: Entire Text

2. In an informal conversation [line excised] told [Assistant Secretary of State for Human Rights Richard] Schifter that (A) Mladenov took a great personal risk in challenging Zhivkov and (B) Soviet Formin Shevardnadze intervened actively in support of Mladenov. [Excision, name] added that the matter was urgent enough for Shevardnadze to intervene quote without extensive consultation unquote.

3. [...] Baker

[*Source: U.S. Department of State, obtained through FOIA. On file at the National Security Archive.*]

660

Document No. 116: Four Soviet Foreign Ministry Documents regarding the Situation in Romania

December 20–25, 1989

The final document in this chronological sequence—a conversation between U.S. Ambassador Jack Matlock and Deputy Foreign Minister Ivan Aboimov on Christmas Eve 1989—is clearly the headline item of this group, which was declassified and published by the Russian Foreign Ministry in 1994 (with obvious public relations benefits in mind). But the whole sequence rewards attention for the evidence the documents provide on the Soviet role in Eastern Europe's 1989 revolutions, and specifically in the lone violent transition—the bloody ending of the Ceauşescu dictatorship in Romania.

The first document below, a note from Foreign Minister Shevardnadze to General Secretary Gorbachev, reports that Moscow is relying on Western telegraph services for news of Romania as of December 20. This is the day the Romanian army ceases its attacks on the mass demonstrations in Timişoara and the protesters proclaim it a liberated city; it is also five days after the first protests sought to protect dissident pastor László Tőkés, and three days after the Securitate (with the army) began shooting. This note suggests the KGB is providing little good information to the top leadership in Moscow, and, contrary to certain suspicions afterwards, probably is not conspiring to overthrow Ceauşescu. (The Yeltsin government, which released this document, would surely have declassified any material derogatory of Gorbachev and his pledges of non-intervention.)

Ceauşescu himself thinks Moscow is behind the troubles, as the second document relates: Romanian Ambassador Bukur calls on Deputy Foreign Minister Aboimov on December 21 with specific allegations from a Ceauşescu speech that the Timişoara protests were "allegedly prepared and organized with the consent of member-states of the Warsaw Treaty Organization" and that "interference in the internal affairs of the SRR [is] allegedly being prepared in the Soviet Union." The reference to WTO members points to Hungary, since the Transylvanian region had been part of Hungary until 1920, and the dissident Tőkés, himself of Hungarian descent, had spoken out for the rights of the Hungarian minority.

The third document shows exactly who has the best information in real time about events on the ground in Romania—Yugoslav diplomats, whose consulate in Timişoara and embassy in Bucharest are witnessing the events first-hand. Yugoslav Ambassador Veres notes succinctly that the causes of the uprising are "rooted in profound popular dissatisfaction with the economic situation in the country accumulated over [many] years, with low living standards, with the lack of basic food and consumer goods, and with the leadership's unwillingness to undertake at least some measures to democratize the political system."

The final document represents one of the most striking examples anywhere of American recognition of the end of the Cold War. After Ceauşescu flees Bucharest on December 22, the provisional government appeals for international support against continuing violence, and on December 23 French Foreign Minister Roland Dumas actually mentions the possibility of Soviet assistance. Secretary of State James Baker, set to appear on a major American television show on Sunday, December 24, and expecting questions about Romania, tasks his ambassador in Moscow (eight hours ahead of Washington time) to query the Soviets urgently about the situation there.

The key exchange between Matlock and Aboimov comes when the U.S. ambassador "hinted at an idea, apparently on instructions from Washington..." that "the military involvement of the Soviet Union in Romanian affairs might not be regarded in the context of 'the Brezhnev doctrine.'" The Soviet diplomat quickly and vehemently declines the invitation: "We stand against any interference in the domestic affairs of other states ... Thus, the American side may consider that 'the Brezhnev doctrine' is now theirs as our gift." This last phrase clearly refers to the American invasion of Panama which has just occurred on December 20, to remove the longtime U.S. intelligence asset and dictator, Manuel Noriega, and reveals the Soviet attitude toward Matlock's (and subsequently Baker's own) invitation as at best "stupid" (Shevardnadze's subsequent characterization), and at worst a provocation to put the Soviet Union on a par with the United States in Panama. The White House would disavow Baker's television statement, but that invitation, together with the Matlock–Aboimov exchange, stand as perhaps the most dramatic American expressions of changed attitudes marking the end of the Cold War.

To Comrade Gorbachev M.S.

Mikhail Sergeyevich:

Regarding the events in Romania in the last few days, we can still only judge on the basis of information from news agencies, primarily Western ones. This information is often contradictory and does not allow one to construct a true picture.

Our attempts to obtain the official version via Bucharest have produced no results. Today, December 20, the Romanian ambassador will be invited to the MFA USSR in order to elicit information from him on this issue.

Until we have complete and objective information, we should not, in our opinion, be in haste to issue a statement from the USSR Congress of People's Deputies. At best we could go no further than to instruct the Commission on Foreign Affairs [of the Congress' Supreme Soviet] to prepare a draft proposal on our possible reaction with all circumstances in mind.

E. Shevardnadze
December 20, 1989

* * *

Memorandum of conversation
with Ambassador of the SRR in the USSR I. BUKUR
December 21, 1989

I received I. Bukur at his request.

The ambassador recounted the address of N. Ceauşescu on Romanian radio and television on December 20, and handed over its complete text.

When I asked if the events in Timişoara involved human casualties and what the present situation was in that region, the ambassador responded that he possesses no information on this issue. He referred to the fact that the address of N. Ceauşescu also says nothing on this score.

I told the ambassador that during N. Ceauşescu's meeting with the Soviet chargé d'affaires in the SRR on December 20 [the former] expressed surprise that Soviet representatives made declarations on the events in Timişoara. Besides, during the meeting it was asserted [by Ceauşescu] that the Romanian side possesses information that the action in Timişoara was allegedly prepared and organized with the consent of member-states of the Warsaw Treaty Organization. Moreover, the actions against Romania were allegedly plotted within the framework of the Warsaw Treaty Organization.

According to our information, officials in Bucharest in conversation with ambassadors of the allied socialist states expressed the view concerning some kind of interference in the internal affairs of the SRR allegedly being prepared in the Soviet Union.

I must declare on behalf of our side that such assertions can only puzzle us; they have no foundation and do not correspond with reality.

Answering the ambassador's question as to whether my words reflected the official viewpoint of the Soviet government, I told him that so far I have no instructions to make any declarations on behalf of the Soviet government, but my words certainly reflect our official position, which is that the Soviet Union builds its relations with allied socialist states on the basis of equality, mutual respect and strict non-interference in domestic affairs. Considering the grave character of the statements by Romanian officials I cannot help tentatively expressing our attitude toward these statements. [...]

* * *

Record of conversation
with the Ambassador of the SFRY in the USSR, MILAN VERES
22 December 1989

I received M. Veres at his request.

He referred to instructions from the Union Secretariat on Foreign Affairs of the SFRY and shared available information on the events in Romania, corroborated by the General Consulate of the SFRY in Timişoara and by numerous Yugoslav citizens who have returned from the SRR. He also reported on Yugoslav evaluations of the developments in Romania.

The beginning of these dramatic developments could be traced to the events of December 15–16 in Timişoara where a large group of people protested the actions of the authorities with regard to the priest, L. Tőkés. This process grew into a huge demonstration by the population of the city against the existing order. According to the estimates of officials of the General Consulate of the SFRY, up to

100,000 people, including workers, university and school students, participated in the demonstration. Protest actions also took place in Arad, Brasov, and Cluj. Large contingents of militia and military were used against the demonstrators in Timişoara. According to the Yugoslavs, during those clashes several hundred people died, and according to certain unverified data the number of casualties exceeded 2,000. In the downtown area, shops, restaurants and cafes were destroyed, and many streetcars and automobiles were also burned. Timişoara is surrounded by troops, but protest actions continue in the city. Workers have seized factories and are threatening to blow them up if the authorities do not satisfy the people's demands. Officials of the General Consulate of the SFRY, the ambassador remarked, noticed that a number of soldiers and militiamen expressed their sympathies with the demonstrators. There were also slogans: "The Army will not shoot at students and school children."

The Yugoslav–Romanian border is practically sealed; its defenses are fortified by troops along its whole length, including check-points. So far the Romanian side has authorized passage only for people with diplomatic and other service passports. The ambassador informed us that the Yugoslavs had evacuated family members of officials from their General Consulate. He disavowed reports by a number of Western news agencies that participants of the demonstration [in Timişoara] found refuge on the territory of the Yugoslav compound, whose premises allegedly were penetrated by Romanian militia.

According to Yugoslav estimates, stressed M. Veres, the main reason for the disorders in Timişoara and for their subsequent spreading to a number of other cities, including the capital of the SRR, is rooted in profound popular dissatisfaction with the economic situation in the country accumulated over [many] years, with low living standards, with the lack of basic food and consumer goods, and with the leadership's unwillingness to undertake at least some measures to democratize the political system.

The ambassador pointed out that the Yugoslav public is very concerned about the situation in their neighboring country. The SFRY mass media are informing the population in detail about the events, including many reports about reactions abroad. On December 19 the Union Executive Vece [executive branch of the Yugoslav state] came out with an appropriate declaration expressing profound concern and regret with regard to casualties during the crack-down on the demonstrations. On December 20, the CC CPY Presidium denounced the actions of the Romanian authorities and laid political responsibility at the door of the leadership of the RCP [Romanian Communist Party]. [The CC] declared a temporary suspension of all contacts with the RCP and repealed an earlier invitation [to the RCP] to send a delegation to the 14th Congress of the CPY (January 1990). Every Yugoslav public organization, as well as both chambers of the Skupcina [parliament], made sharp protests. Late on December 21, the Presidium of the SFRY adopted a resolution denouncing reprisals against the demonstrators, which had led to a large loss of human life.

M. Veres stressed that a particular cause for concern in Belgrade is the situation with Yugoslav ethnic minorities in the SRR. He said that the SFRY supports a peaceful resolution of the situation in Romania and is against any foreign interference in Romanian affairs [...]

Deputy Minister of Foreign Affairs of the USSR I. ABOIMOV

* * *

Record of conversation
with U.S. Ambassador to the USSR J. MATLOCK
24 December 1989

I received U.S. Ambassador J. Matlock at his request.

Referring to instructions received from Washington, the ambassador said that, in the opinion of the American leadership, the Soviet Union and the United States should continue to exchange opinions with regard to the events in Romania. The situation in Romania is still very uncertain. The American side is very concerned by the fact that warfare between the forces of state security and army units continues, and casualties among the civilian population are mounting. In this regard Matlock referred to the positive significance of the fact that the opinions of the Soviet Union and the United States coincided, to the effect that support should be given to the group that is trying to govern Romania and fulfill the will of the Romanian people.

Then the American presented the following thought. The United States took note of the belief expressed by the Soviet Union that military intervention is out of question. The United States regarded with equal interest the declaration of the Soviet government concerning its readiness to lend immediate humanitarian assistance to the Romanian people. The American side would be greatly interested to hear the Soviet assessment of developments in Romania, as well as the opinion of the Soviet side with regard to the most effective ways of supporting the Romanian people and the new leadership of Romania. [...]

I informed the ambassador that earlier, in addition to the declaration of the Soviet government, a TASS declaration was published. This step by our side was necessitated by grave concern over the very tense situation at the residential building occupied by officials of the Soviet trade mission in Bucharest. It turned out to be in the epicenter of combat and for some time was partially under siege by the terrorist forces. Only by the end of the day were they dispersed, and we were able to evacuate the inhabitants from the house. I drew the American's attention to the fact that two of them were lightly wounded, not one, as had been earlier reported. Now these people are on Soviet Embassy territory.

At present the main task is to carry out the evacuation of Soviet citizens from Romania, above all women and children. I informed the U.S. ambassador of the options that are under consideration. [...]

We maintain contact with representatives of the new Romanian leadership, if only via telephone. We have informed them about our steps directed at giving humanitarian assistance to the Romanian population. Several times we inquired of the new leadership of Romania as to their urgent needs. We received no clear answer to our question. It looks like the [National Salvation] Front Council still lacks clear ideas on this score.

With regard to the question raised by the American about the most effective approaches to organizing humanitarian assistance to Romania, I repeated that there is no full clarity about that. The Soviet Union is carrying out measures to prepare such assistance and its practical implementation, according to [the USSR's] own understanding of Romania's needs.

We informed the new Romanian leadership and also the International Committee of the Red Cross and the World Health Organization that we had set up hospitals in border cities of the Soviet Union to receive wounded from Romania. In Moldavia they are already expecting the first group of 600 wounded.

On the means of assistance. The first load valued at a half million rubles (11 rail cars) will be sent by rail. Trains in Romania are still functioning. In addition, we gave instructions to the Moldavian leadership to get in touch with border districts in Romania and clarify two issues. First, what do they need most. Second, what is their advice as to the best way to transport these loads.

To finish our thoughts on the situation in Romania, I remarked that we are in close contact on these questions with our Warsaw Treaty allies as well as with all other states that are approaching us. So we take as a positive sign the desire of the American side to exchange opinions. We consider contacts of this kind very useful.

Reacting to our words, Matlock believed that now the United States was seeking optimal means of cooperation in order to give assistance to Romania. According to Matlock, the United States would be ready to provide assistance with medicine and food as well as with the logistics of transporting this assistance. In this context the American ambassador made the following request. If the Soviet side develops some ideas on this score, the American side will be very interested in being kept up to date.

I responded that naturally we would be ready at any moment to share our considerations with the American side.

Then Matlock touched on the issue that, apparently, he wanted to raise from the very beginning of the conversation. The administration, he said, is very interested in knowing whether the possibility of military assistance by the Soviet Union to the Romanian National Salvation Front is totally out of the question. Matlock suggested the following option: what would the Soviet Union do if an appropriate appeal came from the Front? Simultaneously, the ambassador hinted at an idea, apparently on instructions from Washington. He let us know that under the present circumstances the military involvement of the Soviet Union in Romanian affairs might not be regarded in the context of "the Brezhnev doctrine."

To this sounding out by the American I gave an entirely clear and unequivocal answer, presenting our principled position. I declared that we did not visualize, even theoretically, such a scenario. We stand against any interference in the domestic affairs of other states and we intend to pursue this line firmly and without deviations. Thus, the American side may consider that "the Brezhnev doctrine" is now theirs as our gift.

Developing this thesis further, by way of clarification, I drew the interlocutor's attention to the fact that it was on the basis of these considerations that the Soviet Union was and still is against convening the Security Council (SC) to consider the situation in Romania.

The American, however, immediately inquired what the Soviet reaction would be if the National Salvation Front itself appeals to convene the SC.

I said that we are still not ready to contemplate such a hypothetical possibility.

In the end, both sides confirmed their positive evaluation of the exchange of opinions that had taken place. They expressed support for continuing contacts regarding the rapidly changing situation in Romania.

Deputy Minister of Foreign Affairs of the USSR I. ABOIMOV

[*Source:* Diplomaticheskii vestnik, *no. 21/22, November 1994, pp. 74–79. Translated by Vladislav Zubok.*]

Document No. 117: Memorandum from the CC CPSU International Department, "Towards a New Concept of Relations between the USSR and the States of Central and Eastern Europe"

January 5, 1990

This remarkable critique of Soviet foreign policy would be unimaginable under any regime prior to Gorbachev's (or subsequent to Yeltsin's, for that matter). The clear-eyed realists and new thinkers (Rybakov and Ozhereliev) in the International Department of the Central Committee offer their boss, Georgy Shakhnazarov, a devastating indictment of past Soviet practice as well as then-current Soviet confusion.

The memo opens with the dramatic statement, "the crisis of the neo-Stalinist model of socialism in Central and Eastern Europe has become a general crisis and has broken into the open arena." More candor follows: "during the entire post-war period the USSR systematically interfered in the internal affairs of its neighbors, including through the use of military force." But this was "based on the tacit international acceptance that this region was a sphere of Soviet influence." Yet, complains the memo, Moscow's policy priorities are still not clarified—quite a bold statement given that Gorbachev has been asking for a "strategy" paper since June 1986! And why? Because the "[f]oreign policy of the Soviet state has been paralyzed by a sense of the CPSU's moral responsibility for the current complications the communist parties are facing in Eastern Europe."

The document details a series of "erroneous foreign policy actions" taken "in the outdated spirit of loyalty to a narrow group of party leaders." The most serious such errors include Gorbachev's visit to Romania in 1989 and the awarding of Ceauşescu with the order of Lenin; the failure to change the official interpretation of 1968 during Gorbachev's visit to Czechoslovakia in April 1987; and Gorbachev's failure to tell the truth about the Katyń massacre during his visit to Poland in 1988. In effect, this is an indictment of every major Gorbachev trip to Eastern Europe. Each of these visits provided "[d]emonstrations of loyalty to leaders who had long lost public support and who were simply hated by the people, were steeped in corruption and obscenely violated the principles of communism they publicly advocated, hurt the interests of the USSR and the CPSU..."

And who are the officials in Moscow still working on Eastern Europe? Policy is still "in the hands of people personally responsible for Soviet actions in the spirit of the Brezhnev Doctrine." In addition, all of Moscow's ambassadors are useless; they are "as a rule, non-professional ambassadors who lord over the personnel of Soviet services abroad in their customary command style, and adhere to conservative tenets aimed at preserving the status quo." They "distort[] the real picture of the country" and therefore are unable to forecast events: "Our policy in Romania provides the most stunning example of this."

---

1. ASSESSMENT OF THE SITUATION IN THE REGION

At the end of the 1980s, the crisis of the neo-Stalinist model of socialism in Central and Eastern Europe has become a general crisis and has broken out into the open arena. During 1989, in all the states of the Warsaw Treaty Organization, the accumulated contradictions came together, which led to a change of social order, while in three countries the changes took the form of a chain-reaction (in the GDR and Czechoslovakia they were peaceful, in Romania it was bloody). A palace coup in Bulgaria, although it prevented an open conflict, still came too late.

The most significant element in the new situation, *in the political sphere*, is the end of the era of one-party states in Eastern and Central Europe. Real power is gradually passing into the hands of the leaders of states, governments and parliaments.

Communist parties have lost the leading role in society, both *de jure* and *de facto*, and are continuing to lose their positions. [...]

2. ASSESSMENT OF THE OLD CONCEPT OF RELATIONS BETWEEN THE USSR AND THE STATES OF CENTRAL AND EASTERN EUROPE

Until the middle of the 1980s relations between the USSR and these countries were based on the tacit international acceptance that this region was a sphere of Soviet influence. Although, as a matter of fact, this situation was "sanctioned" in theory only in 1968 in the so-called doctrine of limited sovereignty, during the entire post-war period the USSR systematically interfered in the internal affairs of its neighbors, including through the use of military force.

Until 1985, the priority principle of Soviet foreign policy was to maintain the status quo, and the nature of *political relations* was determined mostly by the special role played by communist parties in the life of the East European countries. The CPSU built channels through which it could influence the formation of party-government elites, and used these on a broad scale until the mid-1980s. Against this backdrop there was an established tradition of strictly observing unquestioned loyalty to those groups of party leaders who were in power at the moment, and also a tradition of keeping secret from one's own [people] and the international public any disagreements within the WTO and the CMEA. This unwritten rule covered, in particular, N. Ceauşescu, who as early as the end of the 1950s broke away from direct Soviet control; limited autonomy [*fronda*] was tolerated since Romanian domestic policy remained neo-Stalinist. Loyalty was no longer observed only in those cases when East European leaders set themselves on the path toward reforms, which were regarded by the CPSU leadership as a departure from the fundamental assumptions and basic laws of socialist construction.

After the beginning of *perestroika,* the CPSU leadership, in accordance with the proclaimed principles of new political thinking, renounced the Brezhnev Doctrine, thereby creating an international climate that favored far-reaching shifts in the countries of Central and Eastern Europe. However, party-to-party relations were not de-coupled from inter-state relations in due time. The nature of relations inside the WTO and the CMEA remained undemocratic (the absence of rotation in the posts of commander and chief of staff of the Unified Armed Forces, secretary of the CMEA, etc.). Other mechanisms of political cooperation, its traditions, and its protocol remained generally the same. Strict controls on the coverage of relations with the East European countries in the mass media did not diminish. These problems lay outside of the policy of *glasnost*. In other words, there were many relics from the past in the system of relations.

Despite the profound shifts that have taken place in the East European states, the priority interests of Soviet foreign policy in this region have not yet been clarified, the main directions of this policy have not been formulated, and a new, adequate set of policy instruments has not been created. Multiple Soviet delegations in the states of Eastern Europe failed to forecast events, even in the short run, and failed to direct the actions of Soviet diplomacy into the correct channel. Our policy in Romania provides the most stunning example of this.

The information that came from the embassies, the central apparatus of the Foreign Ministry, services of the KGB abroad and other Soviet delegations gave grounds for distorted assessments of the internal processes that had been brewing in Eastern Europe. Changes in Poland and Hungary provoked excessive alarm, although as the subsequent turn of events showed those countries managed to carry out a smooth transition to a new social order, and the national-state interests of the USSR have not been impaired in any significant way. As to the leaders of the GDR, Czechoslovakia, Bulgaria and Romania, Soviet services abroad criticized them more for their criticism of *perestroika* in the USSR than for their reluctance to undertake much-needed radical transformations. As a result, an unprecedented power vacuum emerged in those countries, and processes were set in motion, which caught both Soviet and international diplomacy unprepared (for instance, the rapid rapprochement of the two German states).

A series of erroneous foreign policy actions took place in an outdated spirit of loyalty to a narrow group of party leaders. The most serious errors: a visit by M.S. Gorbachev to Romania (1989), awarding N. Ceaușescu with the order of Lenin and sending a very high-ranking party delegation to the last Congress of the RCP. Then we should mention [Gorbachev's] visit to Czechoslovakia (1987), which led to a most serious disenchantment on the part of the population of that country who expected that this visit would bring about changes. During [Gorbachev's] visit to Poland (1988), a chance was missed to reinforce friendly relations with the Poles and to enhance the prestige of the Soviet leadership by giving a clear answer to the question about the perpetrators of the Katyń crime. Another missed opportunity was the delay in acknowledging that the intervention in Czechoslovakia [of 1968] was a mistake.

Demonstrations of loyalty to leaders who had long lost public support and who were simply hated by the people, were steeped in corruption, and obscenely violated the principles of communism they publicly advocated, hurt the interests

670

of the USSR and the CPSU, compromised their policy and *perestroika*, and increased anti-Soviet sentiments that had remained hidden until a given time and are only now budding openly. All these errors can be compensated for only to a certain extent through the successes of Soviet foreign policy on other issues and in other regions of the world.

Other causes of the aforementioned weaknesses and errors should be named:

- The foreign policy of the Soviet state has been paralyzed by a sense of the CPSU's moral responsibility for the current complications the communist parties are facing in Eastern Europe.
- At all stages [the process] of preparing and implementing foreign policy was in the hands of people personally responsible for Soviet actions in the spirit of the Brezhnev Doctrine. Many of them still adhere to old political assessments and preserve personal ties with national governing cadres retaining a conservative neo-Stalinist orientation. They have become the source of less than objective information about events in the country [of their location].
- Principles of staffing and the formation of Soviet diplomatic services in Eastern Europe, as well as the traditions present in the activity of all [Soviet] representations do not correspond to the present complex situation in the region. People who have been sent there are, as a rule, non-career ambassadors who lord over the personnel of Soviet services abroad in their customary command style, and adhere to conservative tenets aimed at preserving the status quo. Messages they send to Moscow get screened through strict ideological filters. Their contacts in the country are almost exclusively with the state-government establishment. All this significantly devalues the information they obtain and distorts the real picture of the country. Obtaining this sort of information does not require keeping so many services in the field; similar conclusions can be drawn in Moscow from an analysis of the official media of these countries.
- The East European departments of the Foreign Ministry are staffed with cadres who have been schooled in corresponding embassies and who rely on the "battle experience" [*zakalka*] they have obtained there in their practical work.

An analogous picture obtains in *the area of trade cooperation*.

After the war, instead of the traditional division of labor in Central and Eastern Europe oriented toward the Western part of the continent, under our strong pressure there emerged a relatively self-isolated economic system under the domination of the USSR. Following the Soviet example, the countries adhere to the principle of autarkic development in their economies. The policy of integration was undertaken only in the 1970s; however, it did not bring the expected fruits because the proposed measures were largely voluntary by nature and hardly reflected the interests of the countries and immediate subjects of economic activity. Cooperation therefore boiled down to centralized barter and commercial and financial relations, and concerns over efficiency played a subservient role. Problems of scientific-technological progress were not resolved; the quality of goods on the CMEA market remained shoddy. For these reasons centrifugal tendencies in economic relations grew stronger, and the CMEA lost its prestige and is now on the brink of total collapse.

In the first half of the 1980s, attempts were made to revive its activity through formalistic bureaucratic programs and face-lifting changes in the mechanisms of cooperation. However, all these measures came to naught because of a lack of coordination between internal mechanisms and the different paths various countries took in their foreign economic policies.

After the beginning of *perestroika*, the USSR proposed a course aimed at the fundamental renewal of forms and methods of economic cooperation. A rigid definition of the main parameters of integrationist mechanisms characteristic of the administrative-command system of management was declared unworkable. A new concept of an integrated socialist market reflected the goal proclaimed in the majority of East European countries: to move to a market economy. However, the achievement of this strategic goal is proceeding in a halting way since in reality market mechanisms do not yet function in any of the member-states of the CMEA. Rather, there is an increasing trend toward bartering in economic relations and even stricter measures to protect market trade from citizens of neighboring states. Under such conditions an integrated market remains merely a distant guideline for restructuring in the sphere of integrationist interactions. [...]

[*Source: Donation of Professor Jacques Levesque. On file at the National Security Archive. Translated by Vladislav Zubok.*]

Document No. 118: Diary of Anatoly Chernyaev regarding German Reunification

January 28, 1990

This record from Chernyaev's diary provides an illuminating portrait of internal Soviet deliberations about German unification. The Soviet general secretary calls together his closest foreign policy advisers, three of whom (Kryuchkov, Akhromeyev, and Falin) would subsequently blame Gorbachev for the "loss" of Germany. But here, all take solace in Helmut Kohl's commitment to keeping the course of German unification within the larger all-European process. They seem to understand, already in late January, that "the process of German unification cannot be stopped. But we need to be present in this process, and see that it does not turn against us." Yet Chernyaev is astonished that the top Central Committee expert on Germany, Rafail Fedorov (deputy head of the International Department), continues to claim "nobody wants unification, especially in the FRG!" At this meeting, the disagreement is only over whether to align with Kohl or with the opposition Social Democrats (the latter seeking to slow down the process); they all recognize, as KGB chief Kryuchkov remarks, that the GDR "is not a real state anymore."

On Thursday, (January 25) M.S. called us to the CC from Volynskoe-2[89] (Yakovlev, Shakhnazarov, and myself) "to discuss the German problem." When we arrived, Ryzhkov, Shevardnadze, Kryuchkov, Falin, Fedorov, and Akhromeyev were already in his office. We sat there for four hours. The conversation was very pointed. I suggested that we should orient ourselves more toward the FRG because we already had no base in the GDR to influence the course of events, and to bet on Kohl, not on the SPD, which is trying to turn unification into an electoral campaign issue.

Kohl, on the other hand, still stands by the theory of unification as part of the all-European process, and besides he is constrained by the allies and is more personally loyal to his relationship with M.S. It is possible that he also understands that in his electoral game on the GDR he would lose to Brandt-Fogel. I am not opposed to inviting Modrow to Moscow, although it would not do us much good, and the question of his visit has already been decided. We should not invite Gizi: why would we stick to the part that practically does not exist? (The others did not agree with me on this).

Later we should gather the "six:" the U.S., Britain, France, the USSR, plus Kohl and Modrow, i.e. the winners and the losers of the war. And we should

---

[89] Volynskoe-2 was another of the working dachas used to draft speeches and position papers. See footnote 17.

come to an agreement [...] because the process of German unification cannot be stopped. But we need to be present in this process, and see that it does not turn against us.

Everybody agreed with the "six." But they also argued that we needed to act through other channels too (Shakhnazarov [suggested] an SPD orientation, Yakovlev supported him). Shevardnadze in general supported me. Ryzhkov was against "giving everything to Kohl." Kryuchkov, as always, was for everything that would be decided; however, he also said that the SED had ceased to exist, and all the state structures in the GDR have fallen apart. It is not a real state anymore.

Ryzhkov said that the only obstacle to unification is the disjuncture of the economies. [...]

Fedorov argued that nobody wants unification, especially in the FRG! And this is the main [Central Committee] expert on Germany!!

M.S. outlined five points for action. We are to orient ourselves toward:

1. The FRG: Kohl, and the SPD.

2. The "six."

3. Modrow and the SED ("it cannot be that among 2.5 million party members there is nobody to constitute a real force").

4. London, Paris—"maybe I should just fly here and there, take one day for each capital."

5. For Akhromeyev—prepare the withdrawal of troops from the GDR: "the problem is more internal than external. There are 300,000 troops, and among them 100,000 officers with families. We need to find a place for them!"

[*Source: Anatoly Chernyaev's Diary, Manuscript. On file at the National Security Archive. Translated by Svetlana Savranskaya.*]

Document No. 119: Record of Conversation between Mikhail Gorbachev and James Baker

February 9, 1990

This Gorbachev Foundation record of the Soviet leader's meeting with James Baker focuses on the question of German unification, but also includes candid discussion by Gorbachev of the economic and political problems in the Soviet Union, and Baker's "free advice" ("sometimes the finance minister in me wakes up") on prices, inflation, and even the policy of selling apartments to soak up the rubles cautious Soviet citizens have tucked under their mattresses. For his part, Gorbachev is careful to explain a key issue on which his top aides (like Yakovlev and Chernyaev) are pressing him—to leave the party and become only the president as a way out of the political mess: "in general I am for separating these posts, but not right now ... [because] two centers of power would form." (Instead, power would actually dissipate from both positions over the next year-and-a-half, leaving Gorbachev holding the reins but without a horse.)

Baker again assures Gorbachev that "neither the President nor I intend to extract any unilateral advantages from the processes taking place," and that the Americans understand the importance for the USSR and Europe of guarantees that "not an inch of NATO's present military jurisdiction will spread in an eastern direction." Gorbachev responds by quoting Polish President (and former dictator) Jaruzelski: "that the presence of American and Soviet troops in Europe is an element of stability."

The key exchange takes place when Baker asks whether Gorbachev would prefer "a united Germany outside of NATO, absolutely independent and without American troops; or a united Germany keeping its connections with NATO, but with the guarantee that NATO's jurisprudence or troops will not spread east of the present boundary." Instead of taking the guarantee, the Soviet leader says only that "[w]e will think everything over. We intend to discuss all these questions in depth at the leadership level. It goes without saying that a broadening of the NATO zone is not acceptable." Baker responds, "We agree with that." Somehow for Gorbachev this is sufficient reassurance, and he never asks for a pledge in writing.

Gorbachev: At the beginning of this part of our talk I would like to add to what has been said about the all-European meeting in the year 1990.

Judging by numerous signs, the situation in Europe is leaping out of our control. That is why this top-level meeting will help to channel the processes. These developments, if directed in democratic evolutionary forms, could bring favorable results for the West and for the East.

I had a thought: our prediction that the world will change, and change dramatically and in many areas, turned out to be correct. And it is a very good coincidence that at the same time relations between the world's two most powerful and influential countries are in a favorable phase. This is important for the present and stock for the future.

We can still do a good deal right now; it will be more difficult later. I have said that our countries are "doomed" to cooperate. We need to make this cooperation stable. There are no insurmountable conflicts between us. We must strive to place the existing conflicts within the framework of cooperation.

Now I would like to say a few words to you about the plenum[90] and the situation in our country.

Baker: Yes, that would be very interesting.

Gorbachev: In addition, we could exchange views on the German question and on Afghanistan. If you would like to discuss something else in this composition, I would have no objection. Perhaps we will discuss Central America.

The plenum was very important for us. We have come to a stage of *perestroika* where it is time to provide answers to many of the questions. Positions are beginning to crystallize in society, movements have become visible, and a major realignment is underway. It is not easy to understand all of this. [...]

From the right and from the left, even with different aims, there is pressure on the center. We have come to the conclusion that it is necessary to accelerate the economic reform.

Before us the problem arose of creating a mechanism that would allow [us] to regulate monetary income more strictly. We came to the conclusion that we cannot avoid reforming the [system of] price formation. We will have to take some unpopular measures.

For that we need to regroup our power, particularly in its highest echelons. A stronger mechanism for implementing decisions is necessary. In connection with this the question arose of creating an institute of presidential power and broadening the government's resources. This is needed to keep the situation in check.

We need to quickly adopt laws dealing with the demarcation of powers between the republics and the Union—laws that must broaden the powers and rights of the Union. The election process and the formation of governmental bodies will almost be complete by March 4. The new governmental bodies must have a legal basis to function. As for relations between the republics and the center, the matter at hand concerns a *perestroika* for our federation. There is a great diversity of approaches to the question of reforming our federation. It must be said that we are behind here and events have preceded our decisions. Much will have to be done. The resolution for all these questions is in the platform that we adopted at the plenum.

There are many discussions surrounding the question of the party and its new role. This issue has stirred strong passions, which is quite understandable.

---

[90] The Central Committee Plenum took place on February 5–7, 1990. Decisions were made to move up the date of the XXVIII Congress of the CPSU, remove Article 6 of the Soviet Constitution on the leading role of the Communist Party, and adopt a platform for the coming Congress, "Toward Humanistic, Democratic Socialism."

In its former role, the party was the framework of the governing structure. And these are not just institutions, these are real living people. That is why the process of realigning power to favor the Soviets and the economic organs, and returning the party to its role as a political organization is proceeding so painfully. The statement that the party renounces its power monopoly and that it will earn its right within a democratic process rather than it being fixed in the Constitution, did not come easily for everyone. But in general we approved such an approach.

Baker: Will article 6 of the Constitution be revoked?

Gorbachev: That is not the plenum's prerogative. However, we decided that the party will produce a legislative initiative to revise this article.

Discussions about reforming relations of production and property questions were also very heated. These are very important links in the *perestroika* process. In the outcome of the discussion, the plenum confirmed and radicalized our approach toward this aspect of *perestroika*. A resolution on moving up the dates for the party congress has also been passed. A realignment and renewal of power is taking place, which allows *perestroika* to continue and develop.

I have been asked what would happen to my posts in the party and in the government. I answer that in general I am for separating these posts, but not right now. If we took this step right now, two centers of power would form. This would not strengthen but weaken the process of *perestroika*. Even with the emergence of new political organizations in the arena, the CPSU will remain a major influence. For now there is a logic to combining the two posts.

Unusual work on the idea of creating presidential power will emerge in the near future. I don't know how it will go. Maybe passions will heat up again. However, the mood in society is favorable to such a decision.

Right now we are going through a critical point on our journey. I mean the economic situation and ethnic relations.

In connection with this, I would like to say that I properly appreciate the president's and your position with respect to the processes going on in our country, your position supporting *perestroika*. I consider this to be very important.

Baker: I thank you for this very condensed, but comprehensive summary.

I already said to Mr. Shevardnadze that we have taken a firm stand in support of *perestroika* and your efforts. We seek to assist you with our policies. In particular, we aim to do everything that we can in order to provide stable international conditions for the fulfillment of your plans. We hope that your domestic policy will continue to be aided by evidence of the productive development of Soviet–American relations, and by [both] sides' achievement of important agreements in the sphere of arms reductions and limitations. You are probably aware that although our administration took it slowly for the first four-five months, now we are not only ready but full of resolve to move the arms limitation process forward.

The proposals we have brought to Moscow are evidence of that. I said to your minister that in conditions of deep and rapid change in the world there is a danger that we may fall behind events and our efforts could be depreciated if we do not act decisively.

Gorbachev: I agree with you.

Baker: Allow me to say a few words on the economic questions.

One aspect troubles me very much, and I spoke about this almost a year ago when speaking with your minister. An economy can be either command or market. There is not some third system that would function effectively.

In connection with this it is very important that you have decided to create a new price formation system. I am glad to hear about this decision. However, it will not be easy to arrive at this system. Before it can be implemented it will be necessary to take certain steps. I have in mind at least two steps. The first is liquidation of the surplus money supply. This can be done in different ways. As I understand, you are already implementing some measures, such as selling apartments to individuals. As far as I know, you are considering the options of a devaluation, of issuing bonds backed by gold, etc. I think all of this should be done before you introduce a new price formation system. Otherwise you risk facing 1,000-percent inflation.

And secondly: before introducing a new price system, it is necessary to create a protective social mechanism that would secure the interests of the poorest layers of society. These steps will reduce, although not eliminate completely, the population's discontent due to the price reform.

I do not want to appear as a lecturer here, but sometimes the finance minister in me wakes up; that is a position I held some time ago. So there is my free advice; I hope it is worth something to you.

In a word, we want your efforts to be successful. And if somewhere in the course of events you feel that the United States is doing something undesirable to you, without hesitation call us and tell us about it. [...]

Baker: [...] This morning I had a detailed discussion of the German question with Minister Shevardnadze. I would also like to hear your thoughts on this matter.

Gorbachev: I would like to hear you [on this issue].

Baker: Firstly, this process is going much faster than anyone would have expected last year, even in December of last year. During the past week I met with the foreign ministers of Great Britain, France, and the FRG. All of them are of this opinion.

On March 18, the people of the GDR will vote in their elections. The overwhelming majority will be for unification, and they will elect leaders who support the idea of German unification. Soon the two German states will start discussions on the internal aspects of unification, such questions as the unification of the governments, parliaments, a common capital, common currency, an economic union. All of this is going on *de facto*.

The Soviet Union's concern is well known to me, I spoke about it with the minister. At the same time we take your recent statement and E.A. Shevardnadze's speech in Brussels in December of last year as the expression of your understanding of the fact that unification is inevitable. The most important thing is for this process to take place under stable conditions and to ensure the prospect of stability. We believe that this requires a framework and a mechanism for resolving questions related to the external aspects of unification. At the same time, creating such a mechanism must be approached very carefully in order not to cause an outburst of German nationalism. Its creation should not be started until the two Germanys begin discussing unification's internal aspects.

With the French and the Germans we have initiated a preliminary discussion of the possibility of creating a "two + four" mechanism, without aiming at an agreement yet.

Gorbachev: I wanted to ask you, what do you think about the possibility of a "four + two" mechanism?

Baker: I think that it would be better to have a "two + four" mechanism. I explained to Mr. Shevardnadze why, in our opinion, a four-sided approach will not work. I think that the idea of using the CSCE process is also difficult to realize since it would be too cumbersome. I would also like to point out that I do not have confirmation from the FRG side that the Germans will agree to the "two + four" approach.

It goes without saying that when developing an approach to the external aspects of unification it is necessary to a certain degree to consider the concerns of Germany's neighbors. Therefore it is quite possible that the CSCE forum could be used for the ratification of agreements developed within the framework of the "two + four" mechanism.

We fought alongside with you; together we brought peace to Europe. Regrettably, we then managed this peace poorly, which led to the Cold War. We could not cooperate then. Now, when rapid and fundamental changes are taking place in Europe, we have a propitious opportunity to cooperate in the interests of preserving the peace. I very much want you to know: neither the president nor I intend to extract any unilateral advantages from the processes that are taking place.

Some other details. We indeed are not speaking in favor of Germany being neutral. The West Germans have also said to us that they do not consider such a decision to be satisfactory. I would like to explain why.

If Germany is neutral it does not mean it will not be militaristic. Quite the opposite, it could very well decide to create its own nuclear potential instead of relying on American nuclear deterrent forces. All our West European allies and a number of East European countries have made it known to us that they would like the United States to keep its military presence in Europe. I do not know whether you support such a possibility. But I would like to assure you that as soon as our allies tell us that they are against our presence, we will bring our troops home.

Shevardnadze: I do not know about your other allies, but a united Germany may demand it.

Baker: If that happens, our troops will return home. We will leave any country that does not desire our presence. The American people have always had a strong position favoring this. However, if the current West German leadership is at the head of a unified Germany then they have said to us they will be against our withdrawal.

And the last point. NATO is the mechanism for securing the U.S. presence in Europe. If NATO is liquidated, there will be no such mechanism in Europe. We understand that not only for the Soviet Union but for other European countries as well it is important to have guarantees that if the United States keeps its presence in Germany within the framework of NATO, not an inch of NATO's present military jurisdiction will spread in an eastern direction.

We believe that consultations and discussions within the framework of the "two + four" mechanism should guarantee that Germany's unification will not lead to NATO's military organization spreading to the east.

These are our thoughts. Perhaps a better way can be found. As of yet, we do not have the Germans' agreement to this approach. I explained it to Genscher and he only said that he will think it over. As for [French Foreign Minister Roland] Dumas, he liked the idea. Now I have given an account of this approach to you. I repeat, maybe something much better can be created, but we have not been able to do that yet.

Gorbachev: I want to say that in general we share this way of thinking. Indeed, the process has begun and is underway. And we need to try to adjust to the new reality. A mechanism is needed that would assist stability in Europe—a very important center of world politics—in remaining undisturbed. Of course we have some differences in looking at this situation. I think there is nothing terrible in that. The most important thing is not to approach this situation in too simplistic a manner.

Firstly, we want the situation in Europe to improve. The situation cannot be allowed to worsen as a result of what is taking place. We need to think about how to act under conditions of the new reality. A question arises: what will this Germany be like? How will it tend to act in Europe and the world? These are fundamental questions. And as we see it, they are perceived differently in, say, Paris, London, Warsaw, Prague, Budapest.

Baker: I understood that.

Gorbachev: Yesterday I spoke with Jaruzelski on the phone. He knows that you are in Moscow right now; he also knows that Kohl and Genscher are arriving tomorrow. Considering this, Jaruzelski expressed his opinions on a number of questions, about Germany in particular. And Germany is a real question for a Pole! He thinks that contact should be maintained and we should consult on this question. He expressed the opinion that the presence of American and Soviet troops in Europe is an element of stability.

In Czechoslovakia and Austria there is apprehension that powers might develop in a unified Germany that would lay claim to the 1938 borders—the Sudeten region, Austria. Of course, today such claims are not being voiced. But what will happen tomorrow? And in France and Great Britain the question arises: will they remain major players in Europe? In short, it is easier for us in this situation due to the mass and weight of our countries. Kohl and his team are speaking to us with an understanding of what that means.

Baker: I agree.

Gorbachev: Thus, it is necessary to proceed delicately and with consideration, understanding the national feelings of the people and not hindering them, but aiming to channel the process. As for a "four + two" or "two + four" mechanism that would rest on an international-legal foundation and provide an opportunity to consult with each other and evaluate the situation, maybe following our exchange of opinions we should continue consultations with our partners in the West and the East—you as you see fit, and we correspondingly. That does not yet mean that we have an agreement, but we should continue to seek one. You said that the FRG did not express agreement with this approach. As for Modrow, judging by our talks with him it seems that he will support such an approach. Tomorrow we can ask Kohl what he thinks about this.

Baker: That would be good. But I would like to voice one precaution. Even if we have a chance to convince the Germans to support the 'two + four" approach, this should only be done after March 18, only after the GDR's self-determination, and after they begin discussing the internal aspects of unification. Otherwise they will say that the four powers' pressure is unacceptable, and unification is solely a German question. Our approach provides that unification's internal aspects are indeed a matter between the two Germanys. However, the external aspects must be discussed with consideration of Germany's neighbors' security interests; they must be acceptable to them. Besides that, we must discuss Berlin's status. If we approach the matter in that way there is a chance that the Germans will agree to the proposed mechanism.

I must once again admit that I did not discuss this at all with the chancellor, and Genscher did not give me an answer. He only said that he will consider this approach. I think that he will approve it. But with the chancellor it is a different matter: he is a candidate in the forthcoming elections.

Gorbachev: This is a very important factor that leaves its imprint on the situation.

Baker: Such are the whims of democracy. He will have to act very carefully in order not to create the impression in Germany that he is handing the question of Germany's unification over to others.

Gorbachev: I would like to tell you about the symposium that was recently organized by the Evangelical academy and which was attended by representatives from all the FRG and GDR parties and groups, with the exception of Modrow's party. As a result of the discussion most of the participants spoke in favor of the confederation. The GDR representatives emphasized that the two Germanys' economic convergence does not have to mean a sell-out or colonization of the GDR. They said they do not want to be spoken to like little children.

The second conclusion was that unification must take place only on the territory of the present-day FRG and GDR, respecting existing boundaries, and keeping the two parts of Germany members of NATO and the Warsaw Treaty.

At the same time there were differences of opinion. Some FRG and GDR representatives spoke in favor of making the future Germany a neutral state. However, the majority of representatives of the two countries spoke in favor of preserving membership in the two unions, which would change from military to new political structures.

[Willy] Brandt's speech was the most surprising. He asserted that no one should hinder Germany's self-determination. He said that the Germans should not wait for the CSCE process, that the all-European convergence should not precede Germany's unification but the other way around—Germany's unification should take place earlier. He rejected a confederation and spoke in favor of a federal German state. At the same time the West German part of this federation must remain in NATO. As for the former GDR—it needs further consideration.

Many FRG representatives criticized Brandt for fueling German nationalism, and for trying to get ahead even of Kohl.

The speech by the renowned scholar, [Carl Friedrich] Weizsäcker (brother of the current FRG president), was very interesting. He said that it is necessary to avoid aggravating German nationalism for many reasons, one of them being that it could lead to a wave of nationalism in the Soviet Union. He understands what a reminder of the past war means for a Soviet person. He also emphasized that an outburst of nationalism in the USSR could become a threat to *perestroika*. The more Germans shout for unification, the more it implicates the neighbors. In Europe, Weizsäcker stressed, Auschwitz has not been forgotten.

The writer Günter Grass emphasized that a unified Germany has always been a breeding ground for chauvinism and anti-semitism. The economic costs of unification were also discussed. A number was given: in the next 8-10 years the economic price of unification will amount to 50 billion marks. The speakers emphasized that when the Germans find out about this they will think thrice whether unification is worth it.

This is the interesting mosaic of opinions. I told you about it in such detail because I think that in the end we should not fall under a wave of emotion, we should not yield to this pressure and move away from considerations and predictions about what all this could mean and how to channel this process. There are powers in both German states that see the danger. This is important. I would ask you to tell the president that we want to stay in contact with you, to exchange information and, if necessary, ideas about this problem.

Baker: I will do that without fail. I would like you to understand: I am not saying that we should yield to a wave of emotion. But I think that soon Germany's internal integration will become a fact. In these circumstances our duty before all people and our duty for the sake of peace in the world is to do everything possible in order to develop external mechanisms that will secure stability in Europe. That is why I proposed this mechanism.

As for the economic price of unification, most likely this question will be discussed during the election campaign. However, I think that it will be swept over by the emotional outburst, by people's striving to unite and be together.

I want to ask you a question, and you need not answer it right now. Supposing unification takes place, what would you prefer: a united Germany outside of NATO, absolutely independent and without American troops; or a united Germany keeping its connections with NATO, but with the guarantee that NATO's jurisprudence or troops will not spread east of the present boundary?

Gorbachev: We will think everything over. We intend to discuss all these questions in depth at the leadership level. It goes without saying that a broadening of the NATO zone is not acceptable.

Baker: We agree with that.

Gorbachev: It is quite possible that in the situation as it is forming right now, the presence of American troops can play a containing role. It is possible that we should think together, as you said, about the fact that a united Germany could look for ways to rearm and create a new Wehrmacht, as happened after Versailles. Indeed, if Germany is outside the European structures, history could repeat itself. The technological and industrial potential allows Germany to do this. If it will exist within the framework of European structures this process could be prevented. All of this needs to be thought over.

Much in what you have said appears to be realistic. Let us think. It is impossible to draw a conclusion right now. You know that the GDR is closely tied to us, and the FGR is our primary trade partner in the West. Historically, Germany and Russia have always been strong partners. We both have the possibility to make an impact on the situation. And we could use these possibilities when we develop a rational approach that considers our and other countries' interests, when we develop a corresponding mechanism. We should not underestimate these possibilities. Of course, right now the matter is complicated by the election campaigns and the intensity of emotions that are heating up society right now. We will watch the situation and think about how to act. [...]

Gorbachev: By the way, with respect to trade and economic collaboration between our countries, it is good that some large-scale projects are being discussed right now. I am speaking about collaboration in using the Baikal–Amur Railroad, in building a fiber-optic communications line, and in the joint construction of aircraft. These are interesting plans. If they are realized, our collaboration will reach a new level. Here once again, it seems, the problem of COCOM will arise. If it does not then we are speaking about the technologies of yesterday.

Baker: Right now we are analyzing the COCOM rules. We intend to reconsider them so that, metaphorically speaking, the walls would be higher but there would be fewer of them. But I would like to say that at the same time we realize the pressure you are facing from some conservatives for your policies.

Gorbachev: Yes, it is a struggle for power.

Baker: I said to Eduard yesterday: in April, May, and June last year, when I started saying for the first time that we want to help *perestroika*, that we trust Gorbachev and Shevardnadze, American conservatives attacked me with criticism. But now, when we are reconsidering the COCOM rules and discussing the possibility of your participation in international financial organizations, the same conservatives are saying: why do the Russians give Cuba MIG-29s? Of course, Cuba is not a threat to the U.S. But it is a certain threat to some small democratic countries in Central America. Castro continues to export revolution. There is only one person he criticizes more often than Bush, and that is Gorbachev. [...]

[*Source: Archive of the Gorbachev Foundation, Fond 1. Opis 1. On file at the National Security Archive. Translated by Anna Melyakova.*]

Document No. 120: Letter from James Baker to Helmut Kohl

February 10, 1990

Courtesy of Helmut Kohl's publication of selected documents from the years 1989–1990, this letter from James Baker to the German chancellor reports on his meeting with Gorbachev (see previous document). It arrives just as Kohl himself is on his way to meet with the Soviet leader. The American briefs the German on Soviet "concerns" about unification, and summarizes why a "Two Plus Four" negotiation, starting with the two Germanys, plus the four powers that won World War II (USSR, United States, Britain, France), would be the most appropriate venue for talks on the "external aspects of unification," given that the "internal aspects ... were strictly a German matter." Baker especially remarks on Gorbachev's equivocal response to the question about a neutral Germany versus a NATO Germany with pledges against eastward expansion, and advises Kohl that Gorbachev "may well be willing to go along with a sensible approach that gives him some cover ..."

Dear Mr. Chancellor:

In light of your meeting with President Gorbachev, the President wanted me to brief you on the talks I've had in Moscow. These were wide-ranging talks, concerning all parts of the US–Soviet agenda. I believe we've made significant progress on all parts of that agenda—arms control, regional issues, bilateral questions, human rights, and transnational matters. I'll have Ambassador Walters brief you on the details of our progress and the character of my extensive discussions with President Gorbachev and Minister Shevardnadze on the recent Plenum and the course of *perestroika*.

For now, I want to report to you about our discussions on German unification. Gorbachev and Shevardnadze were eager to raise this issue with me. I know it will not surprise you that they have concerns. While now accepting unification as inevitable, they outlined a number of concerns:

– They feared unification could create instability and uncertainty in Europe.

– They wondered about the depth of the German commitment to current borders, noting the German court's decision on the border question.

– They evidenced unease over the effect unification would have on any German leadership, saying that reassuring statements from FRG leaders in the current setting might mean little in the context of a unified Germany.

– They emphasized that unification had to be managed and take account of its effects on European security, and that the lessons of history required that the Soviet Union not be passive observers of this process.

I responded that you were sensitive to their concerns, but that no one except the Germans could decide the fate of Germany. I told them that I agreed that unification was inevitable and that events were moving very rapidly in this regard;

indeed, that I expected the internal aspects of unification to proceed very quickly after the March 18 elections.

I suggested that the internal elements of unification were strictly a German matter. I observed, as you have, that the external aspects of unification were a different matter, and that it was important to take into account the security concerns of others.

To that end, I suggested that a framework or mechanism should be developed to address the external aspects of unification. I said the "Four Powers" was an inappropriate mechanism because the Germans could never accept it.

Similarly, the CSCE was far too unwieldy and cumbersome to constitute a timely mechanism for addressing the issue. (The CSCE could, of course, sanction the result of the unification process, but could not be a near-term practical mechanism for helping to shape it.)

As a preliminary idea, I noted that a Two-plus-Four arrangement—e.g., the two Germanys plus the four powers—might be the most realistic way to proceed. I said such a mechanism could begin only after the March 18 elections, only after the process on the internal aspects of unification has begun, and only if the Germans accept it. I mentioned that I had discussed this with Genscher, and he had said it was worth thinking about. I said I had not had a chance to discuss it personally with you, but you had been briefed on the idea.

Gorbachev evidenced some interest in this approach, even suggesting that he thought it might be "suitable for the situation." There was clearly no commitment on his part, and he may be inclined to raise either a variant of this idea or an entirely different approach with you. Whatever he chooses to do with you, I thought it important to outline his response to me.

There is one other point I raised with him, and here again his response was interesting. I told him that the FRG's leadership was strongly in favor of a unified Germany remaining in NATO and not being neutral. I explained that we agreed with this, and thought the Soviets should not reject such an outcome. In this regard, I mentioned that it was unrealistic to assume that a big, economically significant country like Germany could be neutral. And then I put the following question to him. Would you prefer to see a unified Germany outside of NATO, independent and with no U.S. forces or would you prefer a unified Germany to be tied to NATO, with assurances that NATO's jurisdiction would not shift one inch eastward from its present position?

He answered that the Soviet leadership was giving real thought to all such options, and would be discussing them soon "in a kind of seminar." He then added: "Certainly any extension of the zone of NATO would be unacceptable." (By implication, NATO in its current zone might be acceptable.)

In short, I believe we had a very interesting exchange and one that suggests Gorbachev, at least, is not locked in. While he clearly has real concerns about German unification—some of which may be related to the passions this issue evokes in the Soviet Union—he may well be willing to go along with a sensible approach that gives him some cover or explanation for his actions. I suspect that the combination of a Two-plus-Four mechanism and a broader CSCE framework might do that. But it is obviously too early to know, and we will have to see how the Soviet position evolves.

In any case, we will need to coordinate very closely. I will look forward to comparing notes with you after your meeting.

Sincerely yours,
Jim
James A. Baker, III

[*Source:* Deutsche Einheit: Sonderedition aus den Akten des Bundeskanzleramtes. *Eds. Hanns Jürgen Küsters and Daniel Hofmann. R. Oldenbourg Verlag, Munich, 1998.*]

Document No. 121: National Intelligence Estimate 12–90, "The Future of Eastern Europe," (Key Judgments Only)

April 1990

The CIA finally catches up with the march of history in this assessment, five months after the fall of the Berlin Wall. "Communist party rule in Eastern Europe is finished, and it will not be revived." The Soviets have no more leverage in Eastern Europe, and even an aggressive Kremlin leadership will not be able to alter the course of events. "Moscow will seek to replace its lost domination of Eastern Europe with the advantages of a broader engagement with Europe as a whole." Interestingly, the analysis endorses some of Gorbachev's own notions of the mutual dissolution of the blocs and transfer of functions to an institutionalized Conference on Security and Cooperation in Europe (CSCE): "East European events will continue to take place against a backdrop of declining relevance for the Warsaw Pact and NATO. ... Most East European states will aspire to build links to Western Europe and will hope that the CSCE process can provide a basis for such broader security arrangements." The document's final statement provides a hopeful conclusion for the events of 1989—hopeful but premature, given events in the decade or two since this analysis was written, such as the heated debates in Russia over the expansion of NATO, and the controversies over Eastern European countries hosting American military facilities. "In the region where both world wars and the Cold War began, a democratic, prosperous, and independent Eastern Europe would be an element of stability rather than an object of great power rivalry in the borderlands between East and West."

NATIONAL INTELLIGENCE ESTIMATE: THE FUTURE OF EASTERN EUROPE

This estimate represents the views of the Director of Central Intelligence with the advice and assistance of the US Intelligence Community.

- The revolutions in Eastern Europe provide the basis for developing democracy and market economies. But this will not be a linear process, and a number of countries will continue to face political instability, ethnic turmoil, and economic backwardness.
- Even with Western help, East European economies—excluding that of East Germany—are likely to make only modest progress during the next five years.
- The possibility remains of a relapse to authoritarianism, particularly in the Balkans, where the lifting of Communist hegemony threatens to revive old ethnic animosities, civil strife, and interstate tensions. The environmental nightmare will also persist.

- West Europeans are better positioned to lead in shaping the East European future, but the United States has important advantages, among them the desire of East Europeans for a counterweight to Soviet and German influence.

Key Judgments

Communist party rule in Eastern Europe is finished, and it will not be revived. This and the lifting of Soviet hegemony create new opportunities for establishing representative democracies and self-sustaining market economies. The way will also open for new modes of regional political and economic cooperation. The greatest impetus is the resolve of East Europeans and their leaders to achieve reforms by emulating Western economic and political models.

The evolution of the region will make the designation "Eastern Europe" increasingly imprecise, as East-Central European countries—Poland, Czechoslovakia, Hungary, and East Germany—move ahead in closer association with the West, and the Balkans—Bulgaria, Romania, and Albania—settle into a more separate role. Yugoslavia, if it holds together, will continue close ties to the West.[91]

In some East European countries, however, we will see political instability and perhaps even a revival of authoritarianism, amidst lingering economic backwardness and reemerging ethnic animosities. Despite Western aid and investment, the East European economies—excluding that of East Germany—are likely to make only uneven progress during the five-year timespan of this Estimate.

Ultimately, prospects for healthy democracy will be closely tied to the way in which East Europeans resolve their systemic economic crisis:

- Western aid will be essential, especially in the early stages, to make up the "capital deficit" required to cushion any transition to market economies.
- Such aid will have to be linked to private investment, access to Western markets, and long-term programs designed to develop the skills and institutions necessary for a modern economy, as well as to full mobilization of indigenous resources for investment.

The outlook is more promising for the countries in East-Central Europe—particularly East Germany, which will rapidly merge into West Germany's economy. Elsewhere, several countries have good potential as sites for Western-owned manufacturing plants with preferential entree to the European Community. The agricultural sector has the capability for quick turnaround.

But the strains of even successful economic reform that is accompanied by inflation and unemployment will test the patience of people fed up with economic hardship and traditionally cynical about political promises. Lingering economic

---

[91] The Assistant Secretary of State for Intelligence and Research, Department of State, believes that broad regional subgroupings adopted for analytical convenience—such as East-Central Europe and Balkans—at times obscure the differences between countries. [Footnote in the original.]

crises and resurgent ethnic divisions may fuel chronic political instability and interstate tensions, notably in the Balkans:

- The major near-term danger to democratization in East-Central Europe is that the whole process will run out of steam as popular euphoria wanes and little substantial economic improvement has occurred. The result would be a paralyzing political impasse or prolonged "muddling through," as in the Third World.
- The worst case scenario—most likely in Romania and Yugoslavia—will not be a return to Communist regimes but a turn to authoritarianism, growing repression of ethnic minorities, civil strife, and even the onset of greater interstate frictions.

Meanwhile, despite the Albanian regime's readiness to use brutal repressive measures to suppress dissent, it is likely that revolution and reform will come to Albania within five years.

The Soviet Union's size, geographical proximity, security concerns, raw materials, and market will continue to make it a major factor in Eastern Europe. But even an aggressive, post-Gorbachev Kremlin leadership would not—or could not—substantially alter the course of events there. Moscow will seek to replace its lost domination of Eastern Europe with the advantages of a broader engagement with Europe as a whole.

A united Germany, however, will move even more assertively into Eastern Europe as an economic and political influence in the vanguard of the European Community. This will be a source of worry for most East Europeans, particularly the Poles. This concern, however, will be cushioned, because Germany will be democratic and integrated into the European Community. German influence will be somewhat diluted as other Western countries also build economic and political ties to the region. Even so, Germany's weight and occasional insensitivity will raise hackles.

East European events will continue to take place against a backdrop of declining relevance for the Warsaw Pact and NATO. The Warsaw Pact as a military alliance is essentially dead, and Soviet efforts to convert it into a political alliance will ultimately fail. Most East European states will aspire to build links to Western Europe and will hope that the CSCE process can provide a basis for such broader security arrangements.

East Europeans will continue to seek substantial US participation in their development as a counterweight to the Soviets and Germans. In the region where both world wars and the Cold War began, a democratic, prosperous, and independent Eastern Europe would be an element of stability rather than an object of great power rivalry in the borderlands between East and West.

[*Source: Central Intelligence Agency:* At Cold War's End: U.S. Intelligence on the Soviet Union and Eastern Europe, 1989–1991. *Ed: Benjamin B. Fischer, 1999.*]

Document No. 122: Record of Conversation between Mikhail Gorbachev and Wojciech Jaruzelski

April 13, 1990

This warm conversation between Gorbachev and the East European leader he respects the most, Polish President Wojciech Jaruzelski, provides an epilogue to the process of change that started with Gorbachev's first meeting as general secretary with bloc leaders in March 1985. Here, Jaruzelski thanks Gorbachev for the way that Moscow has received Prime Minister Tadeusz Mazowiecki, head of the first Solidarity government (see Document No. 107). The former Polish dictator comments that Mazowiecki is a "realist" who is "pro-West but not anti-Soviet" and that "[h]is positions have solidified as the result of his visit to Moscow. He felt the attention and respect for him from the highest Soviet leadership." Such behavior, Jaruzelski says, is especially important for the leaders of Solidarity, many of whom "were repressed, interned, or just oppressed" so that "now when they see normal, respectful treatment many are quickly changing for the better."

The two leaders commiserate on the economic problems they face, on the "adventurism" of the Baltic nationalists (especially the Lithuanians), on the domestic political pressure in the Soviet Union to solve "present-day conflicts ... through the old forceful methods," and even on the way that communists themselves brought on their crisis (in Jaruzelski's words): "when we tried to treat everybody alike, to make 99.99 percent of the voters vote for us, and to the accompaniment of thunderous applause." Jaruzelski mentions the 50th anniversary of the Katyń massacres, and Gorbachev disingenuously reports that the relevant documents were only recently found "in a place where almost no-one thought to search until now."[92]

Perhaps the most poignant moment occurs near the end, when Gorbachev summons the specter of the "Romanian version" (the violent overthrow of Ceauşescu) to defend his program. "My innermost aim, the chief strategic goal, is to complete perestroika, the democratization of society, and for once to have a renewal take place in Russia without blood, without civil war." In this conversation, it is clear that Poland has become a testing ground for what would come next in the Soviet Union, just a short while later. By December 1990, Jaruzelski had lost his position as president and been replaced by Solidarity activist Lech Wałęsa; only a year later, Gorbachev would in turn disappear from the Kremlin along with the red flag of the Soviet Union. But the red stars on the Kremlin towers would remain, likewise the hammer and sickle on the Russian airline, Aeroflot's, insignia; and in Poland, the young—post-communist—politician Aleksander Kwaśniewski, whom Jaruzelski recommends to Gorbachev in this meeting, would replace Wałęsa for his own two terms as president of Poland.

---

[92] When Boris Yeltsin publicly released the Katyń file it became clear that the documents actually resided in the Kremlin archives and had been seen by Gorbachev himself, who had previously decided against their release.

Gorbachev: A warm welcome to you in the Kremlin. I am glad to meet again. We will have an opportunity to synchronize our political clocks. We are united by many things. It has fallen to our lot to decide a multitude of common and immediate problems.

I think this is a timely visit. We are watching the situation in Poland carefully. I would like to hear your view. We should exchange thoughts on the prospects for the Warsaw Treaty, and about the general situation in Europe. [...]

You could say that right now populism is raging [in the USSR]. And populism multiplied by nationalism produces an explosive mix akin to detonating gasoline. It does not easily lend itself to rational control. In this respect the attitudes in your country's society to some degree resemble the situation [in the Soviet Union].

Jaruzelski: We are all children of one epoch. Mazowiecki, being a rationalist, understands the danger of such a situation. He holds to common sense and realizes [his] responsibility for the situation in the country. In this respect we—the representatives of leftist forces—and he are allies.

Mazowiecki also realistically appreciates the need for normal relations with the Soviet Union. In general, there are two wings in the former opposition. One is pro-West and anti-Soviet, the other is pro-West but not anti-Soviet. By his background and philosophy, Mazowiecki keeps to the Western orientation. But at the same time he is a realist and understands the significance of Soviet–Polish relations. His positions have solidified as the result of his visit to Moscow. He felt the attention and respect for him from the highest Soviet leadership.

I would like to emphasize in general, Mikhail Sergeyevich, that the attention you give to members of the Polish leadership justifies itself completely and yields good political results. Of course, the president of the USSR cannot meet with every Polish leader. But when, for example, [Andrzej] Stelmachowski visited the USSR Supreme Soviet and spoke to A.I. Lukyanov, and E.M. Primakov, he came back to the country elated, ready to contribute actively to the development of a constructive relationship with the Soviet Union. It is important to consider the psychological element here as well. Many of the current representatives of "Solidarity" were repressed, interned, or just oppressed. Of course they reacted negatively to this. And now when they see normal, respectful treatment many are quickly changing for the better.

Public opinion polls conducted in Poland show a high level of sympathy with the Soviet leadership during the last several years. Thus, in 1987, 76 percent of people surveyed stated that they liked M.S. Gorbachev; in 1988 it was 79.6 percent; and in February of this year it was 78.8 percent. Correspondingly, 6.2, 5.2, and 4.9 percent declared their antipathy. And this was at the same time that anti-Soviet attitudes were being disseminated quite persistently, especially with the approaching 50th anniversary of the Katyń tragedy.

Gorbachev: The documents on Katyń that will be transferred to you were recently found in the security archives—in a place where almost no-one thought to search until now.

Jaruzelski: I would like to share with you, Mikhail Sergeyevich, my thoughts on the calculations the U.S. is making for the long-term perspective in relations with the Soviet Union, Lithuania, Ukraine, and all of Eastern Europe. I see two major trends. On the one hand there is a realistic approach that aims at decreasing the number of difficulties the Soviet Union is encountering in the *perestroika* process. On the other hand, there are extremist tendencies. It comes down to [the idea] that since the Soviet Union's difficulties are increasing, there should be as many of them as possible in order to bring about the end of the Soviet Union. It seems the first tendency predominates right now. But the temptation to create a kind of cordon against the Soviet Union is also telling.

Gorbachev: It seems that some people would really like to create a, so to speak, contemporary *cordon sanitaire* that would become the political preserve of the West.

Jaruzelski: I think that a constructive approach should not consist of creating some kind of a cordon but the other way around: [it should consist] of building a bridge between the West and the Soviet Union. After all, the East European countries had and now have traditional ties with the West, especially Poland, Czechoslovakia, and Hungary. But on the other hand, they had and still have economic and other ties with the Soviet Union. Socialist ideas will not disappear without a trace, either. People in these countries often remind me of Moliere's hero, who didn't know he was speaking in prose. In Poland, Czechoslovakia, and the GDR people yell "Away with Socialism!" and at the same time they demand social security, or this or that form of welfare they have had, which is practically a demand to retain the achievements of socialism. With time they will begin to remember and value what had been before: inexpensive books, kindergarten, apartments, the absence of unemployment, etc. In many ways we ourselves provoked the present negative reaction when we tried to treat everybody alike, to make 99.99 percent of the voters vote for us, and to the accompaniment of thunderous applause. For too long we were afraid to accept all the good ideas the West had to offer. But with time there will be a sobering up. It is now already clear that we should not idealize the West's approach to such issues as human rights. It has been supporting Ceauşescu for almost 20 years, while the human rights situation in Romania is far worse than in other East European countries.

Gorbachev: By supporting Ceauşescu the West tried to use him as a Trojan horse against the Soviet Union. That was the most important thing. That is why they practically closed their eyes to the most flagrant violations of human rights.

Jaruzelski: As for Lithuania, I mean to say that it is a matter of the Soviet Union's internal affairs. I think we should not tolerate the adventurism of "Sajūdis."[93] I had some experience in interacting with Lithuanian nationalists. In

---

[93] The Lithuanian Reform Movement, Sajūdis, was formed initially to preserve Lithuanian culture. But after its televised October 1988 founding Congress it quickly developed into a mass political movement that played a central role in the drive for national independence.

1939 I was in Lithuania and made it to Siberia only from there. At that time I already felt how strong the anti-Russian and anti-Polish attitudes were in Lithuania. The nationalist tendencies were especially strong in the Shaulist guard detachments. During the Warsaw uprising they served in the gendarmerie.

Gorbachev: During the period of the German occupation the dirtiest work in the concentration camps was done by the Lithuanian nationalists. More than 700,000 people were killed there. Our press published information about this recently. [...]

Gorbachev: There are aspects related to Catholicism here as well. It is important to keep religious issues from being used by the opposition for political purposes. I reminded Pope John Paul II about this once again in a letter, which I sent recently through V. Zagladin.

Jaruzelski: A Solidarity congress will soon take place in Poland. [Solidarity] has so far appeared in the form of a trade union. While leading it, Wałęsa will have to become involved in a conflict with the government, which is headed by Solidarity. This is stimulating a division within the union. [...]

It is absolutely clear that it is necessary to make unpopular decisions in the economic sphere. For that we need the consent of the majority of the people. That can be obtained only through elections.

Gorbachev: That is also a very difficult question for us. The people who proposed [to introduce] unpopular measures all at once, in one sweep and without the necessary preparation were not taking into account the real state of affairs.

Jaruzelski: In Poland, for at least ten years, we prepared the necessary economic reform and the cadres who would be able to correctly understand and implement it. That is why it is easier for the current administration to make substantial reforms, especially since now it is possible to improve relations with the West considerably. [...]

As for the Polish Roman Catholic Church, after your visit to the Vatican one senses a certain stabilization and improvement in its approach to the Soviet Union. However, in general, the Church is being pushed considerably into the background by Solidarity. Right now it does not need the Church as much as it did before. The Church notices this and is worried. In relation to this, I think, a visit by [Cardinal Józef] Glemp to the Soviet Union would be beneficial; he wants to come. Perhaps Anatoly Ivanovich Lukyanov from the Supreme Soviet could meet with him, and maybe you too, Mikhail Sergeyevich, should spare him a few minutes.

Gorbachev: This should be done. It was good when Glemp was here for the millennium of Christianity in Russia.

Jaruzelski: In the army the situation is good right now. Discipline is better than it ever was before, not to mention in comparison to the situation in the Czechoslovak or the GDR armies. There they vote every time whether they should conduct exercises or not. The improvement in discipline is of course also connected to the reduction of the army. There were attempts by the former opposition to spoil everything; for this purpose they sought approaches to the military men. But in the absolute majority they remained unsuccessful. I pay special attention to this. [...]

We will have to update relations considerably between the Warsaw Treaty and NATO, and take into account the fact that the GDR army virtually does not exist anymore.

In connection with the corresponding statements by E. A. Shevardnadze, as well as the recent statement by the Soviet government, we should start resolving the question of the Soviet troop presence in Poland on a practical level. Their partial withdrawal is already foreseen for this year or next. We should determine the timetable of their further presence in Poland without delay. The fact is that this is a kind of "bomb" that could considerably undermine you and us in the eyes of public opinion. I have in mind the fact that Soviet troops in Poland receive food and services at sharply reduced prices, with major subsidies from the Polish government. I think we need to solve this problem, since we are talking about sums that are, strictly speaking, not too considerable. [...]

One more question, Mikhail Sergeyevich. Across from the Polish embassy in Moscow on Malaya Gruzinskaya Street there is a Polish Roman Catholic Church building, which was at some time built with the money of Polish citizens. Right now it serves as a kind of storage space. It is said that there are plans to refurbish it as a concert hall. But perhaps a compromise decision can be reached—perhaps an organ could be installed there so it could be a church and a concert hall at the same time. It would be good if, let's say, Józef Czyrek discussed this with your qualified colleagues and organizations, and came to a decision on this issue. I think this should also be done in view of the forthcoming visit by Pope John Paul II. [...]

Your last decision regarding the Katyń tragedy was a great support to all the people in Poland who speak out in favor of strengthening friendship with the Soviet Union.[94] This removes the claims some people would like to present to the current Soviet government. Let them not blame us, but the people who are truly guilty. [...]

Gorbachev: Thank you for the interesting and substantive information. Everything that is happening in Poland is of great interest to the Soviet Union, especially since every now and then such facts come up that sharply affect our public opinion. I am talking about all kinds of extremist tricks that touch upon the memory of Soviet soldiers who died during the liberation of Poland. In the decades that we have lived in close collaboration and cooperation, we have grown used to perceiving the Polish people not just as neighbors, but as friends. I will say directly that for us Poland is not of opportunistic but of strategic significance, and we plan to have a corresponding relationship with it, respecting

---

[94] On April 13, Gorbachev presented Jaruzelski with complete lists of names of Polish servicemen executed by the Soviet NKVD near Katyń in 1939, thus establishing Stalin and Beria's responsibility for the killings, and filling in the most controversial "blank spot" in the history of Soviet–Polish relations.

the Polish people's freedom of choice concerning the path and model of its development.

But of course we do not close our eyes to the fact that for years Western stations forged their positions in Poland, as in Lithuania and the Baltic States in general. However, the last word is with the Polish people. There are no politics without respect for the people, their aspirations, and their choice. That does not mean, of course, that we do not have our own assessments of the situations in this or that country, and in Poland in particular. Different circles [in the USSR] are watching the situation in Poland. Some recommend that we copy Polish shock therapy for the economy. We are interested in that, although we have no intention of copying anybody.

We value the realism of Poland's new government, and hope that the normal and friendly development of Soviet–Polish relations will correspond with the mutual interests of our people and countries. This is all the more important right now, during the process of unification of the two German states. On all of these issues we value our mutual understanding and cooperation with Poland. I ask you to communicate this to the head of Poland's government, Tadeusz Mazowiecki.

You touched upon a very important issue in our relations with the Western countries. Indeed, the two directions you spoke about can be traced there. During contacts with Western politicians I always drew their attention to the fact that they should not succumb to the temptation to stir up the situation in Eastern Europe. I agree with you that so far the side of reason has the upper hand in the policies of the West. This is also evident in Western politicians' attitudes toward the situation in Lithuania. But we must be careful.

The situation in Eastern Europe should be judged within the framework of pan-European processes. From this point of view it would be absolutely unrealistic to preserve what the alliance countries had in terms of military-political and economic relations. But at the same time the political commotion—striving to reject absolutely everything at once—would also be most detrimental. This kind of commotion is especially telling in Hungary, and to some extent in Czechoslovakia. Even the West would not be keen on a hurried dismantling of the military-political and economic structures that exist in Europe. It would be much smarter not to liquidate them, but to modify them in consideration of the processes taking place on the continent. And these are exactly the processes that fit into the idea of the common European home. All realistically-minded politicians have to take this into account, including Kohl, as much as he hurried ahead with forcing Germany's unification at first.

I think that your considerations regarding the Warsaw Treaty as well as the position of the Northern Group of Soviet Forces can be calmly examined in the context of Soviet–Polish relations. Here it is important not to send any kind of false signals to anybody. These questions must be examined in the context of the pan-European situation and the changes that are and will be taking place here. The Soviet government's main statement about this was made in February of this year.

As regards our economic relations it is absolutely clear that we have approached a limit where we have to substantially renew them. Right now probably everyone agrees that integration into the world economic associations is necessary. This is a normal, healthy process. Isolation has affected our rates of development quite negatively, and it slows down scientific-technological progress. To be sure, changes in the pricing system and exchange payments are needed. Corresponding changes are necessary in the CMEA mechanism as well. Of course, it should not be done the way it was in Lithuania, where one unbeautiful morning [they] found out that they had been thrown overboard by the Soviet Union. At the same time, the transfer to new prices and a new system of exchange payments cannot be put off anymore. We are in favor of starting this transition no later than January of next year.

I think that we could sign a declaration, which would correctly reflect our evaluation of the current state of affairs as well as the prospects for future developments.

I agree with you about the importance of exchanging cultural objects, which have always had an important place in the relations between our peoples, and I am sure that they will bring us even closer. In this connection, I wanted to consult with you in particular about the proposition by our minister of culture, N.N. Gubenko, who sees an opportunity to return to Poland several cultural objects, which, our scholars say, are from the XV–XVII centuries. Right now they are stored in the Hermitage, where they came as trophies from Germany, which had taken them from Poland during the war. Soviet and Polish specialists could probably evaluate these relics and discuss possible ways of transferring them back to Poland. [...]

To briefly describe the situation in the Soviet Union, [one could say] that its acuteness is generally based on the fact that we have moved away from the administrative-command system and from the party's monopoly on power, but we have not arrived at a new system yet, where economic and political methods of leadership would predominate. That is why the ship of our society and government is rolling and pitching on the waves so much. We have decided to compress to the maximum the transition period from one system to the next. We are speeding up the transition to sovereignty by the soviets [elected councils] and the renewal of the CPSU; we are radicalizing economic reform. This last question we will consider in depth tomorrow at the Presidential Council with the participation of the Federation Council. One may say without exaggeration that decisions of a historical scale await us. The government has reviewed these issues several times. We have to switch to an adjustable market with the full-fledged application of prices, credits, and commodity exchanges. The entire infrastructure must be radically renewed.

Two questions are especially acute: the withdrawal of volatile funds and protection of the poor and low-income layers [of society]. Earlier, we had planned this transition for 1992–1993. But we will have to do it sooner, as early as this year. Tensions in society have reached their limit. It is as if we were in a cellar that has been flooded with kerosene up to our waist. There is the danger of an explosion. We must make a choice, there is no way back. In the past everything was based on using more and more new resources. Now they have run dry. Right now we probably have the most politically loaded society. Extremists are going so far as to call for an assault on the Kremlin, Smolny, Lubyanka. And in some places they are mounting assaults. At one point this would have terrified us, but right now party members are ready to come out of the trenches, although not everywhere by a long shot. In a number of places party leaders have won posts as soviet chairmen in open and honest competition.

Recently, members of the Young Communist League [Komsomol] pressed me on the question of the unification of party and governmental posts. I explained to them that right now, when a realignment of powers is underway, we cannot allow a split in society, we cannot let two centers form. This would ruin everything positive that we have been able to achieve over the last several years. Right now Gorbachev is criticized by the left and by the right; and even among the first *obkom* secretaries there are some who have urged people to vote against me for president of the Soviet Union.

Jaruzelski: I have already had to experience this. Even now I encounter some relatively rude and unjust reproaches. By the way, [former party leader Edward] Gierek says in his just published memoirs that Jaruzelski is a Soviet protégé while he, Gierek, fought for Poland's independence. He even writes that supposedly I went together with [former Soviet Defense Minister Andrei] Grechko on a holiday to hunt in Afghanistan, where I have not been once in my life.

Gorbachev: [...]

A vital question is the renewal of the Federation. The USSR Supreme Soviet recently adopted a law on the conditions for exiting the Union; the question of the distribution of powers between the Union and the republics is under consideration. The point is to give the republics more freedom and to fill the Federation with real substance. It seems we will have to make provisions for different levels of independence for some republics. Even in the tsarist empire, Finland, Poland, and the Caucasus, for example, had a status that took into account their special features.

Regarding your thoughts on the Lithuanian problem, you are right. We want Lithuania to feel independent within the Federation. But if the Lithuanians decide to leave the USSR after all, then, of course, the Union and its republics—Belarus, RSFSR—will undoubtedly have the right to secure their rightful interests to the full extent.

Jaruzelski: How do you see Estonia and Latvia's positions?

Gorbachev: I think they are striving for a different kind of freedom and will not follow the path that the current Lithuanian leaders have started upon.

The difficulty of the situation is that many people in our country do not want to see the new reality. They demand that present-day conflicts be solved through the old forceful methods, and they proclaim the rejection of such methods to be a betrayal of socialist principles; as if socialism today can be spread through blood and violence.

Jaruzelski: They do not want to, and evidently they cannot, understand that the matter at stake right now is the prevention of a catastrophe.

Gorbachev: If the Romanian version [of events] had taken place in Russia, the whole country would have been razed. And considering its strategic power, it is more likely that the whole world would have been devastated as well. My innermost aim, the chief strategic goal, is to complete *perestroika*, the democratization of society, and for once to have a renewal take place in Russia without blood, without civil war. It is very difficult to do right now not only because the problems themselves are very difficult and acute, but also because now that I have been elected president the pressure has increased: [people say] you now have such powers, strike!

Lithuania's leaders are narrowing the field for political maneuver through their thoughtless, adventurist actions. It is shrinking like a wild ass' skin. In connection with this I warned U.S. politicians who are interested in the Lithuanian situation that not everything in this conflict depends on Moscow. We are dealing with adventurists. I told [Sen. George] Mitchell [D-Maine] straightforwardly that if something like this had happened in one of your states you would have imposed order there within 24 hours.

Jaruzelski: At one time they dealt a strong rebuff to the South's attempts to secede, and they still celebrate it annually. [...]

[*Source: Archive of the Gorbachev Foundation, Fond 1. Opis 1. On file at the National Security Archive. Translated by Anna Melyakova.*]

Main Actors

Aboimov, Ivan Pavlovich: deputy foreign minister of the USSR from 1988–1990.

Adamec, Ladislav: prime minister of the Czech Socialist Republic from 1987–1988; prime minister of Czechoslovakia from October 1988–December 1989.

Afanas'ev, Viktor Grigorievich: Editor-in-chief of the newspaper *Pravda* from 1976–1989; socialist philosopher.

Akhromeyev, Sergey Fedorovich: marshal of the Soviet Union; chief of the General Staff of the Soviet Armed Forces from 1984–1988, military adviser to Gorbachev, 1988–1991.

Andropov, Yurii Vladimirovich: general secretary of the CC CPSU from November 1982–February 1984, Chairman of the KGB from May 1967–May 1982.

Arbatov, Georgy Arkadievich: leading Soviet specialist on North America; member of the CC CPSU, deputy of the USSR Supreme Soviet from 1989–1991; founder and head, from 1967–1995, of the Institute for U.S. and Canada Studies (ISKAN).

Baker, James A. III: White House chief of staff under President Reagan from 1981–1985; secretary of the Treasury from 1985–1988; secretary of state from 1989–1992.

Baklanov, Oleg Dmitrievich: Soviet armaments specialist; head of the Ministry of General Machine Building from 1983–1988; secretary of the CPSU from 1988–1991, head of the Committee on CPSU Military Policy.

Biriukova, Aleksandra Pavlovna: secretary of the Central Committee from March 1986–September 1988.

Brandt, Willy: chancellor of West Germany from 1969–1974; leader of the Social Democratic Party of Germany from 1964–1987; originated the policy of *Ostpolitik*.

Brezhnev, Leonid Ilyich: general secretary of the CPSU from October 1964–November 1982.

Brutents, Karen Nersesovich: member of the CC CPSU International Department, 1961–1991, first deputy head of the CC CPSU International Department in the 1980s.

Brzezinski, Zbigniew: national security adviser to President Jimmy Carter from 1977–1981; from 1987–1988 worked on the NSC-Defense Department Commission on Integrated Long-Term Strategy; from 1987 to 1989 served on President Bush's Foreign Intelligence Advisory Board.

Castro, Fidel: prime minister of Cuba from 1959–1976; president of Cuba from 1976–2007.

Ceaușescu, Nicolae: general secretary of the Romanian Communist Party from 1965–1989; president of Romania from 1967–1989.

Chebrikov, Viktor Mikhailovich: chairman of the KGB from 1982–1988; secretary of the CC CPSU from September 1988–September 1989.

Chernenko, Konstantin Ustinovich: general secretary of the CPSU from February 1984–March 1985.

Chernyaev, Anatoly Sergeyevich: head of the consultants' group at the CPSU International Department from 1961–1986; from 1986 foreign policy adviser to Gorbachev; member of CC CPSU from 1986–1991.

Czyrek, Józef: minister of foreign affairs of Poland from August 1980–July 1982, Secretary of the Central Committee of the PUWP.

Demichev, Petr Nilovich: member of CC CPSU from 1961–1989; from June 1986–October 1988 first deputy head of the CC CPSU Presidium.

Dobrynin, Anatoly Fedorovich: Soviet ambassador to the United States from 1962–1986; head of the CPSU International Department from 1986–1988.

Dolgikh Vladimir Ivanovich: secretary of the CC CPSU from 1972–1988; candidate member of the CC CPSU Politburo from 1982–1988.

Dubček, Alexander: first secretary of the Communist Party of Czechoslovakia during and immediately after the Prague Spring, from January 1968–April 1969; supported the Velvet Revolution in 1989, elected chairman of the Federal Assembly on December 28, 1989; re-elected in 1990.

d'Estaing, Valéry Giscard: president of the French Republic from 1974–1981; member of the Trilateral Commission.

Falin, Valentin Mikhailovich: head of the CC CPSU International Department from 1988–1991; member of the CC CPSU from 1989, secretary of the CC CPSU from 1990–1991.

Fischer, Oskar: East German minister of foreign affairs from 1975–1990; from 1971–1989, member of the SED CC.

Genscher, Hans Dietrich: foreign minister of the Federal Republic of Germany from 1974–1992.

Gierek, Edward: first secretary of the PUWP from 1970–1980.

Gonzalez, Felipe: prime minister of Spain from 1982–1996.

Gorbachev, Mikhail Sergeyevich: general secretary of the CPSU from 1985–1991.

Gromyko, Andrei Andreyevich: minister of foreign affairs of the USSR from 1957–1985; chairman of the Presidium of the Supreme Soviet from 1985–1988.

Grósz, Károly: general secretary of Hungarian Communist Party from 1988–1989; prime minister of Hungary from 1987–1988.

Honecker, Erich: general secretary of the Socialist Unity Party of the GDR from 1971–1989.

Husák, Gustáv: president of Czechoslovakia from 1975–1989; general secretary of the Communist Party of Czechoslovakia from 1969–1987.

Jakeš, Miloš: general secretary of the Communist Party of Czechoslovakia, 1987–1989.

Jaruzelski, Wojciech: president of the Republic of Poland from 1989–1990; head of the Polish Council of State from 1985–1989; first secretary of the PUWP from 1981–1989; prime minister of the People's Republic of Poland from 1981–1985; Army general.

Kádár, János: prime minister of Hungary from 1956–1958 and 1961–1965; general secretary of the Hungarian Communist Party from 1956–1988.

Khrushchev, Nikita Sergeyevich: chairman of the Soviet Council of Ministers from 1958–1964; first secretary of the Communist Party of the Soviet Union from 1953–1964.

Kissinger, Henry A.: secretary of state from 1973–1977; national security advisor, 1969–1974; member of the Trilateral Commission.

Kochemassov, Vyacheslav Ivanovich: Soviet ambassador to the GDR from 1983–1990.

Kohl, Helmut: chancellor of Germany from 1990–1998; chancellor of the Federal Republic of Germany from 1982–1990.

Koivisto, Mauno: president of Finland from 1982–1994; prime minister of Finland from 1968–1970 and 1979–1982.

Krenz, Egon: general secretary of the Socialist Unity Party of the GDR from October 1989–December 1989; secretary of the SED CC, member of the SED CC Politburo from 1983–1989.

Kryuchkov, Vladimir Aleksandrovich: member of the CC CPSU Politburo from 1989–1991; chairman of the KGB from 1988–1991; member of the GKChP (State Emergency Committee) that attempted to depose Gorbachev in August 1991.

Kulikov, Viktor Georgiyevich: supreme commander of the Unified Armed Forces of the Warsaw Treaty Organization from 1977–1989.

Kwaśniewski, Aleksander: president of the Republic of Poland from 1995–2005; founding member of the Social Democratic Party of Poland in January–February 1990.

Ligachev, Yegor Kuzmich: member of the CC CPSU Politburo from 1985–1990; head of the Department of Organizational Party Work from 1983–1988.

Lukyanov, Anatoly Ivanovich: chairman of the Supreme Soviet of the USSR from 1990–1991; secretary of the CC CPSU from 1987–1988; accused of participating in the failed August 1991 attempt to oust Gorbachev.

MacEachin, Douglas: head of the office of Soviet Analysis (SOVA) at the CIA from 1984–1989, later Deputy Director of Intelligence.

Matlock, Jack: U.S. ambassador to the Soviet Union from 1987–1991.

Mazowiecki, Tadeusz: prime minister of the Republic of Poland from August 1989–December 1990.

Medvedev, Vadim Andreyevich: chairman of the Ideology Committee of the CC CPSU from 1988–1991; senior adviser to Gorbachev in 1991; member of the CC CPSU Politburo from 1988–1990.

Mitterrand, François: president of the French Republic from 1981–1995.

Mladenov, Petar: president of Bulgaria from April–July 1990; chairman of the Council of State of the People's Republic of Bulgaria from 1989–1990; foreign minister from 1971–1989.

Modrow, Hans: prime minister of the German Democratic Republic from 1989–1990.

Najibullah, Mohammad: president of the Democratic Republic of Afghanistan from 1987–1992.

Nakasone, Yasuhiro: prime minister of Japan from 1982–1987.

Németh, Miklós: prime minister of Hungary from 1988–1990.

Nyers, Rezső: chairman of the Hungarian Socialist Workers Party from 1988–1989.

Occhetto, Achille: secretary-general of the Italian Communist Party from 1988–1994.

Ponomarev, Boris Nikolayevich: chief of the International Department of the CPSU from 1955–1986.

Pozsgay, Imre: deputy president of Hungary from 1989–1991; minister of state of the Hungarian Socialist Workers Party from 1988–1989.

Rakowski, Mieczysław: prime minister of the People's Republic of Poland from 1988–1989.

Reagan, Ronald W.: president of the United States from 1981–1989.

Rusakov, Konstantin Viktorovich: head of the CC CPSU Department of Relations with Communist and Workers' Parties of Socialist Countries, secretary of the CC CPSU from 1977–1986.

Ryzhkov, Nikolay Ivanovich: chairman of the Council of Ministers of the Soviet Union from 1985–1991; member of the CC CPSU Politburo from 1985–1990.

Sakharov, Andrei Dmitrievich: Soviet nuclear physicist, human rights activist; awarded Nobel Peace Prize in 1975.

Schmidt, Helmut: chancellor of West Germany from 1974–1982.

Scowcroft, Brent: national security advisor from 1974–77, and 1989–1993.

Shakhnazarov, Georgy Khosroyevich: adviser to Gorbachev from 1988–1991.

Shevardnadze, Eduard Amvrosiyevich: president of Georgia from 1995–2003; minister of foreign affairs of the Soviet Union from 1985–1990.

Shultz, George P.: secretary of state from 1982–1989.

Sokolov, Sergey Leonidovich: minister of defense of the Soviet Union from 1984–1987.

Solomentsev, Mikhail Sergeyevich: chairman of the CC CPSU Party Control Committee from 1983–1988; chairman of the Council of Ministers of the Soviet Union from 1971–1983.

Stoph, Willi: prime minister of the GDR from 1964–1973 and from 1976–1989.

Štrougal, Lubomír: prime minister of Czechoslovakia from 1971–1988.

Szűrös, Mátyás: provisional president of the Republic of Hungary from October 1989 to May 1990.

Tarasenko, Sergey: main adviser to Soviet Foreign Minister Eduard Shevardnadze from 1985–1990.

Teltschik, Horst: national security adviser to Chancellor Helmut Kohl from 1982–1990.

Thatcher, Margaret: prime minister of the United Kingdom from 1979–1990.

Vorontsov, Yulii Mikhailovich: Soviet ambassador to the United Nations from 1990–1991; ambassador to Afghanistan from 1988–1990; first deputy minister of foreign affairs from 1986–1989; ambassador to France from 1983–1986.

Vorotnikov, Vitalii Ivanovich: chairman of the Supreme Soviet of the USSR from 1988–1990.

Wałęsa, Lech: president of the Republic of Poland from 1990–1995; a founder of the Solidarity Trade Union.

Weizsäcker, Richard von: president of Germany from 1984–1994.

Xiaoping, Deng: de facto leader of China from 1978 until the early 1990s; general secretary of the Communist Party of China from 1956–1967.

Yakovlev, Aleksandr Nikolayevich: member of the Politburo from 1987–1990; senior adviser to Gorbachev from 1985 until 1991; called "the Godfather of *glasnost.*"

Yazov, Dmitri Timofeyevich: minister of defense of the Soviet Union from 1987–1991.

Yeltsin, Boris Nikolayevich: president of the Russian Federation from 1991–1999; first secretary of the CPSU Moscow City Committee from 1985–1987.

Zagladin, Vadim Valentinovich: adviser to Gorbachev from 1988–1991; consultant, deputy director and first deputy director of the International Department of the CPSU from 1964–1988.

Zaikov, Lev Nikolayevich: first secretary of the CPSU Moscow City Committee from 1987–1989.

Zimyanin, Mikhail Vasilievich: secretary of the CC CPSU specializing in ideological work from 1976–1987; editor-in-chief of *Pravda* from 1965–1976.

Zhivkov, Todor: first secretary (1954–1981) then general secretary (1981–1989) of the Bulgarian Communist Party; chairman of the Bulgarian Council of State from 1971–1989.

Selected Bibliography

Baker, James. *The Politics of Diplomacy*. New York: G. P. Putnam's Sons, 1995.

Békés, Csaba. "Back to Europe: The International Background of the Political Transition in Hungary, 1988–1990," in *The Roundtable Talks of 1989: The Genesis of Hungarian Democracy: Analysis and Documents*, ed. Bozóki, András (Budapest: Central European University Press, 2002), 237–272.

Békés, Csaba, Malcolm Byrne, János M. Rainer, eds. *The 1956 Hungarian Revolution: A History in Documents*. Budapest: Central European University Press, 2002.

Beschloss, Michael and Strobe Talbott. *At the Highest Levels*. Boston: Little, Brown and Company, 1993.

Blanton, Thomas. "When Did the Cold War End?" *Cold War International History Project Bulletin* 10 (Winter 1997): 184–193.

Braithwaite, Rodric. *Across the Moscow River: The World Turned Upside Down*. New Haven: Yale University Press, 2002.

Brooks, Stephen G. and William C. Wohlforth. "Power, Globalization, and the End of the Cold War," *International Security* 25, No. 3 (2000–2001): pp. 5–53.

Brown, Archie. *The Gorbachev Factor*. Oxford: Oxford University Press, 1996.

Brown, Archie, ed. *The Demise of Marxism-Leninism in Russia*. New York: Palgrave Macmillan, 2004.

Brown, Archie. *Seven Years that Changed the World: Perestroika in Perspective*. Oxford: Oxford University Press, 2007.

Brown, Archie. "The Change to Engagement in Britain's Cold War Policy: The Origins of the Thatcher–Gorbachev Relationship," *Journal of Cold War Studies* 10:3 (Summer 2008): 3–47.

Brzezinski, Zbigniew. *The Grand Failure: The Birth and Death of Communism in the Twentieth Century*. New York: Scribners, 1989.

Bush, George H.W. and Brent Scowcroft. *A World Transformed*. New York: Alfred A. Knopf, 1998.

Chafetz, Glenn R. *Gorbachev, Reform, and the Brezhnev Doctrine: Soviet Policy toward Eastern Europe, 1985–1990*. Westport, CT: Praeger, 1993.

Chernyaev, Anatoly. "The Diary of Anatoly Chernyaev," National Security Archive electronic briefing book, October 19, 1985. *http://www.gwu.edu/~nsarchiv/NSAEBB/NSAEBB192/index.htm*

Chernyaev, Anatoly. *My Six Years with Gorbachev*. Philadelphia: Pennsylvania State University Press, 2000.

707

Chernyaev, Anatoly, et al., eds. *V Politburo TsK KPSS: po zapisyam Anatoliya Chernyaeva, Vadima Medvedeva, Georgiya Shakhnazarova (1985–1991)*. Moscow: Alpina Business Books, 2006.

Dawisha Karen. *Eastern Europe, Gorbachev, and Reform: The Great Challenge*. Cambridge, UK: Cambridge University Press, 1988.

Dobbs, Michael. *Down With Big Brother: The Fall of the Soviet Empire*. New York: Alfred A. Knopf, 1997.

Dobrynin, Anatoly. *In Confidence: Moscow's Ambassador to America's Six Cold War Presidents (1962–1986)*. New York: Times Books, Random House, 1995.

English, Robert. *Russia and the Idea of the West: Gorbachev, Intellectuals, and the End of the Cold War*. New York: Columbia University Press, 2000.

Evangelista, Matthew. *Unarmed Forces: The Transnational Movement to End the Cold War*. Ithaca: Cornell University Press, 1999.

Falin, Valentin. *Bez skidok na obstoyatel'stva: Politicheskie vospominaniya*. Moscow: Respublika, Sovremennik, 1999.

FitzGerald, Frances. *Way Out There In the Blue: Reagan, Star Wars, and the End of the Cold War*. New York: Simon & Schuster, 2000.

Gaidar, Yegor. *Gibel' Imperii: Uroki dlya sovremennoi Rossii*. Moscow: ROSSPEN, 2006.

Garthoff, Raymond L. *Détente and Confrontation: American–Soviet Relations from Nixon to Reagan*. Washington DC: Brookings Institution Press, 1994.

Garthoff, Raymond L. *The Great Transition: American–Soviet Relations and the End of the Cold War*. Washington, DC: The Brookings Institution, 1994.

Garthoff, Raymond L. "Estimating Soviet Military Intentions and Capabilities," in *Watching the Bear: Essays on CIA's Analysis of the Soviet Union*, eds. Haines, Gerald K. and Robert E. Leggett (Langley, VA: Central Intelligence Agency, Center for the Study of Intelligence, 2002).

Garton Ash, Timothy. *The Uses of Adversity: Essays on the Fate of Central Europe*. New York: Random House, 1989.

Garton Ash, Timothy. *The Magic Lantern: The Revolution of '89 Witnessed in Warsaw, Budapest, Berlin, and Prague*. New York: Random House, 1990.

Garton Ash, Timothy. *In Europe's Name: Germany and the Divided Continent*. New York: Random House, 1993.

Gates, Robert M. *From the Shadows: The Ultimate Insider's Story of Five Presidents and How They Won the Cold War*. New York: Simon & Schuster, 1996.

Gati, Charles. *The Bloc that Failed: Soviet–East European Relations in Transition*. Bloomington: Indiana University Press, 1990.

Goldgeier, James. *Not Whether but When: The U.S. Decision to Enlarge NATO*. Washington DC: Brookings Institution Press, 1999.

Gorbachev, Mikhail. *Zhizn' i reformy*. Moscow: Novosti, 1995.

Gorbachev, Mikhail. *Ponyat' perestroiku ... Pochemu eto vazhno seichas*. Moscow: Alpina Books 2006.

Grachev, Andrei. *Gorbachev*. Moscow: Vagrius, 2001.

Grachev, Andrei. *Gorbachev's Gamble: Soviet Foreign Policy and the End of the Cold War.* Cambridge, UK: Polity, 2008.

Hertle, Hans-Hermann. "The Fall of the Wall: The Unintended Self-Dissolution of East Germany's Ruling Regime," *Cold War International History Project Bulletin,* 12/13 (Fall/Winter 2001): 131–164.

Horn, Gyula. *Freiheit, die ich meine. Erinnerungen des ungarischen Aussenministers, der den Eisernen Vorhang Delete.* Hamburg 1991.

Hutchings, Robert L. *American Diplomacy and the End of the Cold War.* Baltimore: Johns Hopkins University Press, 1997.

Kashlev, Yurii. *Helsinskii protsess 1975–2005: Svet i teni glazami uchastnika.* Moscow: Izvestia, 2005.

Kramer, Mark. "The Collapse of East European Communism and the Repercussions within the Soviet Union" (Parts I, II, III) in *Journal of Cold War Studies* 5, no. 4 (Fall 2003); vol. 6, no. 4 (Fall 2004); and vol. 7, no. 1 (Winter 2005).

Kramer, Mark. "The Myth of a No-NATO-Enlargement Pledge to Russia," *The Washington Quarterly* 32, no. 2 (April 2009): 39–61.

Kusters, Hanns Jurgen and Daniel Hofmann, eds. *Deutsche Einheit Sonderedition und den Akten des Bundeskanzleramtes 1989/90.* Munich: R. Oldenbourg Verlag, 1998.

Kvitsinsky, Yuli. *Vremya i sluchai: Zametki professionala.* Moscow: Olma-Press, 1999.

Leffler, Melvyn P. *For the Soul of Mankind: The United States, the Soviet Union, and the Cold War.* New York: Hill and Wang, 2007.

Legvold, Robert, ed. *Russian Foreign Policy in the 21st Century and the Shadow of the Past.* New York: Columbia University Press, 2007.

Lettow, Paul. *Ronald Reagan and His Quest to Abolish Nuclear Weapons.* New York: Random House, 2005.

Levesque, Jacques. *The Enigma of 1989: The USSR and the Liberation of Eastern Europe.* Berkeley: University of California Press, 1997.

Lundberg, Kirsten. "CIA and the Fall of the Soviet Empire: The Politics of Getting It Right," Case Study C16-94-1251.0, Harvard University, Kennedy School of Government, 1994.

Mann, James. *The Rebellion of Ronald Reagan.* New York: Viking, 2009.

Mastny, Vojtech. *The Cold War and Soviet Insecurity: The Stalin Years.* Oxford: Oxford University Press, 1996.

Mastny, Vojtech and Malcolm Byrne, eds. *A Cardboard Castle? An Inside History of the Warsaw Pact, 1955–1991.* Budapest: Central European University Press, 2005.

Matlock, Jack. *Autopsy on an Empire: The American Ambassador's Account of the Collapse of the Soviet Union.* New York: Random House, 1995.

Matlock, Jack. *Reagan and Gorbachev: How the Cold War Ended.* New York: Random House, 2004.

MccGwire, Michael. "NATO Expansion: 'A Policy Error of Historic Importance,'" *Review of International Studies* 24, no. 1 (1998), reprinted with introduction by Michael Clarke in *International Affairs* 84, no. 6 (November 2008): 1281–1301.

Medvedev, Vadim. *Raspad*. Moscow: Mezhdunarodnye Otnoshenia, 1994.

Medvedev, Vadim. *V Komande Gorbacheva*. Moscow, 1994.

Nation, R. Craig. *Black Earth, Red Star: A History of Soviet Security Policy, 1917–1991*. Ithaca: Cornell University Press, 1992.

Navrátil, Jaromír et al., eds. *The Prague Spring 1968: A National Security Archive Documents Reader*. Budapest: Central European University Press, 1998.

Oberdorfer, Don. *The Turn: From the Cold War to a New Era*. New York: Touchstone/Simon & Schuster, 1992.

Odom, William E. *The Collapse of the Soviet Military*. New Haven: Yale University Press, 1998.

Ostermann, Christian, ed. *Uprising in East Germany, 1953: The Cold War, the German Question, and the First Major Upheaval Behind the Iron Curtain*. Budapest: Central European University Press, 2001.

Paczkowski Andrzej and Malcolm Byrne, eds. *From Solidarity to Martial Law, the Polish Crisis of 1980–1981: A Documentary History*. Budapest: Central European University Press, 2007.

Painter, David S. and Thomas S. Blanton. "The End of the Cold War," in *A Companion to Post-1945 America*, eds. Agnew, Jean-Christophe and Roy Rosenzweig (Oxford: Blackwell Publishing, 2002).

Palazchenko, Pavel. *My Years with Gorbachev and Shevardnadze: The Memoir of a Soviet Interpreter*. University Park, PA: Pennsylvania State University Press, 1997.

Ryzhkov, Nikolay. *Tragediya velikoi strany*. Moscow: Veche, 2007.

Salmon, Patrick, Keith Hamilton and Stephen Robert Twigge. *Britain And German Unification 1989–90: Documents On British Policy Overseas*, Series III, Volume VII (Whitehall Histories). London: Routledge, 2009.

Sarotte, Mary "Elite Intransigence and the End of the Berlin Wall," *German Politics* 2 (August 1993), pp. 270–287.

Sarotte, Mary. *1989: The Struggle to Create Post-Cold War Europe*. Princeton: Princeton University Press, 2009.

Schwartz, Stephen I., ed. *Atomic Audit: The Costs and Consequences of Nuclear Weapons*. Washington: Brookings Institution, 1998.

Schweizer, Peter. *Victory: The Reagan Administration's Secret Strategy that Hastened the Collapse of the Soviet Union*. New York: Atlantic Monthly Press, 1994.

Schweizer, Peter, ed. *The Fall of the Berlin Wall: Reassessing the Causes and Consequences of the End of the Cold War*. Stanford: Hoover Institution Press, 2000.

Schweizer, Peter. *Reagan's War: The Epic Story of His Forty-Year Struggle and Final Triumph Over Communism*. New York: Doubleday, 2002.

Shakhnazarov, Georgy. *Tsena svobody*. Moscow: Rossika Zevs, 1993.

Shevardnadze, Eduard. "No One Can Isolate Us, Save Ourselves; Self-Isolation Is The Ultimate Danger." *Slavic Review* 51, no.1 (Spring 1992).

Shevardnadze, Eduard. *The Future Belongs to Freedom*. New York: Free Press, 1991.

Wohlforth, William C. *The Elusive Balance: Power and Perceptions during the Cold War*. Ithaca: Cornell University Press, 1993.

Wohlforth, William C., ed. *Cold War Endgame: Oral History, Analysis, Debate*. University Park, PA: Pennsylvania State University Press, 2003.

Yakovlev, Alexander. *Sumerki* Moscow: Materik, 2003.

Yazov, Dmitri. *Udary sud'by*. Moscow: Kniga i Biznes, 2000.

Zelikow, Philip and Condoleezza Rice. *Germany Unified and Europe Transformed: A Study in Statecraft*. Cambridge, MA: Harvard University Press, 1997.

Zubok, Vladislav M. *A Failed Empire: The Soviet Union in the Cold War from Stalin to Gorbachev*. Chapel Hill: University of North Carolina Press, 2007.

Index

and Gorbachev, 30, 69, 192, 480, 598, 675–684
  guarantees on NATO, 93–95
  statements on, 111, 200
letter to Helmut Kohl, 685–687
and NSC reform, 67, 197–198
and resistance to *perestroika*, 73, 74, 193, 415, 438–439, 447
and Shevardnadze, 213, 613, 641
and Soviet–U.S. "condominium," 64, 65, 177, 341
and U.S. "pause," 196
and use of force in Romania, 91, 661–662
and "Western" values, 645–646
Balance of forces, 21, 249–250, 494, 509, 586
Balance of power, 2, 45, 64, 199, 566
Balkans, 255, 476, 478, 688–690
Baltic Republics, 27–28, 34, 47, 101, 167–169, 180
  elections in, 450–451
  political instability in, 325–326, 331, 561
  secession of, 180–181, 212, 577, 578
  Soviet nonuse of force in, 145, 165, 326, 451
  U.S. comments on, 508, 635
  Western noninterference in, 561–562, 643
Barcikowski, Kazimierz, 455, 458–459
Batsanov, Boris, 213
Békés, Csaba, 151–154
Berecz, János, 313, 321–323
Berlin Wall, fall of, xxii, 21, 32, 34–35, 44, 49, 82–84, 569, 582–583, 587
  description of, 587–589
Berlinguer, Enrico, 108
Bil'ak, Vasil, 9, 125, 260
Billington, James, 58, 60, 110

Bisztyga, Jan, 454, 455
Blanton, Thomas, xxi, xxiii, 24, 99, 102, 138–139, 159, 174, 194, 204–205, 209
Blatov, Anatoly, 133
Bogomolov Institute, 18, 24, 39, 44, 100–101, 151, 365–381
Bonn Declaration (1989), 33
Bozóki, András, 97–98
Brandt, Willy, 571, 673, 682
Brezhnev Doctrine, xxi, 3–11, 31, 41, 44, 123–124, 130–133, 136, 138, 140–141, 151–152
  origins under Khrushchev, 152
  origins under Stalin, 136, 152
  revocation of, 18, 82, 121, 130–133, 136–137, 139, 217, 268, 463, 466, 525, 527, 561, 614, 632, 669–671
  and Romanian revolution (1989), 91, 662, 666–667
Brezhnev, Leonid, 112, 114, 133, 387, 531, 544
  and comparison to Gorbachev, 149–150, 328, 330
  and Czechoslovakia, 127, 149–150
  and East Germany, 148
  foreign policy of, 23, 114, 127, 129, 133, 148, 166, 286, 330
  and ideology, 108, 328
  and Poland, 129, 133, 136, 147–148
  and reform, 114, 531
  and Soviet economy, 184, 185, 211
  and technology, 544
Brown, Archie, 12, 135
Brussels Summit (1989). *See* North Atlantic Treaty Organization (NATO)
Brzezinski, Zbigniew, 21, 33, 72, 175, 178, 179, 299, 438, 563–568
Bukur, I., 661–663

Bulgaria, 255, 257, 374–375
  See also Zhivkov, Todor
  Communist Party plenum
    (1989), 574–576
  democratization of, 591
  and perestroika, 651–652
  Soviet aid to, 156, 417
  Soviet nonintervention in, 149,
    652, 660
  and Soviet relations, 161
Bush, George H.W., 22, 30, 33,
    36, 46, 51, 75
  See also United States
  administration of, 23, 196–197,
    334–335, 341
    compared to Reagan
      administration, 32, 61–62,
      66, 67, 70, 75, 80, 185, 195,
      463, 601
  on "Common European home,"
    73–74, 96–97
  domestic pressures on, 180, 196–
    197, 464
  and Eastern Europe, 52, 56, 72,
    75, 79–80, 484–487, 527
  on fall of Berlin Wall, 82, 83, 86,
    587–588, 595, 596, 619, 627
  and German reunification, 33,
    36, 46, 53, 73, 86, 89, 190–
    191, 198, 657
  and Gorbachev, 69, 74, 80, 81,
    194, 347–348, 352
    mistrust of, 53, 58, 60, 62, 63,
    193
  NSC monitoring of, 74, 101,
    477
  and Hungary, 76–79
  leadership style of, 75, 96, 334,
    337, 463–464, 465, 497
  and Poland, 71–72, 75–79, 483,
    497, 587
    visit to (1989), 503–505
  policy toward Soviet Union, 23,
    53, 175, 194, 527–529

"pause" in, xx, 20, 23, 29, 32,
    46, 52, 62, 66–71, 78, 98, 192–
    195, 263, 333–334, 347–348
  as president-elect, 57, 334
  and support for perestroika, 504,
    621, 677
  and "the vision thing," 63, 64,
    67, 73, 196

C

Canada, 598–601
Carlucci, Frank, 57, 187
Carter, Jimmy, 52, 61, 99, 141–
    142, 182
Casey, William, 111, 184
Castro, Fidel, 13, 88, 192, 234,
    237, 586, 630–631, 633, 684
  See also Cuba
CC CPSU See Soviet Communist
    Party Central Committee (CC
    CPSU)
Ceauşescu, Nicolae, 5, 10, 31, 49,
    56, 91, 123, 147, 236, 238, 356,
    373, 586
  See also Romania
  criticism of, 217, 226, 253–254,
    409, 478, 490, 499, 586
  and Gorbachev, 144, 218, 227–
    228, 253–254, 476
  overthrow of, 661–664, 691
  and perestroika, 258, 397–398
Central Intelligence Agency (CIA)
  See also Intelligence estimates
    (U.S.)
  destabilization of Soviet Union,
    181–182, 188
  Office of Soviet Analysis, 522
  views on Gorbachev, 110–111,
    261–263, 325–330
Chebrikov, Viktor, 250, 269–270,
    328, 329
  and Congress of People's
    Deputies, 427–428

Chen Jian, 165
Cheney, Richard, 23, 66, 82, 650
Chernenko, Konstantin, 109, 126, 129, 133
  funeral of, xxi, 4, 5, 111, 121, 130, 217–218
Chernobyl nuclear accident (1986), 26, 131, 213, 226, 228, 393, 422, 430
  and *perestroika*, 134–135
Chernyaev, Anatoly, xviii, 7, 12, 17, 35, 92, 99, 120, 199–200, 209
  on the Baltic Republics, 167–168
  on China, 166–168
  diary of, 220–221, 309–310, 331, 542–543, 547, 548–549
    on Berlin Wall, 586
    on German reunification, 673–674
    on Gorbachev's state of mind, 449
  foreword by, xvii–xxiv
  on Gorbachev's ambiguous statements, 163
  on Gorbachev's European policy, 143–144, 163–164
  memoranda from, 222–223, 389
  on nonintervention in Eastern Europe, 121–122, 125, 146, 149–150
  on origins of Soviet "new thinking," 103–104, 108–109
  on Poland, 133–135, 138
  on Soviet–U.S. relations, 189–193
China, 221, 605, 626
  See also Deng Xiaoping
  Gorbachev's visit to (1989), 165–169
  and *perestroika*, 416
  and Soviet relations, 227
  Tiananmen Square protests (1989), 75, 165–166, 169–170
Ciosek, Stanisław, 453, 455, 458

CMEA. *See* Council for Mutual Economic Assistance
COCOM. *See* Coordinating Committee on Export Controls
Commission on Poland (Soviet Union), 130, 157
"Common European home," xxii, 3, 11, 18–22, 33, 45, 96–97, 222, 227, 248, 290–291, 493–495
  See also "New thinking"
Conference on Security and Cooperation in Europe (CSCE), xxii, 20, 35, 495–496, 679
  See also Helsinki Accords (1975)
Coordinating Committee on Export Controls (COCOM), 406, 683–684
Council for Mutual Economic Assistance (CMEA), 4, 7, 14–16, 228, 232, 236, 358–359
  cooperation with U.S., 642–643
  failure of, 265–266
  integration with EC, 8, 14, 45, 495
  and Poland, 603, 697, 536
  reform of, 266, 321
Council of Europe, 20
CPSU. *See* Soviet Communist Party (CPSU)
Crowe, William, 70, 640
CSCE. *See* Conference on Security and Cooperation in Europe (CSCE)
Cuba, 266, 415, 629
  See also Castro, Fidel
  normalization of relations with U.S., 630–631
Czarzasty, Zygmunt, 453, 457, 459
Czechoslovakia, 9, 372–373
  and economic reform, 258
  and *perestroika*, 248, 259–260, 271–272, 373
  and political instability, 436–437, 608–610

716

mass demonstrations, 82
and political reform
personnel changes in, 409, 411
Prague Spring (1968), 9, 127,
133, 149–150, 157, 248, 408–
409, 670
Soviet nonintervention in, 125,
127, 135, 149, 204
and Soviet relations, 229, 245,
247–248, 670
Soviet troop withdrawal, 43–44,
244–246
Velvet Revolution (1989), xxii,
31, 608
Czechoslovak Communist Party
(CPCz), 411
Central Committee of, 608–610
and debate on use of force, 608–
609
Czyrek, Józef, 23–24, 41–42, 453–
455, 461, 695
and Gorbachev, 292–305

D

Danchev, Petko, 575
Davis, John, 81, 482
Dawisha, Karen, 111–112, 149,
155–156, 174
Deng Xiaoping, 166, 169, 227,
586, 605
See also China
d'Estaing, Giscard, 349, 350, 563,
619, 641
Developing countries, 152, 183,
261–263, 327, 328, 350
Dobrynin, Anatoly, 12, 23, 65,
195, 199–201, 203, 206, 228,
234, 239, 250, 311, 329, 345,
346, 637
on Socialist countries and
perestroika, 241
Dolgikh, Vladimir, 217, 288
Dregger, Alfred, 566

Dubček, Alexander, 408–409,
437
compared with Gorbachev, 119,
138, 248, 286, 395
Dumas, Roland, 91, 594, 661,
680

E

Eastern Europe
See also Gorbachev, Mikhail,
Eastern Europe policy
See also Socialist countries
abandonment vs. neglect, 4, 7,
14, 363
democratization of, 29–31, 45,
49, 356, 542–543, 688–689
economic burden on Soviet
Union, 14–17, 156, 265–266,
416–417
and economic reform, 257–258,
281, 366
and political unrest, 284–285,
366–369, 553–554
Soviet military presence in, 251
Soviet nonintervention in
38–41, 45, 121–125, 153–154,
172–173, 203, 234, 259–260,
268
Soviet trade with, 16, 254, 671–
672
Soviet troop withdrawal from,
145, 251, 311, 331, 335–339,
379
Shakhnazarov's proposal for,
555–557
strategic value of, 17
Western aid to, 558–560, 689
Western noninterference in, 465–
466, 477, 497, 532, 564–565,
645, 655
East–West relations, 153, 291, 693
and détente, 555–557
and economic relations, 404–405

and European stability, 64, 80,
206, 341, 377, 503, 504, 530,
675, 688
Environmental protection, 495,
528, 624
Estonia, 168, 331, 451, 561, 577,
698
Eurocommunism, 19, 102–103,
108–109, 152–153, 171–172
European Community (EC), 39,
350, 595
European Free Trade Association,
495
European Union (EU), 46

F

Falin, Valentin, 35–36, 94, 168,
170, 200, 209
Fedorov, Rafail, 673–674
Finland, 561–562
"Finlandization," 376–378
Fischer, Oskar, 515, 517, 518–520
Foley, Tom, 464

France, 477
and *perestroika,* 489
and Soviet relations, 547
Frolov, Ivan, 578
Frost, David, 82, 87

G

Garthoff, Raymond, 59
Gates, Robert, 23, 72, 79, 83, 101,
132, 183, 195
intelligence estimates of, 261–263
on Soviet "new thinking," 55, 60,
68, 111, 261–263, 325, 390,
442, 479
on Gorbachev, 74
Gdula, Andrzej, 454, 456, 459
General Agreement on Tariffs and
Trade (GATT), 406, 622, 628

Genscher, Hans-Dietrich, 36, 85–
87, 90, 159, 482, 597, 680
and Gorbachev, 653–656, 658–
659
Georgia (Soviet Union), 160–161
See also Tbilisi demonstrations
(1989)
Gerasimov, Gennadii, 82, 561
German reunification, xxii, 17, 30–
36, 85–87, 91, 94–95, 191, 200,
566, 593–594
and "2 +4" formula, 679, 681,
686
opposition to, 547, 567, 571, 581,
601, 690
pace of, 648–649, 656, 673–674,
678–679
and Soviet "new thinking," 223,
309
and stability in Europe, 30, 33,
35, 85, 92, 465, 476–477, 590–
592, 593–594, 685–686
and Western leaders, 33, 35–37,
144–145, 175, 648, 649–650,
657 (*See also under* specific
leaders)
Germany (East), 34, 82, 374,
615–616
democratization of, 90, 92, 582–
583
economic ties with West
Germany, 570
emigration from, 155, 515, 517,
518–520, 542, 553
and Hungarian relations, 515–
516
and leadership of, 545–546
mass demonstrations in, 34, 82,
542
and pace of reform, 580–584
political opposition in, 552–
554
and Soviet nonintervention in,
572

Gromyko, Andrei, 111, 201, 249, 286, 288, 328–329, 330

Grósz, Károly, 24, 163, 273, 283, 313–321, 412, 486, 499
and Gorbachev, 409–410, 418–419, 511–514
and Hungarian roundtable negotiations, 470–471

Group of Soviet Forces in Germany, 338

H

Hager, Kurt, 148, 516, 551–554

Haig, Alexander, 141, 183

Havel, Václav, 49, 94, 166, 436, 437, 608

Helsinki Accords (1975), 21, 73, 90, 562, 619, 647, 648
See also Conference on Security and Cooperation in Europe (CSCE)

Hengsbach, Franz, 584

Hermann, Richard, 67, 196–198

Hershberg, James, 130–131, 138, 164–165, 203

Hitler, Adolf, 90, 485, 653, 655, 656

Hodnett, Grey, 522

Honecker, Erich, 10, 30, 32, 34, 42, 82, 122–123, 143–144, 163, 218, 226, 228
assessments of, 222, 476–477, 531–532
Gorbachev and, 127, 146–148, 221, 226, 548–549
perestroika and, 241–243
replacement of, 548, 570–573
Shevardnadze and, 460–462
and Soviet forces, 107

Honecker, Margot, 477

Horn, Gyula, 31, 162–163, 292, 515, 516

Hugo, Victor, 20, 21

Human rights, 45, 288, 312, 361, 401–403, 495

Hungarian Socialist Workers' Party (HSWP), 313–324, 355, 471, 512–513, 565

Hungary, 16–17, 52, 371–372
border opening of, xxii, 24, 34, 72, 82, 154, 159, 162
East German response to, 517, 518–519
Soviet response to, 412–413
debt of, 133–134, 319–320, 322, 572
democratization of, 472–473, 511–514
economy of, 156, 229, 319
elections in (1990), 81
leadership of, 273–276, 314, 319
Political Executive Committee, 511–514
political unrest in, 255, 320, 419
reforms in, 30, 76, 132, 205, 319–323
revolution in (1956), 27, 76, 152–153, 419
Roundtable negotiations (1989), 470–474
Soviet nonintervention in, 39, 129, 419, 465
and Soviet trade balance, 315–316, 321
Soviet troop presence in, 106, 315, 513
and U.S. relations, 76–79, 82, 275

Hurd, Douglas, 47

Husák, Gustáv, 9, 127, 149, 217, 218, 227, 228, 236, 239, 242, 247, 248
and Gorbachev, 271–272

Hussein, Saddam, 162

I

Ignatenko, Vitaly, 122

INF Treaty, 54, 57, 63, 64, 69, 79, 185, 261, 263, 277, 393
Information security, 269, 338–340
Inozemtsev, Nikolay, 113
Institute of Europe (Soviet Union), 20
Institute of the Economy of the World Socialist System. *See* Bogomolev Institute
Intelligence estimates (U.S.), 55–56, 60, 67, 139–140, 183–184, 186–187, 197, 257–258, 325–330
  See also Central Intelligence Agency
  disagreements on, 67, 444–445
  on Eastern Europe, 186
  on Gorbachev, 432–435
  NIE 11-4-89, 442–445
  NIE 11/12-9-88, 280–285
  NIE 12-90, 688–690
  on stability of Soviet Union, 522–524
  "Team B," 182
International Communist Movement, 229, 238
International Monetary Fund (IMF)
  and Poland, 72, 560, 588, 596, 615
Iran and Soviet relations, 317
Iran–Iraq War, 317, 440, 642
Iraq, 188, 208
Iran–Contra scandal, 55, 67, 186–187, 197
Israel
  and Hungarian relations, 317, 412
  and Soviet relations, 413
Italian Communist Party, 108–109, 408

J

Jackson–Vanik Amendment (U.S.), 176, 179–180, 346, 402, 622

Jakeš, Miloš, 9, 42, 148, 203–204, 271, 283, 372, 608
Jaruzelski, Wojciech, 5, 29, 41–43, 77–79, 135, 155, 218, 226, 602, 680
  on American and Soviet troops in Europe, 93, 675, 680
  and "Common European home," 97
  on East European leaders, 238, 461
  and George Bush, 79, 81, 97, 503–505, 619
  and German unification, 571
  and Gorbachev, 97, 127–128, 163, 169, 290, 301–303, 533, 534, 548, 602, 606, 680, 691–699
  Gorbachev's views on, 5, 30, 236, 237, 238, 477, 479, 490, 571, 603, 606
  political strategy of (1988–1989), 204–205, 283, 292–305, 370, 491
  and Polish elections (1989), 76, 81, 452–455, 459, 461, 536
  and Soviet Politburo, 534
  Thatcher's views on, 440, 531

K

Kádár, János, 5, 8, 15, 123, 227, 314
  death of, 512–513
  and Gorbachev, 5, 57, 132, 163, 217, 218, 220–221, 226, 229, 238, 242, 273–276, 545
Karmal, Babrak, 565
Kashlev, Yurii, 21
Katushev, Konstantin, 317, 534
Katyń Forest massacre (1940), 178, 563, 605–606, 670, 691, 692, 695
  See also Poland

Kent, Sherman, 187
KGB (Soviet Union), 40, 46, 74, 212, 214
  and Tbilisi demonstrations, 447–448
Khrushchev, Nikita, 123, 255, 312
  and arms race, 286
  and Hungarian revolution (1956), 136, 152, 153, 242–243
  ouster of, 386, 387, 433
  and reform, 105, 111–112, 114, 118, 242–243, 270, 297, 383, 531
Kim Il Sung, 586
Kimmitt, Robert, 197
Kirilenko, Andrei, 108
Kissinger, Henry, 22–23, 39, 176–178, 337, 352, 468
  and Gorbachev, 63–65, 192, 345–346, 350–351
  influence of, 438–439
  Soviet–U.S. "condominium" proposal, 341–344, 349, 351, 627
Kiszczak, Czesław, 300, 303, 453–456
Kochemassov, Vyacheslav, 143, 517
Kohl, Helmut, xviii, 11, 30, 32, 35
  and fall of Berlin Wall, 53, 77–79, 84
  and George H.W. Bush, 53, 77–79, 84–86, 463–464
    conversations with, 558–560, 587–589, 595–597
    About Gorbachev, 479–481
    letters to, 484–487, 611–618
  and George H.W. Bush, Scowcroft, and Sununu, 647–650
  and German reunification, 85, 89–90, 94, 548, 590–593
  and Gorbachev, 32–33, 35, 74–75, 85, 227, 309–310, 572
    conversations with, 463–467, 475, 476–478, 548–549, 590–593
  and Lech Wałęsa, 580–585
  10-point speech, 36, 46, 85, 90, 209, 617–618, 634, 648–649, 653–656, 658
Koivisto, Mauno, 21
  and Gorbachev, 561–562
Komplektov, Viktor, 195
Komsomol (Communist Union of Youth), 287, 312, 320, 430, 698
Kónya, Imre, 471–473
Kornienko, Georgy, 195, 201, 214
Korotich, Vitalii, 427
Kosygin, Alexey, 114, 118, 148
Kovács, László, 162
Krenz, Egon, 34, 147, 566, 581, 588, 591
  and Gorbachev, 569–574
  and Helmut Kohl, 595
Król, Marcin, 131
Krolikowski, Werner, 143, 148, 516
Kryuchkov, Vladimir, 181, 330, 447, 535
Kukorelli, István, 473–474
Kulikov, Viktor, 158, 277–279
Kvitsinsky, Yuli, 122, 137, 515, 170, 517
Kwaśniewski, Aleksander, 76, 452, 454–457, 691

L

Labor unions, 408
Latin America, 192, 629, 632–633
Latvia, 698
Lenin, Vladimir, 118–119, 125
Levesque, Jacques, xv, xviii, xxv, 1, 14, 101, 117–118, 155
  on Brezhnev Doctrine, 140–141

on Gorbachev's East European policy, 149, 212
on Hungary, 162–163
Ligachev, Yegor, 25, 27, 115, 267, 269, 287, 326, 339
on Congress of People's Deputies, 425–426
Lithuania, 697, 698–699
nationalism in, 694
repression in, 135
Lomakin, Viktor, 416
Lukyanov, Anatoly, 27, 430

M

MacEachin, Douglas, 56, 59–60, 67, 171–173, 186–187, 211–213, 442
on Poland crisis (1980–1981), 139–140
on U.S. intelligence disputes, 182–186
on U.S. reaction to Soviet "new thinking," 110–111, 116–117
McFarlane, Robert, 187
Machcewicz, Paweł, 131, 154
Malin, Vladimir, 152
Malta Summit (1989), 36, 52, 87–89, 192, 596, 599, 606–607
and German reunification, 634–635, 640, 645
and Helmut Kohl, 596, 612, 647–648
transcript of, 619–646
and "Western" values, 643–645, 648, 649
Mao Zedong, 123
Masliukov, Yurii, 430
Matlock, Jack, xxv, 12, 58, 62, 82–83, 95, 180–182, 194–195, 206–208, 337
and Aleksandr Yakovlev, 506–510
cables of, 99, 382–388, 390–396, 399–407

bankruptcy metaphor in, 67–69, 127, 383
on origins of Soviet "new thinking," 109–110, 117
on Poland crisis (1980–1981), 141–142
and Romanian revolution (1989), 665–667
on U.S. "back-channels," 177–179
Mazowiecki, Tadeusz, 42, 81, 154, 164
on "Common European home," 97
and Gorbachev, 157, 602–607
Soviet support for, 537–538, 692
Medvedev, Dmitri, 54, 113
Medvedev, Vadim, 6, 8, 12, 24, 212, 242, 251, 266, 328–329
on Baltic Republics, 450, 578
on Congress of People's Deputies, 424–426
and Kurt Hager, 551–554
Romanian visit of (1989), 397–398
Meehan, Francis, 264
Middle East, 198, 201
Mielke, Erich, 516
Migranyan, Andranik, 18
Military-political alliances, 642
See also North Atlantic Treaty Organization (NATO); Warsaw Treaty Organization
dissolution of, 137–138, 532, 555–557, 567, 571, 690, 696
Miodowicz, Alfred, 205, 295
Mironenko Viktor, 430
Mitterrand, François, 21, 33–35, 389
and George Bush, 75, 491
and German reunification, 571, 593–594
and Gorbachev, 488–489, 490–491, 497–498, 593–594, 657–659

Mladenov, Petar, 149–150, 159, 161, 575, 660
Moisov, Lazar
and Gorbachev, 268, 651–652
Moscow Summit (1988), 12, 51, 56–57
Moynihan, Daniel, 59
Mujaheddin, 142
Mulroney, Brian
and Gorbachev, 598–601
Musgrove conference (1998), xvi–xxv, 99–214
Mlynář, Zdeněk, 9

N

Nagy, Imre, 30, 76, 132, 462
Najibullah, Mohammad, 565–566
Nakasone, Yasuhiro, 120
National Intelligence Estimates. See Intelligence estimates (U.S.)
National Security Directive 23, 71, 175, 525–529
See also Soviet Union, U.S. relations with
Németh, Miklós, 24, 34, 292, 313, 314, 321, 322, 410, 615
and Gorbachev, 412–413
"New thinking," xix–xxiv, 3, 5, 12, 50, 52, 54, 144, 162, 309–310, 311–312
See also "Common European home"
and Eastern Europe, 102, 155–156
evolution of, 118
and freedom of choice, xxi, 4, 6–12, 38, 41, 140, 615, 644
and nonuse of force, 135–136, 144, 199–200
origins of, 103–104, 105–106, 108–110, 117
Soviet military views on, 158

U.S. views on, 110–111, 116–117, 392–393
News media
and perestroika, 287–289, 333, 578
Nicaragua, 88, 631
Nishanov, R.N., 534
Nitze, Paul, 54
Nixon, Richard, 23, 56, 64, 182, 491
North Atlantic Treaty Organization (NATO), 17, 18, 20, 34, 45, 47, 140, 641
See also Military-political alliances
Brussels Summit (May 1989) of, 36–37, 75, 507
Eastern European membership in, 145, 157
U.S. guarantees against, 37–38, 93–96, 208, 683, 686
and German membership, 37, 94, 654, 658, 680, 686
and troop reduction proposals, 70–71, 252
Novotný, Antonín, 149–150, 409
Nuclear deterrence, 279, 614
Nuclear disarmament, xx, 11, 51, 63, 80–81, 200, 309, 508–509
Nyers, Rezső, 314, 315, 518, 519
and Gorbachev, 511–514

O

Obama, Barack, 54
Oberdorfer, Don, 72
Occhetto, Achille
and Gorbachev, 408–410
Oil
prices, 15–17, 25–26, 267
production of, 25
sales to Eastern Europe, 156, 316, 358, 570, 605
Olszowski, Stefan, 147–148

Ortega, Daniel, 632

P

Paczkowski, Andrzej, 127, 130, 204–205
Palazchenko, Pavel, 45
Paris Economic Summit (1989), 483
Patiashvili, Jumber, 28, 447
PCC. *See* Warsaw Treaty Organization Political Consultative Committee
Perestroika, xxii—xxiii, 1–5, 11–13, 18–21, 23, 26 39, 43, 63, 119, 122, 144, 162, 202, 210
    ideological basis of, 383–384
    irreversibility of, 388, 393–394
    limits of, 124–125
    market economy and, 13, 18, 117–120, 206–207, 384–386, 672
    opposition to, 384
    pace of, 421–422, 531, 545–546
    and private property, 124–125, 322, 678
    and socialism, 118–120, 414–417, 500–502
    and Soviet public opinion, 421–424
    U.S. views on, 283, 327, 333–334, 337, 376, 382–388, 391–396, 432–435
    and Western interests, 438–439
Petrushenko, Nikolay, 158
Philippines, 632–633
Piłsudski, Józef, 550
Poindexter, John, 187
Poland, 17, 24, 370–371
    See also Katyń Forest massacre (1940)
    1989 elections, 29–31, 76, 154, 302, 452–459
        Soviet response to, 533–536

and Catholic Church, 294–296, 452, 535, 539, 694
crisis (1980–1981), 133, 136, 139–140, 141, 156, 606
debt of, 134, 305, 572
democratization of, 127–128, 204–205, 695–696
economic reforms in, 604
and *perestroika*, 297
Roundtable discussions, 41–42, 204, 302–303
Soviet nonintervention in, 129–130, 133, 135–137, 550
and Soviet relations, 128–129, 290, 304–305, 533–541, 602–607, 692
    economic relations, 697
Soviet troop withdrawal, 505, 695–696
    George H.W. Bush's comments on, 497, 507
Strikes in, 293
Western aid to, 477, 483, 485–486, 504, 615
    from U.S., 560, 595–596
    from West Germany, 581
Western trade with, 72
Polish United Worker's Party (PUWP), 292–306, 355, 550
    Central Committee of, 155, 452–459
    impact of elections on, 536–537, 604
Ponomarev, Boris, 12, 104, 108
Popov, Gavriil, 194
Porębski, Tadeusz, 301
Portugalov, Nikolay, 36
Powell, Colin, 57, 187, 198
Prague Spring (1968). *See* Czechoslovakia: Prague Spring (1968)
Pravda, 221
Prečan, Vilém, 127, 203
Primakov, Evgeny, 521, 534, 692

Pudlák, Jan, 436–437
Pugo, Boris, 428–429
Putin, Vladimir, 54, 148
PUWP. *See* Polish United Workers'
   Party

R

Rainer, János, 132, 205
Rakhmanin, Oleg, 123–124
   Pravda article of, 5–6, 220–221
Rakowski, Mieczysław, 29,
   127–129, 154, 205, 301, 304,
   454–455
   and Gorbachev, 548, 550
   on Polish elections (1989), 454–
   455, 458
   and Soviet Politburo, 534
Reagan, Nancy, 110
Reagan, Ronald, xxv, 12, 83, 650
   See also United States
   Eastern Europe and, 275
   and Gorbachev, xix–xx, 17, 32,
   51, 61, 96, 189, 192–193, 334,
   628
   and "winning" the Cold War,
   50–51
Reykjavik Summit (1986), 17, 185
Rice, Condoleezza, 69, 74, 476
Ridgeway, Rozanne, 264
Rodionov, Igor, 160
Romania, 229, 373–374, 478
   See also Ceauşescu, Nicolae
   and economic reform, 258
   Gorbachev's visits to, 253–254,
   490–491, 670
   humanitarian aid to, 666
   and *perestroika*, 397–398
   revolution in (1989), 49, 91,
   662–667
   description of, 663–664
   Soviet noninterference in, 663,
   666–667
Ross, Dennis, 67, 197–198

Rusakov, Konstantin, 6, 12, 218,
   220, 221
Russia, 46–47, 97
Ryzhkov, Nikolay, 16, 125
   and Czechoslovakia, 259, 411
   and Soviet economy, 26, 239,
   267, 570
   and Soviet Union's dissolution,
   578
   and Tbilisi demonstrations, 448

S

Sakharov, Andrei, 27
Savimbi, Jonas, 161
Schabowski, Günther, 84
Schifter, Richard, 660
Schmidt, Helmut, 464
Scowcroft, Brent, 23, 62, 69, 78,
   86, 194, 197, 345, 442, 625, 647
SDI. *See* Strategic Defense
   Initiative (U.S.)
SED. *See* Socialist Unity Party of
   Germany (SED)
Semenov, Vladimir, 137
Shakhnazarov, Georgy, xviii, 6, 8,
   12, 16, 21, 43–44, 82, 114–115,
   128–130, 168–171, 188, 200–
   201, 209–210, 269
   and Brezhnev doctrine, 136
   and Gorbachev, 288, 311
   on Gorbachev's East European
   policy, 144–145, 151, 204, 312
   memoranda of, 277–279, 306–
   308, 555–557
   on origins of Soviet "new
   thinking," 105–106
   proposal for withdrawal from
   Czechoslovakia, 244–246
   on socialism, 120–121, 270
   on Soviet economy, 156
Shalaev, Stepan, 535
   and Congress of People's
   Deputies, 429–430